Planning and Design Guide

For Secure Adult and Juvenile Facilities

Leonard A. Witke, AIA, Editor

FOUNDED 1870

American Correctional Association Staff

Richard Stalder, President

James A. Gondles, Jr., Executive Director

Gabriella M. Daley, Director, Communications and Publications

Alice Fins, Publications Managing Editor

Michael Kelly, Associate Editor

Sherry Wulfekuhle, Editorial Assistant

Melissa Dettloff, Administrative Assistant

Production by Morgan Graphics, Takoma Park, Maryland
Prepress Services: Graphic Color Group, Beltsville, Maryland
Printed in the United States of America by IPC, St. Joseph, Michigan

Library of Congress Cataloging-in-Publication Data
    Planning and design guide for secure adult and juvenile facilities /
    Leonard R. Witke, editor
    p. cm.
    Rev. ed. of: Design guide for secure adult correctional facilities. c1983.
    Includes bibliographical references (p.   ) and index.
    ISBN 1-56991-116-9 (pbk.)
    1. Correctional institutions–Design and construction. I. Witke,
    Leonard, R. II. American Correctional Association. Design guide for
    secure adult correctional facilities.
    HV8805.A44 1999
    365'.5--dc21
    99-43095   CIP

ISBN 1-56991-116-9

This publication may be ordered from:
American Correctional Association
4380 Forbes Boulevard
Lanham, Maryland 20706-4322
1-800-222-5646

For information on publications and videos available from ACA, contact
our worldwide web home page at: http://www.corrections.com/aca.

Front cover photographs: Clockwise, starting from bottom left-hand corner.

Wallens Ridge State Prison, Big Stone Gap, Virginia. Photographer: Timothy
Cox. Design/Build contractor: Gilbane. Photo courtesy of Gilbane, Providence,
Rhode Island.

Mecklenburg Jail Central, Charlotte, North Carolina. Photographer: Rick
Alexander. Architect: Little/HOK Joint Venture Architects. Photo courtesy of
HOK, Washington, D.C.

Arkansas Valley Correctional Facility, Crowley, Colorado. Architect: RNL
Design. Photo courtesy of RNL Design, Denver, Colorado.

The Administration/Control building at the Federal Correctional Institution in
Pekin, Illinois. Photographer: Mark Romine Photography. Architect: Phillips
Swager Associates, Peoria, Illinois. Photo courtesy of PSA, Peoria, Illinois.

An open officer's control station inside a typical housing unit in the Portage
County Jail, Ravenna Ohio. Photographer: John Griesen. Architect: NBBJ,
Columbus, Ohio. Photo courtesy of NBBJ, Columbus, Ohio.

Back cover photographs: From top to bottom.

Platte Valley Youth Services Center, Greeley, Colorado. Photo courtesy of
RNL Design, Denver, Colorado.

Paulding Youth Detention Center, Dallas, Georgia. Photographer: Steve
Hornaday. Photo courtesy of Heery International, Atlanta, Georgia.

York Correctional Institution for Women, Niantic, Connecticut. Photo courtesy
of HDR Architecture, Dallas, Texas.

Planning and Design Guide
For Secure Adult and Juvenile Facilities

Contents

3   Inmate and Juvenile Services

4   Inmate and Juvenile Programs

Acknowledgments

I t is with deep appreciation that I thank the authors who contributed to the development of this work. Without their unselfish efforts to bring forth the best possible product, this guide would have fallen far short of its goals. Because of the contributing authors' work, the second edition of the *Design Guide* is a wonderful reference document for anyone who plans to design and build or add to an existing facility.

I am grateful to the American Correctional Association for sponsoring this book. Without the support of the ACA, the corrections' community would not have the benefit of current publications on important issues in our industry. I wish to thank Alice Fins and the staff at the American Correctional Association's Publications Department for their help in putting this work together. As a result of their expertise, and coaching, the book has been made more readable and comprehensive.

I wish to thank the following individuals, agencies, and firms for so generously supplying the photographs and graphics. I appreciate your help.

American Society for Testing Materials, West Conshocken, Pennsylvania

Arrington Watkins Architects, Phoenix, Arizona

Randall Atlas, Ph.D., AIA, CPP

Capitol Communications, Inc.

Carter Goble Associates, Inc., Columbia, South Carolina, especially Stephen Carter

Chinn Planning, Inc., Columbia, South Carolina

Steven Steurer, Correctional Education Association, Lanham, Maryland

Corrections Corporation of America, Nashville, Tennessee

Criminal Juvenile Justice International, Roseville, Minnesota

Federal Bureau of Prisons, especially W. Scott Higgins

Gilbane Building Co., Providence, Rhode Island

William Hamilton, HDR, Dallas, Texas

Heery International, Inc., Atlanta, Georgia

Hennepin County Sheriff's Office, Hennepin County, Minnesota

Hocking Correctional Facility, Nelsonville, Ohio, especially Janis Lane

HOK, Washington, DC., especially James Kessler

HSMM, Virginia Beach, Virginia, especially William Porter

Huskey & Associates, Inc., Chicago, Illinois

Justice Systems, Issaquah, Washington

Kennedy Associates, Inc., St. Louis, Missouri

KMD Justice, San Francisco, California

Little/HOK Joint Venture Architects

Christopher A., Lizza, Ohio Department of Rehabilitation and Correction, Columbus, Ohio

L. Robert Kimball & Associates, Ebensburg, Pennsylvania

LZT Associates, Inc., Peoria, Illinois

Scott Strom, NBBJ, Columbus, Ohio

New York Department of Correctional Services

PSA, Peoria, Illinois

Ricci Associates, New York, New York

RNL Design, Denver, Colorado

James Rowenhorst, Rapid City, South Dakota

Securicor New Century, Richmond, Virginia, especially Charles Kehoe

Without the numerous contributors of photographs, this book would be a lifeless manual. The photographer's descriptive images help bring to mind the meaning of the text and make the book more exciting and enjoyable. They have provided their work without benefit of compensation.

I want to acknowledge Donald Hall Smith, AIA, Keith Goodwin, P.E., and Walter Subey. Each of these men greatly influenced my decision to work in corrections and then tutored and nurtured me to become an effective justice facilities planner. Moreover, they taught me how to listen.

Last, but without question, most important, I want to acknowledge my wife Susann for her patience and support throughout the process of developing this book. She was my mentor, having previously helped publish a technical book. She also volunteered to be my word processor when I could not physically accomplish the task. She always inspired me to stay on task, and without her, I would not have enjoyed the book and my involvement as much as I did.

Leonard R. Witke, AIA
Chief Editor

Foreword

With the explosive growth in the correctional population, the need for new facilities has grown exponentially. This book presents a variety of options and considerations regarding the design and construction of adult and juvenile correctional facilities.

The American Correctional Association (ACA) is proud to present this completely revised version of the 1983 *Design Guide for Secure Adult Correctional Facilities* and to include information relevant to juvenile facilities, as well. The more than fifty contributors to this volume exemplify what is special about our association. They represent a cross section of professionals —administrators, architects, engineers, builders, and programmers, who are working together to benefit the field of corrections. While there may be some philosophical differences among the contributors, these individuals came together to produce a book for ACA that is a landmark in the field.

One of the major purposes of this work is to allow all these types of individuals to talk with one another so the perspective of each can be enhanced and they can work together toward their common goal—building safe, secure, and humane correctional facilities. We hope everyone will read through the entire work, enjoying the excellent photographs and graphics, and learning more about the totality of what goes into a new facility. We urge those in adult corrections to read the sections concerning juvenile facilities because there may be ideas in these chapters that would be useful in their domains and vice versa. Similarly, the chapter discussing lessons learned from other countries provides a useful antidote to any provincialism of readers.

The ten sections of the book discuss the major aspects of planning and design considerations. The first section, "Planning, Design, Construction Process, and Issues" is the longest and sets the stage for the other sections. Section Two, "Inmate and Juvenile Housing," discusses special populations, including housing for sexual predators who have completed their original sentences. The third section, "Inmate and Juvenile Services," describes several service areas from both adult and juvenile perspectives and offers those designing facilities a background that will provide useful questions to consider in their designs. Likewise, the fourth section, "Inmate and Juvenile Programs," presents a description not only of such programs but of the spaces needed to house them.

The fifth section, "Administrative Functions," examines this area and presents a succinct chart on space needs. Section Six, "Service Facilities," discusses the underbelly of the institution whose neglect can be costly. Section Seven, "Security Features," describes the options and goals of such systems. Section Eight, "Opening a New Correctional Facility," fulfills a very important role in suggesting some procedures for preparing the facility and staff after the physical construction of the building has been completed. Section Nine looks at issues of privatization and provides some thoughtful considerations. In the conclusion, Len Witke, the book's editor, wraps up all the ideas and offers some perspective on the future.

This book was a monumental undertaking. Just as no one person has all the answers, so in collaboration with our colleagues, we gain stature and learn new approaches and methods that we may use. This is one of the goals of our association, providing individuals with an opportunity to network and learn from others, whether it is at our conferences, in our training workshops, or through our publications. We welcome the dialog and encourage our members to recruit others for membership so they, too, can grow with us.

James A. Gondles, Jr.
Executive Director
American Correctional Association

Introduction

Leonard R. Witke, AIA

It never seems to end! Every time a new capital budget is passed there is the hope that in fact we may catch up—that we even may build our way out of the bed shortfall; except, it really never happens.

As long as anyone can remember, there has been an overwhelming problem with crowding that has taken precedence over everything else. It has required some correctional agencies to lay off teachers and recreation directors to pay for operating budget increases for new beds. It has diminished the annual budgets of other agencies to enable state corrections and county jails to build more beds. It even has required, in some jurisdictions, that more money be spent on prisons and jails than is spent on schools.

We probably are not any closer to the goal of building our way out of the problem, but we have gained a good deal of experience. From that experience, we learned how to build more with limited dollars and how to build better to insure greater staff and inmate safety.

In the decades preceding the 1980s, there was significant change in the field of corrections as a result of many factors including crowding, inmate riots, antiquated facilities, court-directed improvements, and stricter sentencing guidelines. In facilities design, there was movement from a treatment model for incarceration to a model based on direct staff supervision and delivery of services and programs to the inmates.

Just as significant was the lack of current knowledge, on the part of many people in the field of corrections,

regarding the planning and construction processes used to build new facilities because of limited activities during the period. In Wisconsin, as an example, a new prison had not been constructed since 1966 and the expertise of staff, at the time, regarding correctional planning philosophies, the design process, and state-of-the-art materials and details were minimal.

As a result of these changes, and the need for basic planning information, the American Correctional Association published the first edition of the *Design Guide for Secure Adult Correctional Facilities* in 1983. It quickly became the source book and design "primer" for architects, planners, wardens, and sheriffs who were charged with the responsibility of designing and constructing new correctional and detention facilities. It helped establish typical planning guidelines and standards to be considered in the design of new facilities, and it put into words the process that should be followed to achieve a safe and secure adult corrections or detention facility. The book read as a novel, taking the reader effortlessly from one subject area to the next. Once consumed, the reader had a very clear understanding of the salient issues and steps in the planning and design processes for a new secure adult institution.

For the most part, the 1983 *Design Guide* addressed the specific needs of a medium-security adult facility. It was the opinion of the authors at that time that the majority of state correctional systems and county jail systems had sufficient numbers of maximum-security beds and that the need was really in the area of medium security.

Today, the changes that are occurring in society toward corrections and those who commit crimes are significant. In some ways, these changes are similar to those that had a substantial impact on the planning of correctional facilities in the 1970s and 1980s. It is clear today that the public will not tolerate what it views as coddling of inmates, including unnecessary frills or amenities in the design of facilities or programs offered.

What makes today's task for planning a new correctional facility a bit more difficult is the uniqueness of the inmates that make up the population of most correctional systems or jail populations. These individuals, in many cases, are repeat offenders, more aggressive, with less fear of life behind bars. Others are persons who may have been incarcerated for the first time and are facing their sentence later in life and not necessarily in good health. Still others may have significant mental health problems.

The general public demands that people who commit crimes serve much of their sentence in a secure institutional setting. This can be without the benefit of parole in some states. What this means to those trying to plan a new facility is that many of the inmates who will be incarcerated will be serving longer sentences. Systems will have to address the needs of inmates and offenders, including juveniles that are quite different from those of inmates of the 1980s. Special needs inmates will take up more of the staff's time and more of the institution's operating dollars each year.

Inmates may grow old while incarcerated and, as a result, they may require higher levels of services in the areas of health care and mental health. They may be infirm or require barrier-free accessibility to programs and housing. They also may require special diets and due to their exposure to drugs and alcohol, they may require substantial alcohol and drug treatment while in prison or jail and also on release. They may be more despondent over their situation and as a result become suicidal or aggressive toward staff or other inmates.

This growing problem of the "special needs inmate" has resulted in the development of several new hybrid institutions for correctional systems during recent years. There have been several facilities or parts of facilites designed specifically for the "geriatric" inmate in both the Federal Bureau of Prisons as well as in state correctional institutions. These institutions are unique in that they serve inmate populations that are in some cases infirm due to age and in other cases infirm due to disability

either at the time of incarceration or as a result of things that have occurred during their incarceration. These inmates can be relatively young but clearly in need of services not unlike residents of a typical nursing home or assisted-care living facility.

Another special needs group is female inmates. Many women now are serving longer sentences in facilities as a result of the courts dealing with women on an equal level with their male counterparts for certain crimes. These inmates are often faced with special needs regarding their children, and other family responsibilities. They also tend to require a higher degree of health care services. Parity in services and access to programs is especially difficult to achieve for some jurisdictions and jails due to the small number of female inmates and the need to classify them, which further minimizes their numbers.

With the change in the law for many states to waive all youth at least seventeen years old, who are charged with certain felonies, into adult court, two things occurred. Some of the most experienced, streetwise, gang affiliated, and dangerous juveniles were removed from juvenile detention facilities and systems, which improved the overall nature of the remaining populations. The action also helped to reduce the populations in the juvenile facilities.

The second issue is the additional burden that this action placed on the adult facilities to attempt to segregate this group of individuals and to provide them with access to education and programs in an attempt to help them improve themselves. Some jurisdictions built separate facilities to deal specifically with this special inmate population.

Another special population group that developed during the last fifteen years is the "supermax" inmates. Although there always have been inmates that easily could have qualified as a supermax inmate, it has been the increase in this inmate population and crowded conditions that have made it necessary for some systems to segregate these individuals. It is also becoming more common to build special facilities to handle these inmates.

The unique requirements for incarceration of the supermax inmates makes it most appropriate to segregate them in their own wing, building, or in some states, their own institution. In these facilities, programs are very limited as is staff to inmate interaction. Inmate to inmate interaction is also limited or even eliminated.

The accent is on separation, very few amenities, and a reduced amount of time staff need to interact with the inmate to avoid the potential for injuries to the staff or inmates. Once these individuals have been removed from the general population of other facilities, within a system, or jurisdiction, the other inmates settle down, take direction from staff and generally perform better.

The path to a successful project has become more obscure as a result of a number of choices that did not exist previously. Today, project managers are faced with decisions regarding project financing, bidding, and siting that in most cases were not issues in times past. We have seen the development of design/build/finance proposals that teams of firms are now putting together on major projects. Conventional bidding processes are being put aside in favor of new project delivery methods.

They can enables the agency or jurisdiction to have the facility without spending any significant capital dollars up front. Clearly, there are advantages and disadvantages to these new methods, and the buyer needs to be aware of the pitfalls as well as the benefits of the process.

This edition of the *Design Guide* is aimed at presenting the information gathered from the last fifteen years of justice facilities planning and construction. It is a document assembled by some of the foremost experts in the field of corrections. It provides lessons learned, but in addition, it also offers sensible recommendations for addressing future needs based on the knowledge of these experts. It provides a pathway to follow through the planning, design, and construction process to avoid the common pitfalls and assist your planning team to bring your next project to a successful conclusion.

Planning, Design, Construction Process, and Issues

The urban design of the Chesapeake City Jail in Virginia creates a building that complements the neighboring buildings and public spaces. The curved entry roof reflects its location near the ocean by taking its form from the shape of a wave. It demonstrates the noninstitutional public-side front of the building versus the secure housing on the backside.

Architectural Firm: NBBJ, Columbus, Ohio. Photo courtesy of NBBJ. Photographer: Joe Wiseman.

The photos on the preceding and opposite page show the 413,000 square-foot maximum security facility, the U.S. Penitentiary in Florence, Colorado. It is composed of visitation, administration, health services, educational program areas, chapel, and a gymnasium as well as the personal services of the commissary, laundry, and barber. The housing includes 500 general cells and 75 cells of special housing.

Architectural Firms: LKA Partners, Lescher and Mahoney, and DLR Group, Colorado Springs, Colorado. Construction management firm: Heery Program Management, Atlanta, Georgia. Construction contractor: PCL Constructors, Denver, Colorado. Photo courtesy of the Federal Bureau of Prisons.

General Design and Construction Issues

W. Scott Higgins
Chief, Design and Construction Branch
Federal Bureau of Prisons*
Washington, D.C.

This volume's predecessor, *Design Guide for Secure Adult Correctional Facilities*, published in 1983, was developed largely around the design philosophy and practices of the Federal Bureau of Prisons. Many of the photographs and descriptions used in that book were from the Otisville Federal Correctional Institution in New York, completed in 1981 and other somewhat earlier Federal Bureau of Prisons' facilities.

Since 1983, this author has been responsible for administering the design and construction of new institutions for the Federal Bureau of Prisons. During that time, many dramatic changes have occurred as those facilities evolved. An examination of those changes

shows how impermanent some "planning axioms" can be; yet, it also is a reminder of what remains the bedrock of our program.

What follows is a review of some of the more significant changes that have occurred in the planning of the Federal Bureau of Prisons' facilities and an assessment of what planning elements have survived and continue to be the basis for our operations and design, which may be applicable to the design of other institutions.

* The opinions expressed in this article are those of the author and do not represent the official policy or position of the Federal Bureau of Prisons or the U.S. Department of Justice.

Philosophical Foundation

The earlier *Design Guide* noted that the design guidelines outlined there were based on a specific philosophical foundation, summarized as follows:

- Offenders are sentenced to confinement as punishment; but, not for further punishment by their keepers or by inordinately harsh conditions.
- Inmates should expect to be confined humanely and safely.
- Staff should be able to function professionally and in a safe environment.
- Inmates should be provided with opportunities for self-improvement in areas such as academic, vocational, and social skills.
- Staff should interact directly with inmates to encourage open, interpersonal communications.
- The institutional atmosphere should be as normal as possible for the welfare of both inmates and staff and, ultimately, for the public, as conditions during confinement will likely influence behavior after release.
- A reasonable balance should be struck between the security features of a correctional facility and an architectural environment that allows for a spirit of openness and reconciliation.

This philosophy remains the basis for the management and operation of Federal Bureau of Prisons' institutions and, therefore, is reflected in the new institutions being developed. This is reiterated by the mission statement of the Federal Bureau of Prisons:

"It is the mission of the Federal Bureau of Prisons to protect society by confining offenders in the controlled environments of prison and community-based facilities that are safe, humane, cost-efficient, and appropriately secure, and that provide work and other self-improvement opportunities to assist offenders in becoming law-abiding citizens."

The Role of the Facility

Experts believe that a successful correctional system must be supported by a three-part foundation: (1) a qualified and well-trained staff; (2) an inmate classification system to identify those with special problems or requirements for care or protection and to separate inmate predators from those who can function in a modern correctional setting; and (3) established policies and procedures to deal with the myriad demands of this type of operation. It is easy to forget that even the best designed institution is doomed to fail if such an operational foundation is not in place. The facility itself, and, by extension, its designers and builders, cannot ensure a safe, secure, or humane operation. However, careful thought and planning and high-quality design and construction can contribute in numerous ways to a successful program and assist those professionals who are on the front lines in correctional facilities throughout the country.

Design Direction

Clear direction must be given in the preliminary planning and design effort required to develop a new correctional institution. As with any complex human endeavor, those charged with managing such a facility have widely divergent opinions. If the design of the project is to proceed efficiently and in an orderly manner, these differences must be sorted out and decisions made so as to avoid confusion or costly delays.

As with any complex human endeavor, those charged with managing such a facility have widely divergent opinions.

Even within the Federal Bureau of Prisons, which has been blessed with a high degree of management continuity and philosophical consistency, there are numerous operational issues that continue to surface and must be resolved and often reconfirmed as a project develops. For those fortunate enough to be involved in an ongoing program with a series of projects, this design direction is largely a matter of fine tuning from one project to subsequent projects, with periodic interruptions for significant policy or program changes. The Federal Bureau of Prisons recently has created a Design Criteria Review Committee, made up of senior managers responsible for correctional services, facilities management, and new institutions' design and construction. This committee reviews and approves proposed significant changes to the design criteria for new facilities.

For those involved with development of a new correctional facility for the first time or after a long period of time between projects, determining this design direction can be an enormous and frustrating undertaking. Major decisions must be made that will have ramifications on the project budget, schedule, and operation of the facility for years to come. Predesign analysis and planning are essential to establish the capacity and mission of the proposed institution along with its relationship to the correctional system and its current and future inmate population. This planning should establish security and operational requirements; it should include a projection of staffing requirements and preliminary budget estimates.

This type of early planning is a particular specialty, and qualified consultants should be used to augment in-house resources. These may be retained separately or sometimes through the design entity providing architectural and engineering services for the project. For any project, and particularly for a system's totally new type of facility, planners and designers should strive for a high degree of flexibility for both different uses and for future expansion.

An agency responsible for developing a new facility should establish a system to ensure that a clear design direction is established with the full understanding and support of the agency's top management. It is also essential that a process is in place so that design issues can be resolved and decisions rendered with that same support to avoid serious misunderstandings or surprises as the institution is completed. The authority and responsibility for this design direction should be granted carefully because, inevitably, the most important of these decisions are made long before the warden and any other staff who actually will operate the institution can be identified. Even if some of the initial institution staff can participate in the planning effort, the major decisions will affect their successors for years to come. Therefore, these decisions should be supported or confirmed by higher management.

The authority and responsibility for this design direction should be granted carefully.

Conversely, the designers of an institution should do everything they can to make sure that they are receiving a clear picture of what is expected. When directions are in conflict or issues are not being resolved, the designer may have to take the initiative to find a level of management within the agency to resolve the situation.

While it is critical to have the approval of the uppermost management, it is also extremely important to have the support of the institution administrators and line staff who will operate the facility. For those dealing with ongoing programs, this can be accomplished by maintaining open lines of communication with those in these positions so that concerns and issues can be brought for-

ward, resolved, and incorporated into future facilities, as appropriate. Such a process can be augmented and stimulated by questionnaires sent to institution staff and visits for postoccupancy evaluations of institutions after they have been operational for some period.

For those faced with development of a new project without this previous experience and resource base, the preliminary planning and design effort should involve a wide range of those who will be operating or interfacing with the new institution. Visits to other institutions and their staff can make decision makers and resource personnel aware of the wide variety of solutions available and stimulate valuable discussion and analysis of the needs of the planned facility.

Coping with Population Growth

For at least the past decade, correctional systems at all levels—local, state, and federal—have faced unprecedented population growth. Since the Otisville Federal Correctional Institution was completed in 1981, the number of inmates confined in federal facilities has risen from about 23,800 to a March 1999 level of more than 111,600, with an additional 15,000 inmates now housed in privately managed and contract facilities. Developing new capacity to meet this demand increasingly has been constrained by competition for public resources.

The Federal Bureau of Prisons has responded to this need in four general areas, including (1) increasing use of contract facilities, both secure and community-based; (2) expanding capacity at existing institutions; (3) acquiring military and other facilities and converting them to prison use; and (4) constructing new prisons. Although the first three methods have been used extensively, most of the new capacity has been provided by new institutions. Concern with the high cost of these new facilities and a search for more cost-effective use of resources has resulted in significant changes in the federal system, which were not envisioned in the mid 1980s.

The previous *Design Guide* focused on the type of correctional facility where it expected the largest amount of construction activity—medium-security correctional institutions. The Otisville Federal Correctional Institution conformed to its guidelines, which were presented as the thinking of the leading corrections professionals at that time. These guidelines called for a capacity of no more than 500 inmates housed in individual, single cells.

It is doubtful if any of those involved with the development of either the previous *Design Guide* or the

Otisville Federal Correctional Institution in Otisville, New York, was built in 1983. Contrast this with the recently constructed Federal Correctional Complex in Florence.

Photo courtesy of the Federal Bureau of Prisons.

Otisville Federal Correctional Institution could have envisioned that, within a dozen years, similar facilities within the Federal Bureau of Prisons would be planned for a rated capacity of more than 1,000 and that the rated capacity would be arrived at by allowing 50 percent of the cells to be double-bunked. At that time, double-bunking was considered a necessary, but temporary, solution to crowding.

In response to population pressure and a review of the costs of new capacity, the Federal Bureau of Prisons has implemented changes in its policy on double-bunking. These changes have been made only after careful consideration and were based on its experience with operating institutions under very crowded conditions. The Bureau of Prisons has determined that some levels of double-bunking are manageable. Its current policy for calculating rated capacity allows for 100 percent double-bunking in minimum and low-security institutions, 50 percent in medium-security institutions, and 25 percent in high-security institutions and detention facilities. This change has reduced the projected need for additional capacity by many thousands of beds with a savings of several million dollars.

The development of new low-security institutions by the Federal Bureau of Prisons is also a change from 1983 standards. It was made to provide more cost-effective new capacity. Developments in the Federal Bureau of Prisons' inmate classification system indicated a large number of inmates designated as low security. While these inmates still needed to be in an institution with a secure perimeter, it was felt that they could function in a less controlled environment. New low-security institutions were developed similar to medium-security facilities but with the general population housed in dormitory units instead of housing units with cells. The Federal Bureau of Prisons recently has decided to develop any future low-security institutions with cells.

For similar reasons, the Federal Bureau of Prisons has allowed the development of institutions with larger rated capacities. This has been an evolving development with current standards now allowing for rated capacities of about 1,500 beds for low-security institutions and about 1,150 for medium security.

A final major development for the Federal Bureau of Prisons in the 1990s has been the addition of new high-security institutions. Although the earlier *Design Guide* addressed standards for such facilities, it did not foresee extensive development of new prisons in this category. The Federal Bureau of Prisons also did not then see a need for new capacity in this area, but the enormous population growth of the last decade and the need for more control and security for an increasing percentage of inmates has caused the Federal Bureau of Prisons to develop a number of these projects. They were first developed with 512 general population cells for a rated capacity of about 640. Those currently under development have been increased by about 50 percent, to a rated capacity of about 960. Other design changes related to these high-security facilities are addressed later under specific categories.

The experience with severe population pressures led to another broad category of design program changes from the earlier *Design Guide*. By the mid 1980s, it had become apparent that severe crowding was going to

The desire of the Federal Bureau of Prisons and the design team for the Federal Correctional Complex, Florence, Colorado, was to establish an environment that both acknowledges the nature of the maximum security program and is humanistic in origin. The building forms are sheathed in a field of dark red brick with a buff-colored horizontal striping. There is an intentional balance between respecting the architectural heritage of the area and establishing an identity of its own that is appropriate to the complex.

Architectural Firms: LKA Partners, Lescher and Mahoney and DLR Group, Colorado Springs, Colorado. Construction management firm: Heery Program Management, Atlanta, Georgia. Construction contractor: PCL Constructors, Denver, Colorado. Photo courtesy of the Federal Bureau of Prisons.

The Florence prison camp is a satellite facility of the Federal Correctional Institution on the site of the Federal Correctional complex in Florence, Colorado. Building materials include concrete block with a brick veneer and metal roofs. This minimum-security facility has no perimeter fencing. Inmates are housed in open dormitories. Camp inmates work at the central support facility performing warehousing, vehicle maintenance, landscape maintenance, and UNICOR warehousing for the entire Federal Correctional Complex.

Architectural Firms: LKA Partners, Lescher and Mahoney, and DLR Group, Colorado Springs, Colorado. Construction management firms: Heery Program Management, Atlanta, Georgia. Contractor for the prison camp: Hensel Phelps Construction Company, Florence, Colorado. Photo courtesy of the Federal Bureau of Prisons.

continue indefinitely. Some program and support spaces were increased to accommodate a population level significantly above the rated capacity planned at that time. These increases can be seen by comparing the facilities developed during that period with the standards included in the earlier *Design Guide*. Possibly as a reminder that it is difficult to stay ahead of this growth, within a few years, this contingency-space planning was absorbed by the rated-capacity increases generated by the population increases and policy changes noted above.

Comparing Costs of Institutions

Given the long-range impact of many decisions that are made in an effort to be more cost effective, a word of caution is in order. Comparing costs for new correctional facilities is inevitable. It also can provide useful insights. However, such comparisons should be examined critically before using them as the basis for making major policy decisions. This is particularly true when comparing two different correctional systems. Cost figures should be reviewed to determine which cost elements are included, such as the price of land, site development costs, utility charges, and design or engineering fees. Only then can it be determined that similar costs are compared.

In analyzing relative costs, it is also important to ensure that any comparisons that are made are based on comparable facilities. Cost-per-bed figures can be misleading when comparing institutions of different types and sizes. This can be confusing, particularly when different systems have significantly different ways of determining rated capacity. Such comparisons can be very useful if you compare the cost of facilities with similar security levels, construction type, sizes, and missions. They also can be used to establish budget estimates for future projects.

Unit Management/Direct Supervision/ General Inmate Housing

Probably the two most important concepts underlying the operation of Federal Bureau of Prisons institutions are "direct supervision" and "functional unit management" (*see* Levinson, 1999).

Direct supervision as a management method refers to the use of correctional officers in open and direct contact with inmates within a housing unit, which has been designed to afford good visual supervision of the unit from any point within the open circulation space separating

The housing units shown here and on the facing page feature two levels of cells around an open multipurpose area.

(Above) SeaTac Federal Detention Center in Seattle, Washington. SeaTac Federal Detention Center's Architect/Engineer: NBBJ, Seattle, Washington. Construction contractor: M. A. Mortenson, Bellevue, Washington. Construction management firm: Heery Program Management, Bellevue, Washington. Photo courtesy of the Federal Bureau of Prisons.

(Right) Federal Correctional Institution in Phoenix, Arizona. The Federal Correctional Institution in Phoenix's Architect/Engineer: Leacher and Mahoney, Phoenix, Arizona. Construction contractor: McCarthy Construction Company, Phoenix, Arizona. Photo courtesy of the Federal Bureau of Prisons.

the cells. It is an alternative to correctional management concepts commonly referred to as intermittent surveillance and remote surveillance or indirect supervision. *Intermittent surveillance* is the patrolling of linear cellblocks, which often are on multiple tiers, which allows supervision of only a limited portion of the cell block at any given time. Intermittent surveillance or indirect supervision uses housing unit layouts similar to those of direct supervision models, but it places the correctional officers within secure control rooms to observe the inmates and control their movements to varying degrees by remotely controlled doors and gates.

Direct supervision places a great deal of responsibility on the correctional officers and relies on them to provide control of the unit through constant awareness of and interaction with the inmates. Within the Federal Bureau of Prisons, this use of direct correctional supervision has been expanded to encompass a team of professionals known as the functional unit management staff.

The idea of locating all or most of the staff directly responsible for dealing with inmates within the inmates' housing units originated within the Federal Bureau of Prisons in the late 1960s as a strategy to divide an institution into smaller components to improve interaction between staff and inmates and provide more individualized attention or treatment. This management concept was refined during the 1970s to become a defining force in the way the Federal Bureaus of Prisons' institutions are operated; and it also was a key element of the previous *Design Guide*.

The basic concept of having a team of correctional professionals assigned responsibility for a specific housing unit and located within that unit remains a current idea within the Federal Bureau of Prisons and many other state and county agencies. The staff making up the team includes caseworkers, counselors, correctional officers, a unit manager, and a unit secretary. The responsibility of a unit manager has been expanded so that this position typically oversees two housing units often in separate buildings, each with separate unit staff teams. The design of virtually all general housing units still is based on this commitment to interaction between staff and inmates with a goal of proactive understanding and control of the inmate population. This same concept also has been incorporated into the design of housing units within high-security institutions. The use of unit management has been instrumental in allowing the increases in size of housing units and of the institutions as a whole.

Another example of two levels of cells around an open multipurpose area.

The United States Penitentiary in Florence, Colorado, Administrative Maximum Security facility is the first specifically designed administrative maximum security facility ever to be built in the United States by the Federal Bureau of Prisons. This 575-bed facility is divided into six varying levels of security. Based on each inmate's security classification, support services such as visitation, administration, health services, educational program areas, chapel, and a gymnasium as well as the personal services of the commissary are available.

The design team was challenged to meet the extensive program and highest security parameters set by the Federal Bureau of Prisons and yet present an image appropriate for the local architecture. The exterior materials are integrated in a manner that balances the scale with the massing, establishing a form, which minimizes the visual impact of the facility.

Architectural Firms Joint Venture: LKA Partners, Lescher and Mahoney and DLR Group, Colorado Springs, Colorado. Construction management firm: Heery Program Management, Atlanta, Georgia. Construction contractor of the administrative maximum security facility: Blount, Inc., Florence, Colorado. Photo courtesy of the Federal Bureau of Prisons.

The Federal Bureau of Prisons' designs for housing units for the general inmate population remain very similar in concept to that described in the previous *Design Guide*. A typical unit consists of two housing modules connected by a corridor with two offices for case managers, usually an unassigned multi-use office, a staff toilet, a janitor's closet, storage room, and a unit management suite with space for the unit secretary, unit manager, and inmate files. The housing modules typically have two levels of cells around an open dayroom/multi-use space that contains an open officer's station. Also located around this central space are activity/television rooms, offices for counselors, showers, laundry rooms, and other support spaces. This type of housing unit is used at medium- and high-security correctional facilities and at high-rise detention centers. In a few cases, high-rise detention centers have used three housing modules per floor to form a unit. Although most housing modules have been developed in a triangular configuration, rectilinear layouts also have been used.

Housing modules typically have 64 cells for a total of 128 for the entire unit. With the current policy for establishing rated capacity described above, medium- security units have a rated capacity of 96 beds per housing module or a total of 192 per unit. High-security units have a rated capacity of 80 beds per housing module or a total of 160 per unit. The amount of activity and support space provided has been increased along with this increase in planned capacity.

The changes outlined here have emphasized one particular concern that should not be forgotten. With so much responsibility and potential stress placed on the officers in this type of correctional setting, we must be careful that the demands do not exceed what reasonably can be expected from people in this environment. This has been addressed in a variety of ways by federal, state, and local systems. Additional staff sometimes are assigned to units with crowded conditions and at the most active periods of the day. Work hours of some members of the unit management team often are staggered to bring more staff into the unit in the evenings and on weekends. Additional technological resources, such as closed-circuit television and metal detectors, increasingly are being used or considered to augment surveillance and control of these units. The demands on staff remain a serious issue that requires our continued vigilance.

Segregated Housing or Special Housing

The special housing units now included in Federal Bureau of Prisons' facilities are similar in concept to the segregated housing described in the previous *Design Guide*. They still are divided into Administrative Detention and Disciplinary Segregation wings, although the distinction is now largely operational with the physical characteristics of the wings and cells being virtually identical. A signficant number of changes have been incorporated as these facilities have evolved.

The most striking difference is probably the size of these special housing units. For medium-security facilities, this is largely attributed to the overall capacity increases of the institutions. The previous *Design Guide* called for a total of 30 rooms for an institution with a capacity of 500 inmates. The Federal Bureau of Prisons' guidelines currently recommend a similar ratio of 72 special housing cells for a medium-security facility with a rated capacity of 1,152. The recommended number of special housing cells recently has been increased from 72 to 116 for a high-security penitentiary, with a rated capacity of 960.

Other differences include the provision of stainless steel showers in each special housing cell; a larger outdoor recreation area, subdivided into several smaller "recreation cages" separated by chain-link fencing or woven wire mesh; and areas for storage of personal property and supplies for the unit. A major change made only recently is the use of remotely controlled sliding doors in the special housing units at high-security institutions instead of manually locked, swinging doors.

Administrative Offices

In the area of administrative offices, recent Federal Bureau of Prisons' institutions have striking differences from those developed under the standards described in the previous *Design Guide*. This has been the result of an evolving process as many planning assumptions and operational goals were reconsidered and modified. The earlier guidelines called for all administrative functions to be located within the secure perimeter of the institu-tion. This was advocated to encourage direct contact by executive and administrative personnel with line staff and inmates. It was recommended that the administration building be located close to the front entrance since many people coming to the institution would be there only to visit this building and would not proceed elsewhere.

Over the years, many practicioners recognized that this location required unnecessary traffic through the secure perimeter and created a potential for unwarranted risk in the event of an institution emergency. Now, these institutions have an administration building, located outside the perimeter security, which contains the warden's office suite, business offices, personnel and staff training offices, and some other support and security personnel. This building also incorporates an armory, locksmith shop, and an emergency response squad room. The control center and pedestrian sallyport that provides entrance to the secure compound is connected to this building. Some administrative staff have remained within the compound, including the associate wardens, the captain, and lieutenants; there also are personnel for inmate records and receiving and discharge functions.

Perimeter Security and Site Planning

A basic tenet of planning by the Federal Bureau of Prisons is still that a very secure perimeter enclosing the main portion of an institution allows for more freedom of movement, operational flexibility, and more of a non-institutional environment. These are the philosophical foundations supporting management and operation.

The perimeter security used at the Federal Bureau of Prisons' medium-security institutions remains much as described in the previous *Design Guide*. It still consists of two parallel chainlink fences, twelve-feet high and generally twenty-feet apart, and an array of barbed tape on and between the fences. An electronic intrusion-detection system is mounted on the fence and augmented by infrared or microwave detection systems at entrance points. The perimeter is surrounded by a road used by patrol vehicles with armed officers. Usually there are only two access points through the perimeter security. One is a pedestrian sallyport adjacent to the central control center located between the fence lines and at the front with the central administration building. The second is a vehicular sallyport, usually at the rear of the compound, which provides a service entrance. The perimeter security at high-security penitentiaries is virtually identical but adds guard towers. Recently, a decision was made to use a "taut wire" intrusion-detection

Stacked housing at the Federal Correctional Institution in Coleman, Florida.

Florida's Architect/Engineer: Spillis Candella, Coral Gables, Florida. Construction management firm: Morse Diesel, Edison, New Jersey. Construction contractor: The George Hyman Construction Company, Hollywood, Florida. Photo courtesy of the Federal Bureau of Prisons.

Two-story housing units under construction at the Federal Correctional Institution in Victorville, California.

Architect/Engineer: Kaplan, McLaughlin, Diaz, San Francisco, California. Construction management firm: Morse Diesel International, Philadelphia, Pennsylvania. Construction contractor: J. A. Jones, Los Angeles, California. Photo courtesy of the Federal Bureau of Prisons.

system mounted independently from the perimeter fences at future high-security institutions.

At the campus type of facility, typical of the Federal Bureau of Prisons' institutions for sentenced prisoners, the site layout is similar to that in the previous *Design Guide*. The buildings are arranged within the perimeter fences to form an inner compound where most outdoor traffic occurs. One significant difference that has been incorporated is to arrange the inner compound formed by the buildings to allow virtually all of the area to be seen from any spot on the compound. This reinforces the idea of secondary supervision by staff stationed adjacent to the compound or moving through it. At medium-security facilities, the recreation yard usually is located outside this inner compound and access to outdoor recreation is controlled. Another major change to the overall site layout, brought about by the increase in size of these newer institutions, is the use of "stacked" housing units; in other words, two units of two stories each stacked one atop the other. This was done primarily to keep the compound size within reason, even though the number of housing units increased by 50 percent and secondarily as a cost reduction measure.

This "stacking" of housing units has been done at both medium- and high-security institutions. At high-security instutions, the Federal Bureau of Prisons' practice is to locate all recreation activities within the inner compound formed by the buildings to minimize observation of the outside world. The Bureau recently decided not to stack housing units at future high-security facilities wherever possible to allow for as much observation as possible of this inner compound recreation area from the perimeter guard towers.

Other Service, Support, and Program Areas

While there have been a number of changes to other support and program areas at federal facilities, they reflect the decisions and emphasis of a particular correctional system. The amount of space and its layout to provide for these functions must be determined by the policies and circumstances of the particular correctional system or jurisdiction responsible for the facility. These can be expected to vary widely, and this only emphasizes the importance of the planning efforts and design direction discussed earlier. Perhaps the most important thing to remember is the need to plan for the possibility of future change and growth.

Reference
Levinson, Robert B. 1999. *Unit Management in Prisons and Jails*. Lanham, Maryland: American Correctional Association.

Standards for Design and Operations

Allen Patrick
NBBJ Architects
Columbus, Ohio

The notion of standards for criminal justice began over a century ago in 1870. The application and enforcement of them are an important consideration in the planning and design of facilities. Some standards are legally required, others are voluntary. This chapter will provide a brief history of the development of standards, outline the differences between legally required and voluntary standards, and discuss their use and the standards' compliance process.

A Brief History: Before Standards

The intent and notion of standards and the control of them through the process of accreditation was occurring in other public services, particularly academic institutions and hospitals, long before their appearance on the corrections and detention scene. Educational institutions in the late nineteenth century developed standards to consolidate the educational field's definitions, methods, and goals, and to regularize the policies and procedures for admitting or transferring students. Educators also felt a need to protect themselves from competition from institutions of low quality. Colleges failed to make serious use of the standards and finally regional educational associations determined that they could best succeed in controlling standards through the process of accreditation.

The medical profession similarly saw the difficulty in maintaining integrity due to the lack of standard definitions for quality in medical education. This allowed un-

regulated, low-quality schools to operate. The American Medical Association (AMA) existed more than fifty years before it developed standards for medical education in the early 1900s. The American Medical Association established its Council on Medical Education in 1904. It began testing its first tentative standards in 1906, and after several years, the American Medical Association founded its accrediting body now known as the Joint Commission on Accreditation of Health Care Organizations (JCAHO) in 1933. This program provides accreditation for both medical education and hospital management. These experiences served as valuable historical lessons for the authors of standards and on the effective use of them through an accreditation process.

The intent of the first prison managers in the United States was "reforming" their prisoners. Their guide to operations were individual biases, instincts, and their notion of common sense about how to control and correct prisoners. Many employed a philosophical approach based on religious principles. At that time, those religious principles did not consider criminal personality or the effects that prison life impose on human behavior.

Eventually, in the beginning of the nineteenth century, a new concept of imprisonment with labor was adopted as a better means of punishment than the former harsh corporal penalties. This new concept was profound and humane as compared to previous corporal penalties. The Walnut Street Jail in Philadelphia was adopted for this new penitentiary concept shortly after the Revolutionary War in 1790.

Over time, however, corrections managers and leaders realized that prisons were not reforming inmates and, in fact, severe management problems were becoming more visible. New management concepts began to appear such as a reformatory-type facility for youthful offenders. The introduction and rapid spread of probation and parole programs at the turn of the century brought still another means for managing offenders.

The body of experience in corrections and program approaches was diverse and growing. Some were positive and some negative. However, it was from this body of experience that the notion and creation of standards would begin.

The Beginning of Correctional Standards

There were concerns that there was no organized philosophy or common thinking among prison wardens and managers for dealing with the variety of management concepts and management problems. The Reverend Doctor Enoch Cobb Wines, a preacher and prison reformer organized a meeting, the "Congress of Penitentiary and Reformatory Discipline," which took place in Cincinnati, Ohio in 1870. As a consequence, and after verbose oratory and proclamations by this group of prison wardens and politicians, a "Declaration of Principles" was written and approved. This historic meeting became the organizing meeting for the National Prison Association. The organization continued from that point in time until 1954 when its name was changed to the present American Correctional Association.

The **Declaration of Principles** consisted of thirty-seven statements that ranged from a management philosophy to sanitation issues to comments regarding heating, ventilation, and sunlight. These principles were the first organized and serious attempt to formulate standards for prison facilities. They were diverse, not particularly organized, and lacked a focus, but they were progressive and a bold step in the improvement of prison management.

These principles were the best philosophical guides produced by an organized body that broadly represented the corrections field. They languished for nearly a century with little or no impact. No mechanisms nor any particular urgency enforced their application.

Since the principles were neither precise nor measurable, and with the independent and minimum oversight of prison managers by governors, legislators, or the courts, there also was no pressing need to enforce or even encourage their use. Prison wardens seldom were challenged regarding their authority or practices. Prisons were "hands-off."

In the mid 1900s, the "hands-off" attitude that had kept prisons free from legal challenges began to diminish. A court suit in 1944 was a significant precursor to the change of attitude that wardens, rather than the courts, best knew how to manage their prisoners. In that suit, a prisoner claimed he had suffered injuries due to assaults from "guards" and fellow prisoners. The sixth U.S. Circuit Court of Appeals ruled that "A prisoner retains all the rights of an ordinary citizen except those expressly, or by necessary implication, taken from him by law."

Over the next several years, the courts heard a number of cases that addressed a wide range of prison issues. The resulting decisions began to define the basic rights of prisoners. Wardens no longer were able to operate with unchallenged independence. This new vulnerability generated an interest in having standard, valid operational principles, that would be common to the corrections field in general.

The Standards Movement

During the 1950s and 1960s, administrators realized that standards of prison operations needed to be implemented by some process. Standards had been available but not used. Recognizing that the "principles" developed in 1870 had very little impact, the National Prison Association attempted to achieve greater effectiveness by organizing these principles, rewriting them, and turning them into standards. In 1946, the National Prison Association published *A Manual of Suggested Standards for a State Correctional System*. Later, in 1954, the same year that the National Prison Association changed its name to the American Correctional Association, it published a revised edition, *A Manual of Correctional Standards*. Both the name change and revised manual reflected the change from the emphasis on prisons to a concern for the whole range of correctional services.

Leaders in the field of corrections increasingly recognized that the country's detention and correctional institutions were not prepared to deal successfully with the increasing pressures of crowded prison conditions, obsolete physical plants, court suits, and the growing sophistication and aggressiveness of prisoner advocates.

As a consequence, the American Correctional Association initiated a significant project to develop explicit, defined, measurable standards for adoption by correctional institutions. During the annual Congress of Correction that was held in Cincinnati in 1970, the site of its origination a century earlier, delegates heard a final report on the "Project on Self-Evaluation and Accreditation." The board of directors approved the recommended plan and the general membership ratified it. New standards were to be prepared and made effective by a system for promoting and certifying compliance.

During the 1970s, the American Medical Association also was developing its own standards for jail and corrections populations. The American Medical Association surveyed almost 1,200 jails. In 1972, it reported that there were serious shortages in dental care, nurses, mental health care, and that only about one-third of the jails had a physician available on a regularly scheduled basis. In about half the country's jails, physicians only were available through on-call arrangements. As a result of the survey, the American Medical Association obtained a Law Enforcement Assistance Administration grant to prepare standards for medical services in adult and juvenile facilities, including preadjudication holding and postadjudication incarcerations. The first American Medical Association standards through this initiative were published in 1976. The American Public Health Association also wrote standards that were published in this year.

The American Correctional Association initiated a significant project to develop explicit, defined, measurable standards for adoption by correctional institutions.

Organizations representing specific components of detention and correction services set and wrote standards focusing on specialty areas. These included psychology, prison industries, libraries, halfway houses, and criminal justice education. Similarly, several states developed their own standards for jails, correctional facilities, and youth facilities. These standards typically were written by the membership and staff of the respective organizations and the agencies working as task groups.

Enforcement of the Standards

With the variety of standards being developed by the various focus groups and agencies dealing with components of the criminal justice system, the question of which standards to use, how to apply them, and their true value seemed to be a difficult morass. Also because of the deep interest, need, and various standard writing activities by the components, agencies, and interest organizations, a mechanism was needed to bring a sense of organization and an enforcement process to make the standards meaningful. Certainly, standards with no enforcement are meaningless. Borrowing from the historical lessons of the American Medical Association and the educational field, the American Correctional Association determined that accreditation using standards as a basis for accreditation would create the meaning, measurement, and value for corrections standards.

Beginning in 1968, the American Correctional Association began a movement for an accreditation process. In 1970, the American Correctional Association developed "An Accreditation Plan for Corrections," a result of the "Project on Self-Evaluation and Accreditation." This resulted in a Federal Law Enforcement Assistance Administration grant for a one-year standards revision project to rewrite the manual of standards into a format useful for accreditation purposes. The first American Correctional Association standards manual, *Adult Parole Authorities*, was published in 1976. It was followed by the manual for *Adult Residential Services* and *Adult Probation and Parole Field Services* in 1977.

The American Correctional Association continues to be the body to create, write, and approve the standards upon which accreditation is based. The standards are developed through discussions among experts who typically hold strongly divergent views. These discussions are held through task groups and staff who write, edit, and rewrite the actual text of the various standards. Considerations included are the vast number and complex variations of situations that must be accommodated. Issues of jurisdiction, history, tradition, size, inmate population types, and architecture are considered. Concerns of climates, political realities, and local regulatory requirements are weighed. The end result is a standard that often has a comment that interprets and explains the standard to help those undergoing accreditation.

After the standards have been written, in the American Correctional Association process, they are tested in the workplace. Those that are flawed when applied in the operational setting are rethought and rewritten. In 1978, a state parole board and four community residences were the first agencies to receive accreditation. The first accreditation of a state prison occurred in 1979 and the first jail in 1980. Thus, the implementation of standards as measurable and certifiable requirements for criminal justice facilities was in place.

Legally Required Standards and Voluntary Standards

Standards are developed, used, and enforced for the protection of health and life. They come in a variety of forms and applications. The most essential determination is the recognition of the difference between legally required and voluntary standards.

Local requirements, state standards, and federal standards, where applicable, are legally required standards. Standards promulgated by professional organizations and interest groups such as the American Correctional Association, the American Bar Association, the American Medical Association, the American Library Association, and others are voluntary standards, unless the courts mandate adoption of American Correctional Association standards as a way to redress problems.

Local Requirements

Local requirements, as they relate to criminal justice facilities, deal with the use of land and general construction of buildings. Building codes, zoning regulations, land use covenants, health department regulations, fire marshal requirements, and other local and state regulations are both minimum standards and legal requirements. They typically do not address specific security issues or concerns, and in many instances, criminal justice facilities such as holding, detention, and corrections facilities are exempted from parts of these local requirements.

Local requirements as applicable are required by law and legally enforced. Compliance with these requirements is mandatory. They are enforced by the government agency responsible for their promulgation.

Compliance is recognized by an occupancy permit, health certificate, or other applicable documents that will permit the occupancy and operation of the site, building, or functional area for its intended use.

For criminal justice facilities, these standards are requirements that apply for the protection of health and life, as it pertains to the structural safety, environmental minimums such as air changes, and fire safety such as fire protection, exiting, and other safety issues. In certain instances, where security is an issue, such as in holding, detention, and corrections facilities, exceptions to these requirements are noted with alternative requirements

referenced, which in turn become the minimum standard or requirement. Fire protection and exiting are of particular importance.

State Standards

State standards for holding, detention, and corrections are legal requirements for the design and construction of criminal justice facilities, where applicable. State standards apply to facilities constructed by the state for its own use. These standards are applied as design guidelines during the planning and designing of institutions.

Operational standards are monitored and enforced internally by the state. Several states also have standards for holding and detention facilities that are operated by counties, municipalities, and other government jurisdictions within their state. In those cases, compliance with them is a legal requirement and mandatory. Compliance usually is acknowledged through inspections by the appropriate agency (such as a state jail inspector—typically part of the states' department of corrections or prisons). Compliance is acknowledged by certification that the facility meets state standards and can be used for its intended purpose. States that do have jail inspection and certification programs can and do enforce compliance with state standards by denying certification to noncompliant facilities and ordering their closure.

In some states, state facilities enjoy eminent domain and are excused from local requirements. However, in most instances, state criminal justice agencies make every effort to comply with local requirements as a courtesy, even though legally they are not required to do so. County criminal justice facilities comply with state standards in those states where state standards exist. Designers are advised to contact the state department of corrections or prisons to confirm the standards that are applicable, the enforcement agency, and the specific procedures for certification of the criminal justice facility being designed.

Federal Standards

Federal standards apply to criminal justice facilities designed and constructed for the federal government for its own use. Federal standards closely parallel those developed by the American Correctional Association but are specific for federally owned and operated facilities. These standards are applied as design guidelines for federal institutions and are monitored by representatives of the federal agencies for the type of institution in question. In other words, the Bureau of Prisons, the Immigration and Naturalization Service, the General Services Administration, and so forth, monitor correctional facilties being built for them. During the design process for federal facilities, compliance is acknowledged by the approval and release of contract documents for bidding. Operational aspects of standards compliance is monitored internally by the operating agency involved.

Federal facilities enjoy eminent domain and are excused from state standards and local requirements. However, in many instances, federal criminal justice agencies attempt to comply with state and local requirements as a courtesy—even though they are not legally required to do so. This is particularly so regarding the state fire marshal's approval for fire and life safety.

American Correctional Association Standards

American Correctional Association standards are voluntary. These standards are not legally required for any criminal justice facility, unless cited by a court of jurisdiction as the standards that must be followed. When cited in a court finding, the American Correctional Association standards become a legal requirement.

The American Correctional Association standards are enforced through self-evaluation, self-monitoring, and an auditing process conducted by the Commission on Accreditation for Corrections. Compliance is acknowledged by accreditation of the facility. The standards consist of mandatory requirements, which are relevant to life safety and nonmandatory standards. To be considered for accreditation, criminal justice facilities must be 100 percent compliant with the mandatory standards and at least 90 percent compliant with all others.

Accreditation is valid for a period of three years. As voluntary standards, accreditation acknowledging compliance may be renewed every three years.

All applicable local requirements, state standards, and/or federal standards applicable to criminal justice facilities must be complied with when meeting the American Correctional Association standards. American Correctional Association standards are not a substitute for those requirements, which are separately enforced, as described previously.

American Correctional Association standards and accreditation is an acknowledgment that the facility meets life safety requirements, and it implies a high level of operation. These standards often are used as a defense against lawsuits through documentation and the demonstration of a "good faith" effort to improve conditions of confinement, increase accountability, and enhance public credibility for administrative and line staff, provide a safer and more humane environment for personnel and offenders, to the establish measurable criteria for upgrading programs, personnel, and the physical plant on a continuing basis.

Other Standards

Professional organizations have developed other standards. These include the American Bar Association, the American Medical Association, the American Library Association, the American Public Health Association, the American Association of Correctional Psychologists, the Correctional Industries Association, the National Sheriffs Association, and others.

Compliance with their areas of interest sometimes are acknowledged through accreditation. Separate from the American Medical Association, the National Commission on Correctional Health Care (NCCHC), provides an accreditation process for health care services in jails, prisons, and juvenile custodial institutions.

The American Correctional Association now has an accreditation process for the health care in these institutions, as well. Law enforcement agencies can be accredited though the Commission on Accreditation for Law Enforcement Agencies (CALEA).

Several of the organizations dealing with components of the criminal justice system such as the International Community Corrections Association (ICCA), the Correctional Education Association (CEA), the American Library Association (ALA), the American Association of Correctional Psychologists (AACP), and the American Public Health Association (APHA) do not have accreditation programs.

Designers are encouraged to advise their clients of the possibility that international treaties could include rights for noncitizens and seek written direction on any provisions to be included in the facility design. Detained and incarcerated noncitizens are provided certain rights through international treaties between countries. These international treaties can have a significant impact on every part of the justice system—including federal, state, county, and city jurisdictions. For detention and incarceration facilities, the most important right to be provided to noncitizens may be the prisoners' right to contact their embassy or consulate during intake procedures.

Various treaties may refer to international standards or United Nations' Minimum Rules, which can vary from United States' standards.

Designers are advised to consult with their clients to determine accreditation and certificates desired from professional organizations that have developed written voluntary standards.

The Use of Standards

As outlined previously, certain standards are legal requirements. Use and compliance with them is mandatory, where applicable. Local requirements, state standards when applicable, and federal standards when applicable must be followed to secure occupancy and/or use permits for the beneficial operation and use of facilities. Whereas the application of legal standards is mandatory for the design and operation of criminal justice facilities, the application of voluntary standards is discretionary.

Voluntary institutional standards can be applied for focused areas such as health care services, library services, industries, and so forth. In some cases, as previously discussed, accreditation or certification may be secured for those specific parts of a facility or operation for which standards have been published.

The most comprehensive dynamic standards for holding, detention, and corrections facilities for juveniles and adults are the American Correctional Association standards. These standards have been created and published through a consensus process among corrections administrators, corrections practitioners, and representatives of allied bodies such as law enforcement, the American Bar Association, and the American Institute of Architects. American Correctional Association standards serve as the basis for the only national accreditation program for all components of adult and juvenile corrections.

American Correctional Association's Published Standards

The American Correctional Association has published eighteen manuals of standards for accreditation and two manuals of standards for certification. They are available for purchase.

The American Correctional Association's published standards are organized into a format that deals with the total range of activities and building requirements of a

---

American Correctional Association accreditation standards are available for the following areas:

Administration of Correctional Agencies

Adult Community Residential Services

Adult Correctional Boot Camp Programs

Adult Correctional Institutions

Adult Local Detention Facilities

Adult Parole Authorities

Adult Probation and Parole Field Services

Correctional Industries

Correctional Training Academies

Electronic Monitoring Programs

Juvenile Community Residential Facilities

Juvenile Day Treatment Programs

Juvenile Probation and Aftercare Services

Juvenile Detention Facilities

Juvenile Training Schools

Small Jail Facilities

Small Juvenile Detention Facilities

Juvenile Correctional Boot Camp Programs

Standards for certification of focused areas are for:

Food Service Programs

Health Care Programs

---

facility. They address services, programs, and operations essential to good correctional management, including administrative and management controls, fiscal management, personnel, staff training and development, case records, information systems and research, and citizen involvement and volunteers; physical plant, which includes building and safety codes and emergency procedures, siting, inmate housing, environmental conditions, programs and service areas, administrative and staff areas, security, and institutional operations including food service, rules and discipline, and a variety of subjects that comprise good correctional practice. The American Correctional Association standards are under continual revision to reflect changing practice, current case law, new knowledge, and agency experience. Those changes are published by the American Correctional Association in the *Standards Supplement* that appears every two years.

For the designers of facilities, physical plant standards include requirements such as building and safety codes; specifics on the size, organization, and location of the facility and rooms in it, including inmate housing; environmental conditions; programs and services; administrative and staff areas; and security. Details will vary from manual to manual, depending on the type of facility or the program.

For accreditation purposes, any new architectural design, building and/or renovation of an institution must be in accordance with the edition of the standards current at the time of such design, building, and /or renovation.

American Correctional Association Accreditation

American Correctional Association standards compliance is acknowledged through the Commission on Accreditation for Corrections' accreditation process. Invitations to participate in the American Correctional Association/Commission on Accreditation for Corrections' accreditation process have been extended to all adult and juvenile agencies for which standards have been developed and published. Participating agencies include public and private agencies in the United States and Canadian correctional agencies. The timeliness, requirements, and outcomes of the accreditation process are the same for any agency or facility for which standards have been published, whether public or private, city, county, state, or federal jurisdictions.

American Correctional Association/Commission on Accreditation for Corrections' accreditation is begun by the applicant programs and facilities signing a contract and paying a fee. The agency receives the applicable manual of standards and an organization summary. The agency enters into a candidate status, conducts a self-evaluation, undergoes a standards compliance audit after it meets the required level of compliance, then is awarded or denied accreditation by the Commission on Accreditation for Corrections.

The standards compliance audit is conducted by trained American Correctional Association consultants who form a "visiting committee." The purpose is for the committee to measure the agency's operation and physical plant against the applicable standards, based on documentation provided by the agency, and a tour of the facility.

During the audit, members of the visiting committee review documentation prepared for each standard and interview staff and inmates (where applicable) to make compliance decisions. In addition to auditing standards' documentation, the visiting team will evaluate the quality of life or conditions of confinement, where applicable or conditions of the workplace, where applicable. An acceptable quality of life is necessary for an agency to be eligible for accreditation.

Quality of life includes overall physical conditions, including adequacy of living, support, and program space. It includes institutional maintenance related to sanitation, health, and safety; and adequacy and quality of programs, activities, and services available to inmates and their involvement in turn; and occurrences of disturbances, serious incidents, assaults, or violence, including their frequency and methods of dealing with them to ensure staff and inmate safety. Quality of life issues are very important considerations for planners and designers, as they design and specify types of spaces, quantities, and sizes of spaces, adjacencies, program envelopes, security envelopes, security barriers, equipment, and systems of criminal justice facilities.

American Correctional Association standards and accreditation information is available from:

American Correctional Association
Department of Standards and Accreditation
4380 Forbes Boulevard
Lanham, Maryland 20706-4322
(301) 918-1835.

Other standards and accreditation information may be found by contacting the National Criminal Justice Reference Service (NCJRS) at (800) 851-3420.

Designers are encouraged to confer with their client and the American Correctional Association Division of Standards and Accreditation for the specific publication(s) applicable for facilities in question. Accreditation is awarded by the Commission on Accreditation for Corrections for a period of three years. Agencies may continue accreditation through reaccreditation. The same process is repeated for each accreditation period.

Agencies that do not maintain the required levels of compliance throughout the three-year accreditation period may have their accreditation award revoked. Agencies that are deficient are notified with a specified time to cure the deficiencies. Should the agency fail to correct the deficiencies, the Commission on Accreditation may revoke the agency's accreditation and request that the Accreditation Certificate be returned to the American Correctional Association.

Conclusion

The preceeding information provides a brief overview of the standards and accreditation process. Designers should contact local building and zoning regulatory agencies, state regulatory agencies, and federal agencies, as applicable, to determine the standards and guidelines legally required for the criminal justice project in question. Designers should confer with their client/using agency to determine their desire to comply with applicable voluntary standards. The agencies and organizations that have published standards and corresponding accreditation or certification programs should be contacted directly by the designer to secure specific detailed information and processes required for standards compliance.

References

Keve, Paul W. 1996. *Measuring Excellence: The History of Standards and Accreditation.* Lanham, Maryland: American Correctional Association.

Travisono, Anthony P. and Mary Q. Hawkes. 1995. *Building a Voice: The American Correctional Association— 125 Years of History.* Lanham, Maryland: American Correctional Association.

Predesign Needs Assessment

Bobbie L. Huskey
President, Huskey & Associates, Inc.
Chicago, Illinois

When a jurisdiction decides that a new facility is needed, policymakers should conduct a needs assessment to determine the size and type of facility to be built. The needs assessment is the precursor to the architectural planning and design process.

A needs assessment is a process of gathering and analyzing crime data, assessing the use and impact of current options, and forecasting the need for future bedspace and program service slots. It should assess the extent that the current facility can be used in the future, develop and evaluate the feasibility of facility and program policy options, and build support for implementation.

The ultimate outcome of the needs assessment is to quantify the number and type of secure, special needs, and less secure beds needed to house offenders and the number and type of program options required to supervise nonviolent offenders in lieu of confinement. Non-residential supervision options provide mechanisms to reduce the admissions to juvenile and adult facilities, thus increasing the facility's likelihood of staying within its functional and design capacity.

There are important benefits to conducting a comprehensive needs assessment. Without a clear understanding of past and projected future trends, jurisdictions have a tendency to overbuild or underbuild for their needs. Since incarceration facilities are the most expensive option within the graduated continuum of options, policymakers should not risk building more or less than needed. Being proactive helps policymakers prepare for future trends by being data- and policy-driven rather than crises-driven. Anticipating external community issues and trends allows correctional officials to shape their future direction rather than merely react to forces imposed on them.

The results of needs assessments are often sensitive; they involve siting a new facility or expanding alternative programs. A compelling and well-documented case is required to convince citizens and lawmakers to build a new facility or to expand alternatives to confinement. Jurisdictions have found it is a much easier task when they seek outside technical assistance to develop a case that is driven by facts rather than local or state politics.

Engaging the assistance of an unbiased third party can help jurisdictions successfully adopt and implement recommendations. Many jurisdictions retain the services of a juvenile expert and/or criminal justice planner to lead their needs assessment. A planner is a practitioner with hands-on experience in criminal and juvenile justice planning.

To do a needs assessment requires individuals with knowledge and operations experience of what are the best practices in criminal and juvenile justice, community based corrections, and policy and program development. Special skills are required: posing the right research questions, critically analyzing enormous amounts of information, building consensus, identifing patterns, forming unbiased recommendations, and translating them into easy-to-understand position statements.

Staff typically do not have the time to conduct a needs assessment nor are they considered an objective third party. Jurisdictions should use an outside planner before retaining an architect or contractor because many recommendations relate to a variety of system components that do not yet involve the design or construction of a facility.

The Six Major Steps of Needs Assessment

STEP 1: Formation of an Ad-hoc Steering Committee

To ensure successful completion of a needs assessment, the jurisdiction should form an ad-hoc steering committee. This committee should consist of both implementers and influencers. Implementers are those individuals who will make referrals to or operate the facility. These include judges, prosecutors, public defenders, law enforcement officials, court administrators, probation officers, juvenile/adult detention directors, state corrections directors, public building commissioners, schools, and community service providers (such as, mental health, substance abuse, and other private agencies). Influencers can help mobilize public support and should include local universities, clergy, business and civic groups, citizen advocates, victims, and agencies receiving community service work from offenders.

The role of this steering committee is to guide the planning process and to provide a liaison with the funding bodies. They will review trend information, discuss interpretations of the data and review and provide feedback regarding the feasibility of study recommendations. Often, the steering committee will be engaged in educating the community about the need for the facility by developing communication messages, developing local and statewide public education strategies, and by participating in local and statewide town meetings.

Visual presentations enable an ad hoc steering committee to understand growth trends necessary to guide the planning process.

Photo courtesy of Huskey & Associates, Inc.

STEP 2: Trend Analysis

The first step in documenting the size of your facility is to analyze the historical changes in confined populations. The planner will collect, analyze, and document the percentage change from year to year and the average annual change across years. This trend analysis will serve as a basis for future population and capacity forecasts.

The types of data that should be gathered and analyzed includes the following:

- Information on the general population
- Population at risk
- Referrals by type of crime/gender
- Arrests by type of crime/gender
- Petitions by type of crime/gender
- Admissions to and releases from jail or juvenile detention by type of crime/gender
- Average daily population in jail or juvenile detention by legal status (pre-adjudicated/adjudicated/gender)
- Admissions to and releases from adult or juvenile corrections facilities by type of offense/gender
- Average daily population in adult or juvenile corrections facilities by gender
- Average length of stay by legal status/gender
- Risk factors that lead to delinquency, when dealing with juveniles

---

These data are entered into a specially created database and analyzed using a nationally accepted social service statistical software program, which computes percent change each year and the average annual percent change across all years. The average annual percent change is important since it "smooths" out fluctuations from year to year. This monthly/daily average annual percent change will serve as the basis for population and bed-space projections.

Visual presentations will be critically important in illustrating the historical growth trends in a community. Through discussions with the steering committee, these trends should be explained and factored into population forecasts.

STEP 3: Offender Population Analysis

Trend analysis is important in assessing the growth patterns in the number of adults and juveniles who are processed through the criminal justice system. However, it does not give local officials an accurate picture of the type of offender who is likely to be incarcerated in the future. Knowing the risk and characteristics of the confined population is important in determining the classification of future populations, the types of beds that will need to be planned, and the types of spaces for program services and activities for these populations.

The method for quantifying the risk and need profiles of the population include a snapshot analysis. Areas of examination include demographics, current and prior offense profile, escape potential, prior incarcerations, behavioral need (mentally ill and developmentally disabled), infectious disease status, educational level, employment at time of admission, substance abuse needs, and stability of the population. Using the guidelines of the National Institute of Corrections and nationally accepted research techniques, a sampling methodology is developed to ensure that the conclusions drawn from this analysis are representative of the confined population.

This information can be used to answer several important policy questions. It determines what classifications will need to be housed in the new facility. And, it provides answers to what type of program spaces need to be planned.

For example, a county in Kansas determined that its juvenile population fell into several important classifications that would need to be addressed in the proposed facility. The profile analysis helped this jurisdiction learn that 15 percent of their detained population were special need and thus a special need unit of twenty-one beds had to be planned. Nationally accepted best practices promote classifying inmate populations by gender, risk, assaultive behavior, and special need. This snapshot research enables jurisdictions to quantify these classifications.

The third policy question the offender population analysis answers is—do all these offenders need to be securely confined in the proposed facility or can a portion of them be dealt with in lower security facilities or on nonsecure supervision alternatives to confinement? For example, after analyzing the confined jail population in a county in Iowa, it was decided that 19.2 percent of the adult inmate population were low-risk and could be diverted to other forms of supervision, thus saving the county 127 future beds. Most officials today recognize the potential savings for considering alternatives for low-risk defendants/offenders.

Without a population analysis, it is not possible to answer these questions with a great deal of accuracy. The profile analysis is a critical tool in establishing new policy on the use of future incarceration resources and on the number and type of beds and supervision slots a jurisdiction will need.

STEP 4: Case-handling Process

As many practitioners know, the case-handling process has a direct impact on the length of stay of offenders detained in jails and juvenile detention facilities and may increase the number of beds needed. This analysis includes the following:

- Developing a flow diagram of each step in the criminal/juvenile justice system
- Outlining the functions for each step
- Identifying the time to complete each step
- Analyzing the mechanisms in place to expedite the cases
- Comparing current practices with nationally accepted standards and best practices

If the length of stay in detention can be reduced, even slightly, fewer beds will need to be planned. For example, an Iowa county projected a 13 percent bed savings as a result of hiring a case expediter to track cases from arrest to disposition.

A lengthy case-handling process also has an impact on public safety for those defendants not detained. A California county found that youth brought into custody and released to their home while their case was pending were a risk to public safety. These youth were returned home with no case management oversight while waiting for their cases to be disposed of, which took up to 180 days for youth not detained. During the first thirty days, 15 percent of these youth reoffended. By 180 days, nearly 40 percent of these youth reoffended. Experience in other jurisdictions indicates that case management supervision for those youth returned home and sufficient juvenile detention beds for those who pose a risk to public safety are effective approaches to reducing the risk of future reoffending.

A needs assessment would not be complete without an analysis of the steps in the criminal/juvenile justice case-handling process from arrest to adjudication and from commitment to release.

Step 5: Capacity Projections

A key component of the needs assessment is to assist the agency in developing long-range projections for secure, less secure, and nonsecure beds and both program and support functions. A comprehensive approach that involves both capital and noncapital capacity projections will provide a more effective recommendation for the citizens of a community than a singular approach.

Bedspace projections should forecast the community's need for secure and community-based facilities. Beds should be projected for the following classifications:

- Male and female
- Pre- and postadjudicated
- Security level (minimum, medium, maximum, closed, community-based)
- Special need categories (including, emotionally disturbed, developmentally disabled, physically ill, violent, and aggressive)

Program-service slots for nonsecure supervision strategies (alternatives to detention or to state facilities and transitional and aftercare programs) should be projected.

Most researchers use one of two methods of projection methodologies or a combination of the two. The "growth method" uses the average percentage change in the past to project for future years. The "least squares method" draws a line through the data to minimize the deviations among the data. These two methods are the most widely used in criminal and juvenile justice research. Projections are developed for a minimum of ten years.

Projections are not a precise science. While they are based on actual historical trends on a monthly/daily basis, they are shaped by policies and philosophies of criminal and juvenile justice officials. For example, if a prosecutor is elected on a philosophy of increasing the number of offenders sentenced to state facilities, there will be great pressure to increase the number of offenders sentenced to state facilities.

Forecasts should be based on a number of factors in addition to historical trend data. Current and future philosophies of officials, mandatory sentencing laws, changing demographics, peaking, and classification considerations are all factors that should be reviewed.

A peaking factor accounts for fluctuations in the daily population. An agency should not project its facility size on the highest or the lowest population figures but on an average of these days. The *peaking factor* is a statistical measure to smooth out these fluctuations and provide a more accurate picture of the demand for beds on a consistent basis.

A classification factor allows administrators to have sufficient capacity to deal with special situations that arise on a daily basis. Administrators always are faced with special need offenders who cannot be housed either in the same cell or near other offenders. Special observation rooms or specially designated cells near staffing

Figure 1.3.1
Impact of Alternative Policy Options

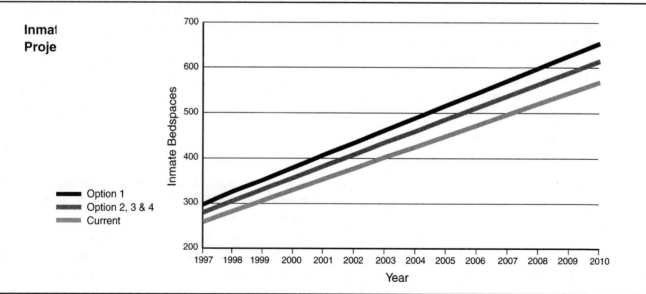

posts are required to ensure the safety of these offenders. Facilities should strive to operate within their "functional capacity" rather than their design capacity. This functional capacity, which is the number of inmates a correctional facility can program and house effectively, ranges from 85-95 percent of the facility's design capacity.

Since projections reflect the policies and philosophies of criminal and juvenile justice officials, it is important to develop several scenarios (*see* Figure 1.3.1). Current trend projections reflect the capacity need if no new policies or programs are implemented. This assumes that the historical growth will continue at the same rate, the length of stay will be constant, and the number of alternative programs will grow at the same rate as in the past.

However, modified projections factor in new policies and alternative programs that could reduce the number of beds the jurisdiction targets over those offenders who have a high likelihood of being incarcerated. These modified projections also should factor in potential failure rates for those offenders participating in these alternative programs. For example, in a county in Iowa, 660 jail beds were projected if no new practices and programs would be implemented. However, this jurisdiction expects a potential savings of 140 beds with the hiring of a case expediter, the expansion of the pretrial supervision program, development of drug court diversion, and a public service program for low-risk sentenced traffic offenders.

These projections become policy options that should be considered by policymakers. Experience shows that when the planner proposes a variety of policy options in addition to building solutions, greater support will be obtained from voters when the facility plan is proposed as a bond referendum.

Step 6:   Facility Assessment and Recommendations

An assessment of the current facility determines the adequacy of the existing facility to meet future demand. The assessment examines the current net area of the facility and each of its operational components.

If a decision already has been reached to build a new facility, the purpose of the facility assessment is to confirm current square footages and to examine how the current facility is used. This information will be important in preparing for facility planning as it identifies how staff currently operate the facility and how they might want to design the space in the proposed facility. It also will be an important educational tool in future public meetings about the facility as it will help the community gain a better understanding of how the new facility compares with the current facility.

On the other hand, if the agency has not yet decided on whether to renovate or expand its current facility or to build a new one, the facility assessment becomes an important step in helping the agency make its decision. Areas to be assessed in this case are the following:

- Current design capacity versus projected population

- Extent to which the current facility complies with local, state, and national standards for acceptable conditions of confinement

- Net usable area for each of the major operational components (for example, intake and receiving, housing, medical, education, programs, dining and food preparation, administration, visiting, laundry, and facility maintenance)

- Life expectancy of the building and its systems (for example, structural elements; heating/cooling; ventilating systems; sprinklers; and security, plumbing and electrical systems)

- Current site usage and legal regulatory zoning issues, such as availability of future site development if expansion is the preferred policy option

- Cost of renovation versus new construction

- Projected time frame for either renovation or new construction

- Ability of the existing facility to be expanded

In either scenario, the planner should use the American Correctional Association standards for facility design and operations, state and local standards and codes, and Americans with Disabilities Act requirements to guide the facility assessment and recommendations. The planner should work closely with the jurisdiction's public works department or the state building commission to ensure that the proposed facility plan meets the guidelines of these agencies.

From this analysis, the planner should offer a series of recommendations. The advantages and disadvantages of renovation and expansion of a current facility or new facility construction will be analyzed and discussed. For example, a county in Kansas determined that new construction on a new site was more viable than using the existing facility because the new facility would provide the most flexibility in housing youth according to a classification plan; it would allow other functions on the current site to expand, and the proposed new facility would minimize exposure to future legal interventions since it would be designed to American Correctional Association and state standards.

Preliminary construction costs for new facility construction should be projected for each option proposed. National experience indicates that the average cost of construction for secure detention beds for adult and juvenile facilities is between $60,000 and $150,000 per bed. Less secure residential cost options range from $20,000 to $40,000. After examining local contractors' cost data, these costs can be projected more specifically.

However, these costs for a new facility cannot be projected in detail until a thorough pre-architectural plan is developed that outlines specific square footages for each space, which identifies the cost of land acquisition, site development, any off site utility system improvements, movable equipment costs, a construction contingency, and architectural and engineering professional fees.

Report and Presentations

All relevant data, analysis, summary of findings, and recommendations are then developed into a draft, and a final report is developed for presentation to the ad-hoc planning committee, boards of county commissioners, state legislatures, policymakers, community groups, and the media. Regularly scheduled meetings with these key groups throughout the needs assessment process will be important for gaining understanding and support for the plan's recommendations.

Conclusion

This discussion highlighted six major steps in conducting a needs assessment. Depending on the needs of the jurisdiction, the needs assessment can either include some or all of these elements. Priorities will be unique to each jurisdiction.

A needs assessment will require sufficient resources to complete it successfully. The fee for a predesign needs assessment usually is based on the elements required: the projected hours spent to complete each task, and projected travel and out-of-pocket expenses.

The building of a new facility is an expensive investment for a jurisdiction. Many administrators will have only one chance in their career to build a new facility. In a real sense, this facility is the legacy of the criminal and juvenile justice system administrators and offenders who will use it and the citizens who will pay for it. Proactive planning will be critical to ensure that the facility will not be crowded the first day it opens or that the system will have adequate population management options to manage its future growth. Citizens and policymakers deserve a well thought out and documented plan to guide them for the future. The needs assessment will serve as the basis for the development of a long-range vision for criminal and juvenile justice services.

Other Recommendations

To assist the agency in developing a comprehensive master plan for facilities and programs, the needs assessment will offer recommendations regarding the following:

- Projected cost of developing and operating alternatives to confinement (National costs range from $3.00 or less a day for regular supervision, $15.00 for intensive supervision, and $48.00 a day for a community residential facility)

- Projected beds saved through the development of alternatives to confinement (National experience shows that a diversion factor of between 5 and 35 percent has been used, depending on the philosophies of policymakers)

- Strategies to build public support for the master plan (National experience shows that specific communication messages need to be developed and these need to be translated into written educational materials, and meetings with key community leaders and editorial boards; also, individual interviews with media are effective)

- Strategies to evaluate the options based on a program evaluation protocol, and performance measures (American Correctional Association and other national organizations promote the development of this process, including intermediate and long-term performance measures to evaluate correctional programs)

1.4

Correctional Facility Site Selection

Dennis Sommers
Nebraska Department of Administrative Services
Lincoln, Nebraska

The site selection procedure is a key component of the development process for a new correctional facility. The location of a new prison project can have a major impact on the initial cost of construction and influence the operational cost of the facility for the future. A variety of methods are used for making the site selection, ranging from simply choosing to add a new facility to an existing correctional complex to the development of a comprehensive statewide competition to provide a host site. No matter how simple the site selection may appear, mistakes made early in the selection process may lead to delays in the construction process, which may add up to years.

Traditionally, the locations of new correctional facilities were selected by lawmakers, based on recommendations of correctional officials, often mixed with a generous portion of political considerations. However, in recent years, regions and communities view new correctional facilities as an opportunity for economic development. A new correctional facility can bring a large payroll accompanied by hundreds of stable job opportunities for community residents. Typically, new prison facilities cannot afford to provide the full range of services required to serve their inmate population, instead preferring to contract for services within the local community.

The "not in my back yard (NIMBY)" attitude toward correctional facilities has not disappeared, however, as an obstacle to the site selection process. To be effective, the site selection process must recognize that there will be a negative perception by some affected community members toward the introduction of a new correctional facility. The development process must identify community concerns early and deal with them by the implementation of a community-based information and educational process. Like any attempt to introduce a change to a community, communication is the key to a successful correctional site selection process.

Methods of Site Selection

There is no single prescription for success in site selection. However, with hundreds of correctional facilities having been built within the last decade to accommodate the nationwide increase in the incarcerated population, some trends have developed. Generally, the methods of site selection can be subdivided into three categories:

(1) Selection based on the use of land currently owned or controlled by state or local correctional jurisdictions

(2) Selection based on regional or political considerations as part of project authorization and funding legislation

(3) Selection based on community or regional competition to provide a host site for the facility

While each of these processes can be used successfully to provide a useful site for a correctional facility, each has advantages and disadvantages. A detailed description of each of the processes, along with their relative merits follows.

Selection based on land currently owned or controlled by state or local correctional jurisdictions

Typically, the departments of correction in states and large communities hold title to sizable parcels of land. Often this is due to the inclusion of major agricultural operations as part of the correctional work programs. While many of the agricultural operations have become less active in recent decades due to changes in correctional programming, the agricultural land often remains under the ownership of the corrections department.

The use of an existing site allows facility planners to make many decisions prior to the request to authorize and fund the facility. The site selection process can become almost entirely internal to state and local officials. Often, the decision to colocate a new correctional facility on a site of a currently operational prison can be justified by initial cost savings and operational cost savings that can be achieved through shared resources, infrastructure, and programs.

Preselection by legislators based on regional political considerations

This might be termed the "old fashioned" method of site selection where the location for a new correctional facility is determined within the lawmaking process as part of the project funding decision. The process may be as formal or informal as the lawmaking body may choose. The input of the department of corrections and the members of the host community might be considered in advance of selection or they may not. The land parcel might be existing state-owned land (other than that currently used for correctional purposes as described above), or the selection of the site within the selected community might be left to a committee of lawmakers or correctional officials.

Like any of the site selection processes discussed here, the degree of success of the political site selection depends on the degree of planning and attention to detail that are included in the process. While this process can be done in a manner very similar to the competitive site selection process in the following discussion, very often it is not. The process described here assumes that many of the steps included in the

---

Potential advantages and disadvantages of the use of existing corrections property for new facilities:

Advantages:

1. There are reduced development costs because there are no land acquisition costs and minimal utilities development costs.

2. There are reduced operational costs due to the sharing of existing ancillary facilities and staff.

3. Negative community reaction is minimal because neighbors have experience and have become comfortable with an existing facility.

4. Site planning is made easier because the topography, soil conditions, and utility capacity are known in advance.

5. Political elements of the site selection process can be minimized.

6. Community zoning and land use issues are not a factor.

Disadvantages:

1. Correctional facilities tend to be concentrated in a limited number of areas where correctional facilities traditionally have existed.

2. There is a potential for negative community reaction to becoming known as a prison town as additional correctional facilities are added.

3. The ability of the new correctional facility to provide an economic development opportunity for communities and to take advantage of enhanced community-based programming opportunities and human resources is minimized.

open-competition process are not done completely or are omitted entirely, resulting in the potential for many pitfalls.

Potential advantages of the political site selection process might include the following things:

1. The selection procedure can be done quickly with a minimum of bureaucratic process. The legislation, which authorizes funding and construction, simply includes a specification of where to build the facility, in terms that either are very specific or are limited to a community or region.
2. The selection of a site might be used as a means to garner lawmakers' votes for a particular project, thereby expediting the passage of the necessary legislation for a correctional project.

The potential disadvantages to this site selection process are numerous:

1. The correctional project may not be well defined at the time of funding, which could lead to later surprises for the selected host community.
2. The cost of site acquisition and development may not be available prior to the selection of the site by lawmakers. Correctional officials may be forced to return to the lawmakers to request increased funding. Selected communities may find that they will incur significant costs to improve the municipal infrastructure to support the new facility.
3. Site acquisition may require extensive negotiation with community planning and zoning authorities. Property acquisition by eminent domain may be involved. Any of these processes can result in costly delays in the development of new facilities.
4. There is an increased likelihood that there will be organized community opposition to the siting of a correctional facility in a town or region that feels it was not adequately consulted and informed before the decision was made. A very extensive program of education and dialog with neighborhood groups and organizations will be required by the department of corrections and community leaders to "sell" a decision that has been made already.
5. The overriding factor in the final decision as to where to site a correctional facility within a selected city may become, "Where is there the least neighborhood opposition?" This can lead to very significant increases in costs for site development and operational support as these factors become secondary considerations.

While site selection by the political process might appear to be a recipe for disaster, it need not be so.

Today, many enlightened lawmakers do foresee the potential pitfalls of making the important decision as to where to locate a major correctional facility without working extensively with corrections officials and community groups beforehand. Hopefully, the process would include many of the factors that are described in the competitive site-selection process that is detailed later in this document.

Site selection based on community or regional competition to provide a host site

Within the last decade, as correctional construction has mushroomed to house the rapidly increasing incarcerated population, the idea that new correctional facilities can be marketed as economic development opportunities has resulted in a new process of site selection. Communities have recognized that a prison facility brings with it many stable, well-paying jobs, and an industry that spends money in the local community to buy goods and services. This approach has helped to offset the negative connotation that the public has always had about correctional facilities.

Communities have recognized that a prison facility brings with it many stable, well-paying jobs, and an industry that spends money in the local community to buy goods and services.

Typically, the process involves the preparation of a detailed "request for proposal" (RFP) prepared by governmental officials for response by regions or communities, which might be interested in being considered as a host site for a correctional facility. The RFP must describe, in detail, the requirements of the proposed correctional facility and should be accompanied by an extensive program statement for the facility, which explains fully what communities may expect to see happening in the facility when it is operational. The RFP also must explain how potential sites will be evaluated and who will make the final decision. While the program statement and typically the RFP are prepared by correctional officials, evaluation of potential sites and decision making can be the responsibility of committees made up of lawmakers, state and community leaders, building professionals, state officials, or a combination of all of these.

The many potential advantages of site selection by this process include the following:

1. If done properly, the process involves lawmakers, correctional officials, and the members of the community in the site selection process. There should be no surprises.

2. All costs associated with the acquisition and development of the prison site are known before the final site decision is made.

3. Corrections officials are given access to community research through the RFP process. The availability of land, human resources, and community-based services are identified by the selection process. Each factor can be weighted according to its relative importance to corrections officials in the decision process.

4. When the selection process is completed, site acquisition and development can begin almost immediately with minimal probability of unforeseen delays and costs.

5. The community can resolve issues of community education, planning and zoning issues, infrastructure financing and construction financing, site sizing, and price before a response to the RFP is offered for state consideration.

Most of the disadvantages to this site selection process relate to the work involved to do it right. They include the following:

1. Lawmakers must be willing to make the decision to fund the project (at least partially) without knowing where it might be sited.

2. The RFP development process can be time-consuming and difficult. It clearly must define the factors to be included in the decision process and require that communities respond with proposals that are complete. The program statement, which accompanies the RFP, must be complete and understandable to community leaders.

3. Intense competition for large correctional projects by communities when combined with an incomplete or ambiguous RFP can result in delays in the selection process and legal action.

Most states that have used the competitive site selection process have met with success. The process assumes that a number of communities will believe that being a host for a correctional facility has the potential to be a positive experience. Even with very favorable economic conditions and low unemployment rates in recent years, communities (especially small rural towns that may not have participated fully in

Site Selection Evaluation Guidelines

The selection of a site for a correctional facility involves a number of areas of consideration. While the needs of various facilities will vary with facility size and level of security, certain general evaluation categories are applicable to nearly all proposed sites. The evaluation process can and should be used no matter what form of the selection process is used to determine the site location.

Prior to establishing the site evaluation process, a number of elements of the proposed correctional facility must be defined. Generally, these items are described in the program statement for the project, which often is completed as a part of the justification for authorization and funding by lawmakers. Key elements to be defined by the facility program are the following:

1. **The mission** of the correctional department and goals for the proposed project

2. **A history** of the project and a justification of the need for the project, which may include inmate population projections and population demographics

3. **A detailed description** of the proposed facility including:
   A. Inmate capacity and security classifications
   B. Potential for future capacity expansion
   C. A definition of the types of inmate programs

D. A description of the management philosophy for the staff and inmates at the proposed facility

E. A physical description of the proposed facility including character of construction, perimeter security, and portions of the physical plant to be placed inside or outside of the secure perimeter

F. The detailed architectural space program listing functions, adjacencies, and square footage assignments

G. Desirable site size and characteristics

H. Project legislation and proposed funding for initial construction and for annual operation

I. A proposed project schedule

4. **Expectations** of the correctional department for ongoing community support including infrastructure requirements, human resources, and community-based programs and services

5. **Summary** of what the correctional facility may offer the community, including a definition of the size and character of the annual operational budget and number and type of full-time employees to be required

the growing national economy) continue to show interest in submitting site proposals for new correctional facilities. The key to the process remains the request for proposal which clearly lays out a decision matrix for all parties involved in the process. The following section describes how such a matrix is used, with minor modifications, by several states, as the keystone of a successful site selection process.

Elements of the Site Selection Process

If the officials who will make the decision as to where to site a correctional facility are to make an informed decision, a number of elements need to be completely defined during the site evaluation process. Each of the key informational elements is identified and described separately below:

Location

The general location of the site should be identified by detailed maps of the proposed site and the surrounding area. Information relating to the surrounding area might include location of churches, residences, schools, and parks or recreation areas. Additionally, the evaluation should identify the proximity of properties, which may cause disruption to the proposed facility. Disrupting properties might generate noise, odor, air pollution, ambient light, or radio transmissions, which would conflict with the correctional operation.

In addition to the assessed value of the proposed correctional site, the evaluation should include the average appraised value for agricultural land, industrial land, residential land, and local taxing rates for each taxing entity.

The evaluation should include information about the zoning of the site and land use plans of the areas surrounding the site. The site's proximity to adjacent communities and nearby metropolitan areas should be identified. The proximity of the proposed site to the department of corrections' central offices and other supporting facilities should be considered.

Site Information

The information relating to the specific proposed site should include maps and aerial photographs in sufficient detail to evaluate the size of the proposed

site, potential expansion area, and the availability of a buffer zone to separate the correctional site from surrounding properties. A survey of the proposed site performed by a licensed surveyor should show the boundary of the land, locations of improvements, highways, streets, railways, creeks, and existing utilities. Information relating to special conditions, such as fault lines, geological data such as the 100-year flood plain, 500-year flood plain, the water table, easements, and rights of way must be considered.

The total acreage of the proposed site should be known. A topographic map identifing site contours, wetlands, and the locations of any existing buildings and improvements, is useful. Information relating to access roads to the proposed site, both permanent and temporary for facility construction are needed.

Finally, information relating to existing site ownership and the required method of acquisition or conveyance of the site is required. If the proposed site will be donated, assurances must be obtained that the method of conveyance will be timely and minimal in cost to the state or other subdivision of government.

Environmental Information

As a minimum, to facilitate the initial evaluation of the site, a Phase I Environmental Site Assessment must be performed. The assessment should be performed by professionals who have experience in conducting environmental assessments. The report should include complete documentation to support any conclusions relating to the environmental conditions of the site. The report also should address any archeological or historical significance issues and provide an assessment of any other hazards present on the site. If the findings of the Phase I Assessment warrant, site evaluators may wish to pursue additional phases of assessment to ensure that sufficient environmental information is available to assess the site adequately.

Utility Information

For large correctional facility projects, the development of water and sewage treatment systems may be included in the construction project. More commonly, proposed new correctional facilities' sites will be situated to allow them to take advantage of the existing utilities' infrastructure of nearby communities. When that is the case, the cost and availability of utilities can have a major impact on new facility development and should be evaluated thoroughly.

Deep concrete caissons, extending to the bedrock, were used in the foundation at the Federal Detention Center in Philadelphia. Extensive archeological research was needed to clear the site. A tunnel connects the detention center to the courthouse across the street, which allows the inside transfer of prisoners. (The detention center is on the left and the courthouse on the right of the photo.)

Philadelphia's Architect/Engineer: Ewing Cole Cherry, Philadelphia, Pennsylvania. Construction management firm: The Temple Group, Washington, D.C. Construction contractor: Keating Building Corporation, Bala Cynwyd, Pennsylvania. Photo courtesy of the Federal Bureau of Prisons.

The utilities evaluation should provide information relating to the adequacy, cost and details of electricity, natural gas, water, elevated water storage, wastewater treatment, solid waste disposal, and telecommunications. Accurate estimates of utility usage and overall utility requirements of the proposed new facility will aid in the evaluation of utilities. The potential need for new housing at the facility to accommodate institution staff also should be considered when looking at utility capacities.

The utilities evaluation should begin with the provision of maps, which depict locations of all utilities along with a scenario of how these utilities will be brought to the prospective site. Public utility commission maps showing electric utility certification plus detailed county and area gas pipeline maps, sizes of lines, pressures, and so forth should be provided. A map of water/sewer lines, sizes of lines, capacity, lift stations, and water tower locations should be included. Any alternative sources and corresponding cost (for example, gas transportation rates, standby liquid petroleum gas, backup water or wastewater systems, solid waste compactors) should be identified, if available.

An analysis of the water supply for the site should be obtained. Information pertaining to the water source and chemical analysis for the Environmental Protection Agency, local health department, or local environmental quality offices should be used. Water should be analyzed for its mineral and chemical content. The availability of water flows at the site for fighting fires, including pressures and gallons per minute, should be measured against the expected emergency requirements of the proposed facility.

The design load and current actual load on community wastewater systems also should be known. The correctional facility's projected wastewater loading parameters should be weighed against the capacity of the local wastewater system. Any potential wastewater surcharges should be identified and evaluated.

Evaluators should obtain commitments relating to all utility rates for the proposed project. The rate proposals must include any debt service repayment for extension of community utilities to serve the new project. Where possible, utility companies should be asked to provide actual rate tariffs, contract forms, riders, utility discounts, power factor correction incentives, and other available rate cost information. The site evaluation and negotiations should identify any incentive rates, which might be available as part of the agreement to locate the facility in the community.

The timing of the availability of temporary and permanent utilities should be provided by local suppliers. The project construction and occupancy schedule should be compared to the utility availability to determine if construction delays may result.

Finally, the availability and cost of telecommunication and radio systems should be evaluated. The location and capacity of local communications, the ability of the system to accommodate future system enhancements, in other words, fiber access, should be evaluated. The location and frequency of the nearest law enforcement and emergency services radio base stations should be identified.

Community/Surrounding Area Conditions and Services

Typically, a new correctional facility will rely on the local community to provide a number of services, which would be expensive and difficult for the facility to provide. Specifics relating to the availability of the community to respond to the facilities' needs are required to evaluate the proposed host site properly.

Most likely, fire protection services will be required from the local fire department. The local fire department often is relied on to provide emergency medical treatment services to the facility. The location of the closest fire protection services should be ascertained along with the number of personnel they have available at all times, and the range of services that they can provide.

Similar to fire protection services, the availability of the local police or sheriff's office should be considered. The location of police stations or sheriff's offices should be evaluated along with expected response times. The number of personnel available and any specialized training and abilities that they have should be evaluated. Also, evaluators should attempt to obtain some sort of commitment from the community indicating their willingness to assist in response efforts at the prison facility.

The proximity of other state and local government offices to the project site should be considered. Potentially important adjacencies include state police offices, parole offices, and other health and human services offices. The proximity of a county attorney's office or other judicial offices, which may interact with the residents of the correctional facility, should be evaluated.

The presence of educational facilities in the community can be an important factor in providing programs for correctional facilities. Community-based academic programs may provide educational programs for inmates, both in the correctional facility setting and in area schools. Ideally, the community should provide access to secondary education, junior college, and college degree programs.

Many correctional facilities work with private industries to provide job training and employment skills for inmates, both in the community and within the correctional institution. The availability of industries within the community, which may have an interest in working in public/private joint ventures to provide inmate jobs, may be a key enhancement to inmate work programs.

Many correctional facilities work with private industries to provide job training and employment skills for inmates, both in the community and within the correctional institution.

Finally, the availability of various means of public transportation and hotel/motel accommodations within the surrounding community are needed to support corrections employees and the friends and relatives of inmates who come to visit. Maintaining contact with family and friends is essential to inmate rehabilitation programs, so means to travel to the location of the correctional facility and a place to stay when there are important, especially if the site is somewhat distant from major metropolitan centers in the region.

Health Services

While many correctional facilities provide health care facilities and staff within the institution, because of the range of services which must be provided and the high cost of maintaining a qualified medical staff, most correctional facilities want to contract with local providers for a range of health services. The availability of an accredited full service hospital in the community may be relied on to provide many of these services. Additionally, the availability of emergency twenty-four-hour medical care should be evaluated.

The number and type of community health care providers in the general area of the correctional site should be considered. A list of area care providers should be developed, and should include physicians, psychiatrists, dentists, clinical psychologists, nurses, certified alcohol and drug abuse counselors, and certified social workers.

Area Workforce and Housing

The major component of the operational cost of correctional facilities is the personnel services budget. Since the great majority of staff who will work in the new facility will live in the surrounding communities, it is very important for site selection groups to evaluate thoroughly the availability of potential employees and housing opportunities for the staff.

In addition to the population of surrounding communities, the demographics of the workforce should be identified and evaluated. The analysis should include average wage data, the unemployment rate, and major area employers. If the area is rural, information should be provided, which may indicate the willingness of the workforce to commute to job locations.

The analysis of local area housing should include the number of single family dwellings that are vacant and information relating to the number of rental units available and the occupancy rates, to indicate the number of units typically unleased. Information should include mortgage rates, rent averages, and the proximity and quality of schools in the community.

Community Support

The failure of the site selection group to accurately assess the level of community support or opposition to the location of a correctional facility in the vicinity can cause delays in project development or even cause a planned project to be abandoned. If the site is being selected as part of competition among communities to become a candidate site, the host community can be required to provide public information and assess community attitudes as part of the proposal process.

Evidence of the degree of local support may include documentation of support from community agencies or organizations. Public informational meetings should be held with times, dates, and number in attendance recorded. Other means of showing support may include letters of support from community leaders, public opinion polls, community surveys, and formal public hearings. In addition, the site selection group should hold formal public hearings as a part of the comparative site selection process.

Site Acquisition Form of Agreement

Prior to making the formal site selection, the site selection team and the host community should have some sort of consensus on the formal agreement, which will be executed by all involved parties. This form of agreement may be prepared by the correctional department or other government officials in advance so that disagreements or misunderstandings relative to terms of the agreement do not needlessly delay the formal development of the project after the final site selection has been made.

Other General Information

Each potential site for a correctional facility may have elements in its favor or against it, which are not adequately described in these categories. Such items might include evidence of support from state senators, county boards, city councils, or other influential public officials. Information might be included relative to the public media network, the court system, or other community features, which might support a correctional facility.

Climatic data may be useful for evaluation in states where the climate may vary widely from community to community.

Since, in most cases, the construction of a new correctional facility can present a very significant construction project, information about the number and capability of construction contractors in the area may be useful.

For projects where the site selection is done under a competitive process, any unique features of a community or special incentives to encourage the location of the correctional facility should be identified completely. Incentives should be offered and evaluated as part of the public selection process.

The Site Selection Decision Matrix

When all of this information has been presented and documented for each of the prospective correctional facility sites, the information should be recorded and rated on a weighted evaluation matrix. In the event that the site is selected as part of a competitive process in response to an RFP, the selection matrix should be prepared in advance and made available to all communities, which may respond to the RFP.

The following is an example of a site selection matrix that was used in an RFP for a 920-bed correctional facility in Nebraska. It demonstrates how all of this information might be aggregated and evaluated in a fairly concise manner.

SITE PROPOSAL EVALUATION FORM

PROPOSER: DATE:

PROJECT: NEBRASKA DEPARTMENT OF CORRECTIONAL SERVICES
           960 Bed Multicustody Correctional Facility

Category	Ph. I	Ph. II	Category Weight	Raw Score	Significance Factor	Weighted Score*
A. LOCATION			10	0-1-2-3-4		
1 ADJACENT NEIGHBORHOOD	X				0.150	
2 OFF-SITE ACCESSIBILITY	X				0.250	
3 PROXIMITY TO ADJACENT COMMUNITY	X				0.250	
4 ZONING CONDITION	X				0.150	
5 OTHER SITE LOCATION ISSUES	X				0.200	
Subtotal					1.000	
B. SITE AND CONSTRUCTABILITY			15	0-1-2-3-4		
1 SITE SIZE	X				0.100	
2 ADDITIONAL EXPANSION AREA	X				0.050	
3 BUFFER AREA	X				0.050	
4 COST EFFECTIVENESS/SITE CLEARING	X				0.070	
5 SOIL CONDITIONS	X				0.030	
6 FLOOD PLAIN	X				0.200	
7 PREPARATION COST	X				0.050	
8 GEOTECHNICAL		X			0.100	
9 ON-SITE ACCESSIBILITY	X				0.050	
10 CONFIGURATION DIMENSIONS	X				0.080	
11 PHYSICAL CHARACTERISTICS	X				0.060	
12 EASEMENTS	X				0.080	
13 OWNERSHIP/CLEAR TITLE	X				0.050	
14 STORM DRAINAGE	X				0.030	
Subtotal					1.000	
C. ENVIRONMENTAL			8	0-1-2-3-4		
1 PHASE I ENVIRONMENTAL ASSESSMENT	X				0.3000	
2 ADJACENT AREA		X			0.100	
3 ARCHEOLOGICAL/PALEONTOLOGICAL/HISTORY	X				0.100	
4 HAZARD ASSESSMENT	X				0.300	
5 ECOLOGICALLY SENSITIVE ENVIRONMENT (e.g. Wetlands)	X				0.200	
Subtotal					1.000	

* Weighted Score = Category Weight X Raw Score X Significance Factor

Category	Ph. I	Ph. II	Category Weight	Raw Score	Significance Factor	Weighted Score*
D. UTILITIES			17	0-1-2-3-4		
1 ELECTRICAL SERVICE AND RATES	X				0.120	
2 WATER SERVICE AND RATES	X				0.150	
3 WASTE-WATER SERVICE AND RATES	X				0.200	
4 NATURAL GAS SERVICE AND RATES	X				0.120	
5 SOLID WASTE DISPOSAL SERVICE AND RATES	X				0.110	
6 TELEPHONE SERVICE	X				0.050	
7 TEMPORARY SCHEDULE OF SERVICE DELIVERY		X			0.100	
8 PERMANENT SCHEDULE OF SERVICE DELIVERY		X			0.150	
Subtotal					1.000	
E. COMMUNITY/SURROUNDING AREA CONDITIONS & SERVICES			14	0-1-2-3-4		
1 FIRE RESPONDER	X				0.180	
2 LOCAL POLICE/SHERIFF'S SERVICES	X				0.080	
3 OTHER STATE OFFICES AND SERVICE AGENCIES	X				0.100	
4 TELEVISION/RADIO RECEPTION & TRANSMISSION	X				0.080	
5 EDUCATIONAL SERVICES	X				0.170	
6 INDUSTRY	X				0.170	
7 MOTEL/HOTEL ACCOMMODATIONS	X				0.100	
8 TRANSPORTATION SYSTEMS	X				0.120	
Subtotal					1.000	
F. HEALTH SERVICES			7	0-1-2-3-4		
1 AVAILABILITY OF MEDICAL PROFESSIONALS	X				0.250	
2 PROXIMITY TO LOCAL HOSPITALS	X				0.200	
3 ACCREDITATION STATUS OF ADJACENT HOSPITALS	X				0.200	
4 LOCAL MEDICAL SUPPORT FOR TREATING INMATES	X				0.200	
5 PROXIMITY TO REGIONAL MEDICAL FACILITIES	X				0.150	
Subtotal					1.000	
G. AREA WORK FORCE AND HOUSING			11	0-1-2-3-4		
1 POPULATION BASE	X				0.350	
2 WORK FORCE DIVERSITY	X				0.250	
3 UNEMPLOYMENT	X				0.150	
4 HOUSING	X				0.150	
5 EDUCATIONAL FACILITIES (K-12)	X				0.100	
Subtotal					1.000	

* Weighted Score = Category Weight X Raw Score X Significance Factor

Category	Ph. I	Ph. II	Category Weight	Raw Score	Significance Factor	Weighted Score*
H. COMMUNITY SUPPORT			7	0-1-2-3-4		
1 COMMUNITY SUPPORT	X	X			1.000	
Subtotal					1.000	
I. LEGAL			5	0-1-2-3-4		
1 NEB. DEPART. COR. SERV. AND COMMUNITY AGREEMENT		X			0.350	
2 BOND/LETTER OF CREDIT/LEGAL COMMITMENT		X			0.300	
3 LAND TRANSFER		X			0.350	
Subtotal					1.000	
J. GENERAL			6	0-1-2-3-4		
1 COMPATIBILITY WITH NEB. DEPART. COR. SERV. OPS.	X				0.150	
2 FACILITY CONSTRUCTION ATTRIBUTES	X				0.150	
3 OTHER UNIQUE CHARACTERISTICS	X				0.700	
Subtotal					1.000	

TOTALS

Total Score

Percent Score

* Weighted Score = Category Weight X Raw Score X Significance Factor

Notes:

Architectural and Engineering Services

Waller S. Poage, NCARB, CCS
Architect/Planner/Consultant
Alexandria, Virginia

Professional Practice

The last half of the twentieth century has produced many changes, challenges, and new opportunities for the modern design professional. Since the end of World War II, building design has become an increasingly complex endeavor involving new technologies, environmental restraints, increasing governmental regulation, and the complications that result from an ever-increasing population and unceasing demand for larger and more complicated high-tech buildings. In the first half of the twentieth century, individual design professionals who achieved a measurable degree of success in their practice enjoyed the distinction of individual name recognition. In the last half of the century, design professionals are more apt to be recognized through their company or as a group or team of interdisciplined individuals acting in concert. It is rare for clients to obtain the services of the lone, strong individual of years past. Such has been the dual effect of increasing competition in the marketplace and the diversity of individual specialization, as modern buildings have become more complex.

Adult correctional facilities have experienced many changes since the beginning of the twentieth century, as well. In 1900, facilities were strong, secure, but fairly unsophisticated in terms of technology. At the end of the century, correctional facilities have become extremely high-tech buildings requiring a number of interdependent security electronics systems, which operate doors, provide surveillance, accommodate communications, and detect improper intrusion or attempted escapes. As facilities have become more complex, they also have become more expensive. Design of correctional facilities has become a specialty for some design professionals. The design professional who is able to shepherd a modern correctional facility to a successful conclusion should be chosen with extreme care.

In the beginning of the twentieth century, the predominant method of project delivery was through a unique relationship between owner, design professional, and contractor. Under the traditional method, the owner selected a design professional who would design the project and assemble documents describing the work to be done and subsequently and separately, the owner would select a (general) contractor, usually by a competitive bidding process, to execute the work. Design professionals, under the terms of their agreement with the owner, would act as the owner's representative in communicating with the contractor throughout the process of building construction. In the second half of the twentieth century, for a variety of reasons, a number of alternative project delivery systems came into general use. It was not unusual for owners to employ methods such as "multiple- prime contracts," "construction management," "program management," and "design/build," all of which are alternative project delivery methods to the traditional owner/professional/contractor relationship.

Alternative Project Delivery Systems

As alternative project delivery systems evolved, the role of the design professional changed as well. For example, under the traditional owner/professional/contractor relationship, the design professional enjoyed the position of being the primary decision-maker and representative of the owner. Under the traditional owner/professional/contractor relationship, the design professional is the entity to which the owner and the contractor turn for both advice and leadership. Under many of the more modern project delivery systems, the relationship of owner, design professional, and contractor has changed. For example, in certain alternative project delivery systems, the owner may not have a direct relationship with the design professional, or even have a direct relationship with one or more prime contractors.

Selecting the Architect/Engineer

The selection of the architect/engineer is one of the most important steps in the process of project development. The owner is served well when the architect/engineer works directly for the owner, as would be the case in the traditional design/bid/build or the design/multiple-bid/build methods of project delivery. If the owner elects to engage a construction manager, the owner's interests may be served better by keeping the architect/engineer in the traditional owner/professional relationship. The owner usually is served best when the architect/engineer remains in a position to advise the owner directly with no allegiance to either the construction manager or to any of the multiple-prime contractors who subsequently may be involved in the project delivery. The owner should be acutely aware that in the program management method or the design/build method of project delivery, others usually hire the architect/engineer, and therefore, have first call on this person's allegiance. In these circumstances, the architect/engineer will not always be in a position to advise the owner in a manner that may serve the owner's best interest.

Direct Selection

For the purposes of this writing, the term *design professional* has been used to describe a number of alternatives that are available to the owner in achieving the primary goal of a finished building designed to meet the owner's needs. The term design professional as it is defined here may be either an architect or an engineer or both. In the early years of the twentieth century, it was common that architects practiced individually or principally, hiring engineers as subconsultants for purposes of the specialized design of the site, structure, mechanical and/or electrical systems for the project. Since engineers tend to specialize by individual disciplines, the architect often employed a civil engineer for site design, a structural engineer for the foundation and superstructure, a mechanical engineer for plumbing and HVAC systems, and an electrical engineer for the design of electrical power circuits and lighting.

At midcentury, architects and engineers began to combine and offer their services under the umbrella of a single architectural/engineering firm. Projects became larger and more complicated in the latter half of the century. Many owners began to have need of more detailed definition and justification of their project needs before either design or construction was justified. This gave rise to the practice of planning. The planner would be hired to perform studies of an owner's needs, including justification of the cost, identification of alternatives including how and where to site a building, alternatives in building program and alternatives in design and construction methodology. At the conclusion of the twentieth century, it was more common to find the typical design professional practicing under a corporate umbrella offering the combined disciplines of architecture, engineering, and planning services. The design professional of the latter twentieth century was often referred to as the architect/engineer or more simply as the A/E.

Owners may wish to select the architect/engineer directly, that is without going through a formal advertisement, review of credentials, development of a "short" list, and interview process to decide which architect/engineer to hire for their purposes. Perhaps the owner and the architect/engineer have a history of working together on previous projects. Perhaps the reputation of the architect/engineer is such that the owner does not see a need or desire to interview a number of architect/engineers.

On the other hand, as is the case with some public owners, law or political decorum may demand that a competitive selection process be employed. In any event, architects/engineers should be selected because of their proven experience, their ability to communicate, and their proven ability to provide leadership in the project delivery process. Secondly, the architects/engineers should be considered because of their ability to design unique and outstanding buildings. Each generation of design professionals has produced a few architects who became celebrated as "Signature Designers." Finally, and most importantly, the architects/engineers should be selected because of their proven ability to recognize and insist on quality of materials and construction methods, which will meet or exceed the needs of the owner and the project.

...architects/engineers should be selected because of their proven experience, their ability to communicate, and their proven ability to provide leadership in the project delivery process.

The design professional, whether this indivdiual is an architect, engineer, planner, or all three, is unique in the assembly of participants who become involved in the project delivery process because the design professional does not have a commodity to deliver. The architect/engineer provides a highly skilled and personally distinctive service to the owner.

While the architects/engineers always should be accountable to the owner for the magnitude, fairness, and basis of their fee, it is seldom constructive or in the best interests of the owner to require design professionals to competitively "bid" their services. When design professionals are asked to compete on the basis of fee as opposed to a qualifications-based selection, the most obvious result is a minimizing of the amount of time that will be devoted to the project. Such minimizing of time may result in:

- Using less experienced personnel and the evaluation of fewer alternatives to better serve the owner's needs

- Developing contract documents with minimal detail that results in increased layout and coordination time and decision making in the field by the contractor

- Selecting systems that require minimum time to design rather than selecting those that may be the most economical and cost effective for the owner during the life of the project

- Providing minimal time in review of submittals of shop drawings and other documentation during construction, leaving the owner vulnerable to lower quality materials and higher maintenance costs during the life of the project

Comparative Selection of Architect/ Engineer Services

While it is not always necessary to do so, there may be good and valid reasons for an owner to select the architect/engineer by a comparative selection process. By comparing the credentials of candidate firms in some form of a formalized comparative selection process, owners have increased confidence that their selection affords the "best" of the best for their purposes. In the case of a public owner, it may be a matter of policy or of law, or certainly it may be in the interest of political decorum, to make opportunity available to a wide number of architect/engineer firms within a particular political subdivision. In these cases, it is advisable for the owner to use one of several comparative processes to select an architect/engineer firm.

The One-step Comparative Selection Process

The one-step comparative process is conducted by advertising a detailed request for proposal (RFP). The RFP establishes a detailed description of the project, establishes detailed criteria on qualifications of candidate architect/engineer firms or architect/ engineer teams that will be acceptable to the owner, and requests a written response from candidates that provide as a minimum:

- A description of the respondent's understanding of the owner's needs and/or the nature of the project

- A description of the respondent's unique qualifications and background experience to serve the owner in the design and related services for such a project

- A description of the respondent's suggested approach to providing the services otherwise, a description of the methodology that will be used in the delivery of architect/engineer service

- A description of qualifications and experience of the personnel that the respondent is willing to pledge for the services to be rendered

- A description of the respondent's current workload and availability of personnel to serve the project

- A list of references or clients for whom similar services have been performed with addresses and telephone numbers

The response to the RFP usually is due to be in the hands of the owner by a specific date and time, after which the owner will review the responses and will make a tentative selection by comparing the various responses. Pending the successful negotiation of fee for the work, the selected architect/engineer firm is contracted for the services with thanks to all participants for their time and interest.

The Two-step Comparative Process

Many owners and architect/engineer practitioners believe that the owner's needs are best served when the comparative selection process is conducted in two or more steps, the second step being the opportunity of a face-to-face interview with the owner's selection personnel. The two-step comparative process is identical to the one-step process, with the exception that the owner, after review of the written response to the RFP, will develop what has become known as a "short list" of three or more of the most qualified firms whose representatives are scheduled for a personal interview. It is helpful to both owner and candidate if the owner publishes in advance the selection criteria and the methodology by which candidates will be ranked to illicit responses that are meaningful but brief in order to conserve the time of the interviewers.

The Three-step Comparative Process

The first of the three steps is to advertise the intention to hire an architect/engineer and to make available a request for qualifications (RFQ). Through the RFQ, the owner may establish general guidelines as to the extent of experience with certain building types, history of practice, size of firm and availability of key staff persons, financial strength, and finally a list of recently completed projects, and owner references from recent commissions. The second step in the three-step process is the development of a "short list" of three or more of the most qualified firms, which are invited to provide a written response to a detailed request for proposal (RFP). The responses to the RFP may follow the general criteria described in the one-step process.

The third step in the process is the development of a second "short list" of two or three candidates selected for a personal interview with the owner. From the interview process, the owner may select the firm that appears to be the most qualified to accomplish the services required. As an optional fourth step in the process, the owner may request in the RFP that each firm which is "short listed" submit a sealed fee proposal along with its general response to the RFP. The sealed fee proposal is opened only after the interview has been conducted and the leading candidate has been identified. If for any reason, the fee proposal of the leading candidate is unacceptable to the owner, the owner may reserve the right to review the fee proposal of the second, and possibly the third candidate to make the final selection.

Competitive Selection of Architect/ Engineer Services

An owner who engages in a process that simply seeks to identify an architect/engineer who is willing to provide the cheapest design is ill advised. The cheap design not only will lead to an inferior product, but may cause a failure in the project delivery process altogether. In approaching a competitive selection process, an owner is better advised to follow the comparative selection process, except that the owner may wish to make certain criteria in the RFQ and/or RFP documents more stringent, thereby creating a more narrow, yet competitive atmosphere in the responses that follow. For instance, an owner may require that the candidate show evidence that the candidate has completed a certain number of projects of a particular type and of a certain order-of-magnitude of cost within a specific number of years in recent history.

If a proposed fee is to be an issue in the selection, the candidates may be asked to provide a separate sealed fee proposal with the response to the RFQ, which may remain unopened until the qualifications have been reviewed thoroughly and a candidate of choice is identified. The reasonableness of the fee then may be the final criteria of the selection process.

The Design Competition as a Method of Competitive Architect/Engineer Selection

Occasionally, an owner may wish to select the design professional (or in some cases the design/build team) on the basis of a design competition. This is seldom either an advantageous method of selecting the design professional nor does it always generate a response from some of the most qualified firms. The cost of a design competition to both owner and design professional can be very high, and therefore, it is not always economical and not always productive. Historically in the United States, design competitions only have been successful where the project has been a highly visible building, which is intended to be a high-profile landmark, where the budget has few if any restraints.

Professional organizations such as the American Institute of Architects have developed guidelines under which design competitions can be conducted on a fair and reasonably equitable basis. First, under such recognized competition models, the owner is expected to prepare a detailed program of design and other documentation that will produce an "apples to apples" or "oranges to oranges" type comparison by which candidate's designs will be judged.

Second, it generally is recommended that a jury of peers (not the owner or the owner's representative) be retained for the purposes of judging the entries. Third, it is usually productive for a series of prizes to be offered as an incentive to the participants in the form of cash awards for the first, and perhaps, up to a fifth place prize in the competition judging. If the only prize offered by the owner is the promise of the award of the commission for the work, experience has demonstrated that winning the commission alone is seldom enough of an incentive to attract the best or most able participants. It is, however, acceptable, even advisable, for the owner to reserve the right to negotiate a professional fee and to award the commission to any participant, the owner may choose, regardless of the outcome of the jury's ranking of the submissions.

In approaching the design/build process, owners have been known to initiate the process by asking the candidates to respond to the request for proposals with a definitive design together with a guaranteed maximum price (GMP). This is, in essence, a form of design competition and should be approached with the understanding that potential design professionals as components of the candidate design/build team competing for this type process may view the risk unfavorably. Consideration should be given to the fact that in responding to the design competition, the design professional component of the design/build team may need to expend from 20 to 40 percent of the typical services required to establish a basis for a guaranteed maximum price.

There are two alternatives in the design/build approach that may overcome the risk problem. The first alternative is for the owner to initiate the process by creating a set of "bridge documents" on which to base the GMP. Bridge documents may consist of a well-defined program of design, a set of schematic design drawings, and an outline of specifications. The program of design establishes fixed parameters of space and function. The schematic design establishes the basic layout and general architectural character of the project. The outline specification establishes the basic materials and methods of construction, all of which eliminate much of the risk that would otherwise fall to the design/build candidate. The second alternative is a procedure where the proposed designs would be judged and awarded some form of a cash prize for the top three to five candidates, thus assuring the design professionals some form of remuneration, for the work that they will have to risk in order to compete.

Primary Responsibilities of the Architect/Engineer

Once the selection process has been completed, the owner may expect that the design professional provide certain basic services that are common to any project, regardless of the method of project delivery that has been chosen. Often, there are issues that must be addressed before the basic services can begin. These elements are often called *predesign* services. Most owners are more completely served if the design professional includes follow-up inspections of the completed building commensurate with the time period established by the several warranties and guarantees that the contractor provides the owner at the final acceptance of the completed building. These services usually are referred to as *post-construction services*.

Basic design services offered by architect/engineering firms include, but are not limited to the following:

Schematic Design

Often called the preliminary design phase, the schematic design phase of the architect/engineer's services is intended to provide a basic project definition illustrating scale and relationship of project components. The schematic design phase usually is limited to studying the site plan and the building(s) plans.

Diagrams may consist of "one-line" floor plans of buildings and site drawn to scale. The architect/engineer may wish to create studies of building cross-sections and prepare conceptual sketches or simple models of building forms and massing. Definition of security

---

Predesign Services

Predesign services offered by architect/engineering firms and planners include but are not limited to the following:

- Special project requirements
- Architectural program development or confirmation of the owner's program
- Design concepts and alternatives
- Analysis of building code requirements and other jurisdictional restrictions that may be applicable to a particular project
- Site(s) analysis and recommendation
- Budget analysis
- Selection of project delivery methodology and alternatives

---

requirements, levels, and systems unique to correctional facilities should be identified during this phase. A review of probable cost is appropriate at the completion of the schematic design phase of service.

Design Development

The design development phase of the architect/engineer's service is intended to expand on the schematic design phase and more specifically to provide definition to such areas as the following:

Design Development Areas

- Exterior design
- Interior design
- Landscape design
- Security systems design
- Mechanical systems design
- Electrical systems design
- Electronic surveillance/control/communications

Drawings may consist of floor plans, building sections, roof plans, wall sections, and exterior elevations. Security perimeters should be identified for both site (exterior) and building (interior). The design development phase should identify all local, state, and federal building code requirements. The special requirements of other agencies with jurisdiction related to correctional facilities should be identified and factored into the design. Basic engineering services may consist of defining site improvements; structural design; determination of plumbing systems, heating and air-conditioning delivery systems, electrical requirements, and security electronic systems and functions.

It is considered "good policy" that the design development phase deliverables will include (1) a design narrative and (2) an outline specification. A written design narrative should be created by each design discipline, and each should describe in some detail the nature of the design that is intended. The combined document is intended to describe the entire project. The outline specification should describe the products to be incorporated in the design. A good "rule of thumb" for the scope of the design development phase of professional architect/engineer service would be that no less than 90 percent of the design decisions for the project will have been made when the design development is complete.

Contract Documents

Contract documents prepared by the architect/engineer complete the design development phase of service. Following the concept that 90 percent of the design decisions will have been made at the completion of the design development phase of service, the contract documents phase of service finishes the description of the work to be done. In other words, during the contract documents phase of service, all of those decisions become fully documented and coordinated to facilitate the construction process. The completed package of contract documents may consist of a number of related components.

The primary effort by the design professional during the contract documents phase of service is expended in the production of construction drawings and the accompanying specifications. The complete package of contract documents also may include the following items: information for bidders, the bid form, any addenda issued during the bidding process, the form of the contract for construction, the general conditions of the contract, any supplemental general conditions of the contract, and any contract modifications that become necessary during the construction process.

Construction Drawings

The construction drawings are graphic illustrations of the work to be done. Drawings represent the relationships between the components and materials, and they generally indicate the location of each material, assembly, component, and accessory. Drawings identify all components and pieces of equipment, and they indicate dimensions of the construction and sizes of field assembled components. Drawings also illustrate details and diagrams of connections.

Specifications

Specifications are written descriptions that establish the requirements for the physical qualities, chemical constituents, and the standards of work associated with the manufacture and installation of materials, equipment, and components of the project.

Assistance During Bidding

The design professional, depending on the type of project procurement, may assist the owner during the bidding process. The design professional may attend and take part in any prebid conferences that may be held. The design professional may prepare any addenda that may be necessary. The design professional may prepare answers to any requests for information (RFI) that may originate with the various bidders.

Observation of Construction

The owner is well served when the designer periodically observes the work of the contractor. The designer of the project, has the best understanding and opinion as to the full intent of the contract documents and, therefore, is the best representative of the owner's interest during construction. Although some projects require full-time representation of the owner, many projects only require that observation of construction by the design professional be periodic.

The general requirements of the specifications will require that the contractors make submissions of information, disclosing descriptions, illustrations and specifications of the materials, methods of construction, equipment, and other components that they intend to furnish under their contracts. The design professional may review such submittals and approve such information that they observe is in conformity with the contract documents and the intent of the design.

Project Record Documents

The contract documents prepared by the design professional are intended to form the basis of the completed building; however, they may not be accurate enough to serve the owner's needs for maintenance in the future. Many of the drawings, particularly the en-gineering drawings, are schematic in nature and do not always provide a reliable basis upon which to accurately locate any number of elements that may require access. Typical building elements such as pipes, ducts, and mechanical and electrical equipment will require maintenance or replacement once the project has been completed.

The specifications may require that the contractor keep accurate records of the locations of embedded items of construction for the owner's permanent record. Often, such project record documents entail preparing a new set of drawings and specifications, based on the original contract documents. Other documents for the owner's permanent records are the manufacturers' product literature, instruction manuals, maintenance data, and warranties and guarantees on materials and equipment.

Optional Additional Responsibilities of the Architect/Engineer

Services that are not normally part of the architect/engineer's services, but that may be required services by the owner, may include the following:

- Demolition documents
- Environmental studies
- Design of off-site utilities
- Design for multiple contract award
- Design for fast-track construction methods
- Life-cycle cost analysis
- Value engineering
- Staffing analysis
- Study of funding alternatives
- Public information assistance

Value Engineering

Alternatives are available to the owner of the project. The key to choosing the "right" alternative is first to identify and then prioritize the factors of the decision. The three primary decision "drivers" that are common to any project are cost, quality, and time.

Cost is defined as total project cost including "hard" and "soft" cost. Hard cost is the total costs of construction including materials, systems, equipment, labor, and the contractor's overhead and profit and other costs. Soft costs total the costs of land, owner's contingencies, professional fees and incidental cost.

Quality is the measure of attributes, properties, life value and other characteristics of a material, system, or equipment that is to be preferred for its excellence of workmanship, manufacture or attractiveness when compared with alternatives.

Time is defined as the period that is required to bring the project to completion including the time to plan the program, the preparation of the contract documents, and the construction process.

It is important to understand that each of these three factors is mutually exclusive. It is also important to understand that any one of these three factors can be the primary basis for decision, but not all three.

Postconstruction Services

Generally, the contractor warrants the completed project to be free of defects and operational flaws or failures for at least one year after the date of the final acceptance of the project. Many elements of the project may have guarantees and warranties that extend for periods of five years or more.

In most projects, the design professional's basic services are complete when the owner accepts the finished project and a date of final completion has been established.

The owner may find it advantageous to employ the design professional to perform inspections and evaluations of the project. This examination can determine if work by the contractor may be required to meet the terms of the established guarantees and warranties.

It is not possible, in most projects, for the factors of cost and time to be controlled with equal priority. When time is the primary decision driver then quality to some extent and cost will be secondary as the result of subsequent decisions made in order to deliver the project in a predetermined time frame. However, the owner may achieve a reasonable degree of quality control by using "value engineering."

The value of a project should be measured in terms of the useful life of the project. Quality should be measured in terms of initial cost plus the predictable cost of maintenance and/or replacement over a period of fifty years. Life value measuring the human resource functions over the life of the project. For example, if the value engineering process identifies a design that reduces staff by five percent, this could pay for the total cost of construction as savings in fifty years.

Value engineering like partnering has been created in response to the lack of control over quality when either cost or time take precedence. It leads to more informed decisions related to value in selecting materials, systems and equipment and is most effective if applied during the development phase of project development.

Finally, the term value engineering may be misleading if it is thought of only in terms of a process to only reduce initial cost. The term Value Management may be more appropriate if the reader is to fully understand what the process of value engineering is capable of accomplishing in the owner's interest.

Summary

The services of the design professional, usually provided by an architect/engineer (A/E), are an essential part of the procurement of a modern correctional facility. The architect/engineer should be selected with great care with investigation into this person's or firm's proven experience with this type of building program. If the institution under consideration has a probable life of half of a century, the owner should be aware of certain facts related to the life-cycle cost that should influence the decisions in the procurement process.

In terms of proportion, it can be demonstrated that the cost of constructing a modern correctional facility will be less than 10 percent of the life cost of the facility. The remaining 90 percent of that life cost will be expended on staff, maintenance, and support services. Of the remaining 90 percent of the life cost, 85 percent of that amount will be expended on staff salaries.

On the other hand, the design professional's fee is less than 20 percent of the original cost of construction. By this reasoning, a correctional facility with a construction budget of $50 million dollars may expect architect/engineer fees to be approximately $3.75 million. One twenty-four-hour staff post requires 5.5 staff persons to operate that post around the clock. If the average salary of a uniformed officer in the year 2000 is $35,000, discounting any escalation of salary, inflation, and benefits, the cost of that one staff post over the fifty-year life of the building will be $9.625 million. Thus, fees paid to competent architectural/engineering firms ultimately will pay dividends in facilities that perform better both from a building standpoint and with regard to operational considerations.

Architectural Program Development for Adult Correctional Facilities

Sandra J. Brand, AIA
Kennedy Associates, Inc.
St. Louis, Missouri

Development of the architectural program is often the most important part of the entire design process. The programming phase is where the planning occurs to determine a new correctional facility's size, function, and other major characteristics, all of which later influence the design. It is also critical in renovations and additions, in that it again focuses concentration on the desired end results, *before* architectural design begins.

Purpose

The net result of this planning process, the architectural program, is the verbal and graphic representation of a project's functional requirements. It contains a problem statement, design criteria for functional purposes, and aesthetic goals. Program development, ideally an interactive process among consultants, owner, and users, is the user agency's initial occasion to identify key components of the building(s) and influence the architectural outcome of the design solution. Development of this progress is the user agency's first opportunity to influence the functional development of the building.

The collaborative environment of the programming phase allows identification of all the necessary and desired components. A diagram that demonstrates the relationships among departments is the ideal arrangement without the constraints of physical boundaries generated by building forms. The program should reflect the epitome of "thinking outside the box." The programming phase is also the time to identify other major elements of a project such as the facility's gross size, and other preliminary site requirements, such as size, utility constraints, public/transportation access, vehicle access constraints, and so forth.

Participants

The input of the user cannot be overlooked. If user input is ignored, the facility may meet industry standard criteria but may not reflect the unique characteristics of the user agency's jurisdiction. Lack of user/owner dialog has prompted the design industry to note that "If you don't tell us how you want to operate your facility, our design decisions will decide for you." The program phase is an opportune time to involve the transition team or warden who will be operating the facility. Otherwise, making changes as the project progresses through each phase of design, and later construction, becomes progressively more costly.

"If you don't tell us how you want to operate your facility, our design decisions will decide for you."

Participants in the programming phase can be exclusively from the user agency or more diverse to involve multiple points of view, expertise, and operational philosophies. A typical project often is funded and developed through the design and construction branch of the government. However, the user agency will maintain and operate the facility. During programming, the user agency may want to identify the life-cycle issues, of the physical environment and the staff environment, which can influence the operation of the facility significantly. An outside consultant(s) often is commissioned to assist in directing and monitoring the progress of program development, or providing the specialized program direction in areas such as food, laundry, and health services.

Program Vocabulary

A basic overview of key terms used throughout the program process is helpful to understand the mechanics of developing the area required for the facility. Each

---

Key Terms

Infrastructure describes the utilities (sanitation, water, gas, electric), telecommunication/data, and site security.

Net or Unit Area, measured in square feet (or meters), is the amount of unobstructed, *usable* space bounded by walls, partitions, or other physical elements (in other words, office = 150 net square feet).

Adjusted Net Area is the net area plus the area required to circulate from one net area to another *within* one department or program service (in other words, office 150 x 1.25 = 188 net square feet).

Circulation Factor is a percentage applied to the total adjusted net area to account for circulation *between* departments or program services.

Gross Area, measured in square feet (or meters), represents the total area required for the facility, including the area required for the structural elements (columns, shafts, wall thickness, and so forth) and nonassignable building elements such as small janitor's closets, small toilet rooms, and small mechanical/electrical rooms or closets. It is advisable to assign net areas to the primary mechanical room, telephone/equipment room, and large public restroom to ensure adequate space within the facility. These items will not require assignment of adjusted net area for circulation.

Net to Gross Ratio represents the efficiency of the building design. Correctional/criminal justice facilities tend to have a lower net to gross ratio than other building types such as commercial office buildings, because of the need for separate but parallel circulation patterns.

Net to Gross Ratio

Net S.F. = Room area = 10′ x 10′ =100 S.F.

Gross S.F. = Room area plus all else =14′ x 11′ =154 S.F.

Gross Factor = $\frac{\text{Gross S.F.}}{\text{Net S.F.}} = \frac{154 \text{ S.F.}}{100 \text{ S.F.}} = 1.54$

Providing adjusted net areas at the programming phase introduces a small cushion of design flexibility. This later may become valuable as the physical constraints of the building may influence the efficiency of a department. It also often accommodates the addition of new spaces during the design development that may have been overlooked (or not in place) during the programming phase.

Programming for correctional facilities also requires determination of *capacity* for the facility. Capacity terms, which are defined below, measure either the correctional system's capacity or the capacity of an individual facility in the system. The capacity terms describe physical plant capacity and do not assess the adequacy of staffing or operation.

Operating Capacity is the number of inmates a correctional facility can program and house effectively. It is based on an analysis of two components—housing capacity and core capacity. Operating capacity is equal to whichever is smaller—housing capacity or core capacity. Operating capacity assumes the physical condition of available space is good and that routine maintenance and repair programs exist to correct deficiencies.

Housing Capacity defines the number of inmates a correctional facility can house based on the occupancy requirements of the user agency (cell size, double/single bunks, dormitories, and so forth) and governing standards such as the latest edition of the American Correctional Association's *Standards for Adult Correctional Institutions.*

Core Capacity defines the capacity to provide nonhousing functions in a correctional facility, such as food service, medical care, recreation, visiting, inmate programs, segregation housing, and facility administration. Traditionally, the operating capacity (often termed *design capacity*) was determined strictly by the housing capacity. It is now more common to invest in core capacity as the facility is designed to allow for easier, future expansion of housing capacity.

Segregation Housing, within a user agency's system, generally should be between 5 and 10 percent of operating capacity. The actual amount required at a specific facility will vary based on the policy of each agency.

---

planner or user agency may have a variation on the descriptive words, but the concepts remain consistent.

Program Process

Depending on the facility's size, the program easily can be developed as two key documents (Part 1 and Part 2). The primary document develops the criteria that will lead to the building's gross size, sizes of key departments, staffing requirements, critical relationships between departments, and spatial relationships within each department. It also should define infrastructure and site-related requirements. From these key elements, the main skeleton of the project is developed. Building/life safety code requirements and correctional standards also should be reviewed at this point.

Steps for Part 1

(Not necessarily sequential)

Information Gathering

1. Identify organizational hierarchy of personnel
2. Determine if facility will use direct supervision versus indirect supervision
3. Determine if program services will be centralized versus decentralized
4. Determine the extent of outsourcing/contract services
5. Determine the boundaries of public movement
6. Determine the level of security within the building(s)/facility operations
7. Identify the spatial relationships of departments/program services
8. Identify relationships within each department
9. Identify and separate circulation patterns of the facility: for the staff, the public, and for secure inmates
10. Identify locations where separate circulation patterns need to overlap/intersect (visiting, court proceedings, shift changes)
11. Develop a questionnaire to discover current operations of key services, existing equipment that may require reuse, and building system parameters (design, temperatures, security systems, and shift limitations)
12. Develop/identify space standards
13. Identify staffing requirements
14. Review the mission statement
15. Tour similar facilities
16. Identify future trends

Kickoff Meeting

Request department heads or key spokespersons(s) to attend the kickoff meeting. It is critical to have one point of contact to schedule future meetings and who will consistently channel key information. At this meeting, discuss the mission statement and develop project objectives. Develop a timetable for meetings and deliverables. Discuss and establish aesthetic criteria and governing standards.

The kickoff meeting is crucial to making sure that everyone is aware of the major elements of the project.

Photo courtesy of Gilbane Building Company. Photographer: Tim Cox.

Department Meetings

Ideally these meetings are conducted with the department heads, and a survey (developed in the information-gathering phase) is distributed for review at the second meeting. Discuss pros and cons of existing operations and review area requirements as they are developed. It is vital to develop area requirements for each department and program area.

Summary of Concepts on Area Requirements

Concepts

Area requirements are a simple listing of each type of space that is needed within a department, the associated quantity of each type of space, and the area required for the spaces. The program area summary reflects the total adjusted net area required by each department. Once the departments are summarized, the net to gross factor (building efficiency) is applied to determine the total gross area.

Table 1.6.1 illustrates a portion of a department summary followed by a program summary in Table 1.6.2 of net area requirements for the facility.

Develop Adjacency Diagrams

Adjacency diagrams (Figure 1.6.1) illustrate the ideal, functional relationships between departments and within a department without the constraints of physical boundaries generated by building forms. Key circulation paths also can be illustrated in these diagrams such as inmate circulation, public access, and staff circulation.

Part two of the program is the detailed description of the individual spaces of the building/facility. This is the detail that each design discipline will rely on as the program is translated into a building design and building systems are developed. This is the opportunity to document special requirements that are necessary for completion of the project but are not germane to the initial design concept. Furniture requirements, specialty finishes, or mechanical, electrical, security and plumbing details can be documented now, with user involvement, and later incorporated as the design team grows exponentially to address the many components of a successful project. A more accurate cost model also can be developed based on the detail provided in this phase of the project.

The architectural program for a new facility is often the most important part of the design process. The construction of Wallens Ridge State Prison, a super maximum security facility at Big Stone Gap, Virginia, required a programming phase not only to determine the facility's size and function, but also to identify its necessary and desired components.

Photo courtesy of Gilbane Building Company. Photographer: Tim Cox.

Table 1.6.1

Area Requirements for Medical/Mental Health Services

| Id. No. | Space/Component | Unit Calculation | | | Requirement | |
		Net Area	Percent Circ.	Adjusted Net	Unit Qty.	Total Net Sq. Feet
08-02-01	Single Patient Room	110	30	143	4	572
08-02-02	Shower/Drying Area	45	30	59	3	177
08-02-03	Isolation Room	220	40	308	2	616
08-02-04	Visiting Booth	40	100	80	2	160
08-02-05	Visiting Room	100	25	125	2	125
08-02-06	Small Multipurpose/Interview Room	200	25	250	1	250
08-02-07	Soiled Utility Room	60	25	75	1	75
08-02-08	Utility Room	100	25	125	1	125

An excerpt of a department summary, courtesy of Kennedy Associates, Inc.

Table 1.6.2
Program Summary of Net and Gross Area Requirements

Program Component		N.S.F.	Gross Factor*	G.S.F.
01. Administration and Training		13,902	1.42	19,741
Administration	(2,423 NSF)			
Business Office	(3,115 NSF)			
Watch Command	(419 NSF)			
Briefing	(2,325 NSF)			
Staff Physical Training	(1,380 NSF)			
Lobby and Reception	(3,390 NSF)			
Show-up/Video Proceedings	(850 NSF)			
02. Employee Facilities		5,645	1.33	7,508
03. Security and Control		500	1.42	710
04. Housing		130,778	1.81	236,708
05. Reception and Diagnostic		14,313	1.42	20,325
06. Medical/Mental Health Services		8,080	1.66	13,413
Clinic	(3,270 NSF)			
Inpatient Unit/Visiting	(4,335 NSF)			
Clinic/Inpatient Support	(475 NSF)			
07. Inmate Programs		2,458	1.42	3,491
08. Food Services		10,268	1.66	17,045
09. Laundry Services		5,195	1.25	6,494
10. Building Maintenance and Storage		6,565	1.25	8,206
Building Maintenance	(2,215 NSF)			
Loading and Receiving	(4,350 NSF)			
Subtotal Net Area		**197,898**		**333,641**
11. Physical Plant				6,700
Mechanical/Electrical Room		5,200		
Public Restrooms		500		
Vehicle Sallyport (if contained within the building)		1,000		
TOTAL GROSS AREA				**340,341**

* Note that the gross factor is based on historical information and specific age and user operational experience.

Courtesy of Kennedy Associates, Inc.

**Figure 1.6.1
Adjacency in Minimum Security Housing Unit**

(Double Cells)

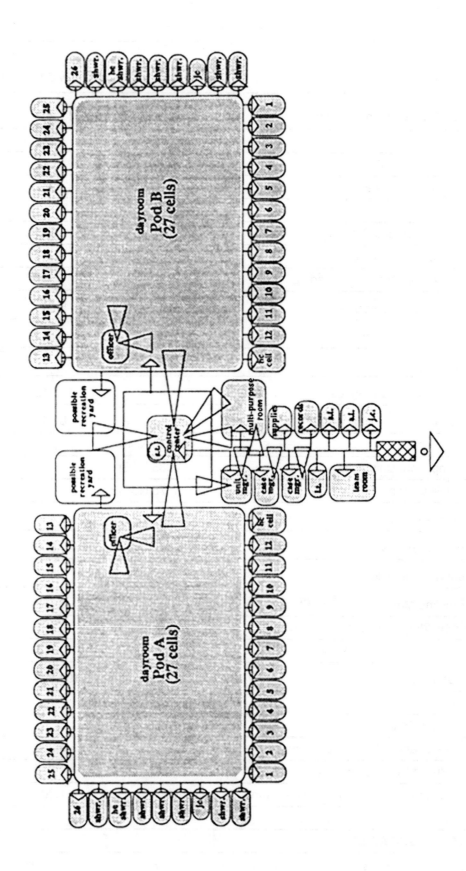

Courtesy of Kennedy Associates, Inc.

Steps for Part 2:

(Not necessarily sequential)

A. Information Development

1. Create a space data sheet for each type of space listed in Part 1 of the program that delineates requirements for the following things: finishes, lighting, plumbing, HVAC, security, communication, furniture, and fixed equipment.

2. Collect manufacturers' information on existing and new equipment to be installed within the facility as either part of the base construction cost or owner furnished. This data is valuable to ensure adequate electrical, data, plumbing, and mechanical services are provided.

3. Generate staffing summaries to verify and relate to the area requirements developed in Part 1 of the program.

B. Department Review

Continue the involvement of diverse groups to allow the expertise of a department to confirm their unique requirements and to gain acceptance of the choices made during the programming process. Initiate development of policies and procedures by the transition team.

Programming for Existing Buildings/Facilities

The program process for an existing building is similar to the process described for a Part 1 and Part 2 program. The information-gathering stage in this case includes an analysis of the existing facility's building systems, life safety constraints, and calculations of available area. Often, an analysis of how the area currently is appropriated will be done to assess the efficiency of the current operation. The process of diagraming the ideal

Partnering sessions at Wallens Ridge State Prison in Virginia, prior to construction. Attendees included Gilbane Building Company, DMJM, Virginia Department of Corrections, Wallens Ridge Economic Development Corporation, Tuck Engineering (site engineer), and major subcontractors. A topographical model of the site is in the plastic case in the foreground. The site is at the top of a 29,000-foot mountain, which was a major issue.

Architect: Daniel, Mann, Johnson & Mendenhall. Photo courtesy of Gilbane Building Company. Photographer: Tim Cox.

design relationships is pertinent to confirm the validity of the existing building and staff's use of the spaces.

The adaptive reuse of buildings originally designed for purposes other than correctional facilities is often the most challenging application of the program process. It is important to assess the operational staff requirements when considering such buildings because the continuing cost of operating a facility can outweigh the initial cost savings presumed from converting an existing building.

Master Plan Models

An outcome of the program process may be a master plan of facility requirements for the user agency. Often, the master plan will generate an "ideal model" of an institution for each security level and any special need, including but not limited to reception and diagnostic, medical/mental institutions, and gender requirements. This will be the basis of program development as funding becomes available for the design of new institutions. Evaluation of existing facilities also can be enhanced by making a comparison to the master plan model.

Summary

Development of a facility program is an organizational method of identifying the many issues, details, and spatial requirements necessary for a successful design project. The outcome of this process is that a user agency will move from very broad issues and multiple user input to a focus on need and building criteria. Conversely, the resulting program document at the beginning is very limited; however, at the conclusion of the program process there is comprehensive documentation that reflects decisions made for an effective, state-of-the-art facility.

Resistance to change can be very strong. Yet, by involvement in the program development process, individuals can develop a sense of ownership and familiarity with the new facility's operating philosophies, which will ease the transition for the user agency's staff. Besides, participation in the process can be rewarding in itself.

Operational/ Architectural Programming for Juveniles

Karen Chinn and Michael McMillen
Chinn Planning
Columbia, South Carolina

Residential facilities for juvenile offenders are becoming more sophisticated due to changes in the character and needs of the population served and increasing demands for safety and security. This occurs in a time of escalating development and operation costs. The long-accepted view that good staff can run a good program no matter what the physical setting has become a less certain proposition as staff increasingly are compelled to divert their attention from interaction and intervention to behavior management and control.

Analysis Needed

In this climate, the need for well-planned facilities has assumed greater importance. Physical environment, staffing, and daily programming must work in concert to ensure safety while providing opportunities for effective responses to juvenile needs. More than ever, the successful achievement of these ends depends on a comprehensive analysis of program goals, daily operations, staffing patterns, and security/environmental priorities as the first step in the facility design process.

Operational Programming

Operational programming establishes the purposes and expectations for the proposed residential program and should involve the participation of diverse local authorities, including representatives of the courts, service providers, related agencies, policymakers, and other key stakeholders. Issues such as protection of the public, internal safety, methods of responding to youth in crisis, program content and opportunities, juvenile rights, positive intervention, and staff involvement with residents, among other issues, frequently are reviewed as the basis for ongoing operational analysis.

The first step in preparing the operational program is the development of a facility mission statement. A mission statement articulates the purpose of the facility and drives the operational concept of the facility. A sample mission statement is shown on the following page.

Once the facility mission is established, specific program and service requirements are established. Daily activities should be structured to ensure the full participation of residents in the widest possible array of productive activities. Experience shows that the greatest benefits to youth, and the most effective behavior management, are achieved when residents are fully involved in structured activities throughout each day. These activities usually include formal education, passive and active recreation, family visiting, counseling, and other services that maintain physical and emotional health. Participation in these activities sets the stage for the provision of continuing services to youth on their return to community settings.

The Mission of the Attention Center for Youth is to protect the interest and safety of the community and the residents by providing a safe, secure, and structured environment for youth and to offer the necessary educational and developmental resources to a culturally diverse detention population.

Guiding Principles

- Safety and security are the priority
- Youth are better able to make positive choices within the context of a structured environment
- Staff emphasize the strengths and abilities of youth
- Initial and ongoing staff training is essential
- Youth deserve to be treated with dignity and respect
- Youth and personnel are more productive within a safe, secure, calm, and healthy environment
- Maintaining a connection with the community enhances a youth's transition upon release

Source: Lancaster County, Nebraska

Operational programming determines when and where activities will occur and identifies related functional components required to support general facility operations, including admissions, food services, administration, central control, medical services, laundry, and maintenance.

Key issues that affect the character, quality, and cost of daily operations also must be examined, including: security/supervision methods, group size, location of activities, support between staff, environmental character, maintenance and repair, and support for future expansion.

- **Security/Supervision Methods**—Will direct or indirect supervision be used? What importance does staff presence make? What types of technological support will be used, for example, door/key control, audiovisual monitoring, communications devices and systems? How restrictive must the construction be? How much access will individuals have? In other words, will there be zone control methods for resident circulation? Will control functions be centralized? If behavior management is used, is there space for emergency responses including time-out, or segregation?

- **Group Size**—Will the housing unit capacity be fixed or of variable size? What space will be needed for activities, for classification, resident interaction/group

maintenance? What provision is made for special needs housing and activities?

- **Location of Activities**—What are the options for housing and the central or dayroom area? What types of residential movement will be allowed? How will this circulation be managed? How much ease of access or freedom of movement will there be during the daytime and in the evening hours? How much flexibility will be built into the space for various uses? What type of public access will there be? What about staff access? What about community linkages?

- **Support Between Staff**—What types of visual and physical connection will there be between spaces? How will staff be able to communicate under normal conditions and during emergency response when there is a need for immediate assistance? How will the space allow for staffing efficiency?

- **Environmental Character**—What type of internal and external images does the facility wish to project? Will it be institutional versus noninstitutional? How will normalization be achieved? Will lighting be all natural or a combination of natural and artificial? What type of furnishings will be appropriate? What type of access will there be to outdoor spaces? How will this outdoor space be structured? Will the facility be single or multiple story? What type of construction materials and finishes will be used? How will sound control be achieved? What about visible hardware?

- **Maintenance and Repair**—For each of the materials chosen, what is its durability. In other words, how much resistance to damage does the material have?

What is the cost of this over the life cycle compared to the initial versus long-term cost? What types of ease will the materials have for daily cleaning? What will the cost of repair and replacement be, and what is the importance of this for ongoing repair?

- **Support for Future Expansion**—What methods are there for expanding the capacity for housing, program areas, and support services? What impact will this expansion have on the initial construction, the design, overall costs, and even on the site selection? How will program disruption be avoided during the facility expansion?

All these issues should be reviewed in detail so that the most effective operational concepts that are responsive to jurisdictional needs and priorities are defined clearly. This will guide subsequent planning efforts.

Staffing requirements also should be analyzed to determine the number of positions needed to fulfill established operational objectives on resident management and the provision of all required direct and support services. Staffing and other operational costs then are projected to provide authorities with a clear understanding of anticipated future operational expenditures, a key concern given the ongoing funding commitment required.

Architectural Programming

Architectural programming, the next step in the facility-design process, draws on all of the material developed during the operational programming phase to generate specific information on the type and number of spaces required to support the operations envisioned for the facility. All subsequent design efforts are derived from this listing of spaces, the associated narrative, and diagrams, which describe the spaces, how they are intended to function, and how they are to be physically related to each other. This spatial analysis further serves as the basis for initial construction/development cost estimation so that jurisdictions can secure funding for facility construction.

Before spatial requirements are defined, however, programming efforts should involve the development of environmental and construction parameters for the proposed facility, including:

- A review of all applicable standards and codes (national/professional standards governing the proposed building type, licensing/certification requirements, state and local building codes)
- Construction/project cost limitations, as applicable
- General internal and external security requirements
- Analysis of existing facility (if applicable) and an existing/proposed site(s), as required to determine suitability

With this foundation, architectural programming of the facility may proceed. A list of all spaces and physical requirements (square feet) for each of the major facility components is developed, with descriptive information (expected activities, spatial character, and materials) typically provided, in the following areas:

- Housing
- Administration
- Staff
- Intake/admissions
- Education/vocational training
- Visiting
- Indoor and outdoor recreation
- Medical services
- Food services/dining
- Maintenance and support services
- Laundry services

Table 1.7.1 illustrates the type of information usually contained in a component space listing. Once the space table has been developed, an adjacency diagram is developed to indicate the spatial relationship of each component listed on the space table. A housing unit adjacency diagram is shown in Figure 1.7.1.

Various options for using spaces, time of use (scheduling), circulation patterns, access control issues, and supervision/staffing requirements are explored in detail with program staff and other authorities to determine the most efficient organization of components and spaces. Spatial diagrams then are developed indicating desired visual and physical connections between spaces (adjacencies), access control points, and resident/staff/public circulation patterns responsive to operational priorities. An overall facility relationship diagram is shown in Figure 1.7.2.

Table 1.7.1
Housing Space

Component Name: HOUSING - 5.000
Subcomponent: General Population Units (10 Beds)
Component Number: 5.100

Space Number	Space/Component	Square Feet	Number	Total Net Sq. Feet	Comments
5.100	Bedrooms (Standard)	70	9	630	single user, toilet
5.101	Bedroom (ADA Access)	100	1	100	single user, toilet
5.102	Quiet Living/Dayroom	500	1	500	10 users, counseling, quiet activities, natural lighting
5.103	Staff Desk	30	1	30	
5.104	Restroom/Shower	70	1	70	single user
5.105	Shower	40	1	40	single user
5.106	Storage/Janitor Closet	80	1	80	

Total Net Square Feet			**1,450**	
Total Component Gross Square Feet (35 percent)			**1,960**	
Six Units (60 Beds) @ 1,960 Gross Square Feet			**11,760**	

Source: Chinn Planning, Inc.

In some instances, detailed descriptions of each room are developed to guide the architectural design process. These room data sheets, as they are commonly known, provide extensive information on the construction and finish materials, lighting, security systems, life safety systems, mechanical equipment, and furnishings to be used in the facility.

Using all of the information previously developed, a summary of all spaces and area requirements is assembled. It is important to understand that the square footage assigned to each room is the *net area* required as usable space for the functions served (*see* "Key Terms" in Chapter 1.6). Grossing factors must be applied to account for circulation within the spaces.

Similarly, the total building area must be increased to account for the space required for wall thicknesses and nonprogrammed functions such as mechanical rooms, electrical closets, corridors, and other things (*see* Table 1.6 for an example). In secure residential settings for juveniles, the actual area to be constructed can be 50 percent larger than the net assignable square footage.

This means that 30,000 square feet of usable space may result in a 45,000 square-foot building.

When all architectural programming activities have been completed, then initial capital cost projections can be prepared to determine if the facility can be accomplished within budgetary constraints. If changes are necessary, the program then can be adjusted to ensure that budgetary parameters can be met with some degree of confidence. It is essential that these efforts are accomplished prior to the beginning of the physical design phases so that fiscal and operational objectives are achieved, and costly changes are minimized as the building design proceeds.

Throughout the architectural programming effort, information should be exchanged between the facility's owners and operators and the programming team. Continual review of materials as they are developed ensures that planning is consistent with established operational objectives and permits modification and refinement, which ultimately will result in the building that best serves the needs of juveniles, staff, and the community.

Figure 1.7.1
Housing Component Adjacency Diagram

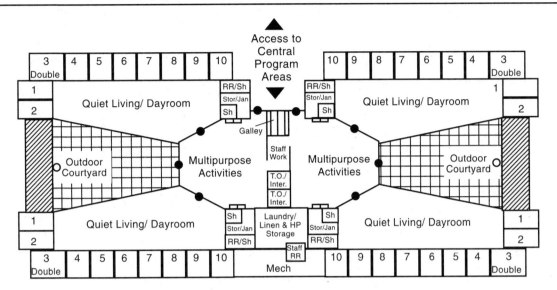

● Secure Access Control

Source: Chinn Planning, Inc.

Figure 1.7.2
Functional Relationship Diagram

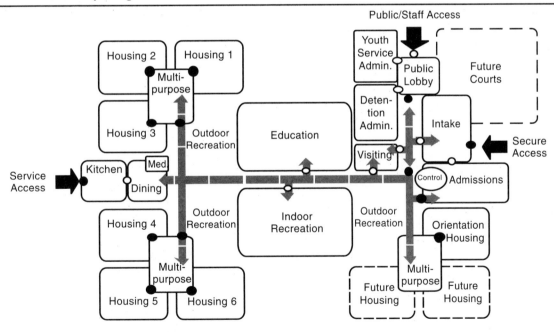

Polk County Juvenile Center Site Diagram

● Primary Security Control Panel
○ Secondary Access Control Panel
◀ Primary Circulation

Source: Chinn Planning, Inc.

Summary

The operational/architectural programming process should be viewed as an opportunity to examine rigorously the values and purposes envisioned for juvenile residential services. Decisions made during this critical first phase of facility development will affect the way juveniles are treated, and the way programs and services are accomplished, long into the future. Equally important, these decisions will have a lasting impact on resources, which must be expended to achieve the level of care desired by the court and/or youth service agencies, and the facility operators.

The design of any facility only can be successful to the extent that it meets the demands and expectations of its users. Given the costs involved in implementing any residential facility, it is essential that the design and the programs it supports be exactly right from the outset: there is no chance to practice, or to make it right later. The comprehensive process of developing an operational and architectural program offers the best opportunity to make decisions that result in the safe, secure, and efficient operation of juvenile facilities.

Staffing New Facilities

Henry Risley*
New Hampshire Department of Corrections
Concord, New Hampshire

The impact of the facility design on staff needs is a critical issue in all phases of planning and design for new construction. Construction costs are a small part of the total life cycle costs of a new prison or jail historically representing between 6 and 10 percent of the total cost of the facility over its life expectancy. However, design decisions that have an impact on staffing can influence the long-term operating costs of the facility significantly. The planning team should carefully consider any design decision that increases staff needs. On the other hand, relatively minor design changes often can reduce staff and long-term costs.

Depending on the particular staffing-relief factor at an agency, one twenty-four hour post can require five staff to cover that post three shifts per day, seven days per week. For illustration, assume an average $30,000 salary and $5,000 benefit cost for a correctional officer. That one post will cost $175,000 per year from the operating budget in salary and wages.

A number of questions should be asked and answered in the early stages of design. The answers will influence staffing levels for many years. Designers of prisons and jails today are familiar with these issues. The owner/operator must ask these questions *before* the design has progressed very far, and while change is relatively simple.

*Commissioner Risley died before the publication of this book.

Direct or Indirect Supervision

One of the basic design questions that affects staffing is the choice between direct supervision, modified direct supervision, or indirect supervision. Indirect supervision offers staff efficiencies. It also minimizes staff-inmate interaction. Officers managing inmate activity are removed from and often remotely located in relation to the inmates. Indirect supervision provides physical barriers separating staff and inmates. Sound and video monitoring are the primary tools used to monitor inmate activity. A policy decision early in the design phase to adopt this model can achieve some efficiency in long-term staff costs. It must be balanced with the loss of staff/inmate interaction and the benefits gained.

Many facilities today have adopted the direct-supervision model. The benefit of direct staff/inmate interaction is considered a major benefit. The positive impacts from the relationship that exists when staff and inmates have face-to-face contact throughout the day outweigh the reduced cost of the indirect supervision model. Inmate compliance with operations of the facility and expectations of staff and overall safety and security are enhanced in the direct supervision model.

One recent variation of the direct supervision design can be called *modified direct supervision*. Glazed walls and doors between inmates and staff characterize this model. Inmates are housed in pods or modules and staff circulate outside the pod in the common areas. Modified direct supervision can retain some of the efficiency of indirect supervision while gaining some of the benefit of direct supervision. It is incumbent on the owner/operator of the facility to provide the design team with a programmatic mandate that is responsive to this issue.

Many corrections administrators have elected direct supervision. In this model, correctional officer workstations are in the same location as the inmate living space. The officer is stationed in the dayroom or common space contiguous to the inmate cells or rooms. A considerable body of thought holds this model is more conducive to managing inmate behavior successfully. It enables the officers to be in direct contact with the inmates throughout their workday. There is the greatest exposure to appropriate modeling of behaviors and resultant positive impact on inmate-rehabilitation efforts. Formal and informal communication between staff and inmates is enhanced.

Operations Policy Impacts

To begin the process of defining posts and staff that are needed to operate the new prison or jail, one first must look to the operational policies that will guide staffing decisions. Policies and operating procedures that exist, or those being developed from ones in use at other facilities, are critical to assessing how many staff will be needed to operate the facility.

Policy questions that one must examine include the following:

1. Does policy dictate the number of officers who must be present for inmate movement? For example, in some jurisdictions, policy dictates that in administrative segregation there must be two officers for every inmate out of his or her cell. Policy may dictate that one officer supervises groups of medium or minimum security inmates.

2. The frequency of cell shakedowns, window and bar checks, inmate pat searches, and other security tasks will drive how many officers are needed in a unit to supervise the inmates there and complete the required security functions.

3. Are the officers relieved for meals and hygiene breaks? Does policy permit them to handle these issues and leave the inmates without direct supervision for periods of time? Policies, which dictate that inmates

must be under constant observation at all times, have a direct bearing on the number of staff required to supervise the inmates in a defined space or area.

4. Does policy establish staff-to-inmate ratios in housing, recreation, dining, and so forth? Are nonuniformed staff counted in those ratios?

This list provides examples of policy issues that have an impact on the number of staff required to operate a facility. The list is not all-inclusive; it emphasizes the merits of reviewing operations policy before embarking on a definition of posts and facility staffing needs.

Facility Design

The next step in the process is to look at schematics of the facility.

- Identify essential control points. These locations may be secure control posts as control rooms, or they may be unsecured posts as inmate traffic control points at doors, at corridor intersections, and so forth. Ask questions: is this a twenty-four-hour, sixteen-hour, or eight-hour post? What activities occur here? Can these activities be done properly by one, two, or more officers? This may vary by shift. Some control posts may be busy on the day shift, slow on the swing shift, and be closed on the graveyard shift.

- Does the facility have towers? Must these all be staffed for twenty-four hours? Can some of the towers be shut down on some shifts and still maintain the level of perimeter security desired? In nontowered facilities, will there be external and/or internal perimeter patrols? Are fewer needed on those shifts when inmate activity is less?

- Look at institution functional areas where inmates are often the primary source of labor. In the kitchen, how many food service workers are needed on each shift? Does policy dictate that correctional officers are assigned in addition to civilian food service staff? Can food service supervisors see inmates working throughout the kitchen? Are there separate working areas that require supervision of inmates? Is the dining area contiguous to the food preparation area? Can it be isolated when dining is not occurring? These same questions need to be asked for all inmate work and program areas.

- Does the facility maintenance staff have responsibility for supervising assigned inmates? Are correctional officers also assigned to maintenance shops? Do sight lines in the shop area permit good work surveillance of inmate workers or require more supervision?

- In inmate program areas, do program staff accept responsibility for supervising inmates? Are correctional officers also needed?

- Are correctional officers needed only at control points into and out of program spaces, or are they needed in every area where there are groups of inmates?

Identifying the Number of Officers Needed

How does one account for all these variables and come up with a comprehensive staffing plan? Computerized spreadsheet software programs make this a simple task, today (*see* Figure 1.8.1). It can be done manually if one docs not have access to a computer or the appropriate software. On the left vertical column, identify all the locations where officers are needed. Each row represents an assignment. Create columns by shift and rank; such as officer, corporal, sergeant, lieutenant, and so forth; three eight-hour (two twelve-hour), and any daytime or special shifts should be included. Doing so provides a tool to identify each officer post for each shift.

Working down the left-hand column, for each assignment, work across the row, and answer each question. How many officers are needed on that assignment? How many supervisors are needed? Do this for each shift and each assignment. When you have finished, you have an accounting of how many twenty-four hour posts are needed, how many eight or sixteen-hour posts are needed, and how many supervisors are needed and where they are needed.

Next, multiply the number of posts by the relief factor determined for each facility. For example, 1.5 to 1.75 are common for 7-day posts, while 1.1 is common for 5-day posts. This relief factor assures adequate staff to cover the post five or seven days per week throughout the year. Weekends, holidays, vacations, average sick leave usage, military-training absences, and other factors that take staff away from their post are accounted for in the relief factor. New facilities will have lower relief factors than those that have been in place a number of years. New staff have vacation opportunities that are significantly less than employees with many years of service.

Those completing this exercise have identified all the uniformed staff needed for the jail or prison operations. In addition to those assignments dictated by the physi-

cal layout of the facility and the operating policies, include other typical operational assignments. Officers for inmate transport out of the facility or inmate escort within the facility are examples. Presuming the design called for space for functions of the inmate disciplinary officer, quartermaster, armorer, and so forth, these, too, need to be included in the spreadsheet.

Administration and Programs

This discussion has focused on the operations staff needed to run the jail or prison twenty-four hours per day, seven days per week. Customarily, this work force consists of uniformed correctional staff. In addition, it is necessary to identify the administrative, program, and support services staff.

Typically, a program statement is developed prior to the design of a new facility. This document will be the primary resource for defining the administrative and program staff needed. Normally, these duties are five days per week and confined to the eight-to-five workday with weekends and holidays off. Therefore, the relief factor does not apply. Relief for vacations and sick leave is accounted for in the determination of how many are needed for each assignment. A table such as that in Figure 1.8.2 listing the functions by job or working title is a useful tool in the development of the staffing needed for administration and programs. A list of all the functions to be performed at the facility is the first step in creating this table. For each operational area, an enumeration of the staff for each of the listed functions can be developed.

This list must account for all the administrative, program, and support functions of the facility. Design of the facility, based on the program statement for the facility, should provide appropriate work space for all functions and staff positions. A review of the schematic design and the program statement should provide necessary information to assure the staffing allocation accounts for all programs and services to be provided.

This guide should provide the basic tools to develop a staffing pattern for the facility. To the extent possible, workload analysis is critical to completing the staff analysis. It may be necessary to conduct this workload analysis after the facility is occupied and all services are operational. Adjustments in staffing are difficult to accomplish once the facility is open. Therefore, a thorough analysis of policies, procedures, the program statement, and the schematic drawings provide the basis for the definition of the staffing needs of the facility.

Figure 1.8.1
Sample Staffing Spreadsheet

Post		7-3 Shift	3-11 Shift	11-7 Shift	8-4 Shift
Captain					1*
Shift Supervisor/Lieutenant		1	1	1	
Sergeant Posts					
Segregation Unit		1	1	1	
Transportation					1
Housing	A		1		
	B		1		
	C		1		
	D				
Total Sergeant Posts		**1**	**4**	**1**	**1**
Corporal Posts					
Central Control	1	1	1		
Visiting			1*		
Segregation Unit	1	1	1		
Housing	A	2	2	1	
	B	2	2	1	
	C	2	2	1	
	D	1	1	1	
Detail Officer					2
Yard/Rover		2	2	1	
Transportation					1
Commissary					1*
Armory					1*
Lock Shop					1*
5-day Corporal posts			**1**		**3**
7-day Corporal posts		**11**	**11**	**7**	**3**
Corrections Officer Posts					
Central Control		1	1		
Lobby		1	1		
Visiting			1*		
Control G.15		1	1	1	
Control F.2.4		1	1	1	
Zone E.1.11		1	1	1	
2nd Flr		1	1	1	
Infirmary		1	1	1	
Seg Unit		1	1	1	
Gym			1	1	
School					1*
Kitchen		1	1		
Loading Dock					1*
Perimeter Patrol		1	1	1	
Yard/Rover		1	1	1	
Warehouse					1*
Vehicle Sallyport					1*
5-day Officer posts			**1**		**4**
7-day Officer posts		**12**	**12**	**8**	

TOTAL SECURITY STAFF					
Captain	1.1				
Lt.		5.1			
Sgt.		11.9			
Corp.			58.8		
Officer				59.9	
TOTAL UNIFORMED STAFF					**136.8**

* 5-day post   For illustration purposes, relief factors of 1.6 for 7-day posts and 1.1 for 5-day posts have been used.

Staffing analysis needs to be an ongoing process. It is not something that one does only once when the facility is being designed and built. Supervisors periodically need do a thorough workload analysis and relief factor review to assure adequate staffing is maintained at the facility. Also, as the facility ages and staff have greater seniority, increased leave usage may require modification of the relief factors. Changes in program definition or mission of the facility can have an impact on staff levels once the facility has been operational for a while.

Remember, correctional facilities being constructed today still will be in operation fifty to sixty years from now. Design decisions made for savings in construction costs can have considerable negative impact on operational costs. Design decisions made for staff efficiencies can create substantial life-cycle savings in the operation of the facility.

Figure 1.8.2
Example of a staff function list

ADMINISTRATION	
Warden	1
Deputy Warden	1
Administrative Assistant	1
Secretary	1
Business Office	3
Records	3
Training	1
Human Resources	2
PROGRAMS	
Programs Administrator	1
Secretary	1
Education Administrator	1
Academic Teacher	3
Vocational Instructor	2

Shared Resources

William G. Porter, HSMM
Virginia Beach, Virginia

Sharing resources between separate institutions near each other or in the same building is a planning goal worth evaluating for operations and construction cost savings (*see* Figure 1.9.1). Shared resources may include services such as food, laundry, waste disposal, emergency services, medical, dental, education, maintenance, and storage. Shared resources also may include utilities such as communications, power, gas, central heating, central cooling, water, sewer, and stormwater management. Roads and parking also can be shared.

Federal, state, local, and private correctional institutions/facilities have been sharing resources with other correctional facilities and other government and private facilities for years. Many federal prison sites combine the main prison (sometimes several), a work camp, and a training facility on the same site. Emergency response plans, maintenance, storage, waste disposal, roads, energy management and control systems, and telephones frequently are shared among the facilities. They often rely on a single water and sewer system, a single electrical power feed, and a single natural gas main. Other resources may be shared to a greater or lesser extent depending on local conditions.

Local governments frequently tie detention facilities into municipal complexes with courts, administration, public safety, emergency operations centers, and so forth. The level of resource sharing is as varied as the number of localities. Recently, there has been an increasing incidence of resource sharing between jurisdictions such as states and localities. Regardless of the circumstances, savings in construction and operating costs through shared resources takes careful planning and negotiation.

There is a greater challenge in sharing resources between adult and juvenile facilities. Most corrections professionals agree that separate administration and staff are required for successful operations of adult and juvenile facilities located on the same site. Mandated sight and sound separation provides additional challenges.

However, successful models operate on the same site (*see* Figure 1.9.2). One of the most highly praised models incorporates a juvenile detention facility and an adult work release facility into one structure. In this model, one continuous structure consists of three "buildings" separated by firewalls. The juvenile and adult facilities each are classified as distinct buildings separated by a third secure link/corridor "building." Internal functions for adult

An enclosed bridge connects the second story of the Federal Detention Center and the courthouse in Miami, Florida.

Architect/Engineer: Wolfberg, Alvarez and Associates, Miami, Florida. Construction management firm: CRSS, Miami, Florida. Construction contractor, Phase I: Turner Construction, Phase II: Cogefar/Impresit USA, Miami, Florida. Completing Surety, Phase II: American Home Assurance Company, New York, New York. Photo courtesy of the Federal Bureau of Prisons.

and juvenile processing, administration, and operations are completely separate, but utilities, food, laundry, and maintenance are shared. Food and laundry are prepared in the adult facility and delivered by adult staff to the secure link/corridor, then picked up by juvenile staff from the secure link/corridor. Neither juvenile nor adult inmates are permitted in the secure link/corridor. More facilities of this type are expected to be designed in the future.

Services

Food

Many state and large local facilities are sharing food services. The cook-chill method of food preparation has gained popularity with facilities in excess of several hundred beds. In this method, food is prepared in large quantities in advance, quick chilled, and stored until ready for final preparation and serving. This method allows food to be distributed over a wide geographic area. As an example, New York State serves all of its correctional institutions from regional food service facilities.

Small and/or adjacent facilities sometimes use rethermalization. In this method, food is prepared at a central kitchen and delivered in bulk to smaller remote warming kitchens. This requires less initial investment in central facilities than the cook-chill method, but is impractical when facilities are separated by long distances due to difficulties in maintaining safe food temperatures.

Laundry

Sheets, towels, and flat goods routinely are laundered in central facilities for distribution to remote facilities. It is not as common for inmate clothing to be laundered centrally. Mesh bags allow inmates to bundle all of their personal clothing. The mesh bag then is washed and dried without taking the clothes out of the bag. This method has reduced problems with sizing and distributing of clothing, but has not been extremely effective for highly soiled clothing.

Caution must be used in planning shared food or laundry services because there is the potential for inmate escape, tampering with an inmate's food or personal belongings, and entry of contraband into facilities. However, there are proven successful models for sharing food and laundry service using staff resources and inmate work programs.

Waste Disposal

Most waste facilities are combined on one site. There is then the potential for use of staff or inmate work programs to deliver waste to a central location on the site. With consolidated on-site pickup, a reduced rate often can be negotiated with a private company. Again, escape and contraband entry need to be addressed carefully. Typically, trash is removed from an institution immediately after a count of all inmates.

Figure 1.9.1

Several facilities and jurisdictions share resources effectively and economically at Beaumont Juvenile Correctional Center, Beaumont, Virginia.

Courtesy of HSMM.

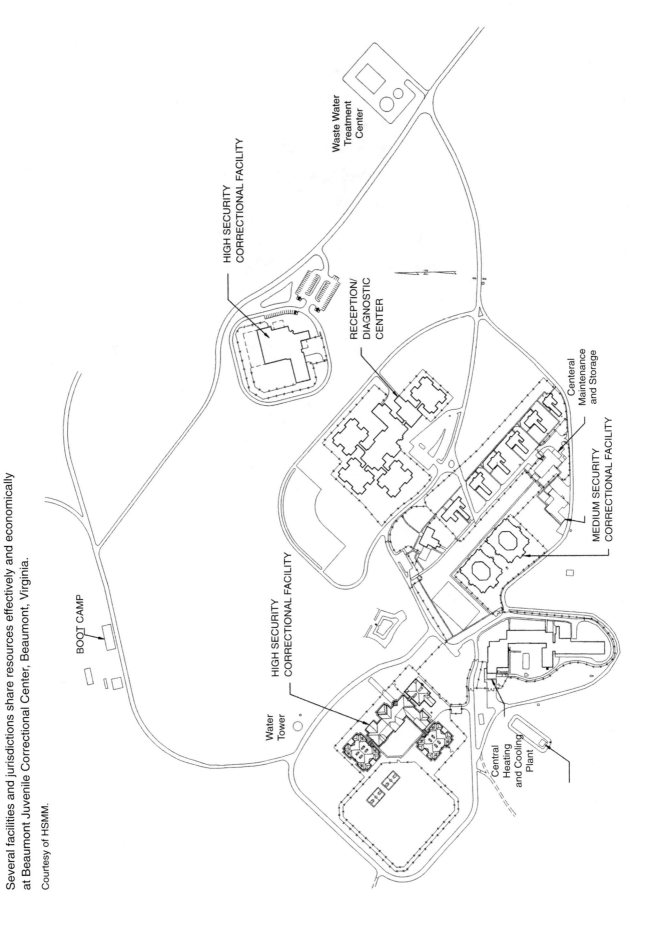

HIGH SECURITY CORRECTIONAL FACILITY

Waste Water Treatment Center

RECEPTION/ DIAGNOSTIC CENTER

Central Maintenance and Storage

MEDIUM SECURITY CORRECTIONAL FACILITY

BOOT CAMP

Water Tower

HIGH SECURITY CORRECTIONAL FACILITY

Central Heating and Cooling Plant

Figure 1.9.2

Juvenile and adult facilities can share resources when carefully planned as seen in this drawing of the Northwest Regional Juvenile Detention Center in Winchester, Virginia.

Drawing courtesy of HSMM.

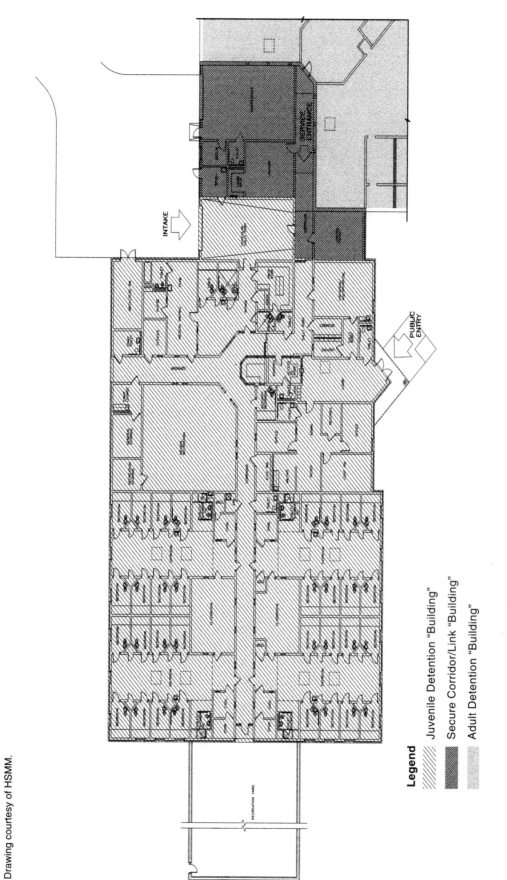

Legend

Juvenile Detention "Building"

Secure Corridor/Link "Building"

Adult Detention "Building"

Emergency Services

In the event of a disturbance, there is a significant advantage in being able to quickly mobilize nonessential staff from adjacent facilities. Optimum efficiency in providing emergency services can be obtained by sharing communications systems. This topic will receive further consideration under the heading "Communications."

Medical/Dental

Smaller facilities often are able to provide higher quality services at less cost through the sharing of medical and dental facilities and staff. A single medical/dental facility can serve several levels of security classifications, if separate waiting areas and patient rooms are provided. Planners need to include a planned, secure route to and from the facilities to the medical/dental center.

Doctors, nurses, and dentists also can serve several small facilities on a part-time basis if travel time is minimal. Some facilities provide most of their medical services by providing nurse and/or doctor visits at remote locations adjacent to each inmate housing area. This minimizes the cost of staff required for moving inmates. Under this scenario, inmates are moved to medical services only for major procedures. Use of telemedicine to deliver medical services further enhances sharing of medical staff and services.

Education

Distance learning classrooms are becoming commonplace for college and correctional education. Colleges have "piped" in educational programs to remote locations for many years. Technology and programming have improved while costs have come down. The same basic interactive videoconferencing technology is being used successfully for court arraignments (*see Best Practices: Excellence in Corrections*). The greatest benefit of distance learning classrooms is sharing specialized instruction with less staff expense. These rooms are usually directly supervised at least part time, but the staff does not need to be as highly trained as in a conventional classroom because the specialized instructor can be at a remote location. One remote instructor generally can handle several distance learning classrooms at a time while retaining an interactive teaching environment.

Security and safety of staff and inmates in the distance learning classroom is still important. At least one security window and possibly closed-circuit television monitoring should be provided for observation from adjacent spaces. This enhances security and safety and also allows the room to be unsupervised for short periods of time. Another staff expense involves supervising inmates leaving the classroom to go to a toilet remote from the classroom. If this is permitted, it is generally good practice to observe inmate movement either with a correctional version of the escort or "hall monitor" many had to contend with in high school. Toilet rooms provided with direct access from each classroom allow the escort or "hall monitor" staff position to be eliminated. The classroom supervisior can oversee movement inside the classroom and into and out of the adjacent toilet area. Between classes, the same staff can supervise movement between classrooms.

Ideally, classrooms should be designed into a new facility. However, most existing classroom spaces can

Educational programs are being shared successfully among facilities through interactive distance learning classrooms as shown here at the Southern Correctional Institution, Troy, North Carolina.

Photo courtesy of HSMM.

The Federal Correctional Complex in Beaumont, Texas, has three major new institutions and a minimum-security camp. In the center of the circle is the central administration building. All the complex shares a central warehouse and use of garage functions.

Architectural firm: HKS, Inc., Dallas. Construction management firm: Morse Diesel International, Philadelphia, Pennsylvania. Construction contractor for the low-security correctional institution: Dick Corporation, Pittsburgh, Pennsylvania. Construction contractor for the medium-security correctional institution and prison camp: Caddell Construction, Montgomery, Alabama. Construction contractor for compound tower: Menendez-Donnell and Associates, Houston, Texas. Construction contractor for UFAS related work: BGI, Beaumont, Texas. Construction contractor for fencing/roads/sitework: W. B. Construction, Beaumont, Texas. Photo courtesy of the Federal Bureau of Prisons.

be converted easily to distance learning classrooms. The only mandatory additions to a conventional space are the communications equipment and power and communications cabling needed for that equipment.

It is a good idea to have hidden conduits pre-installed to run communications and power wiring because exposed conduit and wiring can be used as a weapon. It is also nice to have acoustic design principles incorporated into the original construction, although it is relatively inexpensive to retrofit if acoustics turn into a problem.

Maintenance/Storage

With increasingly complex technology, specialized maintenance staffs are becoming a necessity for security electronics, heating and air conditioning control systems, and so forth. Small facilities cannot afford the special-

ized staff to service this equipment. However, if equipment at nearby facilities is similar, several facilities effectively can share specialized expertise and spare parts inventory. Bulk purchase, storage, and distribution of paper products, cleaning supplies, and so forth, also can provide improved service and savings. Management's challenge is to provide services fairly to all facilities.

Communications

Communications include telephone, intercom, closed-circuit television (CCTV), fire alarm, energy management and control systems (EMCS), maintenance management, educational television, remote arrangements, video conferencing, and emergency response and identification systems for inmates, staff, and visitors. Although these systems are served effectively with standalone equipment, fiber optic technology has provided a sufficient bandwidth to carry all of these signals on one cable or a group of cables. Initial installation of fiber optic cabling between and within buildings and between facilities can provide the flexibility to handle communication signals into the foreseeable future. However, most competitively priced equipment available today requires hardwired rather than fiber optic connections. Fiber optic cable is relatively inexpensive to purchase and install, but the conversion of optical to hardwired signals is still expensive. Larger or more complex facilities with the potential for expansion or connection to additional facilities may prove that fiber optics is a good investment.

Individual systems, such as closed circuit television, fire alarm, maintenance management, and so forth, generally have expensive central processing equipment and high labor costs associated with twenty-four-hour/day, seven-day/week monitoring. Combining the central processing equipment from several facilities into one central point with twenty-four-hour/day, seven-day/week monitoring ability can provide significant savings in hardware and staff costs.

Power

The local power company usually pays for providing electrical service to a site through monthly service charges. However, the facility or the power company can provide power distribution on a site. With proper planning, most power distribution can be located outside of the secure perimeter and can be owned and maintained by the power company.

There is some consideration for providing one metered power feed to a campus with several facilities. The main power distribution system for a single campus feed generally can be sized more economically than separate feeds due to load diversity.

Emergency power also can be shared between facilities, although this is rare. Some facilities warrant some redundancy in emergency generation equipment. If this is the case, there may be the potential for sharing emergency power between facilities. However, the cost of power distribution is highly sensitive to distance. Facilities generally need to be no more than a few hundred feet apart to consider sharing emergency power. Regardless, most power companies have programs to buy power from independent power providers. Some of these programs provide very favorable rates.

Central Heating and Cooling

Years ago, central heating was more common than today's local heating equipment. Reduced initial cost, associated increases in efficiency and improved reliability of local unitary equipment has been the impetus behind this change. In higher security applications, there continues to be strong advocacy for central heating systems due to separation of maintenance staff from inmates.

Central cooling systems in warmer climates generally are providing a better return on investment than in years past. Demand charges by power companies are becoming more common. Central systems have the potential for reducing overall demand charges. Ice and chilled water storage have proven effective in shifting demand and should be considered at large compact facilities with high demand charges and time-of-day rates. Chilled water storage has the additional benefit of providing a ready source of water for fire protection within the institution. The primary advantage of central heating and cooling systems remains the ability to keep maintenance personnel outside of the secure perimeter.

Water/Sewer

Water and sewer service is a critical issue because of cost and the length of time required for permit procurement. When siting a new correctional facility, water and sewer are generally the most important issues after politics. A conservative rule of thumb to use for planning is

Water and sewer are the most commonly shared utilities as seen here at the Peachoid in Gaffney, South Carolina.

Photo courtesy of HSMM.

150 gallons per day per juvenile in a correctional facility. Sewer service generally will consist of only 80 to 90 percent of the water requirement depending on the amount of water used for landscaping, and so forth. Adult facilities use less sewer and water per inmate than juvenile facilities due to the larger staffing ratio associated with juvenile facilities. In adult facilities for men and women, the estimated water usage is 140 gallons per day.

Stormwater Management

Stormwater management has become a significant issue in the last few years. Federal, state, and local mandates to control stormwater quantity and quality have increased the required investment in stormwater management in most jurisdictions. Frequently, it has proved more economical to provide combined stormwater management

facilities. Many jurisdictions are planning ahead and providing stormwater management facilities sufficient to handle all proposed development in an area. This is particularly attractive to areas trying to attract industry.

Roads and Parking

Main entrance and service roads can save construction and operational costs by serving several facilities. Sharing parking generally will require operational adjustments at the corrections facilities and may require jurisdictional approval. Parking peaks generally occur at shift changes and/or during visitations. Where the number of parking spaces is dictated by code, the number of spaces is generally based on a formula associated with the number of occupants or building square footage, and so forth.

The buildings in the middle of the Federal Correctional Complex, Coleman, Florida, share the administrative building and functions, including the business office. They also share warehouses, landscape, and in a few cases, utility buildings. A penitentiary is being built on this site, as well.
Photo courtesy of the Federal Bureau of Prisons.

NIMBY

Experience has shown that combining correctional facilities on a common campus may reduce the overall staff planning effort because of the "not in my back yard" (NIMBY) syndrome. Anyone who has been associated with locating a correctional facility in a locality that has never had one can attest to the time required to deal with NIMBY. Most localities near existing correctional facilities have learned that correctional facilities are good neighbors. Public acceptance of another correctional facility or an expansion of an existing correctional campus may reduce the efforts associated with NIMBY. Rather than dealing with NIMBY, correctional planners can spend their time more effectively evaluating, planning, and implementing resource sharing.

Summary

When carefully evaluated, planned, and implemented, shared resources can save significant construction and operational costs. Each facility's resources must be evaluated in relation to other potential facilities' resources. Planning takes time and persistence, because many agencies, jurisdictions, and private companies may be involved. Implementation requires negotiation and follow through. The result of these efforts can be a significant improvement in cost and efficiency.

At the top of the photograph is the medium-security institution and, in the foreground, is the security camp that provides the workforce that tends the grounds. In between the two facilities is a power plant that serves both facilities, the Federal Correctional Institution and Federal Prison Camp in Sheridan, Oregon.

Architect/Engineer: Zimer, Gunsul, Frasca Partnership, Portland, Oregon. Construction contractor: Hoffman Construction Company, Portland, Oregon. Photo courtesy of the Federal Bureau of Prisons.

Reference

Rhine, Edward, ed. *Best Practices: Excellence in Corrections*. 1998. Lanham, Maryland: American Correctional Association.

Project Budget Development: The First Step to Cost Control

Richard Milliken, John McSkimming, Gregory D. Ridgely, Theodore Sak, Michael D. Tomy, and Clinton Fairchild
Heery International
Atlanta, Georgia

Developing a solid project budget is an essential part of delivering a successful correctional facility project. Jurisdictions have limited funds, and a project that goes over budget delays project development and jeopardizes other needed projects. A well-developed project budget reflects directly on the credibility of both the project and the administration recommending it, and is the first step in responsible management and cost control.

Most jurisdictions employ either staff or consultants who are adept at developing project budgets, but corrections officials need to become familiar with the major components of a good project budget *before* embarking on a building program. The budget must be based on an accurate assessment of program requirements and an understanding of the level of design detail that a jurisdiction expects.

The major components of a complete project budget include clear definitions of the budget process, program, and funding elements, and an understanding of hard and soft costs and contingencies. Design and construction specialists can bring more value to the process and the project if they are consulted in the early stages when they can familiarize jurisdictions with the range of challenges that lie ahead.

Definitions

Defining what is meant by the "project budget" is a critical step in communications. Terminology needs to be defined for the benefit of the entire project team—owner, user, program manager, designer, and contractor. The industry is awash in examples of miscommunication when one team member believes project budget refers to the construction costs, while another believes it covers design and construction costs, and another believes it covers all costs from start to finish including staff costs.

For the sake of simplicity, it is best to develop a complete budget that includes everything it takes to deliver the project. A total budget includes soft costs, such as design, accounting, and staff to manage the project; hard costs for land, construction, testing, furniture, fixtures, and equipment; and a percentage contingency to handle unforeseen site conditions, owner changes during construction, or minor design coordination issues. If costs of ongoing operations will be affected, they must be identified and accounted for early in the process.

Design and construction costs, however, are only a minor part of the total cost a jurisdiction will incur in owning and operating a facility over a thirty-year period.

Once they are analyzed in light of operating costs, short-term design and construction efficiencies often can end up costing a jurisdiction more in the long run. Correctional operations and life cycle concerns should be addressed in the initial project budget and may include a staffing analysis of the design. Good sources include the American Correctional Association, which publishes facility operating costs, and the National Institute of Justice, which publishes construction costs.

When developed at the beginning of the project, the complete project budget often is called a *cost model*. It includes numerous assumptions, which are spelled out in the narrative portion of the model. The cost model can be updated throughout the life of the project as increasing amounts of information are available, thus providing a reasonable budget guide for all members of the team.

The initial numbers in the cost model are macro numbers—general costs based on assumptions that should be listed. In the course of the project, as the drawings are developed and more is known, the model is refined and the numbers become increasingly firm until the project can be bid. A fully developed cost model that has been refined at each design phase allows the designer to make progressive changes during the various phases to keep the project within budget. This helps eliminate surprises on bid day.

Developing the budgets from a preprogram level through a set of bid drawings is more the work of cost analysts than estimators. An estimator typically takes fully engineered drawings and estimates the value of the work shown. A cost analyst can evaluate conceptually what authorities believe will be needed to perform required operations and build an estimate for a complete project. This work can be accomplished at early stages without the need for fully engineered drawings. Later, during the design development process, the estimate becomes a mix of the dollar estimate of the details of work shown on the drawings and conceptual costs of the work remaining.

Funding

No jurisdiction has unlimited funds, but progressive ones are aware of opportunities for matching funds available from states and the federal government. Knowing what is funded and what is not funded are important distinctions in the development of the project budget or cost model. For example, the state may pay for inmate housing, but not for air conditioning the inmate housing. If

your plans call for air conditioning, knowing this limitation before you start design and construction can prevent unpleasant surprises.

To investigate funding options, set up a meeting with your state department of corrections and state legislative committees to discuss your project. States often receive federal funding as part of an effort to relieve crowding of state and federal facilities. For example, Virginia and Maryland have state matching programs that allow counties building correctional facilities to receive matching funds from the federal government to cover a portion of the construction costs. Cities and municipalities often can benefit from state matching programs, as well.

Completing necessary applications and compiling documents for funding sources can be time-consuming tasks. In the development of the project budget, it is important to then keep and meet these deadlines. Meeting these deadlines should be a first priority. State projects require submission of a budgeting form that broadly lays out all costs for developing, designing, constructing, and fitting out of a completed correctional facility. This form, which typically is submitted to the state with projected costs, also helps to identify the various funding sources.

A project budget clearly should identify separate funding sources and budget responsibility to make sure that all necessary funding is secured. A leading source for funding information is the U.S. Justice Department's National Criminal Justice Reference Service (NCJRS) try these sites and see if they are currently at 1-800-851-3420 or www.NCJRS.org. Other sources include the Office of Juvenile Justice and Delinquency Prevention (OJJDP) at www.ojjdp.ncjrs.org, the Bureau of Justice Assistance (BJA) at www.ojp.usdoj.gov/BJA, the Bureau of Justice Statistics (BJS) at www.ojp.usdoj.gov/bjs, and the National Institute of Justice (NIJ) at www.ojp.usdoj.gov/nij.

Soft Costs

Soft costs are intangible expenses associated with developing any facility. They include professional fees for the design consultant, program manager, lawyers, accountants, surveys, tests, feasibility studies, use permits, mitigation measures, if required, and communication systems.

Soft costs vary from project to project, depending on such things as printing costs, staff costs, advertisements, photography, movable equipment, and surveys. Other items affecting soft costs include a jurisdiction's credit rating, and costs associated with operations start-up, training, facility commissioning, and moving of existing equipment and/or furnishings—all of which frequently are forgotten at budget time. Industry averages for soft costs generally range from 20 to 30 percent of the total project budget, but specific project conditions can cause this number to be higher or lower. If the soft costs vary from the average, make sure the explanation for the variance is included in the narrative portion of the cost model.

When building a budget for soft costs, it should include such items as architectural and engineering services, reimbursable expenses for the architect/engineer (A/E), the architect/engineer's equipment; furnishings; a graphics consultant; an acoustics consultant; a food consultant; a security consultant; and consultants on planning, programming, and special systems; traffic analysis; surveys; tests; borings and reports; models and renderings; and any community outreach services required to integrate the project into the surrounding area. In addition, program management consultants will have fees for their basic services and for a reimbursable office and expenses, such as for telephone, computers, printing, copying, relocating personnel, traveling, and living expenses.

Hard Costs

Hard costs often are called "bricks and mortar" costs and are the actual costs of the construction labor, materials, and associated overhead and profit for the contractor. Land acquisition costs, if any, are part of hard costs, as are furniture, fixtures, and the equipment needed to bring the project to occupancy. Hard costs will account for 70 to 80 percent of the total project budget, according to industry averages. Again, any variance should be noted in the cost model narrative.

The facility program requirements provide the basis for developing the project budget. The design consultant usually is responsible for developing a complete list of program requirements that incorporates the expertise of the owner, program manager, and contractor. Complete program requirements include such items as supervision philosophy, capacity, security level, population mix, single and double bunking, expansion needs, and a list of different programs that occur in the facility, such as education, state-use industries, and medical/dental/psychological programs.

A major factor that affects the cost is whether construction is within a secured facility with ongoing operations or "outside the fence." Expansion of existing facilities may require limited access by the contractor and even limited hours of operation. Waiting to be processed through the institution's sallyport can take away forty-five minutes of the contractors' effective work time both in the morning when they come to the facility and again in the evening when they leave. This can result in an additional cost of 15 percent to the project. Also, if a facility is to be remodeled while partially occupied, this, too, will add significantly to the cost of the work.

These conditions directly affect the schedule, overhead, and costs for the contractors, and increase staff costs for the institution. Any cost model should account for the variances of construction within an occupied facility.

Based on the program requirements, agencies can begin to develop some general idea of costs by consulting an index that provides statistics on cost per cell, cost per inmate, and cost per square foot by facility type and region. Several resources commonly are available to provide this information, including the *National Directory of Corrections Construction*, NIJ Construction Cost Indexes, NIJ Square Foot Costs, and R. S. Means. These can provide useful guides, but the real costs of any facility are governed by the site, the program of requirements, local procurement laws, the local economy, and other intangible factors.

Once there is a complete program of requirements, issues like schedule, labor and transportation availability, infrastructure, building technology, and inflation come into play in determining the actual cost of construction. The proposed schedule for constructing the facility is a key component of its cost due to escalation. If court mandate requires accelerated construction, the jurisdiction will pay a premium for the contractor to work double shifts and seven-day work weeks. However, some of these costs will be offset by paying a lower-inflation escalation over the life of the project. For example, if a normal three-year project must be accelerated to be delivered in two years, one year of inflation escalation is eliminated.

One of the single largest potential costs associated with a correctional project is land development. Early identification of subsurface and environmental conditions is essential in establishing a credible budget, while late identification of these conditions may lead to significant project delays and cost overruns. In addition, a rural site's proximity to major interstate highways and airports is an issue for shipping materials and transporting labor to and from the site. Better access means easier construction, which translates to lower costs. Other considerations are adequate utilities and roadways to serve the project and required upgrades. Likewise, an urban site's ability to provide an adequate staging area for construction affects the cost.

Another mitigating factor involves the infrastructure. Is there a local power source to provide energy to run the facility or will the project need to include a small generation plant? Is there a dual feed available for backup power or is there a need for increased generator capacity? Will the facility need its own pumping station and sewage treatment plant? Is there already a road leading to the site? How far away is the nearest concrete plant? How far away is the nearest hospital? These concerns, among others, must be considered at the cost-model level.

To build the construction portion of the cost model, it is important to establish a common format such as CSI or Uniformat to document costs for different categories. CSI breaks the project down into construction activities, while Uniformat breaks it down into building components. Each format has its positives and negatives, but the material point is to make sure that the construction documents request a specific format to help with comparisons during the bid process.

Contingencies: Using the Project Budget to Control Costs

Once the initial project budget is developed, it is important to use the cost model to control costs. Since most mistakes in project budgeting are made up-front during the cost-model stage, it is important to delineate any assumptions about the project in the up-front narrative. Beyond that, adding appropriate contingencies that decrease as more hard design is provided will assist the cost model designer to stay within an appropriate range throughout the design process. Most cost models include both a design and construction contingency.

The design contingency begins at approximately 20 percent during the schematic or concept phase. As the design proceeds and the team makes decisions about specific materials, the contingency continually reduces, first to 15 percent at the end of design development, down to 10 percent halfway through construction documents until, at the point of the completed construction documents, it is gone. In short, as more becomes known, the contingency to handle the unknown no longer is required.

Construction contingencies are extremely important and should not be confused with the design contingency described above. There is no such thing as a perfect set of documents, a perfect site, perfect weather conditions, and owners who do not make at least minor changes to their projects. Construction contingencies are meant to handle the bulk of unforeseen events, but not major issues. Clearly communicating and understanding of the types of changes that the construction contingency is intended to cover can be enhanced by using language in the cost model and documents such as "This contingency is to cover change orders for necessary adjustments to site conditions, minor design refinements, and correction of minor errors and omissions in the documents."

There is no magic number for construction contingencies. A new project on undeveloped property may need only a small contingency of around 5 percent, while modernizations and renovations can have contingencies running upward of 15 percent. Again, if the percentages used in the cost model exceed the averages, the cost model should include a narrative explaining the difference.

Agencies should be aware that modernization, renovation, and additional projects contain more unknown and unforeseen conditions than new projects on a new site. Even with a good set of as-built drawings, there is much that is not known until the walls are "opened up" or the infrastructure "is excavated." It is important on these types of projects to be prepared to deal quickly with issues that arise once an existing condition becomes known.

In situations where modifications are made to an operating facility, emergency contingency funds and processes should be identified with operations staff to handle unforeseen issues, especially those regarding security or electrical operations. For example, a budget may include a line item for a generator to restore power in the event that a line is cut. Such a provision might call for a time limit, such as "reestablishing power within four hours."

Managing the Project Budget

A project development budget, when recast as a cost model and modified throughout the design process, is a living, breathing document that can help a jurisdiction manage its design and construction costs and eliminate surprises. A good cost model reflects positively on the credibility of the project and the jurisdiction. Once the cost model is developed, the jurisdiction is well served to continually check emerging drawings against the model to be sure that the facility can be bid within the budget. Once construction is underway, it is important to monitor change-order costs to keep within the established budget and deliver the project on schedule.

Construction Project Delivery Methods

Glen Gauger
KKE Architects
Minneapolis, Minnesota

Waller S. Poage, NCARB, CCS
Architect/Planner/Consultant
Alexandria, Virginia

Construction project delivery is simply the way in which the players structure their roles and responsibilities, and allocate the risks and rewards among them. A project-delivery system defines the roles and responsibilities of project team members and the sequence of activities required to provide a facility. Design/bid/build, construction management, and design/build are the principal methods of project delivery in the United States today.

Historical Context

During the Middle Ages, the master builders provided a single source of responsibility for design and construction. Since that time, the United States has evolved to a more fragmented way of delivering projects. The now familiar linear, design/bid/build system is the one to which most people are accustomed. After World War II, the construction industry was fairly simple, highly fragmented, and relatively unsophisticated. Since then, building has become much more complex with the fragmentation of the construction process and the rise of specialty contractors. Contracts have become more complex and litigation more commonplace. Understanding the basics of each of the three main delivery methods can help the agency

make an informed choice about which approach is best for their project.

Conventional wisdom on project delivery is changing. We are witnessing a change in the rules and bounds that effect design, construction, and finance. Owners entering into new construction projects traditionally have been guided by three major considerations: quality, cost, and time. Decisions concerning project delivery are dominated by these same considerations.

The various delivery methods affect these same three elements: quality, cost, and time. The roles of the owner, user, architect/engineer, and contractor/contract manager change depending on the method chosen. The contractual relationship an owner chooses is determined by the degree of project definition and the degree of control the owner desires. The more you control, the more you must manage.

One writer has said, "Choosing a project delivery method is a lot like ordering off a menu in a greasy-spoon diner. The good news is, there are lots of choices. The bad news is, you are not quite sure if you will end up liking what you ordered." Each of these methods has differing responsibilities for the members of the team. Each has its advantages and disadvantages.

Security has to be built into the construction and not added as an afterthought. Here, at the Menard Correctional Center in Chester, Illinois, PSA has designed an opening in a security wall.

Photo courtesy of PSA, Peoria, Illinois.

Project Delivery Methods

Most individuals are familiar with design/bid/build. An architect contracts with an owner for the design of a facility. The architect provides complete design documents, which the owner uses to solicit bids from a construction contractor for the work. The relationship with the owner is a fiduciary one—the architect serves as the owner's agent. The contractor, on the other hand, serves as an independent contractor and is paid a sum of money to purchase materials and construct a facility. In its simplest form, bids submitted by a general, or "prime," contractor are based on cost quotations from subcontractors who will perform most of the work for the prime contractor.

Traditional Design/Bid/Build Organization

This process is based on a system of checks and balances. Problems often arise when the participants start to go their separate ways. Many major construction projects become a battleground of charges and countercharges regarding cost overruns, delays, errors, and omissions, lack of responsiveness, and so forth. As a result

of this tendency to do battle, many owners and agencies are looking to a more focused point of responsibility, particularly for justice projects, where time is often a major consideration. This has led to the rise of alternative project delivery mechanisms, including various forms of construction management and design/build.

Traditional Method (Design/Bid/Build)

Advantages

- The architect is advocate for the design intent
- Project investment initially is limited to architect/engineer's fees
- The owner selects the architect/engineer on the basis of ability

Disadvantages

- Shift in prime management responsibilities
- Less control over project costs
- Contractors often selected on basis of low bid rather than management abilities
- Design/bid/build takes the longest time

This is an exterior wall with brick dovetails at the Menard Correctional Center, Chester, Illinois.

Photo courtesy of PSA, Peoria, Illinois.

Figure 1.11.1
Traditional Design/Bid/Build Organization

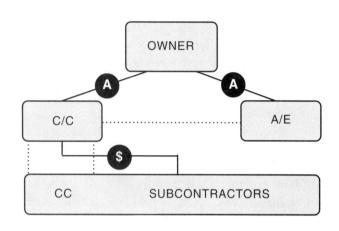

The advantages of the design/bid/build project delivery system include the following:

- The design professional works directly for and advises the owner. The owner/design professional relationship during the design phase provides the owner with reasonable assurance of a balance between economy and quality.

- The owner/design professional relationship is one of trust in that the design professional's advice is free from any consideration except for his or her fee. Ethically, the design professional owes no allegiance to, nor derives any benefit from, the work of the contractor, subcontractor, or manufacturer.

- By competitive bidding, the owner, assisted by the design professional, is assured of a reasonable project cost by a qualified contractor.

- The owner/design professional relationship during construction provides the owner with reasonable assurance of contractor conformity with contract documents.

- The contractor is responsible for coordination and management of the construction process.

- The owner/design professional relationship during the warranty period provides the owner with reasonable assurance of identification of construction defects for timely contractor remedy.

- The contractor provides a bond or bonds giving the owner optimum protection should the contractor default on the contract.

The disadvantages of the design/bid/build project delivery system include the following:

- Confirmation of final cost and date of project delivery is provided late in the process.

- The triangular owner relationship (Figure 1.11.1) can be adversarial and lead to claims and disputes.

Construction Management

Some agencies planning the construction of complex projects may not have sufficient in-house resources to schedule, coordinate, and manage the necessary planning, designing, and constructing of a facility. In these cases, an agency may hire a construction manager or construction management firm to provide these services. Most construction managers have extensive contracting experience in addition to their general administrative skills.

Construction management bears little resemblance to the original form that emerged in the late sixties. It has evolved into a project delivery system, which has taken many forms. Construction management practices can be classified into two distinct categories: agency construction management and construction management at-risk. The roles and responsibilities of the owner, the design firm, the construction management company or manager, and the contractor are different for each category.

Construction management usually involves multiple construction contracts that compress the amount of time needed to complete the construction of a project. If an accelerated time schedule is required, much more intensive planning, scheduling, and coordinating are required in both the design and construction phases than in the other delivery approaches.

The construction manager manages the solicitation and receipt of many smaller trade contracts. Some contracts are issued before the design is complete—such as those for rough grading, foundations, and site utilities. Other long-lead items, such as detention hardware and precast cells, may be bid out early, as well. Design work no longer is done sequentially but is focused on the needs of the early construction contracts so as to shorten the design and construction period. Agencies under heavy pressure to provide additional bed capacity often use some variation of this method. A significant disadvantage is that it may be difficult and expensive to make changes in the later stages of design because of its impact on construction already under way.

Agency Construction Management

This is construction management in the purest sense. The construction management company acts as an agent to the owner throughout the course of the project delivery. The agency construction manager acts in a fiduciary role during the entire tenure on the project (Figure 1.11.2).

Agency Construction Management

Advantages
- Competitive bidding of the prime contract
- The owner selects construction manager on the basis of ability
- The owner has an expert construction advocate
- There is "construction" input early during design phases
- Checks and balances
- Controlled competitive fast-tracking
- Focused management of the owner's risks
- Quick, accurate decision making

Disadvantages
- The owner is most at risk for ultimate construction cost
- The owner retains ultimate responsibility for design quality, cost, and schedule
- The construction management company has no real clout to resolve design/construction issues—can serve only as a mediator

Figure 1.11.2
Agency Construction Management Organization

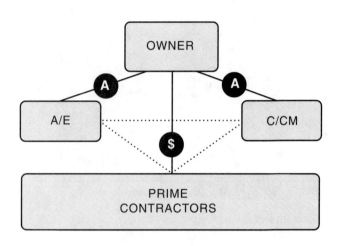

The advantages of the construction management project delivery system include the following:

- In a manner similar to traditional project delivery methods, the design professional works directly for the owner and owes no allegiance to, nor derives any benefit from, the work of construction manager, contractors, subcontractors, or manufacturers.

- Provided that the owner/design professional relationship remains direct, the relationship remains one of trust in that design professional's advice is free from any consideration except for his or her fee.

  The owner/design professional relationship with the assistance of the construction manager during design provides the owner with even more reasonable assurance of a balance between economy and quality.

- By competitive bidding of multiple contractors, the owner is assured of a reasonable project cost by qualified contractors, whose work is coordinated by the construction manager.

- The owner/design professional relationship, in coordination with the work of the construction manager during construction, provides the owner with even more reasonable assurance of contractor conformity with contract documents.

- The owner/design professional relationship coordinated with the work of the construction manager during the warranty period provides the owner with reasonable assurance of identification of construction defects for the contractor's remedy.

- The owner has reasonable assurance of adequate co-ordination of multiple contractors.
- The potential for delay, and claims and disputes are minimized, compared to the design/multiple bid/build method.

The disadvantages of the construction management project delivery system include the following:

- The cost of the project may be higher than project delivery by the traditional owner methods.
- Small projects may not be able to justify the additional cost of a construction manager.
- The services of a construction manager may not be bonded and may not offer the protection of errors and omissions liability insurance.

At-Risk Construction Management

At-risk construction management is sometimes called *contractor construction management.* The construction management company at some point during the design modifies its agreement with the owner to include provisions for a guaranteed maximum price for the cost of construction. The construction management company may hold the contracts or the owner may hold the contracts, as shown in Figures 1.11.3 and 1.11.4.

At-risk Construction Management

Advantages

- Early guaranteed cost of construction management services
- Construction management handles procurement and administration
- Risks focused on construction management as single-source responsibility
- The owner is involved in all decision making prior to cost/schedule commitments

Disadvantages

- Scope of the project must be identified early for construction management to guarantee construction costs
- Scope of construction management services must be detailed to guarantee construction management fees

Figure 1.11.3
At-risk Construction Management Organization

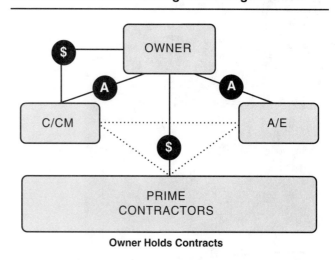

Owner Holds Contracts

Figure 1.11.4
At-risk Construction Management Organization Option

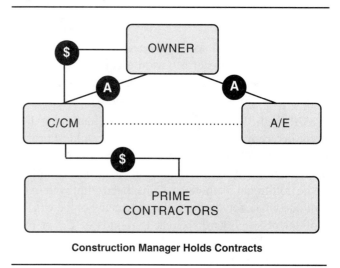

Construction Manager Holds Contracts

Design/build Project Delivery

Design/build is a third category. This is closest to a true master builder concept (that was the normal project delivery method in the Middle Ages). The design-builder contracts directly with the owner to provide programming, design, and construction services guaranteeing cost and schedule. Often, the designer-builder provides the mechanism for financing through assistance with financial advisers or through leaseback arrangements.

The design/build process as it generally is being employed in the United States today can be defined as

This is the foundation of a wall of the Joliet Police Headquarters in Joliet, Illinois. Security wall reinforcing affects costs but is a necessary part of correctional and detention facilities.

Photo courtesy of PSA, Peoria, Illinois.

"one-stop shopping" for the owner. Basically, the process requires the owner to award a contract to a single entity who becomes responsible for designing and constructing the project under a single contract.

Although the design/build process has come into favor in recent years, actually it may be the oldest project delivery system in the history of building construction. The design/build process may appear to be new compared to the traditional methods that have been employed in the United States. Yet, during its history, many of the world's monuments such as the Great Pyramids of Egypt may have been the products of a design/build team centuries ago. While the process may seem to be greatly simplified, the ultimate consequences of the design/build method may have certain risks to all of the parties, especially to the owner.

For more than two centuries of building construction in the United States, perhaps as much as 90 percent of the projects constructed during that period have been delivered under the traditional design/bid/build method. The traditional method usually has assured owners that they stand to have their project delivered for the lowest possible cost.

A second area of assurance is that the design professional, acting on behalf of the owner, being independent of the contractor or the construction process and its po-

tential rewards, can offer reasonable assurance that the owner will receive a quality project at the end. Neither of these traditional safeguards may be fully available to the owner in the design/build process. In approaching the design/build process, an owner is advised to conduct a fair degree of risk analysis before opting to employ the design/build process over the more traditional methods. There is also definable risk for all participants in the design/build process.

The design/build process, by its definition, places both the design process and the construction process under a single contract responsibility. In other words, the design professional is either a permanent part of the design/build contractor's organization or the design professional may "team" with a traditional building contractor to form a design/build organization for one or more projects. The "teaming" method seems to be the more common approach observed in the United States in the latter part of the twentieth century. Figure 1.11.5 illustrates the typical arrangement of the parties in a design/build project.

The advantages of the design/build project delivery system include the following:

- The owner's procurement process is simplified to a "one-stop-shopping" experience.
- Project cost and schedule of delivery is identified early in the process.
- Design documentation is simplified; less detail is required in completing contract documents.
- Delivery of the completed project may occur much earlier than by traditional methods.

Figure 1.11.5
Design/Build Organization

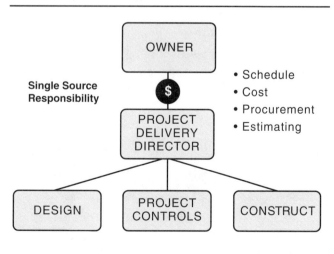

The disadvantages of the design/build project delivery system include the following:

- The owner has little or no control over the quality of materials, equipment, and methodology employed to produce the project.
- The owner cannot rely on the design professional's independent advice or that the design professional will act as the owner's advocate in the project delivery process.
- "One-stop shopping" heavily favors the design/build contractor's interests; therefore, the owner's interests rely on both the integrity and the professionalism of the selected design/build team.

Other Methods of Project Delivery

A number of variations have been tried by government agencies searching for the right approach for them. These include *criteria design/build* (establishing criteria but not necessarily design concept, and similar to Figure 1.11.5), *bridging* (establishing some level of design as shown in Figure 1.11.6), *design/build/lease/purchase* as shown in Figure 1.11.7, where the agency leases the completed facility for a specified number of years before taking ownership, and various permutations of these, and *program management*. Program management is the process in which a single firm acts as the sole representative for the owner and coordinates all aspects of the planning and construction phases of the project.

Criteria Design/Build

Advantages

- Single-source responsibility for design and construction
- Design/build can guarantee cost for design and construction

Disadvantages

- Most construction firms do not have in-house design capability
- No objective architect/engineer to focus on design issues
- Procurement laws may prohibit this method in certain jurisdictions

Figure 1.11.6
"Bridging" Organization

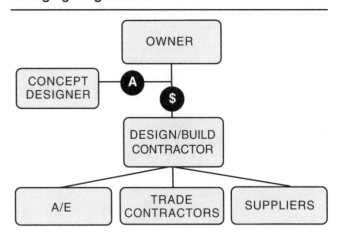

Bridging

Advantages

- The owner selects architect/engineer on the basis of ability
- Project investment limited to architect/engineer's fees
- The owner works directly with the designer to set design requirements
- The design/build team selected to complete the project on the basis of the most competitive proposal

Disadvantages

- The design/build contractor is reluctant to make changes after selection
- Higher cost likely due to risk assumed by the developer
- Original architect/engineer may have little or no involvement/continuity

Design/Build/Lease/Purchase

Advantages

- The owner selects the architect/engineer on the basis of ability
- Project investment is limited to architect/engineer's fees
- State does not have to encumber total construction costs—only lease payment annually

Disadvantages

- Cost of financing higher than if state/county sold general obligation bonds
- Architect/engineer involvement filtered through developer
- More cumbersome process to make changes during construction

Figure 1.11.7

Design/Build/Lease/Purchase Organization

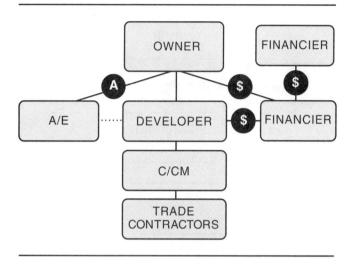

This is the foundation for a wall at the Joliet
Police Headquarters in Joliet, Illinois.

Photo courtesy of PSA, Peoria, Illinois.

Program Management

In the latter half of the twentieth century, some projects have become very large and complicated. Such projects may involve unusually high cost and may require the services of multiple design professionals and multiple prime contractors who must work under conditions of phased construction with multiple and sometimes over-lapping schedules.

In other cases, a project may have an unusual time restraint for delivery, or the owner may wish to occupy certain portions of the project while others are still under construction. For projects of this nature, the owner may hire a program manager for purposes of managing the entire project delivery process. In this instance, the program manager becomes the sole representative of the owner and may be responsible for selecting the design professional(s) and multiprime contractors as well as managing other procurement methods in concert with the project completion. Under this method of project delivery, the program manager establishes and manages the lines of communication among all of the participants. The program manager establishes the scheduling of work and manages the payment of the participants as the project is completed.

Program Management System

Advantages

- The program manager obtains competitive bids from all participants, including the design professional(s), giving the owner the optimum advantage of capturing lower costs
- The single responsibility of the program manager, including the design professional, gives this person the ability to fast-track design by creating multiple bid packages with phased construction, saving time compared to other delivery systems

Disadvantages

- The design professional may not have an independent relationship with the owner
- The owner may not be able to rely on the design professional's advice in matters of quality of materials and methods during construction

Responsibility, Accountability, and Liability Issues

All states have regulations regarding the practice of architecture and engineering. Most states require contractors to be licensed and to satisfy bonding and other financial criteria. These regulations and procurement requirements in various states are often in conflict with each other when design and construction management or construction services are bundled together to provide variations on the design/bid/build process.

The federal government is required to acquire architectural and engineering services by evaluating qualifications and competency rather than price competition under the Brooks Act. The Brooks Act is the pattern for similar legislation enacted by many states. On the other hand, construction services often must be acquired by a process that awards work to the lowest qualified bidder. The interplay of these two regulatory schemes can play havoc with attempts to use guaranteed maximum pricing coupled with design services or design/build.

Much of this confusion stems from the fact that most states do not have specific legislation to reflect the evolution of project delivery in the marketplace for public sector projects. This is changing gradually. Design/build has grown in the last ten years from 4 percent of the nonresidential market to more than 20 percent today, and this figure is increasing.

Inmate Labor

A correctional agency may want to consider using inmate labor and in-house staff to construct some or all of the facility. This can provide meaningful work for inmates, reduce idleness, and eliminate the higher cost of contract labor. Often, however, projects performed by inmates take much longer to complete and may create conflict with the private sector that views the work as unfair competition. To employ inmates successfully on these projects, it is essential that staff are skilled in the various building trades and adept at working and teaching inmates. Designers also must plan a facility that uses easily erected construction components and simple building techniques (Jones, et al., 1998 and Keilin, 1998).

Several factors should be considered before making a decision to use inmate labor:

- Distance of the inmate force from the construction site and on-site accommodations
- Type of work and skills required
- Number of skilled inmates available
- Custody or security requirements
- Availability of staff to supervise
- Cost and time factors involved in use of inmate labor compared to noninmate labor
- Effect of using inmate labor on local employment conditions
- Legal liability
- Equipment and material warranties
- Need for inmate employment
- Ability to maintain the same inmate workers throughout the project and maximize work crew effectiveness

Summary

The agency carefully should consider the advantages and disadvantages of each method of project delivery available to them and their own specific needs and resources. No one method is right for every situation.

References

Jones, Gary D., Steve Anderson, and Willie Dixon. 1998. Work Ethic Camp: Inmates Construct Facility—McNeil Island Corrections Center, Washington State Department of Corrections. In Rhine, Edward, ed. *Best Practices: Excellence in Corrections.* Lanham, Maryland: American Correctional Association.

Keilin, Sharon B. 1998. A Partnership with Habitat for Humanity—Texas Department of Criminal Justice. In Rhine, Edward, ed. *Best Practices: Excellence in Corrections.* Lanham, Maryland: American Correctional Association.

The federal government is a large consumer of various services needed in the construction of prisons and detention services. This shows the foundation being set for a secure building at the Federal Correctional Complex in Coleman, Florida.

Architect/Engineer: Spillis Candella, Coral Gables, Florida. Construction management firm: Morse Diesel, Edison, New Jersey. Construction contractor for the low- and medium-secruity institutions: George Hyman Construction, Hollywood, Florida. Photo courtesy of PSA, Peoria, Illinois.

Lessons Learned from Other Countries

Stephen Carter, AICP
Carter Goble Associates, Inc.
Columbia, South Carolina

An indication of a society's sensitivity to the needs of its citizens can be illustrated through its system of incarceration. Because most societies have used incarceration to punish, incapacitate, and rehabilitate, a review of the forms and methods of building incarceration facilities on a global scale helps illuminate social values. During the past two decades, a worldwide explosion in prison construction has occurred. This offers insight into the differences in approaches to incarceration, and in the core values of nations. The motivation for construction and the architectural solutions are as varied as the cultures they serve. This chapter features some of the international answers to incapacitation and rehabilitation as these are reflected through architecture.

Influence Through Information

From the late Victorian period until the conclusion of the Second World War, the British model for prison design dominated most of the world that relied on incarceration as the principal means of punishment. Examples of the linear, multitiered cell blocks remain as reminders of the influence of the Empire in Canada, India, Australia, Israel, Argentina, and America, to name a few locations.

With the Western nations practicing a measure of isolationism following the end of World War II, no single nation emerged as the trendsetter for prison design until the post Vietnam era in the United States. The social turmoil and judicial activism of the late sixties and early seventies in America led to a new model for incarceration. The architectural expression was critical to the implementation of the rehabilitative model. Also during this period, America began the long ascent to the peak as the world's highest incarcerator of its citizens—a position that has no competitors, save Russia and South Africa.

Since the mid-1970s, the United States has expended more than $50 billion in constructing new prisons and jails. At the peak construction period in the 1980s, America opened the equivalent of a new 500-bed prison every 3 days. This shift to America as the leading prison-builder brought new approaches in management, design, and construction. Some of the most notable innovations have included unit management, podular housing units, therapeutic communities, direct supervision, electronic detection systems, modular cell construction, and high-rise jails, among others.

With the intensity of construction and the role of communication in the global community, America's prison building expansion became the most visible model available for worldwide inspection. Technological systems were developed that detected, detained, and documented the daily routines of prisoners. Low-voltage electronic devices were used to secure the perimeter, control and document access to every space in a prison, identify contraband on a visitor's person, send a silent signal to aid an officer in distress, and visually record the behavior of prisoners and staff, among many other applications. The impact of the explosion in this building approach soon was felt worldwide.

As with all forms of social policy, the success of one culture is not easily transported en masse to another. Although America has led the world in technological advances for prison design, promulgated a set of standards defining prison operation and design, and developed a method of accrediting jurisdictions that follow these standards, other nations also have merged cultural heritage with judicial practice in the care and custody of offenders. The result has been an era of correctional architecture with a universal basis in the search for the best practice.

Diversity in Universal Solutions

Viewed from the global perspective, the term *best practice* in correctional architecture in this context is a subjective acknowledgment of incarceration facilities where cultural sensitivity, humane justice, and restrictive environments blend to offer a physical dimension to incapacitation that provides the offender with access to reconstructive change. This definition is not necessarily universal, but the solutions have design merit that does transcend national boundaries.

Housing Unit Size

In the 1983 version of the *Design Guide for Secure Adult Correctional Facilities*, the housing unit was defined as the "form-giver" in a correctional institution. Fifteen years and 4,000 more correctional institutions on a worldwide scale have not changed this premise. The housing unit remains the distinguishing component of a correctional facility. One of the most significant changes over the last decade and a half has been the size rather than the shape of a housing unit.

Prior to the change in the American Correctional Association standards in 1993, the suggested maximum size for a housing unit was 50 inmates under the supervision of one correctional officer. This number has been expanded to as many as 128 inmates in a single or double-cell housing configuration in several American states. The performance standard has been based on the type of supervision (direct or indirect) and the amount of out-of-unit time as criteria for expanding the unit size. Achieving natural light in each cell continued to define the shape of housing units until the mid-1990s when the American Correctional Association standards were altered to permit windowless cells, if more natural light could be "borrowed" from the dayroom.

Other countries also have experimented with housing unit configurations to match changes in management methods. In the United Kingdom, three-level dayrooms have been used, which effectively reduced the size of the

Dayroom for 256 inmates. Lee Correctional Institute, Bishopville, South Carolina.

Architect: Architectural Engineering Associates. Photo courtesy of Carter Goble Associates, Inc.

Natural light flows into a dayroom at Her Majesty's Prison at Doncaster, Doncaster, Yorkshire, England.

Architect: U.K. Property Services Agency. Photo courtesy of Carter Goble Associates, Inc.

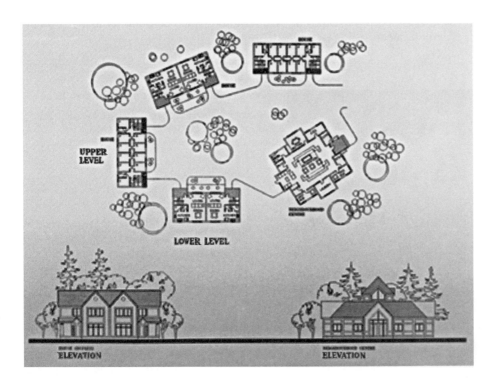

Site plan of Medium Custody Housing cluster, William Head Institution, Victoria, British Columbia, Canada.

Architect: Wagg & Hambelton. Diagram courtesy of Carter Goble Associates, Inc.

unit while maintaining an abundance of natural light and good sight lines in the dayroom. The recent designs for British prisons have indicated a firm commitment to podular, as opposed to linear, multitiered housing of the past. In contrast to America, the housing unit size has remained in the fifty-to-sixty inmate range.

Universally, the concept of a podular housing configuration that began in America in the 1970s has been adopted in various forms by most nations constructing new correctional facilities in the last decade. However, variations are emerging, but the unit remains the "form-giver" regardless of the unit size. During the 1990s, the Correctional Services of Canada introduced a style of housing that combines residential-style rooms with a much smaller unit size. Israel also has abandoned the typical podular format for housing in the most recent facility to be constructed in favor of a "block-of-flats" approach.

Singapore has abandoned the multitiered, Victorian style of housing in favor of the two-level podular approach, but assigns three-to-five prisoners to a cell as a variation on the Western model. Multiple occupancy of cells continues throughout the world as a method of addressing crowding. The institutionalization of dormitory living as a significant form of housing remains a mostly American phenomenon.

Perimeter Security

Most of the world continues to use walls to define the perimeter of prisons, as these establishments often are constructed in populated areas. America did not pioneer the concept of fenced prisons, but has integrated physical barriers of fences and razor ribbon with electronic-detection technology in a manner that has redefined perimeter security. Since the great majority of American prisons are located in rural areas, perimeter aesthetics is a low priority. During the past decade, many perimeter towers were eliminated in favor of roving patrols. Some states have substituted lethal fences for towers as a reported operational cost-reduction solution.

In most other countries, the wall continues to serve as the perimeter of choice. With technological advances in detection and surveillance systems, the walled prison now combines a physical and electronic barrier. The concern for community appearance often has superseded the greater cost for the walled solutions.

The innovations that have occurred in perimeter security design mostly have been associated with electronic detection and surveillance systems, with various seismic devices emerging as the most often used detection systems. However, a single arched fence has proven effective as an alternative to conventional double fences in some community settings where aesthetics and economics are equal priorities. A nonclimbable mesh fence is another alternative to reams of razor ribbon located on and between double fences.

If the housing unit provides the form for a correctional facility, the perimeter establishes the image of incarceration. The past fifteen years have established the prison as an unashamed building type on the American landscape and an emerging walled community in many other parts of the world.

View of Tzalmon and Hermone Prisons, Israel.

Architects: Shmuel Shilo and Planning & Research Ltd.
Programmer: Carter Goble Associates, Columbia,
South Carolina. Photo courtesy of Israel Prison Service.

Double fence, Federal Correctional Institution, Marianna, Florida.

Architects: HLM. Photo courtesy of Carter Goble Associates, Inc.

First use of double fence in the United Kingdom, New Feltham Remand Centre, Feltham, Middlesex, England.

Architects: U.K. Property Services Agency. Photo courtesy of Carter Goble Associates, Inc.

Typical wall configuration, Her Majesty's Prison at Wolds, England.

Architect: U.K. Property Services Agency with UK Detention Services. Photo courtesy of Carter Goble Associates, Inc.

Cells

The most significant change since the 1983 publication of the *Design Guide* has been the degree of crowding that has occurred worldwide. Even though billions of dollars were spent in constructing new institutions at a time that the crime rate began to plateau in most western nations, crowded living environments continue to characterize most institutions. With few exceptions, cells rather than dormitory units, remain the preferred form of housing by managers and prisoners alike. The proclivity to construct cells rather than open dormitories, and an adequate amount of support space, has helped ease the problems associated with crowding in new facilities.

As previously noted, in the United States, the amendment of the American Correctional Association standards to permit windowless cells (if a specific amount of "borrowed" natural light was provided) has introduced new housing unit configurations that reduce the dayroom size and allow plumbing chase access from the rear of the cell. This approach requires a more transparent cell front to access the "borrowed" light and creates a more unencumbered floor area without the traditional plumbing chase. The windowless cell for new institutions is exclusively American and has not yet been adopted by many other nations, which continue to believe that natural light in the cell is a right and not a choice.

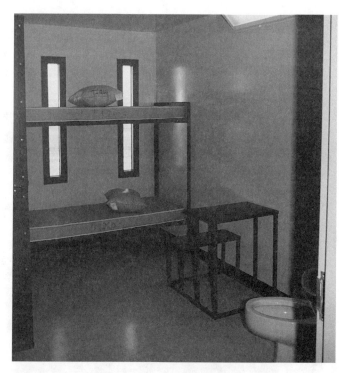

Typical double cell based on 50 square foot per occupant, Lee Correctional Institute, Bishopviile, South Carolina.

Architect: Architectural & Engineers Associates. Photo courtesy of Carter Goble Associates, Inc.

Use of movable furniture in a single cell at the J. Reuben Long Detention Center, Horry County, Conway, South Carolina.

Architect: Timbes/Wilund/Usry/ Carter, Myrtle Beach, South Carolina. Programmer: Carter Goble Associates, Inc. Photo courtesy of Carter Goble Associates, Inc.

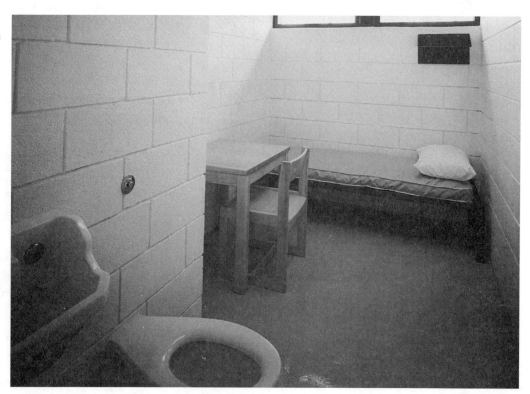

For support areas, construction methods have become more like those for educational or light industrial facilities as lightweight steel or concrete frames with insulated exterior panels and metal stud interior walls have increased construction speed while reducing costs. We may attribute this to the construction of more than 50,000 privately developed bed spaces in the past decade.

Currently, low-voltage electronic surveillance and detection systems are used in most facilities higher than medium custody throughout the world. Beyond the use of electronic perimeters, most new prisons now include closed-circuit television cameras, metal detection, X-ray, personal body alarms, remote access controls, and wide area networks for a variety of computer-based management systems. In America, infrared surveillance, internal prisoner tracking, and bar code identification systems are being used to supplement staff and extend barrier-free security.

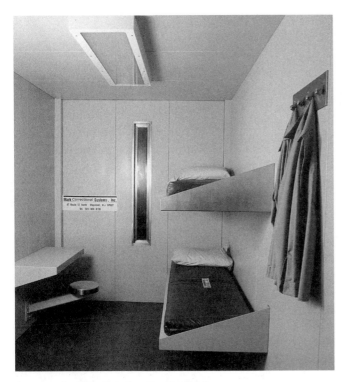

An example of the interior of a steel cell.
Manufacturer: Mark Solutions, Inc., Bloomfield, New Jersey.
Photo courtesy of Carter Goble Associates, Inc.

Although a period of movable cell furniture resulted from the "normalization" era in the 1980s, the 1990s has witnessed a return to fixed metal furniture in the American correctional system. This trend has not been adopted universally as many nations have continued to use wood, plastic, and other similar materials. This persistent difference in cell fixtures and furnishings between America and other westernized nations tends to reflect disparate attitudes regarding the expected behavior of prisoners.

Building Methods

The need for rapid, less expensive prison construction has yielded new building methods worldwide. Modular construction for cells in steel or concrete has become broadly accepted as a method to reduce normal building time by as much as 15 to 25 percent in countries that have this technology available. While the cost of prefabricated or precast assembly has been reduced as more competitors entered the market, in developing nations, conventional construction remains the preferred approach. Improved on-site methods for rapid construction and quality control have offered prison managers a broader range of choices to meet schedule and security requirements.

Modular concrete cell units, Her Majesty's Prison at Altcourse, Liverpool, England.

Architect: TPS/Tarmac Construction Design Build Team. Programmer: Carter Goble Associates, Inc. Photo courtesy of Carter Goble Associates, Inc.

Better communication and greater participation in international conferences and symposia have increased the examples of *best practice,* which has increased the homogeneity in prison design. Even with a similarity in housing unit configurations, applications of technology, and construction methods, most countries have maintained a degree of cultural chauvinism in their individual solutions. Given that cultural differences will continue in methods of care and custody, these cultural differences should be applauded.

Case Studies of International Designs

One of the continued trends worldwide has been the specialization in correctional missions and the concomitant impact on design. While the size of general prisons has increased universally due to operational economies of scale, difficulties in site selection, and capital advantages in large construction projects, at the same time an increase in special mission facilities also has absorbed a growing number of special needs offenders.

General Custody Facilities

The trend toward larger institutions most obviously can be seen in institutions designed to manage general medium-custody prisoners. Most nations have abandoned the linear, multitiered housing units for institutions that are disaggregated into management units of less than 300 prisoners. This has permitted a jurisdiction to gain the economies of scale commensurate with the construction of large institutions, while operating several somewhat autonomous facilities within one perimeter.

Many states, such as California, Texas, Florida, Virginia, and South Carolina, among others, have developed prototype general-custody designs. The consistent theme has resulted in large housing units (up to 128 inmates in a dayroom) and campus configurations. The campus-style institution has also become popular internationally with the United Kingdom, Abu Dhabi, Australia, and Argentina, among others, constructing new facilities based on a podular design for housing units in a campus-type setting.

Tunnel Form Construction Method, Tzalmon Prison, Israel.

Israeli Architect: Poreh-Ya'acovi. U.S. Architect: STV / Silver & Ziskind. Photo courtesy of Carter Goble Associates, Inc.

Open campus for living clusters, William Head Institution, Victoria, British Columbia, Canada.

Architects: Wagg & Hambleton. Photo courtesy of Carter Goble Associates, Inc.

Okimaw Ohci Healing Lodge, Maple Creek, Saskatchewan, Canada.

Architects: Architects Collaborative Maple Creek, Saskatchewan, Canada. Photo courtesy of Carter Goble Associates, Inc.

Tzalmon Model—Division of prison into management groups, Tzalmon Prison, Israel.

Israeli Architect: Poreh-Ya'acovi. U.S. Architect: STV / Silver & Ziskinduch. Photo courtesy of Carter Goble Associates, Inc.

Women's Facilities

America remains the highest incarcerator of women offenders. At the local, state, and federal level, the addition of bed spaces for women has increased at a faster rate than for men. The issues of designing for women are distinct from that of men and represent the opportunity to secure the institution creatively without the high cost and foreboding appearance that characterize many new male institutions. Acceptance of the principle that women should reside in smaller living units is generally universal. This increases the opportunity for reducing the scale and creating a more normalized environment.

The basic design differences in designing for women offenders between the United States and other nations seem to be reflected in an acceptance of less strenuous physical barriers from the international community than in America.[1] Many nations such as Australia, Canada, and Denmark have found that residential-styled design solutions are more appropriate for the majority of incarcerated women.

Perspective of housing cottages, Victoria Women's Prison, Melbourne, Victoria, Australia.

Photo courtesy of Carter Goble Associates, Inc.

Fenceless women's campus, Minnesota Correctional Facility for Women, Shakopee, Minnesota.

Architects: HOK, Washington, D.C. Photo courtesy of Carter Goble Associates, Inc.

Use of daylight and normative materials, Delaware Women's Facility, Willmington, Delaware.

Architects: Grad Associates with Carter Goble Associates, Inc. Photo courtesy of Carter Goble Associates, Inc.

Young Offenders' Facilities

The rapid rise in the incarceration of young offenders has been similar to that of women. The mixed mission of high security and rehabilitation introduces new operational and design challenges. The mission to educate the offender and treat psychosocial problems within an environment that encourages positive behavior requires an architectural expression that blends security features, human scale, and durable materials. While the public anger over heinous crimes by young offenders has caused some jurisdictions to "harden" the purpose-built institutions, no evidence exists that this minimalist approach contributes to the treatment goal. In the United States and abroad, the distinguishing characteristic for youthful offender institutions has been smaller housing units (less than fifty) and a less institutionalized appearance.

Open design with natural light, New Feltham Remand Centre, Feltham, Middlesex, England.

Architect: U.K. Property Services Agency, London, England. Photo courtesy of Carter Goble Associates, Inc.

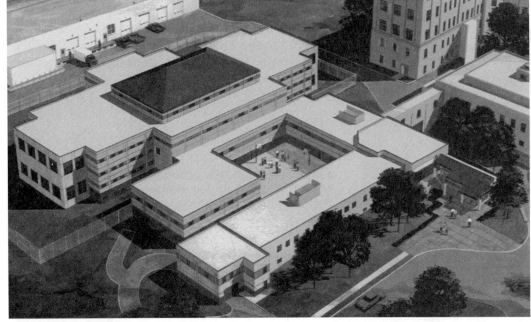

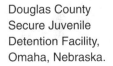

Douglas County Secure Juvenile Detention Facility, Omaha, Nebraska.

Architects: Bahr, Vermeer & Haecker Architects, Omaha, Nebraska. Programmer: Carter Goble Associates, Inc. Photo courtesy of Carter Goble Associates, Inc.

Exterior courtyard, Medway Training Center, Worcester, England.

Architect: Panton Sargent, Worchester, England. Photo courtesy of Carter Goble Associates, Inc.

Pretrial Facilities

Throughout the world, the preadjudication function continues to be the offender's first exposure to incarceration. The United States is one of the few nations that attempts to maintain a rigid separation between pre- and postadjudicated offenders and is also one of the few nations that generally attempts to locate pretrial incarceration facilities as close to courts as possible. This principle, in a time when the electronic transfer of information and images permits instantaneous and accurate communication, has caused the design of many American pretrial facilities to be mid- and high-rise structures. With few exceptions worldwide, the concept of locating prisoners in high-rise structures away from outdoor recreation and horizontal access to programs and services is uniquely American.

Another difference between the American and other international experience is that remanded or preadjudicated offenders in most societies are provided similar access to programs and services as adjudicated prisoners, meaning that the facility includes an adequate amount of area to offer a full range of programs and services. The emphasis is more on interaction than incapacitation.

Exterior view of the Arlington County Detention Facility, Arlington, Virginia.

Architects: HLM, Charlotte, North Carolina.
Programmers: Carter Goble Associates, Inc.
Photo courtesy of Carter Goble Associates, Inc.

View of facility in suburban setting, Prince George's County Correctional Center, Upper Marlboro, Maryland.

Architects: CE McQuire.
Programmers: Carter Goble Associates, Inc. Design Consultant: Gary Mote. Photo courtesy of Carter Goble Associates, Inc.

View of multilevel facility, Allegheny County Jail, Pittsburgh, Pennsylvania.

Architects: Tsao Catelos / L. Robert Kimbell, Edensburg, Pennsylvania. Programmers: Carter Goble Associates, Inc. Photo courtesy of Carter Goble Associates, Inc.

Incorporation of new with existing structures, Metropolitan Remand and Reception Center, Sydney, New South Wales, Australia.

Architects: Public Works Department of New South Wales. Operations Review Team: Stephen A. Carter, Dr. Perry Johnson, and James A. Gondles, Jr. Photo courtesy of Carter Goble Associates, Inc.

Planning, Design, Construction Process, and Issues

Treatment Facilities

Specialization has occurred in corrections as in many fields, and the result has been the construction of institutions that are dedicated to the mission of rehabilitation and treatment. The most predominant types have been medical, mental health, and substance abuse facilities. America also has constructed many institutions dedicated to discipline (boot camps) in the past decade, but these facilities have been distinguished more by the lack of architecture than examples of international best practice.

Most of the medical facilities have focused on the overlay of security requirements on traditional health care environments. This blending of missions has been illustrated best in the new prototype regional medical centers of the Federal Bureau of Prisons. One of the many challenges is the management of cost with the combining of the two most expensive facility types into one institution.

Spiritual lodge—Okimaw Ohci Healing Lodge, Maple Creek, Saskatchewan, Canada.

Architects: Architects Collaborative. Photo courtesy of Carter Goble Associates, Inc.

Entrance to District of Columbia Correctional Treatment Facility.

Architects: Silver & Ziskind / Gilbane Design Team. Programmers: Carter Goble Associates, Inc. Photo courtesy of Carter Goble Associates, Inc.

Institutions designed especially for the care and treatment of substance abuse offenders have been rare since many programs have been incorporated into existing facilities. For the specially built treatment facilities in America, the design solutions have emphasized the programmatic objective of small management groups supported by decentralized counseling and support spaces at the housing unit.

Internationally, the trend has been similar to America with a focus on substance abuse treatment resulting in an emerging building type. The largest such program in the world is currently in design for Singapore. Canada has introduced a new building type for women in extensive substance treatment that emphasizes residential-style living in a secure setting.

High Custody Facilities

The high custody, or "supermax" prison has become one of the most prevalent types of new institutions in America. Almost every state has constructed or requested funds for construction of a facility that is dedicated to the removal of the most difficult-to-manage inmates from the general population for extended periods of time. These facilities are characterized architecturally by double-loaded corridors and electronic control of virtually all movement, activities, and observation of inmates.

Although all nations have inmates that require complete separation from others, the design of a special

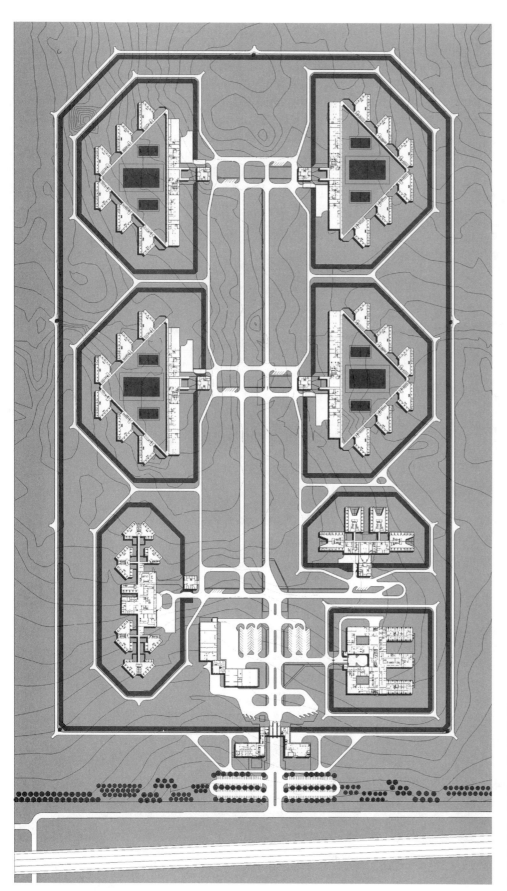

International correctional facilities have been successfully designed to serve as highly secure facilities as shown in this sketch of the Argentine prison complex of Complejo Penitenciario I, Ezezia, in the province of Buenos Aires.

Architects: Spillis Candela & Partners, Inc., Miami, Florida. Engineers/Contractors: Techint Impregilo Iglys Hochtief. Photo courtesy of Carter Goble Associates, Inc.

facility to institutionalize isolation is uniquely American. In many states, assignment to the "supermax" institution means at least twenty-three hours of lock down for a minimum of twelve months. The cost of these types of institutions is much greater than general custody facilities due to the multiple levels of redundancy in security barriers, surveillance, and detection systems.

Low Custody Institutions

At the opposite end of the security scale are specialized low custody institutions, which are characterized by open living units of cubicles or dormitories. These facilities often are constructed of prefabricated materials and can be erected quickly within a fenced or fenceless perimeter. Open dormitories of 100 or more prisoners are an American phenomenon. Minimum-custody institutions in other nations often employ residential, or independent living design solutions as developed in Israel, Canada, Sweden, and Hungary.

Sliding gates for super-maximum prison, Federal Correctional Institution, Florence, Colorado.

Architects: DLR Group-Omaha Office. Photo courtesy of Carter Goble Associates, Inc.

Main circulation walk-in, Hermone, Israel.

Architects: Shmuel Shilo and Planning & Research Ltd. Programmer: Carter Goble Associates, Columbia, South Carolina. Photo courtesy of Carter Goble Associates, Inc.

Rehabilitation and work release facility near Budapest, Hungary.

Architects: Hungarian Prison Service. Photo courtesy of Carter Goble Associates, Inc.

Planning and Design Guide for Secure Adult and Juvenile Facilities

Federal Correctional Institution, Marianna, Florida.

Architects: HLM, Charlotte, North Carolina. Photo courtesy of Carter Goble Associates, Inc.

Private Facilities

The United States will exceed 200,000 privately managed bed spaces by the year 2000, and most of these will be in institutions that have been both designed and constructed by the private sector. Although this management approach was initiated in America, the United Kingdom, Scotland, four states in Australia, and South Africa also have undertaken comprehensive programs of privately offered and operated prisons. Several other nations are seriously considering a similar solution to eliminating crowding and poor conditions.

No other single initiative in prison operation will impact more decisively on correctional architecture in the next decade. Many jurisdictions that are not committing to the private management of prisons will be closely influenced by the capital and operating cost savings that are reported by private firms. Therefore, future government-developed prisons and jails are likely to be highly influenced by the building approaches introduced by private prison operators (*see* the sections on privatization in this book).

Metro-Davidson County Detention Facility, Nashville, Tennessee.

Architects: Corrections Corporation of America, Nashville, Tennessee. Photo courtesy of Carter Goble Associates, Inc.

Of major interest internationally will be the process that the government employs to solicit private solutions. If the operational and design response is left entirely to the private firms, a wide range of design approaches can be anticipated that may be difficult to compare. Thus far, only America has permitted "speculative" prisons in which only life safety and local ordinances must be followed, rather than employing a uniform set of correctional standards or principles to construct the at-risk prison.

Modular concrete cell units, Her Majesty's Prison at Altcourse, Liverpool, England.

Architect: TPS/Tarmac Construction Design Build Team, London, England. Programmer: Carter Goble Associates, Inc., Columbia, South Carolina. Photo courtesy of Carter Goble Associates, Inc.

Aerial view of reclaimed land for prison, Bermuda Maximum Security Prison, Hamilton, Bermuda.

Architects: HLM, Charlotte, North Carolina. Programmer: Carter Goble Associates, Inc. Photo courtesy of Carter Goble Associates, Inc.

Conclusion

As statistics from the Bureau of Justice Statistics indicate, the construction of new correctional facilities in America has been declining over the past three years, even though the number of Americans incarcerated continues to establish new benchmarks each year. This would indicate that citizens have grown weary of paying for new facilities but still demand safe streets. This raises new opportunities for a return to community-based alternatives in line with less emphasis on construction as the only workable answer to criminal behavior.

In many other nations, with the possible exception of Canada and several of the Scandinavian countries, the current focus is on building new institutions. While the combined volume of prison construction of all other nations in one year will never match America's, the hope is that the positive and negative lessons learned from the last decade's most active period of prison construction in history will be readily transferable throughout the world.

Endnote

[1] See a fuller explication on women's prisons in Carter, Stephen A. 1998. Designing Without Glass Ceilings: An Examination of Trends and Opportunities in Designing Prisons for Women, in Joann Morton, ed. *Complex Challenges, Collaborative Solutions: Programming for Adult and Juvenile Female Offenders*. Lanham, Maryland: American Correctional Association.

Inmate and Juvenile Housing

2

The photograph on the previous page shows a crane lifting a twenty-four ton fully equipped precast cell into place on site at Wallens Ridge State Prison, Big Stone Gap, Virginia. Cells were built off site by Tindall Concrete in Lynchburg, Virginia, and transported to the site on flatbed trucks.

Architect: Daniel, Mann, Johnson & Mendenhall. Construction manager: Gilbane Building Company, Providence, Rhode Island. Photo courtesy of Gilbane Building Company. Photographer: Tim Cox.

Direct/Indirect and Podular Design Concepts

James Kessler
HOK Architects
Washington, D.C.

Podular design is based on the understanding that security is as related to inmate psychology as to physical barriers. If physical barriers alone are inadequate for the most basic aspect of incarceration, holding the body, then their use for the more complex aspects of custody such as physical safety, psychological adjustment, and ultimately, rehabilitation, is clearly peripheral. Correctional management that integrates the use of barriers with a strategic staffing plan to achieve the full spectrum of custody goals will prove to be more effective than a less integrated and more compartmentalized approach.

Podular Design

Podular design emerged in the 1970s. The concept sprang not from a design imperative but from the management realization that the goal of rehabilitation rarely was achieved in large undifferentiated groups of inmates without continued personal reinforcement. The podular design subdivides inmates into smaller groups of compatible classifications. The nineteenth century ideal of reform through individual penitence was transformed into contemporary behavioral modification through work, incentives, sanctions, and a more relaxed relationship between correctional officers and inmates.[1]

Podular housing design divides inmates into smaller, compatible groups by classification. Mecklenburg Dayroom: The "inmates" in the picture are really architects in jail uniforms who tested out the facility before turning it over to its owner, the Mecklenburg County Jail in Charlotte, North Carolina.

Photo courtesy of Little/HOK Joint Venture Architects. Photographer: Rick Alexander.

The correctional officer, working in a podular housing unit, is trained to sense negative inmate predilections and inmate's positive potentials. As podular design was refined, the correctional officer was called on to positively influence the behavior and motivation of the inmate. The reduction of behavioral problems results in a more manageable population, which can increase staff efficiency and allow the use of more normative building products in lieu of more expensive, high-security products and materials, which lessen capital costs. There are also potential savings in staff time by bringing services to the inmates at the housing unit rather than in a centralized location, which eliminates staff escort duties.

The reduction of behavioral problems results in a more manageable population . . .

Podular design is associated with two forms of staff supervision: direct and indirect. Indirect supervision places the officer in a secure control room to observe multiple pods. Direct supervision locates the correctional officer within a single housing pod without physical separation from inmates. To enhance supervision, podular design introduced the concept of dayroom space. Direct or indirect housing pods use dayroom space that is directly linked to inmate rooms. The dayroom area provides access for inmates to areas for personal hygiene, recreation, dining, and communication. The location of these spaces within the same security compartment as the inmate rooms is the essence of pod design.

The geometry of the pod is based on achieving a balance between the amount of perimeter wall required to provide natural light to each cell as compared to the area of the dayroom space that is captured by the cell configuration. The recent design concept to introduce natural light into cells through borrowed light from dayrooms has allowed the perimeter wall length to be decreased and in turn diminished the size of the captured dayroom space. This natural light often is provided through the use of skylights. American Correctional Association standards require dayroom space of thirty-five square feet of space per inmate who uses the dayroom at one time. Operational flexibility is maintained when the dayroom is sized for all inmates who are housed adjacent to the space.

Single- and Double-Bunked Rooms

A significant variable in pod design is whether the inmate rooms are double bunked (two inmates per sleeping room) or single bunked (one inmate per sleeping room). Single-bunked inmate rooms require a rigorous configuration to eliminate excess dayroom space. Generally, a triangular housing unit with inmate rooms on two sides and support and entry space on one side provides the most efficient use of space.

The geometry to provide dayroom space for double-bunked rooms is less rigorous, and rectangular configurations often work. Pods in both cases usually employ mezzanine housing to minimize dayroom area and increase visibility for the supervising officer.

Indirect Supervision Pods

The differences between direct and indirect pods are both qualitative and quantitative. Indirect pods allow continuous visual monitoring of inmates in the dayroom for security and safety purposes. The officer in the control room can observe overt nonconforming incidents. The officer, in turn, must alert a response team to take direct action. The officer's knowledge of inmate behavior is based on visually comparing normal or tranquil inmate activities to disruptive or noncooperative behavior and reacting appropriately. The most critical geometry in indirect design is the establishment of clear sight lines from the control room to the entire dayroom of each pod to be supervised. Indirect pods tend to have fewer beds than direct pods because inmate classification is more critical when an officer is not present.

Indirect pods are most manageable when the bed count does not exceed twenty-four. While larger pods have been used successfully, their success depends on a large enough inmate population so as to derive the appropriate number for compatible classifications.

Indirect pods can achieve efficiency through the decentralization of inmate services. Pods are grouped to form a housing unit overseen by a control room and include support space and an outdoor exercise area. Inmates are released from their pods to make use of shared support areas. Units in this configuration should be made up of similar classifications.

Direct Supervision Pods

Direct supervision is a management approach that increases the effectiveness of the correctional officer in influencing inmate behavior. An officer in a control room is limited to observing inmates and activities. An officer located in the dayroom space has the opportunity to become proactive about the demeanor of inmates in the dayroom. Direct supervision is considered by many to be the state of the art for inmate management and housing unit design. The concept is founded on the mutual human respect of the officer and inmate and the imposition of immediate sanctions to the inmate if conflict occurs.

The design of direct supervision pods affords architectural opportunities unavailable in the design of indirect supervision pods. The strict geometry required for sight lines from a control room to multiple housing pods often results in a configuration that requires excess dayroom space. Direct supervision pods, not linked to a control room, may give priority to influences of constructability and practicality. The following issues should be considered when designing direct supervision pods.

Dry Cell Pods

A housing design option usually associated with direct supervision is the use of dry cell pods. These are housing units with centralized toilet and shower facilities versus having toilets and lavatories in each cell. Dry cell pods tend to foster a normalized environment and save money in construction and equipment costs. In these areas, inmates generally are allowed free access from their cells to the dayroom and toilet facilities.

The pod officer will establish the dayroom schedule and maintain a master key or electronic controlled access to all rooms. Cost is saved in the elimination of security doors, plumbing fixtures, and special chases. In some building code jurisdictions, more money can be saved by eliminating ducted air returns in the cells by mixing cell-return air with dayroom air. In wet cells, toilet exhaust must be directly discharged to the outside. It is useful to visualize dry pods as a secure step up from open dormitories where the inmate retains privacy and personal territory, rather than a step down in security from a typical wet cell pod.

A triangular floor plan provides the most efficient use of space in a single-bunked housing unit. Inmates in dry cells use toilets located off of the dayroom. This is a fifty-six bed, single-bunked, direct supervison dry pod.

Courtesy of James Kessler, HOK.

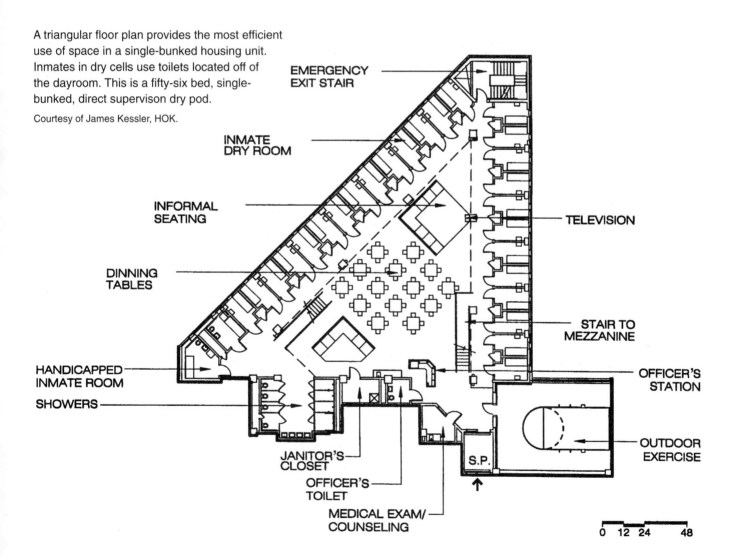

EMERGENCY EXIT STAIR

INMATE DRY ROOM

INFORMAL SEATING

TELEVISION

DINNING TABLES

STAIR TO MEZZANINE

HANDICAPPED INMATE ROOM

SHOWERS

OFFICER'S STATION

JANITOR'S CLOSET

OFFICER'S TOILET

MEDICAL EXAM/ COUNSELING

S.P.

OUTDOOR EXERCISE

0 12 24   48

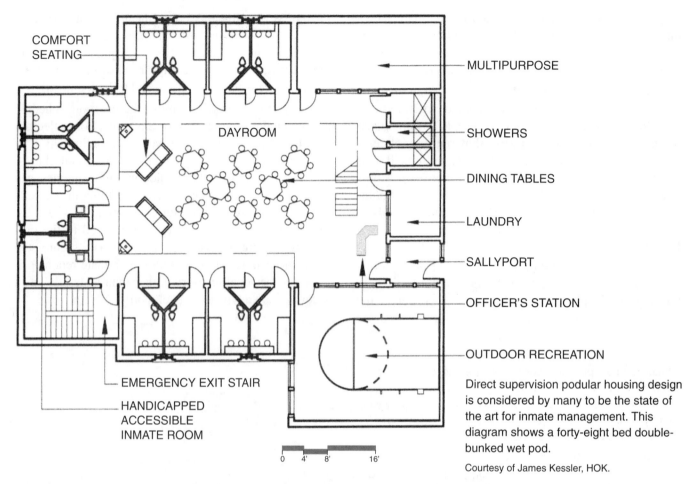

COMFORT SEATING

DAYROOM

MULTIPURPOSE

SHOWERS

DINING TABLES

LAUNDRY

SALLYPORT

OFFICER'S STATION

OUTDOOR RECREATION

EMERGENCY EXIT STAIR

HANDICAPPED ACCESSIBLE INMATE ROOM

0   4'   8'   16'

Direct supervision podular housing design is considered by many to be the state of the art for inmate management. This diagram shows a forty-eight bed double-bunked wet pod.

Courtesy of James Kessler, HOK.

Dayroom

If inmate rooms are like houses, then consider the dayroom as the village green. Inmates view the dayroom as a respite from the isolation of the cell. Security windows that allow views and natural light to enter should be provided. Administrators and staff are able to monitor the inmates' psychological accommodation to the correctional regime by observing social interaction among the inmates. In detention facilities, dayrooms are the focus of decentralized activities, including dining and programs. In correctional facilities, where dining, industry, education, and other programs are centralized, the dayroom becomes important as a nonpunitive default location for inmate passive recreation time.

Officer's Station

Visibility is the basis of control. The design should promote visibility from wherever the officer is in the dayroom. Correctional officers act like police on the beat or teachers in a classroom and know what is going on throughout their area. The direct supervision officer should have a station that is located so that casual observation of the entry sallyport, outdoor exercise area, shower doors, multipurpose space, and all room doors is possible. The floor tile pattern in front of the station may be changed so that inmates know how close to the station they may approach.

Correctional officers, through the use of computers, can supply inmates with information about activities such as visiting, court dates, and the commissary. This establishes not only a relationship of authority between the officer and the inmate, but allows the fruits of a cooperative relationship to be reinforced. The pod officer station should contain a computer terminal, telephone, housing pod door control panel for remote door monitoring, and desk space for report writing. It should not be designed as a safe haven that the officer is uncomfortable to leave.

Outdoor Recreation

A recreation area outside the pod may be designed to allow natural light to enter the dayroom and provide continual access to outdoor activities at the discretion of

An officer's station in a direct supervision pod should be accessible to inmates and provide a workstation for staff. The Mecklenburg County Jail in Charlotte, North Carolina.

Photo courtesy of Little/HOK Joint Venture Architects. Photographer: Rick Alexander.

the pod officer. Thus, the outdoor recreation area can be open all day or shut down, depending on the cooperation of the inmates. The minimum ceiling height should be eighteen feet, and a basketball hoop may be installed with careful consideration given to its misuse as an aid to climbing or escaping. Depending on the climate, large overhead doors used in conjunction with security mesh will allow heating of the space if it is a covered area.

Acoustical Control

Acoustical ceilings and wall panels reduce noise and help the dayroom officer establish control by letting inmates hear the officer's voice. Limited use of carpeting also can greatly reduce the amount of noise in the space. The provision of sound-absorbing materials in housing pods presents particular challenges to the designer. Hard materials by nature reflect sound while soft materials are susceptible to abuse by inmates. Absorptive materials should be used for ceiling areas out of inmates' reach. It also is advisable to place sound-attenuation panels on available wall space that is at least eight feet above

floor level. In a mezzanine configuration, this area often is available over dayroom support space.

If televisions are provided in the dayrooms, provision of either floor jacks for individual headsets, or special wireless headsets should be available to inmates to reduce noise and support better use of the space. These solutions permit classes and other group activities to be conducted using video as a medium within the dayroom while not being disruptive to other inmates who are recreating in adjacent areas of the dayroom. On/off and volume controls for television sets and the inmate telephones always should be provided to staff.

Comfortable Furniture/Television

Comfortable furniture may be viewed as an amenity that can be withdrawn from uncooperative inmates. Inmates appreciate the use of furniture that has backs and at least symbolically implies comfort and variety. The inmates may have worked a full shift in the kitchen or industry, and the association of reward for work is positive. It is useful to create two television seating

Comfortable furniture, television sets, and a relaxed atmosphere allow inmates the opportunity to interact in a positive way with others and not be isolated. The Mecklenburg, County Jail in Charlotte, North Carolina.

Photo courtesy of Little/HOK Joint Venture Architects. Photographer: Rick Alexander.

areas separated to the degree possible for better sound separation. Two areas create viewing options. Television and soft seating are tools that demonstrate to inmates the wisdom of cooperative behavior. Immediate sanction reinforces the authority of the correctional officer. Housing units devoid of dayroom amenities and controlled indirectly must be available without delay for noncooperative inmates.

Showers

Showers are a particularly difficult pod element to design because of conflicting functional goals. Privacy, while important to the normalization of the environment, is particularly critical when considered in the context of gender parity in staffing assignments. If it is likely that officers of the opposite gender will be responsible for supervising inmates, thought should be given to individual shower rooms with associated drying areas. Partial-height doors, designed for both privacy and secure observation, by nature allow steam and condensation into the dayroom. The HVAC system should be designed to mitigate this effect. The floor area immediately outside the drying area should have a nonslip surface and be watertight.

Staff Offices and Program Space

In addition to the officer's station, and in support of a unit-management philosophy of operation, typically the unit manager, clerical support staff, social worker, and other professional staff can have offices on each housing unit or pod. This permits inmate services to be delivered on the pod and helps to reinforce the relationship between staff and inmates. Small group meeting rooms, classrooms, and treatment space can be provided so that inmates in each pod receive service and programming together as a group and do not have to leave the unit for these services, which also could reduce staff escort. The management staff, as a result of their proximity and knowledge of the unit's inmates, act as reinforcement to the correctional officers in keeping an eye on security and the overall temperament of the inmates.

Endnote

[1] Fairweather, Leslie. 1994. Prison Design in the Twentieth Century. In *Architecture of Incarceration.* Iona Spens, ed. London, U.K.: Academy Editions.

Classification and Characteristics of General Population Inmates

John Hultberg and Earl Stahl
HDR
Dallas, Texas

Classification Principles

Inmates classified as minimum security usually are subdivided into two levels within most state systems. The first level includes inmates who can work with little or no supervision inside or outside the compound. Inmates at the second level also can be allowed to work with little or no supervision, but are classified as slight security risks and usually are restricted to activities within the secure compound. Inmates at this level usually can be housed in dormitories or wards with minimal supervision.

Inmates classified as medium security typically are also subdivided into two categories. Although all medium-security inmates are considered to be security risks, some of these inmates are willing to work and participate in inmate programs, all of which are within the confines of the secure compound. Inmates in this classification should be housed in single or double occupancy cells to minimize conflict or disturbance.

Once classified, an inmate receives an orientation and is placed in an appropriate housing unit. Here at a medium-security facility, Virginia Penninsula Regional Jail, Williamsburg, Virginia, the Gilbane Building Company's manager of communications models prison garb with an officer in attendance.

Architect: Daniel, Mann, Johnson & Mendenhall (DMJM). Construction: Gilbane Building Company, Providence, Rhode Island. Photo courtesy of Gilbane Building Company. Photographer: Doug Buerlein.

Inmates classified as close custody are those of a higher security risk due to their noncooperative attitudes. They are prone to mild violence and are more management intensive. Inmates of this category should be housed in single occupancy cells, sufficiently equipped to isolate the inmate from the rest of the population, when necessary for disciplinary reasons.

With these categories of inmates in mind, we next consider how best to house them in a safe environment. Inmate housing is one of the most important elements of any correctional facility. The type of housing conveys to the inmates the philosophy and general attitude of the administration and sets the tone of the facility.

Purpose of Housing

Housing not only must meet the security needs of the inmates, but it also must meet minimum standards of decency and humaneness. How this is achieved depends on the viewpoint of the particular state agency on how to best interact with the inmate. One philosophy is to provide a housing design that strives to minimize tensions and frustrations that result from confinement and institutional living. This can be fostered by providing an atmosphere that encourages self-worth and cooperative behavior, and encourages the use of periods of confinement for personal growth and self-improvement. Another philosophy is to encourage the attitudes of personal growth and improvement by cooperative behavior, but with more of a "hands-off" approach. The latter is normally the preference among the state agencies dealing with large populations and rapid turnover. This issue is further addressed in this section under "Barriers."

Inmate Rooms

Inmates are housed in either single-occupancy private rooms, or multiple-occupancy rooms or dorms. Private rooms best meet the goals of decency and humaneness, and they provide more flexibility and better security. While the initial construction cost for private rooms is higher than that for multiple-occupancy housing, there are significant long-term advantages to this type of construction.

Single rooms reduce the likelihood for conflict that can occur in multiple-occupancy housing. In the event of a disturbance, individual rooms substantially enhance the administration's ability to handle disruptive behavior

Dormitory housing can be very cost effective and works well for minimum and a limited number of medium-security inmates. Use of dormitories in maximum-security should be avoided. Dormitory at North Central Correctional Institution, Marion, Ohio.

Photo courtesy of NBBJ, Columbus, Ohio. Photographer: Randall Lee Schieber.

Private cells best meet the goals of decency and humaneness while providing more flexibility and better security as shown here at the Chesapeake City Jail, Chesapeake, Virginia.

Photo courtesy of NBBJ, Columbus, Ohio. Photographer: Joe Wiseman.

by enabling the officer on duty to lock each inmate in his or her own cell until the problem is resolved. This kind of control cannot be exercised in a dormitory or multiple-occupancy living arrangement. Another benefit that can be derived with appropriate consideration to the size of the cell is temporary double occupancy in single cells to overcome crowded conditions until additional space becomes available.

Thus, private rooms not only are more manageable and safer for both inmates and staff, but staff supervision costs also may be lower. In addition, institutions with single cells are able to be more flexible to accommodate different types and classifications of inmates, a factor particularly important in view of the constantly changing characteristics of inmate populations during the life of a facility. Single-occupancy cells offer the ability to accommodate special needs inmates (youthful, aged, or those of limited mental capacities) by providing privacy, dignity, and personal space. This helps to lessen management problems and control associated operational expenses.

Decentralized Unit Management

A decentralized management system is recommended whereby an institution is subdivided into semi-autonomous living units. The basic elements are as follows:

- Each unit comprises a manageable number of inmates. Ideally the size of units should range from forty-eight to sixty-five inmates; however, units have been successfully operated for up to ninety-six inmates in the direct supervision modality. Although the higher number normally is not recommended, it has been achieved with success. Staff efficiencies and costs are always a factor, at the lower number range (forty-eight to sixty-five). Combining two units under one staff team frequently is necessary.

- Inmates are housed in the same unit for the major portion of their confinement by bringing indoor and outdoor recreation, case workers, multipurpose, legal visitation, medication dispensing, clothing issue, and programming to the housing unit.

- Inmates work in a close relationship with a multi-disciplinary team of staff who is permanently assigned to the unit and whose offices are located in the unit.

- Staff members have decision-making authority for most aspects of institutional programming and living, including disciplinary actions for the inmates assigned to the unit.

- Assignments to a particular unit are based on the inmate's need or classification for the specific level of control or the program offered in that unit.

Decentralized unit management increases contact between staff and inmates, fosters better interpersonal relationships, and leads to more knowledgeable decision making as a direct result of staff dealing with smaller, more permanent groups of inmates. At the same time, the facility can benefit from the economies inherent in centralized service facilities, including one food service facility, one clinic, one education and vocational training complex, and one visitation area.

Generally there are two types of units under the unit management concept: general units and special program units. The program in specialized units is tailored specifically to the common needs of the population housed in that unit. Depending on the needs of its inmates, an institution could have one or more specialized program units to serve inmates who could profit from such things as alcohol or other chemical abuse programs, or pre-release planning. The remainder of the units provide for general programs.

In an institution using a decentralized unit management system, newly admitted inmates are assigned to their unit after being processed through the admissions area. Inmate profile information obtained through pre-sentence reports and other sources is analyzed to determine the appropriate unit assignment. Facilities should be configured to provide at least one general unit to be used to house inmates who are classified as predators (those who bully or prey on weaker inmates). Another general unit can be used to house the weaker inmates who are susceptible of being preyed upon or victimized. It is desirable that there be at least one other general unit where inmates who are neither predators nor potential victims can be assigned. If assigned judiciously, inmates from this group also can be housed in one of the "predator" or "victim" units to balance the populations of those units. However, under no circumstances should known "weak" inmates be placed in units primarily for "predators," or vice versa.

Inmates assigned to one of the general program units sometimes are moved at the discretion of the unit team into a special program or segregation unit. This occurs when the inmate displays offensive or disruptive behavior. Such transfers always should be on a "round-trip" basis. If the inmates amend their offensive behavior, then they usually return to the unit from which the transfer was made.

Centralized Program and Services

Centralizing programs and services requires frequent movement of inmates and is required for medical, education, vocational education, dining, central recreation (gymnasium), and so forth. Yet, movement to these functions can be done to minimize staffing requirements and provide safety for the inmate. If this movement is required within the confines of a building structure, large, wide corridors with frequent access to natural light are necessary. This tends to alleviate both congestion and the feeling of being congested. In the campus aspect, open walkways to these areas are preferred; however, if more control of movement is desired, this, too, can be done efficiently by the provision of economical, yet spatial covered walkways with fenced or screened sidewalls.

Unit Teams

A unit with a stable staff allows an offender's total correctional program plan to be designed and implemented by a single small, integrated group of staff members, the unit team. The unit team is multidisciplinary: for a unit of forty-eight to sixty-five inmates, there should be one unit manager, one caseworker, two counselors, and a secretary in addition to the correctional officers. If staff resources are low and a single unit of up to seventy-two to ninety-six inmates is created, it may be staffed by one unit manager, one or two caseworkers, two or three counselors, and a secretary. In either case, part-time staff members such as education and mental health specialists usually supplement the team.

The team is responsible for all aspects of inmate program planning and monitoring, including assigning inmates to programs, implementing treatment programs, coordinating lectures, participating in disciplinary hearings, making parole recommendations, and conducting prerelease programming. The team is also responsible for sanitation, the physical appearance of the unit, and the custody and control of the inmates.

A unit manager, who is the direct-line supervisor of all facility staff assigned to the unit team, including the correctional officers, administers the unit. The unit manager represents the unit at institution-wide administrative team meetings, this person usually reports to an assistant warden.

Circulation Patterns

Historically, inmate circulation between centralized program/service facilities and housing areas was confined to secure enclosed corridors. This arrangement provided maximum control of inmate movement. With more effective perimeter security and outdoor lighting systems, a "campus" plan is not only viable but also desirable. A variety of outdoor walks or footpaths between the housing units and the central facilities is recommended to diffuse traffic, relieve congestion, and reduce the likelihood of conflict. Separate housing structures dispersed from one another and from major service and administrative functions offer great diversity, provide exercise, stimulate the senses, and help reduce the tensions inherent in institutional living. This more "normalized" environment ultimately contributes to the safety of both staff and inmates.

Conversely, tightly clustered facilities with their limited, congested, and often rigid inmate circulation routes contribute to management problems. They may appear to solve certain problems because there is less area for staff to supervise. Similarly, potential altercations may seem to be more observable and therefore controllable. But overly zealous attention to rigid, tight circulation is counterproductive and may lead to a self-fulfilling prophecy that inmates are prone to disruptive behavior and violence and as a consequence, must be closely watched. Institutions housing the most difficult-to-manage inmates may be an exception, and such facilities may need to be more tightly designed. To the extent possible, the major outdoor circulation routes should be visible from the institution's control center or other officer's posts. Certain staff offices also should be located so that "casual supervision" of most circulation paths is a natural by-product of the staff's regular duties.

Housing structures should be far enough apart from one another so that the interior of rooms in one building cannot be viewed closely by inmates in other buildings. In addition, a minimum of 100 feet should be provided

Centralizing programs and services requires frequent inmate movement. If this occurs in one large structure, wide corridors with access to natural light are essential. York Correctional Institution for Women, Niantic, Connecticut.

Photo courtesy of John Hultberg, HDR.

This multipurpose recreation area at South Woods State Prison, Bridgeton, New Jersey, has been designed to accommodate various types of activities.

Photo courtesy of L. Robert Kimball and Associates, Ebensburg, Pennsylvania.

between the housing structures and the security fence; 125 to 150 feet is preferable. The resulting openness provides sufficient space for proper supervision of the area and creates a no-man's land, an area where inmates should not be.

In contemporary designs based on the unit management concept, the housing structure out of necessity often is composed of two to three modules of forty-eight to sixty-five inmates each. Corridors, common or staff usage areas, which provide managers the flexibility to operate the modules either independently or as a combined unit, should connect the modules. Even when the modules are operated autonomously, this arrangement enables nighttime supervision to be performed by a single officer observing the modules without going outside the building's security.

Multi-use Areas

The term "dayroom" traditionally has been used to describe the space in housing units devoted to general leisure time activities, such as watching television or playing table games. The best application of this space is a plan that combines the dayroom space with the normal circulation area that is located in front of the inmate rooms, providing a central multi-use space around which

all inmate rooms are grouped. Since each room opens directly onto the central area, staff can see the face of each door and into rooms by the use of view panels, either in the doors to the rooms or through sidelights adjacent to the door. This allows staff surveillance to be improved to the extent that it seems almost casual, and becomes more a by-product of other important inmate management duties rather than the predominant concern.

To economize space and dollars and facilitate staff supervision, most of the current housing designs using the multi-use (dayroom) area approach locate the inmates' rooms on two tiers, creating a split-level scheme. This arrangement can be further facilitated for maximum visibility by elevating the area where the staff officer's desk or counter is located.

If the central multi-use space (dayroom) is carefully planned and large enough, and has sufficient sound-absorbing materials (acoustical panels, carpet, and so forth), one or more television sets can be placed in this space. Because of the volume of noise that usually emanates from the television sets, a small room adjacent to the central multi-use area (dayroom) should be provided for quiet activities such as reading. This type of room should have large glassed partitions between it and the larger multi-use area. In addition to providing spaces

The traditional dayroom has become a multifunctional area, observed by staff and capable of serving a wide variety of needs for both inmates and staff. Chesapeake City Jail, Chesapeake, Virginia.

for indoor recreation and other leisure activities, the multi-use areas are suitable for various unit meetings or other unitwide activities.

In addition to the multi-use (dayroom) space in the housing units, many correctional facility designs include outdoor recreation space adjacent to the housing area. This area is usually a small, hard surface such as a half-basketball court or equivalent. Collocating this area within the housing structure offers a means to provide natural light into the multi-use area and provides a variety of recreational activities, including an opportunity for informal unscheduled recreation.

Barriers

One of the controversial issues in correctional facility design today concerns physical barriers that separate staff and inmates. Some authorities believe that secure minicontrol rooms are required in each housing unit for all but minimum-security inmates. The staff in this control room do not come into direct contact with inmates. Instead, the officer operates doors to inmate rooms by remote control. The underlying assumption is that firm controls can be imposed quickly in periods of crisis without endangering staff or innocent inmates and that

potential disturbances can be contained. But establishing barriers between staff and inmates, such as the mini-control rooms, promotes a staff attitude about inmates that too often produces the anticipated disruptive behavior, and strong physical controls, indeed, prove to be necessary.

By eliminating barriers and having all available housing unit staff in frequent, direct contact with inmates, potential problems usually are diffused before they become serious. Staff who are properly suited to and trained for this role establish a rapport with enough inmates in the group to feel the emotional pulse of the unit and address petty issues before they fester and become explosive. In contrast, correctional officers in mini-control stations only can observe activities in the unit, either positive or negative; they cannot supervise inmates directly. Placing officers behind barriers tends to promote complacency on the part of staff, since their duties consist of little more than being "button pushers." This sends out three signals within an institution using mini-control rooms:

• Allows inmates to control the living unit

• Fosters a we/thcy dichotomy

• Portrays correctional officers as "helpless" people

The issue of barriers should be weighed carefully in planning new correctional institutions. Barrier architecture will require additional cost in initial construction, and, if the same level of staff/inmate interaction as in a security barrier-free design is provided, long-term operational costs are also higher. These additional costs can be difficult to justify. Numerous barrier-free facilities have operated successfully for many years with an average number of staff, without the use of minicontrol rooms and related devices. Many correctional authorities recommend that all housing units be barrier-free except, perhaps, those facilities that manage the higher-risk inmates or have a very high turnover of inmates negating the ability to develop a rapport between the staff and the inmates. However, even in facilities using minicontrol rooms and additional security barriers, the diligent use of space and natural light is important and aids in diffusing potential conflict between inmates. Further discussion on these requirements is addressed in "Environmental Considerations" in this chapter.

. . . the diligent use of space and natural light is important and aids in diffusing potential conflict between inmates.

Inmate housing structures should be constructed primarily of fire-resistant materials (refer to the National Fire Protection Association's Life Safety Code). To obtain a residential character, use some "soft" materials such as acoustical panels or loose furnishings, all of which should meet minimum flame-spread requirements. There should be a primary entrance into the housing unit, located so that traffic enters and exits directly into or very near the multi-use space and staff stations or desk. A service entrance used primarily by staff for deliveries to the facility also should be provided. Additional emergency entrances/exits should be provided as needed to meet life safety and fire codes.

Space Requirements

The following spaces should be provided at or adjacent to each housing unit:

Multipurpose Room

This area should accommodate up to 50 percent of the housing unit population or be at least 1,800 square feet. This space can serve as a passive recreation area and meeting room, as an area from which casual surveillance takes place. The area allowance by itself does not satisfy minimum standard allowances for dayroom/leisure-time rooms described below, and additional space is needed to meet minimum standards.

Inmate Rooms

Individual rooms should have from seventy-to-eighty square feet or more, depending on single or double occupancy, and should contain a water closet, lavatory, bed(s), writing surface or desk, robe hook(s), and clothing storage(s) as a minimum. As discussed earlier, the individual rooms often are grouped around the central multi-use space, or dayroom, in a two-tiered or split level scheme. China toilet fixtures are recommended for all but high-security (close-custody or maximum) facilities; their cost is substantially less than the cost of stainless steel security fixtures, and experience has shown that with the unit management style facilities, the more expensive fixtures are not necessary. Each inmate room should have immediate access to natural light, either by a security window in the room, or a glass panel into the multi-use space that allows natural light into the room.

Showers

Individual showers should be provided at the ratio of one per eight inmates in each unit or module grouped at different points to be convenient to the inmates. There should be showers on each floor or tier. The showers should be easy to supervise yet provide for privacy, and have a separate space for drying. Standards require that the water to showerheads be thermostatically controlled.

Office Space

Office space should be planned to allow each housing unit module to operate as a separate autonomous unit. Most offices should be located near the entrance to the module so that staff easily can monitor the traffic in and out of the building without being diverted from their primary duties. The following offices should be provided in each module:

Caseworker's Office. One office, with about 100 square feet, provides adequate room for the caseworker and files, as well as space to talk privately with inmates.

Counselor's Office. Each unit should have a private office for consultations with inmates. The office should provide the same amount of space as a caseworker's. For better supervision, these offices sometimes are scattered throughout the module.

Correctional Officer's Station. An area of about 20 square feet, usually with a stand-up desk and a telephone, should be provided in the central multi-use space.

Multipurpose space should be large enough to accommodate up to 50 percent of the housing unit's population and serve as passive recreation space where casual staff supervision takes place. Note the use of natural light. Hudson County Juvenile Detention Facility, Secaucus, New Jersey.

Photo courtesy of Ricci Associates.

Other Offices. The unit should contain two additional offices of approximately 100 square feet each to be shared by staff who do not work in the unit all of the time, such as psychologists, chaplains, and teachers.

Other Multi-use Rooms. In addition to the central multi-use dayroom space, the unit should contain additional multi-use spaces. These rooms can vary from 150 square feet to 300 square feet, and can be used for training or passive recreation. The rooms should be off the central multi-use/dayroom area for easy supervision.

Beverage Alcove

An area of about eighty square feet should be located in the central multi-use space. A drinking fountain, with a hot water dispenser, and small cabinet with possibly an ice machine or soft drink cooler incorporated into the cabinet should be considered.

Telephones

Two or more pay telephone stations should be adjacent or part of the central multi-use space. These should be located to afford some privacy. Only collect calls can be made from these telephones. Staff should have control of these phones and have a switch.

Storage Rooms

Two rooms, each of about fifty square feet, should be provided for supplies and equipment.

Janitor's Closet

Two janitor's closets should be provided, one on each floor or tier located adjacent to the inmate rooms.

Toilet

A restroom equipped with a water closet and lavatory should be located near staff areas for use by staff and business visitors.

Linear Storage/Washer and Dryer Area

There should be space allocated for these items.

Environmental Considerations

A generous allocation of space is an essential element of the secure environment in a correctional institution, since confined and chaotic spaces tend to exacerbate problems among inmates and between staff and inmates. Moreover, tightly organized, complex spaces will be difficult to oversee and to control. For this reason, the spatial requirements set out in the standards for cell size, dayroom, and so on, should be regarded as minimums, and simple, spacious configurations preferred over the kind of spatial "efficiency," which often is achieved with more complex forms. In many instances, the simpler configurations are more cost effective, even though larger in size.

In housing buildings, in particular, corridors and stairs used by inmates, and the galleries serving the upper tier of cells, should be sized to permit the passing of two persons with a very comfortable margin. In facilities accommodating higher security levels, such passageways should allow three persons to pass abreast—one inmate, possibly in restraints, and two escorting officers. An eight-foot minimum width for corridors and stairs subject to the movement of inmates in groups is not unreasonable, and corridors serving major units of an institution should be up to sixteen-feet wide. A five-foot minimum should be maintained for upper tier galleries, six feet when cell doors are swing doors, which open out.

Natural light is essential in any kind of human habitation, correctional facilities included, and natural light is especially important in housing facilities. Those who cannot believe that deprivation of natural light affects the behavior of inmates should consider the plight of the staff who, it is sometimes said, are sentenced to the institution for life, or at least until retirement. The standards suggest access to natural light should be provided in general population cells through a window of at least three-square feet, either directly to the outside, or through an adjacent space from a source within twenty feet of the cellfront. Also, natural light is necessary in the associated dayroom through glazing of at least twelve-square feet, plus an additional two-square feet for each cell, which gets its natural light through the dayroom, or other adjacent space.

The language of the standards may seem unnecessarily complicated, but they were written in this way to allow for options other than a window to the outside. For example, many versions of the ancient standard cellblock configuration called the "inside cellblock" are still in use today, introducing natural light to the inside cells from the large cellhouse windows across the way. A more recent innovation in cellhouse design avoids the problems associated with outside cell windows in an urban setting. This is done by placing the cell windows on the inside, bringing natural light into the cell from skylights, clerestories, or large glazed openings in the dayspace, which might occur as a part of the unit recreation yard.

Conclusion

Population pressures, at least in the foreseeable future, will continue to require institutions and agencies to stretch every resource and use a variety of inventive measures to house ever-increasing numbers of inmates. The lessons learned during the last twenty years and the American Correctional Association standards should stand as guidelines by which to design and operate correctional facilities and jails.

Segregation Housing

John Hultberg and Earl Stahl
HDR, Dallas, Texas

Whether for disciplinary or security reasons, it is sometimes necessary for correctional administrators to separate certain inmates from the main population. This confinement can vary from a few days to months. The general term used to refer to this type of housing is "segregation," and it will almost always require maximum-security facilities with inmates confined individually in single-occupancy cells. Segregated housing is used to detain inmates who are being investigated for rule infractions, those who are being punished for violating institution rules, and those who would be in danger if they were housed with the main population.

The movement of inmates housed in segregation is sharply restricted and controlled. Most activities involving inmate participation take place in the segregation unit itself. For example, meals prepared in the main kitchen are delivered to the segregation unit and served to the inmates in their cells. Segregated inmates usually can receive visitors in the visiting room, but they must be escorted to and from that area, in some instances in restraints. If their behavior is unpredictable, they may use the special visiting booths located in the main visiting room, which preclude any physical contact between the inmate and the visitor. Today, video-visiting may offer the most effective solution. This technology will be discussed in a later chapter.

The segregation unit is supervised by security staff exclusively. At least two officers are needed to operate these units because they usually are designed for indirect supervision, requiring staff presence in the mini-control room and on the floor (*see* the discussion of "barriers" in the general population housing section). Medical staff must make daily visits to check on the health of each inmate. Inmates' caseworkers and counselors from their regular housing units visit with inmates regularly for counseling. Other staff assist during special activities, such as exercise periods. Good practice also requires that the warden and other administrative staff frequently inspect the units' program and operation.

Single-occupancy cells with very durable finishes and maximum-security equipment are used in segregated housing. The Portage County Jail in Ravenna, Ohio.

Photo courtesy of NBBJ, Columbus, Ohio. Photographer: John Griesen.

Administrative Segregation and Disciplinary Detention

Administration segregation generally refers to the separate housing provided inmates from the main population who, among other things, are being investigated for rule infractions. These inmates are afforded the same privileges given inmates in the main population, except that program and support services such as canteen, mail, education, library, and religious services will be delivered within the cellblock, possibly even in the cell.

The segregation unit at the U.S. Penitentiary at Florence, Colorado, contains both disciplinary and administrative segregation inmates. They spend most of their time confined in their cells for control and separation purposes.

Photo courtesy of the Federal Bureau of Prisons.

In general, inmates are placed in disciplinary detention for a rule violation after some form of due process, such as a hearing by the institution's disciplinary committee. Disciplinary detention should be separate from the area designated as administrative segregation. Most inmates usually are confined to disciplinary detention for relatively short periods of time, but they remain in their rooms or cells most of the day, except for such activities as exercising, showering, and appearing before committees for hearings and reviews.

According to the American Correctional Association standards, inmates in disciplinary detention are extended the same rights and privileges as inmates in administrative segregation with two exceptions. First, unless otherwise authorized by the chief executive officer, their telephone privileges are restricted except for those related to access to the inmate's attorney; and, second, access to counseling, education, library services, and other programs is not required. Like inmates in administrative segregation, however, they must have access to legal services and reading materials, medical care, mail, and basic personal and canteen items.

Segregation housing should be located away from major circulation paths, general inmate housing, and the parking lot. It is best located near the medical facility. Standards require medical staff to check inmates in segregated housing daily, and the medical facility typically is not on a major inmate circulation path. Also, proximity to the reception/transfer facilities is desirable because the segregated inmates often are subject to reclassification, requiring they be moved to another

Confinement, separation from other inmates, and substantially limited privileges are the major features of an inmate's life while in segregation status. Chesapeake City Jail, Chesapeake, Virginia.

Photo courtesy of NBBJ, Columbus, Ohio. Photographer: Joe Wiseman.

institution. Designers should pay particular attention to the orientation of the building. Individual inmate rooms should not face the center of the compound where the general inmate population frequently crosses or the "front" of the institution where visitors enter. If the windows of inmates' rooms do face other nearby inmate housing or activities, an appropriate visual shield should be integrated into the design. Earth berms are sometimes used for this purpose. Otherwise, location of cell windows on the inside, off the dayspace, as discussed in "Environmental Considerations" in the general population housing section, may be used.

Segregation housing facilities often are designed as a single structure composed of two wings, one housing administrative segregation inmates, the other housing the disciplinary detention population. Housing these two populations in a single building conserves resources by allowing the sharing of staff and space, such as offices, recreation, and multi-use areas. Although the two populations can be housed in separate structures, this approach would require expensive duplication of space and staff.

Unlike general housing, there is no need for a large, central multi-use space in a segregation unit because inmates are confined to their rooms most of the time and are not allowed to congregate. Similarly, the typical recreation yard capable of accommodating a large percentage of the unit's inmate population at one time is not useful for segregation units. Instead, a number of smaller yards visually separated from one another should be provided. American Correctional Association standards give a variety of specific size requirements for individual or small groups of inmates. There is also no office space for a unit manager, caseworker, or counselors. Since inmates are housed in segregation only temporarily, caseworkers or counselors from their original unit visit with them in the segregation building, using the hearing room or one of the small multi-use spaces.

This administrative segregation cell at the U.S. Penitentiary facility at Florence, Colorado, contains a shower and a concrete bed. There is a vestibule with a solid door to the corridor and a grille door to the cell interior.

Architectural Firms: LKA Partners, Lescher and Mahoney and DLR Group, Colorado Springs, Colorado. Construction management firm: Heery Program Management, Atlanta, Georgia. Construction contractor: PCL Constructors, Denver, Colorado. Photo courtesy of the Federal Bureau of Prisons.

Out-of-cell time for recreation. Although required by law, it is often limited to individual or very small groups of inmates in segregation. Virginia Peninsula Regional Jail, Williamsburg, Virginia.

Photo courtesy of Gilbane Building Company, Providence, Rhode Island.

Components of a Segregation Building

Sallyport. A sixty-square-foot sallyport should be provided as a security entrance into the segregation housing facility. The outer door is operated by the control center based on both audio intercom recognition and visual recognition through the use of closed-circuit television. The inner sallyport door is opened manually by a segregation unit officer or remotely by the mini-control center officer (or officer's workstation).

Correctional Officer's Workstation. A secure room of approximately 120 square feet should be provided for the unit's lead correctional officer. This room will be equipped with electronic equipment necessary for the remote control of doors, telephones, water supply, and fire water flow and should be situated to provide a clear view of the sallyport and major circulation within the unit. If possible, it also should provide a good view of outdoor recreation yards.

Individual Rooms. For a facility of up to 500 inmates, a unit containing approximately 20 rooms for administrative segregation and 10 rooms for disciplinary detention is often sufficient. However, many agencies require a higher percentage of rooms. The rooms should be of maximum-security construction and have at least eighty square feet as required by American Correctional Association standards for inmates confined to their cells more than ten hours per day. All rooms should be equipped with security light fixtures and ground-fault-interrupter electrical outlets, where permitted, and most should be equipped with combination security toilet/lavatory fixtures. Some agencies do not provide outlets in any cells for security reasons. Ideally, all rooms should be located on one level, although sometimes each wing is designed as a split-level, two-tiered scheme. Some very large segregation units have been designed using three tiers to minimize the distance from the unit control room to the cell front. However, movement of inmates becomes more difficult in a multilevel structure.

Multi-use Rooms. Two rooms, of approximately 150 square feet each, should be located near the front of the building to serve as multi-use space.

Hearing Room. A centrally located hearing room of about 250 square feet serves the administrative segregation population and provides another multi-use room for either population.

Counseling/Interview Room. A room of approximately 100 square feet should be provided to enable program and other staff to talk with inmates privately. This room should be located near the front of the building and be accessible to either population. Staff within the room should be clearly visible to other staff in the facility.

Toilet. A small facility for staff and visitors should be provided.

Meal Distribution Area. Meals are distributed from a centrally located room of about 100 square feet that is equipped with a small refrigerator/freezer, microwave oven, counterspace, sink, and storage. Food is brought from the main kitchen in carts and, if appropriate, heated before being served.

Storage Room. A room of about eighty square feet is useful.

Showers. Experience has shown that inmates in disciplinary detention status are more difficult to manage than those in administrative segregation. Therefore, it is recommended that each disciplinary detention room be equipped with a shower. Even though there is added initial cost, the life-cycle cost will be lower if staff efficiency and control are considered. This provision requires a total room area of at least ninety square feet. A group of three showers is sufficient for the twenty inmates in the administrative segregation wing; each shower should be single occupancy with an adjoining drying area. In many jurisdictions, it will be considered essential to have the capability of locking the inmate in during his or her use of the shower.

Telephones. Movable or portable phone capability should be provided to allow inmates to make phone calls from their cells. A mobile phone unit, wall jacks, or sufficiently long phone lines are alternatives to prevent unnecessary movement of inmates.

Protective Custody

The third major category of segregated housing is protective custody. Inmates generally are placed in protective custody because they would be in danger if they remained in the general population. If jurisdictions have only a few inmates requiring protective custody for short periods of time, it may be appropriate to place these inmates in the administrative segregation unit. Protective custody inmates, like the administrative segregation population, should not be denied any of the rights or privileges allowed the general population.

Before placing an inmate in protective custody, most jurisdictions will explore the possibility of transfer to another institution where the inmate could be housed safely in the general population. If such a transfer is not possible, and there are a substantial number of long-term protective custody cases, then consideration probably will be given to the construction of a separate self-contained protective custody unit or, in some instances, the construction or designation of an entire institution for protective custody inmates.

The protective custody unit should incorporate the same features discussed previously for the segregation building. In addition, since protective custody inmates virtually never go to the main institution where they can be seen by general population inmates or members of the public, a separate protective custody unit in a general population institution must incorporate space for many of the activities that are provided centrally for the general population. These include an admission and discharge area, medical treatment/examination room, visiting area, dining space, vocational and education program, hair care service, and recreational facilities. Most other services such as laundry and canteen can be processed centrally and the items themselves delivered to the protective custody inmates. Some services such as dental care in the medical facility would require the removal of other inmates from that area.

Environmental Considerations

The environmental considerations listed in the section on General Population Housing are even more critical with regard to segregation housing, where inmates may spend well over ten hours each day, and sometimes up to twenty-three hours, locked away in an individual cell. The need for natural light and reasonable acoustics are especially important.

Special Geriatric Housing

Robert G. Falter, Ph.D., FACHE, CCHP-A*
Administrative Officer, Federal Bureau of Prisons,
Federal Medical Center, Devens, Massachusetts

The needs of elderly inmates for health care, life cycle roles, friendships, and security are similar no matter where they may be. However, simply because inmates are chronologically past fifty does not mean that they are in need of special help nor that many younger individuals do not need special help such as that outlined for the "geriatric" set. Inmates need to be classified by their abilities.

According to geriatric criminal specialists, most prisons are built for young offenders who are locked up, taught a trade, and sent back into society. Still, by the year 2000, an estimated 125,000 inmates will be 50 or older, and 35,000 of them will be over 65 (Neeley, Addison, Craig-Moreland, 1999). However, due to the influx of the elderly inmates, prison administrators are beginning to focus on this population and are asking architectural firms to design facilities that address their specific needs.

Additionally, the protections afforded disabled inmates, including the elderly, have been expanded by the Americans with Disabilities Act (ADA), *see* Chapter 2.5. The prevailing view, especially by the U.S. Department

Elderly and infirm inmates require accommodations in all of the areas they use within a correctional facility, including adquate room in the visiting area and noise control. Hocking Correctional Facility in Nelsonville, Ohio.

Photo courtesy of Hocking Correctional Facility.

* The views expressed are the author's and not those of the Federal Bureau of Prisons or the U.S. Department of Justice.

Barrier-free accessibility is mandatory for elderly and disabled inmates. Hocking Correctional Facility in Nelsonville, Ohio.

Photo courtesy of Hocking Correctional Facility.

The inmate's environment can help him cope with disabilities, removing stress and lessening the need for medical care.

Photo courtesy of Hocking Correctional Facility.

of Justice (28 C.F.R. 35.190), is that the ADA applies to prisons and jails. Aday (1994) reported that approximately 65 percent of the states paid at least some limited attention to the special needs of elderly inmates. Eighteen states and the District of Columbia reported providing specific facilities for elderly inmates, including housing options, such as segregated cells, geriatric wings, skilled nursing, and specialized medical services for the terminally ill.

A new federal prison hospital is being designed with a very secure envelope allowing inmates to be able to move around inside it. To lessen possible delays to medical staff caused by necessary security measures, such as locked doors and sallyports, security control centers are being designed to shut down or close each unit separately. The design is intended to make it easier for the staff to get in and out. The results are that medical staff and equipment (such as crash carts, portable x-ray machines, and so forth) can go through the doors more easily.

Some ideas may be helpful for future geriatric prison hospitals. This includes crash carts with microchips to open doors or staff with microchip-encoded badges that allow staff to open doors. Through such a system, the control area can see where anyone is. Based on similar technology, patients who wear such an embedded chip in their clothing or on ankle bands or wristbands, as in common hospital identification badges, can be tracked.

Prison Environments and Their Impact

The environment of the prison has a large impact on the use of health care and consequently, prisons that have a greater amount of self-determination for inmates have lower stress that translates into less need for medical care (Moore, 1989).

Based on analysis and observations, Moore recommended several design implications, namely, (1) to adapt to the physical limitations resulting from chronic diseases, one-story living areas would be desirable, (2) to provide for a small examination room and space near or in the housing unit, (3) to provide rooms with doors for all elderly prisoners that would provide privacy and quiet for resting, and (4) to possibly reduce security measures such as heavy duty prison hardware and building construction in many units housing elderly prisoners, who generally are not considered hostile or aggressive.

Other prison experts suggest the following: "Ramps and subtle grades, with handrails where necessary, [to] enhance access. Doors should be three-feet wide with thresholds one-half inch or lower. Levers should be used in place of knobs, and the pulling force on door closers needs to be less than five pounds" (Neeley, Addison, Craig-Moreland, 1999).

"Restroom facilities can be provided at the ratio of one toilet and sink per twelve male inmates, one per eight for females. Urinals can be substituted for up to half of the toilets in the men's quarters. Showers also should be supplied at a rate of one per eight inmates, and at least one bathtub should be provided. Grab bars are required in the showers and tub areas, as well as for seats, and flexible spray nozzles should be installed. The floor surfaces should be abrasive enough to minimize slipping when the floor is wet" (Neeley, Addison, Craig-Moreland, 1999). Of course, these fixture to inmate ratios are suggestions and local building codes should take precedence if more restrictive.

According to Mike Dinberg, Captain, U.S. Public Health Service and Senior Program Management Officer at the Federal Bureau of Prisons, "Along the walls there should be bumpers so that wheelchairs do not dig into walls. There should be more ramps than stairs. All areas should be wheelchair accessible, so that those in wheelchairs can get in and out of their rooms, reach water fountains, use the toilet, and be able to bathe with staff assistance with a bathtub lift or a handicapped accessible shower."

Special provisions are often needed to address the most routine and basic needs of inmates who are elderly or infirm. Hocking Correctional Facility in Nelsonville, Ohio.

Photo courtesy of Hocking Correctional Facility.

Providing adequate area within a shower and slip-resistant flooring is necessary for those inmates confined to a wheelchair or who have other physical limitations. Hocking Correctional Facility in Nelsonville, Ohio.

Photo courtesy of Hocking Correctional Facility.

Women

A design engineer suggests, "For elderly women prisoners, there are few additional physical concerns. There should not be a mammography unit in the facility because of cost considerations and Food and Drug Administration regulations that are very stringent. These restrictions are so great that it is cheaper to contract with a health care provider to come into the institution to perform mammograms and supply certified technicians and radiologists."

Hearing

On hearing, experts believe, there should be normal noise abatement and for the inmates whose hearing is impaired, there should be hearing aids and staff training for those who must deal with them. In addition, fire alarms with a flashing strobe light attachment will alert those who cannot hear the audio sound of the alarms.

Lighting

Among the elderly, depression is common. In nursing home studies, some depression is due to Seasonal Affective Disorder because there is a lack of natural light. Prisons designed with slit windows may not be providing enough light. Therefore, there may need to be supplements to this light source with light rooms, places where inmates can go several hours a day for additional light that comes from high-intensity fluorescent lights. Additionally, due to declining sight, the elderly inmates may need pinpointed light, or light that is more task oriented, such as a task light by the bed.

Temperature Control

Temperature control is another major issue among the elderly whose bodies may not respond the same as that of other inmates to the temperature. This may be due to their medications and to their disease status. The solution is temperature control and better zoning. The siting of the building is also vital. If the building faces east and west, then some rooms will be cold in the morning and hot in the afternoon. The solution is to have a split heating and ventilation system for individual room temperature control.

Health Status of the Incarcerated Elderly

The events that preceded an elderly individual going to prison are likely to produce a high level of anxiety with outcomes that may be detrimental to their health, according to Booth (1989). Bergman and Amir (1973) found that the strain of incarceration produced an accelerated deterioration in both the physical and mental health status of the elderly.

Persons in older adulthood who are caught, convicted, and sentenced to a correctional facility for nonviolent crimes or acts committed while under the influence of alcohol usually cannot believe what is happening to them. This can be a real shock to their self-esteem and self-image. An outcome is grief and depression that may contribute to their chronic health problems.

Booth (1989) suggests many normal age-related changes that need to be considered with the incarcerated elderly:

Sensation: The elderly have decreased sensitivity to both heat and cold. With decreased subcutaneous fat tissue and sweat gland activity, they do not adapt well to environmental extremes. Warm, light, loose clothing, moderate environmental temperatures (70-75 degrees F.) and activities that require frequent movement are advised measures. In addition, the ability to control the temperature in their environment is critical.

Pain: The elderly respond more slowly to heat and pain or not at all. They may exhibit nonverbal signs of discomfort (restlessness, withdrawal, or reduced level of activity) rather than complain about pain.

Smell and Taste: There may be a decreased sense of smell and taste with aging, which affects the older inmate's appetite. They may demand more sugar and condiments to make their food taste better. Weight loss may become a problem, especially for older males. With reduced salivary gland activity, dry mouth, and reduced muscle strength, elderly inmates are more susceptible to choking. Receding gum lines can contribute to ill-fitting dentures, another problem that can aggravate choking spells and create eating problems. Soft, easy-to-chew foods are recommended. For these reasons, the availability of a small kitchen or microwave is desirable. Caution should be advised concerning inmates with heart pacemakers and their proximity to microwaves, as the microwave may interfere with the operation of the pacemaker.

Touch: Pressure injuries and falls are more likely among the elderly population. Carpeted or highly waxed floors become hazardous. Floors should be designed using nonslip surfaces that have a dull finish. Sensible shoes (rather than nonsupportive loafers) are advised. Velcro closures on shoes will help inmates with arthritis in their hand joints to remain independent.

Cardiovascular Changes: Heart tissue enlarges and becomes less elastic. Valves and blood vessels become thicker, more rigid and less compliant. Blood flow meets more resistance, with less blood being pumped by the heart per minute. The decrease in cardiac output leads to a slower heart rate and pulse, and as a result, less oxygen is delivered to the tissues. Slower rates and decreased oxygen will not adversely affect older inmates unless they exercise strenuously or are under great stress. A pulse rate of 100 or greater at rest, or 120-130 after activity, puts undue stress on the heart.

Shortness of breath with exertion (rather than pain) should be used as an indicator of an older inmate's tolerance. Digitalis preparations used to strengthen the heart contractions have a small margin of safety between therapeutic and toxic levels. Thus, monitoring for signs and symptoms of overmedication is essential. Age-related changes or kidney failure intensifies the elderly inmate's risk for toxic responses to heart drugs. The increased resistance of blood flow against hardened vessels may lead to a rise in blood pressure. Inmates on high blood pressure medications also require close monitoring. Bulging in the neck vein(s) when the inmate is standing or sitting up, or at a 45-degree angle, is a serious sign that requires immediate attention.

Where feasible, inclined ramps instead of stairs may be advisable not only to reduce exertion but to aid elderly inmates who use wheelchairs or walkers. In addition, rooms should be designed to have enough square footage to accept not only beds and chairs, but also wheelchairs. Also, doors should be wide enough to accommodate wheelchairs.

Respiratory Tract: There is reduced lung capacity with increased age. Inmates eighty years of age get only one-third the oxygen as compared with younger inmates. The lower portion of the lung does not expand well; these changes along with others predispose older inmates to lung infections such as pneumonia. Marked fatigue, confusion and persistent coughing, fever, and/or general chest discomfort may suggest infection and should be explored. Wheezing from emphysema may be aggravated by anxiety, fear, cold, exertion, or smoke. Prevention of exposure to infections and administration of influenza vaccines are important. Adequate ventilation is important with a continuous exchange of air in the building.

Nervous System: Elderly inmates respond more slowly to stimuli because their reaction time is decreased. Use of high-speed machinery by the older inmate can be dangerous.

Tremors: Older inmates may develop fine tremors or shaking in their hands and body that may be aggravated by extremes in temperature, exertion, and fatigue. This is in contrast with coarse rhythmical tremors of arms, legs, or trunk when the inmate is at rest that subside with deliberate movements. This second type of tremor is associated with Parkinson's Disease, which also presents with increased muscular rigidity, which leads to changes in gait (for example, shuffling, short steps, or running steps), slow movements, and weakness.

Vision: In the elderly, pupils are decreased in size, and the eyes are less able to adapt to sudden changes in the intensity of the lighting, due to the loss of elasticity of the eye lens. There is decreased accommodation to near objects requiring corrective lenses (bifocals). Peripheral vision is reduced, as is depth perception. Cataracts may form. With extremely bright lights or glare from waxed floors, older inmates with cataracts will have difficulty seeing clear images. Accidents can be prevented by reducing glare, and increasing intensity and constancy of lighting. Providing a contrast of colors in the environment (for example, differentiating edges of steps and painting the steps themselves with contrasting colors), according to Booth (1989), should enhance the older inmate's vision and prevent falls and other accidents. Lastly, consideration should be given to the installation of Braille markers on room doors that allow blind or low vision inmates to navigate their environment.

Hearing: There are two common hearing problems seen with increased frequency as a person ages, particularly in many men as compared with women. These problems include the following: (1) presbycusis or degeneration of the auditory nerve. This problem results in a loss of ability to hear high frequency tones and discriminate between consonant sounds (for example, S and F) and (2) otosclerosis or excess bone cells laid down resulting in decreased movement of movable bones, which conduct sound to the otic nerve.

Sound-absorbing materials in ceilings and wall surfaces will soak in sound and decrease background noise to which the inmate is exposed. The inmate with a hearing loss may become withdrawn and irritable or less communicative. Hearing aids may be needed and if prescribed, they need to be checked for proper fit, for battery changes, and turned on for those older inmates who are forgetful. If the correctional staff faces the inmate and speaks slowly in a normal voice, so the inmate can lip read the speaker, often communications will be successful. However, touch and visual stimuli can be used to speak with the hearing impaired when verbal communication is ineffective.

Sleep and Rest: Patterns of sleep and rest may change as an inmate ages. Since the third and fourth stages (deepest stages) of sleep may be absent, older inmates may require naps during the day since they do not sleep well at night. Inmates who are overweight are particularly susceptible to sleep apnea, a condition where the individual stops breathing momentarily while sleeping. Therefore, some elderly inmates may require single rooms.

Skin: In older inmates, the outer layer (dermis) of the skin thins, wrinkles, and appears more transparent and dry, and is easily irritated. There is an increased incidence of skin cancer, especially among those who have been heavily exposed to the sun. Skin conditions need to be watched for changes in size, color, or lesions. These can indicate potential problems. Changes in the skin and nails are usually nonmalignant but can become a problem, such as fungus infections that attack nail beds. Ingrown nails are common. Foot infections often are preventable with good foot care and proper fitting shoes. Particular attention should be paid to older inmates with diabetes. Many foot problems appear with this condition due to poor circulation in the lower extremities.

Therefore, showers that are accessible to wheelchair bound inmates and grab bars in showers and/or the tub allow the inmates to have control of their personal hygiene and protect them from the breakdown of their skin. For those inmates who are bedridden, the ability to use lift tubs is advantageous.

Extremities: Loss of hair and shiny pale skin on lower legs may be related to circulatory problems. Inmates with poor circulation will constantly complain of cold feet. It may be necessary for elderly inmates to wear warm, lightweight stockings that are nonbinding year round and elevate their legs every two hours to improve circulation, according to Booth (1989). For this population, consideration of other forms of heating and cooling is advisable. This includes baseboard, radiant, or forced warm/cool air depending on the geographical location of the facility.

Muscle and Bone: Despite exercise, inmates may experience decreased muscle strength and some depletion of calcium salts from their bones as they age. With an inadequate calcium intake, lack of regular exercise, and/or changes in estrogen levels, bones are more likely to fracture, and elderly inmates also may experience severe muscle cramping. Because cartilage becomes brittle, the resultant condition is painful and stiff joints are common. A barrel-shaped chest may suggest the presence of emphysema, resulting in breathing problems and in-

creased risk of infection. Ergonomic designed light switches and faucets are advantageous because of the geriatric inmate's strength limitations and lack of fine motor skills.

Gastrointestinal Changes: Since the older inmate's liver may be 50 percent smaller, it affects the metabolism of both food and medication. Constipation is a common problem that can be remedied by increasing fluids and bulk-forming foods and exercises that are tolerated. Prolonged vomiting and diarrhea in the elderly inmate presents a serious situation because they can dehydrate more quickly than younger inmates do and develop a fluid and electrolyte imbalance. Adequate restroom facilities and electric water coolers that are close to or in the inmates' housing unit are desirable.

Pancreas: The pancreas produces insulin when sugars are ingested and metabolized. With age, the pancreas becomes less efficient. Inmates with diabetes may require the ability to eat more often to maintain their insulin level. Consequently, small food preparation areas in proximity to or in the housing unit may be necessary.

Urinary Tract: Kidneys decrease in size with age. The ability to filter waste products is decreased 46 percent, according to Booth (1989), in elderly inmates. As a result, any medication excreted by the kidneys (most are) will take longer to be eliminated from the system. Older inmates, therefore, will need the ability to use rest rooms on an unscheduled basis and, therefore, should be in proximity to the toilet in the inmate housing unit. In addition, in males, an enlarged prostate gland is common over the age of sixty. The enlarged prostate gland and decreased bladder capacity result in increased frequency of urination, difficulty in starting and stopping a stream of urine, nocturnal frequency, and greater potential for infection in elderly inmates.

Females may experience increased frequency of urination with reduced bladder capacity. Incontinence, more prevalent in females, always should be evaluated because many cases can be improved with treatment. Decreased vaginal acidity with aging makes the older female inmate susceptible to vaginal infections.

Cognition and Psychology and Suicide: Unless there are pathological changes in the brain that result in Alzheimer's disease or other dementias, elderly inmates probably can continue to learn. However, elderly inmates have to learn to adjust to declining functions and work through their feelings of loss and grief, reviewing their life, and putting it in perspective, as suggested by Levinson (1978). They have to consider their remaining strengths and achievements and the legacy they have created. Some inmates will become preoccupied with body functions and/or are less accepting of age-related changes than their peers are.

The inmate who is diagnosed with a mental illness requires additional precautions, namely, careful installation of any type of grab bars in the inmate's room, bathroom, or shower since this could be a vehicle for suicidal behavior. Also, any type of hanging device (in other words, coat hooks, fire sprinklers, light fixtures, electrical wall switches, ventilation grilles, and so forth) should be designed to prevent tampering by the inmate or constructed/installed in a way that eliminates the possibility of suicide or injury.

The ability of inmates to enjoy an association with an animal even if only for a short visit can help them deal with their illness and their incarceration. Hocking Correctional Facility in Nelsonville, Ohio.

Photo courtesy of Hocking Correctional Facility.

Call Buttons

All hospitals should be designed to accommodate geriatric patients. For instance, the medical call button should be voice activated rather than push button. This will allow the staff to find out what the patient needs and respond quickly. Such quick response is vital because in geriatric facilities, things change rapidly and the ability to respond quickly is vital.

Conclusion

Other experts, including Faiver (1998), conclude that the number of inmates who are frail and disabled and who require assistance with activities of daily living (dressing, feeding, bathing, toileting, and walking) will continue to increase. Some of them will need nursing home care. Those who are incontinent must be diapered and bathed frequently. Disorders such as Alzheimer's disease and organic brain syndrome resulting from aging will place major difficulties on prison administration.

Compliance with the requirements of the ADA will place greater burdens on correctional systems as the number of elderly and disabled inmates increase. Concerns include many items discussed, such as steps and barriers, width of doorways, handrailings, grab bars, and height of lavatories.

Physical recreation can benefit certain inmates and act both as a physical strengthening tool and a tension reliever.

Photo courtesy of Hocking Correctional Facility.

Bibliography

Aday, R. H. 1994. Golden Years Behind Bars: Programs and Facilities for the Geriatric Inmate. *Federal Probation.* 58 (2, 47-54).

Allen, H. E. and D. E. Simonsen. 1981. *Corrections in America: An Introduction.* New York: Macmillian Publishing, Inc.

Bergman, S. and M. Amir. 1973. Crime and Delinquency among the Aged in Israel. *Geriatrics.* 281, 149-157.

Booth, D. E. 1989. Health Status of the Incarcerated Elderly: Issues and Concerns. In S. Chaneles and C. Burnett, eds. Older Offenders: Current Trends. *Journal of Offender Counseling, Services & Rehabilitation.* 132, 193-214.

Falter, R. G. 1993. Selected Predictors of Health Services Needs of Inmates over Age 50. Unpublished dissertation. Walden University.

Faiver, K. L. 1998. Special Issues of Aging. In K. L. Faiver, ed. *Health Care Management Issues in Corrections.* Lanham, Maryland: American Correctional Association, pp. 123-132.

Flynn, E. E. 1992. The Graying of America's Prison Population. *The Prison Journal.* 7(21 and 22), 77-98.

Fry, L. J. 1988. The Concerns of Older Inmates in a Minimum Prison Setting. In B. McCarthy and R. Langworthy, eds. *Older Offenders: Perspectives in Criminology and Criminal Justice.* New York: Praeger, pp. 164-177

Johnson, E. 1988. Care for Elderly Inmates: Conflicting Concerns and Purposes in Prisons. In B. McCarthy and R. Langworthy, eds. *Older Offenders: Perspectives in Criminology and Criminal Justice.* New York: Praeger, 157-163.

Levinson, D. J., C. N. Darrow, E. B. Klein, M. H., Levinson, and B. McKee. 1978. *The Seasons of a Man's Life.* New York: Ballantine Books.

MacKenzie, D. L., J. W. Robinson, and C. S. Campbell. 1989. Long-term Incarceration of Female Offenders: Prison Adjustment and Coping. *Criminal Justice and Behavior.* 162, 223-238.

Moore, E. O. 1989. Prison Environments and Their Impact on Older Citizens. In S. Chaneles and C. Burnett, eds. Older Offenders: Current Trends. *Journal of Offender Counseling, Services & Rehabilitation.* 132, 175-191.

Morton, J. B. 1992. An Administrative Overview of the Older Inmate. Grant #91P05GHM6. Washington, D.C.: National Institute of Corrections, U.S. Department of Justice.

—. 1999 A Systems Approach to Programming for Older Offenders. *The State of Corrections: Proceedings, American Correctional Association Annual Conferences, 1998.* Lanham, Maryland: American Correctional Association.

Neeley, Connie L., L. Addison, and D. Craig-Moreland. 1999. Addressing the Needs of Elderly Offenders. In *From Aids to the Internet: Correctional Realities.* Lanham, Maryland: American Correctional Association.

Newman, E. S., J. Donald, and M. L. Gervitz. 1984. *Elderly Criminals.* Cambridge, Massachusetts: Gelgeschlager, Gunn and Hain

Pitkins, David W. 1999. March/April. New Millennium-New Dilemmas: Graying of the Prison Population. *Corrections Forum.* 8(2), 50-51.

Reed, M. B. and F. D. Glamser. 1979. Aging in a Total Institution: The Case of Older Prisoners. *The Gerontologist.* 194, 354-360.

Rold, W. J. 1998. Legal Considerations in the Delivery of Health Care Services in Prisons and Jails. In M. Puisis, ed. *Clinical Practice in Correctional Medicine.* St. Louis: Mosby, Inc., pp. 344-354.

Rosefield, H. A. 1993. The Older Inmate—Where Do We Go from Here? *Journal of Prison & Jail Health.* 12, 51-58.

Roth, E. B. 1992. Elders Behind Bars. *Perspectives on Aging.* 25-31. July-October.

Sabath, M. J. and E. L. Cowles. 1988. Factors Affecting the Adjustment of Elderly Inmates in Prison. In B. McCarthy and R. Langworthy, eds. *Older Offenders: Perspectives in Criminology and Criminal Justice.* New York: Praeger. pp. 178-196.

Twaddle, A. C. 1976. Utilization of Medical Services by a Captive Population: An Analysis of Sick Call in a State Prison. *Journal of Health and Social Behavior.* 173, 236-248.

Unger, C. A. and R. A. Buchanan. 1985. Managing Long-term Inmates: A Guide for the Correctional Administrator. Grant FN-6. Washington, D.C.: National Institute of Corrections.

Americans with Disabilities Act and Correctional Facilities

Randall Atlas, Ph.D., AIA
CPP
Miami, Florida

Leonard R. Witke, AIA
Oconomowoc, Wisconsin

The Americans with Disabilities Act of 1990 (ADA) extends comprehensive civil rights protection to individuals with disabilities, including inmates. Title 11 of the ADA, which became effective on January 26, 1992, prohibits discrimination in the services, programs, and activities provided by state and local government entities on the basis of disability. On July 26, 1991, the Architectural and Transportation Barriers Compliance Board (Board) published the Americans with Disabilities Act Accessibility Guidelines to assist the Department of Justice in establishing accessibility standards for new construction and alterations in places of public accommodation and commercial facilities (Title 111). On December 21, 1992, the Department of Justice issued the Proposed Rules for Courthouses (Section 11), and Detention and Correctional Facilities (Section 12).

When the Department of Justice published the proposed Rules for Title 11 facilities, they noted that the Board would be supplementing the Americans with Disabilities Act Accessibility Guidelines in the future to include the comments and suggestions for compliance requirements for justice facilities. In September 1998, the Department of Justice published the amendments for the Americans with Disabilities Act Accessibility Guidelines as revised in the final rules that included Section 11 (Courthouses) and Section 12 (Correctional and Detention Facilities) along with other updates in

Access to programs and buildings must be provided to staff, visitors, and inmates through reasonable accommodations.

Photo courtesy of Capital Communications, Inc.

Building entrances used by the public, visitors, and inmates must be accessible. Designs should permit independent use wherever possible. Entrances and door hardware shall either fully comply with regulations or comply to the maximum extent feasible.

Photo courtesy of Capital Communications, Inc.

definitions, accessible elements, restaurants and cafeterias, medical care facilities, business and mercantile facilities, libraries, transient lodging, transportation facilities, accessible residential housing, and public rights-of-way. In so doing, the proposed rule would establish new ADA standards for facilities covered by the Department of Justice's title 11 regulations.

The law mandates reasonable accommodations and program accessibility for persons with disabilities (an estimated 43 million Americans) who must enter, exit, and pass through a building. The number of inmates in state correctional and detention settings who have serious (full mobility impaired) disabilities varies greatly from state to state. As an example, the Florida Department of Corrections has approximately 8 to 11 percent of its inmate population who are seriously disabled. An additional 20 percent of the population has correctable disabilities (sight and hearing related disabilities). The national average for inmates with serious disabilities is between 1 and 3 percent. These numbers are growing, however, as a result of the aging of inmates, the amount of drive-by shooting injuries that occur prior to incarceration, and the number of cases of HIV and other debilitating diseases among these individuals.

A U.S. Supreme Court decision in June 1999 stated that inmates with correctable disabilities are no longer covered by the ADA but may be covered under other laws and regulations. As a result, agencies that are responsible for incarcerating inmates are not required

under ADA regulations to provide eyeglasses, hearing aides, and other battery-operated aide devices to inmates with correctable disabilities. This decision does not change the requirements for agencies to address the needs of individuals in their charge with serious disabilities. Corrections professionals and architects also must search for cost-effective ways to provide reasonable access for inmates with disabilities in jails and prison facilities without compromising security and safety.

A Statement of the Problem

The proposed Final Rules state that all detention and correctional facilities will comply with the Americans with Disabilities Act Accessibility Guidelines requirements 4.1 through 4.35 (which were formerly requirements of Title III of the Americans with Disabilities Act Accessibility Guidelines).

All common use areas serving accessible cells or rooms, and all public use areas, are required to be designed and constructed to comply with section 4 of the Americans with Disabilities Act Accessibility Guidelines. Common use areas include exercise yards, recreation areas, workshops, and areas of instruction and vocational technical education centers, training, counseling centers, cafeterias, commissaries, medical facilities, and any other rooms or spaces for the use of inmates.

If common use areas are serving only accessible housing areas, then only those common use areas need to be accessible. For example, dayrooms and recreation areas serving accessible housing would need to be accessible. However, this does not diminish those areas used by the public or by employees, which are still subject to the requirements for public use areas and employee work areas in sections 4.1 through 4.35.

One exception in the Americans with Disabilities Act Accessibility Guidelines given to correctional facilities is a waiver of the requirements for areas of rescue assistance in minimum requirements for new construction. A rescue assistance area is one that is a safe haven free from fire and smoke and with access to a communications system. Paragraphs 4.1.3[9], [110], [111] do not apply.

Entrances

Entrances used by the public, including those used by visitors and inmates, must be accessible. The exception is entrances or doorways operated only by security personnel, which are exempt from the Americans with Disabilities Act Accessibility Guidelines requirements 4.13.6, .9, .10, .11, .12. If there are entrances that are used by inmates and not the general public, at least one such entrance, and/or passenger-loading zone, shall comply with Americans with Disabilities Act Accessibility Guidelines 4.1.3[8]. Doors not operated solely by security personnel are subject to security requirements and those that prohibit full compliance with Americans with Disabilities Act Accessibility Guidelines requirements shall comply "to the maximum extent feasible."

Security Systems

Any security systems (metal detection, weapon screening, and so forth) provided at public or other facility entrances are required to be accessible by section 12.2.1, 2 with an accessible route through fixed barriers complying with section 4.3. If the devices cannot be made accessible, an accessible route shall be provided adjacent to the screening devices to create an equivalent path of travel.

Visiting Areas

Noncontact visiting areas shall be located on an accessible route. Five percent, but not less than one cubicle, shall be accessible on the visitor and inmate side. If counters are provided, a portion of at least thirty-six inches in length shall comply with Americans with Disabilities Act Accessibility Guideline 4.32. Accessibility includes provision (section 7.2.3) of voice communication devices, volume control, assistive listening devices, and the opportunity to plug in a TTY. However, if the noncontact visiting areas are not serving accessible cells, then the requirements do not apply.

Fixed seats still can be used in accessible cubicles, if the required clear floor space is provided within the area defined by the cubicle (meaning the cubicle just got a lot larger). Consideration should be given to the placement of grilles, talk-through baffles, intercoms, telephone handsets, or other communication devices, which can be usable from both the fixed seat and the accessible seating area (on both sides of the cubicle).

Inmate Cells or Rooms

The minimum number of inmate cells or rooms that must be accessible is at least 2 percent, but not less than one, of the total number of housing cells provided in a facility (not the entire corrections system). The accessible cells shall be dispersed among all categories, classifications, and types of housing and holding cells. The 2 percent does not require an increase in the minimum number of accessible cells, nor require proportionate distribution. The amount or percentage of accessible cells or rooms to be provided in each available housing category or level of security is not specified, since dispersion is not required to be proportionate to the total number of cells in each category or security classification level.

Placement of accessible cells in housing units that can "shift" classification security level may allow additional flexibility in meeting the requirements for dispersion of accessible cells. In addition to the 2 percent of holding or general housing cells being accessible, if there are special holding or housing cells (protective custody, disciplinary confinement, detoxification, or medical isolation), at least one cell serving each purpose shall comply with the Americans with Disabilities Act Accessibility Guidelines.

An additional requirement is that at least 2 percent, but not less than one housing or holding cell or room, shall be accessible to inmates with hearing impairments. If the cells or rooms are equipped with audible emergency warning systems or permanently installed telephones, then they shall comply with the Americans with Disabilities Act Accessibility Guidelines 12.6 regarding audible and visual alarm systems. If there are no audible alarm systems or permanent phones in the cells, then they are exempt from the additional 2 percent requirement. The minimum 2 percent is based on the number of cells or rooms equipped with these devices, and not on the total number of cells in the facility. This requirement applies only when the alarms or telephones are provided within the individual cells or rooms. If permanently installed phones and alarms are located in common use areas, such as dayrooms, then they fall under the requirements for common use areas.

Medical Care Facilities

Medical care facilities within correctional facilities shall comply with the Americans with Disabilities Act Accessibility Guidelines 6.1, 6.3, 6.4 requirements for medical facility accessibility. Patient rooms or cells are required to be accessible, including medical isolation beds. At least one medical isolation bed per facility is required to be accessible, but it is recommended that all medical isolation cells be accessible. Medical isolation cells cannot be counted as part of the minimum number of required accessible cells.

When holding or general housing cells or rooms are altered in an existing facility, at least 2 percent of the number being altered shall be accessible under the Americans with Disabilities Act Accessibility Guidelines 12.4.1, until the number of accessible cells meets the requirements for the facility requirements of 2 percent. Cells that are required to be accessible must be on an accessible route or path of travel as per the Americans with Disabilities Act Accessibility Guideline 4.3. Doors on that accessible route must be compliant with 4.13, except if operated only by security personnel.

Toilets

At least one toilet facility and one bathing facility shall be accessible. Privacy screens shall not intrude on clear floor space required for fixtures and the accessible route. The requirements for bathrooms and toilets do not preclude the placement of toilet or bathing fixtures within the housing cells or rooms as long as requirements for toilets and bathrooms, such as maneuvering space, are met.

Beds

Beds shall have at least thirty-six inches of space for maneuvering along one side of the bed, and the height of an accessible bed should be seventeen to nineteen inches measured from the finish floor to the bed surface, including mattresses or bed rolls. If there is more than one bed in a cell or room, the maneuvering space of the beds may overlap. Where upper bunks are provided, sufficient clearance must be provided between the bunks so that transfer from wheelchairs to the lower bunks is not restricted.

Drinking Fountains

Drinking fountains and water coolers should be accessible to persons in wheelchairs, in accordance with section 4.15; yet, they also must accommodate persons who have difficulty with bending or stooping. Design alternatives include the use of high-low water fountains, with one fountain at a standard convenient height for those who have difficulty in bending and one at a lower height for wheelchair accessibility.

Fixed Seating and Tables

Fixed seating and tables shall comply with section 4.32 that applies to fixed seating and tables within or serving accessible cells. There is a 100 percent compliance requirement for fixed seating and tables that are provided in adjacent common use spaces such as dayrooms. However, if there are no accessible cells in a housing pod, the seating in adjacent areas is not required to be accessible. Fixed benches shall be between seventeen and nineteen inches high. The prior width requirements for benches were dropped.

Accessible inmate toilet fixtures should be provided with required turning space and grab bars for use by handicapped individuals. Consider making certain grab bars removable to improve use of the cell by inmates without physical disabilities.

Photo courtesy of Randall Atlas.

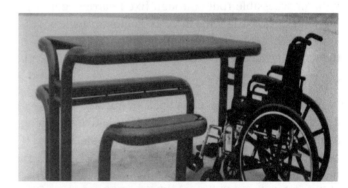

Whether outdoors or within a building, all fixed tables and fixed seating should accommodate use by persons in a wheelchair. This can be done through modification of the seating design or by the use of tables with 45 degree corners that permit wheelchair access without changing the standard design.

Photo courtesy of Randall Atlas.

Storage Facilities

Fixed or built-in storage facilities, such as cabinets, shelves, closets, and drawers located within housing or holding cells or rooms, should contain storage areas that are accessible and compliant with section 4.25. Lockers that are fixed or built-in would be subject to the applicable requirements of Americans with Disabilities Act Accessibility Guideline 4.25. For example, inmate lockers under beds would have to comply with the forward reach requirements of fifteen inches above the finish floor. All control mechanisms, intended for operation by inmates, shall have the required reach requirements and must comply with section 4.27. No changes have been made from the original provision.

Hearing Impaired

Accommodations for persons with hearing impairments is required by section 12.4.3 (if you have audible alarms and permanent phones, then 2 percent of cells must be hearing-impaired accessible). If there are audible emergency warning systems in housing areas, then visible alarms, complying with the Americans with Disabilities Act Accessibility Guideline 4.28.4, must be provided. If there are permanently installed telephones in housing areas, then those phones shall have volume controls complying with 4.31.5.

As a form of equivalent facilitation for alarm systems, it is an acceptable alternative to provide electrical outlets and telephone wiring in the housing areas to enable inmates with hearing impairments to use portable visual alarms and communication devices made available by the operator of the facility. Title II of the Americans with Disabilities Act requires public entities to make available appropriate auxiliary aids and services, where necessary, to ensure effective communication, unless it would result in a fundamental alteration in the nature of a service, program, or activity, or result in undue financial and administrative burdens.

ADA Checklist

The following checklist summarizes some of the major provisions of the Americans with Disablities Act. Of course, it would be prudent to be advised on compliance with the Americans with Disablities Act requirements by a knowledgeable consultant. In the long run, the consultant may be less expensive than litigation brought by inmates, staff, or visitors.

The definition of "alterations" has been interpreted to include resurfacing of streets, sidewalks, parking lots, and other outdoor surfaces, and thus implements the exterior path of travel requirements and accessible parking and loading zone compliance requirements. Guard towers are exempt from the accessibility requirements of 4.1.1(5)(b).

With respect to prison cells on a mezzanine level, the Americans with Disabilities Act Accessibility Guidelines Section 12 requires only that a percentage of cells be accessible. An accessible route is not required for all cells (elevator and stair requirements exempted), including those that may be located on upper tiers accessed only by stairs.

The Americans with Disabilities Act Accessibility Guideline 13 has been revised to allow platform lifts or wheelchair lifts to provide access to raised judges' benches, clerks' stations, jury boxes, witness stands, and to connect levels within an individual housing unit. In the event that a dayroom level is different than the accessible housing, and space does not permit a ramp, a platform lift is allowable.

Entrances

The Board has adopted the recommendation that facilities subject to title 11 of the Americans with Disabilities Act must include all principal public entrances when meeting the 50 percent requirement for accessible entrances in the Americans with Disabilities Act Accessibility Guideline 4.1.3(8)(a)(i). This requirement provides greater assurance that persons with disabilities will have access to the front entrance and avoid excessive travel distances along isolated routes. The provision does not require an increase in the number of entrances planned for a facility. The number of planned entrances will be determined by the design of the facility.

In the final rule, the requirement for access through or around security systems included an exception for doors at such locations. Doors operated only by security personnel were exempt from the requirements for maneuvering clearance at doors, accessible door hardware, opening forces, and specifications for automatic doors, if provided. This exception has been revised to apply to entrances used by the public, and those used by inmates or detainees.

Requirements for door-closers have had the exception broadened to cover not only doors and doorways operated by security personnel, but also those doors and doorways subject to security requirements that prohibit full compliance with these provisions. Where security requirements prohibit full compliance, the applicable specifications are to be met to the maximum extent feasible.

Americans with Disabilities Act (ADA) Accessibility Checklist

❑ Parking is in compliance with requirements.

❑ At least one TTY is in public use areas.

❑ At least one TTY is in secured areas.

❑ There is at least one accessible route through security screening checkpoints. If security equipment is not accessible, then an adjacent accessible route to such security screening devices shall be made to facilitate an equivalent path.

❑ Fifty percent of all principal entrances must be accessible.

❑ Five percent or at least one visiting cubicle must be accessible from both sides. For noncontact visits, accessibility requirements do not apply on the inmate side of the cubicle or counter, but are recommended.

❑ Two percent or at least one housing/holding cell must be accessible.

❑ Dispersion must be within all categories of housing or levels of security.

❑ Accessible cells must comply with the ADA Guidelines Section 4 requirements for barrier-free design.

❑ Doors and doorways on an accessible route shall comply.

❑ At least one toilet shall comply with the ADA Guidelines requirements.

❑ Privacy screens shall not intrude on the clear floor space required for fixtures or accessible routes.

❑ Beds shall have maneuvering space of at least thirty-six inches along one side. Where double beds occur, the maneuvering space at adjacent beds may overlap.

❑ At least one drinking fountain or water cooler shall comply with the ADA Guidelines requirements.

❑ Two percent of housing/holding cells must be accessible to inmates with hearing disabilities if their cells are equipped with audible warning systems and/or permanent telephones. Where permanently installed telephones are provided within housing or holding cells, they shall have volume controls and comply with the reach requirements of the ADA Guidelines.

❑ Visual alarms and strobes are not required where inmates are not allowed an independent egress.

❑ Cells designed as suicide watch or prevention can be designed protrusion-free and are exempt from the requirements for grab bars at water closets.

❑ Ten percent of all patient rooms shall be accessible in medical care facilities in jails or prisons.

❑ At least one medical isolation cell, or special holding cell, shall be accessible.

❑ All fixed seating and tables shall be accessible in inmate, staff, and public areas.

❑ At least one fixed bench shall be mounted seventeen to nineteen inches above the finished floor and provide back support.

❑ Fixed storage, cabinets, shelves, closets, and drawers shall comply with reach requirements.

❑ All controls intended for operation by inmates must comply.

❑ One hundred percent of common use areas serving accessible cells must be accessible.

❑ One hundred percent of all public use areas must comply with ADA Guidelines Section 4.

❑ Requirements for areas of rescue assistance do not apply.

❑ Compliance with the requirements for elevators and stairs are not required in multilevel housing facilities where accessible cells or rooms, and all common use areas serving them including public use areas, are on an accessible route.

Signage

The requirements on building signage 4.1.3 [16] only apply to public use areas. The Board did not make any provisions for government facilities to provide tactile or audible directories, audible signs, or other "way-finding" devices at this time. The Board was asked to consider a revision in signage to include incised characters. The Board confirmed that incised characters are not generally as readable, and, therefore, do not provide an acceptable level of accessibility. No change in the technical provisions for tactile signs has been made.

The current compliance language in the Americans with Disabilities Act Accessibility Guidelines 4.1.2(7) and 4.1.3(16)(a) require that those permanent rooms or spaces that are designated by permanent signs comply with the Americans with Disabilities Act Accessibility Guidelines 4.30-4.30.6. The Department of Justice has reconsidered its policy regarding tactile signs, and whether to include room names in addition to room numbers, exit signs, and so forth. The Department of Justice plans to include names of rooms for Title 11 facilities.

The requirement for signage identifying the accessible cubicle has been deleted in the final rule because the signage is raised and in Braille and can pose a security risk. The signage could be removed from the wall and used as a weapon.

Telephones

The requirement that at least one public Tele-Type-writer (TTY and formerly TDD) be provided in at least one secured area in a detention or correctional facility has been retained. The Americans with Disabilities Act Accessibility Guideline 4.1.3(17)(d) provides that where a bank of phones in the interior of a building consists of three or more public pay phones (as typically might be found in a prison dorm), at least one of the phones in each such bank shall be equipped with a shelf and an outlet (for a TTY). This provision contains an exception for the secured areas of a jail or prison where outlets are prohibited for purposes of security or safety; the Americans with Disabilities Act Accessibility Guideline 4.31.9 (3) allows the use of portable devices. A requirement has been added to the Americans with Disabilities Act Accessibility Guideline 4.11.3.(17)(c) (iv) that at least one interior public TTY be provided in a public use area of a state or local government facility, when an interior public phone is provided in a public area of that facility (like the visitation center, lobby area, and so forth).

Having a volume control on inmate phones is a device that is highly vulnerable to vandalism and can increase the cost of the phone by as much as 66 percent. The compliance requirements would only apply to those common areas serving accessible cells. The requirements for sufficient floor space at telephones (handset cords to be twenty-nine inches) pose design challenges since telephones may be located near cell bars or walls and thus not provide adequate floor space. Security concerns may require that phone cords not exceed fifteen inches. An alternative to the requirements of the Americans with Disabilities Act Accessibility Guidelines is allowed as long as greater or equal access is provided, and may allow flexibility in providing access to inmate-use phones by equivalent means. One equivalent means is by providing hands-free phones.

Security Barriers

Security barriers and equivalent adjacent path provisions were not changed in the final regulations. It was pointed out that weapon-detection screening devices are specifically designed to react to metal, as may be found in braces and wheelchairs. Since the screening devices would be rendered neutral by the metal in these devices, the use of handheld metal detector "wands" and hand searches were supported as an alternative method of delivery. The Americans with Disabilities Act Accessibility Guidelines contains design and construction requirements for accessibility, but they do not cover equipment.

Lighting and Acoustics

The Board was requested to adopt and develop lighting and acoustic standards. These are important issues that affect the accessibility of all facilities. However, the Board did not adopt any guidelines in these areas and is seeking additional information. Professionals in the field in conjunction with the Advisory Council on Corrections and Acoustics prepared a response to the Board with the recommendation that they adopt the Acoustics Design Guide for Corrections (see section 7.9 for this). Jails and prisons are noisy places, and hearing instructions from staff is critical for life and safety. Acoustics and prevention of hearing loss should be part of the Americans with Disabilities Act Accessibility Guidelines for correctional facilities and hopefully will be considered with much greater interest in the future.

Holding Facilities

Courthouse holding facilities are like satellite facilities for the jail. The final regulations have added language to clarify that at least one cell must be accessible where central-holding cells are not separated by age or sex.

Accommodations for security staff who become temporarily disabled should be considered. Areas such as offices and even a secure control room can be made accessible and allow officers to work while recovering from an injury or illness.

Photo courtesy of Randall Atlas.

Grab Bar Design

There was considerable discussion on grab bar design, security concerns, and the potential for suicides in holding cells and correctional facilities. It was stated that grab bars in accessible cells do not pose any more of a suicide or security risk than other cell features, such as cell grilles, bed frames, and air-conditioning vents. Effective suicide prevention is not accomplished solely by rendering a cell protrusion-free. Effective suicide prevention is a function of screening at admission, appropriate classification, adequate staff training, vigilant staff supervision, and physical plant design. The Board felt that grab bars could be properly designed and installed in new construction without posing a security risk. There may be circumstances in an alteration to holding cells where grab bars cannot be securely attached to meet security requirements, due to structural conditions in an existing wall. In such cases, the installation of grab bars would not be required because it would be technically infeasible. However, the Americans with Disabilities Act Accessibility Guideline 4.1.6(l)(j) requires that the alternative provide accessibility and compliance to the maximum extent feasible. In a related issue, an exception for the thirty-six-inch length of the rear grab bar on high-security stainless steel combination toilet/sink units has been granted in new construction or alterations.

Visiting Area

The Board changed the visiting area requirements to include that at least 5 percent, but not less than one fixed cubicle, must be accessible on both sides. Accessibility includes knee clearance and communication devices. In that the secured side of visiting also functions as a common use area among inmates, an exception has been added which states that only those common use areas serving accessible cells or rooms are required to be accessible. Under this exception, noncontact visiting areas serving areas of the facility where no accessible cells or rooms are located are not required to have accessible cubicles on the inmate side.

Mobility Aids

Some correctional administrators noted that inmates with disabilities might present more of a threat to security since mobility aids may be used as weapons or to hide contraband. A study by the California Department of Corrections did not find that inmates with disabilities posed greater security risks. However, the Department has found that inmates with disabilities, as a whole, cannot be considered to be less of a security risk. Rather, the degree of an individual inmate's security risk must be determined by classification on a case-by-case basis taking into consideration all of the normal classification criteria. Inmates with disabilities, though they may appear to be less of a security risk, have assaulted staff and other inmates.

Location of Accessible Cells

A provision was added in the final rule that requires accessible cells to be located in all categories or types of cells. However, this requirement does not specify the amount or percentage that must be provided in each category or security level. Dispersion is not required to be proportionate to the total number of cells in each category or security level. This provision does not require an increase in the minimum 2 percent compliance requirement specified for a facility overall. For example, if a small jail is required under the 2 percent compliance to have one accessible cell, but has four holding classifications, only one accessible cell is required. The minimum number required for the facility overrides the requirement of dispersion among all classifications or types of cells. Likewise, it is now allowable to cluster accessible cells of the same classification level or category to facilitate sharing the same amenities, features, and delivery of service.

Inmate workstations and shelves should be designed with work surfaces at accessible heights. Countertops should be designed to permit use by an inmate in a standard chair or a wheelchair.

Photo courtesy of Randall Atlas.

Medical Care Facilities

Medical care facilities in detention and correctional facilities covered by the Americans with Disabilities Act Accessibility Guideline 12.1 are subject to the compliance requirements of the Americans with Disabilities Act Accessibility Guideline 6.1 (1) that requires that 10 percent of patient bedrooms be accessible in certain facilities. The Americans with Disabilities Act Accessibility Guideline 6.1 requires that in general purpose hospitals, psychiatric facilities, and detoxification facilities, at least 10 percent of the patient bedrooms shall be accessible. This provision does not require jails or prisons to provide medical care units, and thus if these facilities do not contain these types of medical care facilities addressed in the Americans with Disabilities Act Accessibility Guideline 6.1, they would not be subject to that provision.

Toilets

The Americans with Disabilities Act Accessibility Guideline 6.4 requires accessible patient toilet rooms and bathrooms and references sections 4.22 and 4.23. These requirements do not preclude placement of toilet or bathing fixtures within patient cells as long as the requirements for toilets, bathrooms, and maneuvering space are met.

Medical Isolation Cells

A provision has been added to clarify that medical isolation cells required to be accessible under the Americans with Disabilities Act Accessibility Guideline 12.4.2 shall not be counted as part of the minimum number of patient cells required to be accessible under the Americans with Disabilities Act Accessibility Guideline 6.1. Thus, if a medical care facility has both types of cells, at least one medical isolation cell must be accessible under the Americans with Disabilities Act Accessibility Guideline 12.4.2 in addition to the number of cells (10 percent) required to be accessible by the Americans with Disabilities Act Accessibility Guideline 6.1. Experts recommended insuring the accessibility of all medical isolation cells.

Alterations and New Construction

The Americans with Disabilities Act Accessibility Guidelines require a minimum level of accessibility in alterations and new construction. Some administrators may question the practicality of making cells accessible as part of an alteration at a facility not intended to house inmates with disabilities. However, the Americans with Disabilities Act recognizes alterations as opportunities for providing access, and takes advantage of the opportunity to the greatest potential, even if the altered element may not be made fully accessible to, or usable by, persons with disabilities.

Conclusion

While these requirements are the specific issues mentioned for correctional facilities, the implications for full compliance with the Americans with Disabilities Act Accessibility Guidelines is made very clear by the recent U.S. Supreme Court ruling that does not grant exceptions to correctional facilities to comply with the law. This suggests that all areas, especially common use areas, paths of travel, staff areas, public areas, and program areas must comply fully with the law and all of the Americans with Disabilities Act Accessibility Guidelines rules. Accessibility for staff, inmates, and the visiting public must be addressed in the design of all facilities.

The final rules require state and local government agencies that make any alterations to existing facilities to comply with the Americans with Disabilities Act "to the maximum extent feasible." If structural limitations or compliance would drastically alter the function of a program, service, or activity, or pose a life safety hazard, then the agency must do the best it can. If there are areas that do not comply fully with the Americans with Disabilities Act Accessibility Guidelines, then the agency should document which sections cannot be complied with and the reasons for the noncompliance. This documentation should be kept on file in the event of litigation.

It is becoming more apparent with each court proceeding that documentation is the key for agencies and owners in preventing and defending against litigation regarding Americans with Disabilities Act issues. Section 35.105 of the ADA Rules and Regulations states that all public entities are required to do a self-evaluation on the current policies that are in place and identify and correct any deficiencies that are not consistent with the ADA requirements. In addition, agencies that employ more than fifty employees are required to maintain the self-evaluation documents on file for three years. With the need for self-evaluation established by law, conducting the self-evaluation will be critical in defending the agency's position in a lawsuit. Should litigation occur, if the self-evaluation study and corrective measures have not been done, the burden of proof and potential liability to the agency are much greater.

Agencies must take the necessary steps toward full compliance with the law without exception. The time to start is now in the next project or the next capital budget.

Housing of Sexually Violent Persons

Florian Walicki and Steven Radomski
RNL
Denver, Colorado

An increasing number of sexually violent crimes in the United States is encouraging the public and state legislators to reinterpret criminal and civil statutes. Once persons are incarcerated under criminal law for a sexually violent crime and have served their determinate sentence, constitutionally they should be set free. However, many sexually violent persons are serving criminal sentences and then returning to public life only to repeat similar crimes again.

As a result, New Jersey legislators passed Megan's law, which was adopted and modified by a number of states. This law requires that families be notified when a previously convicted sexually violent person moves into a neighborhood. It also identifies individuals deemed to be a menace to society and assists in the effort to have these individuals reincarcerated.

In some cases, a jursidiction's reluctance to let otherwise eligible sexually violent parolees get out on parole stems from the fact that either they did not receive sufficient treatment and therapy or they did not attempt to participate in these programs. Potentially, they could be a menace to society again. Therefore, some states are reincarcerating sexually violent persons based on either revised criminal or new civil statutes that provide indeterminate sentences during which these individuals are provided treatment and therapy.

The states of Washington, Wisconsin, Minnesota, Oregon, and Kansas no longer believe that sexually violent persons who either are eligible for parole or have nearly served their sentences should return to public. As a result of the new statutes, a hybrid facility must be designed to permit incarceration and treatment of sexually violent persons. A number of other states have initiated revisions to their criminal or civil statutes that permit them to move sexually violent persons from a correctional facility to mental health treatment facilities. In most of these cases, sexually violent persons had been relocated to either an inadequate or antiquated mental facility campus and placed in an environment that did not prevent them from preying on other mentally disturbed patients.

In light of this, states now are building new facilities exclusively dedicated to the treatment of sexually violent persons. These new facilities can respond to civil statutes and patient rights; for example, the facility cannot be and should avoid looking like a pure penal institution. The new models must embody the treatment/therapy environment and provide a safe and secure environment for the patient, staff, and general public.

With the advent of these hybrid facilities, the architect is challenged to create a new type of facility that will be dedicated totally to sexually violent persons. The new facility initially may be a smaller facility (less than 300

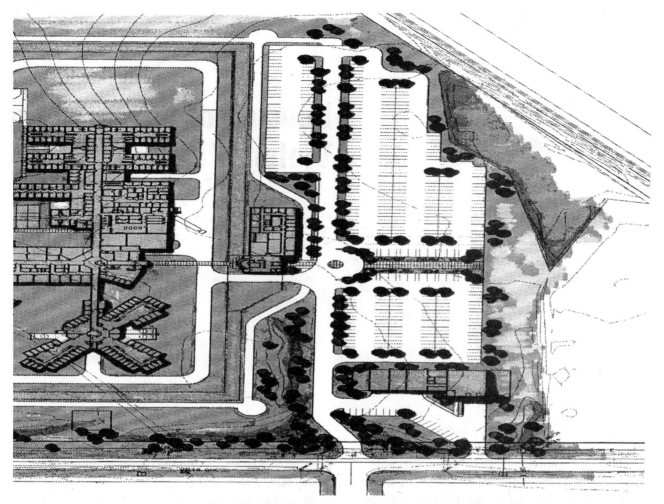

The State of Wisconsin is in the process of developing a new sexual predator institution. The Brewer Creek Secure Treatment Center will house 300 male residents initially with future expansion capability.

Courtesy of RNL Design, Denver, Colorado; Sommerville Architects/Engineers/Builders, Green Bay, Wisconsin; Carter Goble Associates, Columbia, South Carolina.

beds) with housing units for multibehavior classifications. Previously, correctional facility designs usually called for a moderate-sized complex of 100 to 500 beds (except for mega facilities holding 1,000 to 2,000 inmates) and a monoclassification status, either minimum, medium, or maximum security.

Generally, correctional facilities do not mix classifications of residents. However, new hybrid facilities will create a mixture of all behavioral classifications. The new classifications, compared to the former criminal justice facilities classifications are as follows: Maximum security is referred to as low responsibility/high management. Medium security is called medium responsibility/medium management. Minimum security is called high responsibility/low management. These hybrid facilities also require special needs units for residents who

are affected by mental illness and geriatric medical needs due to the aging population that is anticipated in these types of correctional facilities.

Admissions and evaluations of new arrivals may be sporadic in numbers. However, they can be accommodated within an admissions/evaluation unit, which can be incorporated either in the low responsibility unit or the medium responsibility unit, dependent on intake numbers, staffing, and operations of medical personnel. Accommodations for skilled care and acute care units are another function of the design challenge.

Locations of these facilities may present another challenge since they need to be near neighborhood communities that provide accessibility to trained psychological and medical staff for these specific treatment/therapy programs. This challenge to facility design requires the architect to avoid a correctional facility image. To be successful, it is necessary to build a facility that can maintain building and perimeter security and provide the necessary functional elements that will allow for delivery of the rehabilitation treatment programs of a secure treatment center.

With only limited knowledge about a cure for this disorder, an architect's goal is to create a physical environment to try to encourage and foster sexually violent persons to change their cognitive behavioral patterns. By working with behavioral scientists in the field of psychopathy and sexual deviant behavior, architects have begun to explore how to design treatment and housing units in a facility for sexually violent persons.

The facility needs to avoid visual blind spots. The more the sexually violent persons function in the view of other residents and staff, the more the facility environment can draw them out to start recognizing their problems. The design plays into the treatment therapy by helping to take away a sexually violent person's ability to go off into obscure and nonobservable physical spaces. Instead, they are made more aware of their physical interaction with others, and the mental and physiological cycles they go through. They are taught how to recognize when they are starting to fantasize and how to prevent it from reaching uncontrollable stages. Eventually, patients/residents hopefully can turn their thoughts around and redirect them toward recognition and admission of their problems. This is the only result that many professionals contemplate is achievable at this time.

Recognizing the atypical needs for this hybrid facility, designers have found it beneficial to engage the services of behavioral scientists who are well versed in the fields of sexually deviant and psychopathic behavior and treatment. The general perception due to public attitude is that many communities and politicians now perceive that treatment therapy for sexually violent persons is a long-term program and that no recognized cures exist in the psychiatric medical field at this time. Some professionals feel the release rate from these facilities may be as low as 4 to 6 percent based on the willingness and cooperation of the individual residents to participate in programs and the implementation of treatment modules that have the potential to be supported by aftercare programs when and if an individual eventually is released into the community.

The overall facility concept employs a dual circulation pattern whereby specific housing units (low and medium responsibility) are restricted to control and escorted circulation and access to programs versus the high responsibility/lower management units, which employ a "free walk" concept and mall access to programs and treatment facilities. From the initial programming stages into the conceptual design, it was obvious that an increased percentage of support and program space in relation to the housing units should be provided.

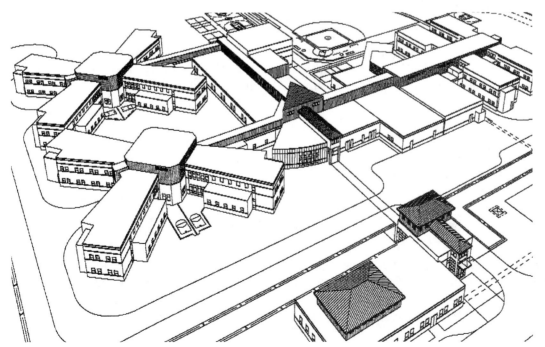

Locating these facilities offers a unique challenge with the need to be near a community for access to services while trying to avoid a correctional institution's appearance. Brewer Creek Secure Treatment Center, Wisconsin.

Courtesy of RNL Design, Denver, Colorado; Sommerville Architects/ Engineers/Builders, Green Bay, Wisconsin; Carter Goble Associates, Columbia, South Carolina.

Specifics of Housing Unit Design

The following requirement for "on-unit" functions are related to treatment, therapy, and conference rooms.

- Restricted circulation is used in high management and medium management housing units where restricted/escorted circulation is employed; the low management units use the "free walk" concept.

- Medical and psychological offices, treatment rooms, and conference rooms are provided on the unit.

- Each housing unit contains a transition unit to the next lower category of management level with the final category being a transition to the community.

- Decentralized dining services occur on all housing wings with the exception of seclusion rooms where food is served to the residents in their room.

- In certain cases, skilled care and acute care inmates require barrier free and oversized rooms as well as oxygen at the bedside. Americans with Disabilities Act compliance is provided in all skilled care and acute care areas, which also are designed specifically with oversized rooms.

- Seclusion rooms are integrated into high management housing units to avoid unnecessary staffing increases.

- Exterior windows on patient rooms are large; however, they are maintained as maximum-security level status where views are controlled to avoid public contact.

Surfaces in Housing and Maximum Units with Restricted Circulation

Hard physical surfaces should be used. Modifying colors promote a more normative psychological environment, conducive to treatment and therapy. Application of sound-absorption materials on walls, floors, and ceilings promote a more normative environment. Avoid noisy sliding security doors, and consider the use of pneumatics or swinging door applications. Provide larger dayrooms for integration of programs, treatment, and passive recreation spaces on the unit. Provide access to adjacent segregated recreation areas and access to exterior large muscle exercise areas as part of the free walk concepts.

The Brewer Creek Secure Treatment Center was designed with the mezzanine configurations to help to reduce the size of dayrooms, plumbing chases, HVAC components, foundation systems, the building envelope, and roofing.

Facility Overview

The Brewer Creek Secure Treatment Center is anticipated to begin operations in January 2001. It will be operated by the Division of Care and Treatment Facilities, Department of Health and Family Services. The Brewer Creek Secure Treatment Center facility will be responsible for the administration and delivery of all phases of the sexually violent person program, including evaluation and reports to the court regarding commitment and progress in treatment, inpatient treatment program and services, case management, oversight of contract and supervised release, community supervision, and treatment services. Periodic examinations will be provided, as required by statute for patients committed to inpatient care in the facility. The facility initially is designed to house 300 male residents and the infrastructure is designed for future expansion, if necessary.

The site has been configured to avoid adverse impacts with adjacent wetlands and specifically is designed to provide landscape buffering from the local community and the major access road along the southern and eastern borders of the facility.

Security concepts include a total building secure envelope serving as the primary security perimeter for low, medium, and high responsibility housing units and treatment and program spaces in the main building complex. An adjacent administration/housing building is integrated with the security perimeter system providing vehicle and pedestrian access through sallyports from controlled points adjacent to a service delivery area. The security perimeter system employs many technologies, including a "stun" electric fence with a warning drift fence and two rows of twelve-foot fencing with nonclimb fabric and razor wire at the top. There is also a mobile patrol road around the entire facility.

Security zones within the building are configured and arranged to control horizontal movement through all major functions of the building. Security zoning also integrates with compartmentalization for fire and life safety zoning.

Overview of Facility Functions

Living units. They are large single-custody level single-cell housing units and include: low responsibility unit/high management (maximum security), medium responsibility unit/medium management (medium security), high responsibility unit/low management (minimum security). The special needs unit is a twenty-bed

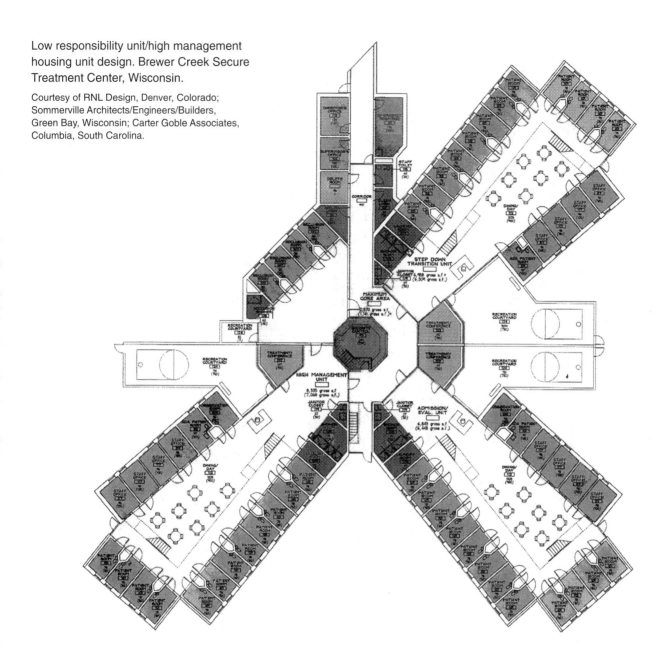

Low responsibility unit/high management housing unit design. Brewer Creek Secure Treatment Center, Wisconsin.

Courtesy of RNL Design, Denver, Colorado; Sommerville Architects/Engineers/Builders, Green Bay, Wisconsin; Carter Goble Associates, Columbia, South Carolina.

skilled care unit with five seclusion isolation beds directly adjacent to the medical infirmary triage area.

Dining. This is decentralized for the living units. Food service is provided by contracted cook/chill operation and rethermalized at the facility.

Recreation. The outdoor segregated units are adjacent to all living units, with high responsibility patients having access to larger outdoor recreation. The facility includes an enclosed gymnasium.

Intake unit. This is part of the low responsibility unit/ high management and has limited scheduled admittance, and also requires escorted inmate movement. Medical

services and evaluation services are provided by the medical staff to the unit. Medical care is centralized in the diagnostic treatment and infirmary unit with triage and services adjacent to acute care and high responsibility unit/low management housing unit.

Programs. There is extensive programming that includes psycho-physiological assessment. Other programs include the following:

— A treatment program for sexually violent persons
— Activity therapy, including therapeutic crafts, therapeutic recreation, physical fitness and health, leisure activities, and open recreation

— Education including adult basic education, general equivalency diploma preparation, special education, and enrichment

— Health and medical services

— Prerelease programs, which cover work skills and living skills

— Religious services

— Staff intern training and development

Visitation. This will occur in a centralized location at the main program treatment building to encourage inmate movement and to control activities. There is only controlled access by visitors to the facility.

Vehicle sallyport. The courtyard is separated from the service yard. The service yard is enclosed by the full perimeter security fencing system that is connected to the guard house building with vehicle and pedestrian sallyport access points.

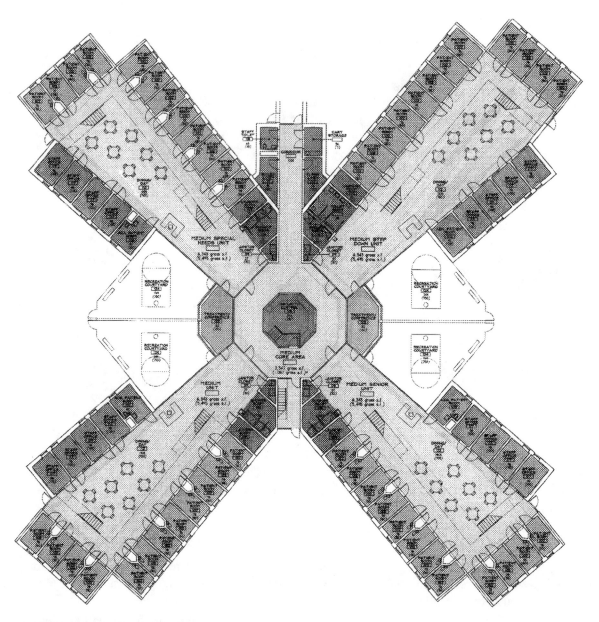

Medium responsibility unit/medium management housing unit design. Brewer Creek Secure Treatment Center, Wisconsin.

Courtesy of RNL Design, Denver, Colorado; Sommerville Architects/Engineers/Builders, Green Bay, Wisconsin; Carter Goble Associates, Columbia, South Carolina.

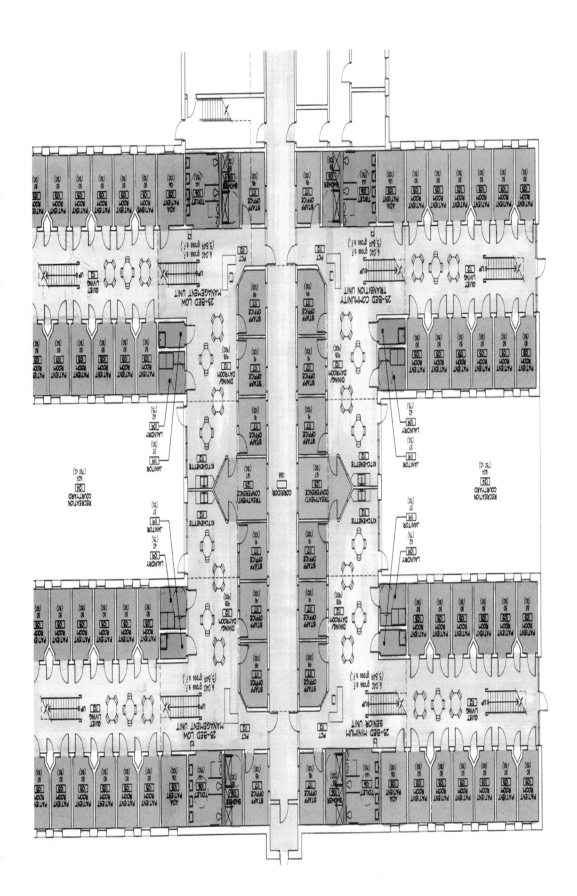

Low responsibility unit/low management housing unit. Brewer Creek Secure Treatment Center, Wisconsin.

Courtesy of RNL Design, Denver, Colorado; Sommerville Architects/Engineers/Builders, Green Bay, Wisconsin; Carter Goble Associates, Columbia, South Carolina.

Supermax Facilities

Jeff Buck, DMJM
New York, New York

Stan Young, Warden, Wallens Ridge State Prison
Big Stone Gap, Virginia

Supermax facilities are often physically remote from other institutions but form an integral part of a growing number of correctional departments' classification and control systems. Wallens Ridge State Prison, Big Stone Gap, Virginia, a super maximum security facility.

Architect: Daniel, Mann, Johnson & Mendenhall. Photo courtesy of Gilbane Building Company, Providence, Rhode Island. Photographer: Tim Cox.

Movement control is absolutely a necessity in a supermax facility. Staff observation and electronic surveillance provide this control. Wallens Ridge State Prison, Big Stone Gap, Virginia, a super maximum security facility.

Architect: Daniel, Mann, Johnson & Mendenhall (DMJM). Photo courtesy of Gilbane Building Company, Providence, Rhode Island, construction manager. Photographer: Tim Cox.

Over the last several years, one of the areas of increased cachet in corrections has been the development of "supermax" facilities as an extension of security classification beyond maximum-security facilities. In dealing with this facility type, the primary questions to address are the characteristics of the intended inmate population and the role the facility plays in the system as a whole. For some professionals, there is an issue as to whether this facility classification is necessary. They ask, what is so special that it cannot be accomplished in a well-designed maximum-security facility?

The architectural adage of "form follows function" is particularly true in the design and construction of supermax facilities. Since the bricks and mortar of construction for this building type are expensive, the real burden is on the using agency to be clear in defining what the purpose of the supermax facility is, how it fits in the over-all system of facilities, and how it should operate, including drafting policy and procedure manuals and staffing plans. Collecting the "worst of the worst inmates" together in one location has definite impacts on facility planning and design.

Population Characteristics

There are two general approaches to the "supermax" designation. One is as a central punitive segregation unit that provides additional systemwide capacity for this purpose. The other is as a high-security inmate classifica-

tion determination to keep high-risk inmates out of the rest of the system. A related approach is collecting the most difficult inmates to handle in one location to minimize transportation around the system or to provide proximity to the courts or other specialized service needs.

A common problem is that segregation units within existing systems of general confinement facilities have been filled to overflowing. In the situation where the supermax population is intended for inmates that have had due process on an offense and have received a punitive segregation sentence of specific duration, the character of the supermax facility is essentially one of a large segregation unit. There has been substantial experience in designing special housing units and a set of specific American Correctional Association standards that apply. The design challenge here is getting a physical design configuration that meets constitutional conditions and is manageable in terms of the total population.

The alternative population for supermax consideration is those individuals who either have demonstrated or potentially could exhibit behavior problems as identified through an objective classification system that identifies high-risk inmates for placement in this setting. This offers the opportunity to divert such individuals from the rest of the system of correctional facilities for a special security setting. In this case, the American Correctional Association standards for general confinement would apply, and the design challenge is getting a physical configuration that minimizes inmate movement.

In examining the question of what differentiates a supermax facility, the following elements can be used as general planning guidelines.

Service Delivery

For both types of inmate populations, as many services as possible need to be delivered to the housing units. Segregation inmates are locked in twenty-three hours a day, with one hour a day out for outdoor/recreation. For supermax classified inmates, movement within the facility needs to be minimized as much as possible.

Housing unit design needs to provide small counseling/interview rooms on each unit as well as direct access to outdoor recreation yards. Medical examination/treatment and food service pantries should be provided for each housing cluster of approximately 250 cells, if not within each housing unit. For general confinement inmates (versus segregation), housing unit clusters also should provide multipurpose small group meeting, academic, and similar activity spaces. In contrast to regular general confinement facilities, supermax facilities tend to reflect the continuing evolution in current jail design where (with the exception of acute medical care, court appearance, or release) there is virtually no movement off the housing units. While maximum security general confinement inmates typically have central dining, supermax facilities provide dining in the cell or on the housing unit.

As part of the planning process, a service delivery matrix should be developed that lists all of the required services for inmates (for example, sleeping, personal hygiene, showers, dining, laundry, attorney visits, and the like), then makes a conscious determination for each one as to whether it is to be provided at the individual cell, housing unit, housing cluster, or central location. As an example, the decision to provide shower capability in each cell instead of a central shower facility in the housing

unit will have an impact on the design of cells (and project costs). The point is that each element must be thought out in terms of how the facility should operate and the "level" to which services are to be delivered. From the service delivery matrix for each housing unit, a determination then follows as to where the space is to handle each required element in the project and how the space should be designed to accommodate them. For example, the decision to provide dining in the cell requires detailing the cell door for a food pass.

Absolute Control of Movement

When movement does occur within a supermax facility, the design must permit absolute control of that movement. Typically, movement will be limited to one inmate at a time, in restraints, escorted by one or two officers, depending on the inmate involved. All movement should

This is the maximum circulation spine of a two-level corridor system seen from the first level and looking up through the grillage floor of the upper level. Inmates are escorted on the first level and armed staff on the upper level oversee that movement. Closed Maximum Security Unit, Tamms, Illinois Department of Corrections.

Photo courtesy of LZT Associates, Inc., Peoria, Illinois, Architects, Planners, Engineers. Photographer: Debbie Franke.

be through secure corridors or channels, monitored and videotaped, and proceed through a series of checkpoints controlled from secure control stations. Preferably, all movement should be visually monitored from secure positions. Control gates, throughout the facility, provide the ability to contain problems that may occur.

In the supermax facility for the Illinois Department of Corrections, the design provided an "officer walk" over the regular corridor constructed of secure welded wire mesh, which permits an officer to follow escorted inmate movement from overhead and to provide a rapid response if a problem occurs.

Limiting the Aggregate Number of Inmates in One Location

In a maximum-security general confinement facility, there is a focus on limiting the aggregate number of inmates who can congregate in any setting, such as no more than fifty inmates at a given time. This would be applicable to housing units, dining halls, escorted movement, and the like. What is different in a supermax is limiting the aggregate number of inmates in a particular housing module. Since there is little or no movement off the housing unit for services, the primary concern is the total number of inmates contained in a single area in case there is a problem. While segregation-type inmates are typically locked in with the exception of an hour a day for outdoor recreation, a potential noncooperative attitude may prevail in the housing unit, in general, when a problem arises.

The real design determinate is the total number of cells that an officer in a housing control room can supervise visually. Typically, this is limited to approximately 125 cells with sightlines to the furthest point of 130 feet or less. This may vary, but the limiting factor is how much activity a single officer can manage; sightlines in excess of 130 feet tend to make it very difficult to recognize specific individuals at that distance. The number of cells in a housing unit should be limited to fifty or less; then, the geometry needs to be worked out for the total number of cells supervised by a single housing control room. This design direction is in contrast to regular general confinement facilities, where due to interest in staffing efficiency in combined direct/indirect supervision models, the trend has been toward getting as many cells as possible around a housing control room.

In the case of the segregation-type supermax, where inmates are basically locked in, there is more flexibility of the housing unit configuration (through the use of closed-circuit television cameras) than is the case for general confinement supermax inmates. Clarity of sightlines from secure control positions is paramount. In some systems, weapons are located in control rooms of high security facilities to put inmates "under the gun." When sightlines become potential shooting lines, they need to be absolutely clear and unobscured. This requirement will dictate the housing unit design configuration and the location of the control rooms in a "superior" noninmate accessible location.

Containment with Reasonable Certainty

For a supermax facility, this element seems self-evident. If you are dealing with the most problematic inmates in the system, there needs to be a real focus on providing appropriate security barriers and devices within the facility. The real impact on design is the concept that everything will be tested by the inmates. The approach then is to use tried and true systems and equipment and

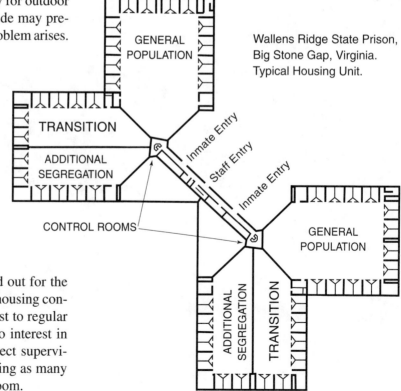

Wallens Ridge State Prison, Big Stone Gap, Virginia. Typical Housing Unit.

to keep the plan as simple as possible. Planning needs to proceed on the basis that staff is the most effective (and expensive) security element and that the entire security, communications, and control system has to be designed to make this resource as effective as possible in carrying out normal and emergency operations. To accomplish this, there needs to be a focused effort on providing a logical and consistent set of barriers to support the intended operation, and everything needs to be designed down to the last detail for durability and serviceability.

Focus on Staff Safety

If there is a setting to be particularly focused on staff safety, a supermax facility is the one to do so. The design and operation of the facility should be developed so that no staff member is in contact with inmates without visual supervision from another staff member. Visual supervision within housing units and circulation has been noted; this planning element focuses concern down to all other activities within the facility. Where an inmate may have direct contact with staff, provision must be made for visual supervision by another staff member. For example, an interview room off the housing unit needs to have a vision panel into that space, which permits visual supervision from outside the space either by an officer on the floor or in the control room. The design guide to bear in mind is "never out of sight of someone else."

Emergency Response Capability

While emergency response capability is germane to design for all secure facility settings, it is particularly important in a supermax, because of the likelihood that it will be needed at some point in time. Provision needs to be made in each housing unit for multiple points of entry, with access controlled from the housing control room. Similarly, each functional component of the facility needs to be designed with the operational requirement of multiple points of entry so that problems may be addressed from various points of access. Provisions need to be made centrally for the equipment and marshaling of emergency response forces, as well as a facility configuration that facilitates their unobserved movement to the scene.

Limitation on Security Penetrations

Due to the nature of the inmate population, this element comes into play to limit the potential introduction of contraband into the facility. The security perimeter needs to be defined carefully and to have as few penetrations as possible. Logically, there should only be three openings: one for the staff/public entry, a second for inmate entry, and a third for reception of goods and materials. Each point of penetration should be remote from the others and needs to have a secure control capability with appropriate screening capacity and sallyports. Ideally, there should be an outside warehouse for vendor delivery and storage, which then permits institutional vehicle traffic only through and within the security perimeter of the facility.

The concept of the supermax facility is likely to be adopted in more systems and locations. It remains to be seen how effective these facilities will be in addressing their mission within correctional systems. The development of additional facilities will clarify their basic intent and operation as time goes by. One thing is clear. The design of a supermax institution requires a clear understanding of the facility's mission, how staff will perform every task, and the specific inmate population of the facility. In addition, the designers must pay special attention to the security and construction of the buildings and use time-proven solutions.

Wallens Ridge State Prison

A recent project to construct a new supermax facility for the State of Virginia, the Wallens Ridge State Prison, has just been completed and is now operational. The following is a description of that facility and the design concepts used in it.

The design of the super maximum-security prison is based on issues of custody and control. Rehabilitative efforts are not of the highest priority, as the inmates assigned to this type prison have demonstrated through their prior behavior that rehabilitative efforts are futile. The use of the "supermax" places the most disruptive inmates in one institution, thereby relieving less secure facilities of these "problems," which enhances their rehabilitation efforts. This design provides an environment where highly aggressive inmates can be controlled with minimal danger to prison staff. The prison design relies on a complex system of cameras, electronic systems, small inmate groups, and strict controlled movement.

The Wallens Ridge State Prison is "home" to 1,200 inmates. The prison consists of four housing units, a gatehouse, a program support building, an administrative/support building, a warehouse, a hazmat building, towers, and a kennel. The program support building divides the housing units. This separation of the housing units better enables staff to control movement with smaller inmate groups. Each side has its own dining hall and recreation yard. A central kitchen supports both dining halls, and the gym is shared by all housing units.

Inmate housing units are divided into six pods. Each housing unit contains two forty-four-cell pods, which are double bunked; and two twenty-two-cell pods, which are double bunked; and two twenty-two-cell pods for administrative segregation, where there are single bunks. A dayroom, showers, and an educational area are provided in all pods except in administrative segregation, where there is no education area. Each administrative segregation pod has a secure recreation area, which allows "open air" recreation.

Each housing unit has two control rooms, which overlook inmate areas. Each control room supervises three pods, the administration segregation recreation area, and the outside recreation yard for the general population. These areas control all aspects of the inmate living areas, such as the cell doors, lights, electricity, telephones, and even the water can be cut off from a control room. The control rooms have the ability to communicate with the inmates and monitor individual cells by "monitoring communication" in the cells.

The administrative/support building houses the institution's administrative and support offices. There are also areas for the library, the law library, staff dining, a security suite, as well as master control. The visiting room consists of ten noncontact visiting stalls and an area for contact visits and is located in the front section of the administrative/support building. Also, in this building are areas for treatment, records, a medical suite, and a training suite for institutional staff.

The medical unit provides both an inpatient and outpatient area. The inpatient area is equipped with seven general infirmary cells, two mental health cells, and two negative pressure cells for airborne illnesses. This area also provides a "secure shower" area where inmates can be secured during their shower period. The outpatient area consists of examination rooms, radiology, pharmacy, dental suite, medical records, and appropriate office space.

The program support building includes the education department and industry area along with a laundry, kitchen, and gym. All academic classes are held through a closed-circuit television system. This building houses two inmate dining halls, which are monitored by two control rooms/gun posts. These control rooms/gun posts also monitor inmate movement and inmates on the recreation yard. Also, in the program/support building is the inmate reception area. Transportation vehicles enter

In this typical cell at Wallens Ridge State Prison, furnishings and finishes are spartan and extremely durable and attack resistant as required in a super maximum-security facility.

Architect: Daniel, Mann, Johnson & Mendenhall. Photo courtesy of Gilbane Building Company, Providence, Rhode Island, construction manager. Photographer: Tim Cox.

through the rear sallyport and inmates are delivered to the reception cells where they are processed.

Two perimeter towers monitor a perimeter, which is surrounded by an outer fence alarmed by a fence-mounted electronic detection system and enhanced with razor wire. The inner fence is a "taut wire" system, which is also alarmed. Both fence systems are monitored by the towers and the perimeter patrol vehicle that uses a mobile map, and an alarm system in the master control. The mobile map is a display of the institution's perimeter security system that indicates to the officer where an alarm on the perimeter is occurring.

The gatehouse provides an area for the search and processing of staff and visitors. This building also houses the institution's armory and key room. The warehouse accepts all deliveries and houses building and grounds shops and the institutional commissary. The kennel contains space for dogs that can be used to search for drugs and assist in inmate control and cell extraction.

Double perimeter fences with security electronic detection on both fences provide a high level of security around Wallens Ridge State Prison, Big Stone Gap, Virginia.

Architect: Daniel, Mann, Johnson & Mendenhall. Photo courtesy of Gilbane Building Company, Providence, Rhode Island, construction manager. Photographer: Tim Cox.

Operation

The Commonwealth of Virginia currently has two "supermax" prisons. The Virginia Department of Corrections uses its supermax prisons for control of its most violent/aggressive inmates. Virginia employs a six-level inmate classification system. This allows the least violent and better behaved inmates to take advantage of more work and treatment programs.

The operation of the Virginia supermax prisons uses less-than-lethal devices, which provide maximum control of inmates, and maximum protection of staff.

All areas where inmates gather (such as dayrooms, dining halls, recreation yard, and gym) are supervised by armed correctional officers in control rooms and at gun posts. These officers are armed with weapons that fire rubber projectiles, which are designed to be less than lethal. Virginia also uses electronic devices such as the Ultron II, Taser, Shield and React Belt. These devices deliver a charge of 50,000 volts, which momentarily

stuns inmates until they can be controlled. Chemical agents such as OC (pepper spray) and CS gas can be used, if needed. The use of these control devices has resulted in a dramatic drop in inmate assaults on staff as well as inmate-on-inmate assaults.

Controlled movement of inmates provides a means of keeping all activities limited to a maximum of eighty-eight inmates. Even though the population is 1,200, there are never more than 88 inmates in the recreation yard, gym, dining hall, and so forth. This method of control and design has proven to be a most effective tool in the management of aggressive inmates.

Housing units are divided by pod based on an inmate's behavior. By abiding by institutional rules, an inmate may progress to a General Population pod (G.P.) and after twenty-four months of positive behavior, he will be considered for a transfer to a less secure facility. However, should an inmate choose to demonstrate negative behavior, he will be placed in administrative segregation until he has demonstrated the ability to control himself. The general rule is that the better an inmate behaves, the more privileges he earns.

Treatment opportunities are provided to inmates willing to participate in an appropriate manner. Academic classes and religious services are provided through a closed-circuit television system, which can be accessed in all housing units. Vocational classes of building sanitation and painting will be available in the program/support building to inmates maintaining appropriate behavior. Individual treatment needs will be met by the use of institutional counselors, psychologists, and a psychiatrist. Recreation will be provided to all inmates; however, the availability of the gym to inmates will be dependent on the individual's behavior.

Inmates are afforded the opportunity of five hours of "open air" recreation per week. The recreation yard for general population inmates is supervised, not only by security staff on the yard, but also by an armed gun post in the program/support building. This gun post can be supported by armed correctional officers posted in housing unit control rooms should the need arise.

Conclusion

Even though it is sad that our society has developed a need for this type of facility, we must not lose sight of our mission and must never forget the types of individuals who are housed at supermax prisons. This design and operation provide a prison system with a tool to "control the uncontrollable." The use of the less-than-lethal devices enables prison staff to ensure the safety of themselves, and inmates in their care. It also provides an outlet to less secure facilities to ensure an environment conducive to serious rehabilitation efforts for the more cooperative inmate. The supermax prison design can provide a safe and secure environment for both staff and inmates.

Female Housing

Larry J. Smith, AIA*
Durrant Architects
Phoenix, Arizona

There are differences between male and female facilities, services, and programs. The issues addressed here are those specifically in the areas that would be different from a typical male living unit within the various inmate classifications. While this topic will attempt to differentiate design aspects, note that in today's political society some may defend providing essentially the same facilities for females as males. For further perspectives see *Excellent Effect: The Edna Mahan Story*, by Mary Q. Hawkes, pp. 176-178 and Miller, 1998.

General

The female inmate population in the 1980s and 1990s has increased significantly across the country. This could be attributed to the justice system's get-tough response with today's criminals. In past years, females were given more leniency in arrest and convictions than males. This country currently is dealing with mandatory sentencing for female criminals who now are coming into the system but who may have been offending for years, with light or no sentences. Therefore, when a female adult is sentenced into the system, she is an individual who most likely has been committing crimes relating to drugs, theft, or forgery for many years.

Staffing

Correctional officers in female facilities may find that female inmates react differently to staff than inmates in male facilities (Albrecht, 1995). Female inmates respond differently than males to the stress experienced due to incarceration and the separation from their children. Consequently, male and female correctional officers must receive training in how to understand and work effectively with female inmates (Cranford and Williams, 1998).

Male staff are subject to allegations of sexual misconduct (Amnesty International, 1999). While female inmates may not be physically abusive toward staff, they may use psychological dependency and excessive acting-out behavior to cope with their incarceration. So, all staff must receive training in how to supervise in the unique setting of a women's prison.

Over prolonged periods of time, these manipulations can cause high levels of frustration in staff and inmates. In these cases, regular rotation of staff is helpful. Female inmates are less physically abusive to staff or other inmates but may be abusive to themselves and suicidal.

---

* With the assistance of M. Tamara Holden, consultant, Portland, Oregon.

In female facilities, the importance of privacy in showers and toilet areas cannot be overstressed. Dividing walls between showers and either punched plate or security screening can be used to give privacy in the entry doors while providing staff with reasonable observation. Virginia Peninsula Regional Jail, Williamsburg, Virginia.

Courtesy of Gilbane Building Company, Providence, Rhode Island.

Environment

The designing of living units for female inmates is a unique opportunity to develop a normalized environment. This has been accomplished in the past for male facilities, but some view this as wasted cost, especially when these "normalized facilities" are destroyed by male inmates. However, in female facilities, whether renovations of old female reformatories or newly constructed, conditions of the physical plants are usually good. This is due to less physical abuse to their environment by female inmates than their male counterparts.

Normalized design features for a female facility can be china toilets, porcelain lavatories, carpeting, wood furniture, curtains, and less restricted access to televisions, recreation equipment, books, and other privileges. However, when designing these features, caution needs to be taken for security by using solid construction and parts not easily removed to make weapons.

In this normalized environment, security needs to be maintained no differently than in a male facility. Sight lines into all areas, control of perimeter access points, and lock-down areas are mandatory. The major security challenge inherent in female facilities is reducing the potential of inmate allegations of sexual contact from staff. This includes not allowing staff easy views into shower areas and toilet areas including cells. This privacy issue may be in direct conflict with security issues.

Typically, in male facilities, security observation prevails over privacy, even where there are female officers. In female living areas, a balance of privacy and security needs to be obtained. The designer must develop creative ways to accommodate this balance and prove its solution to clients in the form of mock-ups and three-dimensional sight line models.

In a male facility, showers could be in open view from an officer's station, and in some cases, from general circulation areas. A solution for females is shower privacy screens that allow vision from the knee down and shoulders up. Other screens can use opaque or screened materials to view silhouettes without detail but allow staff to view what the inmates may be doing.

While cells in male facilities could have toilets without screens and in direct view from outside cell doors, privacy in female facilities for toilets in cells can be obtained with similar screening and orientation of fixtures and chases to develop privacy from viewers outside the door. In one facility, a line was painted on the floor five feet from the front of the door of the cell. In this solution, the facility's policy is for no officer, male or female, to view into the cell any closer than this line unless there is just cause. Other options such as shutter doors, blinds, and so forth do not promote security measures in that inmates can control vision, and soon these will be removed or abused.

Dayrooms should be divided into smaller spaces in female institutions to permit the women to maintain their social groups while still under supervision of staff.

Photo courtesy of John Hultberg, HDR, Dallas, Texas.

Sleeping Areas

Sleeping areas take on different configurations depending on classifications and management desired. Single cells are at a premium cost and should be used for segregation and other isolation classifications. The majority of cells will be double bunked.

In a double-bunked cell, females need to have some degree of privacy from one another at the toilet area; this is unlike a male cell, where in some cases the toilet and lavatory are a foot or so from a bed. The toilets in a female general population cell can be of a nondetention type. A china toilet and porcelain lavatory can be used in place of a security combination stainless steel fixture. This will provide normalized facilities at less cost. In facilities where china fixtures are used, the initial cost saving outweighs the minor breakage replacement cost. The separate toilet and lavatory more appropriately meets Americans with Disabilities Act (ADA) requirements.

It is most appropriate to develop multiple-occupant rooms for general population housing, keeping in mind that an adequate number of single and double occupant cells are needed for other classifications. This small groupings in rooms allows females to develop social groups, have privacy, and some self-discipline from their immediate peers. In many cases, general population groups of three or more to a cell work better than two in a cell. That is, three females may interact without becoming isolated by one cell inmate.

In large female facilities, entire general populations have been housed in six-person multiple-occupant rooms. The benefits to this type of housing is locating toilets, lavatories, and showers in the cell to increase security and privacy without increasing construction cost significantly. A shower in a cell will increase security in that fewer movements of inmates are needed outside of the cell. A bathtub should be available for use by female inmates requiring special hygiene options. Also, it is a good management tool for staff and an opportunity to relax for inmates.

Where dormitories are necessary, a walled separation of sleeping from living areas into small clusters should be used. Groups should be no larger than thirty-two in a

Multiple occupant sleeping rooms provide female inmates with the ability to develop social groups, have privacy, and practice self-discipline.

Photograph courtesy of John Hultberg, HDR, Dallas, Texas.

secured dormitory area. The square footage required for these spaces should follow the American Correctional Association standards for the number of beds in a room or cell.

As in all facilities, a number of inmates—male or female—are disruptive and violent. Therefore, a segregation area is needed. The segregation unit should be single cells of hard design and construction—no different than in a male facility.

Toilet and Shower Areas

Toilets and showers, as discussed earlier, present a major privacy issue. The arrangement of toilets in a dormitory unit needs to provide the balance of privacy and security and also privacy from each stall. Showers should be individual stalls in all types of housing classifications and not gang-type showers.

Individual stalls can be grouped together if desired, but the privacy-security balance needs to be met. As in all inmate showers, special attention needs to be given to designing showers to meet ADA, security, privacy, and basic design for proper wet areas and drying areas with good drainage.

The size of shower stalls and toilet/lavatory areas are dictated by ADA accessibility and the quantity is dictated by American Correctional Association standards and building codes. However, as in any type of facility, the quantity of fixtures should be maximized to provide more time for use by female inmates than in a male facility. Experts recommend that the number of showers and toilets exceed American Correctional Association standards, one for every eight beds.

Dayrooms

Dayrooms should be designed to allow these smaller groups to interact and socialize. At the same time, the configuration needs to be such that security can supervise and view these spaces from one vantage point (the officer's station). Other rooms, such as reading rooms and television rooms, need to be considered. These separate spaces can be multipurpose and also double as rooms for counseling and educational programs. There should be no more than thirty-two inmates sharing a dayroom. The size of dayrooms and activity spaces should follow guidelines of American Correctional Association standards.

Food Service

With the exception of segregation and lockdown, most female inmates should dine in a group. Besides the psychological effect of a normalized eating environment, there can be incentive management obtained with some level of food preparation at the housing unit, whether it is only beverage preparation or a complete kitchenette. Considerations need to be made for prenatal care diets and frequency of meals for other special populations.

Laundry Facilities

A facility of any size will have a central laundry, which is best for linens and general clothing. In the female housing unit, there needs to be at least a washer and dryer the inmates themselves can use for personal clothing. In some female facilities, all laundry except linens are done by the inmates at their housing unit; this becomes a personal hygiene issue as well as a management tool and is highly desirable.

These housing unit laundries can be as simple as a washer and dryer in a corner of the dayroom to a small room with washer, dryer, folding, and ironing areas. The laundry can be done by each inmate for her own personal laundry, or internal assignments as a work detail for the entire housing unit's laundry, or by pods within the unit.

Size of Facilities

The number of beds in a facility is important, and this is especially so in female facilities. Housing of single cells or multiple-occupant cells should be broken down into groups of sixteen to thirty-two beds for inmates and no more than twenty-four beds for juveniles sharing common spaces. These groups or pods can be grouped into a housing unit managed by a unit manager of 96 to 128 beds for inmates.

A juvenile housing unit should not exceed twenty-four beds; however, some creative designs use two separate twenty-four bed units joined to reduce construction cost and security-response time. The housing unit may share satellite kitchen-serving facilities, local laundries, and recreation areas. Typically, it would have inmates with similar classifications in the unit.

Unless security level or climatic conditions require a facility to be under one roof, it is desirable to use a campus-design concept where there is open outdoor space between housing units, support services, and programs. Again, this promotes a normalized environment in that an inmate goes from her house to work, school, and activities. Overall, the facility size should be within the guidelines of the American Correctional Association.

Construction Materials

The construction of housing cells or multiple-occupant rooms needs to be the same as for male facilities in that walls of solid grouted masonry, concrete floors and ceilings, and steel detention doors and windows should be used. The normalized environment additions to this secure infrastructure can be used as incentives and discipline tools. These normalized fixtures such as furniture can be changed or removed.

China fixtures can be installed such that changing to security stainless steel can be done easily. All of these issues promote "build it hard and run it soft." Obviously, construction for minimum security/work release type dormitories do not require the masonry and concrete construction, but if afforded the option, harder construction of housing buildings should be done so that if the populations change, the facility still can be used.

References

Albrecht, Linda. 1995. Facility Programming for Female Delinquents. In B. Glick and A. Goldstein, eds. *Managing Delinquency Programs That Work*. Lanham, Maryland: American Correctional Association.

Amnesty International. 1999. *Not Part of My Sentence*: *Violation of the Rights of Women in Custody*. New York: Amnesty International.

Carp, Scarlett V. and Joyce A. Davis. 1993. *Design Considerations in the Building of Women's Prisons*. Available from the National Institute of Corrections Resource Center, Washington, D.C.

Carter, Stephen A. 1998. Designing Without Glass Ceilings: An Examination of Trends and Opportunities in Designing Prisons for Women. In Joann B. Morton, ed. *Complex Challenges, Collaborative Solutions: Programming for Adult and Juvenile Female Offenders*. Lanham, Maryland: American Correctional Association.

Cranford, Susan and Rose Williams. 1998. Critical Issues in Managing Female Offenders. *Corrections Today*. December. 60:7.

Hawkes, Mary Q. 1994. *Excellent Effect: The Edna Mahan Story*. Lanham, Maryland: American Correctional Association.

Miller, Bona. 1998. Different, Not More Difficult: Gender-Specific Training Helps Bridge the Gap. *Corrections Today*. December. 60:7.

Morton, Joann B., ed. 1998. *Complex Challenges, Collaborative Solutions: Programming for Adult and Juvenile Female Offenders*. Lanham, Maryland: American Correctional Association.

Spaeth, Everett. 1998. A Case Study of the Master Plan and Design of Dr. Lane Murray Women's Prison. In Joann B. Morton, ed. *Complex Challenges, Collaborative Solutions: Programming for Adult and Juvenile Female Offenders*. Lanham, Maryland: American Correctional Association.

Juvenile Housing

Kenneth Ricci, Laura Maiello, and Shelley Zavlek
Ricci Associates
New York, New York

A primary tenet of juvenile justice is the recognition that children are different from adults. To address this difference, a distinct body of law has been developed for dealing with juvenile offenders. Juvenile corrections also recognizes this distinction by securing juveniles in facilities separate from adults. Accordingly, the design of juvenile facilities must reflect a programmatic and architectural response that is different from that developed for their adult counterparts.

This section focuses specifically on the design of housing units in secure juvenile facilities. The housing units are a critical component of juvenile detention or training schools. While juveniles spend a good portion of their day in mandated programs and services taking place in other areas of the facility, it is the housing unit that exemplifies the juveniles' "personal space." It contains the bedroom; sleeping, washing, relaxing, and socializing all take place here. The American Correctional Association's *Standards for Juvenile Detention Facilities* and *Standards for Juvenile Training Schools* both reinforce this, emphasizing that "the [housing] units are the foundation of facility living and must promote the safety and well being of both residents and staff."

State-of-the-art design seeks to meet this goal by providing an environment that is secure, yet normative. Overall, the concept of normative can be articulated through a design that provides residential amenities such as plenty

Bedroom illustrating fixed furnishings including desk, stool, and storage.

Photo courtesy of Earl Stahl, HDR, Dallas, Texas.

of sunlight, acoustical control, familiar materials, color, texture, and a human scale, without compromising security. Specifically, design of the housing unit should focus on the following:

Size

A key distinction between juvenile and adult facilities is the size of the housing units. Large housing units are common in adult jails and prisons, with upwards of fifty inmates residing in a single unit. In contrast, housing units in juvenile detention facilities and training schools should be sized much smaller, to optimize supervision and interaction with youth. American Correctional Association standards dictate that housing units not exceed twenty-five residents, and smaller units are even more desirable, aiming for a capacity of twelve-to-twenty, depending on the population being served. Housing units of this size enhance the ability of the staff to get to know the residents living in their area, to stay on top of things, and to prevent incidents before they happen. Small housing units are also more normative, minimizing the institutionalized feel of large cellblocks or dormitories.

A variety of housing unit sizes and characteristics may be desirable to respond to the special needs of the populations being served. For example, juvenile detention facilities include both boys and girls; pre- and postadjudicated youth; and juveniles accused of crimes ranging from shoplifting to murder. Lengths of stay in detention can range from under one day to several months. The ability to classify juveniles, and then have an appropriate housing unit to assign them to, is key to effective operation and population management. Design flexibility—for example, providing contiguous smaller units that can operate as two self-contained units or one larger one—helps officials respond to changes in population size and classification characteristics.

Configuration

The configuration of the housing unit is also an important design element in juvenile facilities. *Configuration* refers to the physical characteristics and layout of the housing unit, including the sleeping rooms and their relationship to the other elements within the housing unit area. Configuration of the housing units in both detention and training school facilities should consider the following models.

Direct Supervision Model

Direct supervision refers to both the physical design and the management approach of the housing unit. The design of the housing unit is podular, with single rooms organized around a common day space. The design provides clear lines of sight for the supervising officer to all areas within the space. A key element of the design is the absence of an enclosed control station. Rather, the officer is positioned within the housing unit, in the dayroom, in direct contact with the residents. The absence of a barrier separating the officer from the juveniles maximizes contact. By having a constant presence in the unit, knowing the residents, and being aware of the dynamics occurring in the housing unit, the officer is able to *proactively* supervise the population, diffusing potential situations before they escalate. This is in stark contrast to indirect, remote surveillance, where the officer can do little more than *react* to a situation after it occurs.

A good classification system is paramount to the success of direct supervision housing. Juveniles who are not appropriate for this setting—usually between 5 and 10 percent—must be identified at intake and reassigned.

The officer's station is not an enclosed control booth, but rather an open station. A small sitting or standing desk should be provided for completing paperwork, and for accommodating a panel for door controls, and so forth.

Single-occupancy Rooms

While the American Correctional Association standards for secure detention facilities and secure training schools both permit multipurpose housing in up to 20 percent of the facility, a key feature of the direct supervision model is single-occupancy rooms. Single rooms lend themselves to a more normative environment. They afford a degree of privacy and personal space, and they diminish the potential for problems associated with multi-occupancy areas, such as theft, assault, and intimidation.

Rooms should have an open space of thirty-five square feet unencumbered by room furnishings in their operational positions. The space should be at least seven feet in one dimension, permitting some freedom of movement within the room, and thereby minimizing the feeling of confinement in a restricted space. The room must have natural light provided by a window from the room to the exterior or from a source within twenty feet of the room. Security glazing should be used on windows, in place of glass, which could cause injury or be used as a weapon if broken. Ideally, windows should not have horizontal or vertical bars. If bars must be used for security reasons, then a security screen is needed to prevent access to the bars.

Rooms should include a bed, a desk with appropriate seating, and storage for clothing. Some administrators

An individual bathroom and shower with glazing provide privacy, yet allow for visual supervison.

Photo courtesy of Earl Stahl, HDR, Dallas, Texas.

believe that desks and chairs are not essential in the bedrooms, as the room is used only for sleeping (the remainder of the juvenile's time is spent in programs or in the dayroom). Including these amenities in the room, however, provides the sense of a room versus a cell, and affords an element of personal space. If not included in the room itself, appropriate facilities for writing or studying should be provided elsewhere in the living unit (dayroom).

Dry Rooms Versus Wet Rooms

Whether to provide dry rooms or wet rooms is a policy decision that should be made early in the programming and design process. There are several considerations. Wet rooms convey a highly institutional environment, reminiscent of adult jails and prisons. Dry rooms, on the other hand, are more normative, and in keeping with the direct

supervision management approach. The podular design of the housing unit allows officers to supervise residents who need to access the individual bathrooms, which are located in the dayroom area. Residents access the bathroom one at a time, and officers know when they enter and leave the facilities. Individual showers also are in this area. This approach affords a sense of normalcy and privacy and removes the opportunity for altercations that can occur in gang toilets and showers.

American Correctional Association standards require unassisted access to toilet facilities twenty-four hours a day. While this is not an issue during the day, nighttime compliance is difficult to achieve if rooms are dry and kept locked during sleeping hours.

Bedroom Doors

The bedroom door features suggest a variety of safety/ location and security considerations. Doors must have vision panels of sufficient size to allow visual supervision of all parts of the room without opening the door. Glazing should be with secure materials, such as glass-clad polycarbonates, to eliminate the possibility of broken glass that can cause injuries or be used as a weapon.

Opinions differ on the proper direction of the door swing. Doors that swing out prevent the juvenile from wedging the door closed and thus prohibiting staff entry. Time lost in gaining access could be crucial in a suicide attempt or other life-threatening situation. Inward swinging doors provide less opportunity for the juvenile to elude staff members in a struggle and less opportunity for the door to be shoved into an officer's face when it is unlocked. Inward swinging doors are also less likely to suffer damage when being kicked, because the door is forced against the stop of the frame rather than placing the force on the locking mechanism. If doors swing in, it is extremely important that no movable equipment that might be used as a barricade is provided in the room. Whichever direction the door swings, hinge pins must be on the exterior side or unremovable and designed to prevent attachment of a noose in the event of a suicide attempt.

Dayroom

The dayroom is an important element of the housing unit, and its configuration also can promote the direct supervision design philosophy. The dayroom is provided immediately adjacent to the sleeping areas, and is separated from them by a floor-to-ceiling wall. The dayroom must contain at least thirty-five square feet of floor space for each juvenile expected to use the dayroom at one time. Since the dayroom will serve multiple functions, (passive recreation, quiet time, television, unit meetings, and so forth) it may be beneficial to divide the space, setting aside certain areas for quiet activities and other areas for more active programming. Housing units should provide some space for on-unit programming activities to accommodate programming throughout the evening hours.

The design of the dayroom should provide clear lines of sight, so that staff can proactively supervise all juveniles using the area at one time. The layout of the area should encourage rather than hinder interaction between juveniles and staff. Again, remote control stations do not serve this purpose.

The dayroom is the heart of the living unit and should be furnished with durable, but comfortable furniture, receive plenty of natural light, and be well ventilated for climate control. Careful selection of materials to permit varying textures and colors will enhance the juvenile's perception of the space.

Normative Value

While secure adult facilities often have little daylight and few design flourishes, juvenile facility design must recognize the value of a normative, yet secure environment in promoting positive behavior and ensuring safety for residents and staff. Normative value refers to the benefits of providing an environment that, while secure, is as normative as possible in its appearance. Providing a normative, rather than institutional environment can elicit a positive behavioral response from juveniles who must be confined in secure detention centers and training schools. Features to consider in design of the housing units include the following ones.

Natural Light

Natural light should be incorporated into the design of the housing unit. Materials that allow sunlight in improve the aesthetics of the area, and can enhance security by opening up areas for increased visibility. For example,

The Portage County Jail in Ravenna, Ohio, consists of a one-story law enforcement and juvenile center and a two-story male housing unit for 182 beds. Use of sloped roofs complements the area's future housing development. Horizontal bands of brick and color differentiation were used to reinforce the residential scale.

Photo courtesy of NBBJ, Columbus, Ohio. Photographer: John Griesen.

polycarbonate glazing—which ranges in strength from impact resistant to bulletproof—can be used in the housing areas to open up the space visually, while also allowing the officer full view of all areas. Skylights in the housing units also provide abundant natural light in the dayrooms. And, as mentioned previously, natural light must be provided in the bedrooms, preferably through an exterior window.

Acoustics and Noise Reduction

A classic characteristic of adult facilities is the relentless din that comes from poor acoustical control. Noise can be reduced and controlled in the housing units by using carpeting in the dayrooms. This also provides a less institutionalized look than concrete or vinyl flooring. Sound-absorbing security ceilings should be considered in those areas that are accessible to juveniles. In areas that are not accessible and have high ceilings, acoustical ceiling tile can be installed. These can include hold-down clips that keep the panel firm and provide evidence of tampering.

Bedroom doors should use sound-deadening strips or pads on the frame. Metal doors, if used, should be fabricated with sound-deadening cores to reduce noise.

Color and Texture

Materials and finishings that introduce a variety of color and texture into the housing unit promote a more pleasant, noninstitutional environment for juveniles who must be confined in secure facilities. This might include the use of wooden, versus steel doors; glazing as described previously; and furnishings that are both good looking and durable. A variety of colors and textures in the dayroom will provide a noninstitutional atmosphere.

Safety and Security

Both safety and security are important considerations in the design of secure juvenile facilities. In the housing units, there are several issues.

Suicide-resistant Environment

Every effort should be made in the design and furnishing of juvenile detention facilities to provide a suicide-resistant environment. This is especially critical in the housing units, as bedrooms and bathrooms are the two areas where juveniles are not under constant supervision of staff, and therefore most likely to injure themselves.

Furnishings, lights, ventilation, utilities, and other items provided in a juvenile's room must be carefully selected or designed to resist suicide efforts. All elements must be viewed in the context of the potential for attaching a noose, or for inflicting physical damage to oneself. This includes:

— no interior bars or windows
— securely mounted fixtures without slits or protruding objects
— removable or detachable hinge pins in doors
— securely mounted air grilles, which are not larger than one-eighth of an inch with frames flush on the wall
— screen covers on diffusers and vents that permit adequate ventilation but prevent youth from fitting fingers or cloth through them
— recessed shower heads
— beds that do not have openings or projections
— drinking fountains without protruding mouth guards or drain slots
— break-away hooks
— nonbreakable mirrors mounted flush to the wall
— no electrical outlets in rooms
— no access to plumbing chases

Visibility and Clear Lines of Sight

Housing units should be designed to facilitate and enhance supervision and maximize social interaction among youth. Vision panels and interior windows made of security glazing (to avoid breakage) should be used to achieve maximum visibility and optimal staff involvement through direct and indirect supervision of residents. Interior courtyards and outdoor spaces (terraces) built adjacent to dayrooms increase light and a sense of openness. In addition, they enhance programming by allowing secure and easy access to spaces for recreation.

Plumbing

Contemporary direct supervision facilities have moved away from the notion that only stainless steel bathroom fixtures will withstand the rough use of secure facility populations over time. Porcelain fixtures, securely mounted, provide a more normative environment for general population juveniles in which the expectation of respect for property is established. Porcelain fixtures can be purchased at approximately one tenth the cost of stainless steel fixtures. Units that require higher levels of security, such as intake and segregation, require stainless steel fixtures due to their ability to withstand abuse.

Water fountains should be security grade without protruding mouth guards or other elements that can be vandalized easily. Fountains should be securely mounted and access to motors should be securely locked.

Furniture

Classification plays an important role in the assignment of juveniles to various housing units in the facility. Furniture for the dayroom can be selected based on the suitability for the population that is being served. For example, fixed furniture, while very institutional in nature, may be required for residents who have been classified as requiring high levels of security, or for orientation and reception units, where residents have not yet been classified. For the remainder of the population, innovative materials and design provide a range of choices—from heavy, immovable furniture that is near impossible to lift, to lighter weight furniture that is movable and allows for greater flexibility. Natural wood and fabric furniture may be normative, but it is not as durable or long lasting as moduform furnishings.

Specialized Housing Units

In addition to general populations, secure juvenile facilities must accommodate populations with special needs, including medical, mental health, and administrative segregation. For the most part, housing units for these populations will be self-contained. As such, the living units will need to incorporate additional program space, dining area, kitchenette, and recreational space. There is also an emerging trend toward developing facilities for serious adjudicated juvenile offenders that lend themselves to the concept of self-contained units such as these. For specialized populations, furnishings most likely will be fixed, rather than movable. Larger vision panels may be desirable in mental health and medical isolation rooms, which also require special ventilation.

The Americans with Disabilities Act requires that facilities be handicap accessible for both staff and residents. Facility rooms that will house handicapped juveniles must be designed with special attention to their unique requirements. Mounting heights and positioning of furnishings and plumbing fixtures, provision of grab bars and doors and their hardware and approach areas, and the entire path of exit must be designed to comply with local, state, and federal standards. The configuration of unencumbered space is especially important to a juvenile in a wheelchair. Consideration should be given to including one handicap accessible room, toilet, and shower in each of the housing units.

References

American Correctional Association. *Standards for Juvenile Community Residential Facilities.* Lanham, Maryland. American Correctional Association.

___. *Standards for Juvenile Detention Facilities,* Third Edition. Lanham, Maryland: American Correctional Association.

___. *Standards for Juvenile Training Schools,* Third Edition, Lanham, Maryland: American Correctional Association.

___. *Standards Supplement. 1998.* Lanham, Maryland: American Correctional Association.

Glick, B. and A. Goldstein. 1995. *Managing Delinquency Programs That Work.* Lanham, Maryland: American Correctional Association.

Protrusion-free, Suicide-resistant Architecture in Adult Correctional and Juvenile Facilities*

Joseph R. Rowan
Criminal and Juvenile Justice International
Roseville, Minnesota

Effective suicide prevention in correctional facilities must include an environment that is protrusion-free and suicide-resistant. More than 90 percent of custodial suicide deaths occur by hanging. Not all of the sleeping rooms need to be built or retrofitted for this purpose. Experience nationally has shown that single (and double, where they exist) sleeping rooms in the mental health, segregation, and detoxification units and holding cells for short-term detention should be suicide-resistant because of the incidence of suicide attempts and deaths that have occurred in those units.

Obviously, in small- or medium-sized facilities, which do not have mental health units normally containing a suicide observation room, any room in any facility which is used to house suicide risks should be protrusion-free.

* Material presented was adapted from *Suicide Prevention in Custody*, American Correctional Association, 1998 by Joseph R. Rowan.

Suicide-resistant Physical Features

1. Bars on doors and walls in older facilities should be closed off from floor to ceiling, as follows: To allow for good air circulation, better noise and voice pick-up, and clear closed-circuit television viewing, a detention or security screen with openings no more than one-eighth inch should be spot-welded to the bars/frames. Some facilities use sand screen (used in sand quarries to screen out rocks). It is durable, and when properly primed can do a good job at a fraction of the cost of a security screen manufactured for that special purpose. An alternative approach would be to affix one-fourth inch scratch-resistant polycarbonate glazing.

2. Solid steel or wooden doors with small peep holes or panels should be changed to large vision panels of low-abrasion polycarbonate. New construction should include security glazing on the upper half of the door.

3. Existing vents, ducts, grilles, light fixtures and any other similar protrusions should be covered/enclosed with the security screen, as outlined previously. In recent years, a suicide-resistant safety-ventilation device has been built for wall and ceiling installation, which by demonstrations and experience has not been aborted by a noose being attached. The device has been used extensively in retrofitting and in new construction.

4. Door knobs/handles should not exist in rooms. Recessed door finger pull latches are needed, and they cannot be aborted.

5. Steel beds should be replaced with concrete slab beds with rounded edges and painted. A suicide cannot be attempted under them as can happen under steel beds where the noose is run overhead then placed under the neck of the person laying on his or her back. The inmate then turns over on his stomach, and the weight of the head—2.5 to 3 pounds—is all that is necessary to make the inmate black out. In up to fifteen minutes, total asphyxiation occurs and then death.

6. Where four-point restraints need to be used, eye-bolt nuts are anchored in the cement floor to be used when the eye bolt with strap attached is screwed into the nut. Contraband cannot be hidden in this type of bed, and it is indestructible.

7. Shelves, benches, desks, push-buttons in showers and on wash basins, which protrude more than one-half inch and exposed hinges need a sold triangular end plate welded/attached from the wall, sloping down to the end of the flat surface, making it impossible for anyone to attach a noose over the top/corner.

8. Replace solid or so-called collapsible clothes hooks with the ball-in-socket type, which cannot be jammed with a small object, allowing a noose to be attached.

9. Audio monitoring intercom systems for communication between cells/rooms and control centers are required by American Correctional Association standards for emergency/health reasons. Hanging often produces noise such as gasping for breath, gurgling, and a flailing of arms and legs against walls, beds, and so forth.

10. Provide modesty shields or screens with triangular, rounded, or sloping tops. Offenders' feet should be observable when they are behind the screen/shield.

11. Sprinklers should be installed flush with the ceiling. Use breakaway sprinklers which drop down or protrude when set off. Or, place protective cones on old sprinklers. The cones cover the sprinkler except for one-third inch of the tip. This makes the sprinkler suicide resistant.

12. Floor drains should have openings no more than one-eighth inch. Offenders have made a noose from the hem of their shirt or shorts. They affix a slip knot around their neck, place the "rope" over one shoulder and get down on their knees to tie the noose end to the widely-spaced cross bar/fin or cover opening. When the inmate leans into the noose, it tightens and cuts off the flow of blood; the inmate blacks out within thirty seconds and is asphyxiated within fifteen minutes.

13. Illuminate high-risk suicide observation rooms sufficient for twenty-four-hour closed-circuit TV surveillance. Place infrared filters over the ceiling lights; this produces total darkness but closed-circuit television picks up images as if it were daylight. Lighting during daytime needs to be provided separately.

14. Cells/rooms, including bars, should be painted in pastel colors. Also, paint headers above cell doors black or any dark color to reduce camera glare and create contrast. These techniques make closed-circuit television more effective.

15. Combination toilets/wash basins should have a water spout that is flush with the deck or back wall, protruding no more than one-half inch so that a noose

This suicide-resistant fixture has a rounded cabinet, less sharp edges, and rounded housing to the floor, which prevents inmates from fastening material around the fixture.

Source: Acorn Engineering Company, City of Industry, California. Photo courtesy of Joseph Rowan.

cannot be attached. Raised handles should never be used. Hot and cold push buttons should protrude no more than one-half inch. Please refer to item No. 6 for retrofitting push buttons, which protrude more than one-half inch.

16. Correctional officer posts should be located inside the offender housing unit (direct supervision model) or immediately adjacent (podular indirect supervision model) so that officers can respond promptly to any emergency. American Correctional Association standards require this.

17. Suicide-observation rooms not only must be protrusion-free/suicide-resistant, but all parts of the room/cell should be under closed-circuit television monitoring. **Caution**: Two-thirds of suicide deaths occur in single rooms/cells. Closed-circuit television monitoring should only be used to **supplement** direct officer monitoring of suicide risks. American Correctional Association and other national standards require **continuous** or **constant** monitoring of suicide risks. Continuous watching of the closed-circuit television monitor can produce "monitor hypnosis." This has resulted in several legal cases, one in which an officer watched an offender hang for eighty-five minutes, confirmed by the twenty-four-hour filming of the closed-circuit television. If correctional personnel are not aware of this life-safety scenario, informed architects can perform a life-safety public service by acquainting facility administrators with this serious potential problem. Officers should have a five-minute break from closed-circuit television monitoring every half hour to counteract monitor hypnosis.

18. Bath/shower rooms in dormitories should not have steel rods to support curtains. Velcro fasteners are a safe alternative, or a French door, where head and feet can be seen by officers, nurses, and others.

19. Janitor's/utility closets should have locks and a sign posted indicating that, when open, officers shall directly supervise offenders who are there to obtain equipment/supplies.

20. Padded cells should contain no materials that emit toxic fumes, which can injure or kill. Contrary to the past, there are such nontoxic materials available from at least one manufacturer.

21. Suicide attempts and deaths have occurred from mezzanine floors in correctional facilities. Mental health, suicidal, segregation, and detoxification offenders should not be housed on tiers/mezzanine floors.

22. There should be no electric sockets in cells/rooms where at-risk offenders are housed unless ground-fault interruptors are installed.

Conclusion

The ongoing problem of suicides in our correctional institutions and jails continues to be a very serious issue. Designers as well as user agencies must look for ways to reduce suicides in new construction and renovation projects. Some of these solutions will be provided through improved communication and observation. Still others will be made by advances in technology, new construction methods, and better product design.

Inmate and Juvenile Services

3

The photograph on the previous page shows the Federal Correctional Complex in Beaumont, Texas. The central courtyard of the low-security facility is bound on one side by the series of support buildings, which also serve as a security perimeter. The central dining canopy in the left foreground details the materials that link all the support buildings into a "town street," providing clearly defined entry points, protection from the elements, and visual interest. The large circular canopy right of center is the entry to central reception, and the smaller sloped canopies are entries to education, arts and crafts, medical, and other support services.

Photo courtesy of NBBJ, Columbus, Ohio. Photographer: Wes Thompson.

Reception Centers

Larry Hardy
Iowa Medical and Classification Center
Oakdale, Iowa

The reception center can perform a useful role in the correctional system if the design of the center carefully is matched to its precise functions and responsibilities. Reception centers vary considerably from one jurisdiction to the next, and it is important that each jurisdiction specify the responsibilities of the center before beginning the design of the structure that will house the program. The basic concept of the reception center is simple; provide a single point of entry for all inmates admitted to the system to allow for uniform intake processing, record keeping, orientation, and classification. However, even with this seemingly straightforward definition, there are many variables that have an impact on the actual operation and effectiveness of a reception center, all of which must be taken into account in the design.

Anticipated Population

Will the center receive all new commitments only, or will it also receive release violators? Will it receive men and women, adults and juveniles? Will it receive persons with active or unknown medical problems and issues, potential enemies, and others who will need to be segregated from the rest of the population? Are there groups of inmates who might require "special" handling or housing? What about gang issues, sexual predators, the mentally ill, or mentally retarded admissions? Will there be significant numbers of admissions for whom English is not their primary language? What is the anticipated percentage of admissions who have disabilities of one kind or another (blind, deaf, nonambulatory, and so forth)? All these are issues that could have an impact on the operation and effectiveness of the center, and must be considered in the design phase.

Anticipated Population Volume

What is the anticipated number of admissions per day? Per week? Per month? How will the intake be controlled or determined? Will intake be scheduled or left up to the sending jurisdictions? Will the hours of operation be limited (8-5, M-F), or will the door always be open? How quickly does the system need to process incoming inmates, and how will transfers out of the reception center be accomplished?

Role of the Reception Center

Reception centers may be very narrow or very broad in their services to the system. Some may be designed to perform all intake screening, including complete medical, psychological, educational, vocational, substance abuse, and background investigation, as well as complete time computation, preparation of visiting lists, and other records, system orientation, program identification, and security classification. Some reception centers provide limited service, including no more than a brief medical and psychological screen, limited security screening, and an institutional placement decision. Some reception programs may last for several weeks, and others may last only days or even hours. Some reception programs also can serve as "preprogram" placements, conducting "program readiness assessments" or even program preparatory classes and activities. Clearly, the scope of the program will have a significant impact on the design.

All reception centers will share some common elements: a receiving and discharge area; a medical screening area; routine housing; program assessment areas; segregation housing; and a records area.

Receiving and Discharge

This area needs careful attention and planning. Decisions must be made regarding precisely what tasks will be accomplished in the receiving area. The typical receiving process includes verifying identity and commitment, inventorying personal property and storage, fingerprinting and photographing, showering and clothing issues, issuing hygiene materials and other supplies, initiating a system record (both hard copy and automated), and performing an intake informational interview. A well-designed intake area will include separate areas for each of these concerns.

The receiving and discharge area should be organized conveniently so that a minimum number of staff can supervise the area, provide mutual support, and process incoming inmates efficiently. Additional space will be needed if intake medical screening, barbering and grooming, on-site interviews by professional staff, or other functions are incorporated into the receiving area. It is also important to recognize that most likely this same area will be used for inmates being transferred out of the facility, which will require additional "waiting" space.

Some secure "waiting" space should be included, to separate inmates from each other, when necessary, or to isolate inmates who are disruptive. It is highly desirable to locate the receiving and discharge area away from the area that is used for general staff traffic, the public, other general institutional business, and shipping and receiving.

Medical Screening Area

The size and location of the medical screening area should be determined carefully, with extensive consultation with the medical staff, on the precise scope of the screening program. A broad range of health issues must be addressed by the system with each inmate. Administrators must decide if these issues will be addressed as part of the reception process, or if the reception medical screening only will attempt to identify emergent needs. Will a complete health history, including dental, x-ray, laboratory work, and a complete physical, be included in the reception process? If not, then the more broad-based medical services are rendered at the institution to which the inmate is assigned following the reception process.

Will individual inmates having significant medical or dental problems be retained in the reception program until those issues are resolved as best they can be, or will individuals with those problems be moved promptly to another setting and returned to the reception program after their medical issues have been addressed? Will psychiatric issues be addressed as part of reception or separately? Another issue that must be addressed during this process is that of management of inmates with disabilities.

The advent of telemedicine also may have an impact on the medical screening process in reception. Finally, the issue of inmates with infectious diseases such as HIV, hepatitis, and tuberculosis must be addressed, and how the system chooses to approach these difficult issues may have an impact on facility design.

  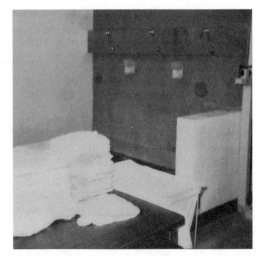

Scenes from the Iowa Medical and Classification Center intake area include the general waiting area for new inmates, the barber room, and the shower area.

Photos courtesy of Larry Hardy.

Routine Housing

Routine housing for reception inmates should be in single cells. While dormitories are easier and less expensive to design and construct, they are not suited to reception programs. The cells should be designed to provide security for staff safety as well as for the inmate (inmates in reception programs can be quite traumatized and sometimes become self-injurious). This means that attention must be paid to both the physical design of the cell space and visibility for staff. Inmates within the first twenty-four hours of their incarceration are at the highest risk for suicide, so the cells for these inmates should be designed with this in mind (*see* Chapter 2.10 on suicide).

Some cells are needed for inmates with disabilities. The routine housing area should include a day area if inmates will be in the reception program for more than a few days, and staff interview rooms (and, depending on how and where health issues are addressed, examination rooms). If the center receives women as well as men, or both juveniles and adults, other issues must be addressed.

Juveniles must have sight and sound separation from adult inmates. This is required for all programming areas as well as housing. The same requirements must be met for female inmates. In addition, processing female inmates and juveniles through the reception evaluation and diagnostic procedures must be done when male inmates are not present. Staffing for these two inmate groups will also be different from that required for adult male inmate processing in the areas of shower and searches.

Segregation Housing

In every reception program, there is a need for segregation space. This is to isolate disruptive individuals, to manage enemy situations, provide additional security for inmates requiring observation, provide an additional level of security for certain medical situations, and immediately isolate individuals who because of their history require separation from the rest of the population.

In general, a useful rule of thumb to use in the design of both routine and segregation housing is to establish what the system considers to be the significant group boundaries that indicate a need for separate housing for different groups. In other words, how does the system as a whole separate and classify its current population? Those same boundaries will have to be considered in one way or another in the design of the reception center, since the center presumably will be receiving inmates who will become members of each of the groups currently defined in the system's population.

Program Areas

Depending on the nature and duration of the reception program, it may be necessary to include larger group rooms for psychological testing, inmate orientation, inmate visiting, recreation, and so forth. This is an area that might be overlooked, only to find later that certain reception functions occur with groups of inmates, but that space is limited, inadequate, or not available.

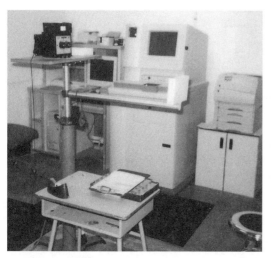 

Reception facilities at the Iowa Medical and Classification Center include automated fingerprint and photo identification systems, and a secure waiting area with a clothing issue window in the background.

Photos courtesy of Larry Hardy.

Records Area

One aspect of the reception process that must not be overlooked is the administrative and records area. Once again, system decisions must be made to determine how extensive the records operation at the reception center will be. Records generation may consist of little more than identification, basic demographics, and "alert" information—similar to a typical jail-booking area.

On the other hand, some reception centers are responsible for generating visiting lists, complete background and criminal history information, psychological and reception reports, extensive custody and program classification materials, and so forth. The record services that will be provided must be decided in advance to determine the size and nature of the records area. For example, where will hard copy and automated records be stored and archived?

It also is important to consider several other factors, such as the provision of clothing and laundry services. Reception centers, with their high volume of new inmate turnover, generate larger than normal amounts of laundry and clothing issues. Will inmates entering the reception center, for example, be provided with only temporary clothing, such as jumpsuits, or will inmates be provided with their full "prison issue?"

The design also must consider the plan for providing food services. For example, will there be a central dining facility or will inmates be served meals in their housing units? What provisions, if any, will be made for inmate visiting? Programs that are brief may not even need to consider this. What provisions, if any, will be made for an inmate canteen?

Staff planning to operate the reception center should consider that many reception activities can be scheduled at times other than "8-5." Doing this can serve several purposes: it can help occupy the time of inmates who in a reception program generally have little to do, and it can allow certain spaces to be used for different activities at different times of the day, efficiently maximizing the use of space. All of these are important issues that will have a significant impact on the facility's design.

Adult Admissions and Discharges

George Yefchak, President
New Jersey Chapter of the
American Correctional Association
Stockton, New Jersey

Mecklenberg County Jail, North Carolina. Controlled access to the admissions area of the facility by staff insures safe and supervised processing of all individuals.

Photo courtesy of Hellmuth, Obata & Kassabaum, Inc. (HOK), St. Louis, Missouri.

One section of the facility that every inmate will pass through is the admission and discharge area. Because each inmate will be processed through this area, a prime concern for an administrator must be the realization that this area will handle both minimum-security and maximum-security individuals as they are processed into the facility. In addition, the administration must be aware that individuals entering this area may be agitated, distraught, unruly, or in a general state of uncooperativeness. Administrators must be mindful of these differences in individuals when considering the design of this area. The objective of this area of the facility is to process an individual into the facility in a safe, efficient, and orderly manner.

Initial Entry

As an individual enters the facility and is about to be processed into the population, the staff must examine the admission documentation and search the individual for contraband. This applies to inmates being transferred from other facilities and for individuals being brought in from court, probation or parole offices, or the "street."

The commitment documentation should be examined and verified prior to the individual being admitted into the secure area of the facility. For this to be accomplished, the individual to be admitted and the accompanying officers should be granted access to a controlled-access entrance room. The correctional officers staffing this room would be located in a control booth and communicate through an intercom and a document-exchanging

Orderly and efficient handling and storage of inmate property avoids problems later. Chesapeake City Jail Renovation and Addition, Chesapeake, Virginia.

Photo courtesy of NBBJ, Columbus, Ohio. Photographer: Joe Wiseman.

compartment. Electronic locking devices controlled by the officers in the booth would control the access to this area. No direct contact would occur between the facility correctional officers and those accompanying the individual being admitted.

Facility design should allow for the same officers who staff the control booth to also control entry to the entrance room. This can be accomplished with the use of surveillance cameras and intercoms located at the doorway, and if directly leading outside, use only low-growth landscaping to permit clear visibility of anyone approaching the facility.

Staffing levels are a concern throughout the entire admission area. These areas usually have spurts of activity and do not operate at high levels of activity throughout the entire shift. Therefore, design considerations and staffing levels that reflect the activity level of that correctional staff post can realize cost savings.

The use of a video that records admission activities and the condition of inmates is a design consideration for this area. A precautionary action, such as videotaping an incoming inmate, may provide exculpatory documentation useful for disproving allegations of abuse or mistreatment. The expense of such video equipment may not pay immediate dividends, but it is a good investment for future legal activities.

Entering the Facility

After determining that the individual has appropriate documentation, that person may be granted admission into the facility proper. Again, security and control remain the prime concern. The individual must be searched for contraband and any inappropriate personal items. This search and confiscation should be done in an expedient manner.

General holding room has spartan finishes and furniture. Direct staff supervision is extremely important.

Photograph by George Yefchak.

This search should occur in a secure room located near the entrance of the facility. An incoming individual should have limited access to other areas and inmates prior to the search. If contraband is found, administrators want to minimize the opportunity for it to be passed onto the general population. A room dedicated to conducting searches located near the entrance and away from general inmates will accomplish this.

Upon completion of the search, confiscated personal property and contraband must be disposed of in a prompt and orderly manner. Locating a property room in this vicinity would allow for this. Contraband could be marked for destruction and those personal items not permissible could be marked for disposal or returned to the inmate's family. Being able to quickly secure these items in an orderly manner is important for security. In addition, inmate claims for lost property are a thorn in every administrator's operation. Securing and storing property efficiently in a property room is an up-front expense with long-term dividends. Leaving property unsecured in a hallway or a search room is an excellent way for it to disappear and property claims to arise.

Consideration should be given for alternate property storage for long-term inmates or general bulk storage away from the property room. Long-term inmates will not need immediate access to their personal belongings and they can be stored elsewhere at the administration's convenience. Also, the property room will need to be maintained in an orderly and neat manner and may not be large enough to handle the inmate population in crowded conditions.

Maintaining the main property room near the entrance is also an efficient placement for the discharge area, as well. The departing individuals can claim their belongings and quickly exit. This prevents the passing and giving away of items to other inmates in the institution.

Temporary Holding Room

Following the documentation check and search of the individual, the person is now ready to begin the formal intake procedure. This process can be time consuming and fraught with many delays. Each step in the admission process is dependent on specialized staff conducting

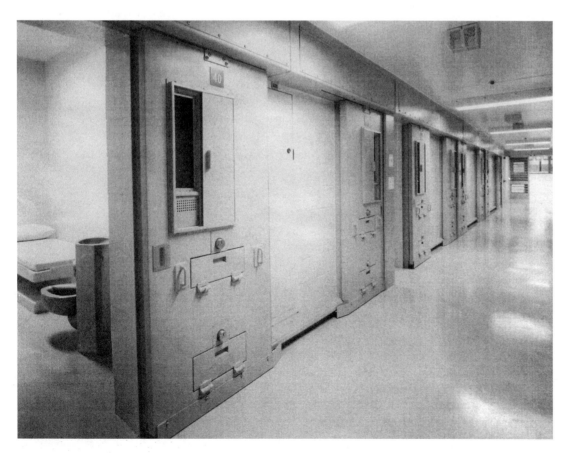

Individual secure housing works best for certain inmates during the admissions process. Oshkosh Correctional Institution, Oshkosh, Wisconsin.

Architect: Venture Architects, Milwaukee, Wisconsin.

Housing dayroom space should be open and observable by staff. The area provides limited out-of-cell time for inmates in the admissions process.

Photo courtesy of Kennedy Associates Incorporated, St. Louis, Missouri. Photographer: Alise O'Brien, architectural photography.

a specific intake function. The time line of this process also is determined by whether this is a short-term or long-term secure facility. A long-term facility may require additional testing or procedures that would not be a consideration in a short-term secure facility. Examples of this would be particular medical testing or educational testing for program placement.

Regardless of the length of the stay of the inmate, certain required procedures must be completed. While the inmate is waiting for the staff to conduct these procedures, the individual must be detained in an appropriate holding area or room. Certain considerations are involved in the use of the appropriate holding room.

By far the most economical is the use of a general holding room. Inmates are placed in the holding room and are brought out when they are ready to undergo a portion of the admission process. While economical, it mixes various classifications of inmates and may not allow the best staff supervision. A video monitor can improve surveillance of the area, but it still allows for potential trouble between inmates to occur. This may be considered best for short-term placement, if used at all.

The use of single-cell housing for admissions is the most efficient and safest method for housing new admissions. This allows for inmates to be housed safely until they can be processed and properly classified for the population of the facility. Intimidation and assaults are less likely to occur in an individual cell situation.

Other considerations for individual cell housing would be to provide a more secure setting for aggressive admissions and for those experiencing mental health problems. Both can be contained more appropriately in this type of a setting with a video monitor as a backup to the correctional staff observation.

Another consideration for administrators in housing new admissions in individual cells is to provide protective custody to new arrivals who may have a degree of notoriety. The embarrassment to administrators who do not have adequate facilities to safeguard against assaults on a person whose case is followed in the media will be very hard to live down.

The waiver of juveniles to adult courts is also a consideration in admission housing. While they may have been waived to adult court because of their offenses, they are still younger than a majority of the inmates being processed and are in the care and custody of the facility administrators. Measures should be taken to prevent any victimization of the younger inmate. Appropriate housing and supervision during the admission process would reduce this liability.

Individuals admitted to a correctional facility are under stress and may react to it in different ways. How they react to this stress is a prime concern to the institutional administrators. Facility design should assume a potential for suicidal behavior or other mental health problems. While it cannot prevent the behavior, it can minimize it through suicide-proof hardware in the rooms, secured beds and furniture, recessed lighting, smoke detectors, and so forth. Video monitoring is also a consideration. It is important to note that while these items may reduce risk, it still is imperative to have a vigilant staff supervise these areas.

Photo Identification and Processing

The process of fingerprinting and photographing a new inmate has undergone significant technological change in recent years. Instead of taking prints and photos and storing them in file cabinets, the process can be done digitally and in minutes. Rather than keeping an inmate in the processing area waiting for a Polaroid picture to develop, digital cameras and computers are used to take photos and store them in a depository, which may even be off site.

A LAN system eliminates the need for any equipment to be present other than a computer, a camera, photo backdrop, and a scanning device for fingerprints. The actual processing can occur in a limited space near the holding area. The files, backup copies, and any other documentation would be stored in a secure location elsewhere in the facility.

An inmate can be escorted from the holding area to the photo and identification section of the facility and processed within minutes. This process is efficient and an effective use of staff. The proximity of these areas to one another reduces escort time and the need of correctional staff to do the escorting.

The use of this equipment reinforces an important point that is related to the overall construction of the facility: namely that technology is a driving force in corrections. It is a lengthy leap from the first electronic locking devices to computer LAN systems, and to facilities operated and controlled by correctional staff in a computerized central control room. Facility design must include wiring for a computer and networking system within the facility. Computer security has improved to the point that all sections of the facility can have some form of access to a computer system.

Medical Evaluations

One of the most important steps of the admission process is the medical examination. Determining any medical problems and the necessity of treatment is a priority for all new admissions. Processing the individuals through a clinic-like setting is both time consuming and requires constant staff supervision. If the evaluations are not conducted in the admission area, staff will be required to escort the inmate to an area outside the admission area and then wait for the evaluation to be completed. This increases staff supervision costs.

Placing an evaluation area in the admission area will reduce escort and supervision time. Technology plays an important role in this area, as well. The area for medical evaluations should be able to accommodate one or two inmates to allow for adequate supervision and a minimum of downtime between evaluations.

Medical personnel other than a medical doctor most likely will conduct most evaluations. The area does not need to be as large as a regular medical office. Rather, it should be of a size sufficient to maintain basic supplies and equipment. It also should be part of a computer LAN system for inputting medical records at the time of the examination.

The area also should be equipped with videoconferencing capabilities to allow for consultations with medical doctors and mental health professionals. It is important to remember that consultations and interviews no longer must be conducted in person. Rather, videoconferencing would be a more practical and efficient method of conducting evaluations.

In addition, the use of outside-service companies to provide radiological services, phlebotomy services, and so forth, reduces the space needed to store the equipment in the facility. Instead, these individuals bring their equipment with them when they provide their services.

The medical area design should include a plan to permit the dispensing of medications. Storage would not be done in this area but medications would be prepared elsewhere and then brought in to be dispensed. The medical area would have controlled access to permit staff to dispense medication to inmates. This area then would be staffed only when in use and otherwise would be closed and secured.

Common Area and Dayroom

The facility must provide space for meals and for recreation of the inmates and allow them an opportunity to spend time outside of their cell. The area available for dayroom use or a common area depends on the admission unit design. The common area in the traditional pod construction is in the center while in more linear construction, there would be a room dedicated for use as a dayroom.

The general visiting area is used by inmates in the admissions process as well as general population inmates.

Photo courtesy of Kennedy Associates Incorporated, St. Louis, Missouri.
Photographer: Alise O'Brien, architectural photography.

Furnishings in this area should be the basic table and chair/stool construction with all items secured to the floor. This would allow passive recreation in the unit. Meals also could be served in this area or in the cells as the administration determines. While it would be the administration's responsibility to set a schedule for use of the dayroom and its use for food service, the facility must provide space for recreation and an opportunity to spend time outside of the cell. There also is a variety of exercise equipment that can be secured to the wall and floor that allows for the exercise of the large muscle groups as required by American Correctional Association standards. Correctional staff would provide direct supervision of this area.

A television can be mounted in this room. Placing it on a wall mount would allow all to view it while not posing a security threat. Televisions would be cable ready and controlled through central control of the facility. This would allow the staff to control the content of the programs and to televise informational programs produced by the facility administrators. Often inmates are able to get orientated to the facility's procedures through the use of a video program viewed on the television monitor.

Food Service

No food would be prepared in this area. It should be prepared in the main kitchen and brought on serving carts to the inmates. Inmates under staff supervision would dispense meals.

Social Services

The admission unit will have social service personnel assigned according to the number of inmates in the unit. American Correctional Association standards provide staffing ratios. Sufficient office space should be provided for all staff to perform their duties. This can be in cubicle-type offices with movable partitions or offices with fixed walls.

Additional Office Space

During the admission process, inmates have numerous meetings with individuals whose official duties require that they meet with inmates in privacy. These include psychologists, lawyers, probation or parole officers, counselors, investigators, and so forth. Meetings with these professionals usually require a degree of privacy in conducting their business. To do so, sufficient office space should be made available for them. Correctional staff frequently has to limit such visitors because of inadequate space. It would be more cost effective to have sufficient staff than to have correctional staff spending an inordinate amount of time shuffling around professional visitors.

To accomplish this, several small rooms should be outfitted with secured table space and chairs. These rooms should handle no more than two to three people and need not be larger than what would adequately accommodate them. Each room should be equipped with a panic button for emergencies and also possibly an intercom. This would allow the offices to be secured when all the participants are inside. Correctional staff then could supervise all offices with visual checks rather than being assigned to observe a specific office.

Outdoor Recreation

Depending on the length of the stay in the admission unit, outdoor recreation may have to be provided. It probably would be most cost effective to use the outdoor recreation area of the main facility rather than to construct a separate recreational space. Of course, if the admission area is in a freestanding building, it may be more efficient and cost effective to construct a recreational area next to the building.

Education/Treatment Space

Some admission units may require that the inmates reside in the unit while they await transfer to another facility, or the unit may require a lengthy stay as part of the admission process. In these cases, education classes or treatment may begin in the admission unit. If this is the case, sufficient education/treatment rooms will be needed. These would be equipped with the usual desks, blackboards, and other related material. Sufficient cabinet space is necessary to secure all material when not in use.

Maintenance Supplies

Routine cleaning and maintenance should be done on a daily basis. Appropriate supplies and equipment must be maintained in the admissions area. American Correctional Association standards should be followed in the storage and accountability for these supplies. To do so, proper storage facilities and areas must be a routine part of the facility design. This is a safety and security issue and should be addressed as such. Conveniently located locking closets for the equipment and supplies should meet this requirement.

Visiting Area

Each administration will develop its own policies regarding individuals in the admission process having visits from friends and family. While in a short-term secure facility, an individual may not be present long enough to have visitors. However, those having a lengthier stay may be able to have visitors.

For security reasons as well as for economical considerations, it would be reasonable to have an inmate receiving a visit to be escorted to the visiting area of the main institution. This would allow the visit to be conducted in a safe and secure manner, outside of the admission area.

Female Admissions

Certain jurisdictions may have only one secure facility and, consequently, will process male and female inmates through their admission unit. There are always inherent problems in commingling inmates. When this is necessary, the concern is to limit contact between the two groups of inmates and to maintain direct supervision. The administration may wish to allow the groups to interact at some point; however, the admission process is not a recommended time.

Female admissions would be escorted through the intake process and then taken to the female housing unit. Design factors should allow for privacy in the medical area and search area.

Discharges

Processing inmates for their departure requires a combination of good procedures and good facility design. The objective of the process is to expeditiously move the inmates and their property from the facility's control to another agency's authority for transfer or release to the community. This should be done with minimal contact with other inmates and with little opportunity to pass off personal property.

Exit photos, verification of identity for release, and a medical examination can be conducted in an orderly fashion with these operations located in close proximity. The departing inmate then can be placed in the holding area until release. At discharge, the individuals can claim their property and leave through the controlled-access room. A proper design of this area will permit a combination of direct supervision and indirect supervision as the inmate is processed and released through the doorway operated by the control room staff.

Medical and Dental Services for Adults

Mary Hardy-Hall
Illinois Department of Corrections
Springfield, Illinois

Federal Medical Center, Butner, North Carolina.
Photo courtesy of the Federal Bureau of Prisons.

Health care administrators shared their wish lists and discussed some of their ideas of what would make their jobs more suitable for quick and efficient service. The following ideas are based on such discussions.

The numbers of inmates we are asked to provide care and custody for continues to rise. This precipitates the need for more bed space; however, that bed space is seldom in the area of health care. New beds are usually for general population inmates. However, as we incarcerate more individuals, health issues increasingly become more prevalent.

Patients in correctional settings are required to be treated similarly to patients with similar ills in the general public. We must treat those with communicable diseases, AIDS, hepatitis, tuberculosis, and sexually transmitted diseases. We also must treat an aging population, female prisoners, juveniles, and others who have special needs.

Health Care Unit Design

The health care unit of a prison should be similar in size and style to that of an outpatient community clinic. Health care administrators' primary request for changes in prison health care units appears to be "larger is better." Increased emphasis on specific treatments creates the need for specific amenities to provide adequate health care. Some amenities beneficial to the caregiver as well as to those receiving the care would include the items on the following page.

How many times have you asked a coworker or a member of your family, "Are you listening to me?" How many times have you wished you could ask the architects designing your correctional health care facilities that question? Didn't they hear you or didn't they listen to you when you requested more space for examinations, more storage space, emergency trauma units that are self-contained, isolation units for contagious diseases, appropriate space to dispose of sharps, suitable security, and so forth, just to name a few issues?

Checklist for Architects and Planners of Health Care Amenities

- **Individual treatment rooms** with amenities such as running water, wall suction and oxygen lines, a small desk area, a small storage area, an examination table, a physician's stool and chair, and good security observation

- **Separate waiting rooms** for male and female inmates easily observable by assigned security staff and health care staff

- **Interview/sick call rooms**—providing privacy and confidentiality for an increasing population in need of particular services—good security observation would be a must

- **Restrooms** to obtain specimens for laboratory work

- A room equipped for a **laboratory** in the treatment area

- A separate area for **dispensing medications**

- Rooms to treat **on-site emergencies**

- An eight-to-twelve-bed **infirmary** with adequate restrooms in compliance with the Americans with Disabilities Act

- **A storage room for clean medical supplies** and an area for dirty medical supplies

- **A storage area for ambulation aids,** such as crutches and wheelchairs

- **A physical therapy room** with a treatment table and parallel bars

- Adequate space for **dental** care

- Adequate space for **mental health** professionals

- An office for the medical **director**

- An additional physician's **office for specialists** on contract

- A separate **nursing office area with a view of the treatment area**

- **Shower and bathing** facilities for health care workers

- An area adequate for **medical files**

- **Pharmacy** space

- **Isolation rooms for communicable diseases** with negative airflow and an antichamber for controlled access and reduced risk of contamination

- **Conference room**(s)

- **Training rooms** for educational purposes

- Approved containers for **bio-hazardous medical waste**

- Panic buttons, off-hook telephone alarms, or other **communications** technologies should be provided in spaces wherever medical staff are alone with an inmate

Requirements

Legislators are becoming more cognizant of the health care needs of citizens. Incarcerated persons' health care needs parallel those same needs. Correctional institutions must provide medical services for inmates with an eye on the level of care (commensurate with community standards) and cost, as well as security implications. With court intervention and the passage of the Americans with Disabilities Act requirements, many alterations to health care facilities in and out of prisons are necessary. Many of these changes, additions, and renovations are beneficial and should be included whenever new health care facilities are constructed.

Grab bars in all areas, accessible bathing, wheelchair accessibility, handrails, step stools, the widening of hallways and examination rooms are just a few of the items needed not only to meet specific requirements but as valuable tools in the care of all patients. Install double swinging doors to the emergency area and enlarge all doorframes from the entrance of the health care unit to the emergency room for easier access. Building the health care unit on the ground floor of a building would ensure access without the need for entrance steps or a ramp.

Traffic Pattern

Control of traffic flow from a central waiting room into individual areas without staff having to pass through the waiting room would make the health care unit more usable. For staff to walk from the nurses' station through the waiting area each time they enter an examination room is an inefficient use of time and a distraction. Patient flow could be improved with the installation of parallel access/egress.

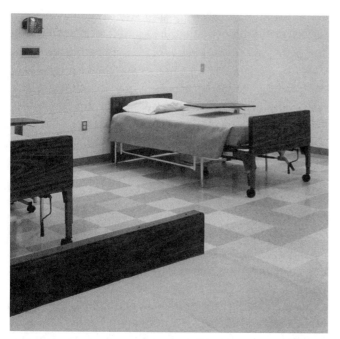

Typical multibed infirmary allows staff to supervise several inmates. However, separate rooms are required for inmates with contagious diseases.

Photo courtesy of Kennedy Associates Incorporated, St. Louis, Missouri. Photographer: Alise O'Brien, architectural photography.

Design should be such that security staff are not required to leave their post to escort inmates to specific clinics and/or examination rooms and still allow staff good visibility down all corridors. Solid doors should be eliminated and a window should be provided in each door. The installation of one-way mirrored windows in a centralized location would permit health care staff and security staff to monitor activities in waiting rooms, emergency treatment rooms, and examination rooms.

Inmate waiting areas should be enlarged and separate from the common entrance for staff and emergency providers. The waiting area should be separate from the patient examination area. The waiting area should be centralized and monitored by video camera. Entrance and exit by inmates to the health care unit should be in two different locations, thus reducing security concerns.

Mental Health Accommodations

Mental health patients need isolation yet constant surveillance. Special features needed for mentally ill patients should include crisis care rooms directly visible from the nurse's and officer's stations. Video monitors should be installed to assist with the required surveillance.

Crisis rooms need to have drains in the floors for ease in cleaning, no linoleum on the floors, vents that would not permit materials to be woven through for construction of nooses, observation windows that are not easily defaced, and water shut-off valves easily accessed for each room.

Geriatric Patient Accommodations

The increased influx of weak and very old inmates, and middle-aged inmates with significant health problems into the nation's prisons and jails, warrants special attention. Most often these inmates are referred to as "geriatric" inmates. Many are maturing adults, but there are also many inmates who are middle-aged adults, who because of their lives on the streets that included significant alcohol and drug abuse, are in physically poor health, and require assistance with activities of daily living and personal care needs. (*See also* Section 2.4).

Needs for geriatric patients must be based on individual cases but may include such things as the need for a lift, sight-impaired and hearing-impaired alarm systems, handrails and seats in showers, risers and/or rails in toilet areas, and dayroom/dining space. The geriatric infirmary room needs to be equipped with a sink, toilet, and shower for easy access. Electric hospital beds should be provided.

Geriatric patients require more intense monitoring. The addition of cameras in ward rooms would greatly enhance the ability to closely monitor these inmates. An observation window in ward rooms would be helpful. Cameras, in particular, would decrease patient falls by allowing staff to visualize an inmate trying to get out of bed. The ability to maintain constant surveillance would decrease the vulnerability of the geriatric inmates to other inmates. The geriatric patients need to be separated from the in-patient/crisis care area.

Emergency Room

Emergency treatment areas must be easily accessible and equipped with essentials. They should be equipped to deal with emergency situations, including emergency medications, x-ray capability, intravenous materials, wall suction and oxygen lines, a triage area, and splints and casting materials.

Installation of one-way mirrored windows between the nursing-supervisor's offices and the emergency room would permit nursing supervisors to monitor activity in the emergency room. During emergency situations, the

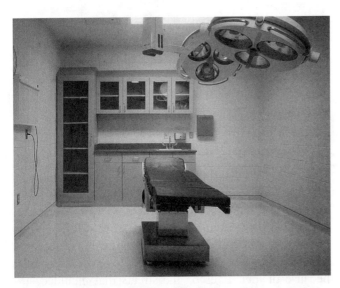

Although spartan finishes are used, the emergency treatment room must be capable of dealing with injuries and medical emergencies initially. Federal Correctional Complex-High Security, Beaumont, Texas.

Photo courtesy of NBBJ, Columbus, Ohio. Photographer: Wes Thompson.

administrative and security staff would be able to monitor activity while reducing the number of persons in the emergency room while treatment was in progress.

Wider halls to the emergency/treatment rooms were consistently requested by nearly all of the health care administrators contacted. Enough room for carts, beds, and other essential equipment to be maneuvered is compulsory. Separation of emergency rooms into individual treatment areas addresses the need for privacy and space.

Conclusion

This chapter addresses only a very small portion of the needs of health care units. There are many other areas that need attention: female offenders, juvenile offenders, inmates with communicable diseases, and so forth. Architects and designers are encouraged to meet with health care administrators when planning a health care unit. **Listen** to what they need, **listen** to what they want, and **listen** to what will work.

Proper Correctional Food Service Design

Richard Hopkins, FCSI, CFSP
Hopkins Foodservice Specialists
Cabin John, Maryland

At first glance, the purpose of inmate food service is to provide the prisoners with nourishing meals that will maintain their constitution. However, behind closed doors, one may find the staff readily admitting that the purpose of food service goes beyond hunger-control to keeping the inmates quiet and happy with the emphasis on quiet.

A sideline to feeding is using food service as an inmate occupation. Depending on the inmate profile (ranging from male to female, youth to geriatric, minimum to maximum security) correctional food service departments employing inmate labor can have widely varying design criteria. For instance, while free inmate labor is often employed, many jails hold pretrial detainees with short-term housing requirements, which results in wild swelling and ebbing prisoner counts. Although there is always more than an adequate supply of inmates willing to work, the turnover at jails all but eliminates adequate time to identify and train cooperative inmates in food service. Transiency and worker mentality are issues that need to be seriously taken into account when designing food service areas for a particular institution.

The use of inmate workers in the preparation of food can help keep food costs down and also reduce inmate idleness. However, kitchen designs must support this mission while providing a safe and secure work environment. As an example, if inmates are classified as maximum security, the need to provide staff observation to all areas of the kitchen is essential. Securing all kitchen

Centralized food preparation in most institutions is commonplace. The choice of centralizing dining versus decentralizing it to the housing units is an important operating decision. Here at the Federal Correctional Institution and Prison Camp in Cumberland, Maryland, inmates walk outside from their housing and program spaces to a central dining area.

Photo courtesy of the Federal Bureau of Prisons.

utensils in locked cabinets at the end of the workday or the use of shadow boards for utensil inventory is also a necessity.

Therefore, the designer of a food service facility in a correctional institution first must consider the inmate profile. By working within the parameters outlined by the inmate profile, the design team can deliver and secure the success of the food service facility.

Architectural Consultant's Perspectives on Food Service Design

Both the client and their architects are well served when an experienced food service consultant is a member of the design team. Consider the perspective of the architectural firm charged with the overall design and oversight of several design disciplines (such as, engineering, civil, security, and fire protection). Their thrust is directed to the big-picture objective of getting the building open on time and within budget.

The overall functionality of the facility is widely determined on an on/off basis. The doors open or close, the cameras hum, the lights go on at dusk and off at dawn with precision. The business of corrections demands such a pass/fail, open/closed, nonsecure/secure condition. There is zero tolerance for less than absolute conditions, such as an almost fully locked door.

However, the production and delivery of food in any environment, including corrections, rarely runs like clockwork. A food service project is judged successful when the operator can respond quickly and easily to a myriad of potential problems. The jail or prison benefits when the architectural team has retained a food service consultant who, while working in tandem with the larger design team, will be skillful enough to foresee all the details of the day-to-day operational requirements and address, by design, the problems and crises that could appear. A good design addresses not only the rare "normal" day, but also the second and third-level backup plans when things do not go right.

These backup plans should be defined in the design program. They should state, for the benefit of the operator as much as for the design team, how meals will be served despite a multitude of labor, inventory, equipment, utility, or security incidents that arise on a "normal" day in the correctional kitchen.

Importance of Food Service Programming

The program is the foundation of a well-designed food service facility. Initial interviews are held with the owner, the architect, and the construction management firm (applicable to design-build projects) to get the basic parameters such as size, number of inmates, future population capacity, meal production system (such as cook-chill/retherm—the reheating and completion of cooking at the location, cook-serve), and meal delivery system (such as central dining, cell, or dayroom feeding), and so forth.

Food production areas must be designed to permit ease of movement, staff supervision, and flexibility for equipment replacement or upgrade with minimal downtime.

Photo courtesy of Gilbane Building Co., Providence, Rhode Island.

The sequence of service then is reviewed with the owner, and the owner is invited to challenge each assumption. For example, beginning at the loading dock, the consultant may pose the assumption that the deliveries from the central institution warehouse will occur five days a week; therefore, the kitchen storage inside the compound will be required to provide enough space to store the nine meals to be served on Saturday, Sunday, and Monday. According to the food service designer, this adequacy of space would allow sufficient time for Monday's meal to be defrosted for cooking on Monday.

Instead, the owner may listen to the theoretical dialog and redirect the consultant. By staging Monday's meals in the warehouse area from the warehouse freezer into the warehouse cooler, Monday's meals still can be defrosted in time, and the design team can reduce costly freezer and cooler storage-space inside the security perimeter by 27 percent. The food service consultant continues to narrate the process from storage to preparation to service and onto clean up.

At each step, recommended security procedures are discussed. The kinds of security features vary according to the security level. For example, at a work camp, where inmates are scheduled to be reintroduced into society, padlocks on food warmer covers are not necessary. Inmates are expected to act responsibly as a condition of their release. On the other hand, in a long-term high-security facility, inmates may want to tamper with exposed controls; therefore, the design justifies specially designed tamper-proof fasteners and locking covers.

In certain institutions, staff are served meals as part of their contract agreement. In other facilities, staff purchase meals. A separate staff dining facility is required. Federal Correctional Complex Allenwood, Pennsylvania.

Photo courtesy of the Federal Bureau of Prisons.

The sequence of service, design parameters, and justifications should be documented in a written program broken down by the same sequence of service (receiving, placing in frozen storage, preparing, delivering the meal, and so forth). This not only will serve as the basis for proceeding but also for evaluating future changes or modifications to the original design.

The justifications are particularly important. Like an engineer's calculation sheets, the justifications "prove" the capacity of the design. On one project, the owner requested three palletized cubes of food storage and pointed to the twelve-foot high freezer used on past projects. The program analysis justified an increase to the walk-in height. Although the three pallets of food could fit in the twelve-foot high storage freezer requested by the owner, an additional twelve inches was needed for the pallet hoist to raise the highest pallet to clear the front edge of the shelving .

The food service program is generally a tool prepared and issued to the client for approval during the schematic design phase. Ideally, the food service program is revisited during design development, updated to reflect the design development plan, and reissued to the owner. The owner then will have the opportunity to reconfirm and track small changes made to the design.

This program resubmission is especially important because the owner is usually not one person but a group of client representatives. The one person typically charged with reviewing food service often is engaged heavily in operations management. This person may not be aware of decisions made by other owner representatives until the design program is reissued as part of the next formal submission.

An owner who shares experiences and successful design solutions with peers in other institutions can be a valuable design ally to the experienced and objective food service consultant. Rather than design by direction, the owner and the designer, in an open and frank discussion, can evaluate all the merits of an idea. It is common for a "design solution" generated in a working operation only to be partially adaptable to new construction. For example, a field recommendation was made to provide thirty-four inches of empty space on the beverage counter. On inquiry, the owner indicated that the additional space was to be reserved for portable insulated beverage carriers that would be used in the event the coffee urn broke down (remember the "backup plan"). Since insulated carriers are notorious for their leaky faucets, the food service consultant suggested extending the drip tray in front of the reserved space.

Inmate Impact on Equipment Selection

Inmates have a lot of time on their hands, which can result in trouble. Regardless of their dispositions, inmates have no altruistic interests in using and maintaining the kitchen for the long-term benefit of the prison system. To keep inmates from removing equipment parts, to ensure durability, and because of incessant use, correctional food service equipment should be of special construction. The philosophical inclination toward rehabilitating through providing residential or normalized appearances clashes with security and maintenance issues in this area.

High-tech equipment solutions also are not justified in this environment. Why for example, compact or pulp trash in a minimum-security facility when there is ample labor to haul it out the backdoor to the dumpster? While high-tech equipment is typically specified to save labor, in the correctional environment, the amount of work required is not the issue; rather, the objective is to maximize the number of workers required in the kitchen.

Circulation space is also very important in food service design to avoid body contact made necessary in a crowded kitchen. The inmate laborer, because of either lack of care or of skill, will maneuver a mobile cart with a pallet into walls, the walk-in cooler, table legs, or hand sinks, particularly in executing turns. Wider aisles and careful layout of equipment can reduce these problems.

Central dining facilities can be extremely spartan or more highly finished. The most important consideration is that selected finishes are easy to clean and maintain. Federal Correctional Complex-Low Security, Beaumont, Texas.

Photo courtesy of NBBJ, Columbus, Ohio. Photographer: Wes Thompson.

Kitchen and servery design must provide the necessary features that eliminate hiding contraband in such areas as in table legs, under counters, behind access panels, in ceilings, and so forth. For example, the manufacturer's correctional package may call for welding the drain screen in place on a braising pan. A better and more secure solution would be to weld the screen to a short length of stainless steel chain that would allow the screen to be scrubbed and sanitized in the well of the braising pan.

Specially designed security features on "correctional-package" food service equipment are as various as the different equipment manufacturers. The American Correctional Food Service Association has begun work on standardizing security devices. The consultant should specify that each manufacturer state the specific components of their security hardware protection, and that the shop drawings show the exact method of fabrication and assembly of these components. For example, one manufacturer shipped a jail a four-inch by eighteen-inch hinged locking control-cover on an oven with the hinge on the four-inch end instead of the eighteen-inch end. The cover had no structural integrity to hold it to the oven and lasted two days under inmate use before the

inmate-operator left it broken in the unlocked position. Not only are well-designed fasteners important, but a consistent manner of tamper-proof fastening of the various pieces of food service equipment is recommended. Multiple types of fasteners delay service and maintenance.

Special security features need to be carefully justified for each piece of equipment. For example, a security feature that disallows regular maintenance may be passed over (in other words, a tamper-proof screen on a washer heater element that probably will require regular repair).

Administrators and designers must consider equipment assembly and subassembly. If components are lost or stolen, the equipment may not function. If the inmate assembles the equipment in the wrong manner, on startup the equipment can be damaged. Fundamentally, the simpler the construction the better. This concept extends to utility connections, as well. Why, for example, mount the electrical outlet under a worktable? Often, the contractor misses the rough-in point. An inmate can use it for a footrest or it can be sheared open by a cart and short circuited. Instead, use twist lock plugs on the mobile cart or processor and lock them into overhead pigtail outlets above the worktable out of water and harms way.

Hot Spots to Avoid

Bringing on the Food Service Consultant Too Late

Early on in the design process, the overall footprint of the building is established by the totality of the departmental requirements and their respective subdepartments. (For example, food service is a department and dry storage is a subdepartment.) The sizes of these spaces can be taken off of previous projects if the other projects had the same inmate profile. The owner may assume that all things are equal and claim to offer the project a prototype design. The design team negotiates reduced fees because the programming conceptually has been completed and embodied into the prototype.

What frequently occurs is that the new project shares only some of the similarities with the prototype. The architect falls into this pitfall. The architect creates the spatial area allocation based on the owner's direction that, in theory, fits the need, but, in actuality, fits neither the equipment nor takes into consideration the nonlinear factor of circulation. When the food service consultant is not brought onto the team until later in the project, and the architect is committed to a facility size and budget at the outset of the project that is not viable, conflict is inevitable. If additional space is not added, the client will face the consequences of building a facility that provides less than the desired capacity or efficiency.

Delaying All Regulatory Reviews to Permit Stage

The owner's food service reviewer and health department reviewer need to be identified and consulted early on in the project and at each submission. Lack of departmental approval of the design may find the design team proceeding to the 65 or the 100 percent level of design completion only to have a torrent of contradictory direction and requirements pour in from the health department or a recently identified operator or department charged with running the facility.

Out of Sequence Value Engineering

Value engineering increasingly is being incorporated into the design process. The key to successful value engineering depends on when it takes place. Once the project is at the 50 to 60 percent level of completion, the design development phase, there is adequate information for a cost estimator to validate the budget. While there is still room for flexibility, the owner can elect to exercise cost-

The kitchen at South Woods State Prison, Bridgeton, New Jersey is organized for maximum efficiency but designed to enable inmates to provide the help.

Photo courtesy of L. Robert Kimball & Associates, Ebensburg, Pennsylvania

cutting options in equipment specification and its method of installation.

The common practice of allowing dealer-recommended substitutions to reduce the cost of food service equipment after the project had been awarded is usually the least cost-effective way to reduce the project cost. There is little or no incentive for any contractor to evaluate the operational impact, long-term maintenance and replacement cost when proposing equipment with a lower-acquisition cost. By the end of design, the design team may have long-since forgotten some of the many factors that led to a particular equipment selection or to an integrated solution to a problem.

A dealer-requested substitution may be successfully considered if the design team has an updated design program or a project log that states key points and the original analysis factors. With this handy information, a sound decision regarding a substitution can be made.

Relying on the Kitchen Equipment Dealer for Equipment Expertise

There is a consistently shrinking pool of qualified food service dealers and installers. Some price-conscious owners and lowest-bid contractors have benefited from price wars and underbidding tactics of food service equipment dealers. The result is that there are fewer dealers able to stay in business; of those, fewer still have a reliable knowledge base, or installation skill base. A proper installation is necessary to uphold warranty claims and to ensure that complex refrigeration, cooking exhaust hoods, and waste disposal systems will continue to operate much past their first year without owner complaints.

Complex systems (for example, dishwashers, remote refrigeration, pulping systems) should be specified to be installed by factory authorized and trained installers. At a minimum, the manufacturer should be required to certify and sign-off on the installation, thereby removing the ambiguity in the manufacturer's warranty language.

For owner confidence in the integrity of the finished project, the interaction among the general contractor, the kitchen contractor, and the manufacturers of major systems mandates some structured communication.

Conclusion

A secure adult or juvenile detention facility is buttressed by a well-run and productive food service operation. Good design is the most basic aspect of good food service management.

Mailroom for Adults and Juveniles

Major Don Bales
Maryland Division of Corrections (Retired)
Gerrardstown, West Virginia

During initial planning for a new prison, the mail-room is usually not a first priority. However, it does not take long after the institution goes on line to realize that the mailroom is not big enough.

Often, a mail and package receiving area is incorporated into the administration building, which is outside the secure perimeter of the institution. This location is useful to provide for electronic inspection for contraband before anything is moved into the institution. As a result of this location, business mail and other package delivery personnel would not have to go through a metal detector before entering the mailroom.

Historically, the mailroom has been responsible for a multitude of tasks, over and above processing the mail for the institution's administration staff and the inmate population. Before the use of computers, inmate mail was received, opened, and inspected for contraband, and the mail clerk had to verify the location (cell number) from a hand-typed roster (that changed every day). Today, hopefully, the typed roster has been replaced by information on computer workstations that allow the mail clerk to verify each inmate's present location. The inmate's location still must be verified before the mail is sent to the cell area for delivery.

In addition to distributing the mail, the mailroom was the place where stamps, money orders, and photographs were logged. The logbooks that the inmate signed verifying receipt of the mail also were kept in the mailroom. The mailroom received packages for inmates and staff.

In many systems, if an inmate received clothing, the mailroom would call the inmate clothing/property room to verify that the inmate was able to legally add to his or her clothing record. In some systems, third-class mail (especially catalogs) completely filled the mailroom.

Today, many systems write policies and procedures to assure the mailroom runs smoothly. At times, the mailroom is the place where there is a fine line drawn between the First Amendment and what is considered "a clear and present danger." The prison mailroom planner still must consider what services the facility wants the mailroom to provide. Typically, mailrooms perform the following tasks:

1. Receive, sort, shake out for contraband, address, and place in containers for delivery, all incoming inmate mail.

2. Receive, sort, address, log, all incoming inmate legal mail.

3. Log all money orders received, if these are allowed. The inmate should endorse the money order, and return it to the mailroom for further processing (to the business office for deposit, and so forth).

4. Sort and deliver or place in mailboxes all incoming mail for prison staff.

5. Process all outgoing mail for pickup by postal authorities. Custody staff on slow shifts could do this or the control center on the second shift might be tasked with this responsibility.

6. Process all prison administration letters and packages for shipment by various carriers, such as United Parcel Service, Federal Express, or the U.S. Postal Service.

7. Process interoffice correspondence, interdepartment, and interagency mail for delivery by special truck.

To do all this without staff bumping into each other, there should be a minimum space of 500 square feet.

Additionally, the mailroom needs the following things:

- Boxes on the wall to sort department mail for easy access by department heads
- Boxes on the wall to sort inmate mail, depending on how the living/cell areas are constructed, for example: housing units 1, 2, and so forth; cell blocks A, B, C; cottage

All institutions need clearly marked inmate letter drops throughout the facility. For the campus style facility, inmate letter drops that look like the metal boxes on the street should be used. A sturdy design that is attack resistant offers security for the mail. If mail pickup by inmates is permitted, the inmate mailroom should be centrally located near other support and program functions. This allows inmates to pick up mail as part of their daily routine. Inmates can purchase stamps, cards, and writing materials from the canteen/commissary using funds from their inmate account or by use of a debit card if that system is in use.

The location of the mailroom varies from institution to institution. In some cases, all mail is brought to one location within the secure perimeter of the facility, sorted there for inmate versus staff mail and then distributed to various parts of the facility, including the housing units. In other cases, institutions have two separate post office boxes for staff and inmate mail. The staff and business mail is taken to the administrative area of the facility, sorted, and then distributed. The inmate mail is taken to a separate locale typically within the secure perimeter of the facility and processed at that location using x-ray and other technology to search for contraband and weapons before distribution.

The mailroom needs good environmental controls, including heating, cooling, and humidity control. There should be a sufficient source of overhead light and avoid workstation desk lamps.

Each mail handler/clerk needs a desk/workstation, with access to the inmate population database. A new facility needs to be prewired for computers, and have sufficient outlets for other electrical equipment. The mail handler/clerk work space should include several four-foot-by-eight-foot tables. Additionally, there should be tables or stands for x-ray equipment for packages, a postage meter, and a mail counter. Many states now require a stamp on all outgoing inmate mail indicating the date it was received in the mailroom. Usually, the facility has twenty-four hours to process outgoing inmate mail and get it to the post office.

Other supplies needed include the following: scales, at least one safe, file cabinets, and carts to easily move mail bags around the room. Mail can be delivered by the postal service but, generally, because of the volume of the mail, a correctional officer typically is assigned to pick up the mail each day. They use a standard small truck to do this task and deliver all the mail initially to the administration building. From there, it is often separated and taken to two locations for processing, as noted earlier. Due to the sensitive nature of the mail, in most institutions either staff distribute the mail or they supervise the distribution.

For an institution with a population of 2,500 inmates, in an average month, more than 78,000 inmate letters (total in and out) would be processed. Mail increases during the Christmas season. This number does not include mail and packages for the prison administration. For a facility of this size, the average number of full-time mailroom staff is three.

The mailroom should not do any of the following:

- Do not answer any telephone, except the one at the workstation.
- Do not have the institution switchboard (PBX) in the mailroom.
- Do not receive anything from visitors for inmates. Other personnel should be used behind a pass-through window if it is the institution's policy to accept any property from visitors for inmates.
- Do not receive inmate packages. This needs to be done by the clothing/property room and can be done in concert with the commissary.
- Do not be responsible for verifying that inmates have sufficient funds in their account to send money from the institution by mail. This should be done in the business office before cutting the check.
- Do not accept stamps. Inmates should buy these from the commissary, with special provision made for indigent inmates.

Once an agency has accepted its building, it is difficult to change the size of any area, including the allocation for the mailroom. Sometimes the law says no changes for a set number of years. For the older institutions that need more space in the mailroom, some other department will have to give up some of its space. The decision about how to do this usually is the responsibility of the managing officer. Good prior planning, and allowing room for growth in the inmate population are the best ways to be sure that the mailroom is adequate for the needs of the expanding population of the facility.

Most county juvenile facilities are small. The mail is delivered by the handful. Larger juvenile institutions, for longer-term confinements, need a mailroom that functions the same as those in the adult institutions.

Mailroom staff usually are not the highest paid staff in the institution. However, they place their hands, sight, and even their lives at risk, every time they open a letter. This provides all the more reason for sophisticated electronic scanning of all incoming mail.

Adult Personal Care Services/Barber Services

John Thalacker
Fort Dodge Correctional Facility
Fort Dodge, Iowa

Being sued by an inmate for a "bad haircut" courtesy of the prison barber, while a nuisance, may be among the least of the difficulties institution administrators face as they provide hair care service to inmates. Barber and/or beautician services, when not planned and administered with security in mind, can lead to deadly situations.

As might be expected, institutions or systems that have experienced a serious injury or death due to misuse of barber or beauty shop equipment or lack of supervision exercise tighter control than those that have not thus far had such an unpleasant experience. Quite simply, the risk to staff and inmates is increased if inmates are allowed to work as barbers. They then have access to sharpened objects and dangerous chemicals. They may work in locations that are not easily supervised, and because they are doing what is considered "routine," they may not be carefully monitored.

Typically, in juvenile facilities, independent barbers are hired to come into the institution to cut hair. Therefore, juveniles' access to barbering tools is minimized.

It is expensive to assign enough staff to supervise a small area to prevent contraband from being exchanged for services, messages passed through the barber/beautician grapevine, or favored treatment given to some inmates at the expense of others. Problems that occur in providing barber and cosmetology services, however, can be decreased by the proper design of facilities. This chapter will address five factors to consider when planning and designing hair care space at a new prison or remodeling an existing facility. These factors are (1) code requirements, (2) philosophy, (3) security level, (4) size of population, and (5) staffing considerations.

Code Requirements

To insure consistent public health standards, state legislatures have created specific laws on the operation of barber and beauty shops. These vary from state to state. Beyond the code, many jurisdictions also have an administrative code, which addresses how a state agency deals with the public. While not having the same authority as law, these rules, as they are commonly referred to, are second only to law in power. They exceed correctional department policy.

Generally, hair care requirements are found as a subsection under public health department rules and give even greater detail about what services, such as sanitation of equipment and the prevention of infectious and contagious diseases, must be available to every customer who gets his or her hair cut or handled in that state. Careful reading of the regulations will determine if hair removal in adult and juvenile correctional facilities must follow all the stipulations required for hair care of the general public.

Philosophy Within the System

All prisons and jails want to insure that weapons and other contraband cannot be concealed in hair. Beyond that, there is broad philosophical difference among jurisdictions about inmate grooming. There also may be differences between institutions in the same jurisdiction.

In some locations, policymakers and legislators believe that the jail/prison experience should be the most demeaning and unpleasant event in a person's life. This is evident by reviewing the personal care products available in the facility canteen or commissary. A very limited number in quantity and variety will indicate little flexibility in what will be permitted. Another example that reflects this philosophy would be the prevalence of or the requirement for a buzz cut similar to the haircut at a military boot camp.

Other leaders believe that an adult inmate's or juvenile's self-esteem and behavior can be improved by permitting at least some choices in self-care. At those locations, attendance at classes in grooming will be encouraged and space provided to support individualized choices in appearance. Commissary lists will have a wide variety of products available in these jurisdictions.

The agency and local institution policy manual, if available, will give direction as to philosophy. In addition, although not standards that absolutely must be achieved for accreditation, the American Correctional Association's standards addresses this issue in its standards for hair care services.

Security Level

The third consideration should be the planned security level of the facility. Among staff, and increasingly the public, the most secure prisons are known as "supermax," the least-secure "minimum," with "maximum" and "medium" in between. There are also lock-up units within all levels of institutions for the temporary holding of hard-to-manage inmates or those confined due to disciplinary action. For planning purposes, lock-up units can be included in the supermax definition. Generally speaking, the higher the security level, the more supervision is provided for each activity, the smaller the variety of activities offered, and the least individuality permitted. At all levels, the first question in planning should be: does the inmate come to the service or is the service delivered to the inmate?

In most supermax or lock-ups within other security level institutions, the barber/beautician delivers their service to the inmate. The usual physical requirements include:

- A location outside the person's cell
- A chair to which the inmate can be restrained either in leg or wrist and belly chain restraints, or both
- Space for attending staff
- Electrical power to operate clippers

Storage space for hair-cutting equipment and hair-washing sinks generally is not required because the barbers/beauticians bring their own tools and equipment with them, and they remove the equipment once they have completed their work.

American Correctional Association Standards for Hair Care Services

For Adult Correctional Institutions:
from *Standards for Adult Correctional Institutions*, Third Edition

Standard 3-4251 under General Conditions of Confinement, requires "Written policy, procedure, and practice provide that inmates in segregation receive . . . barbering, and hair care services . . . on the same basis as inmates in the general population."

Standard 3-4271 under Freedom in Personal Grooming requires "Written policy, procedure, and practice allow freedom in personal grooming except when a valid interest justifies otherwise." The discussion or comment section emphasizes the least-restrictive regulations necessary so long as "safety, security, identification, and hygiene" requirements are met.

Standard 3-4325 under Hair Care services, requires "Written policy, procedure, and practice provide that

hair care services that comply with applicable health requirements are available to inmates." The comment section in its entirety is as follows: "Large facilities should designate a room for hair care services; small facilities can use any multipurpose room. In all cases, hair should be cut under sanitary conditions and in an area that permits observation by staff. Equipment should be stored securely when not in use."

For Juvenile Community Residential Facilities:
Standard 3-JCRF-4C-21 requires "Written policy, procedure, and practice provide instructions and assistance in personal hygiene, grooming, and health care."

For Small Juvenile Detention Facilities
Standard 1-SJD-4B-14 is "There are hair care services available to juveniles."

For inmates in general population maximum custody and all other security levels, inmates have barber services either in their housing unit or at a central location. If space is a premium in a central services building, if movement of inmates is either inconvenient, risky for security, or hampered by weather, or if the unit management concept is in practice, barber/beautician services at the unit are particularly appealing. On the other hand, a central site is preferred if the following conditions exist: movement within the compound is desired, cell housing space is at a premium, and space can be made available for the projected number of people using the service. With both approaches, unobstructed vision of the site is imperative. For certain cosmetology services, the chemicals used may require a site with excellent ventilation.

If the facility has a unit management approach to services, a room with electrical services is needed in the housing unit, pod, wing, or whatever is described as the local living unit. This room will be used for multiple services at different times of the week or even on the same day. For example, if a sink and electrical power is made available, the barber shop or beauty parlor may serve at another time as a group-treatment room, a site for the distribution of laundry or contracted canteen goods, or as a music practice room.

The room can be designed to have either direct or indirect supervision by staff. In a direct supervision mode, a staff member either is present physically in the room or is roving in the general area. This person is responsible for monitoring traffic to and from the site, discouraging loitering, and checking in and out barber/beautician equipment. In the indirect supervision method, the supervision would be from a central control point where the officer would control access through electronically operated doors, view activity through a large window into the room, and decide the order in which inmates or juveniles would be permitted access to the service.

In using a central site to provide barber services, three layouts are most frequently used—linear, circular, and stand-alone. The first two provide for indirect or direct supervision in conjunction with other tasks. The stand-alone layout is used if space for hair cutting cannot be provided in conjunction with other services and direct supervision is required.

In the linear supervision model, there would be a room with direct access to a corridor used extensively by staff with large windows and few blind spots from the corridor. While staff can be encouraged to travel through that area, this method works best if staff MUST use the cor-

ridor at frequent and random times when the barber/beauty shop would be open. It is not effective if the shop is open when few staff are in the area, such as in the evening, on weekends, or on holidays.

In the circular layout, a core of services surround or circle an open area within a building that is patrolled by a staff member. Activities such as laundry, music, group treatment, and barber/beauty services can be conducted simultaneously in separate rooms. Again, large windows from the corridor or dayroom should be provided to permit vision into each area. The advantage of being able to see into all the rooms with a turn of the head also is a disadvantage. That is, the inmates on the opposite side from whatever activity is being observed also can see the direction of the staff's attention.

The stand-alone approach gives the best supervision because if the population size is large enough to support a multichair shop, it can be in a separate room away from other services and heavily traveled areas. This reduces the number of people who would be in the area for other reasons. In a few locales, vocational training is offered in hair care/cosmetology services. In addition to electrical outlets with ground fault protection and sinks with hot and cold water, a vacuum system may be considered as part of the clipping method or for general hair removal. There is a need for locked storage of chemicals used for permanents and hair straightening.

Size of Inmate Population

The fourth factor to consider is the overall inmate population and whether the population is all classified at the same security level. With a population of a few hundred in a central location, no more than one site would be needed to provide hair-cutting services. Generally, one barber can provide at least three haircuts per hour. Whether services are centralized or unitized, the sheer volume of people having their hair cut must be calculated and assessed to determine how much space would be used. Permanents and hair straightening, if offered, take longer, and this should be factored into the consideration. Juveniles tend to be supervised in smaller groups and this group size will help determine the size of the area, including the waiting space.

Staffing Consideration

Administrators always are looking for ways to use available staff better. As indicated earlier, if there has been a serious injury or death in the system due to inmate access to barber equipment, there will be interest in providing a higher level of supervision. Taking into account vacations, holidays, sick leave, and other leaves, an eight-hour post filled seven days a week will require approximately 1.4 to 1.6 staff members on the roster. Obviously, when staff also are supervising other areas, the cost for barber supervision decreases, but at a potential risk for unauthorized use of barber equipment and/or violence.

Conclusion

By considering code requirements, philosophy, security level, size of population, and staffing considerations during the planning and building phases for barber/cosmetology services, the safety of staff and inmates will be increased and enhanced for years to come. As is true in every aspect of prison life, however, how staff manage the inmates in their custody will be the greatest factor in providing safe and secure barber/cosmetology services.

3.7

Personal Care and Other Privacy Issues for Women Offenders and Female Juveniles

Judy C. Anderson
Department of Juvenile Justice
Columbia, South Carolina

Female offenders pose a challenge and present an opportunity to the responsible adult and juvenile agencies that must provide for their care and supervision, usually in multifunctional facilities having multilevels of custody. The rate of growth in the adult and juvenile female offender population exceeds that of the males, at least doubling in the past few years. In 1997, women accounted for 6.4 percent of all incarcerated adults, or almost 80,000 women. Juvenile female delinquency resulting in detention and commitment admissions has increased more than male delinquency from 1989 to 1993.

Historically, adult and juvenile female offenders have comprised a small percentage of incarcerated people. Throughout the years, the varying views on females as well as corrections, and the prevailing conditions in society have made an impact on the type of treatment and programming females received, with a recent emphasis on sameness, but not parity. As noted by Morton (in press), this overdose of equality will continue until administrators, both male and female, begin to understand the complexities of parity.

The unique needs of adult and juvenile female offenders have long been recognized by practitioners. The National Congress on Penitentiary and Reformatory Discipline held in 1870 included in its Declaration of Principles a resolution on female offenders. The American Correctional Association, which evolved from this meeting, endorsed a Public Correctional Policy on Female Offender Services in 1986 and reaffirmed it unanimously in 1991. The policy states, among other things, that the unique needs of the female population must be met through comparable and additional services to those provided for men.

During the past several years, social-behavioral scientists have realized that men and women communicate differently, that men deal in "things" or on a "need to know basis," while women tend to found their actions/reactions on relationships. In other words, adult and juvenile females are not men and boys and cannot be treated as such. Society recognizes that difference and has socialized each sex for different roles. While different cultures have different role expectations, the role model for women and girls in the United States is generally to be mother, wife, and companion as well as partial or sole breadwinner. The first three roles imply nurturing and intimacy, which usually involves some form of privacy and/or small group setting, in other words, a family/social group. Men are conditioned to be one of the team and, thus, appear to be more comfortable with larger settings and less privacy.

Privacy

Women's and girls' biological functions have resulted in a need for privacy, at least in our culture. Additionally, the courts have ruled that women and girls, as well as men, should be afforded privacy, but that the security needs of the facility and equal opportunity rights of the employees also must be protected. Cross gender supervision has been allowed for both sexes. Agencies must be sensitive to women's and girls' needs since many have witnessed or been victimized prior to entrance into the criminal justice system and must not be revictimized by the system, its policies, procedures, and practices and/or its employees.

Privacy is an issue that must be considered when designing or retrofitting a facility for women or girls. Some obvious areas for concern are personal care areas (showers, toilets, and sleeping space). Other less obvious ones include, but are not limited to, dayroom/living space, laundry services, cafeteria/food service, and visiting. Privacy in this context is defined as freedom from total observation of all movement/actions and/or an opportunity to be able to maintain personal space in a larger group setting. The American Correctional Association has addressed these issues through the standards set by the Commission on Accreditation for Corrections in all areas of corrections, both adult and juvenile.

Living Areas and Environment

Living areas for women and girls should be divided into pods or wings, with direct staff supervision. This allows continuous, direct contact by staff and a larger measure of freedom of movement for the women or girls. In addition to allowing the staff to know what is going on in all sections of the living area, it also provides for increased privacy for the offenders who usually can move in and out of their rooms/cells without staff control.

While visibility is important in the rooms/cells and can be provided through use of a window in the door, the offender also is able to not feel that she is in a glass fishbowl. Windows can be unobstructive if they are placed high in the door and are fairly small in size. If a larger window is required, it can be opaque on the bottom, which allows for visibility of movement, but without invading the offender's privacy while changing clothes, using the toilet, sleeping, and so forth. Another alternative would be to allow a curtain at the window during designated short periods of time. As noted earlier, many women and girls have been vic-

timized. It is important that the policies, procedures, and practices of any agency respect that and ensure that she is not victimized again either literally or figuratively. Examples of the latter include feelings of powerlessness, loss of control, and worthlessness.

The environment is important to women and girls who respond to "softer" environments, which include the use of color and respect for privacy. Pleasant, home-like surroundings encourage women to regain control of what they have lost, which helps reduce violence and foster pride. Allowing them to control lighting, have some flexibility in decorating their room/cell, and have some control over the door appear to be positive and therapeutic. Individual control of temperature, which could include opening of a secured window, is extremely important, as a female will experience significant body temperature shifts throughout her life (Carter, 1998).

Bathrooms

If toilets are located in the room/cell, the offender should be afforded privacy by the high or opaque window in the door. She should be allowed to have toilet paper and personal hygiene articles without having to ask staff for them each time she needs them. If this is not possible for some security reason, the staff member should be a female, and the exchange should take place without an audience, especially male staff.

If the toilets are in a common area (gang bathroom), privacy screens, and/or stalls with modified doors, so feet and top of the head can be seen, should be used. Another alternative, though more expensive, would be private stalls with doors opening into a supervised area.

Again, a high and/or opaque window in the stall doors would be necessary. Issuing pajamas/gowns and robes should be standard procedure for all female facilities, which affords both privacy inside the room (sleeping area) and in communal areas. A communal shower area should have individual stalls with either modified doors or shower curtains; gang showers are not acceptable for women and juveniles as they invade privacy and offer opportunities for further victimization by other offenders. Again, a better alternative, though more expensive, would be private showers with doors opening into an area which can be supervised.

A combination shower/bathtub or provision of several bathtubs, which offer privacy, would be optimum. Women frequently prefer tubs and often need to use one for various medical and hygienic reasons.

Sleeping Hours

Care must be taken to ensure that privacy is maintained during sleeping hours. Security checks can be made by using the window; ease in doing this can be improved by the use of night lights in the room/cell. This, coupled with the security dictum that "you must see flesh" will satisfy the security and safety needs of the institution and honor the privacy and safety needs of the offenders.

Since many of the women and juveniles have been victims of abuse, it is important to remember that even a touch on the arm while asleep can trigger posttraumatic stress disorder syndrome (PTSD), which manifests in flashbacks on the abuse and other reactions. Female staff always should be assigned to the living units at least during the sleeping hours.

Hair Care

Since appearance and good grooming are emphasized, rightly or wrongly, in our society, especially for women, hair care and personal grooming areas should be provided. Grooming areas can be available in the room/cell and sink areas by providing good lighting and mirrors. If made of stainless steel for security reasons, mirrors should be of good quality and provide good reflection. An alternative would be to cover mirrors with other material such as clear polycarbonate or similar material, thus allowing a good image, but with safety maintained. Cosmetics should be available through the canteen/commissary with a wide range to offer choices for all ethnic groups.

Optimally, hair care facilities will be available at a centralized location as well as on the living pods. As in the greater society, women and girls should have the opportunity of either doing their hair "at home" or going to the beauty shop.

The hair care facilities in the living quarters should include a shampoo basin, hair dryer, and appropriate equipment. The beauty shop should be a professional shop and should use licensed beauticians, either employees or inmates. A licensed beautician must be provided for juveniles as they are underage for obtaining a beautician's license. An alternative would be to use volunteers from a beauty/barbering school or a licensed person.

Laundry

While central laundering services may be more efficient, "laundromats" are desirable since they allow for separation of clothing and teach/reinforce self-reliance.

Provisions should be made for hand-washing and drying of items since women and girls may stain clothing and linens during menses.

Small Group Seating

Throughout all common areas of the institution, provisions should be made for small group settings, thus allowing privacy. This easily can be accomplished by having tables for groups for four instead of rows of tables in the cafeteria, small furniture groupings in the dayrooms, and individual desks in classrooms. The guiding principle should be to provide a homelike and/or user friendly environment, but one with safety and security factors built-in, rather than improved upon. An example would be having the officer's station elevated so good visibility would be inherent in the area.

Visiting Room

Small group seating is probably most important in the visiting room. Most adult and some juvenile female offenders are mothers and believe that they will be reunited with their children on release. Juvenile female offenders are adolescents, and need a setting to allow shared intimacy (nonsexual) and normal family interactions. Children's centers give opportunities for play and learning while outdoor visiting provides a sense of freedom and normality.

A separate glassed room adjacent to the visiting area allows families greater privacy and an opportunity to work through various issues without fear of others overhearing. The conversation could be monitored by staff through use of microphone links, while actions/interactions would be monitored by sight. Other uses for such a room could be attorney visits and individual and group counseling, all without audio monitoring.

Staff Training

The greatest boon to privacy issues for adult and juvenile female offenders is staff training. All staff members initially, and on a periodic basis, should participate in gender specific training, which emphasizes the needs, goals, and uniqueness of this population. Working with women and girls presents challenges, but it also offers opportunities; correctional administrators and staff must be prepared to meet the challenges while creatively using the opportunities.

References

Bill, Louise. 1998. The Victimization and Re-victimization of Female Offenders: Prison Administrators Should Be Aware of Ways in Which Security Procedures Perpetuate Feelings of Powerless Among Incarcerated Women. *Corrections Today.* 60(7): 106-112.

Carp, Scarlet V. and Joyce A. Davis. 1989. *Design Considerations in the Building of Women's Prisons.* Washington, D.C: U.S. Department of Justice.

Carter, Stephen. 1998. Designing Without Glass Ceilings: An Examination of Trends and Opportunities in Designing Prisons for Women. J. Morton, editor. In *Complex Challenges, Collaborative Solutions: Programming for Adult and Juvenile Female Offenders.* Lanham, Maryland: American Correctional Association.

Chesney-Lind, Meda. 1998. Women in Prison: From Partial Justice to Vengeful Equity. *Corrections Today.* 60(7):66-73.

Cranford, Susan and Rose Williams. 1998. Critical Issues in Managing Female Offenders: Women Offenders Have Unique Needs Which Impact the Ways in Which Staff Manage Them. *Corrections Today.* 60(7): 130-134.

Johnson, Sylvia J. 1998. Girls Are In Trouble Do We Care? *Corrections Today.* 60(7): 136-141.

Morton, Joann B., ed. 1990. *National Public Correctional Policy,* 2nd ed. Lanham, Maryland: American Correctional Association.

—. In press. *Working With Women in Correctional Facilities.* Lanham, Maryland: American Correctional Association.

Morton, Joann B. and Deborah M. Williams. 1998. Mother/Child Bonding: Incarcerated Women Struggle to Maintain Meaningful Relationship with Their Children. *Corrections Today.* 60(7): 98-105.

Miller, Bona. 1998. Different, Not More Different: Gender-specific Training Helps Bridge the Gap. *Corrections Today.* 60(7): 142-144.

Office of Juvenile Justice and Delinquency Prevention. 1996. *Female Offenders in the Juvenile Justice System.* Washington, D.C.: U.S. Department of Justice.

Adult Laundry Services

George Yefchak, President
New Jersey Chapter of the
American Correctional Association
Stockton, New Jersey

The laundry is a vital operation within the institution. It provides the required clean bedding, clothing, and miscellaneous fabric articles used throughout the facility. A properly planned laundry operation provides the required clean items in a secure and efficient manner. The American Correctional Association standards mandate the provision of these articles. The task then becomes how to accomplish this job in a timely and efficient manner.

Most institutions use inmates to work in this area to make it a cost-effective operation. Using inmates under adequate staff supervision and within proper operational design can make this a secure operation and provide a required service in a fiscally responsive manner. It also helps reduce inmate idleness and can be an opportunity to learn job skills as well.

Some facilities have washers and dryers in each housing unit for the inmates to launder their own personal clothing. The advantages of this concept are that inmates are able to learn living skills and take responsibility for their clothing. It also eliminates complaints from inmates regarding lost clothing items. Even with decentralized laundry equipment for inmate personal clothing, a small centralized laundry is needed to do sheets, pillowcases, blankets, institution uniforms for food service, mop heads, and so forth.

Location and Equipment

A design engineer should be consulted regarding the development of specifications for the appropriate laundry equipment for the institution. The inmate population determines the number and capacity of the machines needed to

When choosing equipment for laundry services, security should be kept in mind. Laundry equipment can be used to transport or make contraband.

Photo courtesy of Gilbane Building Co., Providence, Rhode Island.
Photographer: Doug Buerlein.

provide for the laundry needs of the institution. Staffing is also a consideration in this purchase decision. Will the laundry operate in several shifts daily to meet the institutional needs or will an adequate number of machines need to be purchased to complete this task in one shift?

Each shift during which the laundry is operational will require adequate staff supervision. Because soiled items are brought to the laundry from throughout the institution and clean items are brought back, it is an ideal opportunity for inmates to transport contraband throughout the institution. Staff supervision is essential to control this possibility by the monitoring of laundry movements throughout the institution.

Central laundry facilities often employ inmates to clean linens and in certain cases to clean inmate clothing.

Photo courtesy of George Yefchak.

Contraband is a consideration in the purchase of equipment to outfit the laundry operation. The machines used to clean and dry the items, as well as the carts to transport the laundry, all should be carefully evaluated. Proper staff supervision also will prevent the inmates from dismantling the equipment and creating contraband from the dismantled parts.

The design of the laundry area should be considered with staff supervision in mind. Adequate space should be provided so that the laundry equipment can be placed in a floor plan that permits clear observation by staff. Staff must be able to observe the inmates in the operation of their tasks. Space sufficient for a proper floor plan can be accomplished by including the laundry in the initial facility planning rather than fitting it in available space after the building's design is completed.

The use of video monitors to improve inmate supervision in the laundry may be a consideration. The amount of inmate traffic in this area and the access to other areas of the facility make this area a security concern. These considerations should be part of the decision regarding the placement of the machinery, video monitors, and staff supervision.

In a secure facility, a centralized location for the laundry operation may prove easier to control and supervise rather than the haphazard placement of equipment in several housing units throughout the institution. The location of a centralized operation in the institution is an important consideration. The laundry must be in an accessible area as it services the entire institution. It also should have a controlled access because of the movement in the area. As previously stated, its placement should be a prime design consideration and not an afterthought on completion of the overall facility design.

Canteens

Frank Sheridan
New York State Department of Corrections
Albany, New York

A correctional facility is like a small community; all the services required by the inmate population are available within the perimeter including housing, education, recreation, industry, religion, and shopping. The canteen or commissary is where the shopping takes place.

The dictionary defines the two terms this way: *Canteen*: a military shop where soldiers can buy refreshments and provisions. *Commissary*: a store where food and supplies can be obtained.

The *American Institute of Architects'* glossary defines the commissary as: A room within a correctional facility that provides inmates with the sale of personal items such as grooming items, snack foods, radios, and so on.

The American Correctional Association states the requirements for a correctional commissary or canteen in the manual *Standards for Adult Correctional Institutions,* Third Edition.

American Correctional Association Requirements for a Commissary or Canteen

3-4042: An inmate commissary or canteen is available where inmates can purchase approved items that are not furnished by the facility. The canteen/commissary's operations are strictly controlled using standard accounting procedures.

3-4043: Commissary/canteen funds are audited independently following standard accounting procedures, and an annual financial status report is available as a public document.

3-4159: Space is provided for an inmate commissary or canteen, or provisions are made for a commissary service.

In a correctional setting, the canteen, or commissary, offers for sale, items that are not routinely issued to inmates by the institution, such as cigarettes, candy, ice cream, cookies, soap, deodorant, fruit, soda, greeting cards, radios, and shaving supplies. Staff develops a list of acceptable items for sale and each inmate is given a copy of the list. Those items that present a breach of security, or could compromise the safety of inmates or staff, are not available.

When inmates arrive at a facility, they are given an orientation regarding procedures, conduct, and general information about what is expected of inmates and what the inmates can expect. Information on how the canteen functions is part of the orientation.

Inmates are allowed to make canteen purchases on a regular basis and can spend funds from their accounts up to a preestablished maximum amount of money. Before the scheduled purchase, the inmate is given a canteen buy sheet listing available products and prices. Inmates mark their selections on the buy sheet, which is collected and given to the canteen employees who fill each order. The amount of the inmate's purchases is deducted from his or her cash account, which is maintained by the facility, and deposited into the department's canteen fund. The Federal Bureau of Prisons uses a debit card for each inmate and bar coding of items to speed up processing of canteen requests and improve accuracy of charges to inmate accounts. It also allows a current inventory of all items. Funds in the inmate's cash account usually come from wages they earned at the facility and/or money received from family and friends.

At some facilities, inmates work in the canteen. Some of the duties performed by inmates include the following:

- Cleaning all canteen rooms
- Unloading deliveries and stocking shelves
- Receiving inmate buyers' order sheets
- Picking up the items ordered by inmate buyers
- Rotating canteen inventory on receipt of new stock

Just as with a store in the community, there are hours when the canteen is open and when the canteen is closed. Control, movement, and observation of the buying activity and inventory of goods are critical to the operation. Depending on the institution and the inmates' profile, its operational procedures may vary. Inmates move either in escorted groups or to and from the canteen on a schedule, or orders can be submitted by inmates. The orders are received and bagged at the canteen and then delivered by staff to the inmate housing units.

Typical Operation

As the scheduled time for the canteen visit approaches, a group of inmates is escorted from their housing unit by a corrections officer. In the canteen lobby, the inmates stand or sit, and are called individually by the intercom system to one of the slip check windows. At the slip check window, the buy sheets are checked for item approval, item availability, and sufficient inmate's funds. At this point, all adjustments to buy sheets are made.

While the order is being filled, inmates return to their place in the lobby. After the order is assembled, the inmates are called again by the intercom system to one of the buy windows to check and process the order. The inmates then return to their place with the order and wait until all of the inmate orders have been processed. The group then is escorted back to their housing unit. The corrections officer remains with the group at all times and oversees the activity in the lobby area.

Location

The canteen is used by inmates on a scheduled basis. It should be located in a central location within easy walking distance of the housing areas. Location of the canteen also should be related to the central service yard of the facility, where deliveries to kitchen, maintenance, dry stores, and laundry take place. As the canteen receives deliveries of inmate staples, this location makes for ease of operation and efficient officer coverage. The canteen should be a fully secured space.

Functional Areas

Inmate Lobby

This space provides an area for inmates to submit and pick up orders from the canteen. Single lane traffic is required for ease of supervision by officer(s). There should be a counter in front of the buy windows to allow inmates to pack up their merchandise.

Order Make Up Area

This space provides shelves and/or display space for all items. Orders are assembled, checked, and costs are tallied, and items are dispensed from this area. The number of buy windows will vary depending on the size of the facility. This area needs to have controlled heat/humidity and air conditioning. Buy windows should have lockable grilles and doors.

This area needs a lockable access door to the inmate pick up area. Buy windows need counter tops to pass the food items through to the inmates who are receiving the items. The order make up area is where the inmate buy sheets are processed manually and/or by computer.

Product Staging Area

This area is supplemented by the storage area. It is an open area with high shelving around the entire perimeter and either low shelving or low stock pallets in the center area. There will be defined aisles and all items will be clearly identified and displayed. The buy sheets are taken from the slip check windows, filled by the inmate staff, and brought to the buy windows. The toilet facilities, janitor's closet, slip check windows, buy windows, and office are incorporated in the order make up area with clear visibility to each of these spaces from the supervisor's office.

Office Space

This space is required for the staff person who is responsible for the operation of the canteen. The office space should have visibility to the storage and order make up areas.

Storage Area

This space provides for bulk storage and receiving area for all products delivered to the canteen and should be contiguous to the order make up area. This space has a loading dock that conforms to industry standards. The space also has central heat and air conditioning and an exit door to the loading dock.

The storage area should be designed to retain at least a week's worth of supplies, including palletized dry goods.

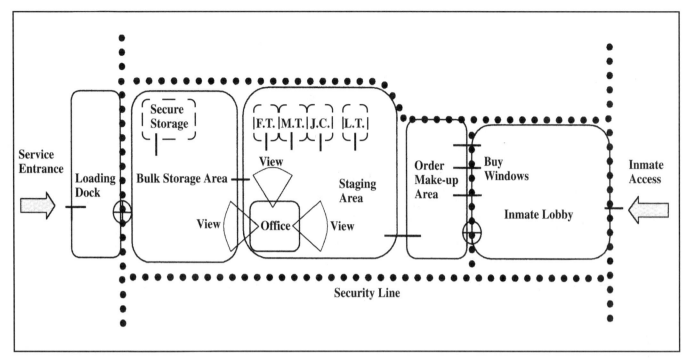

Canteen/commissary adjacency diagram.

Diagram provided by Leonard R. Witke, AIA

Refrigerators and freezers for fresh produce and ice cream also should be provided. There should be a separate room for secure storage.

Secure Storage

This area provides space to secure merchandise such as cigarettes, televisions, radios, and so forth.

Toilets

Toilets and limited locker facilities for civilian males, females, and inmates should be provided. There should be separate inmate, staff, and correctional staff toilet rooms since inmates and staff may work in the area for extended periods of time without being able to leave the canteen.

Janitor's Closet

This area contains a slop sink, mop rack, and locked storage space for cleaning supplies.

Summary of Design Criteria

The canteen should be centrally located near housing units and the central service core. Secure construction should be used for the perimeter walls of the canteen and the lobby and secure storage areas. There should be freezer and cooler space for fresh produce and ice cream. The area should be air conditioned to help preserve perishable food items. Visual supervision of work areas is required. An adjacency diagram similar to the one above should be provided for easy reference when designing these facilities. The size of all areas will vary depending on the size of the institution, scheduling, operational considerations, and how often the stock is replenished.

Services in Juvenile Facilities

Kendal Ball
Department of Youth Services
Columbus, Ohio

Admisssions

The admission of juvenile offenders to the facility is a critical step in the institutional process. Receiving juveniles into a correctional facility, either a detention facility or postadjudicative training school, can be a threatening, fearful, or anxiety-producing event and can result in the juveniles engaging in acting-out behaviors. The facility must be prepared to deal with the juveniles' behavior yet maintain safety and security. At the same time, staff should realize that this is a time to reduce that fear and anxiety for the youths. The best way is to inform the youths about what they should expect and orient them to the process so that they know what will happen next. This knowledge reduces their fear and anxiety, and the process becomes less threatening.

Youth arrive at a facility in a secure vehicle sallyport either fenced or physically enclosed and which has communications with the larger facility. In some cases, where a vehicle sallyport is not required, additional precautions must be taken in moving juveniles from the transport vehicle to the building. The staff in the arrival area, whether enclosed or not, must be able to communicate with the larger facility by intercom, phone, or radio. The facility should monitor the area through direct supervision or closed-circuit television. Generally, the admissions' area is close to the outside perimeter of the facility to allow for a proper transition. The process of securing weapons either in a vehicle or gun locker and moving a youth from the vehicle into the facility is a high-risk event that needs close supervision and clear sight lines. Once inside the facility, the actual admission process begins.

Admission is more than just taking custody of juveniles; it may be the youths' first contact with this type of process. The challenge is to provide an environment and process that ensures the series of events that must occur are done in a manner that is efficient, accurate, and thorough but also provides a level of respect and sensitivity for the individual youth. Some details on this are contained in *Managing Delinquency Programs that Work* by Barry Glick and Arnold Goldstein, eds., Lanham, Maryland: American Correctional Association.

The initial step is to begin to assess the youths' mental and physical condition. Workers, performing this initial assessment of the youths' condition should begin to establish rapport with the individuals, and make the youths feel more comfortable with the process. Then, the first official step in admission is to confirm the legal authority to admit the juvenile. This process includes reviewing court documents or other documents. Once the legal authority to take custody has been established, additional screening can take place. This process must occur in an environment that maintains security.

As part of the intake process, as youths arrive, they should be frisk searched to make sure they have no weapons or contraband that they could use to hurt themselves or others. After they are searched, they may be placed in an observable holding room. It is important that staff talk with the youths so they know what is occurring. This reduces their anxiety and establishes rapport. By staff behaving in this manner, they reduce the risk of the youths engaging in acting-out behaviors against themselves or others. The intake environment can produce anxiety and fear, so the behaviors of staff receiving youth at the intake must be helpful and nonthreatening.

The admission area must provide physical space for (1) conducting the frisk search for contraband, (2) placing the youth in a holding room or area where they can be observed, (3) reviewing records to confirm legal custody and properly completing the paperwork. For planning purposes, administrators and planners should determine the number and types of admissions that will be taking place. This will enable them to define their space needs. If the intake is one or two youth at a time, the spaces required are totally different from what would be necessary if the intake were ten to twenty.

In both cases, the minimum requirement would be appropriate space for frisk searches and secure holding area(s). A space to receive the transport records requires counter and filing space for forms and writing. Such counter or desk space should include areas for personal computers, as most facilities now put their intake information directly into their information system. A minimum of two work spaces should be identified in the plan.

The challenge of custody is to ensure that a series of events occurs in an accurate, thorough, and efficient manner. This process should be in writing and should describe how a youth will be processed out—whether being released, leaving the facility for short-term programming, or for transportation to a medical or psychiatric facility.

Once legal custody is determined, the transporting officer leaves and the admission process continues. This process should be very structured. Staff must be attentive to quick and easy transition allowing the youths to be admitted to the facility in a manner so that the youths' initial adjustment can begin.

The admissions process is the beginning of the youths' orientation program. The youths should be received and oriented into the facility in an orderly, humane, and therapeutic fashion. This transition can be intimidating and threatening, which can result in the youths engaging in acting-out behaviors. Therefore, it is important that the facility have detailed policies and procedures that are closely followed in a structured environment. This process should allow the staff to look for threatening, fearful, depressed, or other behaviors in an understanding and respectful way.

The admission process continues with an interview or more assessment of the youths. The better the rapport the worker has established, the easier this process becomes. If the youths view the staff as supportive, they will be more candid and truthful. In some cases, background information may be available that often can replace a portion of the admission interview. To protect the youths and staff, issues of drug use, depression, suicidal behavior, violence, health, and sexually transmitted diseases need to be discussed and identified. This interview can take place in a more private location later in the intake area, but it should occur as soon as possible.

Early on in the process, a more complete search of the youths should occur to ensure the safety of the staff and youths. This is usually a strip search and is done at the same time as the youths' property inventory is completed. The strip search and inventory process should be structured and detailed in policy and explained clearly to the youths. The youths should be asked to sign the completed inventory and given a copy. Then, the youths should be assigned clothing, toiletries, and bedding. Once the inventory has been completed, the strip search should be completed; the youths should shower and dress in facility clothes.

The admission areas for searches, showers, and the exchange of clothing must provide for observation yet maintain as much privacy as possible. This is especially true if female juveniles are being processed into the facility. Storage space to secure the youths' personal effects, which is adjacent to the admission area, provides for good accountability.

The admissions process includes a health screening by health care personnel or a staff trained in health care. This screening includes observations and interviews to establish and identify any health risks to themselves or others. This screening is preliminary to the medical physical that should occur soon after intake.

More youth facilities are expanding their use of youth identification programs. State laws and local policies are changing and allow or require facilities to photograph, fingerprint, or use modern techniques such as DNA identification. Facilities should be designed to accommodate these programs.

Medical Services for Juveniles

The medical services program should be under the direction of qualified medical personnel. Each youth is required to have a medical screening at intake and a medical and dental examination shortly after. All medications are under the supervision of the medical staff who supervise dispensing and charting of medication. The medical needs of the youths must be communicated with the youths' parents.

Medical care is an essential service for the youths' individual well being and is a basic human right. Consequently, the medical facility should promote good physical and mental health and contribute to the total therapeutic program of the youth. Youth facilities are required to provide an initial medical screening and ongoing medical treatment and emergency care.

The facility must determine the level of medical care they intend to provide, and the design team can ensure that proper facilities are included and the medical facility is properly equipped. Medical facilities for juveniles can vary greatly. They can range from a simple nurse station-examination area to a hospital type atmosphere complete with sophisticated equipment. If the facility elects to have only a modest medical area, then procedures must be in place to transport sick or injured juveniles to an outside medical facility in a timely manner. The design of the facility must accommodate this transportation and provide for a quick, yet secure, entry and exit for emergency staff and equipment.

Depending on the size and security level of the facility, contractual arrangements for the provision of medical treatment may play an integral part of the design of the medical facilities. More facilities are contracting for privatized medical services that occur within the facility. These full-service programs can provide broader services at the facility, eliminating the need to transport.

A medical examination area should be included in even the smallest facility. This area should include spaces where juveniles can be examined and treated in private. As the program grows, the space should be designed to accommodate those program services. Included in that would be any special medical services, dental services, vision care, and mental health services.

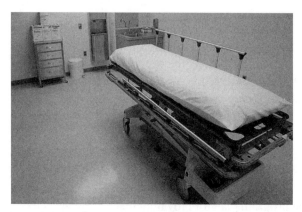

Examination areas as well as infirmary housing should be easily supervised by staff to avoid placing treatment staff or youth in an unsafe situation.

Photo courtesy of Gilbane Building Co., Providence, Rhode Island.

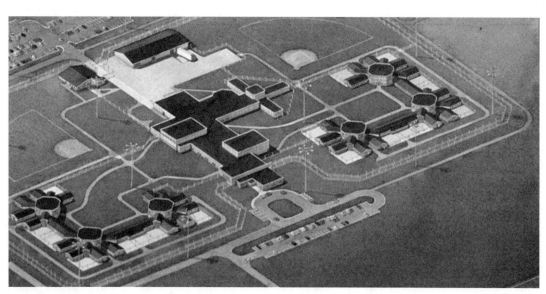

Bon Air Medical Secure Juvenile Correctional Complex—aerial view of courtyard.

Photo courtesy of HSMM, Virginia Beach, Virginia.

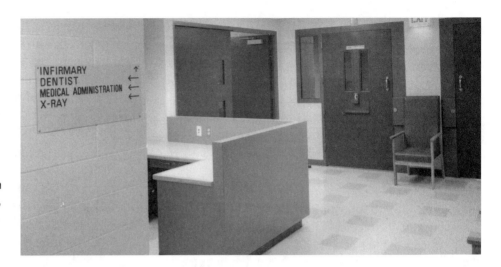

The degree of medical services offered at a facility will vary greatly based on management philosophy and funding. Use of contracted services of professional staff often requires the facility to support their services. The medical reception area of State Correctional Institution, Albion, Pennsylvania is shown here.

Photo courtesy of L. Robert Kimball & Associates, Ebensburg, Pennsylvania.

In evaluating space requirements, the confidentiality and maintenance of records in a secure setting should be considered as well as the security and control of the drug and equipment storage areas. All casework should be locked. Even in a nonsecure facility, these areas must be secure. The two primary adjacencies for medical services generally are intake and housing areas. The medical facility has to be accessible to the youth yet close to good supervision. Medical facilities also should provide for medical isolation.

The program plan for providing medical services must be made early in the planning process. The medical facility must accommodate medical staff or contract staff in a professional environment. Whether or not private providers are used, appropriate spaces must be provided. Telemedicine or video-medicine is now commonplace and provides more extensive services at remote facilities or for high-risk juveniles. Because this type of program is becoming more common and accessible at a reasonable cost, it is being used more universally. The need to provide an increasing number of specialized services to more youths at a reduced cost is important in planning medical facilities. If the facility plans to use telemedicine, planning should include the requirements for the communications systems, proper lighting, and equipment.

Food Service for Juveniles

All youths are to be provided with three nutritional meals and at least one nutritious snack at regularly scheduled hours each day. These meals and snacks should meet standard portion and nutritional requirements. Most juvenile facilities participate in the National School Meal Programs requiring planned meals, according to standards and U.S. Department of Agriculture guidelines. Youths are encouraged to eat their entire meals. These meals should be prepared in a manner that is attractive to the youths. Nutritional education should encourage youths to incorporate healthy eating habits into their personal lifestyles.

Dining Space

The food service program is a very important and integral component of the juvenile facility. The quality and quantity of a tasty and nutritious meal aids in the health, well being, and the conduct of youths in a juvenile facility. Central dining provides for a social time as well as a break time in the general institutional routine. Central dining can be successful with proper supervision, but without such structure, central dining with large numbers of youth in a confined area can pose a threat to the security and control of the facility.

Central dining areas generally serve cafeteria style. Seating can be fixed or not, depending on the security level of the facility. Fixed seating can be more difficult to maintain and clean around and may be less flexible. The dining area provides the opportunity for planners to create a pleasant, attractive, and colorful environment. The appearance of the dining area has an impact on the behavior and attitude of the population.

Transporting Food

Central dining eliminates the logistical problems of transporting food. Transporting food in bulk or in individual serving containers may require reheating for the food to be properly served. Transporting requires keeping hot foods hot and cold foods cold. It is also affected by weather conditions, which can slow deliveries down significantly.

Size

The size of the facility will help determine the size of the dining and kitchen area. The size of the living units and the scheduled time allotted to serve and eat are considerations. The ability of the food service staff to serve the serving line in an efficient manner also will have an impact on the size of the dining facility. Staff and youth should eat together in the same dining room.

Kitchen

The kitchen food preparation area size and layout also depend on the size of the facility, the number of meals to be served, and the type of food service program that will be provided. A full-service kitchen that prepares the full meal must have appropriate food storage, preparation, and serving space, and full service equipment.

The type of food service program can vary greatly from full-service in-house preparation to private contract services. A determination of the type of food service program is critical to early planning. Making changes in the type of program late in the planning phase or after construction can be very costly. Early decisions in this area will provide a clear understanding of the size and type of food storage and preparation equipment that will be required by the facility.

There is also typically a need to prepare trayed meals in every institution. This function can be performed with a minimum of equipment and staff or workers, but adequate space must be provided for everyone and everything to function efficiently. Trayed meals will be provided to juveniles in lockdown status, those who are infirm, and also staff who cannot leave their posts.

Storage space for delivery, dry storage, cold storage, and freezer storage space varies greatly for different types of programs. Clean-up areas like dish washing and cart and can washing are other examples that are impacted based on the type of food service that is provided. All of these spaces need to be evaluated according to the type of preparation. A shared program with another correctional facility or facility preparing meals may need only limited loading space and heating and cooling equipment.

Contract or private providers also may need space for specialized equipment. Even with heat and serve program facilities, equipment must be supplied and be appropriate for that type of program. The facility must be designed to provide for the delivery of a correct and fitting food service program. Proper planning must provide for space and equipment to deliver and serve a nutritious meal at the facility.

Laundry for Juveniles

Laundry program planners have to work closely with the facility planners in evaluating and designing the laundry area of the juvenile facility. Determination of whether the facility will provide clothing or allow youths to wear their personal clothes is a critical decision that must be made early in the planning process. The prime considerations are as follows: contracting laundry out to a private provider, staff providing full laundry services, youths being allowed to wear personal clothes, and youths being allowed to do all or portions of the laundry.

In many facilities, youths receive three complete sets of clean laundry weekly. However, the number of sets of clean laundry that is provided each week is another decision that has to be made. Linens, towels, and washcloths may be washed in a central laundry with commercial equipment while personal clothing may be washed on the living unit with heavy-duty residential equipment.

Equipment Size

The size and type of equipment, the size of the laundry room, and the adjacencies all are relevant to laundry services. Smaller juvenile facilities may contract out the heavier linens and towels and allow youths to maintain the lighter and smaller volume of personal clothing. Combinations of these types of choices are used in several juvenile facilities.

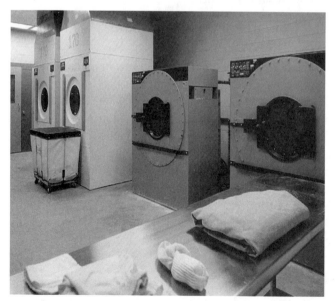

Laundry facilities must provide an adequate area for equipment, carts, and the sorting and folding functions. Beaumont Maximum Security Juvenile Facility, Beaumont, Virginia.

Photo courtesy of HSMM, Virginia Beach, Virginia.

Spaces within the laundry must include areas for sorting, folding, and storing additional linens as well as sets of clothing. Some facilities include a space for a seamstress or tailor for repair and alterations of clothing. The availability of detergents and laundry supplies also must be considered. A modern dispensing system and storage in an area not accessible to youths can increase the safety and security of those supplies and chemicals.

The size and type of equipment and the adjacencies all are relevant to each of the strategies that may be used in providing laundry services. The laundry program should consider how the exchange method for providing clothing and laundry supplies will function.

Canteens/Commissary for Juveniles

Most juvenile facilities offer a canteen or commissary where youths can buy toilet supplies, soap, deodorant, shampoo, food, candy, soda, writing supplies, stamps, or special privilege items like radios, TVs, or electronic games. Detention or very short-term facilities may not have a commissary due to the short length of stay.

The types and amounts of commissary items need to be controlled so they do not become items of barter. Generally, the level of participation is tied into the treatment program. With improved performance or advancement in the program, additional commissary privileges or amounts are provided.

The Commissary as Part of the Program Area

The commissary, as other programs in juvenile facilities, can be a major program area or can be completely nonexistent. The commissary can be like a fast food restaurant serving hot grill items and cold drinks in an area that includes entertainment, such as games or music, and is tied to the treatment program in some form. This type of commissary can operate like a small store and include youths in the operation of the commissary as training or learning experiences. A commissary of this type would require extensive planning and require specific design elements to make sure health codes and security concerns were addressed.

Privatized Commissary Options

Obviously, privatizing the commissary is the extreme end of the option spectrum, as the most common commissary operations involve youths ordering their sundry items from a list and staff filling their orders and returning their requests in sealed packages. Most facilities that choose to provide a commissary program such as this contract with private contractors. By privatizing this type of program, the institution does not have to maintain a large inventory, be concerned with multiple purchases to maintain a varied selection, nor be worried about shrinkage or spoilage. The youths place their orders and staff relay those orders to the suppliers. The purchases are charged to the youths' accounts.

Accountability

In any case, a commissary operation requires very specific policies and guidelines. The accountability for youths funds is a responsibility, and sound accounting principles must be used. The commissary system of ordering and delivering is the simplest. The paper trail that results from the order sheets generally is forwarded to the business office where youths accounts are maintained. Then, the order is filled either by a private provider who uses a sealed container with a receipt for the youths or from the institution itself. The delivery generally is made like most other deliveries to the facility so that security of the facility and the commissary items can be maintained. Youths sign for the commissary items they receive, and accountability is maintained.

Commissary orders delivered to youths must be secured in a holding area until they are received by the youths. Youths making commissary purchases must have a space or locker where they can secure their purchases. Allowing unlimited numbers of commissary items, especially perishables, is asking for a problem of vermin and unwanted bartering among the youths. Storage should be appropriate for the amounts and types of the commissary. For larger institutions, the use of the adult canteen/commissary model and design requirements as outlined in Section 3.9 of this chapter would be appropriate.

Conclusion

The idea of a separate facility or even secure storage for commissary should be planned carefully when designing the facility. The philosophy of the institution may be reflected in the choice of the commissary. In addition, careful planning is necessary to minimize the opportunity for lost or stolen commissary items, because these can be very disruptive. It is important in any commissary program that the lines of responsibility are established clearly. This can occur through thoughtful preplanning.

Outsourcing and Contract Services

Edward F. Tripp
Kennedy Associates
St. Louis, Missouri

Outsourcing of human services is an old concept, dating back at least to the 1920s, when juvenile wards of the city of New York were placed in privately run houses of refuge (Durham, 1989, 1991; Rogers and Mays, 1987, as cited in Mays and Gray, 1996). Traditionally, however, most services and programs provided to adult inmates were provided in-house. Today, expanding inmate populations and a growing need to contain costs have led to outsourcing or contracting out an increasing number of juvenile and inmate services previously performed in-house.

Outsourcing a service can be handled in a variety of ways. Contractor personnel can come into the facility, replace all in-house staff members, and take over the management and operation of the service. Contractor personnel also can provide services from outside the facility. Or, a combination of the two may occur. Finally, in some cases, juveniles or inmates may be moved, and some services provided outside of the facility, either temporarily or permanently.

Regardless of how a service is outsourced, there are generally facility-related design ramifications. Since, in most instances, outside contractors are businesses and profit motivated, they will look for less costly ways to deliver or provide services. They focus on using a smaller staff and have less on-site inventory to manage and secure. They place emphasis on shared equipment and dual personnel responsibilities, where appropriate. This frequently leads to lower space needs.

Outsourcing or contracting out a service also means rethinking location issues. For instance, when medical services are provided in-house, these facilities are located in a highly secure area, accessible to housing and intake areas, but away from routine staff or inmate traffic. If contracted out, consider placing them at a location more quickly accessible to the contractor and emergency personnel, for security and access reasons.

Flexibility must be taken into consideration when planning a facility. This includes the flexibility to convert to an in-house or an outside contractual operation in the event either becomes expedient. Flexibility also is needed to handle contingencies and emergency situations that may arise, such as natural disasters. These concerns, of course, are added to the flexibility that already has to be designed to accommodate population or programmatic changes.

The most logical and frequent services to outsource are medical and dental care, pharmacy, laundry, food service, canteen, and most recently, educational services.

Medical and Dental Care

Medical and dental care frequently are outsourced. Over the years, patients needing care that was too expensive or too infrequently occurring to economically handle in-house have been transported to nearby hospitals for treatment. Also, specialists have been brought into the facility to handle special emergency cases.

Today, inmate services contracts and outsourcing options are increasing rapidly and no longer are considered enrichment by correctional administrators and officers.

Since these companies or businesses frequently provide services to the community and numerous correctional institutions, they can operate on an economic scale not available to government-operated in-house programs. For instance, they may have portable x-ray equipment that can move from facility to facility, using limited space, or freeing up space previously devoted to x-ray use alone.

Other options related to outside medical services also are becoming more common. For example, the use of telemedicine, teleradiology, and radiography are growing. Inmate patients can be "seen" by doctors at remote locations through the use of videoconferencing. X-rays can be taken on-site, scanned by a film digitizer, and transmitted to a remote facility for diagnosis. With these methods employed by outsourced medical providers, access to health care can be quick and transportation costs dramatically reduced. Facilities, however, must be designed for and equipped with high-technology equipment to accommodate this option (*Correctional Building News*, 1998).

While geriatric care has been an issue over the years, it will become even more important in the near future. As our population increases in age, so will the population of our correctional institutions. Increasing age-related health problems may make outsourcing some geriatric care an attractive option. Specialized extended-care correctional medical facilities now are developing specifically to care for geriatric and special needs inmates. Using such facilities will reduce the number of handicapped and accessible accommodations required throughout the facility and thus reduce construction costs related to high-security hardware.

Before reducing space requirements, however, it is critical to build in flexibility. The space must be able to accommodate a change from one vendor to another. Yet, the space should have the ability to support an in-house operation, should that again become desired. Finally, contingency planning is essential to assure that the facility can continue to function and provide essential services in an emergency. For instance, if you are using telemedicine, what do you need to remain functional if communication with the remote site is temporarily lost?

The same concerns apply to outsourced dental care. Contract operators generally will require less space than in-house staff. However, it is critical that flexibility is built in to handle a change in institutional management status, or emergency situations that arise.

Pharmacy

Outsourced pharmaceutical suppliers can provide many of the pharmacy needs of an institution, and keep supplies off-site, thereby significantly lowering storage space requirements and lessening security concerns. At a minimum, medicines for chronic, predictable needs can be provided on an as-needed basis, while maintaining, on-site, some stock of frequently used medications. Or, as previously stated, the entire pharmaceutical operation could be off-site, if the services are outsourced. While this will reduce in-house storage requirements, provision still must be made to accommodate emergency situations. The potential for returning this function in-house also must be considered; thus, adequate space must be available in the general area should this occur.

Laundry

Laundry can be performed totally in-house, outsourced in its entirety, or a combination of the two. Some institutions may want to keep personal item laundering in-house, while outsourcing blankets and bed linens. Others will prefer to outsource all items. However, contracting out the laundering of personal items will require keeping an adequate inventory of personal items on hand to last until the outside laundered items are returned. Reduced laundering programs, however, reduce the space needed for equipment and storage space, along with a reduced maintenance cost.

Food Service

Food service is the program that most frequently is contracted out. A food-service contractor either can fully prepare and serve meals in-house or prepare them at a remote location and transport them to the institution for short-term storage, warming, and serving.

Design features are important to food service contractors; bidding costs depend on which method of preparation is used. A full-service kitchen is needed if the contractor will prepare meals in-house, but primarily warm/chill capabilities will be required if the contractor is to prepare meals at a remote location. Both methods have a serious impact on personnel usage and meal cost.

As with other outsourced services, provision must be made to accommodate out-of-the-ordinary situations, such as late delivery of meals or a natural disaster delaying food delivery for a period of hours or a few days.

Food preparation areas can vary greatly in size and equipment. Sanitation and maintenance of equipment is very important.

Enough capacity must be built in to keep bread, lunch-meat, and other essential food items on-hand to cover such potential occurrences.

Canteen

While many facilities have in-house canteens, many are also turning to outside contractors for this service. Outside contractors may provide order forms for inmates to use. Orders can be faxed to the contractor's warehouse, which will fill the order and deliver it to the institution. Orders frequently are delivered two to three days per week. The amount of storage required for canteens is extensive and the filling of orders depends on the length of time for which orders are placed.

Some facilities and equipment still will be required, such as computers and possibly fax machines for handling inmate accounting functions that call for deducting the cost of canteen items from inmate accounts, transmitting orders to the contractor, and maintaining inventory status. Accommodations should be made for keeping a supply of some items, such as cold beverages and ice cream, in-house at all times. The canteen's supply and delivery can share a sallyport with the food-service operation. The amount of space that is allocated for outsourced canteen services can be reduced significantly from that required for an in-house operation.

How to Structure a Good RFP

When contracting out a service, careful attention needs to be paid to generating a comprehensive Request for Proposal (RFP) and contract for service. The RFP should be structured to outline goals clearly, and specify scope of work and responsibilities. It should limit the liability of the owner to the greatest extent practicable.

Other items that should be included in the RFP include:
- Cost, including incentives for cost containment and disincentives for overruns
- Methods of payment
- Term and renewal provisions
- Performance and indemnification
- Insurance requirements
- Compliance monitoring
- Relationship of the contractor and contractor's employees to the state and the private entity
- Escape clause, stating that the contract is null and void in the event the funding is not appropriated or not appropriated in the full amount

A contract should state the services to be provided, cover unplanned contingencies, and provide for responsibility and liability. It also should state what is not covered by the contract so that issues of responsibility and liability are clearly stated. It should address points of intersection. For example, who pays for transportation and security for an inmate who must be in court? If the inmate has a heart attack while at court, who pays his or her medical expenses (Mays and Gray, 1996)? Careful attention while drafting an RFP and a contract for services, followed by an equally careful review of proposals, will not eliminate all questions and problems, but it can minimize them.

References

Correctional Building News. *Medical Housing and the Aging Inmate.* November/December 1998.

___. Prison Telemedicine on the Rise. November/December 1998.

Durham, A. M. 1989a. Managing the Costs of Modern Corrections: Implications of Nineteenth-Century Privatized Prison-Labor Programs. *Journal of Criminal Justice.* 17:441-455.

___.1989b. Rehabilitation and Correctional Privatization: Observation on the Nineteenth Century Experience and Implications for Modern Corrections. *Federal Probation.* 52:43-52.

___. 1989c. Origins of Interest in the Privatization of Punishment: The Nineteenth and Twentieth Century American Experience. *Criminology.* 27:107-139.

Mays, G. Larry and Tara Gray.1996. *Privatization and the Provision of Correctional Services: Context and Consequences.* Cincinnati, Ohio: Academy of Criminal Justice Sciences and Anderson Publishing Co.

Rogers, J. W. and G. L. Mays. 1987. *Juvenile Delinquency and Juvenile Justice.* Englewood Cliffs, New Jersey: Prentice Hall.

Inmate and Juvenile Programs

4.1 Adult Inmate Programs

4.2 Programs for Juveniles

4

A typical multipurpose space can be used for a variety of functions at different periods of the day. Finishes, lighting, and the introduction of natural light can greatly enhance the use of the space. Shown is the multipurpose area at Virginia Peninsula Regional Jail, Williamsburg, Virginia, a medium-security facility.

Architect, Daniel, Mann, Johnson & Mendenhall (DMJM). Photo courtesy of Gilbane Building Company, Providence, Rhode Island, construction manager. Photographer: Doug Buerlein.

The visiting area of a supermax facility, Wallens Ridge State Prison at Big Stone Gap, Virginia, is shown on the top of the previous page.

Architect: Daniel, Mann, Johnson & Mendenhall. Photo courtesy of Gilbane Building Company, Providence, Rhode Island, construction manager. Photographer: Tim Cox.

Natural light illuminates the gym at the Whatcom County Juvenile Detention Facility as shown on the previous page. This facility is located on the sixth floor of the Whatcom County Courthouse in Bellingham, Washington.

Photo courtesy of KMD Justice, San Francisco, California.

Adult Inmate Programs

Cheryl Fuller
Fuller Koe Associates
Sacramento, California

The objectives of inmate programs in adult correctional institutions are as varied as the number of programs themselves. Inmates can learn to use their leisure time constructively, increase their literacy and job skills, obtain a small income, continue positive relationships with their families, maintain or establish religious affiliations, recover from chemical dependency, learn to prevent relapse behaviors, and increase their physical fitness. In this section of the *Design Guide*, all of the juvenile and adult program areas are grouped separately with the juvenile sections beginning on page 265.

The section on adult inmate programs and a multipurpose area includes: orientation, substance abuse treatment, multiuse areas, education, vocational training, prison industries, religious programs, recreation, and visiting. Larger jurisdictions may offer programs and provide space for all of these programs individually; smaller jurisdictions may provide a single multiuse area, which can serve a variety of purposes.

The range of programs, the amount of space, and the location of the inmate programs depends on a number of factors. These include the philosophy of the correctional jurisdiction, the population of inmates to be served, the mission of the institution, the location of the institution, its proximity to other adult correctional institutions, the security level of the inmates, and other concerns. The size of the population, the size of the spaces that will be allocated to the programs, and the construction budget may be the most pertinent factors that affect space after operating policies and procedures.

Accessibility Requirements

Requirements for accessibility for persons with disabilities must be determined before the design phase. All public spaces and the majority of staff spaces must meet accessibility requirements. Inmate accessibility requirements may vary, and should be determined in conjunction with current case law, state statutes, and prevailing administrative policies. Space recommendations provided in this section do not address accessibility specifically; it is up to the design teams to determine actual requirements.

Summary of Space Recommendations

Table 4.1 lists recommendations for each inmate program and the types, quantities, and sizes of spaces needed. This table is intended as a preliminary room list and guide for beginning the architectural programming process. The space requirements represent the author's suggested minimums. Actual requirements must be calculated based on prevailing standards of practice both nationally and locally, the number of users, budgetary concerns, and other factors. Space recommendations are based on these factors and on a best practice philosophy.

Table 4.1
Minimal Space Recommendations

Program / Space	Quantity	Minimum Net Square Feet	Occupants	Notes
ORIENTATION HOUSING				
Cells	variable	35 SF unencumbered	single	Bunk, desk and stool, 1 toilet/sink combo unit, personal storage.
Cells	variable	25 SF unencumbered/ occupant	double	2 bunks, 1 desk/stool, 1 combo unit, 2 storage units.
Dormitory	not recommended			Dorms are not recommended for newly admitted inmates.
Control desk (direct supervision)	1	variable	1-2 (staff only)	Counter, partially enclosed: work surface, storage, control panel, intercom/phone.
Control room (indirect supervision)	1	variable	1-2 (staff only)	Fully enclosed, secure: work surface, storage, control panel, intercom/phone.
Dayroom	1 per group	35 SF/ occupant	variable	Natural light; movable furniture; multipurpose indoor recreation space.
Showers	ratio of 1:18	varies	single or group	Include drying area, dressing area.
Multipurpose room	1 per housing unit	20 SF/occupant	varies	Provide natural light, wall space for dry erase boards, projection screens, power for TV/VCR, soundproofing.
Examination room	1	120 SF	1-2 medical personnel & 1 inmate	Lockable cabinetry, handwash sink, exam table, counters, work surface for charting, illuminator.
Interview rooms	1-3	80 SF if un-assigned; 100 if permanent space	1 staff, 1 inmate	If this space is unassigned, it may be furnished with a table and chairs. If this is to be a private office, it should contain a desk/chair, file cabinet, side chair, phone, computer.
Miscellaneous	varies	varies	N/A	Other rooms to consider: storage rooms, other staff offices, janitor's closets, staff rest rooms, and conference space.
Dining/food preparation area	N/A	N/A	N/A	Meals may be delivered on carts to dayroom. Alternately, inmates may be escorted to central dining.
Laundry	N/A	N/A	N/A	Laundry may be done by institution. If policy allows inmates to do personal laundry, provide a room in living unit with durable washers and dryers, and ventilation. Enclose to reduce noise.
Canteen/ commissary	N/A	N/A	N/A	Like meals and other services, commissary items (if allowed) can be delivered to living unit, or inmates can place their own orders and pick them up.
VISITING				
Entry/ processing lobby	1	Lobby at 20 SF/ occupant, plus enclosed rooms and processing counter	varies	Located outside the perimeter. Open lobby for queuing line, seating, counter for processing visitors, metal detector, rest rooms, pay phones, vending machines, lockers, pedestrian sallyport.
CONTACT VISITING				
Visitor entry/public rest rooms	2 (separate male and female)	180 SF	3 per room	Secondary lobby (after processing) inside the security perimeter. Locate adjacent to the contact visiting room, not accessible to inmates.
Visiting room	1	20 SF/ occupant plus spaces listed on next page	varies	Movable chairs and tables, free of obstructions for supervision. Good acoustic treatment to reduce noise. Durable surfaces.

Program / Space	Quantity	Minimum Net Square Feet	Occupants	Notes
Vending area	1	150 SF + 50 SF for storage	N/A	Space for 2-3 machines, adequate power outlets. May include cold and hot drink machines, microwave (for warming snacks, baby bottles), snack machine.
Custody station	1	80 SF	1	Elevated, casework; phone/intercom; storage beneath counter; door controls if exits are electrically released; TV monitor.
Children's room	1	300 SF	varies	Carpeting and vinyl flooring; adjustable child-height tables and chairs, shelving, hand wash sink. Natural light. Power for TV/VCR. Enclosed to reduce noise.
NONCONTACT VISITING				
Booths	Minimum of 3	40 SF (for inmate side), 60 SF recommended for visitor side	1 inmate, 1-2 visitors	Fixed stool for inmate, lockable door; security glazing; handsets for talking; visitor side may be open or enclosed, but not lockable, with 1-2 chairs. If used for attorney visits, must be fully enclosed and soundproofed, with paper pass.
OVERNIGHT VISITING				
Apartment	1/500 inmates	850 NSF	1 inmate, spouse, 2 children	Living/dining room, kitchenette, 2 bedrooms, 1 bathroom, small yard.
OUTDOOR VISITING				
Outdoors	1/500 inmates	varies	varies	Paved or landscaped area in view of observation tower or staff control station. Shielded from view of other inmate areas, surrounded by fencing. Benches or picnic tables. Awning, umbrellas or other method of providing shade. Children's play area may be here.
TELEVISITING				
Booth	3/500, if other visiting provided, more if this is only program	varies	1 inmate	Enclosed room designed for video broadcasting to remote location.
PRIVATE VISITING				
Enclosed rooms	2	20 SF/occupant	varies from 2-3 to 6-8 person rooms	Can be used for counseling, family therapy, attorney visits, and so forth. May be located adjacent to contact visiting room, but must be enclosed for privacy and soundproofed.
EDUCATION				
Classrooms	varies	35 SF/student +100 SF/teacher + 45 SF/ inmate toilet	varies	Rooms should contain a desk or study carrel per student, with adequate circulation. Provide rooms with utilities for computer-aided instruction.
Computerized classroom	minimum of 1	50 SF/student + 100 SF/ teacher + 45 SF/ inmate toilet	varies	Dedicated classroom for computer-aided instruction, specialized mechanical/electrical systems to accommodate equipment.
Media center	1	300 SF for broadcast area; 300 for equipment room	varies	Used to broadcast institutionwide announcements and programs, provide in-cell instruction or orientation programs, and so forth.

Continued

Program / Space	Quantity	Minimum Net Square Feet	Occupants	Notes
EDUCATION *continued*				
STAFF AREAS (may be expanded to support vocational training also)				
Administrative offices	varies	120 SF	varies	Number depends on staffing as determined by administration and state or local requirements.
Clerical office	varies	80 - 100 SF	varies	Desk and chair, computer and printer, files.
Records	1	60 - 150 SF	N/A	Size depends on number of inmates in program.
Shared work room	1	350 SF	assumes 4	Workroom shared by up to 4 teachers; increase size of room if more teachers. Includes 4 desks, copier and supplies. Can be used as a break room or conference room.
Conference room	1	20 SF/person	varies	May be provided in addition to staff workroom, if administrative area is remote from classrooms.
Staff rest rooms	per codes	per codes	staff only	Locate centrally for easy access. If classrooms are remote from administrative area, provide staff rest rooms in both places.
LIBRARIES				
General library	1	varies	varies	Include stacks area, offices, copy and supplies, repair area, storage, rest rooms and janitor's closet.
Legal library	1	varies	varies	Enclosed separately from general library, but may be accessible from within general library.
VOCATIONAL TRAINING				
Workshop	varies	dependent on trade chosen	varies	Recommend providing unfinished shell space until program selection completed. Include inmate toilets, sinks, secure storage in each workshop.
Classroom	1:2 programs	35 SF/student 100 SF/teacher	varies	Locate between two workshops so that space can be shared. Centrally locate staff rest rooms for access by all teachers.
Administrative offices and support	varies	varies	varies	If vocational and academic programs are coordinated by the same group, staffs can share spaces. Provide adequate staff offices, restrooms, workroom, and so forth.
RECREATION				
Outdoor recreation	1/500 inmates	15 SF/inmate No less than 1,500 SF	varies	An elevated, sheltered staff observation post may be needed (provide water). Assume these activities at a minimum: baseball or softball, volleyball, basketball, weight lifting, track. Provide paved and grassy areas. Water fountains, toilets within easy access and supervision by staff. Recommend location near gymnasium or other indoor recreation.
Gymnasium	1	8,500 SF	varies	Provide shower/locker areas, bleachers, staff office, equipment storage. May also serve as auditorium for ceremonies, multipurpose.
Indoor recreation	1	15 SF/inmate	varies	Size and quantity depend on administration's policies and preferences for group sizes and availability. Should include storage room. Inmate toilets should be nearby.
Arts and crafts	1	1,200 SF + 150 SF for storage	varies	May need utilities to accommodate kiln, pottery wheels. Provide sinks with plaster traps.

Continued

Program / Space	Quantity	Minimum Net Square Feet	Occupants	Notes
RELIGIOUS PROGRAMS				
Chapel	1	300 SF (seating)	minimum of 15 inmates	Consider locating adjacent to a multipurpose area with a movable partition for larger gatherings. Some faiths may require special accommodations, such as the Muslim faith.
Offices	varies	120 SF for offices; 80 SF for inmate clerk	varies	Minimum of 2 offices recommended, plus inmate clerk. Storage rooms and a dressing room with a hand sink (adjacent to chapel) recommended. Inmate and staff toilets nearby.
Storage	1-2	80 SF	N/A	One large or several small closets may be provided. Locate near chapel.
Dressing room	1	80 SF	1-2	Include 3-4 individual closets with shelves, hand sink, and mirror.
Sweat lodge	1	outdoors	varies	Outdoor space within security perimeter. Needs a water source and a wood storage area.
MULTI-USE AREAS				
Multipurpose rooms	varies	range from 200 SF to 450 SF	varies	Provide several multipurpose, variably sized rooms to accommodate a range of activities. Consider locating adjacent to the auditorium or gym for breaking down larger assemblies.
Auditorium	1	2,000 SF	varies	May be provided in addition to a gym, but for smaller assemblies.
Storage	varies	100 – 300 SF	N/A	At least one room is recommended, but may be increased as needed.
INDUSTRIAL PROGRAMS				
Factory	varies	300 SF/inmate should be adequate for spaces listed	varies	As with vocational programs, shell space should be provided until final program decisions made.
Bulk storage	varies	see above	N/A	Recommend some bulk storage located inside the security perimeter adjacent to factory. Finished products may be stored outside in a warehouse.
Staff space	varies	see above	varies	Provide offices for administrative staff, clerical support, inmate clerks, janitor's closets, rest rooms, and so forth. Staff will provide managerial/ supervision, purchasing, marketing, and so forth.
Warehouse	1	varies	warehouse staff, custody staff, inmate workers	May be located outside the security perimeter and accommodate other functions than industries. Truck loading dock may be required, pallet storage, and so forth.
Corporation yard	varies	varies	N/A	May be located adjacent to the industries complex, inside or outside the security perimeter, or both. Provide adequate paving materials to withstand heat and heavy equipment. Surround with fencing for security.

Continued

Program / Space	Quantity	Minimum Net Square Feet	Occupants	Notes
SUBSTANCE ABUSE TREATMENT				
Living unit	varies	varies	Recommend group size of 40 inmates	Recommend each 40-bed cluster have cells, a dayroom, 1-2 small group rooms, 1-2 interview rooms, shared office on the unit for staff.
Program space	varies	20 SF/ inmate (group rooms)	varies	Amount of program space determined by number of participants. Recommend a variety of variably sized group rooms, ranging from 6 persons to 15 persons. At least one large assembly space (could be a dayroom) should accommodate all residents of a given unit.
Offices	varies	100 – 150 SF	1 per office	Private offices or interview spaces are required for meeting with inmates individually to maintain confidentiality. Administrative offices may be located centrally; counselors should be located on the units.
Staff conference room	1	20 SF/person	varies	Located centrally, for team meeting, staff meetings, and so forth.

The intake/booking area is an open area that enhances circulation and the flow of processing. Rooms for interrogation, classification, medical examination, photography, and so forth, are arranged to facilitate the processing of inmates. A more effective layout allows for higher security by a smaller staff. Portage County Jail, Ravenna, Ohio.

Photo courtesy of NBBJ, Columbus, Ohio. Photographer: John Griesen.

Orientation

After sentencing, inmates are sent to a reception center (*see* Section 3). The reception facility may be a smaller unit within a larger institution, or it may be an entire facility dedicated to reception. The intake process typically includes a phase of data collection and review, medical and mental health screening, and other preliminary assessment activities. This process generally takes between thirty and forty-five days. Once the data has been reviewed, each inmate is assigned to a correctional institution.

Correctional staff take care to place an inmate at an institution that matches his or her custody level with the institution's security systems and procedures. Inmates always should be placed in the least-restrictive environment appropriate to their custody level. On their arrival at their permanent institution, inmates participate in the orientation phase of their confinement.

The orientation phase serves to familiarize inmates with the institution's policies and procedures and helps them make an orderly transition to institutional life. Most orientation programs include lectures, films, and other activities that explain the institution's programs, mission, rules, and regulations. Inmates also receive a comprehensive medical and mental health screening. In addition, staff administer academic assessment tests and conduct in-depth interviews to determine the best programs and work assignment for each inmate. Other data about the inmate also is reviewed, including previous correctional terms, gang affiliations, or special needs.

Housing Options

Many options for housing assignments exist, but most jurisdictions find that some separation of newly admitted inmates from the general population is best for management and custody purposes. One option as shown in the chart on page 242 is to designate a special orientation unit adjacent to the admissions area. A second option is to designate all or part of a regular housing unit for newly admitted inmates. A third option is to provide no special housing, assigning inmates instead to an appropriate housing unit as beds become available. Some jurisdictions may combine two of these options. Smaller jurisdictions may not provide any special orientation housing.

Where staffing and housing availability make it possible, most jurisdictions prefer to separate newly admitted inmates from the general population as much as possible. While some institutions may construct separate dining, recreation, and other facilities, most simply schedule the use of these service areas for inmate management.

Inmates in orientation may be escorted to dining, visiting, medical services, recreation areas, commissary, laundry exchange, and to other services or activities. Another option is to provide a certain amount of multipurpose space within the housing unit itself.

Option 1

Housing units designated solely as orientation housing units can have the most specific spatial requirements. The orientation housing unit may contain only cells, a dayroom, showers, and a custody station. Providing additional program space within the housing unit will decrease the amount of staff escort time and reduce the potential for incidents occurring with general population inmates. Testing, lectures, videos, dining, and recreation all may occur within the housing unit itself.

The number of beds in an orientation unit will vary, depending on that jurisdiction's population projections, regional requirements, and other factors. Most orientation housing should contain single or double cells, to ease management of newly admitted inmates, about whom staff may know very little. While a single-celled arrangement is often the most costly to construct, it is also the safest and most secure option.

Double-celling is somewhat less expensive to construct and staff; however, this arrangement also requires staff to be more cognizant of each inmate to make decisions about who should share a cell with whom. Dormitory-style housing may be appropriate for institutions where all incoming inmates are minimum security, and where the inmates will be assigned to dormitory housing immediately after orientation.

Cells should contain one or two bunks and a toilet/sink combination unit. Other rooms within the housing unit should include a control room or staff workstation, a dayroom, and shower rooms. To minimize escort time out of the unit, or if program space elsewhere in the institution is limited, the orientation housing unit also may contain multipurpose rooms for administering group tests and assessments, delivering orientation lectures, or holding housing meetings.

Depending on the orientation activities designed by the administration, a dayroom could be used for these purposes, thus not requiring a special enclosed space. Providing a separately enclosed multipurpose room, however, would allow the administration to provide orientation activities to newly arrived inmates while offering other activities to those inmates who may be ready for a transfer to permanent housing. Wherever possible, the housing unit should be designed with as much program flexibility as possible.

Providing enclosed staff spaces also decreases the need for escort staff. An examination room (120 net square feet) for medical staff and enclosed interview rooms (80 net square feet) for mental health staff and correctional counselors to conduct private interviews and assessments are highly desirable. If these rooms are not provided on the unit, they must be available elsewhere.

Meals may be served on the unit from carts delivered by the central kitchen, or inmates could be escorted to a central dining room. Laundry exchange also could occur in the dayroom, as could canteen/commissary deliveries and other similar services.

Option 2

If an institution has limited space, or the number of orientation beds is small, the administration may choose to locate orientation inmates in a designated portion of a general population housing unit, adjusting the number of cells occupied by orientation inmates, as needed. While this practice places new inmates with general population inmates, it permits greater flexibility. It adjusts the number of beds available for orientation and makes efficient use of available space. However, mixing orientation and general population inmates within the same housing unit makes the provision of an enclosed multipurpose space even more important than in Option 1.

If program space is not available within the housing unit, orientation inmates would have to be escorted to all services. Some services still might occur in the dayroom for orientation inmates, such as dining, laundry exchange, group testing, and lectures. This is feasible especially if the general population inmates in the housing leave the housing unit for work, school, and other activities at scheduled times, or if the housing unit is subdivided into smaller modules.

Option 3

The third option requires that staff assign inmates to permanent housing immediately upon arrival. This option assumes that staff have sufficient data from the courts, presentence investigation reports, and other information with which to make an informed decision about housing and programming assignments. This option may present the most security concerns for staff and inmates, and relies heavily on an efficient system of data collection and assessment.

Multipurpose area at Virginia Peninsula Regional Jail, Williamsburg, Virginia, a medium-security facility.

Architect, Daniel, Mann, Johnson & Mendenhall (DMJM). Photo courtesy of Gilbane Building Company, Providence, Rhode Island, construction manager. Photographer: Doug Buerlein.

Inmates in a substance abuse treatment group meeting.

Photo courtesy of Corrections Corporation of America, Nashville, Tennessee.

Substance Abuse Treatment

In addition to other educational programs, many institutions provide substance abuse treatment education classes to inmates. Some prisons even have a separate therapeutic community for those who need intensive treatment. An overwhelming majority of correctional inmates have a drug use history, making the information presented in typical education programs pertinent to inmates' lives.

For inmates whose length of stay in a facility is short (less than six months), a classroom substance abuse curriculum may be beneficial by presenting information about making better choices on release. For inmates who have at least one year left to serve, more intense substance abuse treatment programs can have a positive impact on their lives on their return to the community. Outcome studies of in-custody treatment programs, especially those with a duration of longer than six months that are coupled with aftercare community programs, have demonstrated a significant reduction in recidivism rates (*see* Latessa, 1999).

Short-term substance abuse education programs require only a classroom setting. No special design is re-

quired. Long-term intensive substance abuse treatment, however, can be enhanced by a setting that supports the treatment environment. It is this latter program that will be discussed in this section.

Treatment Program Models

The goal of most substance abuse treatment programs is to present offenders with meaningful choices that take full account of the historical experience and perception of the offenders themselves. A typical program provides an environment where these choices are implemented through systematic and worker-like tasks and activities that target irresponsible patterns and cycles of thinking, feeling, and behaving. Some treatment programs also address specific pathologies and deficits.

Programs developed on this model include training in essential life skills, including new cognitive and emotional skills. These are aimed at enhancing the newly released inmate's ability to effectively live and work in the community as a law-abiding citizen.

Treatment typically occurs in four phases, three of which happen during incarceration and one in the community after release. The first phase is the *orientation phase* and may last three to four weeks. Inmates undergo processing and testing, similar to a typical orientation into a larger institution. Then, housing and program assignments will follow. The *residential phase* may last from six-to-nine months. During this phase, inmates learn to identify, examine, and restructure self-defeating patterns of criminal thinking and behavior. Personal relapse cycles are identified, and inmates learn techniques for interrupting the relapse cycle. The third phase is *the pre-release phase*, which typically begins three months from release. Inmates learn specific coping methods for the transition from institution life to life in the community. A personal discharge contract typically is developed with each inmate, which commits him or her to accomplishing social, treatment, training, and work objectives. Parole agent liaisons and correctional counselors work closely with treatment staff during this phase to ensure that linkages with community services are made.

Aftercare, the fourth and final phase, begins upon the inmates' release. On returning to the community, a program graduate may be expected to continue contact with community treatment programs for as long as a year after release. Some individuals in the aftercare phase may live in local residential treatment housing prior to returning to their families. Parolees are encouraged to participate in regular treatment groups at treatment centers, which can provide continuing support and provide early intervention should problems develop.

Staff

Treatment and custody staff are two of the most critical resources for a successful treatment program. Some jurisdictions select and train correctional personnel to provide treatment; others contract with private providers for treatment services. These providers then work cooperatively with custody staff who provide security. Whatever the staffing arrangement, custody staff must fully understand the goals of the treatment program and how it may differ from routine life in a correctional facility. Where contract and custody staff work together, cross-training is critical for both groups to understand the requirements of the security and operational system and the drug treatment goals and expectations. All security issues become treatment issues because adherence to unit rules, respect for the rights of others, respect for the physical environment, and participation in program activities are all important elements of the treatment program.

Daily Schedule

While treatment program models vary, a typical daily schedule for an intensive treatment program involves structured activities from the beginning of the day to lights out. The philosophy of an intensive treatment program is that every aspect of an inmate's day can be considered treatment, from personal hygiene tasks to making a bunk, to attending classes and participating in group counseling. Even leisure time becomes a treatment goal—recovering addicts often have little or no experience in making constructive use of their time.

Group Size

An ideal size for a housing unit is anywhere from twenty to forty. If more inmates are enrolled in the program, the larger group should be subdivided into treatment clusters of a manageable size. Intensive treatment programs focus on learning and practicing daily living skills, getting along with other residents, and holding one another responsible for all behavior. It is important, therefore, that group sizes be kept small to enhance such an intense involvement with each other.

Space

Many jurisdictions use existing living units without changes and designate them for treatment of substance abuse participants. Others construct new units specially designed to promote a therapeutic environment. In addition to living units, other spaces that will enhance treatment goals include classrooms, leisure and recreation spaces, space for religious services, and offices for staff to meet with small groups and individuals. Administrative staff should be located close to the daily operations of the treatment program.

As much as possible, the program participants should be segregated from the general population. Ideally, living units and support services (dining, recreation, laundry exchange, canteen, visiting, and so forth) should be provided separately. If this is not possible, then scheduling these activities to avoid mixing with nontreatment inmates will assist the inmates with the program's goals.

A variety of multipurpose rooms should be provided, sized for small groups from six-to-eight persons, ten-to-fifteen persons, and for an entire housing module. In addition, the living unit should include a large meeting room for daily "house meetings." A dayroom is an acceptable space for this purpose, but does not function well for small group meetings. Instead, each forty-bed cluster should have available a dayroom space, one-to-two small group rooms, and one-to-two interview rooms for individual work. Treatment staff should maintain a constant presence on the living unit, so a shared office where paperwork can be done is recommended.

Another unique feature in a treatment facility may be the abundance of staff offices readily available to participants. Staff are a critical part of the program, and participants need quick and reliable access to counselors and other treatment staff. Individual offices for psychologists and other treatment professionals are required so that they can maintain confidentiality. Staff also require conference spaces for treatment team meetings, which occur with some frequency, often daily.

Program administrators should be located close to the treatment unit, though they need not necessarily be in the same building. If a contract provider has been selected, it is important that staff is provided with adequate offices near custody and administrative offices so that both staffs can work together to achieve treatment and security goals.

Inmate Activities and Services

Institution life is not always structured to make individuals accountable for their daily existence. Mcals are furnished by others, laundry often cleaned, folded, and organized by others, and so forth. Ideally, space should be provided on the living unit for inmates to prepare meals and do their own laundry, just as they will have to upon release. Learning daily living skills such as these can be a valuable component of a treatment program. Other typical activities, such as academic education, vocational training, and prison industry jobs can be the same as for nonprogram participants. Ideally, however, these work and education opportunities would be provided separately from the rest of the population.

Visiting

Visiting is another important component of institutional life. For some treatment program inmates, visits with family members may be antitherapeutic and might be prohibited altogether, at least in the early phases of the program. One of the elements in an individual's relapse cycle is often the still-addicted family members or close friends. In the beginning stages of recovery, participants may need to avoid contact with those persons with whom they may have shared a drug lifestyle on the outside.

On the other hand, families who show a good faith effort or who have no addictive behaviors themselves may serve as a component of an individual's recovery. Once a counselor determines that the family can be helpful, they can be included in the individual's treatment plan by attending family therapy periodically. If the visiting area has some enclosed rooms for six-to-eight persons, these could be used for family therapy. It is important, however, not to mix general visiting for the main population with family therapy sessions. If family therapy rooms are not available, space should be provided for such therapy closer to the treatment unit.

Design Features Enhance the Treatment Community Environment

There should be no question that the treatment program is located inside a correctional facility. A major part of substance abuse treatment programs is to be accountable for one's actions, whether that is taking a drug or committing a crime. However, certain design features in treatment spaces can enhance the program's goals without impeding the general nature of institutional life. For example, the use of durable carpeting in group spaces will reduce the noise factor usually associated with the hard steel and concrete surfaces typical of most correctional environments. In small group meetings, the voice levels of participants can be crucial to the success of the daily meeting or the treatment agenda.

Normalizing the environment in other ways also will enhance the treatment program goals. Inmates will be held accountable for all behavior, including mistreatment of their environment, as they are in all correctional facilities, but here the care of the environment also becomes a treatment goal. Generous amounts of natural light, movable furniture as opposed to fixed furniture, and the ability to personalize spaces all can add to the success of the program.

Multi-use Areas

In some institutions, a centralized area may be provided to serve a variety of functions for both inmates and staff. The provision of a multi-use area may be especially cost-efficient for smaller institutions where budgetary considerations are critical. A broad range of activities may occur throughout the institution daily, including meetings, recreational activities, entertainment, workshops, seminars, and other similar functions. Local volunteer agencies may wish to conduct special meetings or workshops in the institution, augmenting existing programs or creating new ones. Providing a single-use space for each of these functions would be costly and inefficient.

Combining Multiple Program Areas

The number of multipurpose rooms to be provided in a facility will vary from site to site, and should be determined by estimating the number of functions that may occur simultaneously throughout the day. It is important to estimate group sizes, too. It may be possible to provide several multipurpose rooms of varying sizes to accommodate a broad range of activities and group sizes. The spaces should be pleasant and comfortably furnished while also remaining generic enough to maximize flexibility. The rooms may be connected by wide corridors to permit large groups of people to circulate. Rest rooms should be provided separately for each group: inmates, the public, and staff. The multipurpose rooms may be co-located in a single building with other inmate programs such as the arts and crafts area, indoor recreation, and the chapel.

One alternative is to provide a number of differently sized rooms, ranging from 200 square feet to 450 square feet. If located near the auditorium, these rooms could be used as "break-out" rooms following a larger assembly in the auditorium.

Auditorium

As an alternative to a larger, expensive gymnasium, an auditorium could be provided. This space could be used for entertainment, large group meetings, ceremonies, and other functions. Movable seating is recommended so that the space can be used for other purposes. A raised platform is desirable, though not required. If the auditorium is located adjacent to the chapel, a soundproof movable partition would allow the chapel services to expand for special occasions.

The size of the auditorium should be determined based on the administration's preference for manageable group sizes. As a rule of thumb, however, a 500-bed facility might have a 2,000 square-foot auditorium, which would accommodate approximately 300 people. If a gymnasium also is provided, then that space might be used for larger assemblies.

Storage

At least one large storage room of about 300 square feet is recommended for storing chairs, audiovisual equipment, and other stage equipment. Smaller storage rooms of 100 square feet may be used throughout the multi-use complex.

Education

A well-rounded correctional education program provides inmates with a constructive way to spend time and an opportunity to improve their skills. Successful completion of an institutional education program may improve an inmate's chance for successful reentry into the community, including better chances for employment and lower recidivism. In addition, an inmate's sense of self-worth and overall attitude may improve while

Multipurpose area of Portage County Jail, Ravenna, Ohio.

Photo courtesy of NBBJ, Columbus, Ohio. Photographer: John Giresen.

incarcerated, contributing to the inmate's successful re-entry into society as a productive citizen.

Many inmates enter correctional institutions with seriously deficient educational backgrounds. Many lack a high school diploma, and many others have less than a sixth-grade education. A sound education program should strive to increase literacy, provide inmates with remedial education, and possibly allow more advanced students to complete a diploma or even a college degree. Institutions frequently work closely with state education departments and local districts to provide a well-rounded program.

An agency that is responsible for incarcerating young individuals, who must receive an education as required under state law, must provide access for those inmates to educational materials and instruction. This includes meeting an inmate's special education needs, where applicable.

Variety of Programs

A variety of programs should be offered, including Adult Basic Education (ABE) for inmates who have not attained a sixth-grade education; a General Education Development (GED) program offering a high school equivalency degree; and a postsecondary program for those who are eligible. Continuing education courses may be offered for those who want to update their skills and knowledge.

Other programs that may come under the education program's purview include parenting classes, prerelease training, and substance abuse education. These programs may be conducted in the typical classroom setting.

In addition to traditional academic training, an institutional education program also may offer vocational training. Many institutions provide a variety of vocational training programs, which include production work and classroom training.

Education Staff

Staffing should include at least one full-time administrator, assistant administrators, and clerical support, in addition to certified, experienced instructors for the range of academic programs offered. Staff may be hired as institutional employees or as contractors, depending on the availability of qualified persons in the community, budgetary considerations, and other factors. Some jurisdictions have a contract with the local school districts to provide staff, curriculum, and materials. Instructors should be cross-trained so that they understand the demands of a correctional setting in concert with the education program. Educational staff must understand that safety and security procedures, rules and regula-

tions take precedence over the education program. At the same time, custody staff should be cross-trained to enhance their understanding of the demands of the academic classroom.

Academic Classrooms

The size of the academic classrooms should provide approximately thirty-to-thirty-five square feet per student. The number of students per classroom will vary according to the state's teacher-student ratio. Space for a teacher's desk should be added to the total square footage. An inmate toilet in each classroom also is recommended to minimize circulation out of the classroom. Glazing in corridor walls and/or entry doors is recommended for supervision by patrolling custody staff. A source of natural light is highly recommended. Student desks should accommodate the adult learner, and a small number of individual study carrels also may be provided. Depending on the institution's budget, at least one classroom should be designed to accommodate individualized computerized education, with one computer station per student. This classroom should be sized at approximately fifty square feet per person. All classrooms should contain power for other audiovisual equipment such as video recorders and videocassette recorders, televisions, and audio recording equipment.

Education Staff Offices

Administrative staff should have private, fully enclosed offices of approximately 120 square feet. A shared office or work room should be provided for teachers, with audiovisual material storage, paper storage, copier, and other equipment in the room or in a separate enclosed, adjacent space. The administrative area also should contain a records room and clerical area. Offices should be wired for computer equipment, phones, and at least one fax machine. Staff rest rooms should be easily accessible by all staff, and secure from inmates. If a single staff coordinates the academic and vocational programs, the administrative areas should include private offices and support spaces to accommodate all staff.

Libraries

Education programs should include two libraries for inmates. The general library will serve as a learning center and should be centrally located from the classrooms. The legal library will allow inmates to participate in their own legal matters. The legal library collection may be an enclosed room within the larger general library. Both should be designed for computer access.

Where multiple facilities with individual programs and classrooms are located within a larger institution, satellite libraries may be located in each smaller facility, with the central library serving as a repository and distributor for the larger collection. Books may be rotated throughout the satellite libraries or duplicate copies of books may be provided in each satellite. The general library collection should be similar to the library in a public education setting, with a wide variety of books, periodicals, newspapers, and reference materials. Audiovisual materials for education and entertainment purposes also should be available. Materials should be kept relevant to the inmates' needs and should reflect a variety of languages, where the population is multicultural. Materials also should be reflective of the inmates' varied reading levels and interests.

Space Requirements

Spaces within the general library should include the stacks area, at least one enclosed staff office, an enclosed copy and supply room, staff and inmate rest rooms, a repair and staging area, and other support spaces. The layout of the stacks and other areas should ensure that visibility of all areas is unobstructed, with taller shelving units placed along walls and lower-height units in the middle of the floor. A computerized card catalog may be provided.

Library Staff

Library staff may consist of a head librarian who oversees the overall administration of the library system, with support from assistant librarians, and even inmate clerks.

Legal Library

Access to legal materials has been vigorously supported by the courts. The administration must ensure that inmates have access to a legal library seven days a week, especially during evening and weekends so as not to interfere with work and school hours. Each institution should consult the American Association of Law Libraries' materials list to determine the scope of the legal collection that is sufficient for an institution's law library. The lists includes such things as state constitutions and statutes, state court cases, federal case law, court rules and practices, and legal periodicals, digests, and indexes. Much of the material is available on microfilm.

The legal collection should be located in an enclosed room, that is separate from the rest of the general library, with glazing for optimal supervision. An individual, secure study booth is recommended in institutions where maximum-security inmates reside to ensure that these

The learning center is an important element in the education of inmates. Here, access to research information and leisure reading materials help inmates address their school assignments and catch up on recreational reading. Federal Correctional Complex at Allenwood, Pennsylvania.

Architectural firm: The Kling-Lindquist Partnership, Philadelphia, Pennsylvania. Construction management firm: Gilbert Commonwealth, Reading, Pennsylvania. Construction contractor for the training center: Fletcher-Harlee Corporation, Glenside, Pennsylvania. Photo courtesy of the Federal Bureau of Prisons.

inmates have equal access to legal materials without compromising the safety of other inmates and staff.

Another option is to provide a computer system that could give inmates access to the law library data via a dedicated local area network (LAN). Inmates could access the data from their housing units through computer terminals in their dayrooms. This would reduce the amount of area needed for the law library and permit inmates' access to the data without their having to go to the library.

Media Center

An institutionwide closed-circuit television system will allow the administration to broadcast announcements and news. This system also may be adapted to allow in-cell instruction for inmates who otherwise may pose a security risk if they were to be in a classroom with instructors or other inmates. A media room should contain a broadcast room adjacent to an equipment and storage room. These rooms should be designed with high-security features and be easily supervised by staff within and outside the room. A staff and inmate rest room should be included in this area to prevent unauthorized access into other rooms.

Vocational Training

The primary goals of the correctional vocational training programs are to give inmates a chance to make constructive use of their time, to provide marketable skills that will be useful when inmates reenter their communities, and to help them become more productive citizens. A secondary goal of some vocational training programs is to provide a workforce for the institution. Vocational training programs, unlike prison industries, typically are not production-oriented. Inmates usually spend a portion of their day in classroom instruction, learning about safety measures and proper procedures, and a portion of the day in a workshop learning to use equipment properly and practicing their craft.

Ideally, vocational programs should respond to changes in the nation's job markets. Designers should strive to provide adequate and adaptable space that will allow an institution to modify existing space, as needed, to keep pace with technological and marketplace changes.

Types of Programs

Vocational programs range from "dirty" programs such as auto mechanics to "clean" programs such as drafting or copy reproduction. The traditional trades include carpentry, plumbing, welding, painting, auto repair, and electrical work. Other programs may include computer programming, computer-related equipment operation, and office services. In addition, repair of small engines, office equipment, refrigerators, air conditioners, and televisions may be offered. Programs for women and men should afford both groups equal opportunities for employability. Nontraditional trades should be offered to women along with the usual array of programs such as cosmetology and nursing.

Vocational Staff

Vocational training programs typically come under the purview of the education department of the correctional facility. The number of instructors will vary from institution to institution, based on a particular state's mandates for employment and training, available funding, and the availability of local resources. As with academic instructors, staff may be state correctional employees or contract employees.

Some institutions coordinate vocational training with academic training, primarily to increase the literacy of the students prior to their entering a vocational program. Students need to be able to read and follow instructions, learn safety procedures, and read textbooks. Initially, inmates may be assigned to an academic classroom for a specified period. After they achieve an adequate literacy rating, they may move on to a vocational setting. Other institutions place inmates in an academic setting for half a day and a vocational program for the other half. Some institutions link academic education, vocational training, and prison industries with inmates progressing along a continuum to the paid positions of the prison industries.

Vocational training at the Maryland Correctional Institute in Jessup.

Photo courtesy of Stephen Steurer, Correctional Education Association, Lanham, Maryland.

Vocational Training Space

Some vocational programs will require only classroom-type spaces (such as computer programming or office equipment operations), while others will require large open production areas and classrooms. When planning vocational space, programs should be grouped by function, such as placing auto mechanics and auto body repair in a separate building or group of buildings, and locating computer-related programs together in another building.

Where possible, the vocational programs should be located near academic classrooms. Some institutions, however, prefer to keep programs that involve tools and potential weapons stock separate from academic programs, placing the former programs in a zone surrounded by fencing and accessible to truck deliveries.

Students typically attend several hours of classroom instruction and then spend the remainder of the time in the workshop. To maximize use of vocational space, a classroom could be located between two workshops, with access from both. When one group is using the classroom, the other group could be using the workshop.

Support spaces for inmate vocational programs should include toilets and sinks for inmates, which are best located within each workshop or classroom. An industrial-style handwashing sink may be best for shops where oil, grease, or other heavily soiled activities take place (auto mechanics, for example). Classrooms should be glazed so that instructors can see into adjacent workshops for optimal supervision. The classroom may serve as an office for instructors. A staff toilet should be located nearby.

Administrative space should be located centrally, with private offices, storage rooms, a clerical area, records storage, and duplicating equipment. A conference room is recommended also, and may be used as a staff break room. If the vocational and academic programs are coordinated by the same staff, the office areas may be expanded and shared.

Secure storage rooms should be located within each workshop. The amount of materials storage will vary according to the type of program. Some programs will require fenced, covered outdoor space (such as a corporation yard), while others will require temperature-controlled rooms for paper and other supplies (such as for mechanical drawing or computer services).

Finishings, Utilities, and Mechanics

Classrooms should contain some acoustic treatment, and some workshop areas (for example, computer services) may require acoustic tile ceilings. Mechanical and electrical systems should be designed to accommodate a wide variety of programs and should take into account special needs such as dust, odor, and moisture removal. One option is to construct a vocational building as a shell with a minimum clear ceiling height of twelve feet. Later, as program decisions are made by the administration, the most appropriate partitions can be planned. Some jurisdictions have inmate labor work forces that can complete the interior construction.

While adequate utilities should be distributed to the vocational buildings, provisions for secondary distribution systems can be completed after decisions are made concerning specific programs. The required capacity can be determined by estimating the range of vocational activities anticipated for the institution.

An inmate at the Wallkill Correctional Facility prepares eyeglass lenses for distribution to New York State Medicaid clients throughout upstate New York.

Photo courtesy of the New York Department of Correctional Services.

Industrial Programs

The primary purpose of an industries program is to provide employment for inmates, foster good work habits, and provide training opportunities in a range of marketable skills. Work programs reduce idleness for incarcerated individuals and teach them to make constructive use of their time. Earning a salary, however small, and developing a solid work ethic also may help to build inmate self-esteem and eventually make a successful reentry into the community.

Additionally, a functional industry program provides much-needed products and services to the local correctional system. While the total number of inmates who can be employed will vary from location to location, many jurisdictions strive to employ 40 to 50 percent of the inmate population. Nationally, however, less than 7 percent of adult prison inmates are in correctional industries, and this rate is falling according to a study done for the Correctional Industries Committee of the American Bar Association.

Industries programs usually are not provided in local jails. There are some notable exceptions where sentenced offenders may stay only a short period of time and still participate in successful industry programs. Instead, correctional industry programs are primarily found in state and federal institutions.

The range of programs will vary, based on a number of factors. Federal and many state governments have laws that restrict the markets to which correctional industries

Inmates perform industrial activities and learn job skills at the Hennepin County Adult Detention Center, Minneapolis, Minnesota.

Photo courtesy of Hennepin County Sheriff's Department.

can sell their products and services. Additionally, inmates frequently have low skills in certain industries and may require training. (Many institutions develop complementary vocational programs to ameliorate this problem.)

Staff of Industry Programs

Staff should be selected with a wide range of skills and experience. In addition to specialists in a given industry, staff with management and business backgrounds should be chosen to administer the overall program. If marketing studies are done on a statewide basis, the institution may not need individuals with marketing expertise. Staffing requirements will include trainers, supervisors, and support services personnel such as accountants, purchasing agents, warehousing staff, and quality assurance specialists. The ratio of supervisors to inmates will vary from industry to industry. Custody staff will be required to monitor safety and security, but they should not be used as supervisors of production work.

Location

The industrial building or buildings should be located inside the security perimeter, with adequate open space around the building for outdoor storage and staging of materials, and truck deliveries. Larger industries will require a loading dock. A warehouse for raw and finished materials may be needed. Some jurisdictions prefer warehouses to be located outside the security perimeter, thus reducing the risk of contraband and escapes. Locating the warehouse outside the security perimeter also decreases the amount of security fencing, thus lowering initial construction costs.

Space

All industries will require factory or production space, bulk storage space (in addition to warehousing), offices, and separate toilet facilities for staff and inmates. As with vocational programs, the range of programs may vary over the life of the facility, and it may be best to design shell space, which can be adapted for a variety of programs over time. Rapidly changing marketing conditions and the long lead time from initial planning to occupancy often do not coincide in a way that is convenient for designers at the early planning stages.

The ceiling should be a minimum height of twelve feet, and the floor should be left unfinished. Appropriate partitions, utilities, and floor slab can be constructed once decisions are made on the programs.

It is difficult to estimate the actual square-footage requirements, but a good rule of thumb is to assume 300 square feet of space for each inmate who will be working in the programs at any one time. This amount should cover factory, bulk storage, office, and toilet spaces. Offices should contain as much glazing as possible to optimize supervision, and may have raised floors for a better view. It is wise to locate the industrial complex on a part of the site that will allow future expansion.

Joint Ventures with Private Industry

A current trend in the correctional industry field is to forge a joint venture with private industry. In such cases, the prison industries board of a given jurisdiction contracts with a private company to develop an industry inside the prison, using inmate workers. Construction costs even may be borne by the private enterprise. Training, staffing, marketing, and most administrative services also will be supported by the private company. These programs are regulated by the U.S. Department of Justice.

Industrial Program Potential

Once inmates who have worked in an industries program leave prison and return to their communities, they have a job skill as well as good work habits. These traits provide them with a chance to establish themselves successfully and lead a crime-free life.

Religious Programs

Freedom of religious expression is a right guaranteed by the U.S. Constitution. Additionally, the courts have upheld the rights of inmates to be given reasonable opportunities to pursue their personal religious beliefs while they are incarcerated. Correctional facilities, therefore, offer flexible religious programs within the bounds of safety and security.

Religious programs consist not only of the traditional worship services, but also seminars and workshops, prayer meetings, retreats, and observances of special religious holidays. Counseling and family services also may be offered. Most facilities employ at least one full-time chaplain and either contract with local clergy or recruit volunteers, or some combination of these. In addition to the major Protestant faiths, Catholicism, and Judaism, others that often are represented include the Buddhist, Muslim, and Native American faiths.

Chapel

A nondenominational chapel should be designed to accommodate as many faiths as possible, with movable seating and other religious materials. Seating should accommodate a minimum of fifteen persons. If possible, a larger seating area should be provided, to allow more persons to attend on special holidays, including family members. An alternative solution is to locate the chapel adjacent to a larger multipurpose area (such as an auditorium) with a movable partition that can be opened when larger gatherings need to be accommodated. Special accommodations may be required for those of the Muslim faith, with space for prayer and meditation and the foot-washing ceremony.

Support Space

Offices for clergy also should be provided, one for each denomination, if possible. Private offices are more flexible than a shared office, and may be used for individual counseling or consultations. A minimum of two offices of 120 net square feet is recommended. A clerk's office (eighty net square feet) also is recommended. Inmates frequently work with clergy, providing clerical support, so space is needed for this work. Rooms for storing religious artifacts, books, and other items are necessary, as well. One large room with individual closets or shelving units might suffice instead of a number of smaller rooms. A dressing room for clergy is recommended, with closets and a hand sink. Inmate and staff toilets should be located in the vicinity.

Sweat Lodges

A sweat lodge is used by Native Americans for a number of religious ceremonies. A single location should be identified within the facility perimeter for the sweat lodge, which will be constructed by the inmates. In a larger institution, more than one location might be identified. The area may be surrounded by fencing to ensure security. The area must include a water source and a wood storage area. Please see the pictures of a sweat lodge on page 104.

A nondenominational chapel should be designed to accommodate as many faiths as possible, with movable seating that permits a variety of ceremonial activities. The Federal Correctional Complex at Allenwood, Pennsylvania.

Architectural firm: The Kling-Lindquist Partnership, Philadelphia, Pennsylvania. Construction management firm: Gilbert Commonwealth, Reading, Pennsylvania. Construction contractor for low-security correctional institution: Keating Construction, Villanova, Pennsylvania. Construction contractor for medium-security correctional institution: Pizzagalli/Bell Joint Venture, South Burlington, Vermont. Construction contractor for the penitentiary: Centex Simpson Construction, Merrifield, Virginia. Construction contractor for the training center: Fletcher-Harlee Corporation, Glenside, Pennsylvania. Photo courtesy of the Federal Bureau of Prisons.

Recreation

Recreation programs play a crucial role in a correctional facility by providing inmates with constructive ways to channel their energies and relieve tensions inherent in institutional living. A recreation program, consisting of both indoor and outdoor activities, also gives inmates opportunities to use their free time productively, improve their physical and mental health, develop into good sports, and improve morale.

Recreation programs range from highly structured programs to those involving more free choice. Intramural sports may be offered, or inmates may be left more on their own to choose a variety of activities, or a combination of both. Some jurisdictions hire staff specifically to run recreation programs; others provide only custody supervision of activities. Inmates also may be selected and trained to assist with program operations. Community volunteers may be recruited to oversee the program or supplement full or part-time staff.

Outdoor Recreation

Outdoor recreation areas should be near the gymnasium facility and fenced to allow controlled access to this part of the institution. Activities that are popular include softball, basketball, volleyball, and soccer. A walking and jogging track also receives substantial use.

Outdoor recreation fields should be located adjacent to an enclosed space such as a gymnasium, where participants can have access to toilets, locker rooms, showers, and equipment storage rooms. Recreation fields should be as spacious as site and security constraints allow. A minimum of five acres is recommended, which will allow several activities to occur simultaneously. Typical activities may include baseball or softball, handball, volleyball, basketball, weight lifting, and track. Game tables also may be constructed as permanent fixtures outside for chess and checkers. Courts should be constructed of a hard surface that will withstand weather conditions, especially heat and sun. Shade should be provided where possible without impeding supervision.

Water fountains should be placed strategically around the outdoor recreation yard, within easy access for all participants. If a gymnasium is not located nearby with free access to toilets, outdoor toilets (for males) are recommended, designed with modesty screening to provide a measure of privacy.

Female inmates can participate in the same outdoor sports and recreation activities as male inmates. Also,

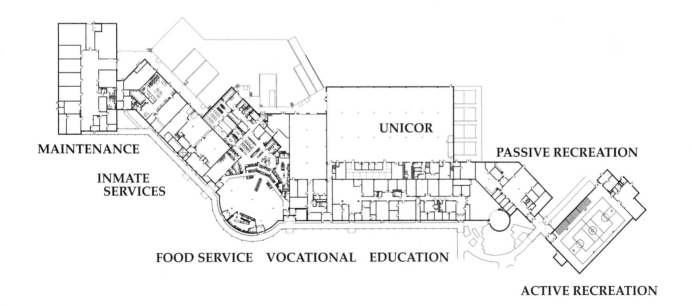

MAINTENANCE

INMATE SERVICES

UNICOR

PASSIVE RECREATION

FOOD SERVICE   VOCATIONAL   EDUCATION

ACTIVE RECREATION

Outdoor recreation areas should be near the gymnasium facility and fenced to allow controlled access to this part of the institution. Activities that are popular include: softball, basketball, volleyball, and soccer. A walking and jogging track also receive substantial use. The Federal Correctional Institution in Greenville, Illinois.

Architect: Phillips Swager Associates, Peoria, Illinois. General contractor: Perini Building Company, Southfield, Michigan. Construction management support services: CRSS Constructors, Chicago, Illinois. Photo courtesy of the Federal Bureau of Prisons.

opportunities for small group interactions should be provided, as many women prefer to gather in small groups. Shady areas with benches and tables are recommended.

If observation towers are not located with a view of the recreation yard, a small elevated staff post is recommended. This post also should be sheltered from the sun and may contain a drinking fountain and toilet. Communications between towers can be handled by radios.

Gymnasium

An enclosed space for active sports is recommended. Depending on the size of the facility, a full-size gymnasium is recommended, with full court basketball, bleachers, showers, toilets, and locker rooms. Approximately 8,500 square feet is recommended, with an unobstructed ceiling height of about twenty-two feet. An auditorium is an alternative solution.

The facility gymnasium also may serve double-duty for orientation meetings, graduations, or for other ceremonies. Providing a gymnasium or some form of sheltered recreation area will allow recreation programs to be continued during inclement weather. Floor finishes should accommodate alternate purposes; in other words, they should be suitable for street-shoe traffic, portable chairs, and other items. The building should be easily accessible from living units, but located away from medical facilities (to minimize noise) and segregation units

(to minimize passing of contraband). If the gym can be located near the main entrance, it may be possible to allow some public access for special events.

Support spaces within the gym should consist of a staff office, an equipment storage room, chair storage space, showers, toilets, and lockers. Two separate shower, locker, and toilet rooms are recommended for competing teams. All areas of the gym should be easily supervised by custody staff while also allowing privacy. The building should contain an intercom or paging system for announcements.

Weight lifting in correctional institutions is currently a controversial activity. Where jurisdictions allow this activity, it is best located outdoors, with a small storage shed located nearby to store some equipment. Indoors, other equipment may be provided, such as universal-type machines, stationary bicycles, and other fitness equipment. Indoor equipment and activities should be provided equally for female inmates, with some alternate activities available such as aerobics.

Supervision

The staff office should be located on an exterior wall with a view of both the gym and the adjacent recreation yard. The floor can be elevated slightly for a better view. Entry doors all should have easy visibility without obstructions. Shower rooms and toilet rooms should be aligned for easy supervision by patrolling staff. If collapsible bleachers are provided, they should include a feature that allows staff to lock them in place.

Indoor Recreation

In addition to a gymnasium, or if a gym is too costly for a smaller facility, at least one multipurpose activity room should be provided. (This room would be in addition to dayrooms on living units.) This room could be used for smaller group functions, such as table tennis, billiards, and similar activities.

Additional furnishings may include a television and card tables for checkers, chess, and other games. The furnishings should reflect the administration's policies

The institution gymnasium serves a variety of purposes at different times in the day. Finishes and sound control are very important to enhance security and multi-functional use.

Photo courtesy of L. Robert Kimball & Associates, Ebensburg, Pennsylvania.

regarding socializing with other inmates. They may include comfortable sofas and chairs for visiting. This room may be located near an arts and crafts area or visiting area and be accessible on special occasions to inmates' visitors and children. As with the gym, toilets should be located nearby. At least one storage room should be provided. A staff office may not be required, since custody staff most likely will provide supervision.

Arts and Crafts

Like active recreation programs, the arts and crafts program can provide inmates with opportunities to build self-esteem and morale and make productive use of their leisure time. Staffing may be provided by community volunteers who specialize in a variety of crafts, or it may be a staffed position. A minimum of 1,200 square feet is recommended, with durable floor and wall surfaces that can withstand constant cleaning and moisture. A lockable storage room of at least 150 square feet should be provided to hold works-in-progress. Another room of 150 square feet should be provided for holding raw materials that are used in the projects.

Mechanical systems should be able to remove odors, fumes, dust, and moisture adequately. Use a shadow board for tool storage for controlling hand tools that might become weapons. Art programs may include pottery, and the room may require electrical service adequate to support a kiln. Sinks with plaster traps also are recommended.

Visits are extremely important to an inmate's mental health and well being. Whether a noncontact visit (as shown here) or a contact visit, the inmates generally look forward to seeing family and friends. Virginia Peninsula Regional Jail, Williamsburg, Virginia, a medium-security facility.

Architect: Daniel, Mann, Johnson & Mendenhall (DMJM). Photo courtesy of Gilbane Building Company, Providence, Rhode Island, construction manager. Photographer: Doug Buerlein.

Visiting Programs

A visitation program that encourages inmates to maintain family and community ties may lessen the negative psychological consequences of imprisonment and reinforce positive attitudes that help the incarcerated individual reenter the community successfully. Visitation programs can strengthen inmate morale and ease tensions and management problems.

Visitation programs also may present security and safety problems to an institution, so it is vital that a clear set of rules and regulations govern the visiting program. Visitors may include attorneys, parole staff who assist in planning for release, clergy, counselors, and family members. Family members may include spouses, children, parents, and grandparents.

Screening and Processing of Visitors

Safety and security must not be compromised by the visitation program. Visitors must be notified of all regulations regarding their visits. Visitors should undergo a preliminary screening to verify their identity, and they should be required to pass through a metal detector or other search process to ensure that contraband does not cross the security perimeter.

No visitor should cross the security perimeter of a prison or jail without being carefully screened and searched. All packages should be inspected, including purses, briefcases, and bags. Identities should be checked against a list of permissible visitors. Visitors should be discouraged from bringing personal items into the institution, except to meet children's needs (for example, diaper bags, bottles, and similar items).

The visitor processing area should contain a processing counter with adequate files and supply storage area, phones, and a metal detector. Vending machines may be provided, and movable seating should be considered for days when visitors must wait a long time to enter.

However, visiting that is confined to specific days and hours may warrant a larger lobby area to contain lines of visitors waiting to be processed or to enter the perimeter.

Entry into the security perimeter must be through a sallyport, and visitors must proceed directly to the visiting room. Locating the visiting area near the pedestrian sallyport decreases traffic to other areas of the institution and prevents unauthorized visitor contact with inmates.

Supervision of Visiting

Supervision is critical to a successful visitation program to ensure the safety of the public, staff, and especially children. At the same time, supervision should be as unobtrusive as possible to allow a measure of privacy.

Frequency and Duration

The visiting schedule is determined by the administration based on the security level of the institution, available staffing, space, and other factors. In general, however, most jurisdictions schedule visiting (except for attorneys) on weekends and holidays. When institutions are in remote locations, visiting hours and days may need to be more flexible to accommodate visitors traveling long distances.

The number of visitors an inmate may receive and the length of visits is determined by the institution's schedule, space, and staff constraints. In addition, the security risks associated with the inmate's current or past behavior should determine the type, frequency, and duration of the visits. Most visits by attorneys are scheduled on demand, whenever possible, so as not to impede the legal process.

Location of Visiting Rooms or Booths

In an institution with a campus-style plan, inmates may travel from their facility to a central visiting location. In a mid-rise or high-rise building, inmates may remain on their living units, and the visitors may travel via public corridors (inaccessible to inmates) to visiting booths on the unit.

Types of Visiting

Most state institutions offer contact visiting, with some noncontact visiting available for high-security inmates. County jails frequently allow only noncontact visiting. Some state institutions allow overnight visiting with spouses, children, and sometimes grandparents.

An alternative is to have inmates remain in their housing units and visit with family and friends through the use of teleconferencing equipment. This process, called "televisiting," uses a computer-based video communications technology to eliminate contact between inmates and visitors and the resulting problems with contraband. It is a technology that is being well received in county jails and it is beginning to find its way into correctional institutions for inmates who are restricted to noncontact visits. All visiting, regardless of location, type, duration, or frequency, is supervised by correctional staff, and also may be monitored or recorded on closed-circuit television.

Noncontact Visiting

As a management tool, institutions that offer contact visiting also may provide noncontact visiting for inmates who present security problems or who otherwise are not eligible for contact visiting. To ensure the safety and security of all concerned, a number of semi-enclosed noncontact visiting booths may be provided. Three booths at seventy net square feet each are recommended at a minimum. These booths often are separated from each other by partitions, with the visitor's side open to the larger visiting room and the inmate's side fully enclosed. Communication is then accomplished through a handset or through perforated window frames. Security glazing allows visitors and inmates to see each other.

In some institutions, only noncontact visiting is allowed. To minimize inmate movement, noncontact booths may be located on the living unit, with public circulation kept separate from inmate circulation.

Attorney visiting may be accomplished in a fully enclosed booth to ensure confidentiality. A paper pass may be provided between the two sides of the booth, designed to permit entry of only a few of pages at a time, to prevent the passage of contraband. Often, this arrangement is used in new jail design so the public defender can review inmate records and discuss a case with an inmate.

Overnight Visiting

A limited number of jurisdictions permit overnight visits by family members. In such cases, a small apartment may be provided, located within the security perimeter and easily supervised by patrolling staff or by staff in an observation tower. The apartment also must be located away from other inmate areas to protect children and to provide a measure of privacy. A visiting apartment typically contains one bedroom (two if children are allowed to visit), a living room, a small kitchen/dining area, and an enclosed, secure outdoor space.

Outdoor Visiting

Outdoor visiting also may be provided as a supplement to indoor contact visiting. The outdoor visiting area, usually adjacent to the visiting room, may be

Family gathering in a women's facility.

furnished with picnic tables, trees or other sources of shade, and a children's outdoor play area. This area should be easily supervised by staff.

Televisiting

When an institution is sited in a remote location, the implementation of a televisiting program may be warranted. Other benefits of a televisiting program include reducing visitor traffic into and out of the security perimeter, minimizing the passage of contraband, which results in potential savings in staffing costs. Televisiting programs essentially are noncontact visiting programs. Cameras are located inside the institution, either at a central location or in each housing area. Inmates are placed in individual booths for the best audio and video broadcasting.

At another location in metropolitan correctional centers or perhaps in the facility's entry gatehouse, booths for visitors are provided for inmates' families, social workers, and other approved visitors. These televisiting sites for families may be located in rural locations also, and may be coordinated, funded, and maintained by the correctional agency, private nonprofit agencies, social service agencies, or prisoner support groups. Screening of visitors and scheduling of visiting hours requires coordination among all participating agencies. The number of custody staff, however, may be reduced. Staff must be able to monitor visits visually and also be able to listen to or record conversations.

In some jurisdictions, these systems have been paid for using revenues generated from inmate telephone use. The system provides inmate families an opportunity to visit with an incarcerated family member when they may not otherwise be able to do so.

Contact Visiting

Contact visiting typically occurs in large open rooms furnished with movable tables, vending machines, and other features. Noncontact booths and private visiting rooms also may be accessible from within the larger visiting area. Public and inmate entries must be provided separately, and an inmate search area is required to prevent contraband from entering the secure perimeter.

Some visiting rooms may offer a separate enclosed room for small children and infants. The design of the space must allow staff optimal supervision, without obstructions or blind spots. Closed-circuit television may be provided for optimal security.

Space Requirements for Visiting Areas

The size of the contact visiting room is determined by the anticipated number of inmates receiving visitors and the average number of visitors at any one time during the visiting period. Arriving at an accurate number of visitors to be accommodated is often difficult, since it may depend on the number of visiting hours established by the institution, the location of the institution, and other factors. A schedule permitting a generous daily visiting time may place fewer inmates in the space at one time, resulting in the need for less space. On the other hand, this visiting schedule may require a higher staffing ratio, and represents a recurring operational cost.

A staff observation station (eighty net square feet) should be located centrally within the room. The station may be placed on an elevated platform to optimize supervision. The visitors' entry, which must be separate from the inmates' entry, should be located near the staff station. Providing an intercom and electrically released door would permit staff to allow entry into the room while not obstructing the view of the visiting room itself.

A separate inmates' entry should contain adequate space for queuing and searching inmates, following their visit. Individual holding cells may be required for inmates who pose security risks and cannot wait in an open area.

Rest rooms for inmates and visitors generally are not located within the visiting room itself to prevent the passage of contraband. Keep inmate and public rest rooms separate from each other if visitor rest rooms are provided in the visiting area. Accommodations for infants and small children in rest rooms are highly desirable. These should include changing tables and child-height toilets and sinks or step stools.

If the visiting room is designed flexibly, it also may be used for other activities, such as small group ceremonies (graduations, counseling sessions, and group meetings). The design should promote informal communication without placing architectural barriers between inmates and visitors or inmates and staff. Seating arrangements, color schemes, and textures should convey a residential character. Privacy can be accomplish-ed by using furniture to form low dividers separating the visiting room into zones without compromising security. Video surveillance should be accommodated to enhance staff observation. Acoustic treatment of the ceiling, walls, and floor will minimize noise and promote a calming atmosphere.

Private Visiting Rooms

Small enclosed visiting rooms will allow a variety of individual sessions to occur. Inmates may visit with attorneys, clergy, counselors, or other mental health professionals, probation or parole staff, and other individuals. Private visiting rooms may be designed to accommodate different numbers of visitors. For example, a six-person room may be provided along with several two-to-three-person rooms.

Children's Areas

Indoor and outdoor areas may be provided for children to play with each other and their parents. These spaces should be designed to allow children to play safely, while also permitting their parents to interact with them and staff to supervise them adequately. Some jurisdictions provide extensive children's areas, with equipment often constructed and installed by the inmates. A minimum of 300 square feet of enclosed or semi-enclosed space is recommended indoors. Outdoor spaces may be as generous as the site and supervision requirements permit. Outdoor areas should be shaded or sheltered from the weather in some way.

Vending Areas

Approximately 150 square feet is recommended for vending machines. The vending area may be located within the visiting room, and should contain a variety of machines offering refreshments. A fifty-square-foot storage room also is recommended for storing replacement supplies. The vending area must be visible from the officer's station in the visiting room. A microwave oven is recommended for warming baby bottles and other food items.

References

Faiver, Kenneth. 1998. *Health Care Management Issues in Corrections.* Lanham, Maryland: American Correctional Association.

Latessa, E., ed. 1999. *Strategic Solutions: the ICCA Examines Substance Abuse—What Works.* Lanham, Maryland: American Correctional Association.

Morton, Joann B., ed. 1998. *Complex Challenges, Collaborative Solutions: Programming for Adult and Juvenile Female Offenders.* Lanham, Maryland: American Correctional Association.

U.S. Marshals Service transports prisoners by plane to a "hub" in Oklahoma City to the Federal Transfer Center. This holding facility enables marshals to bring prisoners from one flight and hold them for another flight to their final destination. Planes are driven to the flyway, which is connected to the building. The Center is designed to hold more than 1,000 inmates.
Photo courtesy of the Federal Bureau of Prisons.

Programs for Juveniles

Charles J. Kehoe
Securicor New Century
Richmond, Virginia

John Platt, Deputy Director
Juvenile Division, Illinois Department
    of Corrections
Springfield, Illinois

Careworker at the Jessup, Maryland, Reception and Diagnostic Center communicates with youth in his care.

Photo courtesy of the American Correctional Association, Lanham, Maryland.

Intake and Orientation for Juvenile Facilities

The Intake Process

Normally, the first contact a juvenile has with a juvenile detention or correctional facility is at the intake area. The purpose of the intake area is to admit the juvenile into the facility safely and efficiently. Several steps are followed regardless of the type of juvenile facility. The first step is to determine that there are legal grounds to take custody of the juvenile. If the juvenile is brought to the facility immediately after an arrest, staff may have to determine if there is probable cause to detain the juvenile. There also may be a court document, such as a warrant, or court order, that directs that the juvenile be placed in the facility.

When the legal authority to hold the juvenile has been confirmed, a complete search of the juvenile and the juvenile's possessions should be conducted. The search should be carried out by staff who are the same sex as the juvenile and in a room that ensures privacy.

The juvenile's personal clothing and property then should be inventoried. The juvenile and intake staff should cosign an inventory slip that lists all of the clothing and property items taken from the juvenile. The juvenile should be given a copy of the inventory list. If necessary, the juvenile's personal clothing should be washed. (Juvenile detention facilities should confirm with the arresting officer that the juvenile's clothing is not needed as evidence, before it is washed.) The juvenile's clothing and property then should be stored in a secure property storage room.

Once the juvenile's clothing and property have been taken, the juvenile should be directed to shower. Before the shower, the juvenile should be issued clean institutional clothing and personal hygiene articles.

Once the preliminary steps have been completed, the intake staff can begin the process of collecting and recording basic personal data and information from the juvenile. Medical, dental, and mental health information should be collected by staff who have been given specific training in the health care area. A risk and needs assessment also should be completed. This will be used to help classify the juvenile.

After this, the juvenile should be assigned a case or admission number, a housing unit, and a room/bed. The juvenile should be given written orientation materials that provide a basic overview of what is covered. A more detailed orientation should be given within the first twenty-four hours of the juvenile's admission to the facility. When all of the necessary data and information have been collected, juveniles should be allowed to inform their family of their new location and mail and visiting procedures.

The Intake and Admissions Area

The intake process can be aided by a design that takes into consideration the various steps in the process. In juvenile detention facilities, the intake area begins with a secure vehicular sallyport. In northern climates, an enclosed sallyport is preferred because of severe winter weather. The sallyport should be high enough to accommodate a large ambulance with parking space for a minimum of two vehicles. A drive-through sallyport is easier to manipulate, but takes up more space. The sallyport should include secure weapons' lockers for police officers' weapons. Some agencies also have installed video cameras in the sallyport area to enhance security.

The juvenile and the police officer or transportation officer enter the facility through a second sallyport that brings them into the intake area. The intake area should include a waiting area, with furniture that is fixed to the floor, a workstation for intake staff, a minimum of two holding rooms (one for males and one for females), showers and toilets, a secure property storage room, a facility clothing room, and a minimum of two interview rooms.

The intake area should be sized based on the greatest number of juveniles to be admitted at any one time. If it is common for several youth to be admitted at one time, the number of holding rooms, showers, interview rooms, and the size of the workstation, will need to be increased. The workstation for staff should be designed to enable staff to monitor shower areas. Although privacy of youth is important, supervision is as well. Selection of appropriate building products such as sand-blasted glass block or perforated metal plate in shower and changing areas can provide a degree of privacy while still giving staff a reasonable degree of surveillance into those areas.

There are several methods for storing a juvenile's personal clothing and property in a secure property storage room. Many facilities have found that plastic bags with a zip lock on them are effective for storing clothing. They can be hung on a clothing rack, which takes less space than lockers. The method that requires the least amount of space, while being secure, is probably the most efficient approach.

The facility's clothing storage room requires enough space to hold the clothing that all new juveniles will be issued at the time of admission. In smaller facilities, all of the facility's clothing will be kept in this room.

Two interview rooms that will seat four will enable facility staff, law enforcement personnel, attorneys, and parents to meet with juveniles. The facility's health care area also should be located adjacent to the intake area and include an examining room, doctor/nurse's office or workstation, file room, and secure storage and equipment room to properly store medications and sharps. A provision also should be made for handling toxic waste and other toxic materials.

Orientation Process

Orientation is a systematic approach used to give the juvenile an orderly transition into the facility. During orientation, the juvenile is given an overview of the facility, including, but not limited to, the facility's mission, services that are provided, daily schedules, verbal and written rules, visiting, telephone and mail procedures, instructions on how to access services, especially health care services, the facility's grievance procedures, and other essential information. In juvenile detention facilities, orientation also provides the facility and court staff the opportunity to assess the juvenile's risk and needs.

Juveniles should receive a physical examination and mental health assessment from a doctor or other licensed health care professional, consistent with national standards. An educational assessment also may be conducted by the educational staff. Additional psychological testing also may be conducted.

The orientation process can take from one day to several weeks, depending on the type of facility and its purpose. Smaller juvenile detention facilities generally can provide a complete orientation in a day. In the larger juvenile correctional facilities, that serve as reception centers, the orientation and assessment period can last several weeks.

Orientation Housing

In smaller juvenile facilities, juveniles are assigned to a housing unit that includes juveniles who have completed their orientation and are considered to be in the general population. Juveniles in the orientation program may be separated from the general population during the day for orientation and testing, but returned to the full group for recreation and evening activities. If newly admitted juveniles are placed in the general population immediately after intake, the staff must determine at intake if the juvenile is at risk of harm from other juveniles, is likely to harm another juvenile or himself or herself. Commingling new admissions in the general population does carry some risk, but for a facility with a small number of admissions in a week, it may be the most efficient use of facility housing.

Another approach would be a dedicated housing pod that would be smaller in size, but part of a larger housing unit. The size of the unit is determined by the number of new admissions that facility receives on a daily or weekly basis and the length of the orientation process. The design of the pod should be the same as other housing pods and include single-occupancy rooms with thirty-five square feet of unencumbered space, sanitation facilities, including access to toilet facilities without staff assistance twenty-four hours per day, a washbasin with hot and cold running water, a bed, a desk, a stool, natural light, and a storage area for clothing.

In a correctional facility, consideration needs to be given to how the sexes will be separated during orientation. It may not be cost effective to have separate orientation pods for males and females. In such a case, a single pod could be designed to handle males and females in separate, single-occupancy rooms. However, because many of the girls and young women have been the victims of aggressive behavior from males, administrators and planners need to be able to supervise all activities and privacy for the females must be provided so that they are not victimized again.

This section does not address the specific design of juvenile reception and assessment centers. However, in a large facility, special orientation housing may be designed, adjacent to the intake area. This will enhance the orientation process. If there are a sufficient number of admissions each day or every week to justify a separate housing unit, pods within the unit can strengthen the ability of the administration to properly evaluate and classify newly admitted youth. The benefit of a dedicated housing unit is that it enables staff, who may know very little about the new residents, to keep them apart from the general population.

In designing a separate housing unit for new admissions, consideration should be given to keeping the movement of the juveniles around the larger facility or campus to a minimum. A self-contained design where the new admission would live, go to school, be interviewed and tested, eat, and recreate makes for a more efficient operation and enhances security. In addition, there should be an adequate number of offices for professional staff and interviewing and testing rooms. The facility also would benefit if the health care offices and examination rooms were adjacent to the orientation unit.

Dayrooms

Dayrooms are at the heart of a good group living design. They provide the space through which access to multiple activities occur, including housekeeping, laundry, showers, and counseling or other office-based functions. Unit or pod dayrooms must be sized to reflect the largest number of youth to be served. The design must recognize their security containment, and provide acoustical control, communications, and excellent sight lines.

A secure staff station, located outside the living unit, and providing indirect supervision of the unit can enhance the unit staff's work with youth. With this staff station providing control of access and egress and the video monitoring for surveillance coverage of the unit, the staff station can help support unit staff who are providing direct supervision of the youth. This design can enhance both staff and youth safety.

Appropriate dayroom furnishings need to be matched to function. This includes fixed security tables, durable table tennis tables, computer desks, and television areas with good acoustics and/or individual floor outlets for plugging in headsets. There also needs to be good visual supervision by staff throughout the dayroom area and staff control of all points of access and egress. Types of floor coverings, colors of furnishings, and lighting as well as access to natural light are critical to the flexibility of the space and its ability to address different functions.

Not every youth wants to do the same thing at the same time. Sufficient design options to permit a variety of activities to be accessed at the same time are important. Locating other features such as multipurpose or group rooms, counselors' offices, and classrooms adjacent to each wing or pod, which are accessible within the extended unit, will increase the likelihood that youth will have access to programs and support services. This avoids the challenge of dressing for inclement weather, moving groups over longer distances, and separating group functions from the unit.

Organizing the architectural design in these ways can support unit team building, strengthen group classification, provide benign control, and integrate multiple functions into the programming. Such objectives can best be done in clustered units that share dedicated program spaces. This becomes more critical in the design of larger facilities and when programming for high-risk youth.

The primary colors of the tables create a dramatic effect against the black and white floor of this dining hall.

Photo courtesy of L. Robert Kimball & Associates, Ebensburg, Pennsylvania.

Daylighting can greatly enhance the appearance of the dayroom space and also help to reduce artificial light of this area during daytime hours. Tidewater Juvenile Detention Home, Chesapeake, Virginia.

Sketch courtesy of HSMM, Virginia Beach, Virginia.

Bedroom   Dayroom   Bedroom

SECTION

8' 4' 0   8'   16'

Educational Program

Since most juvenile offenders are performing below grade level and have histories of absenteeism, behavior problems, and learning disabilities, the educational program is probably the single most important service provided to juvenile offenders in detention and correctional facilities. State laws require juveniles to attend school to a mandatory age. These laws apply to incarcerated juveniles also. Many residents of juvenile detention and correctional facilities are identified as being in need of special education services, which carry additional responsibilities for the educational program. In juvenile detention and correctional facilities, the academic program operates on a twelve-month schedule.

The educational program can include academic classes, tutoring, individual study, and vocational classes. Normally, residents of juvenile detention and correctional facilities are expected to attend school for the same

At the State Correctional Institution at Albion, Pennsylvania, learning to enjoy reading has transformed some inmates. The library may play a major rehabilitative role.

Photo courtesy of L. Robert Kimball & Associates, Ebensburg, Pennsylvania.

number of hours a day as do juveniles in the community. The challenge is to reach these juveniles given a very limited amount of time.

Teachers in juvenile detention and correctional facilities may be employees of the facility or of a local school district. In either case, they need to be consulted and included in the design of the educational area. They need to be cross-trained on the security issues, protocols, and concerns in their facility, as well.

In smaller facilities, the educational area may serve other functions, such as evening activities, religious services, and visiting. In larger facilities, the educational program often will be designed as a separate wing or building. In either case, it is important that the first purpose of the area be identified as a learning area. All other activities must be secondary. Teachers and residents alike deserve an area that is conducive to learning. Designing dayrooms to double as classrooms does not communicate the message to the residents that education is important. On the other hand, participating in several activities in a classroom does identify it as a learning environment.

Technology has expanded the potential for a comprehensive educational program in juvenile detention and correctional facilities. The more the facility's design can access this technology, the stronger the educational program can be for the residents.

The Educational Area

When designing the educational area, architects and designers should follow the state or local school district's standards for design. Classrooms, teacher work areas, and activity areas should meet or exceed state requirements.

Classrooms should be designed for ten-to-fifteen students and have natural light. There should be windows between the classroom and the hallway. Toilet facilities, for the residents, should be accessible from every classroom and may be shared between two classrooms. The access and egress to every classroom must be under staff control. Temperatures in the classrooms should be appropriate to the winter and summer comfort zones. The size of the classrooms may vary depending on class size and activity. Classrooms should be wired to handle the latest computer technology and video conferencing. One room should be designed for videoconferencing and distance learning. This room should be a minimum of

Corridors should allow for ease of movement and permit casual surveillance by staff to see into the classroom. Tidewater Detention Home, Chesapeake, Virginia.

Photo courtesy of HSMM, Virginia Beach, Virginia.

500 square feet and include wiring for lighting and sound systems. The room should include an area for the storage of audiovisual equipment.

The educational program should also include a library for the residents. Again, the state requirements for educational libraries should be followed. In the absence of state standards, the architect or designer should consult with the state librarian or the local library for technical assistance. There should be enough space for a librarian's desk, reading, studying, book stacks, and storage of materials. Book stacks should be restricted in height and arranged to avoid blind spots that impede supervision.

Teachers will need a workroom or work area outside of the classroom. The area should be large enough to serve several teachers at one time. Separate toilets should be provided for the teachers and staff in the educational area. An office for the head teacher also is needed for private meetings and conferences. An area should be provided for the secure storage of educational records of the youth.

A separate storage room for the educational program should be designed into the educational area. This room should include a work table, a copy machine, and storage space for educational materials.

Juvenile Vocational Training

Vocational training usually is considered part of the overall educational program. The purpose of vocational training is to provide juveniles with work skills that will equip them to enter the world of work and earn a living. Vocational programs are found in most juvenile correctional facilities. Juvenile detention centers normally do not offer residents vocational training because they hold juveniles for too short a time to justify the cost.

Vocational programs most often provide training in the building trades, food services, and auto shop occupations. Training in computers and technology areas is increasing. Additional vocational programs include retail sales, printing, forestry and environmental areas, secretarial trades, and laundry services.

Vocational programs must be able to respond to an ever-changing marketplace. Vocational programs will change several times over the life of the facility. This must be considered when designing a vocational area.

Vocational programs should be located where they are accessible by truck. This will facilitate the delivery of supplies and equipment. If possible, the vocational program also should be adjacent to the academic building or area. This will enable the classrooms in the academic area also to be used for vocational classes.

Vocational Program Area

The vocational program area should be designed with change in mind. It also must meet the requirements of the Occupational Safety and Health Administration standards and state and local safety standards. The storage of flammable liquids and toxic materials must conform to fire safety and American Correctional Association standards. Rooms must have proper ventilation and controls.

Vocational areas normally require a ceiling height of twelve feet. The square footage of the area will be determined by the skills that will be taught. Adequate utilities also are needed in the vocational area to support the necessary trades to be taught. If it is difficult to define the need initially, utility stub-ins and/or raceways can be installed to allow for future flexibility. Adequate drainage to handle grease also may be needed.

Access, egress and sight lines that increase supervision are essential. A search room should be located in every vocational room or area. All residents should be searched before leaving the vocational training rooms.

Secure storage for tool and inventory control is critical to ensuring the security of the facility and the safety of residents and staff. The American Correctional Association book: *Guidelines for the Development of a Security Program*, by James Henderson, W. Hardy Rauch, and Richard L. Phillips, 1997, provides a discussion of concerns in this area.

Vocational training rooms also should have adequate windows to the hallways to enhance the security of the area. Closed-circuit television cameras should be located in all vocational areas to supplement overall supervision.

Juvenile Industries

Juvenile industries are generally a part of facilities that project a long-term length of stay for a select population. Use of a small industry in conjunction with a training program can link theory to practice and can join a youth's education to actual work experience.

Product or Service

Great care must be taken in selection of a suitable product or service that is to be manufactured or provided and sold, built, or shipped to a customer. Controlling issues are life safety, Occupational Safety and Health Act standards, the capacity of the youth to handle the tasks, and the status of a program as either a youth training program or an employer of youth. Child labor laws and local statutory requirements must be met.

Industry Space

The design of the industry space is driven by the function and purpose of the industry and tailored to the security needs of those who will work in this environment. Classroom spaces may adjoin the industry area to provide improved access and integrate instruction and supervision from adjacent programs. Spaces should be well lit, uncluttered, simple, and designed to meet Occupational Safety and Health Act standards, be handicapped accessibile, and have noise suppression features. Floor drains should be provided where wet clean up is required. Security of loading docks can be protected with fences, interlocks, or sallyports, and a key and lock schedule that does not permit a single on-site key to open all portals.

The sophistication of the industry product or service and the classification of youth drives the design of the security requirements. Assembly-type industries such as those found in sheltered workshop-type activities require space for storage, loading docks for the material to be assembled, a simple well-lighted production line, quality control, packaging, labeling, and shipping space. Tool control, electrical tool safety shut down overrides, staff control of all points of access and egress, secure tool storage areas, access controlled loading docks, an office space with a raised unobstructed view of all workstations and activity areas are important considerations in the industry program design.

Usually it is the more aggressive and violent offender who receives long-term lengths of stay. Hence, security concerns are a key feature in planning industrial program space. Communications to the central control in addition to a phone, and both interior and exterior video surveillance may be prudent.

Selection of an industry should look to the long-term stability of an appropriate market. Times change. Telecommunications service-based industries such as reservation and travel industries that were located in youth correctional facilities now are impacted by direct customer internet access and may have a limited future.

An example of a long-term industry could be one that microfilms or digitizes public documents and records. Receiving documents, categorizing them, separating them, removing staples, and so forth, copying, quality control, shredding, and packing for recycling are examples of steps in a sequential labor-intensive process that can teach basic skills, which carry over to other work experiences. The number of nonconfidential public records, for example, that require microfilming is enormous and appropriate for various levels of training.

Computer repair services offer a different approach and may reflect a more complex technical training component linked to a secure industry function.

In many states, a Habitat for Humanity linkage to juvenile programming can provide a prefabricated assembly industry that can be linked directly to both vocational training and a positive work experience. These functions are inexpensive to establish and foster links to outside organizations that also may provide materials, expertise, and give youth an opportunity to do something for their community and help struggling families.

Often volunteers and mentors are a part of such a cooperative effort, and the program may carry over to postrelease community programming. The true function of any industry program is to provide a learning experience for youth that supports the mission of the agency and the role of the facility.

Religious Spaces

Spaces for multidenominational religious services or chapel spaces usually are located in the congregate program areas in the facility unless they are stand-alone facilities. These facilities provide a multidenominational

The finishes, furnishings, and overall appearance of the religious space should convey a sense of peace. It is important that the space appears less institutional. Hillcrest Chapel, Hamilton County, Ohio.

Photo courtesy of William Hamilton.

center for worship, faith instruction, counseling, and use by volunteers. The chapel capacity should reflect the maximum number to be permitted to attend a service or activity at any one time including visitors and volunteers who may participate. Access to toilets, drinking fountains, capacity for surveillance, and communications need to be planned carefully.

Interfaith use dictates that the design is flexible. Stacking chairs rather than pews should be considered if security permits, as it increases flexible use of space. Large storage areas should be provided to hold chairs, folding tables, portable altars, lecterns, prayer rugs, blackboards, movable television platforms, and so forth. Larger chapel spaces may have electronic organs, portable choir risers, portable staging, and portable baptismal fonts. Confessional screens and other religious articles may require storage. A multipurpose public address system with features for both music and lectures should be provided.

Chaplains' Offices

The offices for the chaplains should be adjacent to the chapel and provide the chaplains with access to a small counter with a sink and work surface. (Each facility program may require different storage facilities.) Secure storage for sacramental wines, hosts, chalices, candles, and religious artifacts must meet the requirements of different religious faiths.

The offices for the chaplains should be adequate in size for small groups. They may be equipped with closets, a sink, chalkboards, comfortable chairs, a display of religious articles, and storage for instructional materials, vestments, and a lockable secure tabernacle. Officers should be able to view these offices from the outside, but their design should incorporate privacy for conversations. Their location should permit access by parents or loved ones of the child without the visitors going deep into the institution proper.

Modest use of stained glass without images is important. Natural light should flow into this space. A working committee of the religious faith who will use the chapel should give advice on needed features.

As in all congregate spaces, staff should control all points of access and egress. Communication should be provided to a central control and the design should permit multiple points of surveillance. Religious services often provide the only opportunity for groups normally separated by classification to share the same space at the same time. Security issues therefore should be considered in defining the group size to use the space.

Chapel

The location of the chapel is important in the management of volunteers. Its location should take into account the necessity to receive, process, and move volunteers and others into the secure areas of the facility. Staff controlled access to toilets for both youth and volunteers should be considered.

The flexible design should be able to support a variety of religious worship services and cultures. Different service schedules, furniture arrangements, and the actual practice of faith activities are important to the participating faithful and can provide a link to the community.

Recreation

Adolescents have boundless energy. Appropriate correction facility design acknowledges the need for recreational activities and youth involvement in programming up to sixteen hours per day. Youth recreation activities are an integral part of the teaching/learning/growing process. Facilities are needed for quiet times, games, canteen services, physical education, challenge and rope courses, obstacle courses, team activities, and weight training. These all offer different developmental opportunities, but require careful attention to design.

Windows are a source of natural light that enhances a recreational facility and provides access to outside air in lieu of mechanical ventilation. Gymnasium at Northwestern Regional Juvenile Detention Facility, Winchester, Virginia.

Photo courtesy of HSMM, Virginia Beach, Virginia.

Matching Programs to Population

Requirements for security, safety, and control must be matched both to the population to be served by age, sex, and security level and their anticipated length of stay. A short-term detention facility or intake center may have a different configuration of facilities and services than a large training school.

Congregate group program facilities located outside the living unit complexes generally are intended to be accessed according to a scheduled program. This may include dining areas, the visiting room, youth canteen, chapel, vocational and educational spaces, student industries, library, and other multipurpose spaces that serve all housing units. Confinement, medical, and administrative services generally are located in or adjacent to congregate spaces, but separate from housing units.

Facility design should incorporate staff control of access and egress and provide for circulation patterns that permit functional separation. Larger groups should be broken into a more manageable size. The design should provide staff with a continuous surveillance capability through good sight lines, and communication capabilities in all areas that are accessible by the youth.

Natural light is a very key feature of design. It is important to the success of recreation and multipurpose spaces. Choice of window size, type, location, glazing, and operability are key elements. Use of skylights or a clerestory should be considered where direct contact with a window is to be avoided or where there are other considerations such as ballistics protection, limiting youth exposure, or removal of any outside distraction. Spaces that are lit only artificially can be a depressing feature and merit careful review.

The intended use of recreation spaces and their accessibility by youth should define their physical location within the facility plan. For example, a single gymnasium, chapel, visiting center, ball field, and canteen may serve an entire facility. A multipurpose room adjacent to living units may be intended to serve only adjacent living units. Dayrooms may serve only their single wing or housing pods. Residents may see their room as their personal recreation space.

Almost all youth activity is group activity. Organization of spaces, circulation, and room size need to reflect group size and composition. Recreation space design also is driven by the security level, age, and numbers to be served at any one time. A facility for youth who are emotionally disturbed or a facility housing youth with histories of violence, gang activities, and escape may require a different design for access and control. Other considerations include selection of secure furnishings, security circulation, and limits on group size.

A basic rule of thumb is that all spaces are sized to fit the maximum size of the intended user group, are securable, and capable of staff control of all points of access and egress. They should have the capability of being viewed from multiple adjacent spaces or corridors or by surveillance camera and have an adequate communication capability directly to a control center. Access to all youth toilets and showers should be under staff control. Drinking fountains in physical activity areas should be accessible, but not be a hazard to physical activity.

Breaking large groups into smaller groups always improves supervision. In the design of larger recreation spaces, planners should consider movable or folding walls or separation by pull screens to divide activity groups, based on the type of activity and the characteristics of the group.

Multiple purpose spaces designed to support different programming functions at different times are a critical concern when budgets are tight and resources limited. The requirement to provide activities and programs through an active sixteen-hour day requires identification of a master schedule of activities, defining all space requirements, targeting group size, determining circulation patterns, planning access to and supervision of toilets, drinking fountains, showers, storage, and equipment. This planning is critical when designing shared use or multipurpose facilities and for defining the physical relationship of program spaces to living units, school, visiting, medical confinement, administration, and dining.

Generally speaking, the same level of physical security that is built into living units should be reflected in the facilities' program spaces. There is no magic transformation of a behavior when youth leave a high-security unit to enter a gym, recreation yard, classroom, or canteen as part of a group. It is a mistake not to design all program spaces to the highest level of security requirements that youth in the group exhibit. All facilities must incorporate provisions for youth with handicaps and for medical or physical limitations and offer options for large muscle exercises compatible with the needs of youth and security requirements.

Small Fenced Recreation Spaces or Yards

Recreation yards constructed adjacent to living units, whenever possible, should capture exits directly from the unit and be large enough to serve the entire population housed in a wing or pod at one time. They can be equipped

Typical recreation space includes minimal finishes with attention to acoustical control and lighting to address the many functional uses of this area. In addition, video coverage of this space is often used to provide surveillance of, and record, group activities. Beaumont Maximum Security Juvenile Facility, Beaumont, Virginia.

Photo courtesy of HSMM, Virginia Beach, Virginia.

with at least a half-court basketball court, secured yard tables, and a volleyball area. They must be capable of surveillance from a road, a control center, or by surveillance camera. Communication by interactive intercom or other means should be provided to the housing unit control from the yard. The design should consider the location of basketball poles and hoops to the proximity of fencing, windows, roofs, and doorways so they cannot be used as a breaching aid in an escape attempt. Keep poles away from fences! Exterior access for emergencies and maintenance should be provided with gates sized to admit mowers and other items.

Large Recreation Yards

Larger recreation yards for baseball, soccer, or flag football should be defined by gated fencing and may require fixed bench seating or bleachers anchored to the ground. There should be a communication capability such as interactive intercoms or portable radios that enable staff to communicate back to a control center. In addition, a capacity for visual surveillance from a perimeter road or a closed-circuit security camera is important as is staff control of points of access or egress. The area also should be designed consistent with the security level of the population to be served.

These large recreation yards usually are shared between several living units, depending on facility size and capacity. Drinking fountains, storage, and access to toilets are features of design planning. Multifunctional recreation yards can consider providing clustered seating at tables, a sun shelter, and basketball courts, in addition to the traditional volleyball, football, and soccer fields. Running tracks, challenge courses, and use of sidewalks for roller-skating or biking are other options to consider.

Often larger outdoor recreation spaces are placed adjacent to gymnasiums and their fencing captures gym exits with access to the yard space from the gym itself.

Gyms may be used by both education staff and recreation workers. Shared office space, storage, visibility, and control are issues that can be contentious if not properly planned. Also, never underestimate the necessity for adequate secure storage in recreation space design.

Picnic Shelters

Additional shelters with outdoor grills for picnics and other activities may be provided consistent with the security needs of the population to be served. Generally, outdoor furniture is fixed, gates securable, storage lockable, and good lighting provided for night activities. Circulation routes, staff control of access and egress, good sight lines, and communication are prerequisites to a functional, safe, and secure design.

If outdoor visiting is contemplated, the design requirements become more complex with respect to containment, supervision, control of access and egress, and constant monitoring from a point of control. Contraband management, shakedown facilities, and control of bathrooms require the same level of security in the design planning that is present in an internal visiting space. Good design can significantly help to reduce supervision issues.

Swimming Pool

Recreation facilities may include a swimming pool. Pools in youth correctional facilities are often controversial, but can provide a normalizing experience. Public sentiment should be carefully evaluated before a commitment to build is made. Public health regulations can drive both the design and capacity requirements. Consideration should be given to the elimination of diving boards, no pool depth of more than five feet, and a secure location for pool equipment. Outdoor pools can incorporate covers that permit use all year.

Safety and security limitations of the user population dictate that staff controls the access and egress to the pool area. Adequate communication and surveillance capabilities are required. Placement of staff for observation of showers, lockers, footbaths, and toilets and key circulation elements is critical. Secure storage, chemical pumps, and mechanical systems must be isolated and require exclusive staff control. All points of surveillance for staff supervision should have an unobstructed view. Emergency vehicle access should be considered in the event of a mishap. A well-illuminated pool is essential if night use is contemplated.

A determination of the eligibility criteria for youth participation, pool rules, lifeguard certification, and group readiness for swimming lessons must be established. Eligibility for use of pools by youth must be based on a prescreening for hygiene and medical concerns. Identification of nonswimmers must be addressed before enrollment in pool activities. Care needs to be taken to identify security issues in the population that would preclude mixing of individuals in a pool setting and where immediate staff intervention in an altercation is limited by the location.

Visiting

Juveniles rank visiting as the second most important topic in a juvenile correctional facility. For most incarcerated juvenile offenders, maintaining family ties is critical to a successful transition back into their community. As important as visiting is to the juvenile's emotional and psychological well being, it is also a point of concern in most juvenile detention and correctional facilities. Visiting can provide an opportunity for contraband to be introduced into the facility. However, a successful visitation program can offer several hours of visitation each week without compromising the safety of residents and staff or the security of the facility.

Visiting space for some youth requires a secure setting and noncontact visiting. Communication can be through handsets or individual speaker sets. Northwestern Regional Juvenile Detention Facility, Winchester, Virginia.

Photo courtesy of HSMM, Virginia Beach, Virginia.

Visiting Procedures

Every facility should have policies and procedures in place that address all of the steps and points in the visitation program. These policies and procedures must articulate the purpose of the facility's visitation program, who can and cannot visit, the number of visitors a resident can have, and the frequency of visits. Many residents of juvenile correctional facilities are parents. It is important for these young people to learn about their responsibilities as parents, even when incarcerated. The agency's policy should permit visits by children of the residents and see this as a learning opportunity.

Procedures clearly should state what is allowed inside the secure perimeter of the facility and what is prohibited. Winter clothing that visitors bring into the waiting area, and purses and other personal items should not be allowed in the secure area of the facility. Food items also should be prohibited from being brought into the facility.

Agency policy also should specify if gifts and other material items are permitted to be brought to the residents. If clothing items or other material goods are approved by the facility, the items can be kept in the juvenile's locker or bag in the property storage room until the juvenile is released or the staff determines the need for the item.

Money should be received consistent with the facility's policies and procedures on juveniles' funds. Any money received on behalf of a juvenile should be documented and placed in a secure area until the next business day, when it can be deposited.

All staff who have visitation responsibilities should be trained in the procedures for screening and searching visitors and residents, and in supervising visits. Visitors should be made to feel welcome. Their identities should be confirmed, checked against the approved visiting list, and recorded in a facility log. Visitors' personal belongings that are prohibited inside the facility should be stored in lockers in the lobby or waiting room area, or locked in the visitor's vehicle. Visitors should be searched in a private room and instructed to walk through a metal detector. If necessary, a handheld metal detector can be used to check for weapons, after the person has been searched and has walked through the metal detector. If prohibited items are found, the visitors should be instructed to place the items in their vehicle or a locker. Visitors should be warned that if they are found with drugs they are subject to arrest. The search and screening process then is repeated. Only after the visitors have been cleared should they be allowed to pass through the sallyport and go directly to the visiting area.

All residents should be thoroughly searched following the visit before they are allowed to return to their unit or into the program area. Resident searches should be conducted in a room adjacent to the visiting area.

Visitation Areas

In programming for visitation space, the two most important points to remember are access and egress. Staff always must have control over them for visitors and the residents. Staff must be able to see the visitors and supervise the visits and control points. Circulation patterns must limit how far visitors can go into the facility. There must be separate entrances and exits into the visiting area for visitors and residents. No juvenile residents should exit the visiting area through the visitors' entrance or exit.

The visiting area can be in a multipurpose room that is pleasant, informal, and hospitable. The design and acoustics should promote informal communication. Private visiting rooms should be provided near the main visiting area for lawyers, clergy, and noninstitutional counselors.

While contact visits always are preferred for juveniles and their visitors, one or two noncontact visiting rooms should be designed into the facility. These visiting areas should be visible from the visiting area and control room. Agency policy and procedures clearly should state when noncontact visits are permitted and how the noncontact visits are to be carried out.

All visitors should enter the facility through the main public lobby or waiting room, where they register at a staff station or the control room. The lobby area should include lockers for visitors' personal belongings, visitors' toilets, and telephones for public use. There should be separate men's and women's toilet facilities that are compliant with the Americans with Disabilities Act.

A room adjacent to the waiting area should be used to search visitors before they pass through the metal detector. The search room should contain about 120 square feet and insure privacy from other visitors and residents.

The visiting area should be located near the visitors' sallyport and, if possible, in view of the control room. This limits the visitor traffic deep into the facility and prevents problems from developing.

A raised staff station should be designed into the visiting area. This can be a portable or fixed stage that affords good visibility and enhances supervision of visiting.

The size of the visiting area is dictated by the number of residents who will be receiving visitors, the number of visitors each resident may have at each visit, and the visiting schedule. It also will be determined by other uses for the space.

A variety of fixed and movable furniture can enhance the aural and visual privacy of visits without lessening security. Windows into the visiting area from hallways can facilitate security and supervision. The visiting area also should provide separate toilets for males and females, and visitors and residents. These facilities should meet Americans with Disabilities Act requirements. In addition, the visiting area also may include vending machines that dispense soft drinks and snacks. The vending machines can be located behind a secure screen or partition, provided it does not obstruct the staff's line of sight.

Consistent with the security level of the facility, outdoor visiting can be considered, when weather permits. The design of an outdoor visiting area must consider the same issues as the internal visiting area. Supervision, containment, and access and egress must be evaluated carefully. Toilet facilities and search rooms must be designed along with shade and shelter areas.

Before the residents are returned to their rooms or the general population, they should be searched in a room adjacent to the visiting area. The search room should also contain about sixty square feet and insure privacy from visitors and other residents.

5

Administrative Functions

5.1 Administration Offices and Staff Training and Services

5.2 Information Management and Research

The facility pictured on the preceding page, SeaTac Federal Detention Center, Washington, is typical of the federal detention centers with the housing tower above and the support and administrative areas and recreation spaces in between.

Architect/Engineer: NBBJ, Seattle, Washington. Construction management firm: Heery Program Management, Bellevue, Washington. Construction contractor: M. A. Mortenson, Bellevue, Washington. Photo courtesy of the Federal Bureau of Prisons.

Administration Offices and Staff Training and Services

Karen Sicner
Sicner Planning and Design, Inc.
Atlanta, Georgia

The purpose of the administrative program is to provide leadership and support. An effective program ensures orderly operation of a correctional institution. The major components of the administrative program are as follows:

- General administration
- Public entrance and reception
- Business offices
- Staff training and support
- Security administration
- Personnel
- Information management

Each component is interrelated and generally reports to the warden or chief administrator of the institution. The following diagram illustrates the interrelationships among each of the departments.

General Administration

General administration is the hub of the institution. Its primary function is to provide leadership and direction for all staff and inmate programs and activities. The warden of the facility has overall responsibility for the institution, similar to the responsibilities of the CEO in a large corporation. Reporting directly to the warden are assistants, or deputy wardens, who typically are respon-

sible for day-to-day operations of the institution. Their areas of responsibility often are broken down as follows: fiscal management, inmate programs, security, and human resources. Depending on the size of the institution, these management functions may be provided by one or more individuals.

Additional staff in the general administration component may include one or more secretaries, a receptionist who greets the public and answers the telephone during normal business hours, a public information officer, and a special assistant to the warden. The public information officer works very closely with the warden and general

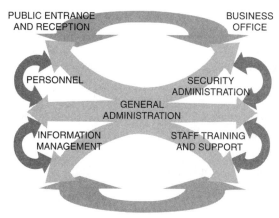

The flow of information and support among staff departments must be understood for effective facility design.

Chesapeake City Jail, Virginia. The lobby, consistent in appearance with other typical public building entries, projects an open, noninstitutional setting for visitors.

Photo courtesy of NBBJ, Columbus, Ohio. Photographer: Joe Wiseman.

administrative staff to ensure clear and concise communication within the institution and between the institution and the public.

General administration space requirements include a private office for each staff member, a space for file and supply storage, a waiting area for the public, an open clerical area, and a large conference room and easily accessible toilets. The waiting area generally is sized to accommodate six to eight individuals and should be located to serve all of the administrative components. Suggested space requirements are shown in Table 5.1.1.

All spaces should have telephones for institution and outside use. These spaces must be handicapped accessible and contain durable office-type finishes and accessories. This area is accessed frequently by the public and will convey the image that the institution wishes to present to the public.

Because these areas are accessible to the public, and generally not to inmates, care should be taken to protect staff from threats by the public. Ballistic-type glazing may be provided at the windows, and push-button-type alarm systems should be available to all staff.

The general administration area needs to be accessible to the public, but with easy entrance to the institution. It is desirable for the warden and his or her staff to spend as much time with staff and inmates as possible. Therefore, at many institutions, this component is located adjacent to the secure perimeter of the institution, either immediately inside or outside the fence. Windows from the warden's and deputy warden's offices should face the institution wherever possible.

Table 5.1.1
General Administration Space Requirements

Space	Occupants	NSF
Warden's office	10	250
Deputy warden's office	3	150
Secretary	1	120
Administrative assistant	3	150
Conference (media) room	12	300
Public information officer	3	150
Toilets	1	50
Waiting	8	150

Public Entrance and Reception Point

The public entrance is the point where all the public enters the institution. In many institutions, all staff and service vehicles enter the facility at the same point. The primary function of this area is to allow staff to screen visitors for weapons and contraband, log them in and out, and direct visitors to appropriate locations within the general administration offices or other parts of the institution. Institution service vehicles enter the institution at this point. They are screened and searched when either entering or exiting the facility.

The staff required depends on the size of the institution and the number of visitors entering and exiting the facility. Generally speaking, one to three security officers staff this area. At night, when visitors typically are not entering the institution, the post may be shut down and control of all doors in the area is relinquished to central control.

Space requirements include room for metal detectors, package screening equipment, visitor lockers and queuing, public toilets, a staff work area, and storage space. If this is a permanently staffed position, a staff office is desirable. Additionally, if this area is located outside the secure perimeter, a secure sallyport will be required to permit entry and exit through the perimeter. Also, where service vehicles enter the perimeter, a secure fenced vehicular sallyport is required that is large enough for a tractor-trailer truck. Outside space may be considered if it is sheltered from the weather. Suggested space requirements are shown in the table below.

Table 5.1.2
Public Entrance and Reception Areas

Space	Occupants	NSF
Staff work area and storage	200	250
Staff office	2	120
Visitor screening	2	100
Package receiving and screening	1 to 2	80
Visitor queuing	20*	300*
Visitor lockers	N/A	120
Toilets	1	50
Sallyport	4	60
Outdoor vehicular sallyport	N/A	2000

* Varies by size of institution and the number of inmate visits scheduled at one time.

The staff station should have telephones for institution and outside use. Closed-circuit television cameras often are used in this area to help monitor both the vehicular sallyport and the public areas. A metal detector is provided in the screening area, and small token-operated lockers should be provided for visitors' belongings. All spaces should be handicapped accessible and contain durable, vandal-resistant materials. This area is accessed constantly by the public and needs continual maintenance.

Because these areas are accessible to the public, and generally not to inmates, care should be taken to protect staff from threats by the public. Ballistic-type glazing may be provided at the windows, and push-button-type alarm systems should be available to all staff to allow them to notify central control if a problem develops.

The public entrance and reception point often is in a small building just outside the secure perimeter fence, called a "gatehouse." When the public reception area is located inside the fence, a camera, an intercom, and remote-controlled gates control the perimeter sallyport.

The public entrance should be located adjacent to or easily accessible to the components that require frequent public access including the business office, personnel office, general administration, and public visiting, which is discussed in another chapter.

Business Office

The business office is responsible for all financial transactions and is staffed by specialists in accounting, budgeting, procurement, contracting procedures, and property management. A business manager generally is assigned responsibility for the business office, with clerical and accounting personnel providing support. The number of staff depends on the size of the institution.

The business office requires space for staff offices, clerical support workstations, secure records storage, a safe, and a transaction area accessible to the public. Conference room and staff toilets should be easily accessible. Suggested space requirements are shown in Table 5.1.3.

All staff spaces should have telephones for institution and outside use. Fax machines, computers, and printers are prevalent throughout the business office. Business office computers should be connected to areas outside of the institution by modem. These spaces must be handicapped accessible and contain durable office-type finishes and accessories.

Because these areas are accessible to the public, and generally not to inmates, care should be taken to protect

Natural light and the use of higher quality acoustical finishes can help make open office plans work better for staff as shown in this clerical support workstation area at the Roanoke City Jail Annex in Roanoke, Virginia.

Photo courtesy of HSMM, Virginia Beach, Virginia.

staff from threats by the public. Ballistic-type glazing may be provided at the transaction window, and push-button-type alarm systems should be accessible by all staff. The transaction area and records room should be secured and monitored.

The business office needs to be adjacent to the public lobby and accessible to the general administration area.

Table 5.1.3
Business Office Space Requirements

Space	Occupants	NSF
Business manager's office	2	120
Clerical workstation*	1	80-
Work area**	1 to 4	120 **
Secure record storage**	N/A	Varies**
Safe	1	25
Transaction area	3	80

* Number of workstations depends on the size of the institution and staffing.

** Size of area depends on the size of the institution.

Personnel/Human Resources Department

The personnel/human resources department is responsible for administering numerous programs related to personnel policy, recruitment, position management, record keeping, and various other activities. This department works very closely with staff training to ensure that staff is competent and capable of performing their duties. A personnel manager generally is assigned responsibility for the business office, with clerical and accounting personnel providing support. The number of staff depends on the size of the institution.

Personnel office space requirements include staff offices, clerical support workstations, secure records storage, and a room available for staff performance reviews and interviews for persons applying for work. Staff toilets should be easily accessible. Suggested space requirements are shown in Table 5.1.4.

All staff spaces should have telephones for institution and outside use. Fax machines, computers, and printers are prevalent throughout the personnel department. Personnel department computers should be connected to areas outside of the institution by modem. These spaces must be handicapped accessible and contain durable office-type finishes and accessories.

Table 5.1.4
Personnel Department Space Requirements

Space	Occupants	NSF
Personnel manager's office	2	120
Clerical workstation*	1	80
Work area**	1 to 4	120**
Secure record storage**	N/A	Varies**
Interview room*	2 to 4	120

* Number depends on the size of the institution and staffing.
** Size of area depends on the size of the institution.

Table 5.1.5
Information Management Space Requirements

Space	Occupants	NSF
Personnel manager's office	2	120
Information management officer	2	120
Workroom*	4	150**
Records storage	N/A	200**
Clerical work station	1	80

* Number depends on the size of the institution and staffing.
** Size of area depends on the size of the institution.

Because these areas are accessible to the public, and generally not to inmates, care should be taken to protect staff from threats by the public. The records room should be secured and monitored.

Due to the volume of records that a large institution may need to have available in an accessible records area, consideration should be given to incorporating movable file storage units that operate on a floor-mounted track system. These systems are very space efficient and easy to operate.

The personnel office should be located adjacent to the public lobby, and be easily accessible to institution staff.

Information Management

Information management is responsible for managing information concerning the admission, release, and transfer of inmates. Information management works very closely with the warden, the deputy warden in charge of programs, and security administration to track inmate movement and activities. Staff size depends on the size of the institution. Generally, staffing consists of an information management officer, and one or two assistants to sort and distribute mail, and manage inmate records.

Information management space requirements include a staff office, a workroom, record storage, and a clerical support area. Conference room and staff toilets should be easily accessible. Suggested space requirements are shown in the Table 5.1.5.

All staff spaces should have telephones for institution and outside use. Fax machines, computers, and printers are prevalent throughout. Provide adequate electrical and data outlets for each workstation or office. These spaces must be handicapped accessible and contain durable office-type finishes and accessories. The record

storage room should be secure with monitored access. The information management office needs to be accessible to staff and security administration offices.

Staff Training and Support

Staff training and support are responsible for providing training, briefing, and support services for all staff. Staff training works very closely with the personnel department to ensure that staff is qualified and well trained. For larger institutions, a full-time training officer is required. Often, this person is also responsible for American Correctional Association standard's compliance and will use the American Correctional Association standards as minimum training standards.

Space requirements include staff offices, a staff library with shelving for training materials and current operations manuals, a training classroom, a storage room for training equipment, and a staff briefing and assembly room used for shift changes. Additional spaces include a staff exercise room, staff lockers, showers and toilets for male and female staff, a break room or dining area, and a workroom and area for receiving and sorting mail. Staff mailboxes should be located in this area and be easily accessible at all hours of the day. Mailboxes that are accessible from two sides make mail distribution easier. Suggested space requirements are shown in Table 5.1.6.

All staff spaces should have telephones for institution use only. Computers and printers should be located in the training office, library, and classroom. Cable and closed-circuit television should be available for training videos in the classroom. There should also be an outlet for the video in this room. These spaces must be handicapped accessible and contain durable office-type finishes and accessories.

The areas for staff support and training need to be easily accessible to all staff at all times. The briefing room and locker rooms should be located near the staff entry to the institution.

Larger institutions also are constructing mock prison cells in the staff training areas to facilitate cell extrac-tion training. This is cost-effective because it has the potential to reduce injuries to staff and inmates.

Security Administration

Security administration is responsible for supervising correctional officers, conducting interviews and holding disciplinary hearings for staff and inmates, writing reports, and meeting with local law enforcement. The exact number of staff depends on the size of the institution. Generally, there is a chief of security and a shift captain in charge of each shift, and clerical support services.

Space requirements include staff offices, a small conference/hearing room, a holding area, an evidence storage room, a clerical area with room for workstations and record storage, and a small waiting area for visitors. Suggested space requirements are shown in Table 5.1.7.

All staff spaces should have telephones for institution use. Outlets for computers and printers should be located in all rooms except the waiting and holding room. These spaces must be handicapped accessible and contain durable office-type finishes and accessories. The evidence storage room should be secure with monitored access.

This area needs to be easily accessible to all staff and inmates and be quickly accessible to all areas of the institution in an emergency. Adjacency or proximity to the staff briefing room and central control is desirable.

Table 5.1.6
Staff Training and Support Space Requirements

Space	Occupants	NSF
Training office	2	120
Library	4	250
Classroom	40	500***
Equipment storage	N/A	150
Staff briefing	60*	800*
Exercise room	8 to 10**	350**
Staff lockers (male and female)	30 to 40**	800**
Staff toilets (male and female)	6**	250**
Staff showers (male and female)	8**	300**
Mail sorting and distribution**	1 to 4	80**
Break room	20**	500**

* One full shift of staff. Number varies depending on the size of the institution.
** Size of area depends on the size of the institution.
***May be larger, depending on the type of staff training desired.

Table 5.1.7
Security Administration Space Requirements

Space	Occupants	NSF
Chief of security office	2	120
Shared office for shift captains	3	300
Clerical area	1	100
Waiting	3	100
Evidence storage	N/A	150
Conference/hearing	5	150
Holding room	1	60

CERT team practices cell extraction at one of the facilities of the Federal Bureau of Prisons.

Photo courtesy of Chris Crawford, U.S. Department of Justice.

Information Management and Research

Steven Chianesi
Rhode Island Department of Corrections
Cranston, Rhode Island

For centuries accurate information has been a vital part of successful management. The manner in which information is retrieved and stored has changed over the years. In the corrections environment, just as in any other environment, managing effectively and efficiently means keeping abreast of all issues relating to the corrections department, both internally and externally. Management Information Systems within the corrections setting have become part of the day-to-day operation. Not only is it a part, rather it is an integral component used to keep the hands of the managers on the pulse of their institution. Information must be available on a "real time basis" to each corrections manager and on an "as needed" basis through "state of the art" Management Information Systems. As we all know, "state of the art" in the information systems' world changes rather rapidly. Nevertheless, information continues to be synonymous with control. Information is no longer at peak value when obtained from manual sources. Information today is considered as valuable a tool of the trade as all other means by which corrections professionals provide security and control within the institution and protection to the public.

Management Information Systems have grown from exclusively jail management systems to executive information systems for all of corrections. Although the "bread and butter" of an information systems' unit remains its ability to maintain and update a variety of information,

including but not limited to admission, transfer, and discharge of inmates, sentence computation and processing of detainers, as well as the ability to maintain court orders, medical and institutional records (some of which are confidential), its importance has been well established over the past ten years. It recently has taken on an even more meaningful role.

New technologically innovative approaches are changing the way corrections professionals handle their business. These technologies include videoconferencing for a variety of uses including arraignment; medical consultations; distance learning; visiting; inmate tracking; bar coding; digital imaging, fingerprints, voice prints; community notification systems; inmate community location devices (such as ankle bracelets and radio frequency transmission); and telephone systems that use artificial intelligence.

Many of these technologies are organized or based on the computer. Door locking controls as well as camera monitoring, and both intercom and radio communications now can be performed by a staff member using a single computer in a control room. This same officer also can call up an information database to help identify the inmate or staff person they have on camera before opening a door or responding to their question.

Also available to this officer is the status of fire and smoke alarm systems, perimeter security, and even the water flow to plumbing fixtures and institution lighting control. This technology is available to report the environmental conditions within a given space or the status of a piece of building HVAC equipment. Malfunctions of systems or individual pieces of equipment are quickly diagnosed and in some cases can be corrected by staff using the computer and its software package. Remote diagnostics through a modem allow a service technician to assist in determining and fixing certain equipment-operating problems without a costly and time-consuming trip.

Increased access to this information and control of security equipment by computers is a function of the cost of this technology coming down in price and the advent of software that is extremely user friendly. These innovations afford the corrections professional with the ability to make a positive identification of the offender and staff, protect the victim, and work in tandem with our colleagues in other criminal justice organizations and keep the general public informed.

Corrections information systems are not limited to use with the client. For example, they also are used in human resources, finance, and policy to name a few other areas.

Requirements of the Unit

The physical requirements for a Management Information Systems (MIS) unit within a department of corrections have changed dramatically. The space needs have decreased. Corrections professionals specializing in Management Information Systems once were concerned with designing computer rooms large enough to hold huge mainframes supported by raised floors. They also needed fire protection systems, miles of coaxial cabling, large uninterruptible power supplies (to maintain the hardware), and tons of memory devices (to support their applications), which were often written in complex computer languages. Added to this were requirements for large printers, miles of green bar paper, huge telecommunications devices, and an area large enough, secure enough, and strategically planned out enough to be cost effective and efficient enough to operate many years. However, these items did not come cheap.

Hundreds of modems were once needed. They no longer are needed because Fractional T1 lines are replacing them. Similarly, routers do not need an enormous amount of room. One strand of fiber is now replacing hundreds of analog cables. Conversion of Legacy or Cornerstone computer applications, which were originally (and painstakingly) designed to run on huge mainframes, are now easily being coded to run on mini personal computers. With the continuing decrease in size of computers, massive MIS offices or space for computer equipment is no longer necessary. A server can be located in a standard size workstation.

Correction professionals are realizing that canned off the shelf, or COTS, applications are more cost efficient. Instead of designing an application to meet the way the institution does business, we are changing the way we do business. The one concern that should be noted is the need to avoid the use and/or purchase of proprietary software if it is not absolutely necessary.

Proprietary software, which is developed by a particular software company to perform very specific tasks, may be needed for special applications. However, there are more and more nonproprietary software programs being developed that can provide users with the required capabilities to manage or generate data without being locked into one manufacturer's product that may or may not be compatible with other software in use by the agency or company.

To be functional, systems and databases need to be tied closely to business objectives and plans. Systems have no meaning unless they remain tied to the mission of what a business does. To be useful as a resource, systems must accommodate the businesses' needs. For example, as state laws change with regard to sentencing, standard operating procedures are affected within the institutions. This leads to modifications that may affect how specific populations are housed within the institution. This type of issue can quickly and efficiently be addressed by the computer.

A correctional department's primary objective is the operation of a full and balanced correctional program, which is consistent with public safety, reflects sound and progressive correctional policy, and is sensitive to the need for fiscal responsibility in the use of public resources. These types of issues can also quickly and efficiently be addressed by the computer. The Cornerstone or Legacy computer systems within the institutions are quickly being recognized as true executive management systems.

Another problem is that technology is changing so rapidly that by the time an organization such as a corrections department orders a faster computer and receives it, something newer is on the market. Departments of corrections need to realize the ramifications of this problem and need to petition budgetary and financial authorities within their state to excuse them from

Medical staff conduct patient consultation by videoconferencing. The equipment can transmit documents such as patient charts and x-rays between sites. Telemedicine has eliminated the need to transport many inmate patients to the Ohio State University Medical Center or the Corrections Medical Center for consultations. This has helped reduce the department's annual transport costs.

Photo courtesy of Christopher A. Lizza, Ohio Department of Rehabilitation and Correction, Columbus, Ohio.

standard procurement processes, which can take many months and add many unnecessary layers of bureaucratic red tape to purchasing technology.

Some things have not changed, however. The environment for the equipment is still something that must be considered seriously but for different reasons. HVAC and space requirements have been reduced drastically. Security is now the key more than ever. Not only is a computer in physical danger of being damaged by negative sources, there are also "bugs," "viruses," and other factors that affect the software code and programs. These are things that may not readily be evident to the correctional professional without special training in knowing what to look for.

A Management Information Systems (MIS) unit should be located in the administrative area of the institution. Off-site backup strategies are very important. This remains true for security reasons. Connection through wire, short wave, telephone, or fiber optics to colleagues in other criminal justice agencies is now more important than ever.

Information is not only helpful to correctional administrators, but it also provides a solid basis for correctional research. New and improved services are the direct result of research. Agreements should be made with local colleges and institutions of higher learning to use stu-

dents who have an interest in technology and criminal justice. This is a valuable source of human resources and benefits not only the student with hands-on experience, but also the institution with new cutting edge technology. MIS is a new and exciting field, and it does not matter whether you are counting widgets, auto parts, clients, patients, or inmates. There is a need to provide more efficient services in both the business world and the human services world.

Blueprints, detailed written information, and standard operating policies and procedures are critical in case of an emergency. Replacing and updating equipment through the implementation of a computerized preventive maintenance system can be very cost effective and can help avoid critical system or equipment failures. Careful analysis should be made to decide whether replacement of equipment supersedes the cost of maintenance for equipment.

Proper security (in other words, firewalls) and systems administrators who delete all accounts and passwords of recently dismissed or disciplined employees also are essential. A firewall is a network component that provides a security barrier between networks or network segments. Firewalls are generally set up to protect a particular network or network component from attack, or unauthorized penetration by outside

The control room of this low-security institution requires computers to track security, and they are used for other administrative purposes. Federal Correctional Institution, Beaumont, Texas.

Architect: NBBJ, Columbus, Ohio. Photo courtesy of the Federal Bureau of Prisons. Photographer: Wes Thompson.

invaders. However, a firewall also may be set up to protect vital institutional data or resources from internal attacks or incompetence. Internal firewalls generally are placed between administrative or security domains in an institutional network.

For example, a firewall might be set up between the network domain that houses the inmate tracking database, payroll, personnel, or financial management databases, and other parts of the institutional network. All traffic to or from the protected network must go through the firewall—it is the "eye" or the "Main Control Center" for the computer, and it is designed to allow only authorized traffic. If the firewall does its filtering job successfully, attacks will never even reach the protected network and more important, the information.

To be effective, the firewall also must be able to protect itself from penetration. To help ensure this, firewalls generally are designed to be special-purpose machines. That is, the firewall will not provide services beyond that necessary to authenticate the user and to decide whether to allow the traffic through. If a received request is legitimate (similar to a security clearance level), the firewall will pass on the traffic to the appropriate database and information can be received.

Like all security measures, firewalls can be useful, but they are not foolproof. They have the advantage of con-

centrating security measures and issues, making it easier to set up and maintain them. Such centralization also provides an Achilles' heel—that is, a point of vulnerability. The firewall's effectiveness depends on the technical correctional professional who works as part of the management team of the correctional agency. That is why it is vital to hire and keep qualified individuals with this area of expertise.

MIS is Technology Hub

Year 2000 technology correction initiatives were placed "on the front burner" in late 1998 and 1999. Information on Y2K appeared daily in newspapers, magazines, and on the television. The general public was saturated with Y2K issues. Complete assurance of compliance could not be given unless every line of code was tested. Although this was true, the situation was not that grim. A strategic and systematic approach to the problem placed most corrections departments in a good position. This potential "problem" has forced corrections professionals to look at things in a manner never before thought possible. It forced them to realize that technology *must* be figured into the equation of corrections. A corrections department with a well-rounded MIS unit is in the enviable position to be poised for entry into the twenty-first century.

MIS in the corrections setting is the hub of technology and should be the focal point of all technology. Isolated pockets of technology are not cost effective and need to be reviewed. A central MIS unit establishes the model of efficiency. Historically, systems were supported by one person and relied on staff who had an interest in computer technology. This procedure offers an unacceptable level of risk due to staff turnover.

It is the correctional manager's responsibility to give staff the tools to do their jobs, the technical knowledge they need, and the training necessary to stay current. Historically, departments of corrections have not allocated sufficient funds for training. Often staff is expected to learn on their own. Imagine if the president of a large automobile company or the CEO of a large computer software or hardware manufacturing company spent less than 2 percent of his or her overall budget on research and development. Where would we be without the advances made as a result of the computer?

Many correctional departments want to run their institutions like a business; however, their hands are tied due to strong labor unions, political influences, and strong lobbying groups. Once administrators realize this, they can devise strategies to help deal with these concerns.

Good news usually does not sell newspapers, and it is more newsworthy to talk about a problem in an institution rather than talk about the positive and innovative strides that correctional professionals are making in the area of technology. Dissemination of good news must be built in as an integral part of the operation. Also, departments cannot depend on staff just learning "on the job." They have to make a larger investment in their staff.

State and local governments should stop competing with private companies for those employees with the technical skills needed. To rectify this situation and to stop the hemorrhaging of employees, the following suggestions might be used: computer-based training in the institutions and the establishment of state-of-the-art computer labs, which teach the correctional professionals at the emplyee's own speed. These are the keys to accomplishing the task of retaining employees and maintaining their commitment to the mission of the department.

The need to address database inconsistencies and proprietary platforms used by several of the criminal justice agencies has forced the State of Rhode Island, for example, to develop a new strategy which has led to a collaborative effort among all of the criminal justice agencies (in other words, the state courts, the attorney general's office, the department of corrections, the department for children youth and their families, state and local police departments, and the public defender's office). This project, known as the Justice Link (J Link), ultimately will result in the establishment of a wide area network (WAN) operating under a common set of standards and protocols for hardware and software applications used by each participating criminal justice agency. The agencies have developed and maintain their own databases based on their specific needs; however, one linking identifier is commonly shared among all participating agencies. To accomplish this, they are migrating to open, nonproprietary systems.

Conclusion

Management Information Systems in the correctional environment have taken on an exciting new integral role. Just as in the private sector, a large percentage of money is allocated to research and development, so too this must be done in the corrections arena. Remember, information means control. Information is as crucial as the consideration to increase the number of correctional officers on the line. Technology is meant to be used as a tool for the corrections professional. Let us maximize its use to our advantage.

Service Facilities

6

Photo on the previous page is a view from the tower of the Federal Correctional Complex in Florence, Colorado, into the service area.

Architects: LKA Partners, Lescher and Mahoney and DLR Group, Colorado Springs, Colorado. Construction management firm: Heery Program Management, Atlanta, Georgia. Construction contractor: PCL Constructors, Denver, Colorado. Photo courtesy of the Federal Bureau of Prisons.

Plant Maintenance for Adult Facilities

Jeffrey Minnerly and Keith Rupert
New York State Department
  of Correctional Services
Albany, New York

In a correctional facility, the maintenance department can be compared to a general contractor. Staff represent various building trades and, in the case of larger institutions, this staff does the majority of maintenance-related work and can do new project work inside the institution if time and work load permit. These staff maintain, operate, and repair the institution's power plant, mechanical systems, equipment, and building systems in a correctional facility. A personal computer-based preventive maintenance system should be used to ensure that the facility's physical plant assets are maintained and that the systems are always operation ready. Typically in many institutions, inmates, as well as civilian staff, are employed in the maintenance department. This work opportunity often translates into excellent on-the-job training and allows inmates to gain very good skills and develop a work ethic. The American Correctional Association standards for *Adult Correctional Institutions* and *Adult Local Detention Facilities* (ALDF), both Third Editions, are shown to the right.

Objective

The maintenance staff will perform work on the building and mechanical systems. This will include but is not limited to the plumbing; electrical; heating, ventilation, air conditioning (HVAC); welding and sheet metal; carpentry; masonry; and painting trades. The staff also will receive training to assist them in dealing with the continuing changes that occur in the technology of each trade.

American Correctional Association Requirements for Maintenance Departments

3-4155: Adequate space is provided for janitorial closets accessible to the living and activity areas. The closets are equipped with a sink and cleaning implements. (This is also ALDF 2E-09)

3-1458: Separate and adequate space is provided for the mechanical and electrical equipment. (This is also ALDF-2E-12)

3-4188: Written policy and procedure govern the control and use of tools, culinary and medical equipment.

3-4206: There is a written plan for preventive maintenance of the physical plant; the plan includes provisions for emergency repairs or replacement in life-threatening situations. (This is also 3-ALDF-3B-08)

3-4314: A written housekeeping plan for all areas of the facility's physical plant provides for daily housekeeping and regular maintenance by assigning specific duties and responsibilities to staff and inmates. (This is also ALDF-4D-05)

3-4398: The institution provides for inmate employment in correctional industries, facility maintenance, operations and to the extent possible in public work and community projects.

A maintenance department is employed to provide for the preventive and corrective maintenance of the facility's mechanical systems. This department is composed of civilian staff and inmates. There is also an administrative branch of the department that is responsible for the facility's administration. This area is composed of various shops from which the individual trades operate. The maintenance area also may be of an open design. This will work, so long as the individual trades have other assigned shop and storage areas. There also should be an area designated for work-order control and administration. The type and classification of the facility will determine the specific layout of the maintenance department.

If the area is of an open design, each trade will have a separate area. Each area will have materials and tools for that trade. If the area is separated into individual shops for each trade, then the shops will have the necessary materials and tools for that trade. Secure construction should be used in this area. Also, individual shops can work as a control mechanism for inmate movement.

Typical Operation

Work should be addressed by the maintenance department in three ways: (1) by scheduling preventive maintenance, (2) by employing normal work order submittal, and (3) by emergency. When work is to be done, the person requesting the work fills out a work request. This is then signed by the area supervisor, to acknowledge that the work needs to be done. The request then is forwarded to the work control center and logged into the computer program for maintenance. The request is assigned a number and a tradesperson to complete the work. The tradesperson picks up the work order, draws the necessary supplies and tools, and completes the work. The work order then is returned to the work control center as completed, and it is closed out of the active file.

Inmates are used in the maintenance area. Those inmates who have the skills of the trade may not need any further training. Inmates who do not have the necessary trade skills will be provided vocational training to enable them to qualify for a maintenance job.

Floor plan of a typical maintenance building shows suggested square footage for both operational and storage areas.

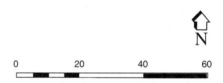

Room No.	Room Name	Net SF
1–15	Electric Shop	620
1–16	Office	170
1–17	Toilets	100
1–18	Carpenter Shop	890
1–19	Storage	240
1–20	Storage	260
1–21	Maintenance Office	490
1–22	Toilet	20
1–23	Passage	0
1–24	Toilet	20

Room No.	Room Name	Net SF
1–25	Toilet	20
1–26	Shower	20
1–27	Plumbing Shop	1330
1–28	Machine Shop	1010
1–29	Parts Storage	250
1–30	Toilets	100
1–31	Maintenance Garage	1700
1–32	Compresser	90
1–33	Office	90
1–34	Office	90

Location

The maintenance area should be centrally located within the secure perimeter. This is needed for ease of access to all parts of the facility. It also should be located close to a loading dock for receiving materials and equipment. An overhead door should be provided and the ceiling height should be twelve feet, at a minimum. Some institutions have this function located outside the secure perimeter for security reasons. The time that staff take to go in and out of the vehicle sallyport should be weighed against the security concerns.

Functional Areas

Plant Superintendent's Office

The plant superintendent is the manager of the maintenance department. His or her office should be located at the front of the maintenance area, with good visibility into the shop area.

Assistant Superintendent's Office

Often, the assistant superintendent shares an office with the document files.

Work Control Office

The work control office should be located next to, or adjacent to, the plant superintendent's office. There should be space for a clerk and several support staff. This staff can consist of civilians and/or inmates. They will process the work requests, issue emergency work orders, process requests for materials by the maintenance staff, and provide the record keeping for the maintenance department.

Shops

Individual shop areas will be set aside for each trade. A dust and fume collection system will be employed in the woodworking and metal-working trades. A separate dust-free shop will need to be provided for the electronic and electrical trades. If a paint shop is provided, and painting is done in the shop, a spray booth should be included.

Tools

Hand tools usually are issued from a secure tool room. Tools are kept on a shadow board. When a tool is issued, the worker will provide a chit/tag to be put in its place. This will allow for the identification of the tool's location. This room will have a secure window or door through which to handle this transaction. This window will be designed so that when it is secured, it will not allow anyone access to the space. There also will be a lockable security door for entry into the tool room. A daily tool inventory will be taken and reported. The security department should be notified of any discrepancies.

Storage

This space is for bulk storage of materials, supplies, and tools. The room is secured when not in operation or attended by the store's clerk. The daily issue of materials needed to complete work orders comes from this room. It should be large enough to accommodate twenty foot lengths of conduit, limited lumber storage, and a wide variety of building materials and equipment.

Toilets

A separate toilet, locker, and shower facility should be provided for both civilian and inmate staff.

Janitor's Closet

A separate slop sink area will be provided to allow for the storage of cleaning supplies to be used in this area.

Summary of the Design

- It should have a central location for ease of access to the whole facility.
- Individual shops should consider access and control of inmates.
- There should be a separate tool and storage area to maintain control and inventory of materials.
- Secure construction should be used due to the nature of the area.
- Designers should provide appropriate utilities to this area to support the varied activities involved.
- If materials are sanded or cut in the area, a dust collection system should be considered.

Plant Maintenance for Juvenile Facilities

Kendal Ball
Department of Youth Services
Columbus, Ohio

American Correctional Association standards govern the maintenance in juvenile facilities, depending on the type of facility. For example, in small juvenile detention facilities, "Adequate space is provided for janitorial closets accessible to the living and activity areas. The closets are equipped with a sink, cleaning implements, and a system of ventilation." And, "Separate and adequate space is provided for mechanical and electrical equipment." Additionally, "There is a written housekeeping plan for the facility's plant." Then, "The institution's potable water source and supply, whether owned and operated by the public water department or the institution, is approved by an independent outside source to be in compliance with jurisdictional laws and regulations." Another standard states that: "The institution provides for a waste disposal system in accordance with an approved plan by the appropriate regulatory agency."

The maintenance department in a juvenile facility can be quite different from that in an adult facility. Juveniles, generally, do not participate in many of the facility maintenance activities that are typical for adult facilities. During the program planning phase(s) for a new juvenile facility, it is important to ascertain the kind of maintenance that will service the facility. Some correctional facilities may have their maintenance support from outside the facility by staff from a central agency or another facility. Even larger facilities may contract out much of their preventive maintenance and have a very small maintenance staff. Once the size and responsibilities of the maintenance section are decided on, designers can adequately plan for the facility inventory and maintenance areas.

An inventory of essential maintenance items needs to be planned whether the maintenance support is in-house or by contract. Spare locks; keys; cameras; heating, ventilation, air conditioning (HVAC); filters; toilet parts; belts; and other items that are not readily available from local or contract sources should be inventoried at that facility. Specialty tools such as screwdrivers for security fasteners also need to be maintained for use by contract maintenance personnel. If an in-house maintenance staff is to be employed, then work spaces and tools will need to be provided. This area should be separated from housing areas and provide for adequate security, including shadow boards for all tools.

Grounds maintenance can be performed by the youth with adult supervision, if desired. A separate area outside the secure perimeter of the facility should be provided for tool/lawn mower equipment. These areas also provide a good contract possibility. Hazardous/flammable materials should be stored appropriately whether in a separate outside storage facility or in appropriately classified cabinets in the general storeroom. Maintenance inventory can be part of the general storeroom or placed in a separate storage area.

Elevators, HVAC systems and controls, fire suppression systems, and security systems maintenance should be handled through private maintenance service contracts. These systems are complicated and usually are beyond in-house staff capabilities unless staff can be hired that has special training and expertise. Generally, in-house staff can supplement the work provided by contract services. Should a facility decide to contract all of their maintenance activities, provisions should be made for escorting and supervising of contract maintenance staff while they are in the facility.

Personal computer-based preventive maintenance software is a useful method for developing and maintaining a good preventive maintenance program. The programs are designed for a wide range of facilities, from very small facilities to an entire system or agency. A computer-based preventive maintenance system allows staff the opportunity to maintain the facility in a preventive rather than fix-when-broke mode, which saves time, money, and downtime. This is critical in a correctional facility because downtime usually presents a risk to safety or security.

A preventive maintenance program also can be used to generate work orders, and keep an inventory of materials and parts on hand that are needed for routine maintenance. It even can be used to justify major equipment replacements based on historical records of equipment problems and repairs.

The success of a computer-based preventive maintenance program requires adequate staff support so that data is kept up to date and accurate. A more efficient maintenance program will result from good preventive maintenance practices, which, in turn, can lower institution operating costs.

Vehicle Garage

Keith Rupert and Jeffrey Minnerly
New York State Department
    of Correctional Services
Albany, New York

In a correctional facility, staff and possibly inmates in the vehicle garage maintain the motor vehicles and other motor-operated equipment. The motor equipment mechanic will maintain, operate, and repair the vehicles and other engine-operated equipment. A preventive maintenance system should be used to ensure that the vehicles are maintained and operational. Inmates, as well as civilian staff, can be employed in the garage and grounds area. A central receiving warehouse will be located in the vicinity of the garage. This complex should be located outside of the secure perimeter of the institution.

The standards for this area are contained in *Adult Correctional Institutions,* Third Edition, as follows:

American Correctional Association Requirements for Garage and Warehouse

3-4188: Written policy and procedure govern the control and use of tools, culinary and medical equipment.

3-4189: Written policy and procedure govern the use and security of institutional vehicles.

3-4398: The institution provides for inmate employment in correctional industries, facility maintenance, operations and to the extent possible, in public work and community projects.

A facility's garage should have access to a vehicle's sallyport as in the Chesapeake City Jail, Chesapeake, Virginia.
Photo courtesy of NBBJ. Photographer: Joe Wiseman.

Service Facilities

Purpose and Objective

The garage is a designated area for the storage and repair work on motor vehicles. Often, equipment for the grounds crew, including lawn care and snow removal equipment is stored in the garage, as well.

To keep the correctional facility vehicles operating and functional on a continuous basis, a motor vehicle equipment mechanic needs to be employed. This person will operate from the garage. More than one mechanic and several inmates may be employed, as well.

Typical Operation

The work done on the vehicles will be scheduled to meet the manufacturers' service requirements and standard practices in this field. A work order will be generated and completed for work done on a vehicle or other motor-operated equipment. The garage, under the direction of the maintenance department, works with the security department. They need to coordinate the many transport trips of inmates to court or to the hospital.

Deliveries usually are made to the facility by vendors. Then, the product is inventoried and a receiving slip completed and attached to the order for verification that it is complete. Then, the vendor will be paid. The daily, weekly, or monthly restocking of the storerooms inside of the facility is done from here. The size, population, and delivery schedule of vendors and normal consumption of consumable items will determine the schedule for these trips.

Location

The vehicle garage should be located outside of the secure perimeter, but in close proximity to the facility. A usual location will be near the vehicle sallyport.

Functional Areas

Garage

The garage should have sufficient space to maintain the facility's motor vehicles. Usually there will be a minimum of two or three bays. Each will have an overhead door for vehicle access. One bay should be equipped with a vehicle lift. An overhead height of twelve to fifteen feet should be unobstructed. Ideally, the garage area should have a water faucet, floor drain, and vent for vehicle exhaust.

Storeroom and Tool House

A storeroom will be provided to keep repair parts and tools. The maintenance work control center will inventory and track the parts and tools on a scheduled basis,

with reports forwarded to the department head. A shadow board and chit system should be used.

Offices

An office for the lead mechanic should be provided. It should allow for the observation of inmates as well as civilian staff.

Toilets

Separate toilets, lockers, and shower facilities should be provided for civilians and inmates.

Janitor's Closet

A separate slop sink area should be provided to allow for the storage of cleaning supplies to be used in this area.

Vehicle Storage Area

In cold weather locations, due to occasional severely cold temperatures and/or heavy snow falls, institutions will have an unheated but enclosed garage adjacent to the vehicle repair garage in which to store patrol, transport, and emergency vehicles out of the weather. These buildings generally are not of a secure construction.

Summary of the Design

- There should be a central location for ease of access to the whole facility.
- There should be a separate secure tool and storage area to maintain control and inventory of materials.
- Designers should provide appropriate utilities to this area to provide support for the varied activities.
- Steel storage shelves are needed for bulk storage of materials.

Vehicle Maintenance Building Description	
A prototypical vehicle maintenance building that has four vehicle bays is situated in a building whose total gross square feet = 4,565 sq. ft.	
Space	*Net Sq. Ft.*
Work Bays	3,525
Office	215
Clerical	190
Lockers	95
Toilet	75
Inmate Toilet	65
Janitor's Closet	60
Parts Storage	100
Mechanical	120
Electric	100
Mezzanine Area*	1,135
Total Net Sq. Ft.	**4,545**
Total Gross Sq. Ft.	**5,037**
* Not counted in building square footage.	

Warehouse Facilities

At South Woods State Prison, Bridgeton, New Jersey, the warehouse is the designated area for receiving, holding, and distributing all materials and supplies necessary for the daily operation of the institution.

Photo courtesy of L. Robert Kimball & Associates, Ebensburg, Pennsylvania.

Leonard R. Witke, AIA
XCEL 4 Associates
Oconomowoc, Wisconsin

Correctional institutions like any other major commercial or industrial facility must have the necessary support facilities to allow them to run smoothly and effectively. Toward that end, most major correctional institutions and jails have a warehouse facility. In that these institutions, for the most part, must be self-sufficient, the warehouse takes on special importance. It serves as the routine storage unit in which all supplies are kept, and from which the institution can draw on a daily or weekly basis to restock consumable items such as food, linens, paper products, personal hygiene items, and building materials.

Objectives

The warehouse facility is the designated area for receiving, holding, and distributing all materials and supplies needed for the daily operation of the institution. Depending on the facility, the warehouse can employ both staff and inmates.

Because it is the destination of delivery vehicles to the institution, it is important that the warehouse be accessible to vehicular traffic at all times. It also should have sufficient loading dock capacity to handle the amount of traffic that it will process during daily operations.

Typical Operation

Supplies and materials are brought into the warehouse on a regular basis. Each item is scheduled based on the use of that item at the institution. Some items, such as dairy products, may be brought on a daily basis, whereas toilet paper and longer lasting food products such as canned goods will come on a monthly or quarterly basis. Upon delivery of goods to the warehouse by the vendor, the warehouse staff will receive the goods, inventory them, and then store them in the warehouse.

In some facilities, the warehouse will have the capacity to store food items for long periods of time in large walk-in refrigerators and freezers. In other facilities, the warehouse does not have this capacity and vehicles that deliver food items are allowed into the secure perimeter of the institution. This practice is not advisable because it places a larger nonsecurity vehicle inside the secure perimeter of the facility that if compromised could aid inmates in an escape attempt. A more middle of the road solution for facilities without food storage capacity in the warehouse is to receive the items and immediately transfer those items to a smaller institution vehicle for delivery to the food service building.

As noted previously, the size, population, and location of an institution as well as the delivery schedule of vendors in the area will determine how often deliveries are received. A trend in some areas of the country is the use of single source vendor agreements. These agreements help the institutions that are more remote and find it difficult to obtain bids from multiple vendors for all consumables. In this case, the institution is allowed to bid out on a group of supplies and materials that are then supplied by a single vendor.

Location

The warehouse typically is constructed outside the secure perimeter of the institution. If a guard tower is part of the perimeter security, then the warehouse is normally in view of that officer. Otherwise, its operation is observed either directly by central control or through surveillance cameras.

Its location should be near the vehicle sallyport entrance to the institution and also on a roadway that is accessible to the main highway or street. The area in front of the warehouse should have sufficient turnaround space for a semitrailer to maneuver into and out of the loading dock area. If after-hour deliveries are permitted, an intercom station should be mounted on a post in front of any control gates that restrict access to the warehouse building. The intercom should be connected to the guard tower or central control.

Functional Areas

Loading Dock

There should be a minimum of two loading dock doors with a dock leveling device on at least one of the doors to handle semitrailer traffic. Adequate drainage and a stairway from grade to the dock level should be provided. A dock seal also will help provide protection from the elements in severe weather conditions.

Receiving Area

This area should be adequate in size to unload a truck and allow the contents to be sorted, weighed, and separated before moving the contents into the warehouse storage areas. Some provision should be made to separate this space physically from the warehouse to control temperature loss in the warehouse and provide additional security for the warehouse storage areas. This area also should contain a large scale to weigh items as they are received.

Manager's Office

This is an office area where staff can maintain files and records of warehouse transactions and conduct business. It needs data and voice connections.

Toilets

Separate toilet facilities should be provided for both staff and inmates if inmate laborers are used in the warehouse. These facilities should be barrier-free. Electric water coolers also should be near the toilet facilities.

Storage Areas

These areas should be designed to permit separation of food items from all other storage to maintain appropriate sanitation. All storage areas should have a minimum clear height (between finished floor and ceiling structure) of fourteen to twenty-two feet. The number of pallets to be stored vertically or the height of steel shelving used to store materials will be the determining factor.

Janitor's Closet

This space should be provided to accommodate all cleaning supplies and toilet room supplies. There should also be sufficient area for any floor cleaning equipment required in the building.

Walk-in Refrigerator and Freezer

These facilities should be premanufactured equipment that is of a standard height with a mezzanine floor above to provide additional storage area and space for cooling equipment. The floor elevation of the units should be level with the floor of the adjacent storage areas. A temperature alarm should be annunciated in the manager's office and central control.

Summary of the Design

- A location near the main vehicle sallyport is most desirable.
- There should be separation of food storage and other commodities.
- Secure construction will insure controlled access and eliminate pilfering.
- The design should be expandable and also convertible to other uses.
- A heating system should be provided to maintain temperatures required for a work environment.
- Separate temperatures may be required in areas that store different consumables.
- Protect all doorframes with ballards to avoid damage from cart traffic.
- A view of the receiving operation by the security staff is desirable.

Utility Systems

John Gromos
SSR
Nashville, Tennessee

As more operational features are automated and computerized, reliability of the electrical system becomes more critical. It is crucial that staff skilled in maintenance and repair of these systems are available to assure minimal disruptions to essential systems.

Both normal and emergency power usually is distributed from a centralized location, which ideally is located outside the secure perimeter. Ready access to equipment is important for utility and maintenance personnel.

An emergency generator is essential to ensure a reliable power supply for vital operations such as the control center, security lighting, and life safety systems. Thus, the generator system should have automatic starting and transfer capability, which will reenergize the electrical system within ten seconds after a utility power outage. Battery backup power should be provided to enable all critical systems to continue in operation during the transition period from normal to emergency power.

The central utility plant in the Federal Prison Complex in Florence, Colorado serves the entire complex of three institutions and the work camp for heating, cooling, and emergency electrical power.

Photo courtesy of the Federal Bureau of Prisons.

The generator is not sized to carry the entire load, but typically provides for building code requirements, security systems including site lighting, automation systems, and partial service for other selected features, such as food storage and preparation. Institutions with electric heat or elevators should evaluate the need for additional generating capacity. For large systems and for facilities in localities which are subject to frequent or prolonged power outages, it is good practice to have more than one generator so that if one is disabled, the other can serve the most essential needs.

In older institutions, all lighting has been controlled by staff members. Increasingly, light switches accessible to inmates are being installed in selected areas, such as inmate rooms and multipurpose rooms in housing units. Where concerns exist about inmates having control of lights, staff override or total staff control is provided.

While the electrical system must meet local codes and the National Electrical Code, there are times when it may be advisable to exceed code requirements. For example, the National Electrical Code requires ground fault interrupters in certain areas to prevent accidental shock. In correctional facilities, it may be prudent to install these devices to minimize the possibility of inmates tampering with the wiring system to injure themselves or others.

Water System

Important concerns for the water system are issues of health, environment, security, and building maintenance. If the local utility company can guarantee sufficient water pressure and volume, no on-site water storage tank is needed. Otherwise, an elevated or pressurized water tank is required on-site. Water usage is usually between 150 and 300 gallons per day per inmate for facilities with kitchens and laundries. If a storage tank is required, at a minimum, the tank should store a five-day emergency backup water supply, not inclusive of fire protection storage.

In addition, provisions must be made to insure sufficient water for fire protection, in accordance with the code of the National Fire Protection Association. Coordination with state, local, and federal officials in addition to plumbing, health, and environmental officials and water treatment facility managers is required early in the design of a new or renovation project. In seismic areas, tiedowns and supports in addition to piping expansion joint requirements should be coordinated with local officials.

In correctional facilities, it is important to isolate the water supply and distribution system by housing wings or dayrooms. This design permits troubled areas to be isolated without shutting off entire buildings. It is recommended that in housing units a bank or wing of twelve to fifteen rooms have a separate water shut-off valve in a secure area to minimize disruption in water service.

Inmate housing units also have special requirements for plumbing fixtures. Depending on security level, fixtures should be vandal proof with no protruding handles that inmates could harm themselves with or break off to use as a weapon. Plumbing fixture manufacturers make china and stainless steel fixtures especially for correctional facilities. China fixtures typically are used in lower-security facilities, while stainless steel fixtures typically are used in higher-security facilities. To prevent inmates from "flooding" the building, lavatories and water closets can be equipped with metering type valves to reduce the number of flushes and the amount of water pressure. Computer-controlled electronic valve systems can be programmed to limit the number of times a toilet is flushed. Stainless steel fixtures can be equipped with combination units consisting of a lavatory, water closet, and drinking fountain.

The Americans with Disabilities Act (ADA) requires that a certain number of cells are equipped with ADA plumbing fixtures. For particular requirements, refer to the ADA guidelines. Special china and stainless steel fixtures including lavatories, water closets, showers, sinks, and drinking fountains are manufactured to meet the ADA guidelines. Clearances and mounting heights also are covered in the ADA guidelines.

Protecting the drinking water (potable water) from chemical or biological contamination is an important concern. Backflow preventers are used on potable water lines to reduce the risk of contamination in one water system from backflowing and contaminating another water system. At a minimum, backflow preventers typically are required at the connection to the municipal system and at the connection to nonpotable equipment, such as HVAC equipment. Some communities have backflow prevention officials who monitor this, and there are special requirements for the backflow preventer installations.

Several factors should be considered in a water heating system. Antiscald protection can be provided with one common mixing valve and/or the mixing valves at the showers. Coordinate the times of showers and durations of showering to the size of the water heater system. Some officials require high water temperature alarms and automatic hot water shut off on the hot water system. Other officials have requirements on hot water storage tanks to prevent the growth of biological contaminants when water is not used for long periods of time. Hot water recirculation systems should be used to provide hot water in short periods of time. Water softeners may be required to maintain the water heating system for water hardness levels more than nine grains.

Because of the higher water temperatures required, it is recommended that a separate water heater be provided for domestic hot water supplied to the kitchen. To reduce utility costs, booster heaters typically are installed at the dishwashers to raise the temperature of the domestic hot water to the temperature required at the dishwasher. The institution laundry usually requires a separate water heater.

Sewage System

Important concerns for sewage and stormwater systems are issues of health, the environment, security, and building maintenance. Maintenance issues include the treatment of the building sewage. Like the water system, it is preferable to connect the facility to a local sewage system, thus conserving the staff time and costs associated with operating and maintaining a separate treatment plant. If this is not feasible, an on-site sewage treatment system must be installed and staffed by qualified personnel who will ensure that the service meets all applicable environmental pollution control standards. The daily sewage flow from a facility to be treated is generally 80 to 90 percent of the total water consumption.

To maintain the sewer system, it is common to have oil separators installed in garages, central plants, maintenance facilities, and security pits for viewing motor traffic and other locations where oil can enter the sewer or storm water system. In addition, lint traps for washing machines in the laundry and separate grease waste systems and grease traps, floor sinks, and solid food traps are required in the kitchen. Dumpsters with kitchen waste also may require area drains with grease traps before connecting to the sewer or storm water. The location of separators and traps in or outside of secure areas should be coordinated for access and serviceability. Local officials may have requirements on tying cooling tower area drains into the storm or sewer system.

Storm water retention may be necessary to comply with environmental requirements. The roof drainage system may be required to connect to the retention area. To prevent inmate escapes, storm sewer pipes crossing under the security perimeter typically are manifolded in multiple pipes not larger than six inches in diameter.

For safety, facilities with flat roofs typically have primary and secondary roof drains with a complete secondary piping system. This secondary roof drain system may be required to connect to the site of the storm water system outside the building or terminate over a doorway or a window.

Some facility managers and sewer companies require a sewage grinder system installed at the end of the facility's sewer line. This grinder should be sized to handle blankets, clothing, or other items inmates flush into the system. The grinder is installed in a pit with a sewer bypass around the grinder pit for maintenance. A bar screen may be required if facility managers require frequent access to the screen to monitor the material inmates flush into the system.

For health reasons, flushing-type floor drains with flush valves located in secure areas sometimes are used in detoxification units. These drains will flush some solids much like water closets and help maintain clean areas. In showers, the water from one shower should not flow into another shower area. This will require a trench-type drain or a minimum of one drain for every two showers.

To keep the facility secure and to prevent inmates from trying to flood an area by clogging the plumbing fixtures, floor drains are recommended in areas outside cells, such as dayrooms. The HVAC requirements for dayroom areas will cause air pressure fluctuations and dry out the traps in these drains. To eliminate sewer gas from entering occupied spaces, the drains should have deep seal traps and trap primers. Waste lines from inmate areas typically are sized at a minimum of six inches to prevent clogging of lines and the potential backup of sewage. Extra cleanouts located in secure areas are also typically provided.

Heating, Ventilation, and Air Conditioning (HVAC)

The most important issue associated with HVAC design of a correctional facility is maintaining the integrity of the facility's security. The HVAC design must consider the security level of the facility for air devices (grilles, registers, and diffusers), and for the installation of security barriers in penetrations of security walls. Security barriers (bars) are installed at all duct penetrations and openings in security walls. Provide security fasteners (tamper proof screws) at all devices and equipment exposed to inmate access.

Space thermostats need to be located strategically to avoid damage by inmates and personnel. Provide security covers on exposed thermostats or locate sensors remotely (in the return air stream) to control temperature.

Local codes may require the installation of a smoke control system for inmate housing areas, and other areas in the facility where inmates may be locked down. These systems typically control smoke by pressure relationships, exhausting the area in alarm and pressurizing the adjacent areas. Air change rates are typically fifteen air changes per hour (four minute air changes) for cell spaces, lock down spaces, and dayrooms, but local, state, and national codes should be observed.

Indoor air quality is another major design consideration, and ASHRAE 62-89 recommendations for minimum outside air requirements should be followed. Local codes may require individual cells with water closets be exhausted, which is a way to receive outside air. When cell exhaust is not required, provisions must be made to relieve air to maintain a slightly positive pressure building. Where smoking is allowed in the facility, outside air should be increased to improve air quality.

Systems controls should follow the "keep it simple" philosophy. It is important to know the level of compe-tence that the maintenance personnel and operator have in the HVAC systems. The design should not be over-complicated (costly). Systems should be serviceable, maintainable, and reliable. Poor servicing of equipment due to lack of a sufficient service area and accessibility will decrease the lifespan of the equipment and increase repair and maintenance costs. Isolation valves should be provided in water systems to strategically shut down only portions of the system, when maintenance does need to occur. These valves should be located in secure locations not exposed to inmate access.

The size and security level of the facility, competence of maintenance staff, budget, initial cost, and operating cost all should be considered when selecting HVAC systems. Smaller, low-security facilities may use only packaged direct-expansion systems, while larger campus facilities may have central chilled water and heating plants. When central plants are used, they typically are located outside the secure perimeter to limit access to authorized personnel. High-security facilities may not allow rooftop equipment so as to eliminate potential hiding locations for inmates, and they may require redundant backup systems for air conditioning. All these issues need to be addressed with the facility operator at the beginning of the design phase.

Power Plant

Jeffrey Minnerly and Keith Rupert
New York State Department
of Correctional Services
Albany, New York

The power plant at a correctional facility can be compared to any local utility company. It usually provides electricity, steam for heat, hot water, and fresh water for drinking. The power plant is a nerve center of a facility whose services either originate at or are distributed from it. The sewage system will depend on a municipality or the facility will have its own wastewater plant.

The *Standards for Adult Correctional Institutions* states the things to be considered in the numbered standards shown to the right.

Objective

The power plant will be used as the main source to provide the utility services to a correctional facility. These services will include, but are not limited to, providing potable water, steam from heat and cooking, electricity, and sewage disposal. Any or all of these services will come directly from, or be supported by, the power plant.

In a correctional facility, the power plant provides the utility services. These services vary by facility. This usually will be a twenty-four-hour operation. Some facilities do not have a power plant. The utilities may be provided for from a neighboring facility.

American Correctional Association Standards for Utility Service

3-4188: Written policy and procedure govern the control and use of tools and culinary and medical equipment.

3-4204: The institution has the equipment necessary to maintain essential lights, power, and communication in an emergency.

3-4207: Power generators are tested at least every two weeks, and other emergency equipment and systems are tested at least quarterly for effectiveness and are repaired or replaced if necessary.

3-4311: The institution's potable water source and supply, whether owned and operated by the public water department or the institution, is certified by an independent, outside source to be in compliance with the jurisdictional laws and regulations.

3-4312: The institution provides for a waste disposal system, in accordance with an approved plan by the appropriate regulatory agency.

Typical Operation

The power plant normally will receive the electrical service from the local municipality. Electricity will be received and distributed, through transformers and switch gear, to the outlying facility. The power received will vary according to the power supply available and the power demand of the facility. If the facility is located in a remote area, then the facility may be able to produce its own electricity, by operation of its own electrical generator system.

An emergency source of electricity always must be available. An automatic transfer switch is employed to provide continuous uninterrupted electrical service. Critical equipment will have a battery backup, just in case there is a complete failure of this system. The emergency generator will be of a suitable size to provide the whole facility with electrical power for critical equipment and system needs.

Boilers usually will be operated to supply the facility with steam for hot water and heat. The steam pressure supplied will be determined by the actual facility makeup. Steam also can be used to operate a steam turbine to produce electricity, if this is the choice. The boilers will need a fuel source. There can be one or more sources of fuel. The boilers typically use oil, gas, coal, or wood for fuel. Many boilers use dual fuel burners so that a fuel source always is available.

The power plant staff usually maintains the potable water system. The receiving and distribution piping is checked for leaks and meter readings are taken daily. This will help to identify an unusual water usage. If the water is received from a local municipality, then the meter reading will be used to verify the billing. If the facility provides itself with water through wells or a reservoir system, then they will be responsible for its treatment, to ensure that it is of a proper quality to consume. A water treatment plant may be necessary. If this is the case, then qualified operators will staff it.

A suitable supply of water will be needed to ensure that the facility will satisfy the National Fire Protection Association's code requirements for fire protection. Additionally, a storage tank will be needed to ensure a positive water supply in case of an emergency. This should be a three-day supply, at a minimum.

Connection to a municipal system is preferred, if at all possible. This is also true for the sewage system. If the facility cannot connect to a municipal sewage system, then it will need to operate an onsite sewage treatment plant. Qualified operators will be required to staff this plant. It also must comply with all codes, rules, and regulations governing the local jurisdiction. The plant should be sized to handle at least 80 percent of the total water consumption of the facility. A bar screen will assist with the removal of debris.

Location

The power plant usually will be located outside of the secure perimeter. It may be located near the garage and warehouse. This creates a small satellite complex of support buildings. They should be centrally located and allow for easy access to the facility.

Functional Areas

Power Plant

The power plant will be of sufficient size to house multiple boilers, pumps, fuel systems, monitoring equipment, emergency electrical generators, switch gear, and related support equipment. There may be several rooms and multiple floors in this building. The rooms and floors will be related to the different parts of the steam cycle and the services provided. An overhead door will facilitate the maintenance and replacement of equipment.

Storeroom and Tool Room

A storeroom will be provided to keep repair parts and tools. The repair parts will be inventoried and tracked by the maintenance work control center. This room will

Prototypical Heating Plant*	
Space Description	*Net Sq. Ft.*
Staff Toilet	90
Inmate Toilet	90
Staff Office	175
Tool Room	390
Boiler Room	5,000
Electric Room	175
Total Net Sq. Ft.	**5,920**
Total Gross Sq. Ft.	**7,326**

* These requirements are based on a building with three boilers and no space for future expansion.

have a secure locking door for entry. The tools will be inventoried on a scheduled basis, with reports being forwarded to the department head. A shadow board and chit system should be used.

Offices

An office should be provided. It should allow for observation of staff and equipment on an ongoing basis.

Toilets

There should be separate toilet, locker, and shower facilities for civilians and inmates. There should be a similar arrangement in the garage and the warehouse.

Janitor's Closet

A separate slop sink area should be provided and space allocated to allow for the storage of cleaning supplies in this area.

Summary of the Design

The following components should be included:

- Provide a central location for ease of access to the whole facility.

- Plan for an overhead door.

- Construct a separate tool and storage area to maintain control and inventory of materials.

- Secure construction due to the nature of the area.

- Provide appropriate utilities to this area to support the varied activities that are involved.

- Use steel storage shelves for bulk storage of materials.

- Design separate rooms for separate utilities.

- Construct water and waste water facilities similarly.

Security Features

The Federal Correctional Institution in Edgefield, South Carolina was designed as a medium-security facility but is used as a high-security facility. Before the fence comes up, bars are used in addition to security glazing. This is the main pedestrian entrance into the compound shown on the preceding page.

Architect/Engineer: Wilkins Wood Goforth Associates, Florence, South Carolina. Construction management firm: Gilbert Commonwealth, Reading, Pennsylvania. Construction contractor for the correctional institution and prison camp: Caddell Construction, Montgomery, Alabama. Construction contractor/fence: Huger, Wanda, South Carolina. Photo courtesy of the Federal Bureau of Prisons.

Security Hardware and Electronic Systems Design

J. Michael Henson
PSA
Peoria, Illinois

To present all design criteria and methodologies of this subject matter adequately, the text required would be many times the volume of this book. Instead, this section presents a view of a project approach, design concepts, and technologies, which have proven successful in planning and constructing secure adult and juvenile facilities.

The Design Approach

The key to any successful project is to achieve the standard of excellence sought as the end result. The class of service and quality of work of all participants should be identified clearly. Unfortunately, this measurement of successful achievement may not be defined and communicated accurately to all design team members at the onset of a project, so false expectations may develop. The path to success is further impeded by not recognizing and articulating negative variables that may occur during the design and construction process, which will cause projects to fall short of their goal at completion.

The owner, the user, the architects, the engineers, and the security consultant must be fully aware of the three critical elements, which govern every construction project. These key elements are quality, time, and cost, and each has a logical cause and effect relationship with the others. For example, if a project has a short time line and a tight budget, the overall quality of that project will be low. If a client is determined to have a high quality facility and maintain a short time line, the client should be told and expect that the project cost will be high.

In other words, all design team members must be fully aware that it is only possible to control two of these elements. The third element is reactive to the definition of the first two elements in establishing an acceptable standard of excellence. If you attempt to control all three elements, successful expectations are flawed, and certain failures will occur. In the design phase, construction documents will be inferior, or redesign will be required to correct exceeded building cost estimates. During the construction phase, many things can occur that will have an impact on any trade, which will lessen the expected quality, planned construction schedule, or overall project cost. To reiterate, the true achievable success of a project is determined by an achievable standard of excellence accepted by the design team.

The Security Consultant

Selection of a qualified security consultant is an important step in the critical path to design and construction of a successful secure facility. In general, the "5 and 5 Rule" should apply to the first qualification phase. This means that a minimum of five criminal justice projects of similar size and scope to the new facility, which have been completed and operational for five years, should be referenced. The facility administrator and architect for each of the five projects should be phoned to verify how the security consultant performed the following:

1. Spent ample time obtaining information on specific needs of the project/program and the user's policies and procedures prior to suggesting design solutions

2. Demonstrated knowledge of the latest proven security technology and presented alternative design solutions based on clearly identified needs

3. Possessed the ability to articulate technical concepts in a commonsense manner and made an effort to communicate to all design team members throughout the project

4. Delivered a security design, which met the program's needs within the schedule

After the direct interview of the security consultant, answer the following questions:

5. Does the consultant understand the importance of defining the specific standard of excellence for the project?

6. When you view examples of published construction document specifications and drawings, do they show quality and completeness?

7. Did you examine the resumes of all key staff members who have been assigned to do the actual work on the project?

8. Did the submitter provide a specific description of deliverables to be provided during the schematic design, the design development, and the construction document process, including participation in scheduled and special team meetings?

9. Did you discover what the consultant will do to provide construction administration, which ensures the defined standard of excellence is reached and project conflicts, poor work, construction delays, and change orders are minimized?

10. Did you find out who the consultant uses at this time to provide services as a detention equipment contractor, security electronics subcontractor, and other significant vendors, fabricators, and manufacturers?

11. Throughout the process, does the security consultant communicate well, articulate technical information in a clear, understandable fashion, and will the consultant be a positive addition to the design team?

The Detention Equipment Contractor

The detention equipment industry historically has been a very high growth and volatile environment, and each detention equipment contractor should be evaluated at least every year or each time for large projects. The dynamics of this industry can cause huge changes in a company's financial position, key specialized personnel, or even the capability to meet the project time line.

The "5 and 5 Rule" applies to the detention equipment contractor, as well. The detention equipment contractor should have experience with a minimum of five criminal justice projects of similar size and scope to the new facility, which have been completed and

Contractor Performance Checklist

- Giving adequate representation at project meetings and maintaining responsibilities for submittals

- Performing product delivery and work in accordance with the construction schedule

- Complying with the construction documents

- Performing quality work

- Responding to repairing punch list items, work that has either not been completed or must be redone to complete the project, and warranty service

- Performing contract change orders of varying sizes and dollar amounts

To further evaluate a contractor, obtain a complete, current picture of the contractor by obtaining:

- Current financial statement

- AIA Form 305A—Contractor Qualification Statement

- Resumes of all key individuals in the company who are responsible for engineering/design, fabrication, project management, and field supervision who will be assigned to work on the project

- Copies of past project shop drawings and product data submittals to verify quality and completeness

- Name of the bonding company and their current bonding capacity

- Chronological listing of all litigation involving the detention equipment contractor and the nature of the settlement or judgment, including fault claims for liquidated damages

operational for five years. Call the facility administrator and the general contractor to verify how the detention equipment contractor performed.

Historically, all detention hardware, hollow metal, and equipment were specified in a separate division of the construction specifications to ensure the detention equipment contractor was the single source of responsibility. That concept is now being revisited by many design teams to consider the "value-added" relationship the contractor has to the services rendered.

An experienced security consultant who can provide special construction details, an intelligent shop drawing review, and properly focused field inspection, can replace the detention equipment contractor.

For example, security glazing was the first special area of work specifications that moved to the general construction area from being in a separate detention division in the specifications. When properly designed and with the appropriate construction details, this work may be included as part of the general glazing package for the building. The security glazing products that have been handled by the detention equipment contractor can be provided, just as easily, by the general contractor at a reduced cost with the same quality. Some recent projects for minimum or low-medium security facilities have been completed successfully without a detention equipment contractor.

However, medium and higher-security projects must have a detention equipment contractor as a single source to coordinate the highly specialized security hardware, such as electro-mechanical sliding door operator cell fronts or sallyports. Any significant renovation work also is performed best by a detention equipment contractor due to the tight time frames, complicated phasing, and specialized work that occurs in an occupied facility.

Security Hardware

The designs of most security hardware and furnishings, used today, have been standardized for many years and, if applied in the security environment for which they are designed, have a successfully proven operational life. Problems with this equipment usually result from misapplication by the security consultant or from inferior installation.

Exciting new security hardware technology uses pneumatics in lieu of electro-mechanical controls for remote device operation. Pneumatics suffered a terrible startup due to an early California Department of Corrections

Architects inspect a pneumatic device for security.

Courtesy of HOK Architects, Washington, D.C.

project where pneumatic locking devices had to be replaced with traditional electro-mechanical devices due to inferior performance. However, on further investigation, the real problem was poor installation, including nonpurged pneumatic lines, lack of proper dryers, duct taped pneumatic line splices, and so forth. Virtually every machine shop in the United States depends on pneumatic systems everyday. There have been design advances in compressors, dryers, storage tanks, and manifolds over the last few years.

One of the best current applications of pneumatic security hardware is the sliding door operator, especially if the project requires a continuous slider cell front design. The design of the pneumatic operator is a large improvement over the electro-mechanical version with the reduction of mechanical linkages, which operate at a much lower tolerance and require an increased maintenance adjustment. The simplified pneumatic slider eliminates the elaborate system of bars, cables, and leverage handles of the electro-mechanical slider emergency release operation. In addition, the maintenance and labor required to support pneumatic sliders generally is less than that required for electro-mechanical sliders with an equal number of openings.

However, when looking at pneumatic swing door locks versus electro-mechanical swing door locks on an equal basis, the argument is less compelling. Although some pneumatic swing locks do have fewer moving parts, the pneumatic system in the purest engineering sense offers additional points of failure. Pneumatic swing locks will complement a pneumatic slider project, but going to pneumatics for a swing-door-only facility should require closer analysis and discussion prior to implementation.

Security Electronics Subcontractor

The security electronics subcontractor's work is typically written to be under the scope of work of the electrical contractor. However, if the project or client requires, the security electronics contractor can be specified as a prime contractor. Specifying the security electronics subcontractor as a subcontractor to the electrical contractor helps to ensure that the critical coordination of conduit and wire comes from a single source and helps to prevent the possibility of having two electrical contractors on the same site with a potential of conflict.

Control Center and Electronic Systems

Paul Allyn and Jack Shetter
Justice Systems
Issaquah, Washington

ACA standards require a control center at each institution to "provide order and security."[1] The main control center generally is responsible for perimeter security, coordinating internal security and communications, inmate counts, key control, and monitoring emergency systems. It must be staffed twenty-four hours per day. Minor or secondary control centers typically support the main control center by regulating inmate movement and monitoring emergency systems within a defined area (for example, a housing unit).

Traditional control centers (including main control and local control at indirect supervision housing) are enclosed, highly secure rooms that often rely on cameras for vision and intercoms for communications. Since the early 1980s, barrier-free open workstations have been employed effectively as direct supervision control centers. Some institutions have eliminated fixed control centers and have promoted staff mobility by equipping control officers with wireless, handheld remotes. These developments have challenged the traditional notion of control centers.

Central control rooms are the brain of an institution with all security functions controlled by its staff.

Photo by Paul Allyn.

After providing guidance on control center planning and design, this section considers the many interior electronic security systems that are integral to control center operations. Modern systems are so thoroughly integrated as to form a single integrated electronic security system, which for purposes of this section are divided into the following three component groups:

- Field devices such as cameras, intercom stations, alarm sensors, and locking hardware located throughout the institution and their associated subsystems. This section briefly covers security controls and alarms, video surveillance, and a number of communication subsystems.

- Operator interfaces, which are located at control centers, such as control panels or video control stations

- Control electronics that perform all logic and control functions and integrate the various subsystems together

Further guidance on electronics issues may be found in the *Standard Guide for Selection of Operational Security Control Systems* published by the American Society of Testing and Materials (ASTM),[2] which is referred to throughout this section.

Control Center Planning

Security Level

It is important to set a level of security for each control center that provides a safe environment for staff that is consistent with the institution's overall security level (for example, intensive management, maximum, medium, or minimum security). For control rooms, the security level will be influenced by the time required to maintain operations before a team can respond. The penetration time of all the materials selected for the room's perimeter should be longer than the expected response time, with an additional comfortable safety factor.

Control Center Type

The type of control center will vary based on its function and responsibility. Examples include the main control center (central control), secondary control centers (support or housing unit control), and open workstations. The combination of security level and type establish the control center's entry-control requirements, including sallyport entry, single door, gate, or open. The entry-control configuration influences the floor plan layout and also affects the selection of materials.

Staff Stations

In the design, determine the number of staff who will be working within the control center who require a fixed workstation (in other words, operator position or desk). What shift will they be working? Will there be relief, or will the control room have to provide for all staff needs? An analysis of control center activities, both average and peak, will help to determine the appropriate staffing levels.

Support Spaces

Support spaces should consider the personal needs of staff, such as for a toilet, food service, coffee bar, and personal storage. Each institution's unique policies will help to determine how these needs will be met.

An equipment room for electronic cabinets and racks should be close in proximity to control rooms and should be secured at the same level. Provide communications between the rooms for maintenance. If a separate room cannot be provided and the control room itself houses the electronics, the room's size and configuration should permit access to the equipment for maintenance without interrupting control room operations.

Equipment Considerations

Items that should be considered in the control center design include key control, paper storage, calendar, clock, working files, clipboards, garbage containers, emergency flashlights, air packs, restraints, fire extinguisher, telephone, radio, and battery charging units, to name a few. Other items can clutter a new control center and detract from its working conditions. Inventories from existing control centers and equipment checklists can be useful design tools.

Control Center Design

Sight Lines

Designers need to consider sight lines to ensure that control operators have maximum vision of areas under their supervision and control. Both horizontal and vertical views need to be investigated. The selection and design of materials, such as structural supports, hollow metal doors, and glazing, also will have an impact on sight lines. For example, structural supports in columns or walls are best located away from the control center to prevent blind spots behind them. Blind spots also can be created by hollow metal mullions that are too large or spaced so as to block vision when viewed at an angle.

If absolutely necessary, supplemental closed-circuit television can provide vision into difficult areas, but direct vision is preferable, wherever possible.

Reflections

Glazing provides vision and light into supervised areas. Reflections from improperly installed glazing can interfere with vision and even produce blind spots. Reflections will increase in proportion to the number of glazing layers between the control center and the supervised area. Methods of controlling reflections include mounting angle adjustment, glazing material selection, and control of illumination levels.

Set horizontal and vertical mounting angles to avoid parallel layers. Select glazing materials that minimize vision problems. Use the highest illumination level at the perimeter of the supervised area and the lowest level within the control center. Step up the illumination level behind each intervening layer of glazing to minimize reflections from that layer. Also, be aware that mirror glass, while it may work under some conditions, is subject to changes in the direction of reflection due to ambient lighting variations from day to night. Each condition will need to be verified.

Materials

The selection of materials should be based on the security level in coordination with the penetration time. This includes the selection of materials for glazing, walls, hollow metal, hardware, and security ceilings. All other materials may be of a normative nature.

Hardware and Hollow Metal

Select hardware and hollow metal to match the control center's security level. Hardware comes in several levels of security ranging from standard, light, medium, to heavy security. Hardware also can be provided in swing, sliding, and power slide configurations. Hollow metal is fabricated with varying levels of detailing, construction, and material gauges to provide different security levels. Protect removable glazing stops by locating them on the secure side of the control room. And if glazing requirements demand a bullet-proof glazing product for the control center, then hollow metal window frames also must meet that requirement.

Consider also the interface between electronic systems and hardware. If the entry door is part of a sallyport, the electronics needs to interlock with the door controls. If the institution does not want the locking controls to be operable with the entry door open, which is relatively common, the electronics needs to interlock the controls with the door hardware. These and similar electronic functions will have a considerable influence on hardware selection.

Control Room Penetrations

For enclosed control rooms, pay attention to all penetrations of the room's perimeter security line, not just the entry doors. Examples of perimeter penetrations include communication devices, package pass-throughs, and mechanical ducts.

Communications to the area surrounding the control room can be accomplished with either electronic intercoms or speak-ports. Both devices may be detailed into either the glazing or the hollow metal. Pass-throughs for both small and large packages may be premanufactured units or custom-detailed into the hollow metal, with or without protection. Select both communication devices and pass-throughs to provide the same level of security as the overall control room. Also protect mechanical ducting that penetrates the room perimeter, when it exceeds the maximum allowable size for a security opening.

Mechanical and Electrical Design

Control room mechanical systems should be independent of surrounding zones, as air movement and controls require different settings for each shift. Since door openings are infrequent, control room zones require a higher level of air movement than a normal room.

Lighting should be supplied in two levels: (1) normal working conditions with low general illumination and localized task lighting on work surfaces and (2) a much higher illumination level for maintenance. Light sources (for example, lamps or bulbs) should be shielded to prevent reflections off video displays and closed-circuit television monitors at typical viewing angles.

Because of the electrical systems used, there should be more outlets and circuits for control centers than for other rooms of comparable size. At least half of a control room's outlets and its equipment room circuits should be supplied from standby power provided by an on-site generator. Life safety equipment (for example, fire alarm, exit lighting, and so forth) requires emergency power from batteries. Consider also one or more uninterruptible power supplies for critical or sensitive circuits to provide power during the transfer to standby power (in other words, a "bumpless" transfer) or if the generators should fail to start.

Also, give attention to cable management between control centers and their equipment rooms. Alternative solutions include raised access floors, wire ducts, conduit arrays, and cable chases.

Workstation Design

Planning and Layout

Workstation design must begin with a complete understanding of each station's intended duties (security controls, data entry, and so forth) and physical needs (material pass, storage, materials needed for normal operations, and so forth). Determine whether the operator typically will sit in a chair, sit on a stool, or be standing. Engineer the operator's position for effective sight lines and a limited range of motion, including close placement of work surfaces and comfortable placement of viewing surfaces.

For security control operations, determine the size and optimal placement of operator interfaces, either hard control panels or video control stations, and other associated equipment, particularly closed-circuit television, intercom masters, and radio base stations. Plan each workstation so that staff can operate all electronics and perform most routine duties from one position. Scattering work areas throughout the control center is bad practice and creates frantic motion between positions during times of peak activity. Consider recessing control panels, monitors, and other equipment into the consoles in situations where their mounting height would obstruct sight lines. Full-scale mockups and computer modeling are good ways to help operators visualize and improve a design with their input.

Console design is very important. Staff operating the equipment must be able to access all control panels and related equipment without undue exertion or long-term fatigue. Whatcom County Courthouse and Juvenile Detention Facility, Bellingham, Washington.

Photo courtesy of KMD Justice.

Console Design

Control console options include prefabricated metal consoles and custom millwork. Prefabricated metal consoles come in fixed widths, slopes, and bends making them difficult to use against walls, in odd-shaped rooms, and with custom panels. For that reason, laminated millwork usually is designed specifically for the control center and its equipment. Carefully detail height, knee space, and other parameters of the work surface for operator comfort. Consider also console access for maintenance while hard control panels or video control stations remain operational.

ASTM 1465 provides guidance for hard control panel or video control station design. Most institutions prefer passive "event-driven" panels and displays that remain dim and quiet under normal conditions (for example, when everything is secure). Indicator lights and tones sound, thereby providing a stimulus, only when a condition is abnormal and the operator's attention is required. Because everything is normal, event-driven interfaces may not even indicate a secure condition (in other words, no green lights).

Consistently and intuitively use colors and sounds. A National Institute of Corrections' survey of institutions[3] found surprising differences in the use of colors. For example, while ASTM 1465 recommends using green for secure and red for unsecure, in 28 percent of institutions surveyed red meant secure and in 21 percent green meant unsecure! Use more rapidly repeating and higher pitched tones to convey a sense of urgency for higher priority alarms. Also consider nonrepeating, single-stroke tones for normal call-ins, and use voice annotation sparingly, if at all, to reduce operator annoyance.

Security Controls and Alarms

Locking Controls

Control staff use locking controls to regulate movement through the institution. The options most commonly employed for locking control include manual remote controls, local key controls, and local access controls.

The manual control option relies on fixed staff at control centers to remotely control locking hardware at cells and movement doors. Control post staffing for this option should consider the quantity of openings and volume of control activity, as well as the time required for the post's other duties. Local key controls allow mobile staff to regulate movement. By providing electric key switches at various cells and movement doors, this option reduces the workload at fixed control centers, encourages staff mobility, and yet maintains control features like electronic interlocks at sallyports. Openings often are equipped with both remote and local controls, allowing them to be operated by either method.

Going one step further, these devices are being replaced with card readers and other automated access control devices. Access controls provide the benefits of local control without the use of keys. More important, access control systems centralize and automate key control and provide an audit trail of movement through the institution. Card coding technologies for access control include proximity and various insertion methods (for example, card swipe). Biometric technologies also have correctional facility application, particularly at very secure locations, such as control centers. They uniquely identify a person using one or more biological features. The most common features are hand geometry, retinal scan, iris scan, and fingerprint scan. The chief drawback to access controls is the relatively high cost of equipping each opening.

The locking controls' configuration must be coordinated carefully with the actual locking systems hardware, particularly the appropriate lock functions (in other words, latch back, half-cycle, and so forth). All controls should be designed to "fail secure" yet accommodate emergency egress (for example, the Life Safety Code[4]). To reduce the hazards of fire and electrical shock, they also must comply with electrical code power limitations and wiring methods (for example, Article 725 of the National Electrical Code[5]).

Personal Alarms

The terms "personal alarm," "panic button," and "duress alarm" are used synonymously for systems to summon assistance in an emergency or duress situation. Fixed reception counters or interview rooms typically employ simple hard-wired panic buttons. Mobile staff often wear body alarm transmitters or carry portable radios equipped with panic buttons. A wide variety of wireless technologies are available for body alarms. They range from low-power radio frequency (RF) transmitters, ultrasonic transmitter/receivers, and RF triangulation systems to various combination technologies. Some combination systems employ the body alarm to receive and store location information as the staff member travels throughout the institution. The body alarm then transmits its stored location to the control center when set into alarm by the person wearing it. Active development is underway for new personal alarm technologies and systems.

Intrusion Detection Alarms

Critical rooms within the institution (such as the pharmacy or property storage) and secure or unoccupied areas (such as rooftops and warehouses) commonly employ intrusion alarms to detect motion or forced entry. At a minimum, status position should be installed on all operable penetrations to the protected area perimeter (doors, windows, roof hatches, and so forth). Glazing can be alarmed with glass breakage sensors. The primary sensor options to detect motion within the protected space include passive infrared (PIR), microwave, PIR/microwave combinations, and video motion detection. Be aware that microwaves are difficult to confine indoors, since walls are largely invisible to its electromagnetic energy.

Electrical/Mechanical Controls

Electronic security systems frequently interface with other electrical and mechanical systems to remotely control various utilities, particularly at inmate housing units. Examples include remote lighting and receptacle control, and shut-offs for sprinklers and domestic water. Dedicated water control systems are available as well.

Video Surveillance Systems

Staff should have unobstructed vision to inmate areas and controlled openings, wherever possible. Since most facilities will be unable to achieve this goal in all areas, closed-circuit camera surveillance is commonly needed to supplement direct vision. Closed-circuit camera surveillance applications include the following:

Movement control: Fixed cameras provide visual identification of persons requesting passage. Most systems integrate camera and intercom selection with locking controls.

Continuous surveillance: Fixed or remotely positioned (pan/tilt/zoom) cameras survey critical areas. The usefulness of continuous surveillance is rather limited, since staff become conditioned to the stimulus from the monitor and frequently are distracted by other duties.

Alarm assessment: This directs staff's attention to the monitors in response to an alarm incident (in other words, "event-driven" surveillance, rather than continual).

Event recording: Alarm inputs also can be used to automate recording of the alarm incident. Closed-circuit camera surveillance recording systems often are associated with fixed movement or surveillance cameras and remotely positioned cameras (for example, dome or track cameras) to document routine operations in the institution. These systems may provide evidence to help defend against litigation by inmates.

Acceptable performance is becoming more affordable as closed-circuit television technology develops. As an example, digital multiplexers have become available to simultaneously display and record up to sixteen cameras on a single monitor and videocassette recorder.

Communication Systems

An institution's communication systems should provide coherent, redundant communication paths to support normal and emergency operations. Two-way radios and a variety of intercom and paging systems usually provide the answer. However, be aware that intercom components are subject to abuse by inmates and the public, so that even the best detention-rated equipment may require frequent maintenance.

Two-way Radio

Typically, handheld radio transceivers are the primary means of staff communication. Reliable radio communication is essential to security and control operations. Channel assignments on older VHF/UHF systems use separate frequencies to separate conversations and signaling methods for privacy. These frequencies often are congested and difficult or impossible to obtain. Newer "trunking" systems support increased traffic by assigning channels on demand from a cluster of frequencies in the 800 MHz band. Channel assignments are computer-controlled similar to cellular telephone technology. Privacy is obtained through "talk groups" that are programmable.

Coverage between handheld radios, or even between handhelds and a base, often suffers due to the steel reinforcement used in correctional facility construction. These problems usually can be solved by an engineered solution of distributed antennas, repeaters, or amplifiers.

Movement Intercom

Intercoms help control centers regulate movement through two-way communications to areas beyond the range of direct speech. Calls from movement stations also notify the control center of movement requests. Many systems automatically answer call requests in the order received using a "next event" function.

Cell Intercom

Most codes and standards require a communication means for cells and inmate living areas to signal a control center for emergency assistance. Within direct supervision housing, consider a simple call button and light at each cell. In remote supervision and close

Noncontact visiting booths are difficult places to communicate. Providing the appropriate communication devices can enhance the function of the space. Portage County Jail, Ravenna, Ohio.

Photo courtesy of NBBJ, Columbus, Ohio. Photographer: John Griesen.

custody housing, two-way intercoms are typical, along with a "mute" function to block inmate nuisance calls. If the local control center is not staffed continuously, unanswered calls will need to transfer to a twenty-four-hour post. Nurse call systems provide a means of requesting medical attention at the infirmary and other medical cells, and take the place of cell intercoms in those areas.

Visitation Intercom

Visitation intercoms provide a speech path across security glazing at noncontact visitation booths. Because of the maintenance that handsets require and the expense of hands-free intercoms, an acoustic path through the frame should be considered. If handsets are used, they can be provided on the visitors' side and a hands-free speaker can be installed on the inmate side.

Voice Paging

Public address and voice paging require forethought and policy to prevent overuse, particularly in the live acoustical environment of a correctional facility. Two-way conversations are usually unintelligible over paging speakers, because of excessive reverberation and ambient noise. The best results are obtained with one-way paging only to defined areas for selective purposes (for example, announcing the end of visiting hours, staff emergency response, and so forth).

Radio Paging

Radio paging is an effective alternative to voice paging, yet few facilities to date have employed this technology. Text-messaging systems are readily added to other radio frequency transmission systems, such as two-way radio or personal alarm, and can be integrated with other electronic systems as well.

Dedicated Staff Intercoms

Many facilities also provide a dedicated intercom exchange for security and control operations between control posts. Other facilities rely on the telephone system for this function. Both systems can provide full-duplex, hands-free communication with reduced digit dialing and are particularly useful for reducing radio traffic between control rooms. Dedicated intercoms have the advantage of not tying up phone lines.

Operator Interfaces

Being the most visible component of the electronics system, there is a temptation to select operator interface technology (hard control panel or video control station) prior to actual design. Instead, do so only after functionally defining the system, including its field devices (in other words, let form follow function). The most appropriate interface generally will become apparent after the following steps:

- Establish each control post's geographic "span of control" (area of responsibility).
- Define the functional span of control for each control center (the control, monitor, and communication functions it performs).

A variety of control panel options are available. Staff who use the equipment should participate in the decision on what type is selected.

Photo by Paul Allyn.

- Divide up each control center's functions by workstation; consider expected staffing and opportunities for work sharing and control transfer.
- Prepare operational sequences and define control hierarchies for each security and control function.

Hard Control Panels

Hard control panel types include miniature push-button panels, oil-tight push-button panels, membrane graphic panels, and push-button graphic panels. In general, hard control panels have the advantage of giving status at a glance, straightforward operation and maintenance, and lower initial cost in some cases. They are compatible with all types of control electronics. Hard control panels' disadvantages include inflexibility and frequent maintenance.

Video Control Stations

Video control stations provide a "soft" control panel by using graphic screens to dynamically display status indicators and activation points to the operator. Pointing devices, such as a mouse, touch screen, or trackball, move a cursor around on the screen, while activation points are selected by depressing pointing device buttons or touching the screen itself. Video control station advantages include their flexibility to be changed through programming, their space efficiency, and the ease with which they handle control transfers and work sharing. Video control stations are compatible with discrete logic, PLC-based, and computer-based control electronics, but not hard-wired or relay logic controls. Speed and response time were major issues in the early systems, but faster hardware, better networks, and software improvements have made it possible to obtain response times similar to hard control panels. Their major disadvantage is the complexity of troubleshooting and maintenance.

Video control station performance and reliability are determined largely by a number of technical design decisions. Guidance about these issues is included in ASTM 1465.

Operator Interface Selection

Ultimately, operator interface selection should be based on a functional analysis by control point. Factors that favor video interface selection include duplication, transfers, or overrides between control posts; limited physical space; use of hidden controls or indicators; planned expansion or changes; and integration between security functions and administrative records.

The staff's ability and willingness to use new technologies will help determine which systems should be selected.

Photo by Paul Allyn.

Overriding criteria may be the staff's technical proficiency and their ability to operate and maintain more sophisticated video control station technology.

Control Electronics

Control electronics is the heart of an electronic security system—integrating various subsystems together (for example, locking controls with intercom and/or video surveillance) and providing the system's logic. They control how a system functions and are largely responsible for its reliability, response time, and other measures of performance. Usually located in a secure equipment room, the control electronics are less visible than the rest of the system, but certainly no less important.

Control Electronics Options

Control electronic systems may be broadly divided into the two categories of hard-wired and programmable.

Hard-wired systems use relays, integrated circuits, and other discrete logic components to provide rudimentary logic and control functions. Programmable systems use microprocessor-based controllers that execute a program stored in the controller's memory. Whereas the operation of hard-wired systems is determined by the configuration of its components and is not readily changed or expanded, programmable systems provide more flexi-

bility and allow more sophisticated control functions. Programmable system options include programmable logic controllers, dedicated detention controllers, commercial access controls, and general-purpose models including IPC-based, distributed control systems.

Programmable logic controllers (PLCs): These general-purpose controllers, first developed for manufacturing plants and later applied to corrections, have become the most common controller type in recent years. PLCs are well-supported reliable systems, but they must be programmed for security applications by trained and knowledgeable personnel.

Dedicated detention controllers: Various controllers are manufactured only for use in correctional facilities. Their software is detention-specific and more readily understood and modified than other systems. They also are designed to interface with other security subsystems, such as closed-circuit surveillance camera controls. However, these controllers are supported by only one vendor and may not function with equipment from other manufacturers.

Commercial access control: Many access control (in other words, card reader) systems have characteristics of distributed control systems. Although designed primarily to integrate security systems within commercial and industrial establishments, they also are being used in correctional facilities. Access control systems have many of the same benefits and drawbacks as dedicated detention controllers.

Industrial computers and distributed control systems: Manufacturing plant controls are shifting away from PLCs toward networked industrial personal computers (IPCs) and field device networks. This evolving technology is more economical and less proprietary than traditional PLCs. For each component and network, there are numerous manufacturers to choose from, and functionality among manufacturers is assured by industry standards. Advances in controls software are propelling this evolution as well.

Infrastructure Considerations

Raceways, wires and cables, connectors and cable terminations, racks, enclosures, and grounding accounts for at least one-half of the initial cost of an electronic security system. In addition, this "infrastructure" is very expensive to replace and is able to last the entire thirty-to-sixty-year life of a facility, if properly designed and installed. In contrast, the expected life of field devices, operator interfaces, and even control electronics is only ten-to-twenty years, meaning these system components should be replaced two or three times over the facility's life. As a result, obtaining qualified engineering support to design and oversee these critical infrastructure components is extremely important.

Inmate Systems

Communications

A number of communication services frequently are made available to inmates or provided on their behalf. Toll-restricted telephone access, recreational and educational television, and even music distribution are communication services often made available to inmates. Videoconferencing systems also are finding wide application in correctional facilities for telemedicine, remote court and parole proceedings, and video visitation.

Movement Tracking Systems

Systems also have become available to track the movement of inmates throughout the institution. The most common technology uses bar-coded wristbands to establish identity and bar-code scanners at control points to record inmate movement to and from each controlled area. The system, for example, will generate alarms whenever inmates do not travel to their approved destination within a preset time.

Systems are also under development to establish a radio frequency detection grid throughout an institution and have inmates wear radio-coded wristbands. By continually recording the location of all inmates at periodic intervals (for example, every three-to-ten seconds), the system automatically would count inmates, identify escapees by their absence, document inmates in the vicinity of an incident, and perform similar tasks that would not be feasible without such a system. If successful and secure, such systems possibly could be used even to automate inmate movement through an institution. The field of technology is evolving so rapidly that new advances of this type, both expected and unforeseen, may be commonplace by the time this volume is next updated.

Notes:

[1] *Standards for Adult Correctional Institutions,* Third Edition. 1990. Lanham, Maryland: American Correctional Association.

[2] ASTM 1465, *Standard Guide for Selection of Operational Security Control Systems.* 1998. West Conshohocken, Pennsylvania: American Society for Testing and Materials.

[3] National Institute of Corrections. 1993. *Correctional Technology: A User's Guide.* Washington, D.C.

[4] National Fire Protection Association 101, *Life Safety Code,* 1997 edition. Avon, Massachusetts.

[5] National Fire Protection Association 70, *National Electrical Code,* 1999 edition. Avon, Massachusetts.

Perimeter Security Systems

Alan R. Latta
Latta Technical Services, Inc.
Plano, Texas

Consideration of perimeter security in any application requires an approach that includes an assessment of threat and an evaluation of risk. Only after a definition of this threat and risk can the user or designer develop potential solutions using perimeter security systems.

A perimeter security system consists of a physical barrier and a detection system. The barrier typically consists of single or multiple fences and razor wire. Detection systems range from an officer in a tower to fiber optic mesh providing a barrier and electronic detection.

Multiple levels of security including electronic detection and physical barriers are used to create the secure perimeter of an institution. Wallens Ridge State Prison, Big Stone Gap, Virginia.

Photo courtesy of Gilbane Building Co., Providence, Rhode Island.

Threat and Risk

The search for a solution begins with a definition of a threat. There may be an assumption that the threat is similar for similar types of facilities, which is not usually the case. Threat definition is very much based on perception in addition to physical conditions.

A threat can be defined as what is perceived to be the likelihood of an attempt to penetrate the perimeter security. The threat includes the willingness of an inmate to attempt escape, the difficulty should such an attempt be made based on restrictions (operational and physical), and the tools or support the inmate will have available.

As an example, while an escape attempt is the simple threat, the threat is increased with such conditions as assisted escape from the outside and close proximity to the perimeter. Assisted escape from outside has become a larger threat, especially in juvenile institutions where gang activity is prevalent.

Another determining factor is the risk of penetration. This assumes a penetration is successful and attempts to evaluate the resulting cost. An evaluation of risk requires consideration of the surrounding environment. While a facility with surrounding acreage, mountain range, and so forth may have minimal risk, a facility with adjacent residential or commercial properties is a substantial and immediate risk. The custody level of the escapee also will generate a level of risk. These are some of the factors to consider in creating perimeter security systems that can range from minimum to maximum.

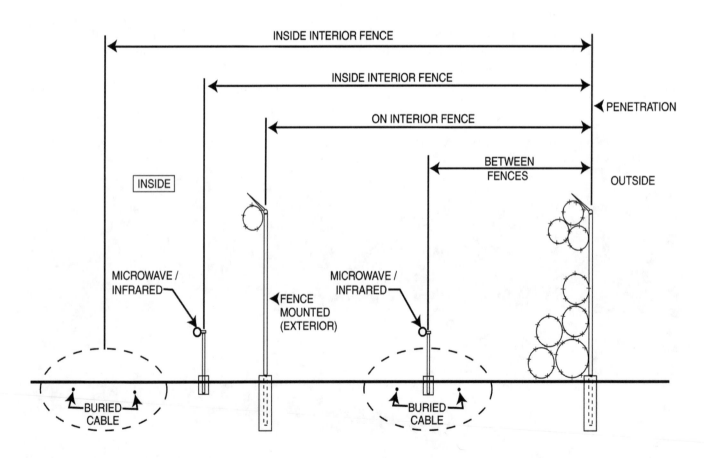

An integrated perimeter security system consists of both a physical barrier and a detection system.

Courtesy of Alan Latta.

Mission of the Perimeter Security System

The mission of the perimeter system is to deter, detect, and delay. Each is a component of any solution.

Deter   To provide deterrence is to provide information as to the futility of an attempt. Visual information is provided by the barrier itself, such as the typical dual fence with a razor wire perimeter. The visual information presented is that you will likely get injured seriously should you attempt an escape. An armed officer in a tower is a similar deterrent. A perimeter with an electrified stun or lethal fence with appropriate signage is a similar visual deterrent. Some perimeter barriers will convey the futility of the attempt while not conveying the likelihood of injury.

Detect   An important consideration is the available response time provided by a perimeter security system. The available response time is the period of time from detection until successful penetration. To start the response time, a detection system must be involved. The sooner the detection is made, the greater the likelihood of terminating the escape attempt. Previously, the official detection system consisted of an officer in a tower. Today's facilities incorporate electronic detection systems in most facilities using various technologies and levels of sophistication. Placement of detection will have an impact on the available response time. While placement on the interior fence is most common, systems on the interior of the perimeter offer additional time to respond, and systems installed between fences minimize the available response time.

Delay   The physical characteristics of the system will be the sole defining component of delay. The exception will be with electric stun or lethal fences. The more formidable the barrier, the longer the available response time. In the case of electric stun, and especially lethal fences, the available response time may be considered to be infinite.

Detection Systems

When considering electronic intrusion detection systems for the "detect" portion of the equation, the options are plentiful. To boil it down to a manageable number, start with a consideration of the physical barrier. That component is static and can be defined in both initial cost and maintenance costs.

When selecting a system, designers must recognize that each system has its own strengths and weaknesses. As an example, a fence-mounted system often has some susceptibility to wind, ice, and snow. Buried cable systems usually are susceptible to pending and/or running water. Advances in technology are addressing these issues as time progresses.

To understand and evaluate the sales literature available for detection systems, it is important to understand a few definitions. Alarms fall into two categories: intruder alarms and false alarms. False alarms include "nuisance" alarms and "environment" alarms. Consider these definitions.

Intrusion Alarm: The annunciation of an alarm that results from the detection of a target specified to be detected and which represents an attempt to intrude into the protected area.

False Alarm: The annunciation of any alarm, excluding nuisance and environmental alarms, where there is no intruder.

Nuisance Alarm: An annunciation of an alarm resulting from the detection of the specified target to be detected, but it does not represent an attempt to intrude into the protected area.

Environmental Alarm: The annunciation of a false alarm during environmental conditions that exceed those specified.

Often the information presented in sales literature and presentations will treat nuisance and environmental alarms separately from false alarms. An acceptable level of false alarms should not exceed one false alarm per month per zone. Thus, the definition of false alarms is critical to the performance evaluation of any system.

Microwave systems can be used to detect movement between perimeter fences and are protected from inmate contact.

Photo courtesy of Alan Latta.

While space will not allow a description of each available system, the following types are the most common.

Audio Cable

The typical system consists of a continuous sensor cable placed on the fence fabric. The cable "listens" for selected frequencies of noise that are representative of climb and cut attempts while discriminating against frequencies that represent horizontal movement, which may be caused by wind. Some newer systems have electronic intelligence that can discriminate against such conditions by comparing information along the length of the cable. Advantages of the system include low cost and ease of installation and repair. Disadvantages include susceptibility to environmental conditions, such as wind, ice, and blowing debris.

Buried Cable

The typical system consists of a single or double leaky cable(s) installed below grade at a depth of approximately eight inches. The system creates an invisible field of detection above (and below) grade that will detect an intruder passing over it. There is no visual indication of its location so it is difficult to defeat. The system provides early detection when installed inside the interior fence. Some applications have included installation between the fences. Installation requirements include good drainage

of the site and avoidance of subterranean liquid-bearing piping systems. Advantages of the system include early detection, invisible detection, and medium-range cost. Disadvantages include susceptibility to ponding and/or running water.

Capacitance

The typical system consists of an array of wires (spacing of six inches to eight inches) mounted on a structure attached to a fence. The system provides an alarm when the wires are separated or when an intruder comes in close proximity to the wire array. The system does not provide a physical barrier and must be placed on an existing fence structure or on a free-standing series of posts. This system type also can be used on an outrigger mounted on a wall to detect a climb. An advantage of the system includes its relatively medium cost. Disadvantages include susceptibility to environmental conditions, such as wind, ice, and blowing debris.

Infrared

The typical system is used for short-distance detection to close electronic detection across vehicle or pedestrian sallyports. Some installations use it for complete perimeter protection. The system uses infrared light beams to create a curtain-type detection zone above grade. The system detects and alarms a penetration of

The fence-mounted sensor, known in the industry as a "shaker" system, is easy to install and detects vertical motion in the fence.

Photo courtesy of Alan Latta.

Taut-wire system in stand-alone array. This system has an extremely low false alarm rate and presents a physical barrier.

Photo courtesy of Alan Latta.

this curtain-type zone. This system is line of sight and is not terrain following. This may require multiple zone pairs to cover a distance if the terrain is not flat. Sometimes these systems are used for roof or building wall protection. An advantage of this system is its low cost. Disadvantages include a medium to high false alarm rate depending on applications, and it does not follow the terrain.

Microwave

The typical system is used for short distance detection to close electronic detection across vehicle or pedestrian sallyports. Some installations use it for complete perimeter protection. The system creates an elliptical detection zone above grade that detects a disturbance in the area. This system is line of sight and is not terrain following. This may require multiple zone pairs to cover a distance if the terrain is not flat. These systems sometimes are used for roof or building wall protection. The advantage is its low cost. The disadvantages include a high false alarm rate and the fact that the system does not follow the terrain.

"Shaker"

The typical system consists of a sensor placed periodically on the fence fabric. The sensor is a device that detects vertical motion such as a climb or cut attempt while disregarding horizontal movement, which may be caused by wind. These systems may be susceptible to environmental alarms relating to wind. Some newer systems have electronic intelligence that can discriminate against such conditions by comparing information from adjacent sensors. Some systems require custom fabricated cable/sensor assemblies requiring field verification of the installed fence prior to assembly. Advantages of the system include low false alarm rates and medium range. Disadvantages include susceptibility to environmental conditions such as wind, ice, and blowing debris.

Taut-wire

The typical system consists of a physical barrier with an array of barbed wires of variable (six inches to twelve inches) spacing over the height of the barrier. The system provides an alarm when the wires are separated or when a downward force is exerted on a wire. The wires are

Video motion detection using pole-mounted cameras to cover the perimeter.

Photo courtesy of Alan Latta.

under tension and will alarm on a wire cut. The system provides a physical barrier and an electronic detection system. This system type also can be used on an outrigger mounted on a wall to detect a climb. Advantages of the system include low false alarm rates and a physical barrier. Disadvantages of the system include required maintenance for retensioning the wires and a higher initial cost.

Video Motion Detection

The typical system includes video cameras mounted on posts or building walls to view a selected area for detection. Detection occurs when a change in the video image is noted. Low light level performance is a critical consideration. There is a wide range of sophistication among available systems that cause the results and costs to vary significantly. Advantages of the system include video assessment/recording and supplemental video for periodic and/or general surveillance. Disadvantages include a higher initial cost and infrastructure (lighting and support) requirements.

Summary

These are general descriptions of just a few of the systems available to those interested in perimeter security systems. More systems are coming on the market and the existing systems are improving. The challenge to the person making decisions regarding perimeter security is to find the optimum balance of components to create a perimeter security system that meets the requirements of the defined threat and risk. Each installation has its own unique combination of requirements that must be addressed for a successful result.

Access Points/ Biometrics/X-Ray/ Heartbeat

David Musacchio
Corrections Consultant
Cookeville, Tennessee

The normal and usual breaches of the security perimeter of a correctional facility occur at three points: (1) the public entrance, (2) the official or prisoner entrance, and (3) the service entrance. Each of these entrances requires specialized methods of identifying those individuals requesting access and egress and thus ultimately controlling that access and egress. The effectiveness of the operations and procedures at these access points may be of ultimate importance to the security of the facility because, in addition to all of the internal controls, the perimeter is the final control between the facility and the public.

Access Points

Effective control of the access points is an interface between very specialized security equipment and the facility staff. The security equipment functions as a hard barrier or a detection and annunciation system that, when alarmed, requires an appropriate response from the staff. Theoretically, these principles apply equally to facilities where the exterior wall forms the security perimeter and those where there is an elaborate system of exterior fences and gates. Each of the three access points poses differing challenges for observation, detection, and control.

Public Entrance

This is where the general public enters the facility for purposes ranging from visiting prisoners to the salesperson calling on the business manager. This entrance requires close coordination between the staff and the visitor. Since this is really the "front door" of the facility, it is important that the proper image be projected. As a part of this entrance, proper directions and identifications must be effected at appropriate locations. The inmate visitors and the administration visitors require different processing and thus need to be separated for the processing.

Official or Prisoner Entrance

Since prisoners are transported in the custody of some official agency, the identification and control of this entrance is somewhat simpler than the public entrance. Customarily, the transport vehicle, escort, and prisoner are processed through the security perimeter by way of a sallyport with interlocked gates.

Service Entrance

While the majority of the traffic through this entrance deals with supplies being delivered and refuse being removed, the security challenges can be difficult. Even though this is primarily a vehicular access point, of necessity, there is some attending pedestrian traffic. This is also the most dangerous access point for escape attempts from the standpoint of concealment in either cargo or refuse. Due to the types of materials being moved through this access point, it is also the most time consuming to process.

Identification and Access

When an individual or a vehicle approaches an access point, the first task of the staff is to identify that individual or vehicle and thereby determine authorization to pass the access point. Traditionally, such tools as photographs, physical descriptions, tokens, passes, or other methods of written material have been used to assist the staff in making the identifications.

Direct voice intercoms and closed-circuit television have augmented observation and personal interaction. This has allowed remote locations surrounding an access point to be monitored and controlled from one central point. This has resulted in an efficient use of staff.

As an attempt to add further efficiency to identification and control of access points, devices such as card readers have been used. A serious limitation to this form of identification and control is that if the individual card is out of the control of the intended user, then anyone possessing the card could gain access. There is no guaranteed connection between the identification card and the intended user.

A method of connecting the identification directly with the intended user is through biometric measurements specific to the individual being identified. This type of identification can be computer-based and coupled with other identification systems, such as photographs and physical descriptions. These combined systems can be used in connection with trained staff to provide a high level of security.

Almost everyone is aware of the individuality of the human fingerprint. Historically, the difficulty of using fingerprints for identification purposes was the necessity of having a trained expert read the individual prints and comparing them with a known set to establish positive identification. The use of computer optical links has increased the development of the Automated Fingerprint Identification System (AFIS). This system has become so efficient that it generally is accepted by the courts in criminal procedures and has been adapted for use in correctional facilities.

Another method of identification, which is quick and highly reliable, is the hand geometry reader. This consists of a series of positioning pins, which allows the reader to measure an individual's palm. Once an individual is enrolled in the system, the hand automatically is recognized and the individual identified each time it is inserted in a reader. Currently, this system is being used for visitor identification with a great deal of accuracy and staff efficiency.

Another biometric identification method, which is so accurate that banks are currently using it for identification at automated teller machines, is the scan of the iris of the individual's eye. This requires the individual being identified to place his or her eye to a scanner, which reads the iris under normal light conditions. A similar eye scanning system uses the retina of the eye for identification, but this system requires the introduction of a bright beam of light into the eye. The retina scan can cause discomfort to the individual being identified and, therefore, does not appear to offer the potential of the iris scanner.

Some attempts have been made to use the uniqueness of an individual's voice graph or voiceprint. While each individual's voice is identifiably unique, the limitations of the acoustics available in the field have been difficult to overcome in adapting the equipment for efficient use at the access points of correctional facilities.

Security Equipment

To assist the staff in processing individuals and materials through the access points, certain types of security detecting equipment have been developed for correctional application. Rather than being used for identification of the individual, these devices and equipment are used to detect the introduction of contraband into the facility.

The simplest form of this security detection equipment is the metal detector. This device can be provided in either fixed position units where the individual walks between two components of the sensing device, or a handheld unit can be used where the individual remains still and the tester passes the device over him or her. In either system, the device sounds an alarm whenever metal is detected. The system has limitations related to the body mass of the individual being tested and the types of metal detected. The system is effective for rapid processing of large numbers of people in a short period of time.

Another form of detection currently in use to detect contraband is the x-ray. This is available for processing packages, such as purses, which are being brought into the facility. Another form of x-ray is one which provides a full body scan of an individual. Both of these forms of x-ray offer identification of any mass, including metal, which is hidden in a package or on the person involved. An obvious limitation of this type of screening is the exposure to x-ray by both the individual being scanned and the staff performing the scan. However, when properly employed, this can be a valuable tool for use in screening for contraband.

With the continuing concern about individuals concealing themselves in vehicles leaving the facility, some relatively new methods of detection are being tested. One method is the use of listening devices placed on the vehicle, which is situated on a pad with the motor and all operating devices off. This device is capable of detecting the beating of the human heart. Obviously, this would reveal the presence of a person and then the staff would search the vehicle. A similar use of infrared detection is being experimented with, but to date has had only limited success.

Issues Relating to Detection and Identification Equipment

For the identification systems to function, the individual whose identity is being questioned must first have been enrolled, or entered, into the system. The computer compares the questioned individual with a data bank of known individuals and connects the questioned individual with a known identity. With the card access reader, this enrollment is simply the issuing of a card to the individual, which could be done by mail. In the case of the biometric readers, the individual must be physically present for the system to make an initial reading and enter it into the data bank, while connecting the reading with other known data. All future inquiries then will be compared with the entire data bank to establish if a match is made and the results reported to a staff member which will result in access permitted or denied.

A more efficient system is where a verification of identity is requested rather than a total database searched. With a verification request, an identifying entry such as a Personal Identification Number (PIN) is entered along with the biometric read of the individual. The system then compares the biometric read with the data belonging to the PIN. If there is a match, the staff member is notified or access is permitted or denied.

Either of the biometric systems could be used with staff, inmates, or visitors. The significance is the initial

step of actually enrolling the individual. The enrollment process can be staff intensive depending on the amount of information being entered into the database. In very elaborate systems, photographs, identifying data such as social security numbers, dates of birth, and physical descriptions all could be entered and used in comparison. The more parameters that are used, the more accurate the identification process. However, an elaborate identification process is time consuming and could slow the flow of traffic if used in a high volume area such as visiting. Some jurisdictions, however, have had a great deal of success with such things as routine comparison of the visitors with an outstanding warrant database.

In selecting a system, the validity and reliability of the system and equipment must be evaluated. The validity means that it measures and compares the required parameters accurately. The reliability means that the valid comparisons are made consistently over multiple uses. Simply stated, the user must have confidence that the system is accurate over many uses.

An important part of the system reliability is the speed at which it functions and the number of false alarms. The importance of staff and equipment interaction cannot be overstated. With all tools of this type, there is the possibility of the staff becoming complacent and relying too heavily on the equipment. The staff must be vigilant and continually check the calibrations and the manufacturer's required procedures. Staff training in the use of the equipment is equally important since untrained staff will be unreliable in their use of the equipment.

The standards of the industry and reliability of the equipment manufacturer also must be considered in selecting identification equipment. Since this is a relatively new industry with a limited demand and market for the equipment, there may not be a considerable amount of experience of usage in the marketplace. Additionally, with such a small marketplace as the correctional field, a potential system user may have to look to other security fields such as the banking industry in the case of the iris scan reader.

Often the industry standards are only established when many manufacturers are producing the same or similar equipment. For example, the use of biometric readers is a new field and has only a few suppliers. In some cases, the potential user has only the manufacturer's statement as to the equipment. There just is not anyone else to ask. In that case, the potential user should establish the manufacturer's past experience with quality control and customer service. Since this is a new and expanding field, the lack of experience with the individual product may not be negative but must be considered as a part of any decision relative to the equipment.

Finally, a question of required maintenance and the amount of down time experienced must be considered. Maintenance is both routine, which can be scheduled, and unanticipated, when something breaks. In either case, the availability of service technicians and replacement parts is important. In some instances, the owner's staff can be trained to maintain the equipment. Where that is available, a stock of spare parts should be available.

Any of these systems and equipment does not exist in a vacuum. The most important component is a well-trained staff who has been provided with clear policies and procedures. When this is in place, secure access and egress exist.

Armory and Locksmith

David Musacchio
Corrections Consultant
Cookeville, Tennessee

The armory and lockshop are two of the most vulnerable areas of any correctional facility. The armory is the repository of the main body of weapons at the facility, while the lockshop contains the keys that operate all of the locks and the mechanical overrides for the security operating devices in the facility. Anyone gaining access to either of these areas conceivably could control the entire facility.

Because of the critical nature of security in these areas, the highest level of construction (physical barriers) and surveillance is required. While these areas must be secured from unauthorized access, staff must be able to quickly access both areas, whenever necessary, for routine and emergency operations.

In one form or another, all correctional facilities contain both armories and lockshops. Large facilities may have several separate rooms, connected in a suite, devoted to these services, while small facilities may function out of secure cabinets. Facility size, level of security, and staff will dictate the amount of equipment required. Additionally, agency policy and statutes will govern certain aspects of equipment and operations of the armory.

The armory provides a place for storing and issuing weapons, ammunition, and the chemical agents of tear gas and other forms of crowd control. In some facilities, riot gear also is stored in the armory. Since this equipment requires periodic inspection, cleaning, and mainte-nance, a separate area generally is provided where the facility armorer can work and store the required records.

Another space that often is provided, adjacent to the armory, is a training room. It is an area where tactical training can take place, and such placement allows equipment from the armory to be used in the training.

Since the security requirements are the same for both the armory and the lockshop, and since, in some facilities the armorer and locksmith are the same person, these two services may be located together. Conversely, the armory may be located adjacent to central control and the lockshop located in the maintenance area. Generally, if the armory and locksmith are not located adjacent to central control, they are located in either the base of a security tower or an entry building where they are under direct staff surveillance.

Armory

It is generally more convenient to have an exterior door and/or pass window to the armory. This allows for the delivery of supplies and provides a place to issue weapons and ammunition from outside of the security perimeter. In a large facility, weapons and supplies would be routinely issued from this location. This could occur during the change of shifts, while arming of staff for prisoner transport, or in the event of an emergency, such as a riot or an escape.

A properly equipped armory will require weapon racks designed to store securely the various types of weapons used by the facility. The most time-sensitive procedure conducted from the armory is issuing weapons in an emergency, which requires rapid access to the weapons, some method of recording which staff member has which weapon, and the ability to safely transfer the weapon from the issuing staff to the receiving staff. In addition to issuing the weapon, a supply of ammunition also is dispensed, most conveniently in a pouch. This entire procedure is reversed when the equipment is returned to the armory.

In addition to the weapons, other items, such as tear gas or other chemical crowd control agents may be dispensed. These agents may be more conveniently issued inside the security perimeter, which would require another door or pass window. The most efficient and secure method of dispensing weapons and equipment is through a pass window rather than a door. If a door is opened, there is the possibility of staff entering the armory and removing weapons without the proper record of who was issued which weapon.

Pass windows are of multiple designs, but the safest and most efficient ones are devised so that the issuing and receiving staff can communicate while facing each other across the security barrier but with the weapon being passed through a unit, which can be opened on one side only. This method allows for one weapon transaction at a time and provides a method of transfer where weapons are not pointed at either staff member during the transaction.

The armory should have adequate space for the storage of all weapons. This storage should separate the weapons ready for issue from those requiring service or repair. In some facilities, weapons used for staff training are separated from the regular service weapons.

Record storage and processing space is essential in the armory. All weapons should be recorded and tracked by the use of their serial number. This is a standard number provided by the manufacturer on each weapon that allows the weapon to be traced from the date and point of manufacture to its current status. This is essential for compliance with statutory requirements for weapon controls. Internally, this facilitates an orderly method of weapon rotation and replacement.

Since the weapons and the records are stored in the armory, this is a secure and convenient location for weapon inspection, service, and repair. For this purpose, a workbench and storage space should be provided for the armorer. It is also important to provide adequate lighting and ventilation. General and task lighting is important and should be located where work is to be performed. Proper storage for the fresh and used solvent also should be provided. As this solvent may be flammable, it is particularly important that approved containers be provided. One additional convenience is a stainless steel sink that is long and deep enough to submerge a rifle barrel for cleaning.

Ammunition storage falls into two categories: (1) issue stock and (2) reserve stock. Most facilities have an established procedure for rotating the ammunition stock so that the freshest stock is stored in reserve and issued while the older stock is used for training. Generally, the stock that is issued routinely is contained in pouches or other easily transported units. The reserve and training stock can be stored on shelves in its original shipping containers. Proper temperature, humidity, and air circulation must be maintained in the storage area.

Tear gas and other chemical crowd control agents require storage in sealed containers in the event of leakage occurring in the individual canisters or projectiles. Again, this storage is divided between issue and reserve stock. As with the ammunition, older stock of these agents can be used for training. Adequate ventilation of areas that contain tear gas and other chemicals is absolutely essential for staff safety.

Due to the potential of an explosion of the ammunition and chemical agents, the building codes in some jurisdictions and agency policy require that blast or blowout panels be provided in the armory and storage area. Also, smoke exhaust and automatic fire detection and suppression may be required in these areas.

Locksmith

The locksmith shop is separate from the control room function of the normal and emergency issuing of individual keys and key sets. The locksmith maintains all pattern keys and records pertaining to key control. The locksmith must maintain records of all keys in the facility. These records may be computerized or duplicate files maintained, but the primary responsibility for updating these files generally is reserved to the locksmith.

The locksmith makes all new and replacement keys. The design and construction of a new correctional facility should include provision of a key cutting machine and adequate key blanks to sustain initial operation. Because each institution will have a restricted keyway established by the lock manufacturer, only the key cutting equipment supplied to the institution and the manufacturer should be able to cut keys that can open locks at that institution.

The locksmith maintains a stock of parts and replacement hardware for all security and commercial applications in the facility. In coordination with the facility safety officer, the locksmith is responsible for developing plans for routinely testing the emergency aspects of the detention/security hardware and equipment. The locksmith also maintains records and certifies that the tests have been conducted in accordance with the life safety plans for the facility.

The locksmith, in conjunction with the security staff, establishes and maintains all sets of emergency keys and routinely tests them to determine that they function as intended. If the locksmith does not aggressively follow up on the emergency key tests, it is possible that locks could be changed without proper keys placed on the emergency set.

The locksmith is responsible for developing and implementing all key codes and changes to these codes for the facility. These codes are to conform to the parent agency, institution, and other regulatory agency policies.

In the event of a failure of a lock or locking device, the locksmith is responsible for assisting the security staff in reestablishing proper functions in a timely fashion. In the event of a personal safety and/or life-threatening situation, the locksmith must be prepared and equipped to take necessary action.

Security Control and Monitoring

Agency and facility policy should establish the procedure for controlling and monitoring of both the armory and locksmith area. At the very least, this control and monitoring should include an annunciation and alarm system to alert central control whenever the doors or pass windows are unsecured for either of these areas.

In the case of the locksmith area, there will be little need for any person other than the locksmith to have access. Since the locksmith area may contain keys or information required by the administration, some means must be in place to gain access whenever the locksmith is not available. This can be accomplished either by providing remote access controlled from the central control or by providing a duplicate key at either central control or in another secure area. This is also a wise precaution in the event that the locksmith becomes incapacitated while locked in the shop.

For the armory area, a wise precaution for both the issuing and receiving staff is to have a closed-circuit television camera placed so as to cover the transaction and surrounding areas. A recorder can be attached to this system, and it will act as an additional record of all transactions and provide protection for the staff outside of the security perimeter.

Wherever there is the possibility of a door and pass window being opened simultaneously, an interlock should be provided either to prevent both being open at once, or to alert a supervisor that the event has occurred. These may appear to be trivial items, but a firm operations procedure, which is closely followed, is the best prevention against compromising the facility security.

With the tasks and responsibilities placed on the armorer and the locksmith, it is apparent that highly qualified and trained staff should fill these positions. Even when highly qualified and trained staff are present, there also should be a system of checks in place to catch any failures in security. Internal and external audits should be conducted routinely to identify any problem areas or security failure.

Roads and Parking

David Musacchio
Corrections Consultant
Cookeville, Tennessee

Correctional facility road use can be separated into the two categories of entry/access and internal circulating. This is true for either rural facilities located on large sites or for urban facilities located on tight intercity sites. A major concern regarding roads used by the two types of facilities is ownership and responsibility for ongoing maintenance.

Rural facilities tend to have extensive road systems, both for entry/access and internal circulation that were designed and built as part of the initial construction. All or any part of this road system must be repaired and maintained either by the facility or the governmental agency having responsibility for roads and highways. This applies to tasks like snow removal, pothole patching, and complete resurfacing.

Urban facilities generally are located on, or adjacent to, major streets and roads. In these facilities, the roads are more like driveways and access paths rather than true roadways. Often the roads are part of a parking lot or service yard. While there is less roadway involved than in rural facilities, the same requirements of snow removal and so forth exist.

Serious thought and planning must be given to the initial design and construction of these roads. Otherwise, considerable traffic circulation problems and significant maintenance costs can occur.

Access Roads

Vehicular access to correctional facilities falls into three categories: (1) public or visitor accesses, (2) official or prisoner access, and (3) service access. To provide efficient functioning and traffic flow, each of these access points and roads should be separate and easily monitored and/or controlled.

The public access generally is located at the formal, or "front" entrance to the facility. This serves as a combined entrance for inmate visitors and visitors to the institutional officials. Often, this entrance also serves as the staff entrance and is used extensively during the regular shift changes. Unless special planning and scheduling is implemented, this road could become quite congested if a large group of visitors is attempting to enter or exit during shift change.

Since the most frequent and potentially the most congested road would be the public entrance, the access for official or secure prisoner transport vehicles should be separate. This road should lead directly from the public thoroughfare to the vehicle sallyport.

Service roads also should be separate from either the public or prisoners' roads. The breach in the security perimeter for the service entrance is usually in the immediate area of the kitchen, central warehouse, or industries facilities. Some facilities have all deliveries made to the central warehouse with further distribution made by the facility staff using the facility's vehicles.

Access for emergency vehicles could be required at all of the above-identified entrances. Ambulances often are required to transport sick or injured prisoners so the ambulance entrance should be accessible to the infirmary or hospital area. Fire equipment would require access to the vehicle sallyport and onward into the institutional compound. Obviously, proper access for emergency vehicles would supersede any other institutional traffic requirements. However, institutional vehicles generally are required to accompany the emergency vehicles as they travel throughout the facility, so proper planning is required to handle this traffic.

To facilitate entry and exit, adequate signage must be provided as necessary along the public roadways. Presume everyone is entering the facility for the first time. Provide signs so that the visitor is able to determine where he or she is to go and how to get there. Place these signs in conspicuous locations. They should be highly visible and give clear directions. These signs should be lighted for convenience after dark. The signage at the visitor's entrance should clearly identify those items which will be allowed into the visitor's room. This is so visitors will not need to make multiple trips to their vehicle to deposit items not allowed in the visiting room.

Entry to restricted areas should be clearly identified with signage, and where necessary, physical barriers should be in place. Physical barriers are locations that require either a staff position or an audio and video station for surveillance, monitoring, and control purposes. Often it is necessary to provide a staff post at such locations either because remote monitoring and control are not possible or because interaction between the visitor and a staff person is required by the complexity of the situation. This is particularly true in areas with large volumes of traffic, where physical screening or searching is necessary, such as the delivery area for the kitchen or warehouse.

The width of the access roads and the type of construction are dictated by the intended use of the roadway. Service roads, for example, have daily traffic consisting of heavy delivery trucks and even heavier trucks such as garbage compactor trucks. To sustain this weight of traffic on a regular basis, the roadway needs to be constructed of suitable base materials, properly compacted and finished with a surface which will withstand heavy traffic and usage. In most instances, heavy highway-type construction is necessary to meet the weight requirements. As for the roadway width, design and traffic patterns will dictate whether one or two-way traffic is required. Sometimes if adequate pull-off's and queuing areas are provided, a single lane is sufficient. Volume and frequency of traffic using the particular roadway dictate this.

Circulation or Patrol Roads

Large rural facilities often will be provided with a series of perimeter security and patrol roads. This is particularly true where the fence(s) is equipped with in-trusion detection devices. These roads are placed at the exterior of the fence and located at a sufficient distance from the fence so that on receiving an alarm of intrusion in a specific zone, the patrol officer and vehicle will have the opportunity of intercepting the intruder from the outer side of the fence. This situation then requires a significant clear space between the road and the fence for the staff to have line-of-sight control of the space for purposes of identification and apprehension. This also applies to a cleared space on the side of the patrol road— away from the security fence.

Some facilities have found it advantageous to have a patrol road on the inside of the fence for patrol and fence inspection purposes, only. While this road would have limited benefits during an escape attempt, it is quite helpful for interception of contraband. If recreation yards are adjacent to the perimeter fence, this road would be of great value in facilitating a mobile sweep of the fence prior to allowing inmates to enter for recreation.

In larger facilities, a number of additional roads might be required for support and supply purposes. Older facilities located on very large sites usually have a network of roads, which were originally farm roads. These roads may be impossible to control and monitor due to the area that they cover. Since they do not breach the security perimeter, the lack of control and monitoring is of little consequence.

Large facilities require the distribution of supplies and equipment throughout the security perimeter. One of the most effective methods of providing access is to construct the major sidewalks and streets of sufficient strength to support the vehicles used to transport the supplies and equipment thus getting dual use of the same pavement. This circulation network is essential in providing access to the individual portions of the facility for emergency vehicles.

Parking

Parking is the usual adjunct to the access roads. The two largest groups requiring parking are the staff and the visitors. Both of these groups need to park as close as possible to their point of entry. Serious planning is required to establish the number of vehicles which will have to be accommodated at any specific point in time. Some calculation will have to be made as to the number of visitors' vehicles to be parked at any specific time. When evaluating the parking requirements for an existing facility, consider the visiting patterns and the number of visitors per individual visited. This information can then be used to calculate the number of parking spaces that are required and the time frame for their use.

Facility staff parking requirements are determined more easily. During the normal business hours, there will be a need to accommodate the administrative staff in addition to the security staff required for the shift. Maximum parking space would be required at the afternoon shift change. Parking would be required for two security shifts plus the parking for the administrative staff who work the normal business hours.

Parking also is required for the institutional vehicles. These vehicles range from staff cars to the trucks and heavy equipment necessary to operate the facility. Staff cars need to park in or near the staff parking area since this is closest to the staff entrance. Prisoner transport vehicles should be parked conveniently near to the intake and receiving area. All institutional emergency vehicles such as ambulances and fire apparatus should be parked, or housed, so that they are conveniently located for the staff who will be using the equipment. Also space may need to be set aside to park buses that bring groups of visitors to the facility.

Facility support equipment should be parked in, or near, the service area. Maintenance vehicles should be parked in, or near, the maintenance shop areas. In facilities where there is a large internal area within the security perimeter, the security staff often will require some form of vehicular transportation. Often, golf carts or other forms of industrial vehicles will be used. If these are battery powered, recharging stations will be required in the parking area.

In a facility where there is a great deal of traffic from outside law enforcement agencies, some special parking will be required to free the security sallyport or vestibule of congestion. Since these law enforcement vehicles may contain firearms, the special parking area must be secured from inmate access.

Road and Parking Issues

Design and construction of both roads and parking is a complicated and extremely expensive component of any correctional facility. The initial expense is often so great that only the absolute minimum number of roads and parking spaces are constructed as part of the original construction. This is not necessarily a negative situation, since final road and parking requirements may not be identified until the facility is in operation for some time.

All of the principles of good roadway and parking design should be used. These principles include the following: ease of access, line-of-sight visibility at intersections, proper width of the roadway to carry the anticipated traffic load, adequate drainage to avoid ponding of water during heavy rain, proper base and surface materials, sufficient lighting, guard rails where necessary, and appropriate signage for traffic and security control.

A rather unique question regards the direction of travel on any or all of the roadways of a particular facility. In certain circumstances, it would be more efficient to have traffic flowing in one direction, only. This could be true of the visitor and staff parking lots. Another consideration is the number and location of the entrances to these same parking lots.

The base material and final paving are of great significance in the design and construction of roads for correctional facilities. The roadways that will carry heavy loads and large volumes of traffic should be designed and constructed to standards which have been tested and approved for heavy capacity. Some jurisdictions require that the prevailing highway standards for the jurisdiction be used when designing the primary roads in a correctional facility. In northern climates where snow removal is a frequent problem during the winter months, a smooth hard surface works well. In other climates where the existing ground is firm, proper grading and drainage and markings will be sufficient to establish the roads. Often, the light traffic roads are constructed of surfaces such as gravel to control cost.

On all of the roadways and parking, handicapped accessibility must be respected. This means that specialized drop-off and parking areas must be provided and properly marked. This is especially true for the public and visitor parking areas. The staff parking areas also should be provided with handicapped parking in compliance with the applicable local codes.

Fences, gates, and barriers are a significant component of design and construction of correctional roadways.

Wherever any of these items are used, some form of monitoring and control must be provided. This has great implications for security staffing patterns. The design goal should be to identify the crucial access or traffic control points and provide the appropriate security at these points. A few well-placed security points are much better than many random points.

Finally, flexibility is required in approaching roadways and parking. During the lifespan of a facility, the demands and security requirements change. If new roadways, parking, security barriers, and so forth are planned, they should be integrated into the overall security. Security functions best when the physical and staff components interface smoothly. The staff is the nucleus of any security system.

Terrain and Berms

David Musacchio
Corrections Consultant
Cookeville, Tennessee

The site terrain of correctional facilities is a critical component of the operational programs and the security of the entire institutional complex. The site terrain features can seriously affect the size, shape, and locations of buildings within the complex. Modern technology provides the means and methods of modifying terrain that previously had been perceived as unsuitable for correctional facilities.

A level or slightly crowned site generally is preferred since this allows all of the buildings in the complex to be on the same plane while providing natural drainage to the site. This level plane enhances surveillance of the area and provides for ease of movement of inmates during program activities.

The level terrain allows for an efficient layout of the complex. In addition, it provides additional opportunities for security control from both perimeter security towers and road patrols. The ideal security situation is one in which nothing is interposed between the observer and the individuals and activities being observed.

Terrain has a strong influence on the drainage of the facility site. There are usually large compromises between designing drainage to follow the natural lay of the land and that required to meet the operational, security, functional, and construction constraints. Two goals of any drainage scheme are to minimize the number of drainage pipe penetrations of the security perimeter and avoid the discharge of surface drainage through the perimeter fence. Meeting these goals often requires the installation of complex drainage schemes, which can be complicated by difficult terrain conditions.

Examination of the site and terrain of existing major correctional facilities in the United States reveals a broad spectrum of terrain types. The terrain would range from tight level urban sites to vast rolling or mountainous sites. This means that some of the sites are not optimum, but in every instance accommodations have been made in order to use the site.

Several existing facilities are located in congested urban areas where the interior of the security perimeter is plainly visible from either tall buildings or hills surrounding the perimeter wall. Simply viewing the interior of the facility is not generally a problem; yet, anyone interested in helping an inmate to escape or in introducing contraband would be greatly assisted by this view. However, these institutions have implemented policies and procedures that extend the surveillance perimeter to cover these observation points. Also, inmate movement is controlled so that any advantage of observation is minimized.

Urban sites can have traffic congestion problems caused by the hilly terrain where a facility is located. This congestion often is complicated by lack of visibility at points where the entry/exit to the facility occurs. Clear line-of-sight often is not possible to achieve, and this can distract the drivers and security officers who staff the secure prisoner transportation vehicles. While the officers are thus distracted, their vehicle would be an easy target for anyone attempting to assist prisoners in escaping.

In the large rural facilities, the staff generally uses existing terrain features to the advantage of security. Large clear areas between the perimeter fence and the outermost buildings provide an ideal area to search for any unauthorized movement. This can be effected either directly by staff or through the use of remote audio-visual monitoring and control equipment. Some facilities have interior activity yard areas located on several different elevations. These facilities have made the yards usable by erecting internal fences, which control inmate movement and separate the various elevations into usable space.

In some facilities, the interior terrain is so uneven so as to require a series of steps and ramps to make the hilly terrain usable. With current regulations relative to handicapped circulation requirements, facilities have installed lifts or elevators to meet these requirements. Obviously, these conditions are far from ideal, but the historic location of some of these facilities makes them impossible to relocate.

One facility has such unusable terrain that a series of subterranean circulation corridors have been constructed to provide secure circulation. Some other facilities have constructed above-ground enclosed security corridors for secure inmate and equipment movement over the multilevel terrain. Both of these solutions require that elevators or lifts be employed to accommodate the handicapped and material being moved.

So far, the effects caused by terrain have been described relative to existing correctional facilities. It is easy to understand that the limits of transportation and technology played a major role in the location, design, and construction of many older correctional facilities. However, similar situations exist with facilities presently being constructed.

It seems ridiculous to say that there are no ideal sites on which to develop a modern large-scale facility, which is available at a reasonable cost. The real question, however, is the cost of site acquisition and preparation. Factors like closeness to the source of inmates and inmate visitors, availability of qualified individuals to fill staff positions, and other operational considerations are important. These considerations are more likely to affect site selection rather than terrain. The true effects of rough terrain are felt in the high cost of sculpting the site to provide suitable building pads.

Initial cost of site acquisition, preparation, and the total construction cost is typically less than 9 percent of the total life cycle cost of the facility over a thirty-year period. Saving in long-term operational costs if the design results in the reduction of the total number of security posts could offset large site preparation costs.

A modern correctional complex requires that there be specific amounts of relative level land for purposes such as recreation fields, vehicle access and support, parking, and service areas. Some buildings of the complex are large and require level sites. Some of these buildings are the gymnasium, industries, and food service and dining. Buildings such as housing units occasionally can be designed to take advantage of sloping terrain, and therefore control some of the building cost. In the final analysis, there is still a great deal of site preparation work on any major prison project. If the site can be properly selected and the amount of major site reshaping limited, a reasonably cost-effective project can be delivered. Conversely, if the site development costs are high due to an extensive amount of earth moving, one can expect to have an unusually costly total project.

Often, sites are selected due to political realities or conditions other than operations, security, or cost efficiency. However, the selection process must recognize the impacts of the site environment and terrain on project development costs, and more important, on long-term operational conditions. This analysis requires a careful identification of the terrain/site conditions and an understanding of the potential constraints these conditions may impart on the correctional facility. With this full knowledge of the physical development and environment impacts, officials then can make informed project decisions.

Major facilities require large sites, which are easily accessible from several sides or locations simultaneously. The terrain most often is the limiting factor, which dictates the points of access. Roads can be constructed to the various access points, but alterations to the terrain are not always possible so as to allow the roads to access the site. Since the operational programs require the access points, the site must be graded to accommodate the access requirements.

When the designers of the Federal Bureau of Prisons' U.S. Penitentiary facility in Lee County, Virginia began the task of placing the proposed facility on the site, they were faced with an enormous task of earth moving. The terrain sloped from a ridge line at one corner to a slight depression at the opposite lower corner. Additionally, certain environmental elements restricted building on other areas of the site. Further requirements stated that the compound of the U.S. Penitentiary be on the same level as the housing units and other program and service buildings. There was no single area on the entire site which would accommodate these requirements. Consequently, some section of the site would have to be altered to create a suitable platform on which to place the main compound.

A suitable site was created by cutting into the face of the ridge, at the rear of the property, and filling the low areas at the front with the material removed from the ridge face. This resulted in locating the base grade at a lower level than originally anticipated, and this caused the changing of the grade of the administration building and the power plant. Also, the entrance road was moved to a different location than originally intended. A considerable saving in site development cost was effected by this planning effort. The poor terrain was altered to develop an acceptable site for the facility. All program requirements were met by the final site work.

Berms

Berms essentially are mounds of material, which result in reshaping the surface of the ground and are an important component of most major prison sites. Berms serve many purposes from creating visual barriers to defining pathways for water to follow as it drains from the site. Berms can be used in conjunction with fences and other barriers to prevent vehicles from breaching the barrier. An example would be where a mound or moat is created to restrict vehicles from crashing into either a fence or gate and thereby providing an avenue of escape for inmates in the area.

Site grading, including the installation of berms, must be done with an understanding of the potential impacts on operations, maintenance, and security. For instance, low, depressed areas, which are desirable for efficient site drainage, can provide blind spots in the electronic surveillance system. Berms should be kept outside of the clear zones and not be potential locations for observation/intrusion activities. Problems have occurred with improper grading/drainage in relation to recreational facilities. Large open flat areas require special attention and detailing to prevent nonstandard surface results.

Berms can be used in conjunction with the security perimeter as a means of preventing the general public from having visual access to the facility. Conversely, the berm also could restrict the vision from the inside so that individuals on the outside of the facility could not communicate with the inmates. When landscape material such as trees and shrubbery is added to the berm, visual privacy either is created or increased.

When placed outside of the security perimeter, a berm could prevent vehicles from penetrating the perimeter fence by absorbing the force of the vehicle. To maximize the effectiveness of the berm, it must be placed parallel to the fence and at a sufficient distance from it so as to prevent attack on the fence while not obscuring surveillance. The size and shape of the berm must be carefully designed to maximize the effect of the force absorption.

Another effective use of berms is to contain specific areas. Berms very effectively contain any spilled or leaking material from hazardous material storage facilities. This could be gasoline or diesel fuel from tanks or more toxic materials used in the industries' operations or from the facility's utilities. Many of the requirements for the containment of hazardous material leaks or spills are clearly defined in the various building and life safety codes. While the codes control these materials from the standpoint of life safety, it is quite clear that these materials are also a security threat and important to control.

It is quite important that the placement, design, and construction of berms be coordinated with and integrated into the overall security planning for the facility. Poor design and placement of berms can create more problems than they solve if there is any interference with the security objectives.

Proper analysis of terrain features must be accomplished before site development can be properly addressed. These terrain features can be either assets or detriments to the design and construction of a correctional facility. Modifications of the terrain could be quite costly, even when all economies of design and construction are effected. In some instances, it could be more cost effective to select another site if the site development costs are excessive. However, skillful use of the existing terrain could provide savings if the designer is fortunate enough to combine the operational and physical plant requirements of the correctional facility.

ASTM F 33's Standards Process

Vijay Ruikar
Intertek Testing Services
Antioch, California

As astronomical sums of public money are spent on the construction and rehabilitation of detention and correctional facilities, the design and engineering professionals working on these projects are under the microscope to reduce waste and to get the "best bang for the buck." Budget crunches and the enormous responsibility for public safety put these people in a difficult situation. How does one decide which building product is the best value in a given situation? How does one choose a good product objectively, from a bewildering array of claims and counterclaims by salespeople of vendors?

Obviously, a product or a system that has been tested and certified by an independent, third-party laboratory with nationwide recognition and accreditation will be a good choice, when compared to a product whose sole claim to fame is from its salesperson. However, to be able to test competing products objectively, a testing laboratory must have a set of nationally accepted test standards, which define the tests and the results unambiguously. The tests must focus on the product performance that comes as close as possible to the real-life situations the product will face. Furthermore, the standards must be reasonable, and the requirements must be

clear so their users can understand them and find them relatively easy to conform to within the constraints of costs and standard industry practices.

Do such standards exist for detention and correctional institutions? If so, where can they be obtained? Who creates them? What is the process that is used in creating them? This chapter will address these questions.

The architects, design professionals, correctional facility managers, and other concerned people are the natural choice as the creators of such standards. Obviously, they will want a neutral platform, free from the heat of the day-to-day competition, where they can come together, voice their concerns, and create technically sound, practical, and implementable standards to solve their problems. The American Society for Testing and Materials (ASTM), founded in 1898, with current membership exceeding 65,000, provides the ideal platform and atmosphere for this purpose. ASTM standards are recognized with great respect all over the world. The aim of this chapter is to explain the nature of the ASTM process, and, in particular, the work of the ASTM F 33. We will focus on the latter, which is a group dedicated to standards for detention and correctional facilities.

Statistics on Size and Scope of the Corrections Problem

On December 31, 1996, 5.5 million people were on probation or in detention—nearly 2.8 percent of the adult population of the United States. At midyear 1997, the state and federal detention facilities had 1.2 million inmates. Another 0.6 million were inmates in 3,304 jails in the country. The jail inmate population increased by 9.4 percent over the preceding twelve months, at nearly double the average annual rate of increase of 4.9 percent observed since 1990.

By mid 1997, the jails were filled to 97 percent of capacity. The jails increased their capacity by 19,713 beds in 1997. More than $74 billion was spent by federal, state, and local governments on criminal justice in 1990 (Bureau of Justice Statistics, and FBI press release, January 1998).

Response of the Society

With such stunning magnitude of unlawfulness, it is only natural that local, state, and the federal government have responded by enacting tough laws, such as the "three strikes and you are out" law. Threats of severe punishment may deter some criminals, but for the short term, large increases in the inmate populations are seen. To comply with the laws about crowding, and to be able to bring some semblance of order, additional correctional facilities have to be built. Rehabilitation of older detention facilities is also on the upswing. While the dollar volume of the business is always subject to fluctuations, the overall trend over the long term indicates a substantial increase in detention-related construction.

Harnessing the Standardization Process As the Solution

Suppliers of building materials and the design professionals, as well as the owners/managers of the detention facilities were hard pressed in the mid 1980s due to the dearth of benchmarks, design guidelines, and standards. While there were hundreds of standards available for the general construction, there were very few national standards in the security field, and none of them was focused specifically on the needs of detention and correctional facilities.

As the correctional institutions began to feel the heat in the early 1980s, the American Correctional Association, the prominent association in the field of corrections,

came out with the first edition of the *Design Guide*. This was a unique, first attempt to take on the fast-growing problem. Since then, a number of new developments have taken place, and several new technologies as well as laws have come into being. This second edition of the *Design Guide*, addressing these developments, is, therefore, very timely.

When a product has to meet certain defined performance requirements, its engineers know how to design it for optimal performance. For example, if a piece of glazing is to be used in a detention facility, it must withstand an attack by a sledge hammer from a youthful, muscular inmate attempting to escape. The performance standard will require the glazing to be tested to see if it withstands that kind of attack, and if so, for what duration. If the design engineer knows the magnitude of the force exerted, he or she can come up with a laminated glazing product design that will pass the test. If a known design passes the test, all other materials of the same design also will have a high likelihood of passing it. To add objectivity to this process, all products from several manufacturers are subjected to the same attack under the same test parameters by an independent, neutral, third-party laboratory that is accredited by appropriate authorities to perform such tests.

Competition among manufacturers gives owners and designers an objective way to specify and compare the performance of the products vis-a-vis their prices. A small or medium-sized manufacturer, through good engineering, can produce a product that matches the performance of the expensive product of the large company, and compete effectively; the standards provide a level playing field where big companies no longer can dominate by sheer virtue of their size alone. Thus, the task of the ASTM F 33 is of special importance to society in general and to the detention/correctional industry in particular.

ASTM as an Organization

In 1988, the American Society for Testing and Materials formed the ASTM F 33 Committee with a specific focus directed toward meeting the standardization needs of detention/correctional facilities. With more than 65,000 members operating in 171 technical committees, and with thousands of published standards recognized and respected worldwide, the ASTM certainly may be the best qualified organization to handle the task of setting these complex material standards. As soon as the committee was formed, more than 100 members joined it, signifying the popularity of its mandate.

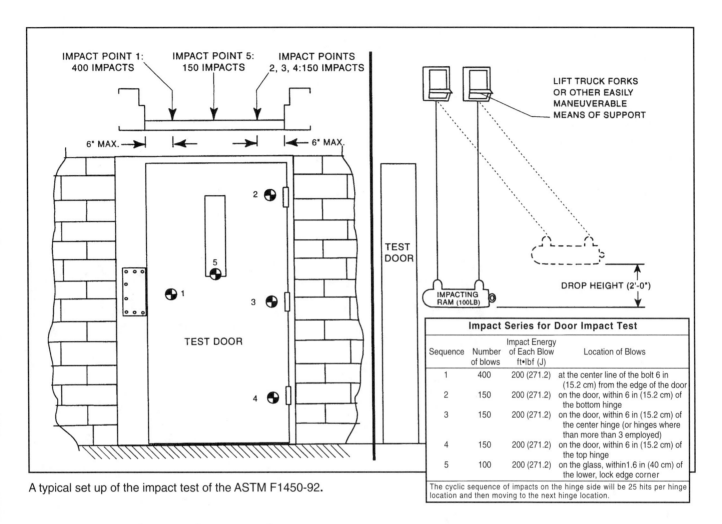

IMPACT POINT 1: 400 IMPACTS
IMPACT POINT 5: 150 IMPACTS
IMPACT POINTS 2, 3, 4: 150 IMPACTS

6" MAX.   6" MAX.

2
5
1
3
4

TEST DOOR

LIFT TRUCK FORKS OR OTHER EASILY MANEUVERABLE MEANS OF SUPPORT

TEST DOOR

DROP HEIGHT (2'-0")

IMPACTING RAM (100LB)

A typical set up of the impact test of the ASTM F1450-92.

Impact Series for Door Impact Test			
Sequence	Number of blows	Impact Energy of Each Blow ft•lbf (J)	Location of Blows
1	400	200 (271.2)	at the center line of the bolt 6 in (15.2 cm) from the edge of the door
2	150	200 (271.2)	on the door, within 6 in (15.2 cm) of the bottom hinge
3	150	200 (271.2)	on the door, within 6 in (15.2 cm) of the center hinge (or hinges where than more than 3 employed)
4	150	200 (271.2)	on the door, within 6 in (15.2 cm) of the top hinge
5	100	200 (271.2)	on the glass, within1.6 in (40 cm) of the lower, lock edge corner

The cyclic sequence of impacts on the hinge side will be 25 hits per hinge location and then moving to the next hinge location.

All ASTM standards are created with the spirit of a voluntary consensus, a freely arrived at agreement. A main committee such as the F 33 deals with all the different needs of a specific, broad-based industry field, such as the field of detention/correctional facilities. Within this main committee, several subcommittees and task groups are formed to deal with various products or systems that require standards.

Members of a task group put their ideas together in several meetings, agree on the requirements, and create a draft copy. This draft then goes through the subcommittee ballot, main committee ballot, and the society ballot before it becomes a standard. At each stage, the voting members are free to express their concerns through comments or negative votes. Progressive ballots ensure that the draft standard is reviewed by members with completely differing viewpoints. Also, members of other committees study and review the standard for a particular product or system so that it does not have conflicting requirements that may nullify its compatibility as a subassembly of a larger system.

The ASTM process of voting on a standard requires that every negative vote must be accompanied by the engineering or logical reasons leading to it. Then, each and every negative vote is discussed by the concerned subcommittee or the main committee. All legitimate concerns are fully addressed. If a negative vote is found to be persuasive, the standard draft is modified to correct the problem. If this correction is of a technical nature that changes the operation of the standard, then the corrected draft goes back for reballoting. If the changes are of an editorial nature that does not change materially the intent or the functioning of the standard, the draft standard goes on to the next stage. All standards are written in accordance with the ASTM manual on form and style, which ensures clarity and uniformity.

ASTM regulations ensure that manufacturers and nonmanufacturer members are in a certain balance in voting so that the results of the ballots are eminently fair. For example, a large company may have five members in a committee on doors, but it gets only one vote. Also, if there are twenty-five manufacturers but only fifteen architects in a given committee, only fifteen manufacturers get to vote. Thus, balance is achieved in every ballot.

After a draft standard has been voted in the affirmative through a ballot, it is published as an ASTM standard. Throughout the balloting process, people who are not ASTM members but have an interest in the standard are free to offer their comments and criticisms. All input is gratefully received and carefully considered. Sometimes, seminars and symposia are conducted, and articles are written by the committee members to attract greater participation. Every published standard is available for correction/revision from the day it is printed. All standards are subjected to at least one review every five years, per ASTM regulations.

The membership of the ASTM is open to all people regardless of their nationality, race, religious affiliation, gender, or citizenship. Typically, the ASTM committees consist of the representatives of the manufacturers, end users, regulating authorities, architects/specifiers/design professionals, testing laboratories, and so forth.

This is the fire-exposed face of a door-fire test assembly after three hours of the fire endurance-test, ASTM E-152 (1981).

This test standard is issued by the ASTM E-5 committee. The ASTM F 33 committee modified the test procedure to include "positive pressure," radiation measurement, and other items so that the test combined the most severe features of several international standards such as ISO 3008. This was futuristic foresight on part of the ASTM F 33 in 1995 when testing to "positive pressure" was still in the discussion stage. In addition, this test had door assemblies including the overhead slider lock and a food pass mechanism, both of which are commonly used in detention facilities, but neither had ever been tested.

With an increasing number of detention facilities being situated in densely populated urban areas, the fire rating of the door assemblies, as tested by this ASTM F 33 test procedure, is of paramount importance.

In this test, the face of the test assembly faced 1,000 degrees Fahrenheit (538 degrees Celcius) at five minutes into the test, and the temperature steadily increased to 1,925 degrees Fahrenheit (1,052 degrees Celcius) at three hours into the test.

ASTM F 33

This committee works on the standards and other documents specifically focused on the detention/correctional facilities. The committee meets four times a year. Every meeting is usually on the Saturday prior to a major convention in corrections, such as the summer American Correctional Association Congress of Correction. Since its inception, this committee has pursued an aggressive agenda and to date has published more than ten standards, and several others are in the making. The ASTM F 33 has taken great pains to come up with an interlinked matrix or a family of standards that relate to one another and make a harmonious whole system. Thus, security doors, locks, and the walls in which they are installed, along with the windows and glazing and so forth, all must conform to the same level of performance requirements that is defined by the interlinked standards.

Even though the standard for a given type of product may address the special needs or features of that product, the overall performance levels established by the

The outside (unexposed) face of the same test assembly at three hours. Notice the deformation of the door assemblies.

This test door has undergone 950 impacts in the impact test to ASTM F1450-92. Each impact had an impact energy of 200 foot pounds (271.2 joules). In comparison, a healthy, muscular male attacker (25 years of age, 6 feet/182.8cm height, 220 lb/100kg weight), wielding a 20 pound (9.09 kg) sledge hammer with a three-foot (0.91 m) handle has been estimated to deliver a blow with 140 foot pounds (189.8 joules) of impact energy.

The exposed face of the test assembly is pictured after it was exposed to the impact, erosion, and cooling effect of the hose stream test, which immediately followed the three-hour fire endurance test. The hose stream test means that within a minute after the three-hour fire exposure as described on page 352, the exposed face was impacted by a stream of water from a nozzle 1.125" (28.58mm) in diameter, with a 45psi/310kPa water pressure for four minutes. This test is mandatory per ASTM E-152 (1981).

ASTM F 33 standards harmonize the performance levels. This makes it possible for the design professionals to combine several subsystems that may have been designed by different companies and tested separately to result in an overall system that addresses all of their special needs and concerns.

A brief sampling of these standards is as follows:

Standard Test Methods for Physical Barriers:

ASTM F 1450: Hollow Metal Swinging Door Assemblies for Detention Facilities
ASTM F 1592: Detention Hollow Metal Vision Systems

Standards for Operational Systems:

ASTM F 1465: Guide for Selection of Security Control Systems Part III–Defining the Operator-System Interface

ASTM F 1576: Guide for Selection of Security Control Systems Part II-Defining the Central Control System

ASTM F 1577: Test Methods for Detention Locks for Swinging Doors

ASTM F 1643: Test Method for Detention Sliding Door Locking Device Assembly

Furnishings and Equipment:

ASTM F 1534: Standard Test Method for Determining Changes in Fire-Test Response Characteristics of Cushioning Materials After Water Leaching

ASTM F 1550: Test Method for Determination of Fire-Test Response Characteristics of Composite Mattresses or Furniture for Use in Correctional Facilities After Exposure to Vandalism, by Employing a Bench Scale Oxygen Consumption Calorimeter

Test Methods Under Development:

Detention Security Glazing
Walls in Detention/Correctional Facilities

Practical Use of ASTM F 33 Standards

To generate a functional, safe, and easily usable standard, merely theoretical work and discussions are never enough, even when done by "experts." Putting the standards themselves to test, to determine if they are safely and easily usable, and to see if they could deliver results usable in day-to-day decision making, is indeed an acid test of the test standards themselves.

On October 11, 1995, ASTM F 33 members sponsored a fire test and an impact test on detention security door assemblies at Intertek Testing Services (Warnock Hersey) in Pittsburg, California to put their standards to test on their own products. Unbelievable as it may seem, the detention security doors had never been fire tested with a slider lock mechanism or with a food pass mechanism. Attendees at this historic event included seventy-seven members of the Committee of Architects for Justice (CAJ) of the American Institute of Architecture (AIA), and several international guests from Canada, Australia, and other countries. The outstanding success of these tests assured everyone that the ASTM F 33 standards are technologically sound and that they can be easily used to test conventional assemblies and for breaking new grounds. The test results were crystal clear in assessing the conformity of the products to the standards.

Conclusion

When huge sums of public money are being allocated and spent on detentions/corrections, even when other budgets are being cut, it is absolutely essential to make the public dollars go the farthest possible distance in enhancing public safety. One of the best ways to achieve this is to use tested and certified products and systems. Current technologies, when used in product design, production, testing, and certification will yield rich dividends. Testing and certification by an independent, unbiased and competent engineering organization will provide the objective assessment of the products, systems, and assemblies to the national standards. Voluntary consensus standards created by the ASTM F 33 for detentions and corrections are the bedrock, the technological foundation, on which the process of conformity assessment rests. Thus, knowledge and awareness about ASTM and active participation in its process are definitely the first steps in making our society safer and more secure in the twenty-first century.

For a full list of published standards and standards being developed, please contact the ASTM F 33 staff manager, at (610) 832-9737.

Coping with Acoustics

Jerry P. Christoff
Veneklasen Associates
Santa Monica, California

The third edition of *Standards for Adult Correctional Institutions*, prepared by the American Correctional Association states, "Noise levels in inmate housing units do not exceed 70 dBA (decibels) in daytime and 45 dBA at night." This standard should be considered as a minimum level of acceptability. It is generally understood that 47 dBA is the upper limit of sound levels which will produce undisturbed sleep. Therefore, this should be the limiting sound level for continuous noise produced by the ventilation system.

Another concern is reverberation time. Reverberation relates to the "decay" in sound level that occurs after a sound source is turned off. We speak of reverberation in terms of "live" and "dead" rooms. What is the significance of reverberation time in terms of a correctional institution? It relates to the ability to understand speech, either direct conversation or amplified sound over a public address system. As the reverberation time increases, speech becomes less intelligible; and communication becomes strained and eventually deteriorates. For dayrooms, the reverberation time should not exceed 1.5 seconds for general use and 0.75 seconds if the dayroom will also double as a classroom. Room layout, wall and ceiling surface design, material selections, and the choice of furnishings all can help to reduce reverberation time

and thus improve the ability of staff and inmates to hear and understand one another.

Relationship Among Acoustical Materials, Background Noise Levels, and Reverberation Time

The amount of sound absorption in a room will control its reverberation time. The number of sound sources, their sound power output, and the amount of sound absorption in the room will determine the background sound level. It is very difficult to predict actual sound levels accurately, because of the so called "cocktail party effect," which has been studied analytically by acousticians. We are all familiar with it. Imagine a reception in a "live" room. When only a few are speaking, normal conversational levels are used. As the number of guests increase, one has to increase one's speaking effort to overcome one's neighbor, and so forth. This increase in speaking effort continues to rise, as the number of guests increase, until everyone is shouting to be heard. Obviously, everyone gets tired, people give up talking, and the levels drop. The whole process begins again! Sometimes the inability of people to communicate due to noise can lead to confrontations. See the Wisconsin Department of

Corrections' study that discusses the problems related to noise in correctional facilities that follows this section.

Acoustical Materials for Correctional Institutional Dayrooms

The first principle guiding noise reduction methods for dayrooms is that normal communication and low background noise levels are desirable and beneficial to a more effective operation of the correctional environment. The historical view of a jail—as a multitiered, open cell front, noisy facility—has changed dramatically with the advent of direct supervision forms of management, and its influence on design, construction materials, and furnishings.

A second principle to be considered to reduce the noise levels in dayrooms is that the use of sound absorption materials does not have to increase the capital or maintenance cost. Life cycle costing for correctional facilities has shown that neither the initial nor long-term maintenance cost is higher when sound absorption materials are used in dayrooms in lieu of the more traditional concrete floor and masonry construction. The choice of materials needs to reflect an integration of noise control and security objectives, with cost objectives in mind.

Acoustical Design of a Typical Dayroom

A Review of Dayroom Acoustical Objectives

Since a dayroom will often be used as a classroom, the design objective for reverberation time should be 0.75 seconds maximum. During activities in this space, the noise levels should not exceed 70 dBA.

General Acoustical Design Principles

- Irregularly shaped rooms are preferrable to rectangular spaces.
- Acoustically finished materials should be distributed on ceiling and wall surfaces.
- Use acoustical materials with high noise reduction coefficients (NRC).
- Locate acoustical materials near sound sources for maximum effectiveness.
- Limit the volume of television sets.

A Dayroom Design Example

The noise level and reverberation time has been predicted for a housing unit incorporating fifty-six inmates in individual cells. To compute the noise level, it was assumed that one quarter or fourteen of the inmates are talking simultaneously using normal conversational effort. A summary of the results is as follows:

A Dayroom Design Example

Scenario	Area (sq. feet)	Noise Level (dBA)	Rev. Time (sec.)
1. No Acoustical Treatment		76	5.60
2. 5/8" Acoustical Tile (0.55 NRC)	2,000	69	2.00
3. 2-1/3" Security Ceiling System (0.95 NRC)	2,730	65	0.75
4. — 2-1/2" Security Ceiling System (0.95 NRC)	2,730	63	0.75
— 5/8" Acoustical Tile (0.55 NRC)	2,000		
— 1" Acoustical Wall Panels (0.80 NRC)	250		
— Commercial Carpet (0.35 NRC)	3,640		

What the Architect Needs to Do

What is the architect's role in all of this? The publication, *Acoustics in Corrections, A Guide to Addressing Acoustical Problems in Correctional Facilities,* actually contains enough information for an architect to perform some straightforward calculations to predict reverberation time and sound levels in dayrooms. Armed with the acoustical characteristics of the actual materials that the architect is considering, individuals can proceed rather swiftly through the computation of the reverberation time and the room noise levels. This will furnish guidance in terms of sounds generated by activities within dayrooms, but it will not solve such issues as noise control requirements for the HVAC system. For this, the advice of professional acousticians is advisable. Obviously, they also can assist in evaluating the acoustical design of the dayroom in more detail.

Summary

Modern detention facilities of all classification levels require careful attention to the acoustical design, since there is a direct relationship between relatively quiet, relaxed surroundings and improved morale, less stress, and consequently greater security. The achievement of low noise levels is not an accident. It requires conscious acoustical design using appropriate materials selected by the architect and prison administrators that create a quiet, nonthreatening, and secure facility.

Wisconsin Department of Corrections' Noise Study

A study seeking to determine the impact of noise levels on corrections staff and operations

August 17, 1996

Committee on Acoustics in Corrections
Wisconsin Research Team

Knut A. Rostad
Wendy S. Meister
Richard Wener, Ph.D.

Wisconsin Department of Corrections
Noise Study Project Team

Client
**Wisconsin Department
of Corrections**

Committee On Acoustics Project Team

Knut A. Rostad
Managing Director
Committee On Acoustics
Project Director

Dr. Richard Wener
Polytechnic University
Technical Advisor

Wendy S. Meister
University of Wisconsin—Milwaukee
Director of Research

Shiner & Associates Consultants
Acoustical Consultant

Environmental Interiors, Inc.

Epic Metals Corporation

Hunter Douglas Architectural Products

Wildeck, Inc.
*Co-sponsors, Committee On Acoustics
in Corrections
Acoustic Materials Suppliers (Phase II)*

The Big Deal About a Little Noise

*Donald W. Gudmanson, Warden
Oshkosh Correctional Institution*

Corrections administrators have a myriad of "front-burner" issues which demand our attention. Other issues get to the "back-burner." It's part of our business. Noise is usually pushed to the "back burner" issue. This report should put noise on each of our front burners.

Why? The findings in this report show how noise can be a significant security issue, and can put our entire program and treatment delivery system in jeopardy.

Noise can jeopardize the security and safety of staff and inmates. As corrections professionals, experience has taught us that excessive noise levels can be used to mask aggressive inmate behavior in the housing unit, or "background" noise forces our staff and inmates to raise their voices just to be heard, and the ability to maintain a secure and safe operations is jeopardized. Correctional staff rank "reducing noise levels" as a vitally necessary strategy to deal with their concerns of safety and assault.

Noise can jeopardize the delivery of programming and treatment. Our staff have worked hard to develop effective programming. Results require that we get through to inmates. If unit managers, social workers, counselors, and teachers must compete with the amplified noise of normal unit operations, what they have to give inmates is lost. This might explain why in this study corrections program staff rank noise as a significant contributor of tension and stress. In fact, noise is comparably ranked with the issues of "crowding" and "threat of assault."

Noise needs to be on our front burner. As this study demonstrates, noise significantly impacts our staff; noise can play a weighty role in our ability to provide a safe and secure environment. I encourage you to move noise to your "front burner," and reading this report is a good first step.

If you have any questions about this study or the issues it raises, please contact me or the Committee on Acoustics in Corrections.

Wisconsin Department of Corrections'
Noise Study
Summary of Findings

Introduction

The Committee on Acoustics in Corrections research team set out to address a basic question about how noise affects corrections officers and staff. The question was outlined in the original project scope: The issue is whether and/or to what extent corrections officers, staff and operations are impacted by a poor acoustic environment.

The methodology through the first two phases of the project entailed four steps. First, we conducted in-person interviews with line staff members from two Wisconsin Department of Corrections' (WDOC) institutions; i.e.: Racine and Oshkosh. Secondly, based on the results of these interviews, a questionnaire was developed; and data was collected and analyzed in its totality and by four housing-unit clusters created on the basis of the level of acoustical treatment in the units. Thirdly, noise levels were taken in three of the nine Oshkosh housing units by an independent acoustical consultant.

While these two phases provide important insights into the significance of noise in a prison environment, additional work remains to be completed.[1]

Major Conclusions

1. The issue of noise in security and operations is substantially "hidden." While high noise levels are often not identified as a "problem," controlling noise is often identified as a "solution."

Noise is frequently not directly identified as a problem by corrections staff because the staff seem to believe that it is an integral part of the physical environment. Like stress, noise is *just part of the working environment in a prison* and is outside their control. Consequently, silence over noise does not necessarily mean noise is not important to staff. It simply means staff believe it can't be changed.

This phenomenon is evident in the results from different phases of the research. In the first phase during the initial open interviews, noise was *rarely volunteered as* an important issue. However, in the second phase of research, noise is ranked relatively high—compared to other conditions—as a condition causing stress and concerns for safety, assault and control (see Findings A and B).

In the next phase, the *reduction* of noise levels is explicitly offered as a viable "change" in the physical environment (and so identified as a part of the environment which can be controlled). To address the concerns for safety, assault and control of the facility, noise reduction ranks very high relative to other changes which are offered (see Finding C).

2. Staff seem to relate noise levels with their control of housing units.

In the housing units with the least amount of acoustical treatment, reducing noise levels is perceived to be a somewhat more effective method (compared to more "staff training") for gaining a feeling of control over the housing units (see Finding E). This contrasts with findings from the other housing units where staff training is ranked somewhat more effective than is noise reduction.

In their totality, these findings seem to imply that at some point, staff in housing units no longer feel that staff training can address their concerns of control. The importance of these findings can be tied to existing research on loss of control and "learned helplessness." This research indicates that once individuals feel they have no control over a situation, they view other situations as outside their control. In our findings, staff on the housing units with the least amount of acoustical treatment are beginning to exhibit signs of learned helplessness.

3. The impact of noise is very "visible" to the staff at Oshkosh.

Noise contributes significantly to concerns of safety, assault, and a feeling of a lack of control of the housing unit; it also contributes significantly to stress and tension. While the factors which contribute to stress and concerns for safety are numerous and interrelated, the staff at Oshkosh perceive noise to be important, relative to other well known stress/security factors. The relative importance of noise is evident when compared to many issues which are normally considered important causes of stress and tension; i.e.: inmate behavior, crowding, idleness, staffing levels, staff training and/or programming/work assignments (see Finding B).

When the data from the housing units are clustered by the amount of acoustical treatment within the dayrooms, additional associations with noise levels are evident. Concern with inmate behavior and inmate space increase with noise levels (see Finding D) and the importance of staff training and programming increases with noise levels (see Finding E).

Major Findings

The findings from this study are divided into two parts. In Part One, the summary data is analyzed. In Part Two, the data is divided into four subsets, created to group together housing units with similar acoustical material applications.

Part One—Summary Findings

A. Inmate behavior is the most important "condition" which corrections staff relate to their concerns of assault, safety and control.

Several conditions were ranked by staff on the basis of how they contributed to their concerns of safety, assault, and control of the housing unit. (These conditions were explicitly identified by staff members during the initial phase 1 interviews.)

Throughout the data, there is a clear pattern in how different conditions were ranked. "Inmate behavior," "number of inmates for the amount of space" (inmate space), "staff to inmate ratio" (staffing levels) and "difficulty hearing inmate activity" (noise) are the conditions which are of greatest concern to staff. "Co-workers inmate management techniques" (management techniques) and "design or layout" cause less concern. (See Table I).

The most important condition or variable linked to concerns of "safety," "assault," and "control" is "inmate behavior."

Safety. When it concerns conditions felt to affect the corrections staff personal safety (as ranked on a nine-point scale where a 1 signifies the greatest cause for concern and 9 the least cause for concern) the responses are clustered fairly closely between 3.7 and 5.9. Inmate behavior leads at 3.7, while inmate space and staffing levels follow at 4.5. Noise is ranked 5.2. (See Table I) It is interesting to note that management techniques of co-workers is ranked least important of all the variables, and scores a 5.9.

Assault. When it regards conditions which corrections staff feel contribute to their concerns of assault, the most important factor, again, is inmate behavior, ranked 3.2 (on a scale of one to nine where one is the highest and nine is the lowest). Inmate space and staffing levels follow at 4.1, and noise is ranked 5.1.

Control. When the issue shifts to concerns of lack of control, the issues of inmate behavior, inmate space, and staffing levels are more closely ranked (as ranked on a nine-point scale where a 1 signifies the greatest cause for concern and 9 the least cause for concern) at 3.6, 3.9, and 3.8. The issue of noise follows, on the nine-point scale, at 4.7.

TABLE I
Contributors to Concerns of Safety, Assault and Control

	Safety	*Assault*	*Control*
Inmate behavior	3.7	3.2	3.6
Inmate space	4.5	4.1	3.9
Staffing levels	4.5	4.1	3.8
Noise	**5.2**	**5.1**	**4.7**
Design or layout	5.2	5.2	5.1
Management techniques	5.9	5.5	5.1

B. Corrections staff rank noise a significant contributor to tension or stress.

Among several situations which "contribute to tension or stress," "inmates with behavior problems" and "confrontations with inmates" ranked as the greatest contributors (see Table II below) at 5.8 and 5.6 (on the nine-point scale where 9 is the highest score.) These factors were followed by "overcrowding in the housing unit" at 5.3, "threat of assault" and "gang problems" at 5.1, and "noise" at 4.9. Following, were "not enough staff on the housing unit," "lack of program resources," and "co-workers' inmate management techniques" at 4.8, 4.7, and 4.4 respectively.

TABLE II
Contributors to Tension or Stress

	Stress Level	
Inmate behavior	5.8	
Confrontations with inmates	5.6	
Crowding	5.3	
Threat of assault		5.1
Gang problems		5.1
Noise		**4.9**
Staffing levels		4.8
Lack of program resources		4.7
Meeting inmate demands	4.6	
Co-workers' management techniques	4.4	
Mass movements	4.4	

C. What changes do corrections staff believe would best address their concerns of safety, assault, and control? The most important "change" is more staff training. Still, *reducing noise levels is also ranked high*.

Safety. The four most highly ranked changes are clustered closely together between 6.5 and 7.4. "More staff training" is the highest ranked change at 7.4; "reducing blind spots" follows closely at 7.1. "Increasing programming and/or work assignments" is scored at 6.9, and "reducing noise levels in the dayroom" at 6.5. "Stricter rules and regulations" follows at 5.9.

Assault. On this issue, all the responses were clustered between 6 and 7 (again where 9 is the highest). Staff training led at 7.0, and programming/work assignments and reducing noise levels followed at 6.7 and 6.2, respectively. Rules/regulations followed at 5.9.

Control. The rankings concerning the issue of control are even more closely clustered, with staff training, programming/work and reducing noise levels ranked at 6.9, 6.5, and 6.4, respectively.

TABLE III
"Changes" to Address Concerns of Safety, Assault and Control

	Safety	Assault	Control
Inmate behavior	3.7	3.2	3.6
More staff training	7.4	7.0	6.9
Increase programming and/or work assignments	6.9	6.7	6.5
Reduce blind spots	7.1	6.2	6.4
Reduce dayroom noise levels	**6.5**	**6.2**	**6.4**
Stricter rules/regulations	5.9	5.9	6.2

Part Two—Housing Unit Clusters by Acoustical Materials

The data was then analyzed in four clusters of housing units based on the amount of acoustical materials present in each unit. The clusters were developed by the research team, in collaboration with the staff at Oshkosh.[2] Noise levels were also measured by an independent acoustical consultant in three housing units,[3] and thus provided benchmark data as to the acoustical environments.

The significance of these "clusters" as distinguishable acoustical environments is further evidenced by the association between the amount of acoustical treatment in the housing unit, and the corrections' staff agreement that the housing unit "is usually too noisy." On the nine-point scale, from the best acoustically treated to the worst acoustically treated housing unit, the cluster rankings range from 2.9, 4.1, 5.4 to 6.6 (See Table IV).

TABLE IV
Housing Unit Clusters, Noise Levels, and Agreement that the Housing Unit "Is Usually too Noisy"

Housing Units	dBA[a]	Agreement that the housing unit is "usually too noisy"[b]
CC, K	—	2.9
MC, OC	63	4.1
Q, R	67	5.4
U, V	69	6.6

[a] Noise levels were measured in Middle Center (MC), Q and U.
[b] The scale from one to nine, where a "one" was "strongly disagree" and a nine "strongly agree."

D. Concerns with inmate behavior and inmate space increase with the noise levels of the housing units.

At the outset we note that the staff do not believe there is a relationship between the housing unit clusters and inmate behavior problems in the housing units. This is based on their own evaluation ("the housing unit I work on has more behavior problems than the other housing units").

However, even though "more behavior problems" are not associated with housing units with different noise levels, the data do indicate that staff concerns with safety, assault and control tend to increase as acoustical treatment is reduced and noise levels increase.

Concerns with inmate behavior and safety increase with rankings of 4.1, 4.2, 3.7, to 3.4; assault: 4.3, 3.4, 3.0, to 2.4; control: 4.3, 3.9, 3.4, to 3.3. Concerns with inmate space also increase; safety: 5.6, 4.3, 4.6, to 3.7; assault: 5.4, 3.9, 4.3, to 2.9; control: 5.3, 3.4, 4.0, to 2.8.

TABLE V
Staff Concerns Increasing with Noise Levels

	Inmate behavior contributing to concerns of			Inmate space contributing to concerns of		
	Safety	Assault	Control	Safety	Assault	Control
CC, K	4.1	4.3	4.3	5.6	5.4	5.3
Mc, OC	4.2	3.4	3.9	4.3	3.9	3.4
mean	*3.7*	*3.2*	*3.6*	*4.5*	*4.1*	*3.9*
Q, R	3.7	3.0	3.4	4.6	4.3	4.0
U, V	3.4	2.4	3.3	3.7	2.9	2.8

E. The most important change for staff in the housing units with the highest noise levels is reducing noise.

In the housing units with the highest noise levels, reducing noise levels is more important than is staff training—the most highly rated change overall. For the staff in these housing units, this is the best way to address concerns of safety, assault and control, as seen in Table VI below.

TABLE VI
"Changes" to Address Concerns of Safety, Assault and Control

	Safety	Assault	Control
Inmate behavior	3.7	3.2	3.6
More staff training	7.4	7.0	6.9
Increase programming and/ or work assignments	6.9	6.7	6.5
Reduce blind spots	7.1	6.2	6.4
Reduce dayroom noise levels	6.5	6.2	6.4
(In housing units U and V)	**7.6**	**7.3**	**7.4**
Stricter rules/regulations	5.9	5.9	6.2

F. The importance of staff training and programming/work programs—as changes which will improve staff safety, concerns of assault and control, increase with the noise levels of the housing units.

Staff training is the most significant "change" which staff believe will positively affect these concerns. The staff working in units with the worst acoustics and the highest noise levels generally believe most strongly in staff training.

When it concerns safety, the rankings increase from 7.0, 7.7, 6.6 to 8.2; assault: (in reverse scale) 3.4, 3.0, 3.0 to 2. 1; control: 6.8, 6.9, 6.9 to 7.4. When it concerns programming or work programs, a similar trend is seen with the issue of safety (from 6.7 to 7.7); assault (in reverse scale, 3.3 to 2.3); and, finally, the issue of control (from 6.7 to 7.1).

TABLE VII
Staff Training and Programming/Work Programs and Noise Levels

	Staff training increases in importance			Programming/work programs increase in importance		
	Safety	Assault	Control	Safety	Assault	Control
CC, K	4.1	4.3	4.3	5.6	5.4	5.3
MC, OC	4.2	3.4	3.9	4.3	3.9	3.4
mean	*3.7*	*3.2*	*3.6*	*4.5*	*4.1*	*3.9*
Q, R	3.7	3.0	3.4	4.6	4.3	4.0
U, V	3.4	2.4	3.3	3.7	2.9	2.8

NOTES:

1. There is reason to suspect that noise can directly and indirectly affect correctional officers' and inmates' behaviors and perceptions. Through our in-person interviews and questionnaire we have collected data that sheds light on the contribution of noise in its totality. Many variables contribute to noise and some relationships are more obvious than others. Thus it is important to note that, due to indirect relationships, noise may not always be the variable officers identify as the primary contributor to the problem. It is for these reasons that the data in its totality is as important as the relationship between noise and individual contributors.

2. The clusters were grouped as: 1) Close Center and Southwest Center, 2) Middle Center and Open Center, 3) Q and R, and 4) U and V.

3. Shiner & Associates, Chicago, Illinois, "Oshkosh Correctional Institution Dayroom Sound Pressure Levels," May 1995. Measurements were taken at the housing unit correctional officers' station at different times; the measurements applied in this table were taken in the evening (not during dinner) when the unit was partially occupied.

COMMITTEE ON ACOUSTICS IN CORRECTIONS

The Committee on Acoustics in Corrections is comprised of leading architects, corrections administrators and acoustical consultants. Committee members represent many of the most well-known architectural firms active in the corrections market. It is chaired by Robert A. Broder, AIA, President, Monacelli Associates Architects and Planners, Cambridge, MA.

The mission of the Committee is to educate the corrections industry on the importance of acoustics. In fulfilling this mission it has published *Acoustics in Corrections—A Practical Guide for Administrators and Planners*, written numerous articles for trade publications, and conducted briefings at industry conferences.

The work of the Committee is funded through contributions and sponsorships from private companies and agencies. The four founding sponsors are Environmental Interiors, Inc., Epic Metals Corporation, Hunter Douglas Architectural Products, and Wildeck, Inc.

Planners and administrators who have questions regarding acoustics are encouraged to call acoustical consultants and *Acoustics In Corrections* editors, Jack E. Randorff, Ph.D. (in Houston at 713/521-2205) or Jerry P. Christoff (in Los Angeles at 213/870-9268).

For a free copy of *Acoustics in Corrections,* contact Knut A. Rostad, Committee on Acoustics In Corrections, 1899 L Street, NW, Suite 500, Washington, D.C., 20036; 202/466-7001 (fax) 202/466-7002.

Robert A. Broder, Chairman, *Monacelli Associates*

James E. Aiken, *James E. Aiken Associates*

Tom L. Allison, *Orange County Corrections Division*

Louis A. Austin, *HSM&M*

Jacob D. Bliek, *Pennsylvania Department of Corrections*

Stephen A. Carter, *Carter Goble Associates*

Jerry P. Christoff, *Paul S. Veneklasen & Associates*

Michael H. Frawley, *HOK*

Dee Halley, *National Institute of Corrections*

Scott Higgins, *Federal Bureau of Prisons*

Stephen J. Ingley, *American Jail Association*

Dale E. Kostner, *Sverdrup Corporation*

Peter Krasnow, *DMJM*

Morton J. Liebowitz, *Rappahannock Security Center*

Rod Miller, *CRS, Inc.*

Terrence P. McManus, *Voinovich Companies*

Frederic D. Moyer, *Moyer Associates*

Dale A. Nederhoff, *HOK*

Allen L. Patrick, *NBBJ*

Thomas G. Pinkerton, *HOK*

Bob Price, *Henningson, Durham & Richardson*

Jack E. Randorff, *Randorff & Associates*

Knut A. Rostad, *Committee on Acoustics in Corrections*

Frank Sheridan, *New York Dep. of Correctional Services*

Harvey H. Siegel, *Phillips Swager Associates*

Karen M. Sicner, *Sicner Planning & Design*

Wantland J. Smith, *HOK*

Jeffrey Washington, *American Correctional Association*

Opening a New Correctional Facility

Proper planning ensures a smooth opening and operation.

Photo courtesy of HOK Architects, Washington, D.C.

On the preceding page, the Federal Detention Center in Houston, Texas.
For a view of the completed building see page 391.

Architect/engineer: 3D/International, Inc., Houston, Texas. Construction contractor:
Hensel Phelps Construction Company, Houston, Texas. Construction management firm:
CRSS Constructors Inc., Houston, Texas. Photo courtesy of the Federal Bureau of Prisons.

Opening a New Correctional Facility

James A. Rowenhorst
Correctional Consultant
Rapid City, South Dakota

The last phase of the correctional facility development process is the actual opening of the facility. This phase is no less important than the planning, designing, or building phases of the project. There are many examples of well-planned and designed facilities experiencing serious operational problems after opening because inadequate attention was given to the opening phase of the project—missing equipment and supplies; inadequate policies, procedures, and post orders; not enough staff; poor staff training; escapes; facility damage; low staff morale; and high staff turnover. However, there are many examples where a well-planned opening of a new facility overcame planning and design deficiencies. Such planning helps ensure that the facility development process will end in success.

The opening of a new facility sometimes is referred to as *activation* in that the facility operation is started. Others call it *commissioning* likening it to the shake down and commissioning of a naval vessel. Still others refer to it as *transition* because it is a transition from the old to the new. The author's experience is with the term *transition*, which is used throughout this section.

Why Is Transition Important?

The best way to answer this question is to look at what happens when insufficient attention is given to transition. In some cases, there has been inattention to specifications for supplies, equipment, and bidding time.

For example, the equipment was not what was wanted or needed and sometimes arrived too late for the scheduled opening. In other cases, supplies and equipment were never identified and the building could not be opened on time.

Without a good transition process, staffing requirements can be overlooked or early preliminary staffing projections are relied on even though conditions change. The result may be not enough staff being available to operate the new facility. If the facility is opened without adequate staff, considerable damage can be done to the facility because the inmates are not adequately supervised. In addition, planned services and programs to alleviate boredom and better manage inmate behavior simply cannot be implemented.

Staff training requirements also may be overlooked if there is not a good transition process in place. New facilities have opened only to find the staff did not know how the facility was supposed to function, or how to operate the new, more complex systems. In one instance, inmates were able to simply walk out the front door of the new jail because staff did not fully understand the door status indicator lights. In fact, most escapes from new facilities are due, in part, to staff error in operating the new facility.

Where the transition process is inadequate, facility systems have been improperly or inadequately tested and failed soon after occupancy, causing major facility disruption and posing threats to safety and security. Ultimately, the result of a poor transition is low staff morale, a loss of faith in management to solve the problems, and high staff turnover.

Although the author is unknown, the following quotation makes a very important point: "All of these problems could have been avoided or mitigated in these facilities if the local officials had recognized that the transition process is an essential part of the overall building process—no more or less important than, for example, having a good functional program prior to design."

The Process of Opening a New Facility

The opening of a new facility is a well-tested process. It is a series of major work tasks, subtasks, and activities directed toward having the new building and an adequate number of trained staff ready at a given point in time. Major work efforts include the following actions: writing new policies, procedures, and post orders; procuring dozens of equipment and supply items; hiring and train-

ing staff; and thoroughly testing all systems in the new building. The list of tasks, subtasks, and activities varies from facility to facility but will be several hundred items long.

The tasks are interdependent. In other words, each task builds on the previous task. Therefore, each task in the process must be done well before proceeding. If a task is not done correctly, it will likely have to be done over, wasting time and resources. Shortcuts are dangerous and should be avoided.

Organizing the Transition

The first step in the transition process is to "get organized." It involves identifying the major work tasks associated with transition and then developing a strategy for completing the tasks. *Strategy* refers to how the work will get done, by whom, and when. Time elements must be pieced together into a time line for the process, which will coincide with the completion of the facility.

Definition and Principles of Transition

Transition is defined as the completion of a set of post-design activities to occupy a new facility successfully. It ensures that an adequate number of properly trained staff are ready to operate the facility and that the facility, equipment, and supplies are ready for occupancy. A well-planned transition ensures that the staff and building are ready at a prescribed point in time.

There are several important principles associated with the transition process:

- **People Support What They Help Create**

  This principle highlights the need for line staff to be involved in the transition process. If involved, they are likely to take "ownership" of the new operation and thereby do their best to make it work. If left out of the process, staff can take a negative position of "it won't work," which may become a self-fulfilling prophecy.

- **Take Time to Do It Right**

  This principle addresses the issue that once the facility is opened, it is difficult to back up to correct mistakes. Therefore, the new operation must be thought out very carefully to anticipate and mitigate potential problems.

If extra time is needed to complete the transition, it should be taken. Too often, officials stick to an arbitrary opening date regardless of the consequences.

- **New Facilities Do Not Solve All Problems**

  It is important to remember that new facilities simply provide more and probably better space for correctional operations. Operational problems, such as staff not having adequate inmate supervision skills, easily can be transferred from the old to the new facility. Thus, the problem of a dirty facility or inmate damage to property can be just as prevalent in the new facility as in the old.

- **The Opening of the New Facility Provides an Opportunity for Change and Taking Control**

  Usually change is very slow and incremental in an organization. Staff will accept only a little change at a time. However, when a new facility is being opened, both staff and inmates expect—almost demand—major "changes for the better." Thus, the opening of the new facility provides an opportunity to scrutinize the existing operations and correct as many problems as possible.

The author, James Rowenhorst, and Captain George Bradshaw, the transition coordinator, review the transition progress for the opening of the Mecklenburg County Jail, in Charlotte, North Carolina.

Photo courtesy of James Rowenhorst.

Transition Budget Items

Introduction:
A transition process also costs money. Thus, a transition budget should be prepared showing the cost of the transition process. The budget should show *all* of the cost of the transition process including the costs that may be absorbed in existing budgets. In this way, policymakers have a clear understanding of the amount of resources required.

Personnel:
Agency Administrator (part-time)
Facility Administrator (part-time)
Transition Manager (full-time)
Transition Team Members (full-time)
Clerical Staff (full-time)
Fringe Benefits

Furnishings, Equipment and Supplies:
Desks, desk chairs, file cabinets, etc.
Computers, printers, copier, fax machine, etc.
Stationery, copy paper, legal pads, etc.

Other Office Expenses:
Office rent, telephone, postage, utilities
Printing policies, procedures, post orders and training materials

Travel:
To national conferences and to tour other facilities

The strategy, time line, and budget become the transition "plan," which will guide the transition process. The plan should be approved by the agency administration and funding/governing bodies. If not fully funded, the strategy may have to be adjusted to stay within the approved budget. The funding body should be notified of any repercussions from reducing transition funding and be made fully aware of the potential risk.

The process of opening a new detention facility will require a significant commitment of personnel. The transition manager or coordinator that is selected must be a good organizer, motivator, and supervisor. This individual must be someone who is capable of researching the facility opening process and developing a detailed plan. Then, the individual also must be capable of implementing the plan, including managing the process to accomplish tasks and adhering to time frames established in the plan. The manager must be capable of making adjustments to compensate for changing conditions and of supervising a team of individuals who actually will complete the transition tasks. Since the process involves interaction with other agencies, the transition manager must be well respected.

The transition team is a group of staff selected for their ability to complete the tasks, subtasks, and activities in the transition plan. Several transition staff will be required depending on the workload of the transition. Even a small jail will require a transition team composed of several members to complete the tasks. Large facilities may require a transition team of ten to twelve individuals. The transition planning function is a full-time job and staff assigned to the transition team should not be expected to perform the duties of their regular job. Temporary staff will have to be hired to address those job responsibilities that the transition team members did previously.

Transition team staff must be knowledgeable about modern correctional operations. They must have good oral and written communication skills. They must be self-starters and hard workers. They also must be respected by their peers since their work products must be accepted by their peers.

Office space also must be provided. At a minimum, the office must include a work station for each transition team member and a spare work station for others who may work on transition on a part-time basis. To the extent possible, office space should include a waiting area for persons waiting to see transition team members or to attend meetings, a meeting room, and space for files, a copier, a fax machine, and so forth. Good work space is absolutely essential to the efficiency and productivity of the transition team because of the amount of work that must be accomplished in a short amount of time.

Transition office equipment and furnishings also will be needed. These may include the following items:

- Desks/Workstations
- Desk chairs
- File cabinets
- Side chairs
- Copier
- Bookshelves
- Telephones
- FAX machine
- Computer terminals
- Wastebaskets
- Printer(s)
- Liquid chalkboard
- Conference/Meeting table and chairs

Furnishings being purchased for the new facility can be purchased early and used in the transition office. Thus, there is no additional cost.

Assembling Resource Documents

The transition process requires access to a number of resource materials. At a minimum, the transition team needs copies of facility planning documents and building specifications, applicable state statutes and codes, and state and national jail standards. These documents are routinely used by the transition team to identify and address operational issues. Several sets of the documents may be necessary since several staff may need access to them at the same time.

Training the Transition Team

Prior to undertaking the transition process, the transition team will require some special skills and knowledge to carry out a successful transition. This includes training in the following areas:

- Developing operational scenarios
- Developing a master facility activity schedule
- Writing policies and procedures
- Developing post orders
- Developing a staff training plan
- Training for the new facility
- Operating of similar facilities

The first five training subjects are covered in the National Institute of Corrections' "How to Open a New Institution" program. Facility training, including a thorough briefing on the design of the new building, should be provided to the transition team by the project archi-

tect. It is important to know and understand how various spaces were intended to be used. Also, visits to other facilities of a similar size and configuration should be made by the transition team to provide the team with a broader frame of reference from which to develop the operational procedures for the new facility.

Completing Major Work Tasks

Most of the transition effort surrounds the completion of a series of major work tasks. To a great extent, each task builds upon its predecessor; thus, each step must be done well before moving to the next task.

The most time consuming of these tasks is scenario development. During scenario development, the transition team carefully analyzes and describes every task or activity that takes place in the facility. For each task, the transition team must write a step-by-step description of how that task is done. Later, the written description will become the step-by-step procedures in the policy and procedure manual.

In scenario development, the transition team also will record equipment, supplies, and materials associated with each task, which will be used later for procurement purposes and as a final checklist to ensure everything is in place just prior to moving the inmates. Information concerning persons involved in each task is also recorded and used later in the transition process to prepare a staff training plan.

It is easy to see that many later tasks in the transition process are aided by scenario development; thus, sufficient emphasis must be placed on this task. An estimated 125 to 175 scenarios will be written for the new facility—some less than one page, while others will be several pages in length. Some simpler scenarios take only one or two hours, while others may take several days.

Scenario development is a combination of group and individual activities. Small groups (two or three staff) discuss how each activity will take place in the new facility. They should brainstorm the steps in the activity, list the equipment and supplies that will be needed, and specify who will be involved in the activity. One member of the small group takes notes and prepares the first draft of the scenario. Using floor plans, each scenario is tested by walking through each step and determining whether it will work. The scenario should be consistent with the functional program for which the building was designed and the architect's explanation of the use of various spaces. When facility spaces are available, the

In the construction of the Mecklenburg County Jail in Charlotte, North Carolina, the transition team moved to a construction trailer on the site to improve access to the new facility while developing scenarios, policies and procedures, post orders, and deciding on equipment furnishings and a supplies list.

Photo courtesy of James Rowenhorst.

scenarios should be tested on-site. The group reviews the first draft before submitting it for review and approval by the transition and agency administration.

Once the scenarios are completed, a number of other major tasks can take place. Since the transition team becomes intimately knowledgeable about the minute details of the new operation, they can construct a detailed master daily activity schedule for the facility. Since equipment, supplies, and materials were identified for each scenario, procurement lists can be created. For each item on the list, bid specifications must be developed and procurement procedures initiated.

Because the transition team develops a clear understanding of staffing requirements during scenario development, they can finalize the facility staffing plan. The staffing plan identifies staff positions or posts that must be filled and the hours the post must be covered. The plan's narrative should provide a justification for each position. A "shift relief factor" also must be calculated to provide sufficient staff to cover days off, holidays, staff vacations, sick days, military leave, training, and staff breaks. The shift relief factor is applied to the number of positions that must be filled to determine the total number of staff needed to operate the facility.

In addition, a staff activation plan must be developed. This plan identifies *all* the steps in the staff recruitment, hiring, and training process. Many months are usually needed to complete the staff activation process. Prior to hiring new staff, the completion date of the facility should be confirmed. If there are delays, staff hiring should be delayed.

The staffing plan and staff activation plans have significant budgetary impacts. Therefore, both will require approval by the funding body of the facility. If the staffing plan and staff activation plan are not fully funded, the transition team must adjust both plans while keeping the funding body fully informed of the repercussions of changes that are made to reduce costs. One alternative for reducing the cost of staff activation is to open the facility in phases. Phased opening may allow some new staff to be hired and trained after the initial opening of portions of the new facility.

Another major effort is the development of new policies and procedures describing the operation of the new facility in detail. This may require the writing or rewriting of 75 to 100 policies and procedures. Although the step-by-step description of an activity in the scenarios is the major part of policy and procedure development,

The Federal Medical Center at Butner, North Carolina, with a rated capacity of 763 beds, is scheduled for opening before 2000.

Architectural firm: Urbahn Associates, New York. Completing construction contractor: Lehrer McGovern Bovis, Inc., New York. Construction management firm: CRSS, Brooklyn, New York. Completing surety: American Home Assurance Company, New York. Photo courtesy of the Federal Bureau of Prisons.

considerable time is required to draft policy statements and translate the step-by-step description of how an activity is completed into the format and content of a policy and a procedure.

The transition team also writes post orders for every staff post or position in the new facility. A post order provides a chronological list of duties by time of day for a specific staff post. It also provides a list of unscheduled or continuous duties for which that post is responsible. Thus, staff assigned to a post know exactly what is required of them.

Staff Training

Two types of training are associated with the transition process. The first is the training required for new staff. New staff require the usual basic and on-the-job training of all new recruits. Since they must fill in for the existing staff when the existing staff are being trained to operate the new facilities, new staff must be fully trained in the operation of the existing facility. They also may need to complete the basic academy training to receive state certification. Completing this training may take twelve to fifteen weeks.

The second type of training is new facility operation training. Both the new and existing staff will require training concerning the new operation. Since the existing facility must continue to operate while staff are being trained, training must be done in several groups. For example, if a new detention facility requires 50 percent

more staff, the new staff could replace half of the existing staff at one time in the old facility while existing staff receive training in the operation of the new facility. Therefore, training to operate the new facility would be done in three groups. Typically, it will require eighty hours of training for staff to become proficient in the operation of the new facility. Therefore, in this example, it will take six weeks to train all of the staff in the operation of the new facility.

To ensure timely and adequate training, the transition team must develop a training plan identifying who has to be trained, what training is needed, how the training will be provided, and who will provide the training. A training schedule must be included in the plan. Subsequently, the transition team will develop classroom training materials and a field training manual. Training should be conducted as close as possible to the opening of the new facility to maximize staff retention of the knowledge and skills.

Building Preparation

In addition to getting the staff ready, the transition team must ensure that the building is ready for occupancy. This involves obtaining possession of the building and then thoroughly shaking it down, in other words, checking and testing everything over and over. Once possession is obtained, the building must be secured and access controlled by correctional staff. Typically, at this time, master control becomes operational to control entrance and movement within the facility. This allows for training of control room operators and thorough testing of security electronics. An entrance checkpoint also is established to check contractors in and out of the facility while they are correcting punch list items.

Building preparations include repeated testing of detention electronics, doors and locks, and fire response systems. As these systems are repeatedly checked, system failures are likely to occur and can be rectified prior to inmate occupancy. Building preparations also include:

- Receiving and installing owner-supplied furnishings and equipment (tag and inventory)
- Stocking supplies
- Arranging all necessary inspections
- Completing a thorough building search
- Arranging full mock operations to put the building systems under a load

All building preparations should be completed at least one week prior to the move of the inmates to allow time to resolve unforeseen last minute problems.

Making the Move

The move into the new facility must be planned well in advance of the move date. The transition team is responsible for drafting a move plan that specifies *how* the move will take place, *who* will be involved in the move, and *when* the move will take place. The transition team must determine the following things:

- The mode and route of transportation, both internal and external, for the move of the inmate population
- Personnel, transportation, and moving equipment needed for the move
- The types of personal property inmates will be allowed to take into the new detention facility
- What information will be provided to the inmates regarding the move and when it will needed
- Documents and contracts for movement of equipment and supplies
- What information will be released to the families of inmates and the general public regarding the move of the inmate population

Truckloads of supplies are stored at the Mecklenburg County Jail in Charlotte, North Carolina in preparation for the arrival of inmates.

Photo courtesy of James Rowenhorst.

The transition team must develop the following items:

1. Procedures for the reclassification of inmates just prior to the move based on the new facility's classification plan
2. A strategy for the disposition of personal property items that inmates will not be allowed to take into the new facility
3. Procedures for searching all inmates before they are moved to the new facility
4. Procedures for handling escape attempts, riots, and other disturbances or threats to security, which may occur during the move
5. Procedures for providing emergency medical services during the move
6. A strategy for serving meals during the move
7. A plan for the staffing of two facilities during the move

In addition to moving the inmate population, the transition team must include strategies for moving equipment and offices in the move plan.

Postoccupancy Activities

After the inmate population is moved, operations must be monitored carefully to ensure everything is operating as it was intended. When problems occur, timely corrective action must be taken. In some cases, this may require timely changes to policies and procedures or

additional staff training. Neglecting postoccupancy activities leaves a leadership void, which is filled by individual staff and inmates—neither of which is desirable.

Time Required for Transition

Transition literature indicates the following time requirements for a successful transition process:

Pretransition activities .... 2 to 4 months

Transition activities .... 15 to 18 months

Occupancy .... 1 to 2 months

Posttransition activities .... 1 to 12 months

The time required for transition depends, in part, on the amount of resources (staff) directed to the transition effort. Fewer resources necessitate an earlier start on the transition process. However, time frames depend on when certain work products must be completed. For example, training materials, which are derived from the scenarios,

policies and procedures, and post orders must be ready at the scheduled start of staff training.

The issue of time can best be handled when developing the transition plan. To ensure an appropriate start date, the plan should be completed at least eighteen months prior to obtaining possession of the building. Most transition processes take at least twelve to fifteen months. Part of it depends on how soon material/work products have to be done to meet the requirements of the staff activation schedule.

Conclusion

When undertaking the planning of a new correctional facility, it is important to recognize transition as a crucial part of the facility development process. Completing a thorough transition process ensures the successful opening of a new detention facility. Officials should start early and plan carefully.

Figure 8.1

Example of Staff Activation and Training Schedule

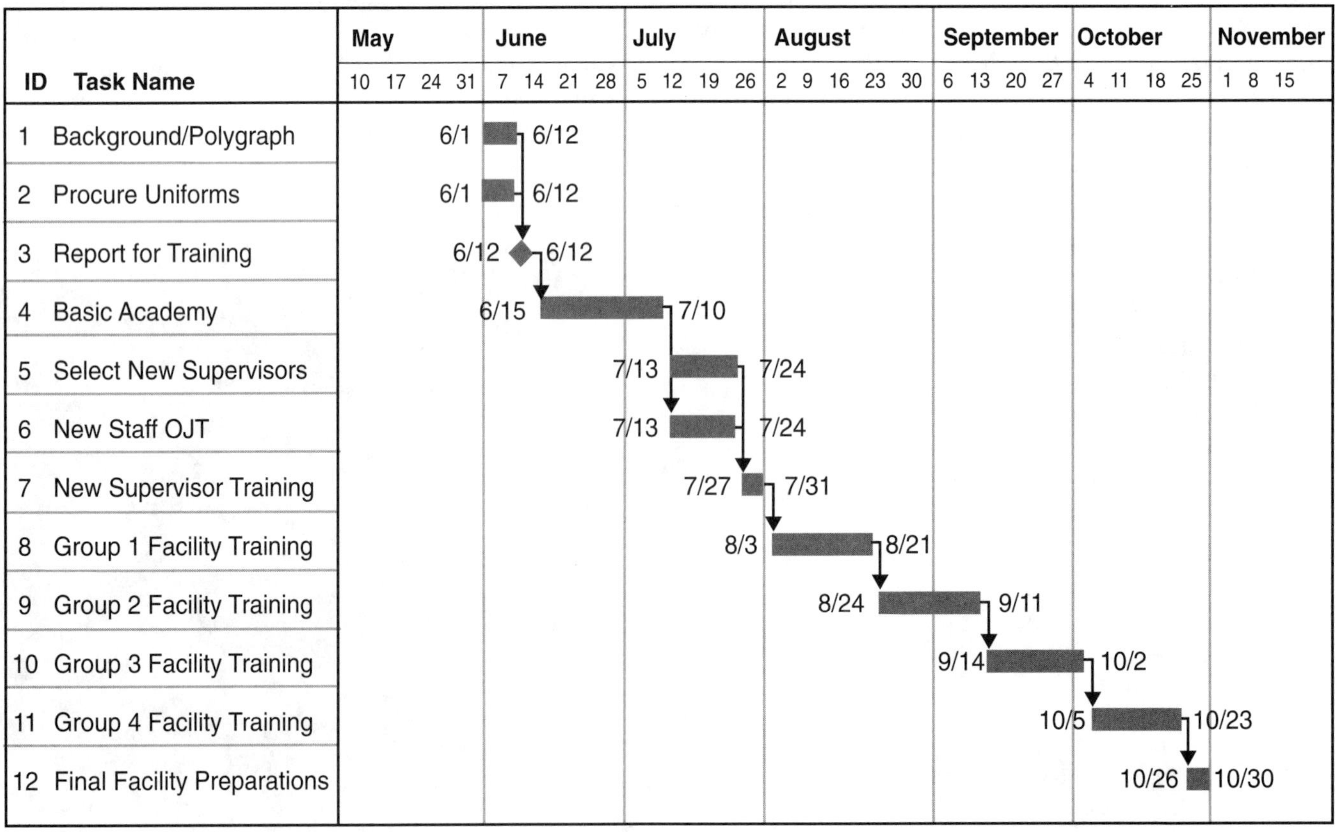

ID	Task Name	May	June	July	August	September	October	November
		10 17 24 31	7 14 21 28	5 12 19 26	2 9 16 23 30	6 13 20 27	4 11 18 25	1 8 15
1	Background/Polygraph	6/1 ▮ 6/12						
2	Procure Uniforms	6/1 ▮ 6/12						
3	Report for Training		6/12 ◆ 6/12					
4	Basic Academy		6/15 ▬▬ 7/10					
5	Select New Supervisors			7/13 ▬ 7/24				
6	New Staff OJT			7/13 ▬ 7/24				
7	New Supervisor Training			7/27 ▮ 7/31				
8	Group 1 Facility Training				8/3 ▬ 8/21			
9	Group 2 Facility Training				8/24 ▬ 9/11			
10	Group 3 Facility Training					9/14 ▬ 10/2		
11	Group 4 Facility Training						10/5 ▬ 10/23	
12	Final Facility Preparations						10/26 ▮ 10/30	

Chart courtesy of James Rowenhorst.

Figure 8.2

Example of Facility Transition Time Line Chart

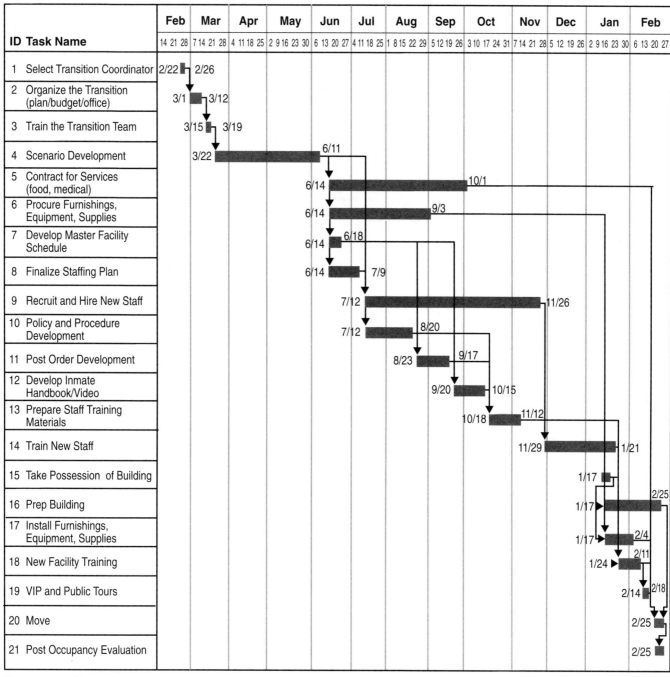

Chart courtesy of James Rowenhorst.

Privatization Versus Public Sector Development

The photo on the previous page shows an aerial view of the Lawrenceville Correctional Facility in Lawrenceville, Virginia. The facility was financed by the Corrections Corporation of America.

Architect: Arrington Watkins Architects, Phoenix, Arizona. Construction management firm: Canam Construction, Edmond, Oklahoma. Photo courtesy of Arrington Watkins Architects. Photographer: Bob Greene.

Privatization and the Delivery Process

Norman E. Wirkler
Durrant Group
Denver, Colorado

The recent history of privatization of secure detention and correctional facilities starts in the 1980s; however, by 1985 only 1,345 adult beds in correctional facilities were privatized. The use of privatization grew as the federal government began to experiment with the privatization of detention beds for the U.S. Marshals Service and the Immigration and Naturalization Service. These services did not have a tradition of running their own detention facilities, and most frequently, they contracted for beds with local or state agencies.

The move to contracting with a private company was therefore a rather simple step of expanding the contracting authority to private agencies rather than a government agency. Privatization efforts before the early 1980s were exclusively in areas considered to be more appropriate for private operations such as areas of prelease and community residential treatment centers and were not viewed as true privatization of corrections and detention by the corrections community.

The use of privatization, however, has a much more lengthy history in the United States and the world, for that matter, than most people realize. England contracted with early private plantation owners in the Colonies to send prisoners from England to the New World, where the privatization contracts often allowed or required the prisoner to stay in the Colonies after the sentence and the privatization contract were completed.

The early prison system in the United States also involved two distinctly different philosophies of detention and corrections. One philosophy (the workhouse concept) assumed that punishment for offenses should involve hard work as punishment, and various government entities contracted with private companies to provide work and housing for the prisoners. The second philosophy was that of the penitentiary, where individuals were isolated and locked up to ponder the seriousness of their misdeeds and to be penitent for those deeds. Thus, penitence is the source of the word *penitentiary*.

It is important to realize that privatization is not a completely new concept and has been, in and out of favor, with government, social philosophers, and the general public since before the start of our independence. The current trend, however, is part of a broader acceptance of privatization of all types of infrastructures in the United States.

The following discussion addresses several aspects of privatization in the United States. The lines are not clearly drawn, but to provide help to allow readers to understand the issues, we will discuss three different aspects of privatization of secure detention and corrections facilities. Remember, the three may be combined in a variety of ways. The three aspects involve (1) privatization of operations, (2) privatization of the real estate, and (3) privatization of supporting operations.

Privatization of Operations

In correctional privatization, the privatization of operations of secure detention and corrections facilities is the most common perception of the meaning of privatization. However, housing for pretrial, sentenced, prerelease, and community corrections for adults and juveniles all may fall within this general description. The private operator of the facilities may be a large public company or a private company. The private company may be a "for profit" or a "not for profit," but if the facility is not operated directly by a government entity, commonly it is considered to be privatized. The growth of privately operated facilities has been extremely rapid, at least in terms of percentage growth, from literally no secure beds privatized in 1980 to approximately 10 percent of all secure beds privatized at this time.

Some optimistic forecasts predict 20 percent or more of secure adult beds will be privatized in the next twenty years. The growth is even more remarkable when the overall growth of secure beds is considered. The total number of private and public beds has grown at a rate of almost 10 percent per year. Projections forecast 1,500,000 adult secure beds by the year 2005. In spite of the remarkable growth, it does not seem likely that private corrections ever will exceed, in number of beds, that of publicly operated secure facilities. Certainly, there are no predictions at this time that private facilities ever will completely replace the public sector beds.

Political factors and public sentiment currently keep some limitations on the growth of private corrections. Public employee labor unions, in some cases, have objected to privatization, which they see as a threat to their public employees' union membership. The pressure from the public employees or their elected representatives at local, state, and federal government levels continues to restrict some of the growth. Some states have laws prohibiting prisoners to be placed in private facilities in their state.

Jails (adult local detention facilities) have been the least privatized (in terms of the percentage of facilities or beds privatized) of all the various types of secure correction and detention facilities. There are several reasons; the majority of jails are small. There are approximately 3,201 jails in the United States, and 50 percent of all jail facilities are less than 50 beds, and these are not economically attractive to privatization interests. The pretrial aspect of the jail population also makes it difficult to maintain the jail occupancy population at steady levels. The requirements of movement of pretrial prisoners to court for appearances and the relatively short length of a stay make all but the larger county jails unattractive for the economies of privatization.

Privatization of Facilities (The Real Estate)

Several alternatives to public ownership of jails and prisons have been in place for a number of years. A quasiprivate alternative has been the establishment of a not-for-profit corporation to hold, own, and lease the facility to the government agency. There are also building authorities that own and lease jails and prisons to the states, counties, and municipal agencies. The financing of these facilities is accomplished by the sale of bonds or equivalent financial instruments, which often can be approved as tax exempt, in some cases double tax exempt —avoiding taxes at both the state and federal levels.

The owning entity builds and leases the facility to the government agency with a lease that is the same length as the term of the financing, and the facility lease often is designed to transfer the facility to the government entity at the end of the lease and financing period for a nominal sum, such as $1.00. The financing costs for this method of financing are slightly more than a full faith and credit general obligation (GO) bond but still relatively economical as the lease will be based on a tax-exempt financing instrument.

Privatization of jails and prisons also can be accomplished by the private sector as a straight lease or lease-purchase by a private company or developer. It is not at all unusual for cities, counties, states, and the federal government to lease facilities from private developers. Many of the rural post offices have been built and leased for years. The General Services Administration has had an aggressive program to place government agencies (including federal courts) in privately developed office buildings. State and local governments also extensively used this method to provide space for a variety of uses. There are also a number of privatized roads and sewer and water facilities, which are critical infrastructure facilities, for the communities they serve.

If the government is comfortable contracting for or leasing space for a wide variety of uses, why has the move to privatize facilities for jails and prisons been as slow as it has? The answer appears to be the specialized use of jails and prisons and the difficulty of converting these facilities to other uses at the end of the leases. It could be argued that post office facilities are also very specific uses and those building are not easily adapted to alternative uses. Whatever the reason, the reluctance of government agencies to consider leasing jails and prisons is being overcome rapidly. On the other side, developers and investment bankers see the projections and proof of continuing demand for correctional facilities, and they are more confident that the need and demand will continue for the term of the lease and financing, thus assuring a reasonably secure investment for the owner.

The third alternative is to have the private corrections operator provide both the facility and the lease. This can be accomplished directly by the facility operator or through a sister company that owns the real estate in a holding entity separate from the corrections' operating company. Real Estate Investment Trusts (REITs) are companies organized under specific Internal Revenue Service rules that allow for the ownership of real estate by companies that can distribute available revenues as dividends without first paying corporate tax prior to the distribution. Several REITs have been organized to own and lease correctional facilities to either private correctional operators or to government entities.

Some government agencies are more comfortable with the separation of the real estate from the private operations. It allows some future flexibility for the government to consider returning the facility to public operation from private operation or contracting for a change in the private operators without the accompanying risk of the private operator offering the facility to another entity and leaving the original government agency without the availability of the beds.

A government agency may choose to privatize its real estate for a number of reasons. One of the main reasons concerns putting the issue to the voters. For local governments agencies, cities and counties, funding a new facility often requires a referendum on a bond issue, and bond issues for jails for cities and counties are often very difficult to pass. Some states allow leases to be accomplished without a referendum.

The private sector also usually delivers a project quicker than it can be accomplished through the public process. For example, a bond issue for a county would involve a process that would start with the selection of a corrections planner and architect to develop a program and budget, then the process often would involve a public information process to educate the public on the need and the process. It would not be unusual for this process to take at least a year and often more than one year. After the bond issue referendum is approved by the voters, the design would be developed, the project bid, and construction completed.

Depending on the project size, at least eighteen months usually would be the minimum time to place the facility in operation. The total elapsed time would be at least three years. A fast-track privatized design-build-lease solution probably would cut that time in one-half. For an average project with a private delivery time of eighteen months, expect it to take three years to do the same project in the public sector. Time is a very important factor when considering crowding in our nations corrections facilities.

Privatization of Supporting Facilities

The privatizing of supporting facilities is a very prevalent and a much used form of privatization; yet, it often is overlooked as even being privatization. Government agencies use privatization of a wide variety of services in jails and prisons. The following are just some of the services that are privatized for a variety of reasons: food, laundry, medical, telephone, information, housekeeping, mechanical and electrical system maintenance, security system maintenance, and so forth. There are not a lot of statistics available on the amount of privatized support services but the level of privatization here is considerable. Some government agencies that do not consider themselves to be privatized may have only the detention and corrections officers provided by the public entity. The private corrections companies also further contract to other private companies for some of these services, making this the privatization of privatization.

Summary

Privatization is here to stay. The United States and state and local governments are accepting privatization of a wide variety of services. Privatization of corrections is also here to stay. The maturity of the private companies providing services for correctional facilities has allowed them to establish a track record of good service at a reasonable price.

Recently, a number of studies, most notably the Louisiana State University study *Cost Effectiveness: Cost Comparisons of Private versus Public Prisons in Louisiana* found that both public and private prisons could be effective in serving the need for prisons. The final conclusion noted that private prisons probably have a definite place in any state's total prison system. It also concluded that "No state should consider a totally privately operated prison system, nor should any state do business exclusively with only one vendor. To do so would result in the loss of dynamic competition." There is room for excellence in operating both public and private prisons, and the balance is healthy and will promote a higher level of design excellence and efficiency, creative solutions of operations, and competition for providing better measurable outcomes in reducing recidivism.

The Owner's Perspective and Goals

W. L. "Kip" Kautzky
Department of Corrections
Des Moines, Iowa

Although barely newsworthy in most detention or correctional institutions, the merger of Corrections Corporation of America (CCA) and Prison Realty Trust on January 1, 1999 raised important questions for correctional agencies. The merger raised the toughest question for corrections—Who is in charge? Within that question is the highly charged issue of state liability for offenders assigned to the care of private providers. The policy question of how correctional agencies could position themselves where a private company could show up on Monday morning and advise a state correctional agency that a new and different company now owns their contract for private prisons is an important issue. If you are still a disbeliever, ask those states who were doing business with the U.S. Corrections Corporation in Louisville, Kentucky but now are owned by Corrections Corporation of America.

In the business world, profitability speaks louder than any other variable.

To correctional administrators, this is a foreign language. Yet, understanding business strategy will improve an agency's success in structuring private sector deals. Lincoln's guidance about measuring twice and sawing once is practical guidance for carpentry and for crafting private sector deals. Both legislators and the private sector use other people's money. As a result, due diligence is in order whether the legislature authorizes the agency or is forced to consider private sector options when the Federal court is at the door. In either case, it is important for the user agency to understand and craft the rules of engagement.

Rule One: Define What Private Sector Firms Are Expected to Do

Although Federal court orders make a difference in budget negotiations with legislators, correctional agencies are typically like dependent families. Their financial destiny is mired in the public policy debate that typically adds or takes away resources based on variables that most businesses would find unreliable. Whether other state needs are met is of little or no concern to business. Private operators are interested in their own deal. The liability of Federal court takeovers may be equally unpersuasive since it suggests policymakers may not control their own destiny. After all, looking after kids by putting money into school is more marketable during November elections.

Business understands correctional agency dependency. By deploying proposals not bound by such standards, they offer policymakers a way to neutralize the policy stalemate. If you do not want to put state money into more prisons, let the private sector take the risk. Business lobbies policymakers heavily on being able to provide correctional services quicker and cheaper. The prospect of not requiring the state to fork over capital funds to build the facility is a marketing strategy. Underneath this transparent strategy lurks the long-term bonds and the equivalent mortgages.

To improve success, correctional administrators must approach the project as a business proposal. If the legislature authorizes private facility development, the agency must know both operating and financial issues including:

1. Does the state want a private firm to design and build a facility?
2. Does the agency want a private firm to operate the facility?
3. Will the state authorize bond funds to build the facility?

If the legislature does not authorize a facility for state use, will the state limit speculative prison development through a licensure process? Particularly when private development is deferred due to labor union pressures, the Ohio question of whether another state's correctional clients should be placed in your backyard should be considered as a practical matter. Both Ohio and Arizona can provide practical guidance on this matter.

Rule Two:
Correctional Agencies Should Control the Contract Specifications

Because the state is the funding source, the rules of engagement are particularly critical. In some jurisdictions, there are reasons to choose a Request for Qualifications over a Request for Proposal if the agency wants to find the best firm. A Request for Proposal assumes legislative authorization and a greater level of precision and control during the procurement process. A Request for Qualifications assumes the agency will select the best firm and rely on their judgments to complete the project. However, both processes require the agency to specifically understand what they want the private firms to propose.

Recommended Questions and Issues

- Organization structure for the project
- Experience of the person responsible for the project
- Five years of audited financial records
- Corporate status--publicly or privately held
- Unresolved legal liability in last five years by specific case
- Experience in managing security level of facility in Request for Proposal /Request for Qualification
- The general contractor used by the firm
- Experience in selling bonds to pay for capital projects

Under building specifications, the following items should be included:

- Capacity—number of cells or dorm beds
- Security level of each housing unit, such as maximum, segregation, medium, minimum, and so forth
- Single cell or multiple cell occupancy
- Staff efficiency requirement (for example: a minimum of 30 percent of the housing will be configured in double tiered single cell configuration of not more than twenty-four cells to a unit. Units may be grouped for efficiency around a single control indirect supervision control room supervising no more than three units of twenty-four each.)
- Administrative segregation space
- Medical housing—inpatient or infirmary space requirement
- Program space—educational, vocational, religious,
- Administration housing including the department of correction on site monitor
- Private sector work program
- Requirements to use state prison industry
- Requirements to provide schematic level architectural drawings

The following operations requirements must be included:

- A table of organization and equipment
- Staffing pattern analysis by custody position, shift, and post assignment
- Salary range for each separate classification
- Medical staffing requirements for inpatient and outpatient
- Subcontracted services--medical, canteen, private sector labor
- Offender work program criteria—number of offenders working by category and location
- Educational contract with local educational agencies--community college
- Vocational staffing and building structure
- Disposition of canteen funds and telephone rebate funds for inmate use
- Records management--confidentiality and agency requirements
- Information technology compatibility

Making the final decision to hire a firm requires legislative, executive, and judicial involvement. Evaluation requires outside involvement by architectural and planning firms who understand the state requirements. The several thousand dollars in evaluation costs can save the state large sums by defining the areas for negotiation prior to execution of the contract. Key players always will include the state procurement agency, state attorney general, key legislators in the correctional appropriation process, and architects and engineers from the agency with construction oversight. With a defined process, state agencies can achieve exactly the items that they are willing to negotiate.

Privatization from the Developer's Perspective

Lynn Arrington
Arrington Watkins Architects
Phoenix, Arizona

As was discussed earlier, the recent developments in the privatization of jail and prisons started in the early 1980s. Developers of facilities have been faced with changing and evolving procurement and contracting formats. Many contracting methods have been used in the past ten years, but two types of contracting formats have dominated the private development process.

The first, most frequently used and all encompassing contracting format is for a developer to finance, construct, and operate a facility at a fixed rate to the agency, in most cases based on a per-diem per-inmate basis. The second and less frequently used type of contract is for facilities to be financed, developed, and leased to the agency. This option includes operation of the facility by a private operator or operation by the agency.

Both contracting approaches have been used, with the owner/operator companies holding the largest share of the private market. But the trend in private development of facilities is changing with governing agencies looking more toward self-operated leased facilities. This section will address, from the developer's perspective, why this trend seems to be developing, and provide some insight on how each contracting method has affected the end product, "the facility."

Private Developments in the Early 1980s

The majority of privately operated jail and correctional facilities developed in the United States are facilities owned and operated by companies that provide both development and operation services. These companies provide complete corrections and detention services on a contract basis based on an inmate per-diem rate structure. Typically, the process for selection of these companies has been through the solicitation of competitive per-diem cost.

The Request for Proposals soliciting these facilities were very "loose" in defining the requirements of the facility in terms of operational requirements, space needs, and security requirements. Request for Proposal requirements were in effect only requiring the developers to provide a specified number of beds and to meet American Correctional Association standards, and federal, state, and local code requirements. Developers were left to determine the facility space requirements, facility configurations, and the quality of the level of construction.

In addition, the operational aspects of the facility were left to the companies to develop and propose. The structure of facility administration, training of staff, security procedures, and many, many other aspects were in total control of the proposing company. The facilities developed in the early to the mid 1980s were developed by owner/operator companies, and the quality of the facilities for the most part was of equal quality to their counterpart facilities developed by the governmental sector.

As more agencies requested proposals for privatization of their populations, and competition grew, the private operators were faced with the challenge of reducing costs to remain competitive. Staffing was and is the largest cost of operating a facility, and the private sector began to reduce staffing levels at existing facilities and proposed fewer staff for new facilities.

By the late 1980s, several agencies were facing difficulties with privately operated facilities being run with too few and, in some cases, with minimally trained staff. This problem later would be addressed by a new contracting method, the separation of contracts for facility development and operations.

Private Developments in the 1990s

By the mid 1990s, most Request for Proposals were asking for a separation of the costs for the physical facility development contract and the operations contract. Contracts for the facilities were being developed with long-term lease rates for the facilities with buyout language. Operational contracts were being written for two-to-three year duration, with renewal clauses and minimum staffing level requirements. This contracting method was used to try and get better control on the operations of the facility. If the private operator could not do the job, the agency could take it away and operate it themselves or contract with other private operators. Monitoring of facilities' operations by governmental agencies, became an integral part of private facilities' operations.

The split contract format (lease contract/operations contract) did have an effect on the type of facility being proposed by facility developers. This type of contract opened the market to a different type of proposing team. Owner/operators could not be assured of recovering construction costs from the operation contract and vice versa. Each aspect would be required to stand on its own. The market was opened further to developer contractor/operator team combinations. Operation groups that did not have access to development funds now could join with the developer and contractors and compete for contracts. The split contract format, however, would introduce a new set of concerns for the development of private facilities.

The private market had responded to the lowering of construction costs, but as the number of competitors increased, so did the pressures to reduce costs and be competitive. The developers under this new contracting format, not being directly responsible for operations and maintenance of the facility, tended to see most facilities as overdesigned and sought to reduce the facility to its minimum size. The operations groups felt that facilities needed to address operational conveniences and allow for the most cost-effective operation. Subjects like the size of warehouses, the need for vehicle maintenance, the capacity of freezers to allow bulk buying, all were issues that created hardships for one or the other of the groups. Incorporating these features raised the cost of the facility. Not providing them raised the cost of operation.

Many of the competitors entering the market were not owner/operator companies, but were associations of developers/contractors and operation companies. Because response times to Request for Proposals were relatively short, the design presented and the operations proposed did not always complement one another. Even though the Request for Proposals described in more detail the requirements for staffing levels and stating policy and procedures, the facility's physical requirements were largely undefined and open to developer's interpretation.

As developers interested in developing facilities with long-term leases, the pressure to develop the most cost-effective facility sometimes outweighed providing some important functions, low maintenance high front end cost equipment or security features. From the using agency's perspective, the minimal program definitions and facility space requirements in the Request for Proposals has allowed the developer to cut corners and develop facilities that agencies feel would not meet their needs. But, in fact, price, schedule, and the ability to avoid capital funds commitments have allowed contracts to be written and facilities to be built.

The Latest Development Trends

The latest trend in privatization of facilities may allow the government agencies to get the best of both contract formats. In the past several years, a few developer/contractors have emerged with the experience and ability to finance and construct speculative facilities and offer them for lease to the federal, state, and local agencies. They have proven their ability to design and construct quality facilities, which meet and exceed the type of facilities being developed by the government agencies. They are able to secure financing that is competitive and complete

Corrections Corporation of America financed, designed, built, and manages the Shelby Training Center in Memphis, Tennessee for the Juvenile Court of Memphis and Shelby County. Opened in 1987, the Shelby Training Center provides a secure residential alternative for juvenile males, ages eleven through twenty-one.

Architect: Nathan, Evans, Taylor, Coleman, and Foster, Memphis, Tennessee. Photo courtesy of Corrections Corporation of America.

construction of a facility several years ahead of the government sector.

These developers now are engaging in the development of speculative facilities, designed to meet the needs of specific inmate populations, and the operational needs of the agencies. Their desired contract format is a long-term facility lease with the agency providing the operation or contracting for private operation. Speculative development is an aggressive approach but from the developer's perspective—one that has many advantages for all involved: the governments, the department, the building authorities, and the developer/contractor.

Politically, the state or local governments have little or no risk in the venture until they can evaluate the facility's performance and quality. Even though the facility will be offered at a lease rate, which was not competitively bid, the agency has a very good negotiating position, because there are a limited number of potential users. The agency's position is equal to but opposite that of the developer, and this will result in a fair and equitable negotiation for both parties. Contracts most likely will be developed with buyout clauses, which would allow the governmental agency to benefit in the long run. Use of this method means that the delivery time for the facility is far better than what could be achieved otherwise with little or no time lost in the procurement process. Thus, facilities will be on line to meet the current needs.

For the department, facilities developed for operation by the agency will eliminate the disparity in policy and procedures experienced when facilities are both privately operated and agency operated within one system. The agency will have total control of the operations, with policy and procedures defined by the agency. Treatment of inmates or prisoners will be consistent. The department will experience less competition for staff with the elimination of the disparity of pay between the private operator and the agency

There also are benefits for the building authorities. Agencies will be able to maintain control through the permit and inspection process. In some cases, they can provide some development standards and guidelines to the developer.

Certainly there are benefits for the developer/contractor. For the developer, the speculative approach presents several advantages. Developing a project with low risk and minimal competition is important. Controlling construction cost and monitoring the design approach minimizes risks taken during design and construction. The ability to select proven subcontractors and use the contractor's buying power reduces construction schedules and costs. Constructability issues are controlled, land acquisition cost is in the developer's favor, without inflated pricing due to agency-imposed site location restrictions.

The pressure to develop a facility that will meet the agency's needs, be used by the agency, and be cost-effective enough to lower the agency's cost, is a better incentive for a developer to build a quality facility than the competitive bidding process. Allowing the developer to take full advantage of the free market conditions will

Corrections Corporation of America financed, designed, built, and manges the Kit Carson Correctional Center in Burlington, Colorado. Opened in late 1988, the facility houses adult male inmates for the state of Colorado.

Architect: DLR Group, Omaha, Nebraska. Photo courtesy of Corrections Corporation of America.

improve their margins and still allow them to deliver a cost-effective facility, maintain a good return for investors, and profit from the risk taken.

If the speculative developer goes too far in either direction, cutting corners or raising costs, the results will be a facility that is either too expensive to lease to the agency or one which does not meet the needs of the governmental agency. The market for private development is limited by the willingness of investors to take risk and the government agency's willingness to turn over control of design and construction.

Private development and operation of jails and correctional facilities have come a long way in the past twenty years. The industry has experienced many problems and has weeded out many companies that were not competitive or competent. The remaining companies are very responsive and cost effective. Traditional procurement methods for facilities and services will need to change to take advantage of the opportunities the private market has to offer. Refinement without over control will be necessary if the private market is to be given a chance to prove its abilities. The future is exciting and will be challenging for all involved.

Conclusion

As shown on the previous page, the Federal Detention Center, Houston, Texas, is ready to begin its commissioning before it accepts any inmates. This facility has a rated capacity of 670 beds.

Architect/engineer: 3D/International, Inc., Houston, Texas. Construction contractor: Hensel Phelps Construction Company, Houston, Texas. Construction management firm: CRSS Constructors Inc., Houston, Texas. Photo courtesy of the Federal Bureau of Prisons.

10

Conclusion

Leonard R. Witke, AIA
XCEL 4 Associates
Oconomowoc, Wisconsin

"Stone walls do not a prison make nor iron bars a cage." These words were written by Richard Lovelace, 1618-1658, in his letter, "To Althea from Prison." For individuals working in the field of corrections, these words hold a variety of messages.

For some, Mr. Lovelace's words may refer to the separation of prisoners from their loved ones and the anxiety of being in prison. For others, the statement may address the feelings of loss that inmates experience when they realize they have given up so much as a result of their incarceration and the need on staffs' part to help those individuals regain an interest in life and themselves while serving their sentence. Still others look at Mr. Lovelace's poetic line as a reminder that as planners, designers, builders, and users, we must take our roles very seriously in the planning and construction of new corrections and detention facilities.

When elected officials ask the citizens of this country if they should be tough on crime, the answer that routinely comes back is "yes!" The average taxpayer does feel strongly that people who break the law should be punished. What that person often does not understand is that these same individuals someday will be back on the street and could be their neighbors. When presented with that scenario, the same taxpayer probably would suggest that the criminal justice system do something to rehabilitate the individuals while they are incarcerated so that they can be more productive, law-abiding citizens on release. If we want our next construction project to make a positive difference in the lives of the inmates, we must commit to discharging our responsibilities as good planners effectively and without bias.

The responsibility of agencies to effectively address the requirements of special needs inmates and still maintain appropriate levels of services and programs for all inmates is very challenging. Generally, it is easier to accomplish these tasks in larger institutions or systems. However, every facility shares a responsibility to manage inmate populations and provide equal opportunities for services and programs and to classify inmates in an effort to maintain a safe and secure environment.

Addressing advances in technology and providing access to new learning tools, including computers and distance learning video systems, are clearly important to the rehabilitation of inmates. However, we must go further if our correctional system, jail, or juvenile detention center is going to make a significant difference in the lives of inmates or juveniles assigned to our facilities.

Programs and space must be provided to train inmates in trades and skills that will enable them to gain good work habits and reestablish their self-respect and sense of responsibility to themselves and others. Institutions can continue to be places where society separates those who have committed crimes but at the same time, prison or jail sentences should not be a period of unproductive time with regard to the inmate. Our society, if judged by the quality of our prisons, cannot afford to simply punish inmates for the time of their incarceration. Rather, we must commit to doing better by these individuals so that we all will reap the benefits from the time that they spend behind bars.

The end result should be a facility that provides a secure and safe environment, for both staff and inmates, supports rehabilitation, adheres to national and local building design standards, and maintains human dignity. It should be flexible and capable of change to meet the new and still undefined needs of the future. It should be a facility that both the staff and society can be proud of based on a mission statement that includes improving the inmates or juveniles who are in its charge.

Biographies
of Authors

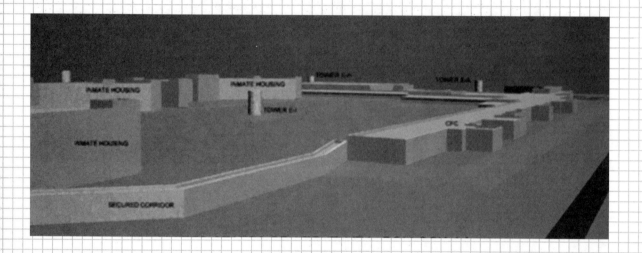

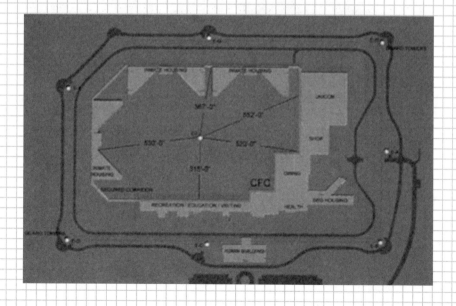

The computer graphics on the previous page show a three-dimensional model and the layout design from which it was rendered. The model enables planners to see the views from the tower locations before they are built. This enables planners to trace the light source and see the shadow lines.

Images courtesy of the Federal Bureau of Prisons.

Planning and Design Guide for Secure Adult and Juvenile Facilities

Biographies of Authors

The biographies were supplied by the authors and edited for style and consistency. The address and phone number of the authors is at the end of their paragraph so that you can contact them.

Leonard R. Witke, AIA, Editor of *Design Guide*

Leonard Witke is a registered architect with more than twenty-seven years of experience in the practice of architecture. For the past twenty years, he has focused his career in the areas of public service and institutional facilities design, planning, construction, and management. He was an employee of the Wisconsin Department of Corrections where he held the positions of director of facilities management and staff architect. He was responsible for the development and management of the capital budget. During his tenure there, he was responsible for an annual capital budget program of $100 million and a prison expansion program that added roughly 6,000 prison beds to the system at a cost of approximately $350 million. System expansion included adult male and female as well as juvenile beds. In 1995, Mr. Witke created the consulting firm of Witke Planning Associates, in Madison, Wisconsin. The firm specialized in correctional facilities planning, security systems design and architecture for juvenile and adult correctional facilities. As principal of this firm, Len participated in the planning, design, and construction of several county and state justice facilities. In January 1999, Mr. Witke, in partnership with fellow architect and construction manger Ludwig Ridder, established XCEL 4 Associates, Inc. This firm also specializes in the planning, design, and construction management of justice facilities. Mr. Witke is a member of the American Correctional Association's Tech-

nology Committee and the Facility Design Committee. He also has been a member of the National Institute of Justice's Corrections Technology Advisory Committee. He is a regular speaker at the University of Wisconsin on Justice Facilities Planning, Programming and Design. XCEL 4 Associates, Inc., P.O. Box 1060, Oconomowoc, Wisconsin 53066-6060, (262) 369-0600 Fax: (262) 369-0800, e-mail at lrwitke@execpc.com

Paul Allyn

Paul Allyn is a principal of Justice Systems Corporation, consulting engineers who partner with criminal justice agencies to design upgrades and replacements of their security electronic systems. Mr. Allyn holds a Bachelor of Science degree in Electrical Engineering, graduating cum laude from the University of Washington, Seattle, and is a licensed electrical engineer in the states of California, Washington, Oregon, Nevada, Texas, and Hawaii. Paul founded Justice Systems in 1994 and has overseen its growth to nine employees and three offices. In all, sixteen years of Paul's twenty-year career have been devoted to detention electronic systems. He is a member of the American Correctional Association, American Jail Association, and the National Fire Protection Association. Mr. Allyn recently has authored guide standards for touch screen security systems as a member of the ASTM F-33 Committee for Detention and Correctional Facilities. Justice Systems, 1495 Northwest Gilman Blvd., Suite 4, Issaquah, Washington 98027, 425-392-2328

Judy C. Anderson

Judy C. Anderson has a Bachelor of Science degree from the University of Southern Mississippi and a Master of Arts degree from the University of South

Carolina. She has completed all course work for a doctorate degree. She has worked with women and girls and other special needs offenders for more than twenty-five years, serving as a warden for the South Carolina Department of Corrections for sixteen years. Presently, she is Chief of Institutional Operations, South Carolina Department of Juvenile Justice. In 1998, she received the American Correctional Association E. R. Cass Correctional Achievement Award. South Carolina Department of Juvenile Justice, Operations Division, 4678 Broad River Road, Columbia, South Carolina 29212, 803-896-9753

Lynn Arrington

Lynn Arrington was graduated from Kansas State University in 1973 with a Bachelor of Architecture degree. Since that time, he has been responsible for the planning, design, and construction of major projects in the areas of criminal justice, high-tech, and office buildings. He is registered with NCARB in fifteen states, including his home state of Arizona. He has designed more than $850 million worth of state and local criminal justice facilities, ranging from juvenile facilities to maximum-security facilities. These facilities represent more than 26,000 beds and include two 4,200-bed prison complexes for Arizona and California's Pelican Bay Prison. Mr. Arrington has completed six major design-build projects in the past five years, totaling 7,100 beds. In addition to his knowledge of security electronics and detention hardware, Mr. Arrington has developed many innovations that allow facilities to be built economically and run at very efficient staffing levels. Arrington Watkins Architects, 5240 North 16th Street, Suite 101, Phoenix, Arizona 85016, 602-279-4373

Randall Atlas

Randall Atlas, Ph.D., AIA, C.P., of Atlas Safety & Security Design, Miami, Florida serves on the American Correctional Association's Design and Technology Committee and serves as technical assistant and consultant for the National Institute of Corrections and the U.S. Department of Housing and Urban Development. Dr. Atlas is both an architect and a criminologist. He has been involved in the design of more than fifty correctional facilities. He has authored numerous articles on prison and jail security, inmate suicide prevention, and compliance with the Americans with Disabilities Act. For more information contact him at: www.CPTED-security.com. Atlas Safety & Security Design, 770 Palm Bay Lane, Suite 4I, Miami, Florida 33138, 305-756-5027

Major Don Bales

Major Don Bales, U.S. Army, retired, Maryland Department of Corrections, retired, was a custody shift commander for twenty-two years. He now serves on the adjunct faculty at Hagerstown Community College, and is a consultant/trainer, for the Maryland Police and Corrections Training Commission. He was the editor of the American Correctional Association's *Correctional Officer Resource Guide,* Third Edition. P.O. Box 144, Gerrardstown, West Virginia 25420, 304-229-2143

Kendal Ball

Kendal Ball is a corrections consultant for the Ohio Department of Youth Services. He is a recognized leader in planning, developing, and implementing correctional and detention facilities and programs. He has guided the planning of more than fifty facilities in numerous states, several of which have received recognition, including the American Correctional Association's "Best Practices" award. Mr. Ball has worked with state, county, local governments, and private providers. For more than twenty years he served as an institutional administrator in several correctional facilities with the Ohio Department of Youth Services. He is a member of the American Correctional Association's Juvenile Corrections Committee, the Facility Design Committee, and serves as an American Correctional Association Auditor. Mr. Ball is also the Executive Director of the Ohio Public Facilities Association. Ohio Department of Youth Services, 3833 Overdale Drive, Columbus, Ohio 43220, 614-457-4860

Sandra Brand

Sandra Brand is a project manager with Kennedy Associates Incorporated, a St. Louis based architectural and engineering firm. Ms. Brand has more than seventeen years of experience in the planning and design of judicial and correctional facilities. This includes managing the design of a new 1,500-bed state prison in Southeast Missouri and a new 732-rated bed, direct-supervision Justice Center for the City of St. Louis. She is the 1999 Citation Award winner in the American Institute of Architect's Committee on Architecture for Justice and the American Correctional Association's Justice Facilities Review. Ms. Brand is a graduate of the University of Michigan College of Architecture and Urban Planning, from which she received a Bachelor of Science in 1982. She completed her Masters of Architecture from the University of Colorado in 1989. Kennedy Associates, Inc., One Metropolitan Square, 211 North Broadway, Suite 1900, St. Louis, Missouri 63102, 314-241-8188 X275

Jeff Buck

J. Alan Buck (Jeff) is an architect who has specialized in program planning for criminal justice facilities for more than twenty years, getting his introduction to corrections as Director of Facilities Planning and Development for the New York State Department of Correctional Services from 1978 to 1982. Subsequently, he has had his own program planning firm and has been a principal in major architectural firms doing justice work. Jeff is presently justice planning principal for Daniel, Mann, Johnson, & Mendenhall. Working out of DMJM's New York Office, he is involved with client agencies defining facility programs and developing operationally effective conceptual designs across the country. Jeff got his Bachelor of Science in Architecture at the University of Cincinnati (1968), and his Master's Degree in Architecture at Rensselaer Polytechnic Institute (1970). He has been involved in the planning, design, and/or construction of more than 120,000 prison and jail beds in the United States. DMJM Architects, 300 East 42nd Street, 10th Floor, New York, New York 10017, 518-281-7948

Stephen Carter

Stephen Carter, AICP, is the founder and president of Carter Goble Associates, Inc. His Bachelor's Degree in Architecture is from Clemson University. His Master's diploma in Urban Design and Planning is from the Architectural Association, London, England, with additional postgraduate studies in economics. He has served on the faculty of the College of Architecture and Planning at Clemson University, and other colleges, including as a trainer at the National Academy of Corrections in Colorado. Since 1995, he has been an instructor in the Harvard Graduate School of Design. He has assisted more than 35 states, 300 countries, and several foreign countries in formulating public policy and plans. He is involved in technical studies in the areas of needs assessment, operational and architectural programming, design review, program management, and policy evaluation. Carter Goble Associates, Inc., 1619 Sumter Street, Columbia, South Carolina 29201, 803-765-2833

Steven Chianesi

Steven F. Chianesi, MSW, ACSW, was assistant director for Rhode Island's judicial information systems. For eleven years, he administered the MIS Unit, Records/ID/Bail operation of the Rhode Island Department of Corrections. Previously, he was the assistant administrator of the state's juvenile correctional institutions. He is a member of the American Correctional Association and on the Northeast Regional Chapter of the National Law Enforcement and Corrections Technology Council of the National Institute of Justice. He also serves on the Technical Advisory Committee for the Rhode Island Governor's Justice Commission and the Infrastructure Working Group of the Global Criminal Justice Information Network Advisory Committee of the U.S. Department of Justice. His psychology degree is from Rhode Island College. He also holds a Master's Degree in Social Work. Mr. Chianesi is now with Rhode Island Judicial Systems and Sciences, Supreme Court of Rhode Island, Rhode Island Traffic Tribunal, 345 Harris Ave., Providence, Rhode Island 02909, (401) 222-5055.

Karen Chinn

Karen Chinn is the founding principal of Chinn Planning Inc., a consulting firm in Columbia, South Carolina. Ms. Chinn has wide experience in needs assessment, program evaluation, operational analyses, system master planning, and facility programming for criminal justice, law enforcement, juvenile justice, human services, health care, and general government agencies. She is a member of the American Correctional Association, the American Jail Association, National Juvenile Detention Association, American Planning Association, National Association of Counties, and the International Association of Chiefs of Police. Ms. Chinn holds a Bachelor of Arts degree and a Master of Urban and Regional Planning from the University of Illinois. She also attended the George Washington University, School of Government and Business Administration, Department of Urban and Regional Planning in Washington, D.C., with a concentration in policy analysis and program evaluation. Chinn Planning Partnership, 1314 Lincoln Street, Suite 214, Columbia, South Carolina 29201, 803-779-1999

Jerry P. Christoff

Jerry Christoff is a member of the Committee on Acoustics in Corrections. He is a president and principal of Veneklasen Associates with more than forty-one years experience in architectural acoustics. One of his specialties is the acoustical design of detention facilities. His projects include the Lynwood Regional Justice Center, Los Angeles Metropolitan Detention Center, and the Los Angeles County Jail Expansion. Mr. Christoff also lectures on acoustics at Woodbury University and the Art Center College of Design. Veneklasen Associates, 1711 16th Street, Santa Monica, California 90404, 310-450-1733, jchristoff@Veneklasen-assoc.com

Clinton Fairchild

Clinton Fairchild has provided services for more than twenty-five years as an architect on dozens of prisons and jails delivering 21,000 beds for juveniles and adults, males and females. Mr. Fairchild's experience is further broadened with past jobs including those at all security custody levels with project budgets ranging from $2 million to $180 million. Currently, he is working with Heery International, 999 Peachtree Street, NE, Atlanta, Georgia 30367, 404-881-9880

Robert G. Falter

Captain Robert G. Falter, USPHS, Ph.D., FACHE, CCHP-A, is the administrative officer at the Federal Bureau of Prisons Federal Medical Center, Devens, Massachusetts. This 986-bed correctional facility with an adjacent 150-bed satellite prison camp houses medical, mental health, and low- and medium-security general population inmates. From 1991-1999, he was the chief, of the Budget and Management Support Branch, Office of the Assistant Director, Health Services Division, Federal Bureau of Prisons, Washington, D.C. He began his career in 1977 as the first nonphysician director of the United States Public Health Service Outpatient Clinic, Centers for Disease Control in Atlanta, Georgia. Captain Falter received a Bachelor of Arts degree in Speech from St. John's University in 1967, an M.A. degree in Audiology from Kean University in 1973, an M.B.A. degree in Health Services Administration from Cornell University in 1976, and a Ph.D. in Health Services from Walden University in 1993. Federal Bureau of Prisons, P.O. Box 880, 42 Patton Road, Ayer, Massachusetts 01432, 978-796-1000

Cheryl Fuller

Cheryl D. Fuller is President of Fuller, Coe & Associates, Inc. (FCA) of Sacramento, California. Ms. Fuller is a skilled facilities planner and programmer, having worked for more than sixteen years with a broad range of both state and county public sector clients in the criminal justice field. Her resume comprises needs assessments, master plans, operational and architectural programs, and postoccupancy evaluations. Her range of experience includes planning and evaluating both juvenile and adult facilities and programs for all custody levels of male and female inmates and wards, with particular expertise in populations having special medical, mental health or substance abuse treatment needs. Fuller, Coe & Associates, 2750 Gateway Oaks Drive, Suite 300, Sacramento, California 95833, 916-648-6545

Glenn Gauger

Glenn Gauger, AIA, is Senior Associate and Director of Government and Justice Facilities Planning and Design for Korsunsky Krank Erickson, Architects, Inc. (KKE), Minneapolis, Minnesota. He is responsible for directing the resources, planning, and design of justice projects for KKE. Over the last twenty-five years, he has directed or participated in the planning, programming, design, or construction of more than 100 justice facilities in 30 states and Australia. During that time, he directed justice design and construction for two of the nation's most prominent firms specializing in justice facilities. Several of Mr. Gauger's justice projects have been recognized for exemplary design by the AIA Committee on Architecture for Justice/American Correctional Association Exhibit Program. Mr. Gauger is Past Chair (1997) for the American Institute of Architecture Committee on Architecture for Justice. KKE Architects, 300 First Ave. North, Minneapolis, Minnesota 55401, 612-336-9621

John Gromos

John Gromos is a 1990 graduate of Vanderbilt University where he earned a Bachelor of Science in Mechanical Engineering. He is a registered professional with nine years of experience at Smith Seckman Reid, Inc. Mr. Gromos is the Division Vice President of the Corrections Group having worked on such projects as the Federal Correction Complex in Beaumont, Texas. Smith Seckman Reid, Inc., 3319 W. End Avenue, Suite 700, Nashville, Tennessee 37203, 615-383-1113

Larry Hardy

Larry Hardy is currently deputy warden at the Iowa Medical and Classification Center, Oakdale, Iowa, the state's reception center for all inmates entering the Iowa Prison system. Hardy has worked at Oakdale since 1970, beginning as a correctional officer, and was involved in the planning and development of the reception program, which opened in 1984. He has Master's Degrees in History and Public Administration and serves as a trainer and facilitator for quality management efforts in the Iowa State government. Deputy Warden, Iowa Medical and Classification Center, P.O. Box A, Oakdale, Iowa 52319, 319-626-2391 X472

Mary Hardy-Hall

Mary Hardy-Hall currently serves as administrator of Accreditation and Standards for the Illinois Department of Corrections. Mrs. Hall has served the Illinois Department of Corrections in various capacities:

warden of several adult prisons; superintendent of a youth center; and, chief administrative officer of community correctional centers. She is a member of the American Correctional Association, is a trained American Correctional Association auditor, and serves on the Affirmative Action Committee (Vice Chair), Women in Corrections Committee, and the field Advisory Committee to the Standards Committee and Commission on Accreditation for Corrections. Mrs. Hall is a charter member of the Illinois Corrections Association. She has been active in the National Association of Blacks in Criminal Justice, serving as a regional representative to the board of directors. She was a founding member of the Illinois Chapter of NABCJ. She is President-Elect of the Correctional Accreditation Managers Association. Illinois Department of Corrections, 1301 Concordia Court, P.O. Box 19277, Springfield, Illinois 62794, 217-522-2666 X3003

J. Michael Henson

J. Michael Henson, Vice President of the technology group at Phillips Swager Associates (PSA) received his Bachelor of Science degree in 1980 from Illinois State University. He is licensed as a security consultant in Texas and Illinois with more than sixteen years of experience in the criminal justice industry. The PSA Technology Group provides physical security, electronic control systems, and telecommunications systems design expertise nationally through their offices located in Peoria, Illinois; Chicago, Illinois; Dallas, Texas; and Washington, D.C. Phillips Swager Associates, Inc., 3622 N. Knoxville Avenue, Peoria, Illinois 61603, 309-688-9511

W. Scott Higgins

W. Scott Higgins is chief of design and construction of the Federal Bureau of Prisons. He has held a variety of architectural and management positions in their central office in Washington, D.C. and their Dallas Regional Office. He is a graduate of the University of Oklahoma with a Bachelor of Architecture and is a registered architect. Since 1983, he has been responsible for the design and construction of all new institutions for the federal prison system. During that time, 38 major new institutions have been completed, representing a planned capacity of more than 40,000 beds. Projects currently in some stage of development or planning include an additional 20 major new institutions that will provide approximately 22,000 additional new beds. Chief of Design and Construction, Federal Bureau of Prisons, 320 First Street, NW, HOLC Building, Room 654, Washington, D.C. 20534, 202-514-5942

Richard Hopkins

Richard Hopkins is vice president of Hopkins Foodservice Specialists, Inc., which has offices in New York and Washington, D.C. It plans kitchens and meal distribution systems for local, state, and federal correctional facilities nationwide. Mr. Hopkins sits on the board of governors of the Certified Food Service Professional (CFSP) program, which qualifies food service professionals. Mr. Hopkins is a nationally recognized authority on Hazards Analysis Critical Control Point (HACCP) programming, a regulation adopted by many states, which requires a study of the paths of foods from receiving through service to identify and eliminate points in which food risks contamination. His most recent project was for the new Federal Correctional Institute and Camp in Lee County, Virginia, which will be serving more than 1,200 high-security and up to 250 medium-security inmates. He is a long standing member of the American Correctional Foodservice Association. Hopkins Foodservice Specialists, 7906 MacArthur Boulevard #100, Cabin John, Maryland 20818, 301-320-9200

John Hultberg

John C. Hultberg, AIA, is a senior project manager with HDR Architecture, Inc., located in Dallas, Texas. Since joining the staff of HDR's Justice Design Group in 1979, he has carried the primary responsibility for the design and management of more than 20 correctional facilities projects totaling more than 28,000 beds. HDR Architecture, Inc., 12700 Hillcrest Road, Suite 125, Dallas, Texas 75230, 972-960-4000

Bobbie Huskey

Bobbie Huskey has conducted needs assessments in twenty states, won four national awards for her contribution to corrections including American Correctional Association's E. R. Cass Award for Outstanding Achievement. She is past president, vice-president, and treasurer of the American Correctional Association. For further information, contact her at 773-348-3852 or bhuskey@ huskey-associates.com, Huskey & Associates, Inc., 1417 West Berteau, Chicago, Illinois 60613.

Kip Kautzky

W. L. "Kip" Kautzky has been the director of the Iowa Department of Corrections since 1997. Appointed by Governor Branstad and reappointed by Governor Vilsack, Mr. Kautzky came to Iowa with extensive credentials as a top corrections administrator. He was the deputy secretary for the North Carolina Department of Corrections. He also served as executive director of the Colorado Department of Corrections, as director of prisons in Washington State, and in command roles at military prisons in Vietnam, Thailand, and the United States. Mr. Kautzky holds a Master's Degree in Criminal Psychology from Florida State University and a Bachelor's Degree from Regis College in Denver, Colorado, and has done additional postgraduate work at the University of North Carolina School of Business Administration and at the Harvard University Kennedy School of Government. Department of Corrections, 420 Keo Way, Des Moines, Iowa 50309, 515-281-7345

Charles J. Kehoe

Charles J. Kehoe, ACSW, began his career in corrections in 1964 as a correctional officer in Illinois. Since then, he has worked in community-based and institutional programs in the public and private sector. From 1989 to 1994, he was the first director of the Virginia Department of Youth and Family Services. He is presently the vice-president of Securicor New Century, a private corrections operations and management company. He began helping architects to plan and design correctional facilities in 1970. From 1994 to 1999, he worked for HSMM assisting architects and conducting feasibility and planning studies. He has been directly involved in the design of more than 3,500 correctional beds in 12 states and the territory of Guam. He is an active member of the American Correctional Association and has served as the association's vice president and treasurer; he has served on the Standards Committee, the commission on Accreditation for Corrections, and the Board of Governors. Securicor New Century, LLC, 9609 Gayton Road, Suite 100, Richmond, Virginia 23233, 804-754-1100

James Kessler

James Kessler, AIA, a senior principal at Hellmuth, Obata & Kassabaum, P.C., is the director of HOK's Washington, D.C. Justice Focus Group. During his twenty years at HOK, he has taken particular interest in the design of large urban detention facilities. Mr. Kessler has served as the principal designer on numerous major correctional facilities, including the 1,800-cell Mecklenburg County Jail Central, Charlotte, North Carolina; Wake County Public Safety Center, Raleigh, North Carolina; Baltimore Central Intake and Booking Facility, Baltimore, Maryland; Fairfax County Adult Detention Center, Fairfax, Virginia; Fluvanna Correctional Center for Women, Troy, Virginia; and Montgomery County Detention Center, Clarksburg, Maryland. Mr. Kessler currently is designing the 1,000-cell North Carolina Close Security Prototype that will be site adapted at multiple locations throughout the state. Mr. Kessler is a graduate of Yale University School of Architecture. HOK Architects, 3223 Grace Street, NW, Washington, D.C. 20007, 202-339-8700

Alan R. Latta

Alan R. Latta, P.E., is President of Latta Technical Services, Inc. (LTS) with offices in Texas and Missouri. He has been responsible for the design of numerous electronic security systems for federal, state, county, and municipal justice facilities. As a member of American Correctional Association, American Jail Association, and ASTM, he has participated as presenter in seminars, training, and workshops. He can be reached at 972-633-5850 or arlpe@ airmail.net. Latta Technical Services, Inc., 701 East Plano Parkway, Suite 400, Plano, Texas 75074

Laura Maiello

Laura Maiello is senior associate and justice planner for Ricci Associates. In her fifteen years with the firm, she has led a variety of juvenile and correctional planning projects. Her expertise lies in system analyses, facility operations and programming, facility transition and planning, and procedure development. Ms. Maiello designed and implemented a national training seminar on Planning and Design of Juvenile Detention Facilities for the University of Wisconsin, held annually. She is a technical assistance provider for the National Institute of Corrections. Ms. Maiello has a Master's degree in Criminal Justice from Rutgers University. Ricci Associates, 130 West 30th Street, New York, New York 10001, 212-563-9154

Michael McMillen

Mike McMillen, the principal of his own firm, has specialized in juvenile justice facilities planning and design since 1978. He has provided operations analysis, architectural and operational programming, and facility design services in more than seventy-five youth-related projects nationwide under both federal and private contracts. For the U.S. Department of Justice, he co-authored *Residential Environments for the Juvenile Justice System,* and helped develop the American Correctional

Association's *Handbook on Facility Planning and Design Guide for Juvenile Corrections*. He was an editor for *The Juvenile Justice System: Change as Constant* (American Institute of Architects) and coauthored the forthcoming Office of Juvenile Justice and Delinquency Prevention's Best Practices Monograph, *Juvenile Detention and Corrections Facilities*. Mr. McMillen has developed and taught seminars for the National Institute of Corrections' *Planning of New Institutions for Juveniles (PONIJ)* program. 2091/2 West Clark Street, Champaign, Illinois 61820, 217-355-8173

John McSkimming

John W. McSkimming is a project director with Heery International, Inc. He is a registered architect and engineer with twenty-five years experience in the design and construction industry specializing in corrections and educational and governmental projects. John has a Bachelor of Science degree in Architecture from Ohio State University. Heery International, 999 Peachtree Street, NW, Atlanta, Georgia 30367, 404-881-9880

Richard Milliken

Richard L. Milliken is senior associate and project director with Heery International, Inc. He has managed the programming, design, bid/award, and construction phase of ten county detention centers in eight different states. Mr. Milliken has also served as the on-site construction manager on two Federal Bureau of Prison projects located in Beckley, West Virginia and Seattle, Washington. Heery International, 999 Peachtree Street, NW, Atlanta, Georgia 30367, 404-881-9880

Jeffrey Minnerly

Jeffrey Minnerly was born and raised in Highland, New York. He served in the U.S. Navy for five years with training in advanced engineering programs. He currently works for the New York State Department of Correctional Services in the division of Facilities Planning and Development. His role is to assist their seven New York City facilities with the planning and implementation of capitol projects, minor rehabilitation, and daily maintenance procedures. He has participated in several initial accreditations and reaccreditations of these facilities. Division of Facilities Planning and Development, Department of Correctional Services, State Campus, Building #2, 1220 Washington Avenue, Albany, New York 12226, 518-435-9477

David Musacchio

David E. Musacchio entered the field of corrections in 1961 as a social worker at the Kentucky State Reformatory. He subsequently held positions as the director of reception and orientation and deputy warden at this same facility. He later served as corrections and state police planner with the Kentucky Crime Commission, director of adult and juvenile corrections in Jefferson County (Louisville) Kentucky and Orleans and Jefferson Parishes in Louisiana. From 1975 until the present, Mr. Musacchio has been a private practicing consultant. He has developed a comprehensive knowledge of detention/security hardware and electronic communications, surveillance, and control systems. In 1994, he was brought in by the governor of Ohio to provide advice on the riots at the maximum-security Southern Ohio Correctional Facility (Lucasville). He then worked with the team of architects, engineers, and contractors to redesign and install security upgrades at this facility. Corrections Consultant, P.O. Box 5001, Cookeville, Tennessee 38505, 931-528-6342

Allen L. Patrick

Allen L. Patrick is recognized nationally and internationally for the planning and design of the entire family of criminal justice facilities, including detention, corrections, adjudication, and law enforcement for adults and youth. He graduated from the University of Cincinnati with a Bachelor of Science degree in Architecture and is a registered architect licensed in seventeen states. He is a member of the American Correctional Association's Standards Committee and a past commissioner for the Commission on Accreditation of Corrections. He is on both the American Correctional Association International Relations Committee and the Facility Design Committee. He is a member and past chairman of the AIA Committee on Architecture for Justice and immediate past chairman of the American Society of Testing and Materials' Committee F33 on Materials and Equipment for Security Applications. He is a member of the American Jail Association, and other justice related associations. URS Greiner Woodward Clyde, 33 North High Street, Columbus, Ohio 43215-3076, 614-464-4500, Fax: 614-464-0588

John Platt

John R. Platt is a career corrections professional. He completed his undergraduate and graduate education at Northern Illinois University. He has served as a line level youth supervisor, a correctional educator and as the superintendent or warden of ten institutions, two of these twice. He has served as the program administrator for the Illinois Department of Corrections and administered the juvenile division's parole, licensing, and construction planning. Mr. Platt was named the deputy director of the juvenile division in 1998. He has provided consultant services related to juvenile corrections programming, security, and design to many jurisdictions nationally and has been an American Correctional Association auditor. He is past president of the Illinois Correctional Association and has an abiding interest in the future of the American Correctional Association and in strengthening correctional services. Illinois Department of Corrections, 1301 Concordia Court, P.O. Box 19277, Springfield, Illinois 62794, 217-522-2666

Waller Poage

Waller S. Poage III, NCARB, CCS, is a consultant. He was formerly project manager with Hayes, Seay, Mattern & Mattern, Inc., Architects, Engineers, and Planners. His experience of thirty-four years includes principal in associated architectural practice in both private and public sectors. His public clients include federal, state, county, city, and municipal governments. Public sector work has included state prisons, county jails, law enforcement facilities, juvenile detention facilities, municipal police facilities, jails, and judicial facilities. Other experience includes emergency communication and response centers, municipal and county fire stations, and various projects for agencies of the federal government. In recent years, he has served on design/build teams for projects ranging from $5 million to $100 million in construction value. He is the author of *The Building Professional's Guide to Contract Documents*, published by R.S. Means Company, currently in its third edition. 7060 Gatton Square, Alexandria, Virginia 22315, 703-922-0045

William Porter

William G. Porter, P.E., was national director of HSMM's judicial and corrections division since its inception. In February, 1999, he was appointed manager in charge of HSMM's Tidewater Office. He retains responsibility for judicial and corrections projects in this position. Mr. Porter is an experienced principal, project manager, and project engineer specializing in planning prisons and juvenile correctional facilities. He has planned, designed, and/or managed corrections projects in twenty-five states and overseas. These projects have been recognized with local, state, and national awards. He is also a member of the American Correctional Association and the National Juvenile Detention Association. Mr. Porter has a Bachelor of Science in Business Administration from Virginia Polytechnic Institute and State University and a Bachelor of Science in Engineering Science from the University of North Carolina at Charlotte. HSMM Inc., 448 Viking Drive, Suite 145, Virginia Beach, Virginia 23452, 757-306-4000

Steven Radomski

Steven J. Radomski, AIA, is a senior associate and senior project manager with RNL Design and the studio designer for RNL Design's Institutional Studio. With a total of twenty-one years experience, he has fourteen years of specialization in adult and juvenile justice system planning, programming, and design. His focus on special needs populations includes facilities for youth offenders, adult and juvenile females, forensic patients, and sexually violent persons. Ten of his projects have received citations or recognition from the National AIA Committee on Architecture for Justice. RNL Design, 1515 Arapahoe Street, Tower 3, Suite 700, Denver, Colorado 80202, 303-395-1717

Kenneth Ricci

Kenneth Ricci, FAIA, is president of Ricci Associates, an architecture and planning firm in New York City. Mr. Ricci's thirty year career has focused on the planning, programming, and design of juvenile justice and correctional facilities. He has conducted more than 100 juvenile justice and correctional projects nationally, from master planning to award-winning facility design. A nationally recognized leader in the field, Mr. Ricci is a frequent speaker on justice planning and design at conferences, seminars, and universities. He is a member of the faculty for the National Institute of Corrections, as a seminar designer and lecturer for the Planning of New Institutions (PONI) program. He recently designed and implemented a new national PONI program for juvenile facilities. Mr. Ricci has a Bachelor of Architecture from Pratt University. He is a fellow of the American Institute of Architects and is a member of the AIA Architecture for Justice Committee. Ricci Associates, 130 West 30th Street, New York, New York 10001, 212-563-9154

Gregory Ridgely

Gregory Ridgely is manager of cost estimating for Heery International's East Region. He has experience in supervising preconstruction estimating services, having done so for three prisons/jails in the past two years. Heery International, 999 Peachtree Street, NE, Atlanta, Georgia 30367, 404-881-9880

Henry Risley

Henry Risley, the Commissioner in New Hampshire until his death in September, 1999, had worked in adult corrections at the state level since 1970. He held a Bachelor of Science and a Master of Science degree from Michigan State University. He majored in corrections administration in the School of Criminal Justice, College of Social Science. His career included work in adult facilities and state departments of correction in Michigan, Montana, Delaware, Texas, Kansas, and New Hampshire. He was involved in and responsible for managing large prison expansion projects in six states. He served on the Technology Committees of the American Corrections Association, Association of State Correctional Administrators, and was a member of the National Law Enforcement and Corrections Technology Advisory Council. Department of Corrections, P.O. Box 1806, Concord, New Hampshire 03302, 603-271-5606

Joseph Rowan

Joseph R. Rowan, President/CEO of Criminal and Juvenile Justice International, when presented the E. R. Cass Award in 1992, was described as "the chief architect of the American Correctional Association medical/mental health standards." He has worked in the criminal justice field for fifty-eight years in numerous positions across the nation in adult and juvenile detention facilities, probation and parole agencies, and law enforcement. He was director for two state and four national private correctional agencies and programs. He has provided service in sixteen foreign countries since 1988. Mr. Rowan has received outstanding service awards from the American Correctional Association, the International Association of Correctional Officers, the American Jail Association, the National Juvenile Detention Association, and the National Commission on Correctional Health Care. Mr. Rowan is the author of three national suicide prevention training manuals. Since "retirement" in 1984, he has worked full time providing survey, consultation, train-ing, and expert witness services. Criminal and Juvenile Justice International, Inc., 381 South Owasso Blvd., Roseville, Minnesota 55113, 612-481-9644

James A. Rowenhorst

James A. Rowenhorst is a nationally recognized criminal justice consultant specializing in the planning and opening of new institutions. He has more than thirty years of experience in law enforcement and corrections. Mr. Rowenhorst has held such positions as chief deputy sheriff and jail administrator. He has participated in more than ninety projects in thrity-three states involving correctional facility planning, transition to new facilities, and corectional staff training. Mr. Rowenhorst's expertise includes identifying and mitigating factors having adverse effects on jail crowding, determining pretrial and sentencing alternatives to reduce the jail population, projecting inmate housing needs, preparing pre-architectural programs, determining staffing requirements and operations costs of facilities, and writing policies, procedures, and post orders. He also has conducted jail facility audits for jurisdictions experiencing management and facility problems. Mr. Rowenhorst co-authored the *Jail Design Guide* and also serves as a consultant for the National Institute of Corrections in the "Planning of New Institutions" and "How to Open New Institution" programs. Corrections Consultant, P.O. Box 9695, Rapid City, South Dakota 57709, 605-342-5781

Vijay Ruikar

Vijay Ruikar has been associated with the detentions and corrections industry since 1986, as a testing and certification engineer. He joined the ASTM F33 in 1988, at its inception and has been the chairman since January, 1994. During this period, the committee has produced numerous test standards, all of which are directly focused for use by the detentions and corrections community. Mr. Ruikar has a Bachelor's and a Master's degree in Mechanical Engineering and he is a Professional Engineer registered in California. He works as a senior project manager with Intertek Testing Services, at their Antioch, California facility. Intertek Testing Services is the largest testing and certification organization, with operations in sixty-six countries. Intertek Testing Services, Antioch Industrial Park, 2200 Wymore Way, Antioch, California 94509, 925-756-6606 X215

Keith Rupert

Keith D. Rupert, P.E. is the supervisor for technical services for facilities planning and development for the New York State Department of Correctional Services. Mr. Rupert received a Bachelor of Science degree in Mechanical Engineering from Syracuse University and a Masters of Science in Managerial Systems from Clarkson University. He is a licensed Professional Engineer in New York State, serves on the Northeast Regional Advisory Council for the National Law Enforcement and Corrections Technology Center is a member of the American Correctional Association, the Northeast Wardens Association, the Construction and Management Institute, and several professional organizations. Division of Facilities Planning and Development, Department of Correctional Services, State Campus, Building #2, 1220 Washington Avenue, Albany, New York 12226, 518-435-9477 X2450

Ted Sak

Ted Sak, a vice president with Heery International has nearly twenty-five years of experience in design, engineering and construction management. He has provided inspection, management supervision for design, construction, and closeout/turnover activities for numerous correctional facilities. Mr. Sak has worked on projects with city jails, county detention centers, courthouses, and federal detention centers. Heery International, 999 Peachtree Street, NE, Atlanta, Georgia 30367, 404-881-9880

Frank Sheridan

Frank Sheridan is the director of facilities planning and development for the New York State Department of Correctional Services. He has held this position for the past seventeen years. Mr. Sheridan oversees one of the largest correctional construction programs in the world. This program costs more than $1 billion, and concerns range from 23 prisons and 14,000 inmates to 70 prisons and 70,000 inmates. Division of Facilities Planning and Development, Department of Correctional Services, State Campus, Building #2, 1220 Washington Avenue, Albany, New York 12226, 518-435-9477 X2457

Jack Shetter

Jack Shetter brings more than thirty years of experience in security systems and justice facility planning, design, and evaluation to the KMB Justice Facilities team. His extensive experience in law enforcement, courts, detention, and correctional facility projects is based on a comprehensive knowledge of standards, and the operational and functional needs of secure facilities. Careful attention to the project budget is also a priority. As director of security, Mr. Shetter is responsible for all aspects of security design. His career includes lead designer responsibilities for more than 200 projects in 34 states. The size of projects he has been involved with has ranged from small local facilities, to large and complex projects such as the Harris County, Texas $85 million 4,000-bed addition. KMB Justice Facilities Group, 2311 W. 16th, Suite 79, Spokane, Washington 99204, 509-744-0515

Karen M. Sicner

Karen M. Sicner is an architect with a specialty in criminal justice design and programming. She obtained a Master's Degree from the Georgia Institute of Technology, in Atlanta, Georgia, in 1986 and is a registered architect. Ms. Sicner is president of an architectural firm located in Atlanta, Georgia and has spent the last ten years of her career involved with the programming design and construction of criminal justice projects; including prisons in Georgia, Wisconsin, and Michigan. She is a member of the American Correctional Association, American Jail Association, and the AIA Architects for Justice Committee. Sicner Planning & Design, 182 Hilderbrand Drive #202, NE, Atlanta, Georgia 30328, 404-303-7755

Larry J. Smith

Prominent in the justice field, Larry J. Smith, AIA, has nearly twenty-five years of experience programming and designing female, juvenile, and adult facilities for agencies throughout the United States. Currently vice president of Durrant Architects, he specializes in criminal justice design and is a member of the American Correctional Association, the American Jail Association, the American Institute of Architects, and the ASTM F33 Committee for Developing Security Standards. His specialties include female detention facilities. Having designed such projects as the 2,200-bed female state prison in Madera, California and the 96-bed, maximum-security female prison in Taycheedah, Wisconsin, he understands the special needs of these facilities. His attention to detail, knowledge, and security operational design issues, have created some of the nation's most innovative and efficient justice projects. Durrant Architects, 426 North 44th Street, Suite 300, Phoenix, Arizona 85008, 602-275-6830

Dennis Sommers

Dennis Sommers is currently employed as the planning and construction manager for the Nebraska Department of Administrative Services, State Building Division. Prior to moving to this position, he was employed by the Nebraska Department of Correctional Services from 1975 to 1997, first as a construction project manager, then as the manager of facilities engineering. Project experience, while at corrections, included the replacement of every adult male correctional facility in the state with new institutions as well as the programming, planning, and construction of several additional new complexes. Mr. Summers received his Bachelor of Science degree in Construction Management from the University of Nebraska in 1971. Department of Administrative Services, One Metropolitian Square, 521 North Broadway, Suite 1900, St. Louis, Missouri 63102, 314-241-8188 X275.

Earl Stahl

Earl M. Stahl is a senior project manager with HDR Architecture, Inc. in Dallas, Texas. One of the founding members of HDR's Justice Design Group in 1975, he has been a major contributor to the planning, design, and construction of countless prisons and jails across the United States. HDR Architecture, Inc., 12700 Hillcrest Rd., Suite 125, Dallas, Texas 75230, 972-960-4000

John Thalacker

John Thalacker is the first warden of the Ft. Dodge, Iowa, Correctional Facility, the newest prison in Iowa. This facility has a population and capacity of 750. Construction will bring the capacity to 1,162 by January 2000. He has been a warden since 1978 in four Iowa prisons ranging from 150 to 1,500 minimum to maximum custody. He also served as an auditor of twenty-three institutions for the Commission on Accreditation for Corrections of the American Correctional Association. He also has reviewed books for the Association. He is active in community development. He holds a BA and MSW in social work. He is married and has two grown children. Fort Dodge Correctional Facility, 1550 L Street, Ft. Dodge, Iowa 50501, 515-574-4700 X4711

Michael Tomy

Michael D. Tomy, vice president of Heery International, has more than twenty years of experience in architecture, with extensive expertise in the design and construction of new and renovated judicial and correctional facilities (federal, state, and county), as well as courthouses. He has served as the project director for three state juvenile facilities, a U.S. penitentiary, two courthouses, and a law enforcement facility. In addition, he has provided design reviews, project management, and design for numerous other correctional facilities. Heery International, 999 Peachtree Street, NE, Atlanta, Georgia 30367, 404-881-9880

Edward Tripp

Edward F. Tripp is vice president of Correctional Facility Planning at Kennedy Associates Inc. with more than forty-five years of correctional system operational and management experience. In various positions with the state of Missouri and the city of St. Louis, he has managed and rennovated traditional indirect-supervision facilities and was instrumental in initiating the design of St. Louis, Missouri's soon-to-be constructed direct-supervision City Justice Center. He has served as a field auditor and consultant for the American Correctional Association's Commission on Accreditation for Corrections since 1978. He is also quite active in university-level corrections education. He is a recipient of the American Correctional Association's highest and most prestigious E. R. Cass Award. Kennedy Associates Incorporated, One Metropolitan Square, 211 North Broadway, Suite 1900, St. Louis, Missouri 63102, 314-241-8188.

Florian Walicki

Florian Walicki is a principal and head of the Institutional Studio for RNL Design. His experience includes twenty-five years of institutional projects with ten years specialization in hospitals and mental health facilities. Furthermore, Mr. Walicki has spent fifteen years specializing in planning, programming, and design of criminal justice projects, to include courts, correctional, detention, juvenile facilities, special needs, forensics, mental health, and special commitment centers (SVP). RNL Design, 1515 Arapahoe Street, Tower 3, Suite 700, Denver, Colorado 80202, 303-295-1717

Norman Wirkler

Norman Wirkler is a nationally recognized architect in the field of justice and public safety, with extensive experience in all types of projects through more than thirty years with the Durrant Group. He has served as project director or principal-in-charge and has offered significant design and/or administrative input on projects ranging from small county jail facilities to very large correctional institutions. He is active in the American Correctional Association and is a past member of the Standards Committee. He also was actively involved in developing the second and third editions of the American Correctional Association's Adult Local Detention Facility amd Adult Correctional Institution standards. As a past member of the Board of Commissioners of the Commission on Accreditation, he contributed to the writing of the prior *Design Guide* and has written numerous articles for corrections journals and magazines. He has also been involved in research and projects with the Institute of Continuing Legal Education and the National Institute for Correction, involving a variety of law enforcement, court, and corrections projects. Durrant Group, 3773 Cherry Circle North Drive, #240, Denver, Colorado 80209, 303-377-2900

Leonard Witke *(see first entry in this section)*

George Yefchak

George Yefchak, who holds Master's degrees from both the University of Pennsylvania and Kean University of New Jersey, has been involved in the field of corrections for twenty-seven years. Mr. Yefchak started his career as a parole officer and later served as a hearing officer for the State Parole Board. He is presently with the Division of Parole and Community Programs in the Department of Corrections. He was the superintendent of the McCorkle Training School for Boys and Girls, Skillman, until its closing in 1992. Mr. Yefchak is the president of the New Jersey Chapter of the American Correctional Association and chairman of the Ethic's Committee for the American Correctional Association. He is a member of the Governor's Juvenile Justice Delinquency Prevention Committee and the state Parole Advisory Committee. Mr. Yefchak is also on the board of directors of the American Probation and Parole Association. In his local community, he is an advisory member of the planning board. New Jersey Branch of the American Correctional Association, 967 Sergeantsville Road, Stockton, New Jersey 08559, 609-777-1891

Stanley Young

Stanley K. Young, warden at Virginia's new super-max prison, Wallens Ridge State Prison in Big Stone Gap, is an eighteen-year veteran of the Virginia Department of Corrections. Mr. Young is a 1975 graduate from Tazewell High School, in Tazewell, Virginia, and a 1979 graduate of Emory and Henry College in Emory, Virginia, with a Bachelor's Degree in History and a minor in Education. He was a former teacher/football-wrestling coach in Buchanan County, Virginia from 1979 to 1981. Wallens Ridge State Prison, P.O. Box 759, Big Stone Gap, Virginia 24219, 540-523-3310

Shelley Zavlek

Shelley Zavlek has more than twenty years of experience in juvenile justice administration and planning, law, and special education. Currently, as senior juvenile justice planner for Ricci Associates, Ms. Zavlek specializes in juvenile justice system analyses, long-range physical planning, and operational and space programming. In addition, she served as project manager under a contract between Ricci Associates and the National Institute of Corrections to develop and implement a week-long curriculum on Planning of New Institutions (PONI) for Juvenile Facilities. As of June, 1999, three Juvenile PONI workshops were successfully delivered. As executive director of capital and operational planning for the New York City Department of Juvenile Justice, Ms. Zavlek managed and monitored the agency's capital budget and projects, which included project management for the construction, outfitting, and transition to two new 124-bed juvenile detention facilities. Ricci Associates, 130 West 30th Street, New York, New York 10001, 212-563-9154

Index

Photo on previous page shows the entrance to the Dare County Jail, Manteo, North Carolina.

Photo courtesy of L. Robert Kimball & Associates, Ebensburg, Pennsylvania.

Index

Note: Items in boldface indicate a photo or graphic.

A

Allenwood, Pennsylvania, Federal Correctional Complex, **258**
Hillcrest Juvenile Facility, Hamilton County, Ohio, **271**
  juvenile programs and services, **271**, 272
  space requirements, 245
Charlotte, North Carolina
  Mecklenburg County Jail, *See* Mecklenburg County Jail, Charlotte, North Carolina
Chesapeake City Jail, Virginia
  lobby, **280**
  multi-use dayroom space, **127**
  noninstitutional front of building, **2**
  private cells, **123**
  segregated housing, **132**
  storage and handling of inmate property on admission, **194**
  vehicle garage, **299**
Chesapeake, Virginia, Tidewater Juvenile Detention Home, **268**
Chester, Illinois
  Menard Correctional Center, *See* Menard Correctional Center, Chester, Illinois
Chianesi, Steven, 285-289, 399
Children of female inmates, xii
  inmates, as, *See* Juveniles and facilities
  prenatal care diets, 175
  visitors, as, *See* Visitors and visiting areas, children as visitors
China fixtures *versus* steel fixtures, 128, 173, 175, 181
Chinn, Karen
  Chinn Planning, 55-60, 399
Christoff, Jerry P., 355-363, 399
Circulation patterns and movement control
  definition of circulation factor, 48
  food services, 207-208
  health care facilities, 202-203
  housing units and centralized facilities, between, 125-126
  intercom systems used to control, 322
  roads, 342
  segregated housing locations, 132
  sexually violent person housing, 157
  supermax facilities, need for absolute control of movement in, **164, 165,** 165-166
  tracking systems, 325
  video monitoring to control, 321
  Wallens Ridge State Prison, Big Stone Gap, Virginia, 169
Classification of facilities
  high security, *See* High-security facilities
  low security, *See* Low-security facilities
  maximum security, *See* High-security facilities
  medium security, *See* Medium-security facilities
  minimum security, *See* Low-security facilities

super maximum security, *See* Supermax facilities
Classification of inmates, 121-122, 156
  abilities rather than age, classifying older inmates by, 137
  accessibility issues, 147
  contingency-space planning, 24-25
  Federal Bureau of Prisons
    low-security facilities, development of, 6
    operational foundations for, 4
  females, xii
  food services, 205
  high security, *See* High-security facilities
    housing and, 121-130
  juveniles, *See* Juveniles and facilities
  low security, *See* Low-security facilities
  maximum security, *See* High-security facilities
  medium security, *See* Medium-security facilities
  minimum security, *See* Low-security facilities
  moving into the new facility, 373
  needs assessment, 24-25
  perimeter security requirements and, 328
  segregated housing, inmates in, 132-133
  sexually violent person housing, 156
  supermax facilities, 164
Climatic concerns and site selection, 34
Close custody
  classification principles, 122
  high-security facilities providing, *See* High-security facilities
Closed-circuit television (CCTV), *See* Video monitoring
Code requirements, *See* Building/safety code requirements
Cogefar/Impresit USA, Miami, Florida, 68
Coleman, Florida, Federal Correctional Institution
  foundation setting, **90**
  shared resources, **74**
  stacked housing units, **12**
Color
  female inmates' response to, 220
  juvenile facilities, materials used in, 181, 268, **268**
  visiting areas, design of, 264
Colorado
  Florence, Colorado, Federal Correctional Institution, *See* Florence, Colorado, Federal Correctional Institution
  Kit Carson Correctional Center, Burlington, **390**
Commercial access control
  control electronics, 324-325
Commissaries, *See* Canteens and commissaries

Commission on Accreditation for Law Enforcement Agencies (CALEA)
  standards and accreditation programs, 17
Commissioning new facility, *See* Transition process
Common areas
  ADA requirements, 146-147
  dayrooms, *See* Dayrooms
  female inmates, small group seating areas for, 221
  lavatory and washroom facilities, *See* Lavatory and washroom facilities
  multi-use, *See* Multi-use common areas or dayrooms
  recreation areas, *See* Recreation areas
Communicable diseases
  admissions screening for, 190, 230
  juveniles and facilities, 230
  medical isolation units for patients with, 202, **203**
Communications systems, 322-324
  control centers, entry into, 319
    inmate systems, 325
    intercom systems, *See* Intercom systems
    noncontact visiting booths, intercom systems for, 322, **322**
    paging, 322-323
    public address systems, 322
    radio paging, 323
    radio transceivers, 322
    voice paging, 322
Community-based alternatives, 109
Community concerns, *See* Public attitudes
Community resources, making use of, *See* Sharing resources
Competitive selection procedures
  design competitions, 42-43
  fee-based competition, problems with, 41, 42
  privatization, 387, 389
  public requirements or political considerations requiring, 40, 41
  site selection, 29-31
Complejo Penitenciario I, Ezezia, Buenos Aires, Argentina, **105**
Computer systems
  control electronics, *See* Control electronics
  education programs
    distance learning classrooms, **71**, 71-72, 253, 254
    media rooms, *See* Media rooms
  growing importance of, 393
  information management, *See* Information management
  IPCs (industrial personal computers), 324, 325
  maintenance and repair, 294, 298
  media rooms, *See* Media rooms
  operator interfaces, *See* Operator interfaces

Marianna, Florida, Federal Correctional Institution, **95, 107**
medium-security facilities, *See* Medium-security facilities
Miami, Florida, Federal Detention Center and Courthouse, enclosed bridge between, **68**
mission statement, 4
office and meeting space, 10
operational foundations for, 4
Otisville Correctional Institution, New York, 3, 5-6, **6**
perimeter security, 11-12
Philadelphia Federal Detention Center, **32**
philosophical basis of planning and design, 4, 11
recreation areas, 12
sallyports, 11
SeaTac Federal Detention Center, Seattle, Washington, **8, 9, 277**
segregated housing, 11
staffing
    housing unit management, 9, 10-11
    operational foundations for, 4
supervision
    direct supervision, 8-9
    functional unit management, 8-9
taut-wire intrusion-detection systems, 11-12
Victorville, California, Federal Correctional Institution, 12
Federal government
    funding match programs, 78
    project delivery regulations, 78
Feltham, Middlesex, UK
    New Feltham Remand Centre, **95, 101**
Female inmates, xii, 171-176, 219-222
    abuse or mistreatment, 171, 220, 221
    admissions/reception/evaluation, 191, 199
    beauty shops, 221
    campus-style facilities, 100, **100,** 175
    cells, 173
    children of
        prenatal care diets, 175
        visitors, 221
    common areas, small group seating in, 221
    construction materials for facilities for, 175
    cross-gender supervision of, 171, 220
    dayrooms, **173,** 174, 221
    Delaware Women's Facility, *See* Delaware Women's Facility
    direct supervision, 220
    dormitory living, 173-174
    double bunking, 173
    environmental (surroundings) concerns, 172, 220
    food services, 175
    geriatric inmates, 140
    health care, xii
    housing units, 171-176, 220

increase in number of, 171
international considerations, 100, **100**
kidney problems and changes, 142
laundry, 175, 221
lavatory and washroom facilities, 172, 173, 174, 220
minor children of
    prenatal care diets, 175
    visitors, 221
National Congress on Penitentiary and Reformatory Discipline, Declaration of Principles by, 219
Niantic Women's Facility, Connecticut, **125**
normative materials and residential-style design, 100, **100,** 172, 173, 220
podular design, 220
posttraumatic stress disorder (PTSD), 221
prenatal care diets, 175
privacy, 172, 174, 219-222, 230
psychological factors, 171, 219
recreation areas, 259-260
sexual abuse of, 171, 220, 221
showers, 172, 173, 174, 220
single bunking, 173
size of facility for, 175
sleeping areas, 173, 221
small group seating areas for, 221
staffing
    cross-gender supervision, 171, 220, 221
    sleeping hours, use of female staff only during, 221
    training for special needs, importance of, 221
substance abuse treatment facilities, 104
Victoria Women's Prison, *See* Victoria Women's Prison
Virginia Peninsula Regional Jail, Williamsburg, **172**
visitors, 221
vocational training, 255
women's facilities, 100
Fencing
    capacitance (wire arrays), as mounting for, 330
    double fencing, 94, **95**
    Federal Bureau of Prisons, 11-12
    international considerations, 94-95
Financial issues, *See* Budget and finance issues
Fingerprinting
    access point control, 334
    admissions/reception/evaluation, 197, 230
    juvenile inmates, 230
Finland
    new *versus* existing facilities, 109
Fire prevention
    armory, 338
    ASTM testing standards, **352, 353**

housing units, use of fire-resistant materials in, 128
    water supply, 304, 308
Firewalls and information management, 287-288
Fletcher-Harlee Corp., Glenside, Pennsylvania, **254, 258**
Flexibility
    outsourcing and privatization of services
        health care, 236
        planning and design, 235
    parking facilities, 343-344
    planning and design, needed in, 235
    religious spaces, 272
    roads, 343-344
    visiting areas, design of, 264
Florence, Colorado, Federal Correctional Institution
    aerial shots, **1, 7**
    general exterior shots, **1, 3, 10**
    guard tower, view from, **291**
    satellite facility, 7
    segregated housing, **132, 133**
    sliding gates, **106**
    utility plant, **303**
Florida
    Coleman Federal Correctional Institution, *See* Coleman, Florida, Federal Correctional Institution
    general custody facilities, prototype designs for, 98
    Marianna Federal Correctional Institution, **95, 107**
    Miami Federal Detention Center and Courthouse, enclosed bridge between, **68**
Food services, 51, 205-210
    admissions/reception/evaluation, 192, 198
    Beaumont, Texas, Federal Correctional Complex, **208**
    beverage alcoves, 129
    Brewer Creek Secure Treatment Center, Wisconsin, 159
    canteens and commissaries, *See* Canteens and commissaries
    circulation patterns, 207-208
    classification of inmates, 205
    contraband, introduction of, 208
    deliveries, 206
    equipment selection, 207-208, 209-210
    female inmates, 175
    geriatric inmates, 140
    hot water supply, 305
    inmates employed in, 62, 205
    juveniles and facilities, *See* Juveniles and facilities
    orientation, 248
    outside consultants, use of, 206, 209
    outsourcing and privatization of services, *See* Outsourcing and privatization of services

programming, importance of, 206-207
purpose of, 205
review and resubmission of program, 207, 209
security, 205, 206, 207-208
sequence of service, organizing, 206-207
sharing resources, 68
staff, for, **207**
staffing needs, effect on, 62, 205
value engineering, 209
Foreign countries, *See* International considerations
Foreigners, *See* Aliens
Fuller, Cheryl, 241-264, 400
Fuller Koe Associates
Fuller, Cheryl, 241-264, 400
Functional unit management, *See* Unit management
Furniture
ADA requirements and accessibility
fixed seating and tables, wheel-chair accommodations for, 148, **148**
heights of workstations and shelves, **153**
significance of, 148
ASTM standards for furnishings and equipment, 354
comfortableness of, 117-118, **118**
juveniles and facilities, 178-179, 182, 268
movable cell furniture *versus* fixed furniture, **96,** 97
segregated housing, 134
soft costs, as, 79
space requirements, 128

G

Gaffney, South Carolina
Peachoid water and sewage facilities, **73**
Garage, 299-300
Gauger, Glen, 81-90, 400
Gender-sensitive issues
cross-gender supervision, 171, 220, 221
female inmates, *See* Female inmates
showers, 118-119
General custody facilities
international considerations, 98
Generators, 303-304
George Hyman Construction, Hollywood, Florida, 12, 90
Geriatric inmates, xii, 137-144
abilities rather than age, classifying inmates by, 137
accessibility issues, 138-139, 143
ADA protections, 137-138, 143
Alzheimer's disease, 142, 143
animals, association with, **143**
bone changes and problems, 142
brain pathologies, 142, 143
call buttons, 143

cardiovascular changes and problems, 140-141
circulation problems, 142
diabetes, 142
environmental (surroundings) concerns, 138
female inmates, 140
food services, 140
gastrointestinal changes and problems, 142
health care and hospital accommodations, 140, 203
call buttons, 143
Federal Bureau of Prison's hospital design, 138
normal age-related changes, list of, 140-143
outsourcing and privatization of services, 236
hearing impairments, 140, 141
Hocking Correctional Facility, Nelson-ville, Ohio, *See* Hocking Correctional Facility, Nelsonville, Ohio
increasing problem of, 143
kidney problems and changes, 142
lavatory and washroom facilities, 139, **139**
light requirements, 140
muscular changes and problems, 142
need for, 137
nervous system changes and problems, 141
noise and sound control, 140, 141
pain response, 140
pancreatic changes and problems, 142
percentage of prisons and jails addressing special needs of, 138
psychiatric problems, 142-143
recreation areas, **143**
respiratory tract changes and problems, 141
sexually violent person housing, 156
showers, 139, **139**
skin changes and problems, 142
sleep and rest needs, 142
smell, sense of, 140
suicide, 142-143
taste, sense of, 140
temperature control, 140
touch, sense of, 140
tremors, development of, 141
urinary tract problems and changes, 142
vision impairments, 141
visitors, **137**
Gilbane Building Co., **50, 53, 112, 121, 163, 206, 223, 231, 239, 248, 261, 327**
Gilbane Design Team, 104
Gilbert Commonwealth, Reading, Pennsylvania, **254, 258, 311**
Gondles, James A., Jr., ix, 103
Grab bars, **148,** 151, 202
Grad Associates
Delaware Women's Facility, Wilmington, **100**

Greenville, Illinois, Federal Correctional Institution, **259**
Gromos, John, 303-306, 400
Gross area
defined, 48
juvenile facilities, 58
net to gross ratio, 48-50
program area summary reflecting, 51
Guard towers
Federal Bureau of Prisons, 11
recreation areas, 260
staffing needs, effect on, 62
Wallens Ridge State Prison, Big Stone Gap, Virginia, 168
Gudmanson, Donald W., 357
Gymnasiums, 260, 274, *See also* Recreation areas

H

Hair care, *See* Barbers and beauty shops
Hallways, *See* Corridors, stairways, and walkways
Hamilton, Bermuda, Maximum Security Prison, **108**
Hamilton County, Ohio
Hillcrest Juvenile Facility, **271**
Hand geometry, 334
Hanging, 183. *See also* Suicide
Hard costs, 79-80
Hardy, Larry, 189-192, 400
Hardy-Hall, Mary, 201-204, 400-401
HDR Architecture, Inc.
dayrooms for female inmates, **173,** 174
Hultberg, John, 121-130, 131-135, 401
Niantic Women's Facility, Connecticut, **125**
Stahl, Earl, 121-130, 131-135, 407
Health care, 104, 201-204
ADA requirements and accessibility issues, 148, 153, 202
admissions/reception/evaluation, medical screening area for, 190, 197
area requirements, 50, 51
Beaumont, Texas, Federal Correctional Complex, **204**
Brewer Creek Secure Treatment Center, Wisconsin, 160
budget and finance issues, 236
checklist of required amenities, 202
circulation patterns in health care facilities, 202-203
communicable and contagious diseases, *See* Communicable diseases
emergency services, 203-204, **204**
Federal Bureau of Prisons, *See* Federal Bureau of Prisons
females, *See* Female inmates
geriatric inmates, *See* Geriatric inmates

architectural program development, staff involvement in, *See* Architectural program development

barbers and beauty shops, 215, 217-218

barriers between staff and inmates, 127-128, 131, 167

budget and finance issues, planning and design affecting, 61

continuing process, analysis of needs, 65

control centers, *See* Control centers

determining needs and requirements, 371

direct supervision, 61-62

disabled staff, reasonable accommodation of, **152**

education programs, 71, 253, 269

escort staff for inmates undergoing orientation, 248

Federal Bureau of Prisons
　housing unit management, 9, 10-11
　operational foundations for, 4

female inmates, *See* Female inmates

food services
　staff dining facilities, **207**
　staff to run, 62, 205

functional lists, 63, 65

guard towers, effect on staffing needs, 62

housing availability for, 32, 34, 36

housing unit teams and managers, 124-125

identification systems, 336

indirect supervision, 61

information management offices, 283

inmate labor and staffing needs, 62

intercom systems, staff-dedicated, 323

jobs created by new facility
　area workforce, 34, 36
　public attitudes affected by, 27, 29, 30

juveniles and facilities, *See* Juveniles and facilities

lavatory and washroom facilities, 130

libraries, 254

mailrooms, 211-213

maintenance and repair, 62-63, 293, 294

managers of housing units, 124-125

modified direct supervision, 61-62

needs assessment, 21-22, 61-65

new facilities, 61-65
　facility design, effect of, 62-63
　jobs created by, *See* Selection of site
　number of officers needed, determining, 63, 64
　operational policies, 62
　supervision, type of, 61-62

noise and sound control, views on, 353-363

number of officers needed, determining, 63, 64

offices
　administrative offices,
　　See Administrative offices

private meeting space for staff and inmates, *See* Office and meeting space

supervisory officers, stations for, *See* Officers' stations

operational policies and, 62

operator interfaces, skill and comfort levels of staff as determining factors in choosing, 324, **324**

parking facilities, 343

personnel/human resources department, 282

planning and design, effect of, 61

post orders, 372

programs and services needs, 62-63

public entrances and lobbies, 281

reasonable accommodation of disabled staff, **152**

relief factor, 61, 63

security administration, 284

security needs, effect of, 62-63

segregated housing, 131

spreadsheets, 63, 64

substance abuse treatment, 250

supermax facilities and staff safety, 167

support for planning and design, importance of, 5

team management systems, 124-125

training for staff, *See* Training

transition process, *See* Transition process

vehicle garage, 299, 300

visiting areas, observation rooms for, 264

vocational training, 255

Stahl, Earl, 121-130, 131-135, 407

Stairs, *See* Corridors, stairways, and walkways

Standards, 13-20
　AACP (American Association of Correctional Psychologists), 17
　ABA (American Bar Association)
　　consensus process with ACA, involvement in, 18
　　development of standards by, 17
　　voluntary nature of standards, 16
　ACA (American Correctional Association) standards
　　accreditation, standards as basis for, 15, 17, 18, 19-20
　　AIA, involvement with, 18
　　allied bodies, 18
　　barbers and beauty shops, 216
　　canteens and commissaries, 225
　　cells, 178-179
　　comprehensiveness of, 18
　　control centers, 317
　　creation, writing, and approval of standards, 15
　　dayrooms, 174
　　electrical power, 307

　　enforcement of, 17
　　health care, 18
　　information on, 19
　　lavatory and washroom facilities, 174, 179
　　light requirements, 92, 96
　　maintenance and repair, 293, 297
　　needs assessment, 25
　　noise and sound control, 355
　　number of beds in room or cell, 174
　　original project to develop standards, 14-15
　　privacy, 220
　　process for accreditation, 19-20
　　publication of standards by, 14, 18-19
　　revisions, 18
　　segregated housing, 132, 133, 134
　　showers, 174
　　utilities, 299
　　vehicle garage, 299
　　voluntary nature of standards of, 16
　　warehouse, 299
　AIA (American Institute of Architects) standards
　　ACA, involvement with, 18
　　design competition guidelines, 42
　ALA (American Library Association)
　　accreditation programs, lack of, 17
　　development of standards by, 17
　　voluntary nature of standards, 16
　aliens, 17-18
　AMA (American Medical Association) standards
　　accreditation standards for medical education, significance of, 13
　　development of standards, 15, 17
　　voluntary nature of standards of, 16
　American Public Health Association, 15, 17
　approval of, 15
　architectural program development, 49
　ASTM, *See* American Society for Testing and Materials (ASTM) standards
　budget and finance issues, 349, 354
　CALEA (Commission on Accreditation for Law Enforcement Agencies), 17
　canteens and commissaries, 225
　cells, 178-179
　contact checklist, 20
　control centers, 317
　Correctional Education Association (CEA), 17
　court involvement in, 14
　creation of, 15
　dayrooms, 174
　electrical power, 307
　eminent domain
　　federal facilities exempt from state and local government requirements, 17

Notes

Notes

Notes

Notes